HISTORY OF RELIGIONS

BY

GEORGE FOOT MOORE, D.D., LL.D.

PROFESSOR OF THE HISTORY OF RELIGION IN HARVARD UNIVERSITY

I

CHINA JAPAN EGYPT BABYLONIA' ASSYRIA INDIA PERSIA GREECE ROME

NEW YORK

CHARLES SCRIBNER'S SONS

1913

The International Theological Library.

EDITED BY

CHARLES A. BRIGGS, D.D., D.Litt.,

Sometime Graduate Professor of Theological Encyclopædia and Symbolics, Union Theological Seminary, New York;

AND

STEWART D. F. SALMOND, D.D.,

Sometime Principal, and Professor of Systematic Theology and New Testament Exegesis, United Free Church College, Aberdeen.

HISTORY OF RELIGIONS.

By GEORGE FOOT MOORE, D.D., LL.D.

PREFACE

THE plan of this work embraces only the religions of civilised peoples. What are miscalled "primitive" religions are a subject for themselves, demanding another method, and much too extensive to be incidentally despatched in the prolegomena to a History of Religions. Nor is an investigation of them necessary to our purpose; the phenomena which occur in the higher religions as survivals are just as intelligible in Babylonia or in Greece as in Africa or Australia.

The present volume comprises the religions of China, Japan, Egypt, Babylonia and Assyria, India, Persia (Zoroastrianism), Greece, and Rome (including the religions of the Empire). A second volume will be devoted to Judaism, Christianity, and Mohammedanism—three religions so intimately related in origin and history as to constitute a natural group.

In the presentation of the several religions, the endeavour is made, as far as the sources permit, to show their relation to race and physical environment and to national life and civilisation, to trace their history, and to discover the causes of progress and decline and the influences that have affected them from without. Prominence is given to religious conceptions, as they are implicit in myth and ritual or are thought out by poets, philosophers, and prophets; and particularly to the higher developments in theology, ethics, and religious philosophy, especially where, as in India and in Greece, these developments are of great intrinsic interest

v

and of abiding consequence. In the case of the Greeks there is another reason for fuller exposition: Christian, Jewish, and Moslem theology are so largely in debt to Greek philosophy that these chapters lay the foundation for much of the second volume.

The limitations of space forbid the multiplication of illustrative extracts and of citations from the sources or from modern writers, as well as the discussion at length of controversial points. The annotated bibliography may be taken in partial compensation. To facilitate comparison of institutions, observances, and ideas in different religions, the index has been prepared with especial reference to this use (see, *e. g.*, such entries as "Eschatology," "Ethics," "God," "Sacrifice," "Salvation").

All the peoples with whom this volume deals emerge upon our knowledge in a relatively advanced stage of development, when compared with ancient or modern savages. The days are past when the *"Juventus Mundi"* was pictured for us from the pages of Homer, and the Hymns of the Rig-Veda were thought to lisp the *"parler enfantin"* of religion.[1] Most of the religions appear upon the scene of history as national polytheisms, to a considerable degree moralised; what went before that lies as completely beyond the horizon of history as the beginnings of civilisation. But they carry on many survivals of a prehistoric stage of culture, embedded in the ritual and myth of public religions, or as superstitions among the masses. These features persist with the tenacity of an organic inheritance; in times of demoralisation or decadence they revive and prevail. At bottom they are all alike, being in fact the one inextirpable religion of the race, entailed by remote ancestors. Such phenomena enable the historian to prolong his vision beyond the confines of history: in these survivals he recognises antecedents and di-

[1] This characteristic phrase is Max Müller's.

vine origins. Their inveteracy explains, too, the inertia with which the progress of higher ideas has to contend, the violence of reaction against reforms, the swiftness of decadence. But only in so far are these elements the object of the historian's concern; their origin and affinities belong to the anthropologist with the religions of modern savages.

Upon the higher plane of the natural polytheisms, also, there is much that is common. But on this level national individuality begins to count for more in all spheres of culture, and in religion it becomes more distinct with every step of progress. In this respect there are wide differences among religions of comparable advancement: some have developed independently, according to their own genius, while others early came under the influence of higher civilisations by which the native development was arrested or turned into new channels. Such fusion has occurred repeatedly—Rome and Japan at once present themselves as instances. In the Hellenistic and Roman world a massive syncretism, favoured by political and social causes and cultivated by pantheistic philosophies, is the signature of the age.

In religions as in civilisations it is not the generic features but the individual characteristics that give them their highest interest and, we may say, value. It has accordingly been the author's aim, without exaggeration, to bring into relief the individuality of the several religions as it expresses itself in their history. In the religions of India and Persia, for example, the background of common Indo-Iranian cult and myth is of great moment to the student of Indo-Germanic origins; but in the historical religions themselves the striking and instructive thing is the diametrically opposite directions of the development, notwithstanding the close kinship of the two peoples and their common inheritance.

The student who attentively surveys the whole field can hardly fail to discern a unity in the diversity, a general trend of evolution, which warrants the more comprehensive conception of a history of religion. Local and natural religions fuse in national polytheisms; the progress of civilisation in varying degrees moralises religion; mythology and nascent philosophy take up the problem of cosmogony, and are led to unify the creative power or the first principle; the demand for unity in the moral order of the world also tends toward monotheism; vague notions of continuance after death give place to more vivid imaginations; the lot of mortals appears more dismal in contrast to that of the gods; the belief in divine retribution or in the inexorable consequence of deeds is extended beyond this life; man struggles to escape his destiny, and demands of religion that it shall show him the way and give him the assurance of deliverance. Thereupon a new kind of religion arises in which men ask, not to be satisfied with the good things of this life, but to be exalted above the limitations of humanity or to be saved from the consequences of deeds, and, positively, to share the blessedness of the gods or to attain to union with the godhead. Salvation may be sought—to adopt the Indian analysis— by the way of works, or of knowledge, or of faith; and the methods vary accordingly. Religions of this type address themselves to the individual, and are therefore, logically, ways of salvation for all men, without distinction of nation or race; they often form organised religious communities and spread by missionary effort; the teachings of the founders are collected in a canon of authoritative scriptures and systematised in a body of doctrine, practical or philosophical.

The great religions of this class have their beginnings in the centuries from the eighth to the fifth before the Christian era. This is the age of Taoism in China; of the Upanishads, of Buddhism, and of the precursors of Hinduism in India; of Zoroaster in Iran; of the Orphic-Pythagorean movement in Greece; and of the Hebrew prophets. The coincidence is more than curious; it is an instance of that simultaneity in progress and decline, comparable to geological epochs of upheaval and subsidence, of which the history of civilisation has other striking examples—we think of the centuries about 3000 B. C. in Egypt, Babylonia and Elam, Crete, and China, the first maximum in this strange and unexplained periodicity. In like manner, whatever the cause, the eighth to the fifth centuries B. C. witnessed a maximum in the tides of religion. The religions of civilised peoples in our own time are almost all of this type—Buddhism and Hinduism, Judaism, Christianity, and Islam—though the actual religion of the peoples who profess these faiths contains large survivals of earlier stages, down to the level before the dawn of civilisation.

The field of this volume is much too wide to be covered with first-hand knowledge by any one scholar. Most recent works of similar scope are consequently the co-operative product of several authors, each of whom writes on that part of the subject with which he is especially qualified to deal by knowledge of the language, literature, and history of the people, and sometimes by actual observation of their living religion. The advantages of such a division of labour are too obvious to need a word. But it is difficult, not to say impossible, in this way to secure unity either in method of treatment or—what is more important—in point of view. The result is almost inevitably a series of monographs, individually, perhaps, of high authority, but related to one another only by being bound in the same covers. A general history of the religions of civilised peoples can, in the nature of the case, be only an introduction to the subject; for more extensive and detailed knowledge of any particular religion recourse must be had to works on a larger scale written by scholars of special equipment. And for the uses of such an introduction, unity of method and of point of view, and the wider outlook gained by the comparative study of many religions, may perhaps to some extent offset the greater independence and authority obtained by collaboration.

To enable the reader to pursue the study of individual religions or of special aspects of them, the literature has been given with some fulness (see pp. 603–616), and to many of the titles brief notes are appended, indicating the scope and character of the work.

One of the minor perplexities of a volume like this is how to spell the foreign words, especially proper names, from a variety of languages. The principle adopted is to give familiar names in the most common English form, and to write the rest in a way approximating as nearly to the pronunciation as our alphabet permits; the refinements of diacritical points are intelligible only to the scholar, who does not need them. The vowels are meant to have their so-called continental sounds; the consonants are to be pronounced as in English, with one or two exceptions: In Indian and Persian words *c* is pronounced like English *ch*, and *ç* nearly as English *sh;* the German *ach* sound is represented by *kh*. In Chinese words the aspirate, which is often distinctive, is written with a turned apostrophe ('); ĕ (as in Chuang-tszĕ) is a very short neutral vowel. In the chapters on Buddhism some difficulty is made by the fact that many names have become established in English in the Sanskrit, or artificially Sanskritised forms of the texts in which the Buddhist scriptures were first known, and Sanskrit forms are still generally given in versions from the Chinese, while the Pali forms of the southern canon are preferred by many recent scholars. It is believed that the compromises adopted will be easily understood; in some less obvious cases the identification is made in the index. Convenience has throughout been given precedence over consistency.

In conclusion I wish gratefully to acknowledge the counsel and assistance I have received in the long course of these studies from many scholars; and in particular to Mr. E. B. Drew, of Cambridge, formerly Commissioner of Chinese Imperial Maritime Customs, who was kind enough to read the chapters on China and lend me his aid about Chinese names; to Professor A. V. Williams Jackson, of Columbia University, who gave the chapters on Zoroastrianism the benefit of his most competent criticism; and to my colleague, Professor Charles R. Lanman, to whose wide and exact learning I have often appealed—never in vain—and who was so good as to submit the chapters on India to his painstaking scrutiny, and to suggest numerous improvements. I am much indebted also to Mr. Albert H. Moore, of Washington, D. C., who assisted me throughout in the preparation of the manuscript, and whose close observation detected many inaccuracies and obscurities which might otherwise have escaped me, and to my wife, who has helped me in many ways both in making the book and in carrying it through the press.

CAMBRIDGE, MASS., *October* 12, 1913.

Judaism p. 531

Good

CONTENTS

CHINA ✓

JAPAN

EGYPT

BABYLONIA AND ASSYRIA

INDIA ✓

ZOROASTRIANISM

THE GREEKS

THE ROMANS

HISTORY OF RELIGIONS

HISTORY OF RELIGIONS

CHAPTER I

CHINA

THE RELIGION OF THE STATE

Origins—Canonical Books—Nature Worship—Divination—Ancestor Worship—Modern Cultus—Veneration of Confucius—Religious Ideas—The Gods—Heaven and the Moral Order—The State—Heaven and the Life of the Individual—Moral Obligations—Ceremoniousness and Reverence.

THE scene of the mythical history of the primitive Chinese is in the north-western corner of China proper, in the present provinces of Kan-su and Shen-si. Thence the progenitors of the dominant race pushed eastward along the line of the Yellow River (Hoang-ho), and spread out in its basin (Shan-si, Shan-tung, Ho-nan) to the sea, gradually reaching south to the valley of the Yang-tse Kiang, which was, even under the Chou dynasty, the extreme south of the empire. The myths of the origins of Chinese civilisation in the Shu-king carry its development along with this expansion, and the provinces named above are the stage of the legendary history of the early dynasties. There is no hint of an antecedent migration from Mongolia or Tibet. So far as tradition knows the people was native in its earliest seats and its culture was autochthonous; and, notwithstanding the attempts that have been made to connect this civilisation with that of Egypt or Babylonia, Western scholars generally concur on the latter point with the Chinese.

The country which in the course of centuries they made

their own was not an uninhabited wilderness. The classical texts in their accounts of historical times as well as of the prehistoric ages have much to say about barbarous tribes in all quarters, whom they qualify by such designations as "big bowmen," "dogs by the fire," "huddled vermin." These barbarians do not seem to have presented any serious obstacle to the Chinese occupation, and they certainly made no contribution to Chinese civilisation.

Chinese history presents a long array of dynasties, ascending to remote antiquity, accompanied by a precise chronology which, leaving Fu-hi and Shen-nung out of the reckoning, brings the first "historical" emperor, Huang-ti, to the throne in 2704 B. C. These dates were, however, computed under the Han dynasty (206 B. C.–8 A. D.); another system, considerably shorter, is found in the "Bamboo Books," according to which Huang-ti acceded in 2491 B. C. The attempt to find a fixed point in an eclipse mentioned in the Shu-king in the reign of Chung-k'ang has not led to any assured results; the first astronomically ascertained date is the year 776 B. C. The historian Szĕ-ma Ts'ien (ca. 163–85 B. C.) does not undertake to give an exact chronology before 841 B. C., with which year the second period in the history of the Chou dynasty begins.

The traditional dates of the early dynasties to which we shall have frequent occasion to refer below are as follows: Hia, 2205–1766 B. C.; Shang, 1766–1122; Chou, 1122–841, 841–249; (interregnum, 249–221); Ts'in, 220–206; Western Han, 206 B. C.–8 A. D.; Eastern Han, 25–220 A. D.[1]

In China certain books have for many centuries been accepted as regulative in religion, morals, and government. They are not regarded as revealed or inspired: their authority is due solely to the prescription of antiquity or to the wisdom and virtue of their reputed authors; but no professed revelation has exerted a more absolute supremacy

[1] These dates are taken from Arendt, "Synchronistische Regententabellen zur Geschichte der Chinesischen Dynastien," in Mitteilungen des Seminars für orientalische Sprachen zu Berlin, Jahrgänge, II–IV.

over the minds of men or more completely dominated a whole civilisation. These books are the five Canonical Books (*King*) and the four Classics (*Shu.*[1]) The Canonical Books are the *Shu-king*, or Book of Historical Documents; the *Shi-king*, or Book of Poetry; the *Yih-king*, or Book of Permutations (a manual of divination, in whose unintelligible oracles speculation has discovered occult philosophy); the *Li-ki*, or Rites and Ceremonies; and *Ch'un-ts'iu* (Spring and Autumn), a meagre chronicle of the principality of Lu from 722 to 481 B. C. The four Classics are the *Lun-yü*, Conversations of Confucius (Legge, "Confucian Analects"); the *Ta-hioh*, or the Great Teaching; the *Chung-yung*, or Doctrine of the Mean; and *Meng-tszĕ*, the teaching of the philosopher Mencius.

All these books are associated in one way or another with the name of Confucius (551–478 B. C.). He is commonly regarded as the compiler of the first four Canonical Books and the author of the fifth; the Analects are a collection of his sayings, chiefly in intercourse with his disciples; the Great Teaching and the Doctrine of the Mean are attributed to disciples of the sage or to his grandson; Mencius (372–289 B. C.) is the greatest of his successors. Criticism—native as well as foreign—demands some qualifications of this comprehensive attribution, but does not impugn the right of this whole literature to be called in a general sense Confucian.

The emperor Shi-huang-ti (246–210 B. C.), who in 220, after long years of war, brought all China under one rule and erected on the ruins of the anarchic feudalism that had prevailed for centuries a firmly centralised empire, recognising in the veneration for the past fostered by the Confucian literature a grave peril to the new order of things which he had established, and being convinced that nothing short of extirpation would avail, issued in 213, an edict ordering that the official chronicles of the states, except

[1] The enumeration and classification is comparatively modern, perhaps from the time of the Sung dynasty (960–1127 A. D.).

those of his own country, Ts'in, should be destroyed; all
copies of the Shu-king and the Shi-king in the hands of
private scholars were to be burned within thirty days; to
possess these books, or even to talk about them with other
scholars, was forbidden under penalty of death. The only
writings exempted by this decree were works on medicine,
divination (to which class the Yih-king belongs), and agriculture.[1] The persecution, though severe, was not long continued; the emperor died in 210, and his short-lived dynasty
fell in 206. Under the following dynasty, scholars set themselves with all diligence to recover the treasures of antiquity,
which had acquired an enhanced value from the effort to
annihilate them. The existing texts of the ancient books
proceed from this restoration and recension by the scholars
of the earlier Han period (206 B. C.–8 A. D.). The Li-ki was
compiled in the same age from various memoirs on rites and
customs, chiefly representing the usages of the Chou dynasty (1122–249 B. C.). From that time on these writings
have possessed canonical character; in particular the Confucian teachings have enjoyed an authority which had not
before been universally conceded to them.

The religion of China may be summarily defined as a
union of nature worship and ancestor worship. At the most
remote time of which any record is preserved it appears fully
systematised and regulated, and its character has remained
substantially unchanged to the present day. Worship is
offered to heaven; to the heavenly bodies, and to the weather-
gods—cloud, rain, wind, and thunder; to the regents of the
seasons; to earth; to mountains, rivers, and seas; to the spirits of the soil and the crops; to the tutelary deities of the
empire and its subdivisions and of cities and towns; to the
spirits of former sovereigns, statesmen, and sages, the inventors of the arts of civilisation (including the first match-

---

[1] The text of the decree may be found in Legge, Life and Teachings
of Confucius, pp. 7–9: Scholars do not learn what belongs to the present
day, but study antiquity. They proceed to condemn the present time,
leading the masses of the people astray and into disorder.

maker), the patrons of various industries, and to the penates of the household.

All these powers are conceived as spirits. They are classified as celestial, terrestrial, or human, but this distinction of sphere does not imply a difference of kind. The relative rank of the spirits is defined in a kind of table of precedence patterned after the organisation of the feudal monarchy. At the head stands Heaven, the Supreme Emperor, followed by Earth, with the titles of a great feudatory prince. The deceased emperors of the reigning dynasty come next, outranking the sun and moon.

The public cultus is a function of the state; the sacrifices, minutely described in the liturgical works, are offered at stated seasons or on particular occasions by persons of suitable rank in the government; there is no other priesthood. Worship is performed for the people, not by them. Only at the sacrifices at the village altar to the local spirit of the soil is the presence of representatives of each family presumed, and at the clan sacrifice to the spirit of their own fields. The worship of the family ancestors constitutes the private religion of all classes. Besides the offerings to the manes, the common people had by law but one sacrifice; some reared their altar to the guardian of the door, others to the guardian of the cooking furnace.

The emperor, the Son of Heaven, is the religious head of the nation, and the worship of powers on which the welfare of the whole empire depends is his exclusive prerogative; for a subject to sacrifice to Heaven was open declaration of his purpose to seize the throne. It is in the emperor's power to enlarge the pantheon, to promote or reduce the spirits in rank, to establish or abolish sacrifices, and revise the ritual. If the spirits of the soil and crops, after having received the proper offerings, allow floods or drought, he can remove them and designate others in their place, exactly as he removes princes who do not do their duty by the altars of these spirits. The inertia of ancient custom and the conservative force of antiquarian tradition stood in the way of too free a use of these attributes of religious sovereignty; yet in the course of time very considerable changes have been made in the public cultus.

According to the Li-ki, the emperor sacrificed to Heaven and Earth, to all the famous mountains and great rivers, and to the spirits of the soil and the crops of the whole empire; the vassal princes to the tutelary genius of their region, to the spirits of the soil and crops of their states, and to the mountains and rivers in their territory. In the centralised monarchy the same principle prevailed: the governors, prefects, and magistrates offered sacrifices to the spirits of their provinces, departments, or districts.

The ancient books do not often give detailed descriptions of the worship, and the particulars which may be gathered from them represent the usage of different periods, chiefly of the later centuries of the Chou dynasty. The general features are, however, sufficiently distinct. The imperial sacrifices to Heaven and Earth were offered in the southern and the northern suburbs of the capital respectively. When a new capital was laid out the locations were determined by divination, and the altars were inaugurated by sacrifices. The stated annual sacrifices were at midsummer and midwinter. The account of the worship of Heaven in the Li-ki, ix, 2, 2, emphasises the simplicity of the ancient ritual.

At the great suburban sacrifice the Son of Heaven welcomed the arrival of the longest day. It was a great act of thanksgiving to Heaven, and the sun was regarded for the occasion as the seat of the Spirit of Heaven. The space marked out was in the southern suburb, the place most open to the brightness and warmth of the heavenly influence. The sacrifice was offered on the ground, which had been swept for the purpose, to mark the simplicity of the ceremony. The vessels used were of earthenware and gourds. The victim was a single red bull calf, "to show the estimation of simple sincerity"—not the costliness of the victim, but the spirit of the worshippers is regarded. The road that the emperor was to traverse on his way from the palace to the suburb was sprinkled and swept by the people, who also kept torches burning in the fields near by. The emperor, arrayed in ceremonial robes, rode from the palace "in the plain carriage, because of its simplicity." The victim, which had been kept in a clean stall for three months, was brought out, and, after inspection, was killed with a knife to the handle of which bells were attached, and burned on a blazing pile of wood.

The great annual sacrifice was not the only occasion of worshipping Heaven, nor was the capital the only place. In the second summer month was held the great summer sacrifice to the Supreme Emperor (Heaven) for rain. An autumn sacrifice of a ram to the Supreme Emperor, and to King Wen, "associated with Heaven," was offered in the Brilliant Hall. When about to set out on a tour of inspection, the emperor made a sacrifice with the usual forms to Heaven, offered the *I* sacrifice at the altar of Earth, and the *Shou* sacrifice in the fane of his father. In an imperial progress to the four quarters of the empire, Shun offered in each a burnt offering to Heaven, and sacrificed in order to the hills and rivers. Before setting out with his army to depose the last Shang emperor, Wu offered special sacrifice to the Supreme Emperor, presumably at his own residence. The worship of Earth was performed in the northern suburb of the capital, where a great mound was raised; the victim, a young bull, was not burned but buried in the mound, being thus made over directly to the Earth. Sacrifices to the sun were offered at an altar east of the capital; to the moon, in a pit or hollow on the west.

No worship appears in the canonical books so closely associated with the worship of Heaven as that of the mountains and rivers. It is repeatedly recorded in the Shu-king that the emperor sacrificed to Heaven and to the mountains and rivers. It is believed that these control climatic influences—both the physical climate and what may be called the spiritual climate, the *Feng-shui*. Especial mention is made of the four mountains, one in each quarter of the empire: T'ai in the East, in the modern province of Shan-tung; Hua in the West, in Shan-si; Heng in the South, in Hu-nan; and another Heng in the North, in Chih-li. Later a fifth was added to these famous mountains, Mount

Sung, in Ho-nan; and with the expansion of the empire four "frontier mountains" in the new provinces were added. Under the late Manchu dynasty fifteen mountains and hills, in three groups of five, had a place in the imperial worship. The four great rivers, upon which a large part of the country depended for its prosperity, but whose devastating floods were a constant menace, had a rank among the gods corresponding to their power for weal or woe. The four seas, which according to mythical geography bound the earth, or, what is the same thing, the dominion of the Son of Heaven, follow the great rivers in the sacrifice to the waters. The princes of the states—in later times the governors of the provinces—sacrificed to the mountains and rivers within their territory.

Of scarcely inferior importance was the worship of the spirits of the soil and the crops. The imperial altar to them stood under the open sky, "to allow the influences of heaven and earth to have full development upon it," at the right of the palace, while the ancestral temple was on the left. In the capital of each state there was an altar to the territorial spirit of the soil, and the offering of sacrifice to these spirits was the highest religious function of the ruling prince. The villages had their altars to the local spirit; while heads of clans offered to the spirit of their fields on the altar in the court of their houses, "all recognised in it the source of their prosperity." The season of this sacrifice was the second spring month. In the emperor's sacrifice three victims, a bull, a ram, and a boar were offered; the princes offered only the last two. A hymn supposed to have been used in an autumnal thanksgiving to these spirits is preserved in the Shi-king.

Another sacrifice having reference to the success of the tillage is that to the Father of Husbandry, a mythical emperor of the remotest antiquity, Shen-nung by name, who first taught men how to plough and plant; with him were associated in worship the worthies who introduced the various kinds of grain, and many others who in different ways had contributed to the development of agriculture, such as the inventors of dikes and irrigating canals.

An ancient agricultural ceremony fell in the first spring month, when the emperor, attended by his ministers and high dignitaries, proceeded in state to a field in the southern suburb, and there, with his own hand guiding the plough, ran three furrows across the field; the ministers followed him, turning up five or nine furrows according to their rank. The object of this ploughing, according to the texts, was to provide the materials for sacrifice, on the principle that the worshipper should present only what he had raised or made. We should be inclined to connect the ceremony with the prince's ploughing in India and elsewhere, the religious inauguration of the ploughing season, and still more primitively a performance of magical efficacy. As the emperor thus not merely superintended the tillage of the country, but formally participated in it, so the empress took part in the nurture of silk-worms, the gathering of the cocoons, and the spinning and weaving of the silk from which the sacrificial vestments were made.

Mention must be made, finally, of the household sacrifices to the five penates, offered, at different seasons of the year, by the emperor, the vassal princes, and the highest officers, to the guardians of the door, the furnace, the central court, the gate, and the path. Common people, as we have seen, had but one of these altars, making their choice between the first and second.

The spirits which have a place in this nature worship are not all nature spirits. The regents of the seasons, for example, are kings or ministers of mythical antiquity; the earth-god, Hou-tsi, is said to have been a scion of the line of Kung-kung, who was able to reduce the nine provinces to order; Shen-nung, who taught men how to grow cereals, was the genius of husbandry; in summer, at the season of the imperial sacrifice to Heaven for rain, sacrifices were offered throughout all the districts to the various princes, high ministers, and officers who had benefited the people, with prayers that there might be a good harvest of grain. At the suburban sacrifice, the successive dynasties designated some worthy of more remote antiquity as "the mate of Heaven"; in the time of the Chou dynasty, for example, this position was held by Chi, the progenitor of the house; under the late Manchu dynasty the five predecessors of the reigning emperor were worshipped on the altars of Heaven and Earth with equal honours. The wise and good sovereign, indeed, in life "forms a trinity" with Heaven and Earth, and stands side by side with spiritual beings; "in power of his goodness he is their match, and his benefits extend at once to all things"; he is the fellow, the equal of Heaven; he employs the agencies of nature—the seasons which are produced by Heaven and the sources of wealth which are produced by Earth—as well as those of human society. In Chinese philosophy as well as in Chinese religion man's nature is not separated by impassable limitations of kind or degree from that of the other intelligent forces at work in the world, nor is he the least among them. The deification of great men is not, therefore, to the Chinese mind what it appears to us, elevation to another kind of being. It is to be observed also that the spirits of men become tutelary divinities of families, cities, provinces, or of the whole empire, or the patron divinities of arts or occupations in which they excelled in their lifetime, thus continuing in the spirit state their former functions.

The religion of China had no oracles, but divination was resorted to on all occasions—the designation of ministers, the selection of a capital or a spot for a tomb, the choice of an auspicious day for sacrifice or for any business, the infliction of the five major punishments "according to the judgment of Heaven"; to forecast the character of the coming year, the issue of a campaign, the outcome of an illness, the luckiness or unluckiness of a sleeping chamber. There are two chief modes of divination, by the stalks of the yarrow (Chinese, *shi*) and by the tortoise-shell. The details of the manipulation have not been handed down, but it is known that a coating of some thick black pigment was laid on one side of the tortoise-shell and fire applied to the other side until cracks appeared in the coating which the diviner interpreted according to the rules of his art; and that a bunch of yarrow stalks was handled in such a manner that they formed diagrams. The Yih-king seems to be a handbook for the latter form of divination; the hexagrams with the interpretation of which that book is occupied may originally have been certain combinations of whole and broken lines formed by the falling of the stalks.

The two methods were practised by different classes of diviners. The tortoise-shell was regarded as the nobler, and was used by persons of higher rank and about greater matters. On some subjects either might be employed; but if one of them had given an unfavourable response, it was not proper to consult the other. The conjunction was most propitious when the results of the divination confirmed the judgments of the sovereign, the counsel of his ministers, and the opinion of the people; this was called the great concert. The tortoise-shell and the yarrow stalks are means by which the mind of Heaven is disclosed, or that of the ancestors; in the latter case the divination takes place in the ancestral temple. In the words of the Shu-king, through them the intelligence of Heaven is brought into connection with man.

Prognostications were taken also from dreams, the interpretation of which was the business of special diviners; and it appears that incubation was practised. When dreams coincide with divinations the auspicious omen is double. For the common people there were weather signs in the stars: "Some stars love wind, and some love rain; the courses of the sun and moon give winter and summer; the way in which the moon follows the stars gives wind and rain." Portents of divers kinds were noted: a crowing pheasant lighting on a sacrificial tripod, the appearance of fabulous beasts and birds, particularly the "phœnix" (*feng*) and the "unicorn" (*kiĕ-lin*).

The worship of the ancestors of the family is the prime religious obligation of all classes, from the highest to the lowest. The higher ranks have temples for this worship; the common people only a shrine in the living-room of the house.

According to the Li-ki, the ancestral temple of the Son of Heaven, in the time of the Chou dynasty, had seven shrines: that of his "great ancestor" facing the south; at the right and left of this shrine those of Wen and Wu respectively;[1] then, facing each other, the four immediate ancestors of the reigning emperor, beginning with his great-great-grandfather. The temple of a vassal prince had five shrines, lacking those of the dynastic founders; high officers had three—for the "great ancestor" (the founder of the house), grandfather, and father; lower officials but one.

When an emperor died and his soul-tablet was placed in the temple, his predecessors were moved up one place, and the tablet of his great-great-grandfather was transferred to the temple of the more remote ancestors, which was a depository for the tablets as they were displaced. If upon some particular occasion prayer was addressed to one of these remoter ancestors, a space was marked off, an altar set up, and sacrifice offered. The tablet of the "great ancestor," the first of the line, always kept its place. A similar rule applied to the ancestral temples of the princes and high officials. The tablets of the wife were set beside those of her husband.

When a new capital or a new palace was built, an abode must be provided for the spirits of the ancestors before the habitations of the living: "When a man of rank is about to engage in building, the ancestral temple should have his first attention, the stables and arsenal next, and the residence last." When completed, the temple and the sacrificial vessels were consecrated by pouring or smearing

[1] Wu-wang, first emperor of the Chou dynasty; Wen-wang, Duke of Chou, father of Wu. Wu ascended the throne, according to the Chinese chronology, in 1122 B. C.

upon them the blood of the victims in the dedication sacrifice, "to show how intercourse with the spirits was sought." The ancient hymns in the Shi-king, many of which were composed for these ceremonies, give vivid pictures of the worship in the emperor's ancestral temple. Many additional particulars may be gathered from the different books of the Li-ki. The rites were similar, though less splendid, in the temples of the vassal princes and of the high officials. Sacrifices were offered in the ancestral temples regularly at the four seasons of the year, and at other times as occasion might require—for instance, at the end of a war or in time of drought. A quinquennial (or triennial) sacrifice to all the ancestors is also mentioned. At the seasonal sacrifices the princes of the reigning house assembled, and many of the provincial nobles came up to the court, contributing by their presence to the splendour of the ceremonies. Those who were to take part in the sacrifice prepared themselves by fasting and various purifications.

The ancestors to whom worship was offered were represented by "personators," living descendants of the same surname, the impassive solemnity of whose demeanour as they sat in their places in the temple neither moving nor speaking is proverbial: a ruler who neglects all his duties is said to sit "like a personator of the dead." The spirits of the ancestors they respectively represented, having been solemnly invoked, were believed to be for the time embodied in the personators, who ate and drank of the offerings as those in whose place they sat would have done, received the prayers through the medium of a "prayer officer," whom we may perhaps call the prophet of the ancestral oracle, made known the will of the ancestors, and pronounced to the "filial descendant" their blessing on the sovereign and his line.[1]

The ancestral sacrifices were family feasts for the living

---

[1] The employment of personators was discontinued by Shi-huang-ti (died 210 B. C.); since that time the ancestors have been represented at the sacrifice only by their tablets.

and the dead; viands were set out in profuse abundance and variety, and all the art and mystery of Chinese cookery was brought into use. The smaller dishes (sauces, condiments, cakes, and the like) were prepared by the wife of the "filial descendant" by whom the sacrifice was offered and the ladies of the household. Cups of divers liquors made from millet went around. The service, conducted with minute and ceremonious observance of ritual, continued for many hours, sometimes outlasting the day; and all who took part in it were, it is naïvely said, much exhausted before it was over. At the close, the "prayer officer" announced to the filial descendant the satisfaction of the ancestors and promised him their blessing: "Fragrant has been your filial sacrifice, and the spirits have enjoyed your liquors and viands. They confer on you a hundred blessings, each as it is desired, each as sure as law. You have been exact and expeditious; we will confer on you the choicest favours in myriads and tens of myriads." The blessings oftenest specified are long life and fortunate posterity. The bells and drums now signalised the completion of the sacrifice; the "prayer officer" announced that the spirits had drunk to the full; the personators of the dead rose from their seats, and, escorted by the music, withdrew. The spirits, who had come at the beginning of the service in response to invitations, "tranquilly return" to their abode—that is, according to the commentators, to heaven. The servants and the women removed the dishes and trays to an apartment in the temple behind the hall of the ancestors, where a feast was spread for the near kinsmen of the sacrificer; on the next day, after a supplementary sacrifice, a feast was given in the temple to those who had personated the dead.

Music had a large place in the liturgy of the ancestral temple; various percussion and wind instruments were stationed in the open court of the hall; in the hall itself stringed instruments were used. Dances were also performed on these occasions. "The dancers move with their flutes to the music of the organ and the drum, while all the instruments perform in harmony. All this is done to please the meritorious ancestors, along with observances of all ceremonies." The dances, which were taught by the director of music, were pantomimic, and were accompanied by singing. The favourite one represented the evolutions of Wu's army on the night before his victory over Shang. The ruler himself, with shield and battle-axe, took part in it, "to give pleasure to the august personators of the dead." The sacrifices to the ancestors were clearly distinguished from the food which was set out beside the corpse while it lay in the house and by the grave at the funeral. The latter is merely a pious provision for the needs of the departed; after the interment a personator was designated, a stool and a mat for viands placed before him, and the "sacrifice of repose" performed—"the service of him as living is over, and that for him in his ghostly state begins." Following this ceremony the spirit tablet of the deceased was set in its place in the ancestral temple, next his grandfather and opposite his father. The custom on the last point varied; but the significance of the distinction is not affected.

The character of the Chinese state religion has remained through all the centuries essentially unchanged. The cultus, however, has long outgrown the "simplicity" which the idealising compilers of the Li-ki attribute to the antique ritual. The imperial sacrifice to Heaven in recent times was one of the most grandiose acts of worship ever performed by men.[1]

The altar of Heaven stands in an extensive walled park in the southern suburb of Peking. It is a circular structure of pure white marble, rising in three concentric stages,

[1] The following description of the sacrifice according to the ritual of the late Manchu dynasty is taken chiefly from an article by Henry Blodget, "The Worship of Heaven and Earth by the Emperor of China," in the *Journal of the American Oriental Society*, XX (1899), pp. 58–69; and from John Ross, The Original Religion of China, pp. 295–312, where diagrams of the park and altar will be found. Since the abdication of the emperor (Feb. 12, 1912) there has been no one to offer these imperial sacrifices, and the present administration has apparently allowed the whole official cultus to lapse.

surrounded by richly carved marble balustrades, to a height of about eighteen feet. The lowest stage is two hundred and ten feet in diameter, the second one hundred and fifty, and the highest, the flat top of the altar, ninety feet. The ascent is by steps at the four cardinal points of the compass. In the vicinity of the altar is a small round temple, in which the tablets of Heaven and of the imperial ancestors are kept, two smaller temples for the tablets of the deities of lower rank which have a part in the cultus, repositories for the sacrificial vessels and other apparatus of worship, a slaughter-house for the victims, a furnace or pyre for burning the holocaust, and the hall of abstinence in which the emperor spends the night before the sacrifice, fasting.

The ceremonies begin some time before dawn. The emperor, in azure robes (the colour of heaven), attended by a procession of princes and dignitaries of the state, takes his place at the southern gateway of the precincts surrounding the altar; the tablets are brought from the temples in which they are housed and set in their proper places on the altar. On the top of the altar on the north side, facing south, under a canopy of blue silk, is placed the tablet of Heaven, bearing the inscription, "Throne of Sovereign Heaven, Supreme Emperor"; on the east and west, facing each other, are the tablets of the imperial ancestors, the place of honour, on the left of the tablet of Heaven, being occupied by that of the founder of the dynasty. These tablets also stand in canopies of blue silk.

On the second stage of the altar are the tablets of inferior deities who are associated with Heaven and the imperial ancestors in this worship. On the east, facing west, in a blue tent, is the tablet of the sun, and by its side, under one canopy, are the tablets to the seven stars of the Great Bear, the five planets, the twenty-eight constellations of the lunar zodiac, and to all the stars of heaven collectively. On the west, facing east, is the tablet of the moon, and by its side, under a common canopy, tablets to the four "heaven spirits," viz., cloud, rain, wind, and thunder. Before each tablet are placed the carcases of the proper sacrificial victims (calves, sheep, swine) and a great array of food— soup, fish, flesh, vegetables, rice and rice-cakes, dates, nuts, wine. During the ceremonies upon the altar, a bullock is burnt as a holocaust to Heaven on a pyre below.

The emperor, attended by the princes and high dignitaries of state, having ascended the altar, burns sticks of incense on small stands before the tablets, to Heaven and his ancestors; then, kneeling, he lays before each a jade stone and a piece of silk, and presents to each a bowl of broth. A libation of rice wine to Heaven follows, while an official reads aloud a prayer. The ministrants now ascend to the second terrace and offer before the tablets incense, silk, and wine; a second and third libation by the emperor follow; further offerings are presented to the deities of the second terrace; the emperor elevates before the tablet of Heaven a chalice of wine and a dish of meat. Genuflexions and prostrations mark the progress and completion of the rites, which are directed and announced by a master of ceremonies; classical music and hymns accompany the whole ceremony.

The objects which have been offered to the spirits, including the silk and the written prayer, are now removed by attendants to a furnace and burned. The tablets are ceremoniously returned to the temples from which they were taken, and the emperor is escorted back to the palace.

The altar of Earth, in a park north of the city, is a square structure of dark-coloured stone, twelve feet high, in two stages, the lower one hundred and six feet square, the upper sixty feet. It is surrounded by a stone-walled trench six feet wide, which at the time of sacrifice is filled with water. Temples for the tablets, treasuries for the sacred vessels and utensils, and the hall of abstinence correspond to those near the altar of Heaven. The great sacrifice is at the summer solstice. On the top of the altar, on the south side, facing north, under a canopy of yellow silk, is set the tablet of Earth; on the east and west the tablets of the imperial ancestors, also under yellow canopies—the colour of earth.

On the lower terrace on the west and east are the tablets of the great mountains—fifteen in all—of the four seas, and the four great rivers. The offerings to Earth and the ancestors are the same as in the sacrifice to Heaven, except that the jade and the silks are yellow instead of blue, and the ritual is throughout closely similar; but at the end the objects offered to the terrestrial spirits are buried, not burned.

A definite symbolism is manifest in the circumstances of this worship. The sacrifice to Heaven is at the winter solstice, when the powers of light and warmth begin to prevail over the cold and dark of winter; the sacrifice to Earth at the summer solstice, for the contrary reason. For in the dualistic physical philosophy of the Chinese, Heaven belongs to the *Yang*, the bright, warm, male principle; Earth to the *Yin*, the dark, cold, female principle. For the same reason the altar of Heaven is south of the city; that of the Earth, north; the former is white and round, like heaven; the latter dark and square and surrounded by water, like the earth; Heaven has a round blue jade stone, Earth a square yellow one; the canopies of the tablets and the vestments of the emperor are of corresponding colours.

A characteristic feature of the modern state religion is the veneration of Confucius. As if in amends for the attempt of the Ts'in emperor, Shi-huang-ti, to annihilate the whole Confucian literature, the first ruler of the Han dynasty, in 194 B. C., visited the tomb of the sage and offered a bullock there; half a century later a temple to Confucius was erected at his home in K'ü-fou. A decree issued in 267 A. D. ordained that four times a year a sacrifice of a sheep, a hog, and a bull should be offered to Confucius both on the imperial altar and at his home, and in 555 it was prescribed that a temple should be erected in honour of Confucius and his favourite disciple, Yen Hui, in the capital of every prefecture. To-day there is not a city in the empire which has not one or more such temples. The tomb of Confucius is one of the holiest places in China; on the left and right of it are the tombs of his son, Poh-yü, and his more famous grandson, Tszĕ-szĕ, and near by those of the heads of his family, K'ung, for seventy generations.

The temples throughout the empire are on the same general pattern. Through a series of courts access is gained to the temple proper, the Hall of the Great Perfection, at the end of which is the tablet of Confucius, inscribed "The Blessed Sometime Teacher, Master K'ung," on the left and right of which stand the tablets of two of his immediate disciples, Yen Hui and Tseng-Ts'an, his grandson, Tszĕ-szĕ, and Mencius. On the side walls are the tablets of the disciples, the Twelve Sages, who stand next in repute, eleven being pupils of Confucius himself, and the twelfth the great interpreter of Confucianism, Chu Hi (1130–1200 A. D.), while on the sides of the principal court are galleries containing the tablets of seventy-two others of minor fame.

The ritual is minutely prescribed: offerings are made at each new moon and full moon, and with greater pomp at the beginning of the second month of spring and the second month of autumn. At the capital these sacrifices were offered by the emperor either in person or, more commonly, by his representative; in the provinces the civil magistrate of highest rank officiates, assisted by other civil and military mandarins, the whole being under the direction of a master of ceremonies. Dishes of various kinds of food, cups of wine, incense vases, and lighted candles are set out on three tables before the tablets. In the middle of the hall is laid a roll of white silk, and before it the three victims stand. The officials take their proper stations, and the rites proceed in four stages: the greeting of the spirits, the presentation of the offerings, the removal of the offerings, and the parting salutation to the spirits. The several liturgical acts are accompanied by the singing of appointed hymns and instrumental music by a chorus and orchestra posted on the terrace before the sacrificial hall; boys in antique garb, carrying a flute in one hand and a pheasant's feather in the other, go through stately dances in the court. At the end of the service the roll of silk is burned and the flesh of the victims distributed among the humbler ministrants. The celebrating mandarin then makes a last obeisance before the tablet and with his train retires.

The liturgy contains no prayers in the proper sense, either of petition or thanksgiving, but praises of the sage; it is, so far as that goes, an act of veneration rather than divine worship. In 1906, however, in connection with the educational reforms, an imperial edict raised Confucius to the same rank with Heaven and Earth, the motive being, it is said, to assert the supreme value of moral education.

The state religion of China, at the time when the canonical books were written, was not only highly organised and in the possession of an elaborate ceremonial, but it had definite and in some respects advanced religious ideas.

The tutelary and departmental deities, whether by origin objects or powers of nature or human beings, are all distinctly conceived as spirits, a stage of development far removed from that which sees in the sun or the river a living being. These powers have no plastic, dramatic individuality, like the gods of Greece; no mythology recites their exploits. They have definite functions, and by these alone they themselves are defined. In this, as in other respects, the religion of China strikingly resembles that of the Romans; for a practical people it is enough to know what the gods do, and what their worshippers have to do to secure their favour, without trying to imagine what they are like.

The powers operate in their own spheres: the mountains and streams, the gods of cloud, rain, wind, and thunder, control the weather; the spirits of the soil and crops give the increase to the husbandman's labours; the guardian genii of the empire, the state, the city, protect the inhabitants; the spirits of the fathers watch over and bless the family. For these good gifts men approach them with sacrifice and prayer. If neglected, they may desist from the beneficent activities on which the welfare of all depends.

But above this natural religion rises the conception of a

sovereign and moral rule in the world which is intimated in a king's plaint: "Oh! what crime is chargeable on us now, that Heaven thus sends down on us death and disorder?" Heaven (T'ien) is literally the sky, "the azure vault," and is addressed in prayer, "O thou distant and azure Heaven," "O bright and high Heaven, who enlightenest and rulest this lower world." It is not, however, as the firmament or the void that Heaven is thus appealed to, but as a spirit—the highest of spirits. The pre-eminence of Heaven in Chinese religion is a feature which it shares with the Mongol religions generally, in which the heaven-spirit (called in some dialects "Tengri," a name etymologically cognate with T'ien) occupies the same rank. But the superiority of Heaven has developed in China into supremacy. Heaven is the Emperor (Ti), or more commonly the Supreme Emperor (Shang-ti), the ruler of the world and of men. Heaven is not merely the cause, mediate or immediate, of natural phenomena, but the source of the order of nature (the Tao, or Way). It is, however, particularly as ruler of men that the idea of Heaven becomes more definitely personal. "Great Heaven is intelligent, and is with you in all your goings. Great Heaven is clear-seeing, and is with you in all your wanderings and indulgences."

The personality of Heaven is moral not mythical; of anthropomorphism in the proper sense there is hardly a trace. "The toe-print of the Lord (Ti)," where the mother of Hou-tsi miraculously conceived—apparently an allusion to an ancient myth—is almost a solitary instance in the canonical books. In the same ode we read: "We load the stands with offerings, the stands of wood and earthenware. As soon as the fragrance ascends, the Most High Lord (Shang-ti), well-pleased, smells the sweet savour." But such language, common in the Old Testament, is very rare in the Chinese sacred books. Even the expression, "the Lord (Ti) said to King Wen," is so unusual that Confucian scholars, with whom it is a dogma that Heaven does not speak, are moved to explain it away.

In an ode to the great Wen it is said: "King Wen is on high, Oh! bright is he in heaven. . . . King Wen ascends and descends on the left and right of the Lord," the divine sovereign in heaven being imagined seated in state, like the emperor, the Son of Heaven, on earth. But, again, a representation as inevitable as this stands almost alone. There is no celestial court with ministers of various ranks; no angels bringing to God in heaven reports from the world below, carrying his message to men, and executing his will on earth in nature and history.

But, none the less, Heaven is, in the ancient Chinese religion, a personal god. This appears most strikingly in odes in which the poet inveighs against the injustice of Heaven. Thus, a victim of intrigue and slander appeals: "O vast and distant Heaven, who art called our parent, that without crime or offence I should suffer from disorders thus great! The terrors of great Heaven are excessive, but indeed I have committed no crime." In a period of misgovernment and disorder another exclaims: "Great Heaven, unjust, is sending down these exhausting disorders; great Heaven, unkind, is sending down these great miseries." "O unpitying great Heaven, there is no end of the disorder." "From great Heaven is the injustice." "Great and wide Heaven, how is it that you have contracted your kindness, sending down death and famine, destroying all throughout the kingdom? Compassionate Heaven arrayed in terrors, how is it that you exercise no forethought, no care? Let alone the criminals—they have suffered for their guilt. But those who have no crime are indiscriminately involved in ruin." In another ode, written in a similar situation, an officer admonishes his countrymen: Heaven is sending down calamities; Heaven is exercising oppression; Heaven is displaying its anger; revere the anger of Heaven. Heaven in anger plagues the people with famine and bad rulers—ignorant, oppressive, negligent. The outcries against the injustice of Heaven, like those of Job, derive all their force from the belief that God is not unjust nor capricious; and this is the constant teaching, the fundamental assumption, of the Chinese books: the rule of Heaven is moral.

The moral rule of Heaven is seen in the political sphere. The emperor reigns by the appointment of Heaven. But he must not presume on his divine right: the appointment is not irrevocable. Government was instituted by Heaven for the good of the people, and if the sovereign abuses his powers or neglects his duties for his own profit or pleasure, saying, "the people is mine, and the appointment is mine," Heaven annuls its mandate. When a royal house becomes corrupt or effete, Heaven seeks out a suitable man to execute its judgment of deposition, and confers on him its appointment to found a new dynasty. Heaven is, indeed, patient, it gives warnings which should lead the offender to examine himself and mend his way; but if these are unheeded, the doom falls.

The emperor is responsible for the acts of all his subordinates, who hold their appointment from him, and toleration of their misdeeds is imputed to him as his own evil doing. The sovereign is doubly responsible for his subordinates, because, according to Chinese theory, if he is virtuous and upright, they will be so by the force of his example, and *vice versa*. It is especially the outcry of the misgoverned people which provokes the divine intervention, for "Heaven loves the people, and the sovereign should reverently carry out this mind of Heaven." The leaders of the revolutions which overthrew successively the dynasties of Hia and Shang, in the indictment of their sovereigns by which they justify rebellion, proclaim that by dissoluteness, neglect of religion, and above all by perpetrating and permitting oppression, the emperor has forfeited his right to the throne, and that they have been commissioned to carry out the sentence of Heaven.

The appointment, or decree, of Heaven is recognised also in the life of the individual: it is destiny. It determines his allotted span of life and his fortunes in life. In this decree there is no partiality, no hatred, and no mistake. It is a mark of the "superior man" that he stands in awe of the ordinances of Heaven while the "common man" does not know them, and therefore does not stand in awe of them. The superior man is quiet and calm, waiting for the appointments of Heaven, while the common man walks in dangerous paths, looking for lucky occurrences. For the individual, as for the state, the decrees of Heaven are not arbitrary, they are congruous with man's character. Good and evil do not wrongly befall men, but Heaven sends down misery or happiness according to their conduct. The way of Heaven is to bless the good and make the bad miserable. In its inspection of men below, Heaven's first consideration is righteousness, and it bestows on them accordingly length of days or the contrary. On the appointment of Heaven in the life of private persons the Shi-king and Shu-king, from their character, cannot be expected to say much; Confucius and the philosophers are reticent for a different reason. Of the beliefs of the common man about the ordering of his life we have no indication.

The course, or order of nature (Chinese, *Tao*, literally, 'way, principle')[1] is Heaven's Way. The operations of nature are attributed sometimes to the spirits which preside over the several departments of nature, sometimes to Heaven directly; the latter always when these operations are thought of as not merely physically effected but morally determined. The relation of Heaven to the inferior divine powers seems, however, not to have been reflected upon. There is no intimation that these powers are the agents of Heaven's will or that Heaven works through them; that they should ever work at cross-purposes with Heaven is doubtless inconceivable. Like the princes of the feudal empire, they had a considerable measure of responsible independence in their own sphere, subject to the intervention of higher authority: if the spirits of the soil and crops did not do their duty, the Son of Heaven, the vicegerent of God, might depose them and give their offices to others. Historically, the gods of

[1] See below, pp. 49 *f*.

this class, guardians of regions and localities, genii of fertility, belong to the land and its agricultural civilisation, while Heaven and the manes are elements of the older religion of the nomadic Mongols. The lack of complete co-ordination is thus explicable.

The old Chinese religion has neither a doctrine of creation nor a cosmogonic myth. Heaven and Earth, themselves the two greatest gods, produce all things by the interaction of the opposites, heat and cold, light and dark, male and female.[1] The processes of nature which men see every day went on through all the past as they do at present; that they had a beginning—and when and how—was as little in men's minds as that they were eternal; they are simply accepted. Equally little did it occur to them that if Heaven and Earth accounted for all the rest, they themselves remained to be accounted for. Chinese philosophy, indeed, early raised the metaphysical problem of the ultimate principle; but it did not, as in Greece, find an anticipation of the problem in religion.

The moral standard of the religion is high. The anger of Heaven is provoked not only by the vices and crimes of the mighty—by drunkenness and lust, by idleness and dissipation, by arrogance, oppression, and cruelty, by the luxury which lays heavy burdens on the masses—but by the indolent self-indulgence which neglects the welfare of the people. The ruler, as the parent of the people, is responsible for the prosperity and happiness of his subjects; a discontented people voices the disapproval of Heaven. He must surround himself with wise counsellors, and must employ in the government none but intelligent and virtuous men; must see that order is maintained and the laws enforced with a justice tempered by mercy. He must himself be reverent in his relations to the gods and sincere in his dealings with men, setting an example of love to his fellows and respect

---

[1] Yih-king, the root of the later Confucian physical philosophy. See Grube, Geschichte der chinesischen Litteratur, pp. 333 ff. Of this dualism there is no trace in the older literature.

to his elders, and showing kindness to the distressed and suffering as if they were his children. More than by command and punishment, he should govern by education; and the most impressive of teaching, the most potent influence, should be his own character. Mindful of his responsibility rather than his prerogative, he must feel that "a place of difficulty is the Heaven-conferred seat." In a proclamation announcing the beginning of his reign, T'ang, who overthrew the dynasty of Hia, says:

It is given to me, the One Man (monarch), to secure the harmony and tranquillity of your states and clans; and now I know not whether I may not offend against the Powers above and below. I am fearful and trembling, as if I were in danger of falling into a deep abyss. Let me be reverent! Let me be reverent! (The Way of) Heaven is evident, and its appointment is not easily preserved. Let me not say that it is high aloft above me. It ascends and descends about our daily doings; it daily inspects us wherever we are. I am like a little child, without intelligence to be reverently attentive to my duties; but by daily progress and monthly advance, I will learn to hold fast the gleams [of knowledge] till I arrive at bright intelligence.[1]

Humility is the mark of true greatness as well as of true goodness. "Indulging the consciousness of being good is the way to lose that goodness; being vain of one's ability is the way to lose the merit it might produce."

The princes and magistrates, the officials of every grade, have, in their narrower sphere, similar duties to their inferiors, with the added obligation of loyalty to their superiors.

The moral obligations of all classes are defined by the "five relationships," namely, those between father and son, elder brother and younger, husband and wife, ruler and subject, friend and friend—the cardinal doctrine of Chinese ethics. "From Heaven are the social relationships with their several duties; we are charged with the enforcement of those five duties." More detestable than robbers and murderers are the unfilial and the unbrotherly, "the son who does not reverently discharge his duty to his father,

[1] Shi-king, III, 3, 3.

but greatly wounds his father's heart, and the father who does not love his son," the younger brother who does not respect his elder, and the elder who is not friendly to the younger. The state must punish those who thus violate the principles of human nature and the constitution of society.

To an external view, ceremonious formalism character-ises the ancient Chinese worship. In the apprehension of the worshippers themselves this ceremoniousness is the natu-ral expression of reverence, and "reverence" is, as in the Old Testament ("the fear of the Lord"), the word which most adequately expresses the religious frame of mind. Rev-erent should be man's thought of the powers of nature, above all, of the great moral power, High Heaven, and of the spirits of the wise and good of former generations; reverent his feeling and demeanour in their presence; reverent all his conduct as in the sight of these unseen witnesses.

Without reverence there is no worship; without sincerity no use in sacrifice: "The spirits do not always accept the sacrifices that are offered to them; they accept only the sacrifices of the sincere." Similar utterances occur in the ritual books, for example: "Sacrifice is not a thing laid on a man from without; it issues from within him, and has its birth in his heart." The truly filial son offers sacrifices to his fathers without seeking anything to be gained by them. It is not the costliness of an offering that gives it value, but the simple sincerity of the offerer—a single bull-calf was the ancient sacrifice to Heaven. "Officiousness in sacrific-ing is called irreverence; and multiplying of ceremonies leads to disorder."

The moral effect of the sacrifices on the worshippers is more often dwelt upon than their influence on the spirits. Sacrifice to the gods not only expresses but engenders rev-erence: no one can perform the ceremonies in the right spirit without being more reverent, that is, a more truly religious man. Sacrifice to the ancestors cultivates filial piety and cements the bond of the family.

CHAPTER II

CHINA

MORAL AND POLITICAL PHILOSOPHY

Confucius—His Career—Attitude Toward Religion—Gods and Spirits
—Heaven—Ethics—Conflicting Doctrines—Yang Chu and Moh
Tih—Mencius—Political Theory—Wang Ch'ung—Neoconfucian-
ism: Chou Tun-i and Chu Hi—Religious Aspects of the Sung
Philosophy.

THE orthodox religion of China, the religion of the state
with all its officials and of the whole literate class, is by
Western scholars commonly called Confucianism.[1] The
name must not, however, be understood to import that
Confucius stands to this religion in the same relation in
which Buddha stands to Buddhism or Mohammed to Mohammedanism. Confucius was not the founder of a religion,
nor even a reformer in the ordinary sense of the word. In
no sphere is his own estimate of himself, "a transmitter, not
a maker, believing in and loving the ancients," truer than
in that of religion; and nothing could have seemed to him,
with his exaggerated veneration of antiquity, more irreligious than any innovations in the ceremonies that were instituted in the most remote times by the model sovereigns,
Yao and Shun, and had been piously observed by all their
worthy successors. His utmost thought was to revive customs that had fallen into desuetude and to conform everything to the ancient pattern. This was part of his general
plan for the restoration of the good old times; but it does
not appear that he had much opportunity to achieve practical results in this direction, nor were his efforts to inspire

[1] The Chinese name is *Ju-kiau*, "School of the Learned."

in his stiff-necked generation the reverence for Heaven and its decrees, which was the inwardness of the old religion, much more fruitful. The religion which has left its monuments in the oldest hymns of the Shi-king as well as in the documents of the Shu-king, as it has been described above, is substantially the religion of Confucius and of modern official China.

In another sense, however, it is not improper that it should bear his name. For Confucius has been through more than twenty centuries in China the great authority in religion as well as in ethics and politics; the entire body of canonical and classical literature is attributed to him as editor or author; the whole education of China has been in this literature, and almost bounded by it and works based upon it. Furthermore, Confucius unquestionably impressed on his disciples the non-committal, and in some respects agnostic, disposition toward theological questions which was characteristic of his own temper; and in the later Confucian schools, especially in the renaissance of philosophy under the Sung dynasty, this tendency is still more strongly marked. On the other hand, though Confucius was no more original in the field of ethics than of religion, he and his successors, the authors of the Great Learning, the Doctrine of Mean, the Book of Filial Piety, and above all Mencius, gave to Chinese ethics classical form and authoritative finality.

Confucius was born in 551 B. C., in the little state of Lu, within the bounds of the present province of Shan-tung. Of his early life almost nothing is known; but he had at least such opportunities of education that at twenty-two he began to teach. It may be assumed that in the following years, while giving instruction to the pupils who in increasing numbers resorted to him, he continued his own studies of history, literature, and ancient customs (especially ritual, in which he early acquired the reputation of an expert), and at thirty, he tells us, he "stood firm," that is, had settled opinions.

An incident of considerable importance in his life was a visit, in 517 B. C., to Loh-yang, the capital of the empire, where he had a long-desired opportunity to see the places where the great sacrifices to Heaven and Earth were offered, and to inspect all the arrangements of the ancestral temple of the reigning dynasty of Chou and of the imperial court, and perhaps to pursue researches in the archives. The following years were a period of great disorder in the state of Lu. At the beginning of it, in 517, Confucius followed his exiled sovereign to the neighbouring state of Ts'i; but, finding the then ruling duke little disposed to profit by his counsels, soon returned to his native country, where he kept steadfastly aloof from the strife of factions, declining public employment. In this period, probably, fall the collecting and editing of the ancient literature with which his name is inseparably connected. In the year 501, however, he was appointed chief magistrate of a city named Chung-tu, and put his theories of administration into practice with such effect, we are told, that in a twelvemonth Chung-tu was a model town. This transformation was noted with surprise by the duke, who asked Confucius whether the same principles could be applied to the government of a state, and being assured that they could, he made Confucius assistant superintendent of public works, and shortly after minister of justice; whereupon, according to his eulogistic biographers, laws against crime fell into disuse, because there were no criminals.

He strengthened the ducal house and weakened the private families. He exalted the sovereign and depressed the ministers; a transforming government went abroad. Dishonesty and dissoluteness were ashamed, and hid their heads. Loyalty and good faith became the characteristics of the men, and chastity and docility of the women. Strangers came in crowds from other states. Confucius became the idol of the people, and flew in songs through their mouths.

But this Utopian Lu excited the jealous apprehensions of its neighbours, and by liberal presents of horses and dancing-girls they distracted the ruler's mind from the counsels of the sage, who, finding himself disprized, surrendered his office, and sadly—and slowly, hoping that the duke might at last repent—shook the dust of the ungrateful state from his feet. Thus ended Confucius's one brief experience as a practical statesman. For thirteen years, accompanied by a band of disciples, he wandered from court to court, offering his counsel and exhortations to princes and ministers; sometimes consulted by them, but not establishing any permanent influence; yet never losing confidence that if one of them would but employ him, "I would effect something considerable in the course of twelve months, and in three years the government would be perfected." In 483 he was recalled to Lu, where he spent the last years of his life in labours upon the ancient literature, particularly the Shi-king, in finishing the Ch'un-ts'iu, and in the study of Yih-king, of which he is reported to have said, "If some years were added to my life, I would give fifty to the Yih, and then I might come to be without grave faults." He died in 478 B. C., at the age of seventy-three years.

In all the externals of religion Confucius was extremely punctilious. As a child, we are told, his favourite play was arranging sacrificial vessels and practising postures of ceremony; and as a man he showed the same predilections by antiquarian researches into the ritual of former dynasties. The apparatus of worship at the capital drew from him the exclamation, "Now I know the wisdom of the Duke of Chou, and how the house of Chou attained to the imperial sway." The ancient music of Shun, the tradition of which was preserved in Ts'i, so ravished him that for three months he did not know the taste of flesh: "I did not know," he said, "that music could be made so excellent as this." He believed that the virtue of the people and the welfare of the state depended upon the reverent observance of the sacrifices to the gods and the spirits of the ancestors. He himself "sacrificed to the dead as if they were present; he sacrificed to the spirits as if the spirits were present"; and the crowning proof to him that the Duke of Lu was incorrigible was the indecorous haste with which he despatched the solemn sacrifice to Heaven in order to hurry back to his dissolute pleasures.

Confucius, who was never weary of discussing the minutest points of ritual, had very little to say about more vital religious matters. Too much stress has perhaps been laid by Legge and others upon particular utterances, such as his reply to a disciple who asked him about serving the spirits of the dead: "While you are not able to serve men, how can you serve the spirits." "I venture to ask about death," the inquirer continued: "So long as you do not know life, how can you know about death?" To another, who asked what wisdom is, he answered: "To give one's self earnestly to the duties due to men, and, while respecting spiritual beings, to keep aloof from them." It is not so much single sayings of this kind as the absence of any teaching about the nature of these "spiritual beings" and their relations to men that is significant.

The belief that the destiny of states and individuals is ordained by Heaven was accepted by Confucius without question. Faith in his own mission sustained him in critical moments of his life. When his life was threatened in K'uang, he said: "After the death of King Wen, was not the cause of truth lodged here in me? If Heaven had wished this cause of truth to perish, then I, a feeble mortal, should not have got into such a relation to that cause. While Heaven does not let the cause of truth perish, what can the people of K'uang do to me?" Yet one of the subjects on which he seldom spoke was the appointments of Heaven. He scarcely ever uses the name Shang-ti, Supreme Lord, and it has been surmised that he consciously avoided it because it more distinctly implied the personality of God, preferring the impersonal, or at least ambiguous, T'ien, Heaven. Here, again, the inference is uncertain. T'ien occurs with increasing relative frequency in the later hymns of the Shi-king and the later documents of the Shu-king; and Confucius may well have employed it in conformity with the prevalent usage of his times, rather than from any prejudice of his own.

Confucius was not a speculative thinker; the problems of the origin of the universe, the nature of being, the one and the many, which exercised the early philosophers of Greece and India, lay beyond the horizon of his mind. His common-sense philosophy dealt exclusively with the practical questions of ethics and politics. To him, as to other thinkers of this type, God was essentially the moral order of the world, an order energising in the phenomena of nature as well as in the course of history and the destiny of individual lives. The more uniform, that is, the more unvaryingly moral, this order is, in the interest of ethics, conceived to be, the more impersonal the conception becomes—the something, not ourselves, that makes for righteousness. If in the unvarying moral order the destiny of men is determined in strict accordance with their conduct, it is obviously futile to importune Heaven to change it: "He who offends against Heaven has none to whom he can pray." Once when Confucius was ill his disciple, Tszĕ-lu, asked leave to pray for him. He said, "Is that proper?" Tszĕ-lu replied: "Yes. In the Prayers it is said, 'Prayer has been made to the spirits of the upper and lower worlds.'" The Master said, "It must be a long time since I prayed."

Expressions which imply a more personal thought of God are, however, not lacking in the sayings of Confucius. "Heaven produced the virtue that is in me. Huan T'ui —what can he do to me?" "The Master said, 'Alas! there is no one that knows me.' Tszĕ-kung said, 'What do you mean by thus saying that no one knows you?' The Master replied, 'I do not murmur against Heaven. I do not grumble against men. My studies lie low, and my penetration rises high. But there is Heaven; that knows me.'" Such language shows that Confucius's ethical rationalism was not incompatible with a real religious faith.

In the ethics of Confucius filial piety is, as it has been in China in all ages, the cardinal virtue. The son who loves, respects, and obeys his father, anticipating his wishes while he lives and regarding them when he is dead, will make a kind brother, a sincere friend, and a loyal subject; men who are filial and fraternal seldom offend against their superiors. Beyond the "five relations" of the family and the state are the relations of men to their fellows in society, and these are to be ruled by the same principle. Filial piety and fraternal love are the root of benevolence, which Confucius defined as love to all men.

The one word "reciprocity" may serve as a rule of practice for a man's whole life: "What you do not want done to yourself do not do to others." Benevolence must not, however, transgress the limits of equity. When asked what he would say about the principle enounced by his older contemporary, Lao-tse, that injury should be requited with kindness, Confucius's characteristic answer was: "With what, then, will you requite kindness? Requite injury with justice, and kindness with kindness." Men should deal with one another as Heaven deals with men, according to their deserts. If the duty of blood vengeance for the murder of a father or mother devolve upon a son, he should sleep on straw, with his shield for a pillow and his weapon at hand, "he must be determined not to live with the slayer under the same heaven."

A fundamental doctrine of the Confucian ethics is that the nature of man is good. In the Shu-king, T'ang says: "The Most High Lord has conferred even on the inferior people a moral sense, by obeying which they obtain a nature constantly right." "Heaven, in giving birth to the multitudes of the people, annexed to every faculty and relationship its law. The people possess this normal nature, and they consequently love its normal virtue." In this respect all men are similarly endowed. Hence if men do wrong, they cannot lay the responsibility on the nature which Heaven has given them.

But though all are good at the beginning, few prove themselves to be so at the end. Through parental neglect to inculcate filial piety, through faulty education and bad example, the most deteriorate, and by habit unrighteousness becomes second nature. The good nature bestowed by Heaven must be developed into a stable good character by man's own effort. To achieve this it is necessary to have not only the steadfast will but the true ideal. It is the end of education to set forth this ideal and inspire men to strive after it. Accordingly, the burden of Confucius's teaching is the character of the "superior man"—the man who in every situation knows the right thing and does it, a man not only of faultless virtues, but of faultless propriety.

The age of Confucius and the two following centuries were a time of great intellectual activity in China; conflicting theories of ethics were enunciated and controversy was rife. Yang Chu, who lived about the middle of the fourth century, was a pessimist. Life is short and full of trouble; death is the end of all. The only profit in this evil world is to enjoy the pleasures of sense while we can, without sacrificing a hair to the interests of mankind or the welfare of the state, and regardless of the praise or blame of men. None is more famous than Shun and Yü, Chou-kung and Confucius. Those heroes of virtue never had a day's enjoyment in their lives; and though their fame endure ten thousand generations, what is that to them? The dead know nothing of the praises bestowed upon them; they are no better than a stock or a lump of clay. None is more infamous than Kieh and Chou; yet those tyrants in their lifetime enjoyed to the full riches, power, and honour, and what do they care now for the curses of posterity? The ancients knew this, and followed their natural inclinations; they did not make a virtue of denying themselves the pleasures that came in their way, nor let themselves be urged by ambition for fame to put constraint on their natures.

At the opposite extreme from this cynical egoism is the radical altruism of Moh Tih. One who inquires into the cause of the ills of society and the state as a physician inquires into the cause of a disease will find that all those ills have one origin: men of every class and condition love themselves and do not love their fellows; hence they wrong others for their own advantage. There is therefore but one remedy—mutual love. For if men loved one another as every man loves himself, there would be no more crime. If each regarded his neighbour's house as his own, who would then steal? If each regarded his neighbour's person as his own, who, then, would rob? If princes regarded foreign states as their own, where would there be occasion for wars? All the misery in the world—the overpowering of the weak by the strong, the oppression of the minority by the majority, the defrauding of the simple by the shrewd, the haughtiness of the eminent toward the insignificant—is due to the making of distinctions between men, whereas universal love embraces them all, without making such differences. If it is asked how this millennium is to be brought about, Moh Tih answers, with characteristic Chinese faith in the influence of the ruler, that if princes would only show that they delighted in the love of all for all, the people infallibly would cultivate it.

The teachings of both Yang Chu and Moh Tih are vigorously combated by Mencius. The individualism of the former—"every man for himself"—is anarchism; the altruism of the latter—"love all men equally"—is unfilial: both strike at the roots of human society. If they should prevail, they would reduce men to the state of the beasts, who acknowledge neither king nor father; benevolence and righteousness would cease, and men would devour one another. If this is to be averted, these false doctrines must be stopped, and the sound principles of Confucius reaffirmed.

The Confucian doctrine of the inborn goodness of human nature was impugned by more than one philosopher. One affirmed that the nature of man is morally indifferent; it is like water, which will run in whatever direction a channel is opened for it. Others maintained that it can be made good or bad by influences from without, as in the times of the good kings Wen and Wu the people loved goodness, and under the cruel kings Yü and Li they loved cruelty. Others, again, that the nature of some is good, and of others bad; a virtuous father may have a wicked son, or the converse. Against all these Mencius argues. From the sentiments which are proper to human nature it is evident that it is constituted for the practice of what is good; this is what is meant by saying that man's nature is good. Such feelings, common to all men, are sympathy and pity, shame and abhorrence, respect and reverence, approbation and disapprobation. From these spring benevolence, righteousness, propriety, and knowledge, which are therefore not implanted but innate; only we do not think of them. Hence it is said: "Strive for them, and you will attain them; neglect them, and you will lose them."

The controversy continued. Siün K'uang, a younger contemporary of Mencius, maintained in opposition to him that man's nature is evil. His spontaneous impulses are all selfish: the hungry man is prompted by nature simply to satisfy his appetite; if out of consideration for the rights and interests of others he resists this impulse, it is by a conscious effort and because he has been taught that he ought to do so—not therefore by nature, but against natural impulses. Uncontrolled by education and moral discipline or by the law and its penalties, there would be a state of universal strife—every man's hand would be against his neighbour. That man has to strive to become good is proof that his nature is evil. A later philosopher, Yang Hiung (53 B. C.–18 A. D.), took an intermediate position: human nature is a mixture of good and evil; he who cultivates the good side of his nature becomes a good man, and he who cultivates the evil a bad man. In the end, however, chiefly through the influence of Mencius, the native goodness of man became the orthodox dogma, which is to-day laid down as a fundamental proposition in every elementary text-book of moral instruction.

To the exposition and defence of Confucianism against opposing doctrines no one contributed so much as Mencius, who thus earned the place he has long held next in honour to the Master. Mencius was born in 372 B. C., and died in 289. He seems never to have held office, and, unlike Confucius, it does not appear that he sought to do so. Like many others in his day, he passed from city to city, teaching the disciples who followed him in his migrations or who in any place resorted to him, expounding to rulers, as occasion offered, the enlightened principles of government on which the prosperity of states depends, and giving sound advice on the ethics of private life and the conduct of affairs, as a kind of consulting philosopher to princes, after the manner of the wandering sophists among the Greeks. His works. consisting largely of such discussions, surpass the Confucian Analects in logical acumen and in orderly presentation. He employs the form of dialogue with much skill to refute an opponent or to constrain assent to his own proposition by superiority in dialectic in a fashion which at times reminds us of Socrates.

A Chinese scholar, comparing Mencius with Confucius, said: "Confucius spoke only of benevolence, but as soon as Mencius opens his mouth we hear of benevolence and righteousness. Confucius spoke of the will or mind, but Mencius enlarged also on the nourishment of the passion-nature"—the cultivation of the emotions.[1] In the conversation with Hui of Liang, with which the book begins, the prince salutes the philosopher:

"Venerable sir, since you have not counted it far to come here, a distance of a thousand *li*, may I presume that you are likewise provided with counsels to profit my kingdom?" Mencius replied: "Why must your majesty speak of profit? There are benevolence and righteousness, and these should suffice. If your majesty say, 'What can I do to profit my kingdom?' the great officers will say, 'What can we do to profit our families?' and the inferior officers and the common people will say, 'What can we do to profit ourselves?' Superiors and inferiors will try to snatch this profit the one from the other, and the state will be endangered. . . . There never has been a man trained to benevolence who neglected his parents; there never has been a man trained to right-

[1] See Mencius, II, 1, 2, 9 *ff.*

eousness who made his sovereign an after consideration. Let your majesty say: 'Benevolence and righteousness, and these only.' Why must you use that word 'profit'?"[1]

The state exists for the people, and its stability depends on the welfare of the people. The conditions of public welfare are ultimately economic. The government must preserve peace abroad and order at home; it must not burden the people with forced labour on public works by which they are withdrawn from their fields, nor harass them with a complicated system of taxes and imposts; it must instruct, encourage, and, if necessary, assist the tillers of the soil, for on agriculture the prosperity of all depends. To reduce the people to starvation by misgovernment or neglect is sheer murder.

"If the people have not a certain livelihood, they will not have a fixed heart. And if they have not a fixed heart, there is nothing which they will not do in the way of self-abandonment, of moral deflection, of depravity, and of wild license. When they thus have been involved in crime, to follow them up and punish them—this is to entrap the people. Therefore an intelligent ruler will regulate the livelihood of the people, so as to make sure that, above, they have sufficient wherewith to serve their parents, and, below, sufficient wherewith to support their wives and children; that in good years they shall always be abundantly satisfied, and that in bad years they shall escape the danger of perishing. After this he may urge them, and they will proceed to what is good, for in this case the people will follow after that with ease."

In the contrary case, "in good years their lives are continually embittered, and in bad years they do not escape perishing. In such circumstances they only try to save themselves from death, and are afraid they will not succeed. What leisure have they to cultivate propriety and righteousness?"[2]

This insistence on the economic conditions not only of prosperity, but, consequently, of righteousness and good order, is characteristic of Mencius; and he discusses at large the practical measures by which the end is to be achieved. *Vox populi, vox dei*—"Heaven sees as my people sees;

[1] Mencius, I, *cf.* VI, 2, 4.   [2] Mencius, I, 1, 7, 20.

Heaven hears as my people hears." The common voice of the people about a man's character, his fitness for office, or his desert of death, is more to be trusted than the advice of courtiers or high officials.

Mencius explicitly asserts the right of revolution: "If a prince have grave faults," he told a king to his face, "the nobles and ministers who are of his blood ought to remonstrate with him, and if he do not listen to them after they have done so again and again, they ought to dethrone him." The murder of a tyrant like Chou was not the putting to death of a sovereign, but the cutting off of a base fellow; by his crimes he had forfeited all right to a better name than ruffian and robber or to different treatment. But only a "minister of Heaven" may presume thus to execute its requirements.

Wang Ch'ung, who wrote toward the end of the first century of our era, occupies in some respects a place apart in the history of Chinese thought.[1] He may be described as a materialistic monist, and his physical philosophy somewhat resembles that of Epicurus and Lucretius. At the beginning there was a homogeneous vaporous or nebulous chaos. Out of this the lighter and the heavier elements "spontaneously"—that is, without intelligence or design—separated; the warm and light (elemental fire) above, the cold and dark, represented by water, below. So he adapts the old doctrines of Yang and Yin, fortifying himself by quotations from the Yih-king and the Li-ki. The Taoist Lieh-tszĕ developed a similar theory; but Wang Ch'ung, as pure materialist, has no use for the mystical Tao nor for the primal intelligence of Chu Hi and the Sung Confucianists. From the combination and spontaneous interaction of these principles all things arise. Man's body is of coarse matter, Yin; his vital spirit and intelligence are of the fiery nature of the Yang. Heaven—that is, the sky—is material just as truly as the earth, only of a different composition, and

[1] See A. Forke, Lun-Heng: Philosophical Essays of Wang Ch'ung. 1907.

its operations are equally without design. It does not take note of men's doings to punish the bad and reward the good. Heaven does not speak, nor does it hear what men say; divination is absurd—how can the shell of a dead tortoise or the stalks of a withered weed elicit a response from Heaven! "Some people think that Heaven produces grain for the purpose of feeding mankind, and silk and hemp to clothe them. That would make Heaven man's farmer or mulberry-girl!" The philosopher is fond of pricking man's self-importance. To this vast frame of nature we are no more than insects crawling on a human body. The struggle for existence is proof that there is no wise and good purpose in creation. "If Heaven had produced its creatures on purpose, it ought to have taught them to love one another, and not to prey upon and destroy one another"—precisely the argument of Epicurus.

The vital spirit, or soul, is a particle of the cosmic principle of warmth and light; it is born with the body, grows and decays with it, and at death returns to its source. It is an individual soul endowed with intelligence and activity only through its union with the body. There is no consciousness before birth and none after death. If souls were immortal, they would give some sign of their existence. He combats the notion that the dead become ghosts and can harm men. Ghosts are not the spirits of the dead, they are the creatures of morbid fancy. "When sick people are haunted by fears, ghosts appear; their fears set their imaginations to work, and their eyes have visions." By dispelling these beliefs, he, like Lucretius, would deliver men from the fears to which they are in bondage.

Sacrifices are useless; there are no personal beings such as people imagine to enjoy them, nor can the spirits do anything for man or against him. At most, offerings are symbolical acts expressing the gratitude and piety of the offerer; but no evil consequence can follow from omitting them. Exorcism is equally unprofitable; the spirits cannot harm man; and if they could, they certainly would not let themselves be driven away, but would resent the attempt and would make it the worse for the exorcist.

In his ethics Wang Ch'ung does not depart so widely from the current doctrine. On the much-debated question of the native goodness of man he holds that some are good and some bad, just as some are intelligent and some stupid. Good fortune is not the reward of virtue, nor misfortune the punishment of vice; both depend on fate. "Profound philosophy does not procure riches, and the highest accomplishments do not get a man into office."

Not the least striking pages in these essays are those in which the author roundly denies that the former times, whose praises everybody sang, were better than the present. This superstition is of a piece with the notion that in antiquity people were all tall and strong, good-looking and long-lived, while nowadays they are little and ugly, feeble and short-lived. Human nature has been the same in all ages; there were unprincipled characters in the past and there are to-day men of the keenest sense of honour. Wang Ch'ung has no reverence for his predecessors because of their antiquity. He has an essay on Taoist untruths, and is particularly hard on the political theories of Han-feï; but he freely criticises Confucius and Mencius, whose authority their followers did not dare to question, pointing out obscurities and contradictions in their teachings.

In the following centuries Confucian orthodoxy prevailed, and became as stagnant as undisputed orthodoxies are wont to be. The great expansion of Buddhism falls in this period, and what thinking was done in China for a thousand years was chiefly done in Buddhist monasteries, and on metaphysical and theological questions with which Confucianism had never concerned itself. In the eleventh and twelfth centuries of our era, however, in the brilliant renaissance of all branches of literature, new life was breathed into the dry bones of philosophy. Buddhism had been reduced to low estate by the great persecution under the emperor Wu Tsung (in the middle of the ninth century) and by a succession of repressive measures under later rulers; it was, moreover, intellectually in decadence. Taoism had long since degenerated into magical quackery. The field was clear for a revival of Confucianism. The revival could, however, not be a mere repristination of the teachings of Confucius and Mencius. Taoism and Buddhism had raised metaphysical problems which never entered into the mind of those worthies, but which, when once they were raised, could not be ignored.

The founder of the Neoconfucianism of the Sung dynasty, or, as it called itself, Sing-li, Philosophy of Nature, was Chou Tun-i (1017–1073 A. D.). His system is based on the Yih-king, whose occult meaning he was, according to Chu Hi, the first to fathom. From our point of view his significance lies in the fact that he endeavoured to transcend the dualism of Chinese cosmic philosophy with its two forces, Yin and Yang, whose reciprocal operation explained the universe and all its phenomena, by positing a "Great Ultimate," or first principle, from which both proceed—a species of monism. The Ultimate in motion generates the Yang, or active principle, at rest, the Yin, or passive principle, and this alternation repeats itself eternally, motion tending to rest and rest passing over again into motion, "each is the cause of the other." Yang and Yin coming together generate the five elements and the five corresponding meteorological phenomena, and the four seasons begin their rotation. The male and female principles are evolved, and generate all things. Man occupies the highest place in nature, being of a more spiritual constitution. By contact with the world, the five cardinal virtues are called into action; good and evil are discriminated; different types of conduct emerge. The virtuous man governs himself by moderation, straightforwardness, humanity, and righteousness, and thus realises the idea of manhood. Cultivating his character, the virtuous man is happy, while the common man, living in conflict with it, is unhappy.

The greatest name in the Confucian revival is Chu Hi

(1130–1200 A. D.). His recension of the classical texts and his interpretation of them in his commentaries became authoritative, and his manuals of domestic rites and of morals and manners, chiefly based on the Li-ki, have done more, perhaps, than any other books to educate the Chinese people in correct Confucian conduct and ceremonial. In his philosophy he called himself a disciple of Chou Tun-i, but he departed from the teaching of that thinker in some important particulars. Chu Hi finds in the universe two principles, a primal matter (K'i) and an incorporeal immanent intelligence which he identifies with the Ultimate of Chou-tszĕ. Both are eternal, so that it cannot be said that intelligence is prior in time, but only that it is logically prior, as in rank it is superior. The Ultimate is not a being existing independently before heaven and earth; it is only a comprehensive name for the rational principle in heaven and earth and all things. In the terms of Western philosophy, matter and form are correlative; there is no pure form without matter, as there is no matter without form. Chu Hi's relation to Chou-tszĕ is therefore somewhat like that of the Stoics to Aristotle, as, indeed, the Sing-li philosophy has many other resemblances to Stoic physics. The Yang and the Yin, active and passive, warm and cold, light and dark, are modes of matter, whence proceed the five elements and all sensible objects. Humanity, righteousness, moral ideals, and wisdom are qualities of the rational principle.

Western critics often call this philosophy materialistic; but inasmuch as Chu Hi's eternal matter is informed and directed by an immanent intelligence, it is evident that Neoconfucianism is a materialism only in the sense in which Stoicism may be called a cosmological materialism. Indeed, the name is in one sense less properly applicable to it than to Stoicism, since for Chu Hi the immanent intelligence is incorporeal. With atomistic mechanical materialism such as Epicureanism and the Indian system of the Carvakas it has no affinity, and as little with the modern materialistic monism which makes mind a function of matter. In fact, like Stoicism, it might with quite as much propriety be called pantheism.

It has been remarked that Confucius, in speaking of God, avoids anthropomorphic expressions, and hardly ever uses even the title Shang-ti. Chu Hi explicitly rejects the notion of a Heavenly Emperor, with ministers on either hand like an earthly monarch; and it is obvious that his philosophy has no place for a sovereign of the universe ruling it from without. Concerning death Confucius preserved an agnostic reticence—when you do not know about life, how can you know about death? Chu Hi, like the sensualist Yang Chu and the materialist Wang Ch'ung, though from different premises, denies a conscious existence after death.

It is not strange that, on the ground of these negations, Neoconfucianism has been declared essentially irreligious by those to whom belief in a personal God and the immortality of the soul are the essence of religion. There is no question, however, that it has been the religion of multitudes of scholars in China, and its introduction into Japan in the seventeenth century greatly quickened the religious interest of thinking men. Its conception of the "infinite and eternal Power which is not ourselves, and yet constitutes the very essence of our being," has been thus defined: "It is not God—that is, an individual like a man; it is not material, it is not dynamic, it is not like our passions, nor like our knowledge, nor like our spirit or mind or soul; it cannot be described in terms of cause and effect; it preceded even the negative and positive principles by whose interaction the universe has been formed. Formless, from it has come all form; powerless, from it has come all power; it remains through all change changeless, and yet is norm and governor of it all. This supreme, which we cannot yet call object, nameless and adjectiveless, may yet be best defined by that which stirs in the soul of man as righteousness." [1]

[1] G. W. Knox, Development of Religion in Japan, pp. 176 f.

CHAPTER III

CHINA

TAOISM

Lao-tse and the Tao-teh-king—Metaphysics—Ethics—Politics—Lieh-tzsĕ and Chuang-tzsĕ—Relativity—Mysticism—Practical Taoism—Alchemy—Taoist Monasteries and Temples—Deities—Rewards and Punishments—Morals.

THE only independent system of native Chinese philosophy which ever seriously disputed the supremacy of Confucianism is Taoism. The founder of this system was Lao-tse, an older contemporary of Confucius,[1] of whom almost nothing credible is related except that he filled the post of librarian, or keeper of the archives, at the court of Chou.

An anecdote narrated by the historian Szĕ-ma Ts'ien relates that Confucius, on his visit to the court of Chou at Loh-yang, tried to get some information about ancient usages from the aged keeper of the archives, and got instead a pointed rebuke of his antiquarian curiosity about men whose bones had long since mouldered to dust, of his lofty airs, his extravagant aims, and his multifarious activities. The interview made such an impression on Confucius that he compared Lao-tse to the dragon, whose mysterious flight through the sky on wind and cloud baffles comprehension. The story, which evidently comes from a Taoist source, is historically worthless; but it expresses well enough the bewildering effect of the teachings of Lao-tse on the Confucian mind. "The adherents of Lao-tse reject the school of K'ung-tse (Confucius), and the adherents of K'ung-tse

[1] The date of his birth is given as 604 B. C.

48

reject Lao-tse. At variance in fundamental principles, they cannot agree."

To Lao-tse is attributed the Tao-teh-king, which holds the place of authority among the Taoist books. The legend of its origin is that as Lao-tse was abandoning the sinking state of Chou, the warden of the frontier pass persuaded him before his departure to commit his principles to writing. This he did in a compass of little more than five thousand words, and, leaving the book with the keeper, wandered on and disappeared from mortal ken. Some critics have not only rejected this story, but have denied that the Tao-teh-king is the work of Lao-tse at all, though it may contain some sayings of his preserved by oral tradition. More conservative scholars regard the book as substantially embodying the teachings of Lao-tse, perhaps set down by a disciple rather than by the master himself, and not without interpolations by later hands.[1]

The Tao-teh-king consists of two parts, entitled respectively Tao and Teh, and has been divided by commentators into eighty-one short chapters. The first part is predominatingly metaphysical, the second ethical and political; but no logical plan is followed. The book is very obscure, in consequence partly of extreme conciseness, but still more because the author is struggling to express ideas for which the language provided no terms—ideas, moreover, of a kind for which words are at best an inadequate vehicle.

The fundamental problem of interpretation confronts the translator in the very title of the book. *Tao* is literally 'way'; then, like corresponding words in many languages, 'course, method, order, norm.' In the Confucian literature the word is used of "the way of Heaven," especially in its dealing with men, the moral order of the world, which is manifest also in the physical order. It is used also of the right way of human life, the way which Heaven approves, the path of reason, of principle, of truth. Finally

[1] See Grube, Geschichte der chinesischen Litteratur, 1902, pp. 141 *ff.*

it denotes the rational and moral principle by which conduct is guided.

The Taoist writers sometimes employ the word in similar senses; for example: "The way of Heaven is to diminish superabundance and to supplement deficiency. Not so the way of man; he takes from those who have not enough to add to his own superabundance"; but in general *Tao* has in this school a different and distinctive meaning. It is not a descriptive or circumscriptive name, but a symbol for the nameless. "The Tao (way) that can be trodden is not the enduring and unchanging Tao. The name (Tao) that is named is not the enduring and unchanging name." The nearest approach to a definition of what it stands for is in the twenty-fifth chapter of the Tao-teh-king:

> "There was a Something, undifferentiated and yet perfect, before heaven and earth came into being. So still, so incorporeal! It alone abides and changes not. It pervades all, but is not endangered. It may be regarded as the mother of all things. I know not its name; if I must designate it, I call it Tao. Striving to give it a name, I call it great; great, I call it transcending; transcending, I call it far off; far off, I call it returning. . . . Man takes his norm from earth; earth from heaven; heaven from Tao; the Tao from itself."

Chinese thought had hitherto taken the world as it found it, without asking how it came to be. In Lao-tse a speculative thinker appeared who tried to penetrate to the ultimate reality behind the world of appearance, the one beneath the many, the changeless being from which all becoming proceeds. Before the Most High Lord (Shang-ti),[1] is a first principle (the 'αρχή of the Greek philosophers), which in its essential being is unknowable. As source of all being, *ratio essendi*, it is itself beyond being: "All existences in the universe sprang from Being (Tao, as active); Being itself sprang from Non-Being (Tao, as absolute)." It produces and nourishes all things, "by its outflowing operation," and to it, as to their origin, all things, when

---

[1] Tao-teh-king, 6, 3—the only place in the book where this name of God occurs. *Cf.* Chuang-tszĕ, VI, 1, 6, 7.

they have run their course, return. It is the end as well as the beginning of all existences. "We look at it and do not see it, and we name it 'the Equable'; we listen to it and do not hear it, and we name it 'the Inaudible'; we try to grasp it and do not get hold of it, and we name it 'the Subtle.' With these three qualities it cannot be made the subject of any descriptions;[1] and hence we blend them together and obtain the One."

Though the Absolute in itself is unknowable, its operations in the phenomenal world are within men's knowledge. Intelligent observation discovers in these operations a constant characteristic, a way, or method, of nature, in which we may discern to the character of the Being from whom nature and all its operations proceed. It is this which makes *Tao* the most appropriate word for the unnamable.

The quality which most impressed Lao-tse in the orderly operations of nature was that they are accomplished without effort or purpose. The Tao does everything without doing anything. It is the way of Heaven not to strive, yet it overcomes. It produces and sustains all, yet claims nothing to itself. Heaven and Earth endure because they do not live of, or for, themselves. Equally little are they prompted by benevolence: "they treat all things like grass-dogs."[2] This method of the universe is the norm for man. He should not merely take example from it and pattern his conduct after it: he should make it the inner law of his life, from which conduct spontaneously flows. Then he not only knows the Tao, but has it; the cosmic principle is in him ethical principle; his life is nature. This is the foundation of Taoist ethics and politics, which form the subject of the second part (Teh, 'Virtue') of the Tao-teh-king.

The corner-stone is the doctrine of "not doing," inaction (*Wu-wei*). The common man thinks that for his own im-

---

[1] The qualifications are pure negations.
[2] These puppets were thrown away after the sacrifice. Chuang-tszĕ, XIV, 2, 7, 4.

provement or the bettering of the world he must always be doing. He reflects, plans, toils, strives, defeats himself, and knows not why. The wise man takes the opposite course: he will have no desires or ambitions, no aims, no purposeful and energetic activities; then everything will go right of itself. When man, with his conceit of wisdom and his selfish will, ceases to interfere with the order of the world and impede it, he will find that it goes on perfectly without him. The "practical" reformer, with his schemes for saving society, was therefore the most impractical of men; Confucius would have seemed to Lao-tse a fussy meddler in the affairs of the universe, while Lao-tse would have been, in the eyes of Confucius, a paradoxical dreamer.

The ethics of such a system are necessarily quietistic. The Taoist cultivates inaction; he is silent even about the Tao; he teaches without words; he renounces learning and wisdom; he has an air of indecision and irresoluteness, a vacant and stupid look. Gentleness marks his dealings under all circumstances; it is one of the three jewels of character, and overcomes where violence fails. He has learned that weakness is strength and strength weakness. "There is nothing in the world more soft and weak than water, yet for attacking things that are firm and strong nothing surpasses it."

The wise man humbles himself and is exalted, while the aspiring man asserts himself but is not honoured. "There is no guilt greater than to sanction ambition; no calamity greater than to be discontented with one's lot; no fault greater than the desire for gain. The sufficiency of contentment is an enduring and unchanging sufficiency."

The third jewel, with gentleness and humility, is frugality; and as by the way of opposites true courage springs from gentleness and humility leads to honour, so the counterpart of frugality is liberality. "The wise man does not accumulate. The more he expends for others, the more does he possess of his own; the more he gives to others, the more does he have himself."

As gentleness overcomes force, and weakness strength, so evil is overcome by good: "To those who are good I am good; and to those who are not good I am also good, and thus all get to be good. To those who are sincere I am sincere; and to those who are not sincere I am also sincere, and thus all get to be sincere." [1] "To recompense injury with kindness" is the way of the Tao. [2] This principle, which rises as high above the Confucian "reciprocity" [3] as Matt. 5, 44–48 does above the "Golden Rule," is not an *obiter dictum* of Lao-tse, but is the logical consequence of his fundamental axioms.

Benevolence and righteousness and filial piety, which are for the Confucian school the highest ethical notions, represent in the eyes of Lao-tse the decay of morals. "When the Great Method (Tao) was abandoned, benevolence and righteousness came in; wisdom and shrewdness arose, and there ensued great hypocrisy. When harmony no longer prevailed throughout the six kinships, filial sons became known; when states and clans fell into disorder, loyal ministers appeared." The virtues owe their existence, under the law of contrariety, to the prevalence of the opposite vices; in a perfect state of nature there would be neither. Virtue, therefore, is the result of a fall. "If we would renounce our sageness and discard our wisdom, it would be better for the people a hundredfold. If we could renounce our benevolence and discard our righteousness, the people would again become filial and kindly. If we could renounce our artful contrivances and discard our scheming for gain, there would be no thieves and robbers."

The following are sentences selected from the indisputably genuine remains of Lao-tse, to be found scattered here and there in early Chinese literature: [4]

All the world knows that the goodness of doing good is not real goodness.

[1] Tao-teh-king, 49, 2. [2] *Ibid.*, 63. [3] See above, p. 36.
[4] Giles, Chuang Tzŭ, Mystic, Moralist, and Social Reformer, Introduction, pp. vii *ff.*

When merit has been achieved, do not take it to yourself. On the other hand, if you do not take it to yourself, it shall never be taken from you.

By many words wit is exhausted. It is better to preserve a mean.

Keep behind, and you shall be put in front. Keep out, and you shall be kept in.

What the world reverences may not be treated with irreverence.

Good words shall gain you honor in the market-place. Good deeds shall gain you friends among men.

He who, conscious of being strong, is content to be weak, he shall be a cynosure of men.

The Empire is a divine trust, and may not be ruled. He who rules, ruins. He who holds by force, loses.

Mighty is he who conquers himself.

He who is content has enough.

The wise man's freedom from grievance is because he will not regard grievances as such.

To the quietist ethics of Taoism corresponds a political nihilism. In the primitive state of nature "the people did not know that there were any rulers; in the next age they loved them and praised them; in the next they feared them; in the next they despised them." The chief evil of the present times is overgovernment. The state meddles with everything; it multiples laws; it cultivates arts and industries; it reduces the people to starvation by taxes. The best government is that which governs least; in a perfect state the operation of the political order would be unobserved, like the course of nature itself.

"There is no calamity greater than lightly engaging in war," not alone because of the loss of life and the devastation of the land, but because in its violence the jewel of gentleness is lost. Capital punishment is a failure because the people do not fear death as they are supposed to do, and because it is not possible always to seize the wrong-doer. Moreover, to put a man to death is to presumptuously usurp the place of the One who presides over the infliction of death. Other maxims of government, though no less logical on Taoist premises, have a more paradoxical ring: "The difficulty in governing a people arises from their having too much knowledge. He who tries to govern a state by his wisdom is a scourge to it; while he who does not do so is a blessing." "The truly wise man, in the exercise of government, empties the people's minds, fills their bellies, weakens their wills, strengthens their bones. He constantly tries to keep them without knowledge and without desire; and where there are those who have knowledge, to keep them from presuming to act on it. Where there is abstinence from action, good order is universal." Popular education, on which Mencius put such great hopes, was in Lao-tse's eyes the greatest mistake a state could make, for it sophisticates men, and leads them farther and farther from the state of nature in a return to which is the only salvation of the state and the individual.

Of religion in the common acceptation of the word Lao-tse says nothing. Forms of worship, to the correctness of which Confucius attached so much importance, in so far as they were an effort to influence the course of nature in man's favour, were, upon Taoist principles, like the efforts of the practical statesman and reformer, vain and impertinent; they arose from ignorance of what nature is and how it works. Not to bring the universe, by activities of any kind, into harmony with man's desires, but by pure passivity to be in harmony with the universe, is the way to be blessed.

Heaven is for Lao-tse no personal God, not even a personification of the moral order of the world; it is a part of nature and takes its laws from the Tao. Shang-ti is mentioned only to say that the Tao is more ancient than he. The spirits, to which religion attributed specific operations of nature, are ignored altogether. The spirits of the dead have power to harm men; but the way to keep them from exercising this power is not to propitiate them by offerings, but to govern the state according to the Tao; then they will not manifest their spiritual energy in any way.

Yet though, from the point of view of the established religion primitive Taoism was pure irreligion, it was itself a religion in a higher sense—a way by which man might attain perfect blessedness. When the universal law is the law of his being, he is one with the universe; having emptied himself, he is filled with the fulness of the transcendent Tao. There is a glow of mystic emotion in the contemplation of the Tao which shows that in his metaphysics Laotse found the eternal satisfactions of religion.

It is obvious that such philosophy made no appeal to the masses of men; its adherents were either speculative thinkers of mystical tendency or contemplative recluses such as existed in China before as well as after Lao-tse. It was not until much later, and after great changes, that Taoism became a popular religion.[1]

The authors who contributed most to the dissemination of Taoist principles were Lieh-tszĕ, who flourished probably in the second half of the fifth century B. C., and Chuang-tszĕ, a century later. The former is the more philosophical thinker, and speculates on the nature of the ultimate principle and on the evolution of the cosmos; he also discusses for the first time the problem of the infinite and the finite. An interesting part of his work is the refutation of Yang Chu, the sensualist.

Chuang-tszĕ, a contemporary of Mencius, is one of the most brilliant writers that China has produced and one of the most fertile, if not one of the most original minds. In his second chapter he develops the doctrine of the identity of subject and object in the unity of the Tao: "When subjective and objective are both without their correlates, that is the very axis of Tao. And when that axis passes through the centre at which all infinities converge, positive and negative alike blend into an infinite One." In a note on the philosophy of Chuang-tszĕ prefixed to Giles's translation, Mr. Aubrey Moore remarks on the affinity of this chapter with the teachings of Heracleitus, whose One is also the unity in which all opposites are resolved. But, unlike Heracleitus, Chuang-tszĕ develops the mystical side of the doctrine. "The universe and I came into being together; and I, and

[1] See below, pp. 61 *ff*.

all things therein, are One." "The revolutions of ten thousand years leave his [the sage's] unity unscathed. The universe itself may pass away, but he will flourish still." Man, in his empirical existence, is an emanation of the divine; the way of return to his origin is the overcoming of selfhood. "He who knows what God [Heaven] is, and who knows what man is, has attained. Knowing what God is, he knows that he himself proceeded therefrom." "The pure men of old did not know what it was to love life or to hate death. . . . They did not forget whence it was that they had sprung, neither did they seek to hasten to return thither." They were merely channels through which the Tao flowed. "They acted without calculation, not seeking to secure results. They laid no plans. Therefore, failing, they had no cause for regret; succeeding, no cause for congratulation." They were absolutely free; in harmony with all creation. "What they cared for could be reduced to One, and what they did not care for to One also. That which was One was One, and that which was not One was likewise One. In that which was One they were of God; in that which was not One they were of Man. And so between the human and the divine no conflict ensued." "A man looks upon God as upon his father, and loves him in like measure. Shall he then not love that which is greater than God (*i. e.*, the Tao)?"

As in most mystical systems, the secret of the Tao could not be communicated by teaching even to one who had the qualifications of a sage. But there were methods through which, stage by stage, the goal might be reached. An adept describes these thus:

"I imparted as though withholding; and in three days, for him, this sublunary state had ceased to exist, with all its paltry distinctions of sovereign and subject, high and low, good and bad. When he had attained to this, I withheld again; and in seven days more, for him the external world had ceased to be. And so again for another nine days, when he became unconscious of his own existence. He became first etherealised, next possessed of perfect wisdom, then without past or present, and finally able to enter there where life and death are no more —where killing does not take away life, nor does prolongation of life add to the duration of existence.[1] In that state he is ever in accord with the exigencies of his environment."[2]

One or two other characteristic quotations follow:

"How do I know that love of life is not a delusion after all? How do I know but that he who dreads to die is as a ch.ld who has lost his way and cannot find his home? . . . Those who dream of the banquet, wake to lamentation and sorrow. Those who dream of lamentation and sorrow wake to join the hunt. While they dream, they do not know that they dream. Some will even interpret the very dream they are dreaming; and only when they awake do they know that it was a dream. By and by comes the Great Awakening, and then we find out that this life is really a great dream. Fools think they are awake now, and flatter themselves they know if they are really princes or peasants. Confucius and you are both dreams; and I who say you are dreams,— I am but a dream myself. This is a paradox. To-morrow a sage may arise to explain it, but that to-morrow will not be until ten thousand generations have gone by."

The same idea recurs at the end of the chapter:

Once upon a time, I, Chuang Tzŭ, dreamt I was a butterfly, fluttering hither and thither, to all intents and purposes a butterfly. I was conscious only of following my fancies as a butterfly, and was unconscious of my individuality as a man. Suddenly, I awaked, and there I lay, myself again. Now I do not know whether I was then a man dreaming I was a butterfly, or whether I am now a butterfly dreaming I am a man. Between a man and a butterfly there is necessarily a barrier. The transition is called Metempsychosis.

The Taoism of Lao-tse and Chuang-tszĕ was a speculative mysticism. Its metaphysics were incomprehensible to the common mind, and its mysticism alien to the common experience. It therefore speedily succumbed to the degeneration which is the historical fate of mysticism when it has cast its pearls before swine. Its transcendental teachings

[1] In Tao life and death are one.
[2] The resemblance to Indian mysticism is obvious. See, e. g., Warren, Buddhism in Translations, p. 109.

found as little interest as intelligence; but the supernal bliss of the mystical attainment was converted by the crass imagination of the multitude into very mundane realities—a misinterpretation for which the hyperboles and paradoxes of the Taoists opened the door. If they spoke of an eternal life over which death had no power, that was taken to mean that they had discovered the secret of immortality. If they said that he who had attained the Tao was superior to nature, that must mean that he possessed supernatural powers. The hermits who in their mountain solitudes cultivated the method of kenosis—practised doing nothing, saying nothing, thinking nothing—until they attained the perfect vacuity in which was the pleroma of the Tao, were believed to possess such powers. But there were other ways of working wonders more comprehensible to the mass of men; plants of such unmixed spiritual essence that an elixir of life could be concocted from them, minerals of such potent virtue that by them base metals were transmuted into gold. The adepts, who possessed the secrets of longevity and riches, were believed to be able to use their attainments for the profit of others, and their services were naturally in great demand among a people which has always counted long life, wealth, and numerous offspring the three chief goods of human existence.

Fables of the ancients were current in the fourth century of islands somewhere in the Gulf of Chih-li, whose immortal inhabitants dwelt in palaces of gold and silver, and where grew the ambrosial plant which yielded the elixir of life. Many attempts were made to reach these islands, but though they had often been seen by mariners like clouds on the horizon, on nearer approach they sank into the depths of the sea, or violent winds drove the vessels away. The most famous attempt to find these islands was made by the emperor Shi-huang-ti (221–210 B. C.), who sent on the expedition hundreds of young men and maidens—the immortals having a natural partiality for youth—under the guidance of a magician. They reported that they had seen the islands, but had been turned back by strong head-winds. A second attempt had no better fortune.

In the following century and later the operations of Chinese alchemists were directed to the production of the philosopher's stone, which had the double property of making gold and prolonging life. The process, which, like the development of the fœtus in the womb, occupied nine months, during which the preparation underwent nine transformations, could be conducted to success only by those who were spiritually fit, and was attended with such difficulties that few who attempted it achieved their end. Those who did, chiefly Taoist recluses, not only attained immortality, but were able to free the soul from the body and ascend to heaven, and again at will resume their bodily form. Charlatans won the patronage of rulers by promising to make for them this potent remedy for mortality, and at least one emperor in the Middle Ages invited his death by too free indulgence in the elixir of life, which is not strange, considering that the active ingredient in it was cinnabar!

At first sight it seems the pure irony of history that Taoism, with its lofty indifference to life and worldly goods, should have devoted itself to these ends as if they were the *summum bonum*. Theosophy has, however, always evinced a strong affinity for magic; and alchemy in the West, throughout its entire history, was intimately associated with pantheistic mystical philosophies.

Under the Ts'in and Western Han dynasties alchemical Taoism flourished rankly; several of the emperors were completely under the influence of its professors, notably the emperor Wu Ti (140–87 B. C.); and men of all classes neglected their business and squandered their substance in the pursuit of the philosopher's stone. In later centuries the system, under royal favour, enjoyed more than one revival, and never became extinct, gradually blending with the mass of superstition and magic which constitute popular Taoism.

The Taoist holy men were originally hermits who in mountain solitudes cultivated nature's method of doing nothing with purpose or effort, thus becoming one with the universal and eternal cosmic order. Preternatural longevity and various transcendental powers were attributed to the adepts of the Tao; for vulgar apprehension such saints were gods (*shen*). Many of them had their cells or caves on certain especially "spiritual" mountains, and it is possible that, as happened with Christian ascetics under similar circumstances, communities of hermits developed into cœnobite societies; but it is more probable that this change was promoted by Buddhist example. Whatever the beginnings may have been, it is certain that the Taoist monasteries and nunneries were modelled closely after the Buddhist pattern. Temples, idols, and, indeed, religious worship of every kind were alien to primitive Taoism; [1] but it borrowed all these from its rival, Buddhism. The imitation is so frank that in place of the triad of images of Buddhas the Taoist temples exhibited the images of the "Three Pure Ones." In modern times Taoist nunneries have almost if not altogether disappeared, and the number of cloistered monks is very small. The head of the Taoist clergy is a pontiff, bearing the high-sounding title T'ien-shi, "Heaven-Master," who resides upon a mountain in the province of Kiang-si, in a palace surrounded by temples and monasteries. The office is hereditary in the family of a certain Chang Tao-ling, who is said to have lived in the first century after Christ. This so-called "Taoist pope" has no great authority; besides his functions as chief exorcist, he nominates the tutelary gods of cities (gods of the walls and moats), usually dead mandarins who have merited well of the community in their lifetime; but his candidates have to be approved by the ministry of worship at Peking and appointed by the emperor to make their worship legitimate.

In the popular religion, as will appear hereafter, the

[1] Taoist gods are first heard of in the fourth century A. D.

priests who officiate in the temples call themselves Taoists, and there are also gods of Taoist origin, or who, at least, have been appropriated by the Taoists. Among these is Lao-tse himself, to whom sacrifices were first ordered by the state in 156 B. C., and about whom myths, matching the stories of Buddha and often imitating them, cluster. The Taoists fable that when Lao-tse disappeared from China he journeyed to India and was reborn there as Buddha —an invention the obvious motive of which is to assert priority for the Chinese religion in the features which in fact it borrowed from Buddhism. With Lao-tse in the group of the Three Pure Ones are associated T'ai-shi, the "Great Original," the personification of a metaphysical principle, and Yü-huang-shang-ti, commonly called by foreigners the "Yellow Emperor," better rendered, "the divine, exalted, supreme ruler." In what is told of this deity a basis of nature-myth may perhaps be discerned; but Buddhist influence is manifest in the story of the young prince, of supernatural birth, who out of boundless compassion distributed all his treasures among the poor, and resigned the throne to withdraw to the mountain of endless light and devote himself wholly to the study of the Tao, till, having become adept in it, he ascended to heaven, whence he rules the world. In the last capacity he is the sectarian equivalent of Shang-ti, the Supreme Emperor of the state religion, a correspondence which appears also in the name T'ien-kung which he bears in southern China. He is the most popular of the Taoist great gods, and is not only worshipped in the temples, but has a place in the humble domestic cult.

There are also the five classes of genii, out of whose uncounted multitude a group of the eight genii are among the most universally venerated figures in the popular pantheon. Among the deities which Taoism has appropriated, the foremost place belongs to the tutelary gods of cities and walled towns, the "fathers of the walls and moats," whose rank corresponds to that of the places over which they preside. They not only protect their inhabitants from foes and natural calamities such as drought and fire, but observe and record their good and evil doings, and report them to the lords of heaven and of hell respectively. In the temples of the city god representations of the ten regions of hell, the prisons in the heart of the earth, are frequently found. Each of these regions has its own prefect and its own tribunal, before which the souls are tried according to the nature of their offences. The punishments also are appropriate to the sin; for example, ecclesiastics who neglect to read the masses for the dead for which they have been paid are sent to a dark room, where, by the feeble light of a poor lamp, they have to read the mass from a book written in a minute and illegible hand. It need hardly be said that these post-mortem retributions are of Buddhist origin.

The worship of the gods of walls and moats is recognised by the state, and the sacrifices are conducted by the prefect of the city and his staff. But the popular religion, with its mixture of Taoist and Buddhist elements, has asserted here its right and interest in the cultus with greater effect than at any other point in the official system.

The highest good of vulgar Taoism is immortality, or at least prodigious longevity. This was the goal of its alchemical aberrations, and it is also the motive in its moral teachings as represented in such popular writings as the Book of Rewards and Punishments and the Book of Secret Blessings.[1] In the former we read, for example: "Lao-tse taught that the bad and good fortune of man are not determined in advance; man brings them on himself by his conduct. The recompense of good and evil follows as the shadow follows the figure. It is for this that there are spirits whose duty it is to search out the faults of men, and who, according to the lightness or gravity of their

---

[1] The "Sage Edict" quotes with approbation the word of Chu Hi: "The teaching of Lao-tse concerns itself alone with the conservation of the vital forces."

offences, reduce the length of their lives by periods of a hundred days. . . . There are three spirits which dwell in the bodies of men. At fixed periods they mount to the palace of heaven and render account of the crimes and faults of men. On the last day of the month the spirit of the hearth does the same. When a man commits a great fault, twelve years are deducted from his life; when he commits a slight fault, a hundred days. There are several hundreds of great and little faults. Those who wish to gain immortality should avoid them in advance." "He who wishes to become an immortal of heaven must do a thousand and three hundred good works. He who wishes to become an immortal of earth must do three hundred good works." This is the specifically Taoist conception of retribution.

The morals inculcated in these popular and widely disseminated manuals are sound and humane: Do not seek your own advantage at the expense of others. Do not give up the public good for private motives. Do not suck other men's brains. Do not conceal the virtue of others. Do not expose the defects of others. Do not reveal private affairs. For substance they are the immemorial precepts of Chinese moralists, expressed in pithy and homely form.

CHAPTER IV

CHINA

THE RELIGION OF THE MASSES

Relation to the Religion of the State—Spirits of the Soil—Holy Mountains—Various Gods—Temples and Images—Festivals—Priests—Domestic Worship—Feng-shui—Divination—Salvationist Sects—Buddhist Influences—Ancestor Worship—Tombs and Burial—Modern Funeral Ceremonies—Demon-lore.

In the official religion of China the worship of the spirits of the soil and grain fills a large place.[1] They rank next below the imperial ancestors in the hierarchy of divine powers, above all the nature gods except Heaven and Earth. The emperor sacrifices to the spirits of the soil and grain who preside over the fertility of the whole empire, the provincial governors to those of their provinces, and so on down through the administrative subdivisions of the state. To the people themselves are left only the offering to the local spirit of the soil and grain at the village shrine, in which a representative of each family is presumed to be present, and the offering of the clan to the spirit of their own fields. This worship doubtless goes back to the time when the ancestors of the Chinese established themselves in the land and settled to till the soil; and the clan and communal sacrifices perpetuate its oldest form, while the offerings of rulers for their states, and of the emperor for the whole country, and of his vassals or officials for the provinces and districts, is a subsequent development and systematisation.

The same thing is true of the mountains, which govern wind and rain, hold down the earth when it is upheaved

---

[1] See above, pp. 8, 10.

by earthquake, and restrain the violence of floods, and of the rivers whose floods have so often been the ruin of vast regions: the local worship of these powers is far older than the state religion, older than the state itself. Nor has the appropriation of this whole sphere by the state and its assertion of an exclusive right, through its officials, to sacrifice to the mountains and rivers of the whole empire and its several provinces ever supplanted or suppressed the ancient local cults. When it is said, therefore, that the religion of the Chinese people consists in part of the worship of the gods of the state religion—a worship not recognised by the state—the facts are not seen in their historical relation. The truth is, rather, that the state has attempted, with incomplete success, to take a large part of the religion of the people out of its hands. To the local spirits of the ground, or the spirit of the earth and the soil, temples or shrines are erected everywhere, especially by the country people. As giver of the fruits of the earth, the spirit of the soil is the god of wealth, and as such is worshipped by shopkeepers and artisans whose gain does not come directly from the earth.

Besides the mountains of each region, some of the great mountains of the systematised state religion are the object of a wide-spread popular worship, in particular T'ai-shan, the Eastern Summit.[1] Prayers are made to this deity in the spring that he will favourably influence the growth of the crops, and thanksgivings in the autumn for his benefits bestowed; he is appealed to to restore the stability of the earth in time of earthquake and to restrain the violence of flood. Dominating the East, it is from him that life arises; in his flanks are lodged all the souls that await their birth, and to T'ai-shan all souls return at death—a popular belief which can be traced back to the early centuries of our era. Inasmuch as all souls issued from him and returned to him, he determined the duration of life. Finally, when the

[1] E. Chavannes, Le T'ai Chan, 1910. See also "Le dieu du sol dans le Chine antique," *ib.*, pp. 437 *ff.*

Buddhist doctrine of retribution after death became part of popular belief, T'ai-shan became the judge of the dead, and the old Elysian Fields in his depths were transformed into seventy-five hells, whose ingeniously varied torments are represented in as many chambers surrounding the court of his temples. With the god of the Eastern Summit is associated the goddess of the rosy clouds of dawn, whose temple to-day is the most splendid of those which crown the top of T'ai-shan, and who has many other temples in northern China, where she holds a place similar to that of Kuan-yin in the south; her attendants are functional deities who preside over maternity and children. To T'ai-shan thousands of pilgrims annually resort, and he, with his satellites, have temples in all the cities of northern China.

Multitudes of gods not acknowledged in the state religion are worshipped among the people. The various trades and callings have their patrons, commonly supposed to have been men who invented the art or first practised the occupation, or such as achieved the highest skill or fame in it. The principle is the same as that which gives such figures as the Father of Husbandry, the First Physician, the God of War, their place in the state religion. There are gods who are specialists in curing different diseases as well as general practitioners of healing. Besides gods who are worshipped in all parts of the empire are others whose cult is more restricted. A temple of no matter what god may acquire fame as a place where the desires of worshippers are signally fulfilled and wonders are wrought; when this happens men will throng to it in quest of like boons. After a time its repute may wane, or be eclipsed by another of which more marvellous things are told, so that the first is little frequented and falls into neglect.

The nature gods of the old Chinese religion had neither temples nor idols. The local genius of the soil was worshipped at an altar or mound of earth reared around the foot of a tree. In the official cultus to-day the gods are represented only by tablets on which their names are inscribed,

and the great sacrifices take place under the open sky. In
the modern popular religion, however, doubtless in imitation of Buddhist example, the gods are represented by images and housed in temples. The idol of the chief deity
of the temple, commonly a seated human figure with distinctive attributes, occupies a wooden shrine or tabernacle
facing the main entrance; other gods, his associates or ministers, have their places near him or in side chapels. Large
idols are of wood or pottery, smaller ones of the same material or of metal. Not only the deities who are believed to
have been men, but the gods of mountains and rivers are
thus imaged. Before the god is a table for offerings, on
which stand permanently lamps, vases for flowers, and a
vessel filled with the ashes in which the lighted sticks of
incense are set up. The temples are built and repaired by
public subscription, and the most liberal contributors become trustees or directors, on whom devolve also the arrangements for the celebration of festivals and extraordinary
services. The officials, who are responsible for the welfare
of their districts and should not neglect any means that may
conduce to it, are expected in their personal capacity to put
their names down for respectable sums; but the government
as such does nothing for the support of the popular temples,
which are indeed, in strict view of the law, illegitimate, and
always liable to be closed by the authorities.

To these temples individuals resort with their private
needs. A couple of incense sticks set burning in the vase
before the image, a prostration, and a simple and direct request for help, are the commonest approach to the god, but
other offerings are brought in greater affairs, or the prayer
may be accompanied by a vow to be fulfilled if the petition
be granted. The vower may pledge himself to offer the
flesh of an animal, most commonly a pig, or to supply oil
for the lamps or objects for the decoration of the temple;
contributions to the celebration of festivals are often promised, also gifts to the poor, and works of public benefit such
as the repairing of roads and bridges.

Every temple has its festival seasons, which bring the worshippers together, often in great numbers, for public services. In the case of the gods which are recognised by the state, these seasons generally follow the calendar of the official cultus; for the others each temple has its own custom. Besides offerings on a larger scale, plays are enacted on a stage within the temple precincts or adjoining them; the smaller shrines content themselves with a puppet show. Processions, in which the images of the gods are carried through the streets of the quarter, also occur at these festivals. Similar ceremonies are performed on divers special occasions, as when a new temple is dedicated or an old one restored, or when some public calamity such as an outbreak of disease is to be stayed. In the last-named case, the images, in which reside the spiritual substance and power of the gods, are believed to dispel the demonic influences that cause sickness. The processions are frequently held at night, when the power of the spirits of darkness is greatest, and a great uproar of gongs and drums and horns and the firing of guns aid in putting the demons to flight.

Such exercises, as well as the ceremonies at festivals, are usually conducted by priests hired for the occasion. These priests (Wu) are frequently mentioned in the old books, and the description of their doings makes it clear that they were successors of the Mongol shamans: they had the power of inducing possession, that is, of causing spirits to enter into them and speak and act through their bodily organs; in this state they not only revealed the efficacious means of making the gods work for men's ends and of thwarting the demons and driving them away, but were able, with supernatural power, to perform the acts thus indicated. The official religion eliminated these "mediums," and the laws prohibit their dealings with "heterodox spirits," but, notwithstanding the law, some of them still practise possession according to the ancient model; such exhibitions are particularly to be seen in processions to drive away the demons of plague.

The priests live among their countrymen and engage in ordinary occupations, to which many of them add as a side branch exorcism, the preparation of amulets, and magical hocus-pocus of various kinds. These arts are handed down in certain families, and the calling is thus hereditary, but the Wu do not in any other sense constitute a sacerdotal class; they are not permanently attached to the temples and have no regular income from them. On their ceremonial robes, which they wear only when engaged in sacred functions, they embroider the sun, moon, and stars, mountains, rivers, and seas, indicating their character as nature priests, and with these the symbol of the dual forces, Yang and Yin, which together make up the Tao, or one universal order. They like to call themselves Tao-shi, "Taoist Scholars," and regard Lao-tse as the patron of their craft; what they have of Taoism, besides the pretentious name, is, however, not the metaphysical mysticism of Lao-tse or Chuang-tszě, but a magical philosophy of nature which is much more indebted to the Yih-king than to the Tao-teh-king. It may be surmised that it was partly the reputation of the later Taoists for magic, including alchemy, which led the Wu priests to assume the title "Taoist Doctors," partly, perhaps, that under that name they might escape the laws against shamans.

The gods of the popular religion are worshipped not only in the temples, but in the homes of the people, where they are represented by pictures on the wall or by small images set on the shelf with the tablets of the ancestors, sometimes enclosed in a shrine. Almost any god may be thus honoured. The favourites are the god of the soil or of the earth, in his quality as the god of wealth, the fire god, the Buddhist goddess of compassion, Kuan-yin, the war god of the Manchu dynasty, Kuan-yü, who by reason of his reputation for uprightness and learning is chosen as a patron by many tradesmen and students. The patron deities of the various callings are also frequently found in shops and houses. Offerings of food and wine are set up before these gods on their calendar days. On great occasions in the family, well-to-do people sometimes call in a so-called Taoist priest to hold a special religious service similar to those in the temples at festivals, and the exercises may be enlivened by a play or puppet show.

The Chinese philosophy of nature, with its two polar forces, Yang and Yin (light and darkness, heat and cold, activity and receptivity), on whose working everything depends, makes the choice of the right time for any undertaking essential to its success. If the favourable conjunction be utilised, nature works with man and brings his enterprise to a happy issue; if otherwise, he goes counter to nature, which thwarts and defeats him. One of the most important functions of the government is the calculation of an almanac by the use of which the auspicious moment may be seized, the disastrous avoided. Individuals, also, before embarking on any undertaking, consult experts in the art of determining lucky and unlucky days. It is no less necessary to know whether a spot is so situated that, for example, a dwelling erected there will enjoy in full measure the beneficent influences of nature or will be exposed to the forces which work ruin. This kind of divination is called Fengshui, literally, "Wind and Water"; we might say, climatic influences, but should have to note that the climate with which it is concerned is not that with which our meteorology deals, but the operation of the dual principles, Yang and Yin, and of spirits of nature and of dead men. Chinese climatology—in the sense just indicated—is an imposing pseudoscience, whose effect on the whole civilisation is incalculable. For a time it declared itself obstinately against railways and telegraph lines, which by disturbing the Fengshui threatened to involve in disaster the regions through which they ran, but the ingenuity of its professors presently discovered—for a consideration—methods of averting such calamities.

Nowhere is this science more necessary than in fixing on a site for a tomb; the repose of the dead, and by consequence the welfare or even the life of their families, depend upon the choice of a favourable location. Great difficulty and corresponding expense are sometimes encountered in finding such a spot; meanwhile the body remains, perhaps for months, unburied. If misfortune overtakes the family, this may be attributed to the bad Feng-shui of the tomb, and experts with high fees called in to find a better place. Not only the natural configuration of the surroundings, hills, watercourses (superficial or subterranean), and the like, affect the "climate," but buildings, especially on conspicuous sites; for which reason Buddhist monasteries and temples in such situations were sometimes spared by the authorities and even rebuilt by them.

In the ordinary concerns of life the outcome of which men desire to foresee they have recourse to a divining apparatus usually found in the temples. A common form consists of two wooden lots, half prolate spheroids divided in the plane of the major axes, which are cast, and an omen taken from the way they lie; or a slip of wood with a number on it is drawn from a bunch, and an oracular sentence bearing the corresponding number taken from its pigeonhole and read. The two methods may of course be combined, the lots being cast to try the oracle.

The briefest sketch of the religion of the Chinese masses would be incomplete without some mention of the salvationist sects. The popular religion which we have been describing, like the official religion, is a religion for this life; the good things sought in it are mundane goods. In the sects of which we have now to speak, on the other hand, the end is the salvation of the soul. In this end, as well as in the ways in which they pursue it, they show that they derive from Buddhism. Buddhism had taught the Chinese to ask the question, What must I do to be saved? Tens of thousands of seekers of salvation entered the order; its adherents among the people were numbered by hundreds of thousands. Apprehensive of the growing power of the church, the government repeatedly broke up the monasteries and sent back the monks and nuns to the secular life. These measures, contrary to their intention, probably contributed not a little to the leavening of the masses with Buddhist ideas. The laws restricted the number of religious establishments and put many obstacles in the way of admission to the order, but they could not keep the laymen from trying to save their own and their neighbours' souls, or from associating themselves for this purpose. Teachers appeared among them, founders of sects, apostles, who gathered companies of believers in many places. Some of these sects spread widely through the empire and had many thousands of members; some maintained themselves for centuries, others flourished for a time and disappeared, merging perhaps in stronger ones or surviving under other names.

All these societies, or churches, were under the ban of the law, and were thus compelled to take refuge in secrecy. As secret societies they were doubly obnoxious to the government, since they might easily become centres of political agitation; in fact, they have not infrequently been so used. On the other hand, severe repressive measures have repeatedly goaded the sects into revolt; some of the most obstinate rebellions in modern Chinese history have been of this character.

While the Buddhist strain in the beliefs and practices of these sects is predominant, elements drawn from Taoism and Confucianism, as well as from the popular religion, are not lacking, and in the T'ai P'ing books there are even phrases picked up, perhaps at second-hand, from Christian sources. An outward sign which connects them all with Buddhism is their abstinence from animal food, whence they speak of the brethren as "vegetarian friends," and in official rescripts are often designated as "vegetarians" and their places of assembly as "vegetarian halls." The five Buddhist commandments for the laity are in general the foundation of their morals, curiously combined, however, with Chinese dualistic philosophy and the Confucian "relations"; and selected Buddhist Sutras constitute the greater part of their religious scriptures. Besides these they have books of their own, which they diligently conceal from the malevolent inquisitiveness of the authorities, and few of which have come under the eyes of European scholars. They meet in private houses, or, when the vigilance of the mandarins is relaxed, in halls.

One of them, the Lung-hua, of which we possess somewhat more detailed knowledge than of others, has nine degrees, from the patriarch of the sect who bears the title K'ong-k'ong, or "Supremely Empty," down to the most recent novice of the "Little Vehicle" degree. The initiations are patterned after the Buddhist (Mahayana) ritual for the ordination of monks. This sect is strongly ritualistic; another, closely related to it in origin, is addicted to the doctrine of Wu-weï, or quietism, in which Buddhist notions of the attainment of Nirvana by contemplation and inner concentration are fused or confused with Taoist conceptions of the sublimity of living without reason or intention. It is not the specific methods of salvation employed by the sects, however, that concern us so much as the fact that in these oppressed churches multitudes of Chinese have found the satisfaction of their religious needs.

The worship of ancestors was, as has been shown above, a large part of the old Chinese religion as we know it from the classical books, and it has lost none of its importance in the modern religion of the people. The spirits of the dead watch over the living to protect and prosper them, and the living cherish and honour their dead. Parental love and filial piety are not dissolved by death; the relations and obligations they involve reach beyond the tomb. The strength of the family bond in China has its most significant expression in the family cult; and, reciprocally, this cult, more than anything else, cements the family and gives it the consciousness of its unity and perpetuity through the passing generations. It is also a most effective means of cultivating the filial piety which is the first principle of Chinese ethics. Inwrought thus into the whole structure of

society and of thought, it has survived, substantially unchanged, the great changes in notions about souls and their
destinies which Buddhism introduced, and presents the
most difficult problem to Christian missions.

The main features of the cult of the ancestors in China,
as in other countries, are of immemorial antiquity. The
existence of the dead can only be imagined as a continua-
tion of their existence among the living; they have the same
needs, they do the same kind of things, they are prompted
by the same motives. The survivors, therefore, provide
habitations for them furnished with articles of use and luxury appropriate to their rank and calling on earth. The
tombs of the rulers in China are on a grander scale than
any except the Egyptian pyramids. The crypt was a vaulted
chamber in the heart of an immense mound of earth, connected with the outside by a gallery or tunnel. In some
periods an avenue leading to the tumulus was lined on
both sides by stone images of men and animals—elephants,
camels, and mythical nondescripts—such as guard the approaches to the mausolea of the Ming emperors north of
Peking and to the tombs of the Manchu dynasty. The treasures hidden in the tombs were a temptation to robbers; and
the emperors not only surrounded them with walls, but
established garrisons, or military colonies, for their protection. The grandees imitated their masters and lavished
fortunes in erecting huge mausolea till the law stepped in to
regulate the dimensions of the tombs according to the rank
of their owners.

In former times objects of great value were deposited in
the burial-chamber, rich silks, works of art, precious stones,
and quantities of gold and silver, besides weapons and armour, musical instruments, vases, mirrors, parasols, fans—
in short, the house of the dead was as completely and lux-
uriously furnished as the palace of the living; it was also
stored with a profusion of food of all sorts. Horses are
known to have been buried in the imperial tombs, and in
the historians are numerous records of the entombment of

men and women with their lord to serve him in the life beyond. Thus in 619 B. C. a hundred and seventy persons, including three high ministers, followed to the grave their master, Mu, ruler of the state of Ts'in. Instances are credibly reported from times so recent as the first century of the Ming dynasty, e. g., in 1398 A. D., and—on more doubtful authority—of an emperor of the Manchu dynasty in 1661. Such records occur only sporadically, however, and give the impression that the burial of the living with the dead was an unusual event rather than a settled custom. It is certain that from an early time wooden puppets in human likeness were deposited in the tomb in place of real men. Confucius condemned even this, on the ground that it might lead to the use of living victims, or, as we should interpret the situation, this reminiscence of the custom might serve to revive it.

No doubt in ancient time the poor also equipped the house of the dead according to the measure of their ability with real things; but as puppets were substituted for men and women, so toy imitations of furniture and utensils, or block-print pictures of them, replaced the objects themselves, and pasteboard covered with tinsel does duty for bars of gold and silver. Another change of custom is significant; the burial-chamber is no longer stored with provisions, but food is set out before or on the tomb; and the bamboo and paper furniture is not deposited in the grave but burned. The assimilation to the offerings made to the powers above is obvious, and involves a shift in the point of view: the things given to the dead are not now, as in the beginning they were, a provision for physical needs, but an offering to the manes.

While the body is carried to the grave in a catafalque, the soul is supposed to go along in a provisional tablet or in a streamer on which the name of the deceased is inscribed. When the interment is over the permanent tablet is brought out, and solemnly "dotted," if possible by a mandarin of rank, completing the inscription. The effect of this ceremony is that the soul takes up its seat in the tablet. It is thus reconducted to the house, where it is given a place on the shelf with the other ancestors in the principal living-room. A table standing before this shelf receives the periodical or occasional offerings of the family. To the ancestors all important happenings and concerns of the family are dutifully announced—for example, a projected journey or the return from one, a business venture, a marriage engagement. Before the tomb also there is a table of brick or stone, on which offerings are made at certain times in the first year after the death, and thereafter annually in the spring.

With the classic funeral rites recognised or prescribed by the state religion people of all degrees, even the lettered classes who most affect to despise everything unclassical, combine Buddhist masses for the dead, which are performed for the most part, not by members of the cloistered brotherhood, but by unordained secular "priests"—whose principal function, indeed, is the reading of these masses; in the case of the sects the service is conducted by some of their members.

For Confucian philosophy the term of a man's life is fixed by the decree of Heaven; popular religion may confer this office on another deity; for example, on T'ai-shan. But the mourning customs, classical as well as popular, bear witness to the persistence of the more primitive belief that death is the work of demons. The lingering demonic influence makes the house in which a death has occurred and the persons who have come in contact with death or are akin to the dead dangerous to others; the funeral rites and the rules of mourning are in great part precautions against demonic infection.

Demons, ghosts, vampires, werwolves, populate China as densely as its human inhabitants, and are the subject of a vast folk-lore, not a little of which has got into writing. They do all sorts of harm, from swallowing up the sun in an eclipse to making a blank of a candidate's mind in an examination, and life is an incessant battle with them; man defends himself by magic and enlists the gods as allies by religion. Mental and nervous disorders are universally attributed to possession by evil spirits, and the only cure is exorcism.

The religion of the Chinese people to-day thus presents in many ways a more primitive aspect than the official religion of the classics. The latter, indeed, bears plain marks of a reform from above in a spirit which we may call Confucian, though it is older than Confucius. The assumption of all the functions of religion by the state and its minute regulation by law is itself sufficient evidence of such a reform in an age which for us lies beyond the historical horizon; and this inference is confirmed by the elimination from the legitimate religion of the empire of many things which unquestionably belonged to the actual religion of the time and have been conserved in the religion of the masses to this day.

CHAPTER V

CHINA

BUDDHISM

Introduction and Spread—Character of the Religion—Two Great
Branches of the Church—Reasons for Its Success—Persecutions
and Restrictions—Charges Against Buddhism—Status under Later
Dynasties—Modern Chinese Buddhism.

THREE foreign religions have in different ages established
themselves in China: Buddhism, Mohammedanism, and
Christianity. The last two have remained essentially
foreign, and have exerted little influence on Chinese thought
or life; but Buddhism has been so fully naturalised that it is
commonly counted one of the three religions of the country,
and it has contributed in large measure to the composite,
or conglomerate, religion of the masses, as well as to the
teaching and practice of various heretical sects.

It is related that the emperor Ming-ti, in the year 61
A. D., in consequence of a dream in which he had seen hovering above the palace a golden image which was interpreted as a statue of Buddha, sent to India for Buddhist
teachers and copies of the Buddhist scriptures. The story
implies some previous knowledge of Buddhism; and we have
other grounds for believing that, through trade with India
and Chinese military expeditions to the westward, the
Chinese had come into contact with Buddhism as early
as the second century B. C., if, indeed, Buddhist missionaries had not already imported their religion into China
itself. Ming-ti's envoys returned after six years, bringing
with them Indian scholars who made the first Chinese
translations of Buddhist books.

During the three following centuries Buddhism made gradual progress in China, but, although temples were built in the chief cities, it was not until 335 A. D. that it was made lawful for subjects to receive the tonsure. In the latter half of the fourth century many large monasteries were erected in northern China—a writer of the sixth century mentions no less than ten in the capital, Loh-yang, and thirty-six more in the neighbourhood—and the native historians report that a large part of the people had embraced the foreign faith. In the beginning of the fifth century a considerable body of Buddhist literature was translated into Chinese by Indian scholars under royal patronage. About the same time Chinese Buddhists began to make pilgrimages to India for the purpose of visiting the sacred places and studying the doctrines of their religion in its home, and brought back their precious collections of books. The most famous of these pilgrims in this period was Fah-hien, who left China in 399 A. D., and returned home by sea after an absence of fourteen years. His descriptions of the countries through which he passed on his way and of India itself are of great interest.

It would be hard to think of a religion with which the Chinese mind and temperament had less affinity than with the doctrine of Buddha. The Indian religion was born of a profound pessimism: to exist was to suffer, and the sufferings of the present life were multiplied by infinity in lives past and lives future with heavens and hells between—the eternal series of rebirth—in the inexorable causal nexus of the deed and its consequence (Karma). The cause of this misery lay in desire—ultimately, in the will to be; the only salvation, in the extinction of desire. To accomplish this, man must sever the ties of kindred and affection, renounce all social and civil obligations, and become a member of the mendicant brotherhood, practising under its simple rule the art of dying to the world. The goal was the endless peace of Nirvana, freed from the illusions of self and soul, from desire and dislike, from the consequences of deeds done, from the wheel of rebirth—a state of which the master declared it profitless to ask whether it was existence or non-existence.

In the centuries between the rise of Buddhism in India and its introduction into China it had undergone a development comparable to that through which Christianity passed in the first five centuries of its history. In both, besides the thinking out of the implications of the original teaching, two factors principally contributed to this development: the construction of doctrine in the concepts of an alien metaphysics, and the influx of popular paganism from the religions of the converted peoples.

Buddha himself put aside metaphysical questions as unprofitable—the one thing which concerned man was his own salvation—but his followers, by the necessity of their own thinking, and in controversy with thinkers of other schools, were constrained to face the problems which the master had declined, and, under the influence of the dominant type of Indian speculation, superimposed upon the primitive plan of salvation a philosophy of the Absolute. The missionary success of Buddhism brought into the church as adherents or as members of the order multitudes whose religious needs primitive Buddhism, without god or worship, did not satisfy; and the void was filled by adoration of the Buddhas and by the introduction, in the guise of Buddhist holy ones, of the popular gods of India or of the regions beyond whither the religion spread. To them temples were erected, images set up, and a sumptuous liturgical worship paid. Not only the religion but the superstitions of the masses found their way into the new faith. The common Indian belief that the contemplative life, at the furthest limit of liberation from the earthly and the individual, results in supernatural powers, very early—if, indeed, not from the beginning—found a place in Buddhism, and opened a back door for various forms of magic.

Controversies over points of discipline and doctrine had divided Buddhists into many schools and sects. The most important of these divisions turned upon the end which the religious man should set before himself. The goal of the older and more conservative school was sainthood, the attainment by the individual of his own salvation. The younger and more progressive school proposed a greater end: not to become an *arhat* (saint) and save himself alone, but to be a *bodhisattva*—one of those who in a succession of existences are perfecting the character by which a man is fitted to be in future a Buddha, a saviour of all living beings.

As the goal which this school set before itself was higher and more remote, so the means by which it was to be attained were more various, and in the consciousness of its superiority it called its doctrine Mahayana, a "Great Vehicle" of salvation, and named the teaching of the conservative party in depreciatory contrast Hinayana, "Little Vehicle." In philosophy, also, the Mahayana school was the more progressive: it was by Mahayanist thinkers that the great coherent system of Buddhist absolutism was developed.

In this development there would seem to be little to make Buddhism more acceptable in China. The existence of Taoism should, indeed, warn us against assuming that either the metaphysical or the mystical strain is wholly lacking in the Chinese temperament; but, as a race, the Chinese are active rather than contemplative, eminently practical in their aims and endeavours, well satisfied with mundane goods, and industriously bent on getting them in satisfying measure. Buddhism not only denied all worth to the objects which the Chinese most highly valued—life, wealth, children—but declared attachment to these things to be the very root of evil; it offered in exchange for them deliverance from a world-misery which the Chinese, in the innocence of their souls, were quite unaware of—a remote and intangible good in place of the concrete and actual. It was, in short, a radical "Umwertung der Werte." Its metaphysics were incomprehensible to the ordinary mind; the idle, unsocial, and uncivil life of its monks conflicted with the fundamental principles of Chinese morals.

Yet, as we have seen, Buddhism spread rapidly in China, and took root so deeply that no violence of persecution was afterward able to eradicate it. The cause of this success lay in part in its teachings concerning what is after this life. The Chinese believed that the spirits of the dead continued to exist; that the spirits of ancestors, sages, and rulers watched over later generations, receiving their offerings and bestowing prosperity upon them; but beyond this their thought had not gone. The Buddhist teachers described with much detail the state of the departed spirits; the blessedness of the good in heaven and the torments of the bad in hell. The Chinese had not conceived of any difference in the lot of the dead except between those whose filial descendants provided abundantly for their wants and the neglected ghosts; but the doctrine of posthumous retribution, once presented, was convincing to a people who had well-developed ideas of retributive justice in the earthly sphere. The missionaries also knew not only how men could put themselves in the way of salvation, but how they could minister to the welfare of the departed, and to the present day Buddhist masses for the dead are an ordinary part of Chinese funerals even in circles which have otherwise no Buddhist proclivities.

The rites of the state religion, as we have seen,[1] were performed by the rulers and officials for the benefit of the people of the empire or its divisions; to the people themselves was left only a simple domestic sacrifice and the offerings to the family ancestors. It is hardly conceivable that the actual religion of the masses was ever limited to the acts of worship thus legally recognised. The popular religion of modern China doubtless preserves much that has come down from remote antiquity. It is safe to affirm, however, that the ancient popular religion was of a simple form, and directed, like the religion of the state, to practical earthly ends. The powers to which it was addressed were shapeless and colourless spirits, defined only by the

[1] See above, pp. 7 f.

functions they fulfilled. Buddhism, on the other hand, had a rich cultus; images of Buddhas and Bodhisattvas, of genii and protecting demons, wrought in precious materials with an art hitherto unknown, filled its imposing temples; priests in splendid vestments murmured their holy texts amid clouds of incense and prostrated themselves before the images. The goodness and mercy of these gods—for such they were to common apprehension—were the subjects of innumerable narratives. Buddhism thus appealed to the emotional and æsthetic sides of man's religious nature, to which the native religion offered little, and it awakened the soul to a need which the old religion could not satisfy. Here were powers who not merely worked nature for men, but loved men; gods to whom man could come not only with his wants, but with his hopes and fears, his aspirations and his sins. From Buddhism the Chinese first learned a religion of the inner man.

On its side Buddhism, with the power of accommodation which it everywhere displayed, made no attack upon the established religion, and found no difficulty in admitting to its capacious pantheon the native divinities; for Buddhas had come among men to enlighten them and lift them up in many lands under many names. It is no wonder, therefore, that multitudes of all classes embraced Buddhism. Many of the rulers openly cultivated it, and it seemed on the highway to complete success.

This flourishing period was succeeded by vigorous attempts to suppress the foreign religion by force. In the years 444 to 446 A. D. the emperor, T'ai-wu Ti, of the Wei dynasty, who had previously favoured Buddhism, issued a series of edicts proscribing it, ordering that the temples and pagodas should be burned, the images and sacred books destroyed, and the monks put to death, and forbidding subjects of every rank, under the same penalty, to harbour or protect them. The motive for this sudden outburst is said to have been the discovery that Buddhist monks in Ch'ang-an (the present Si-an-fu) were giving aid to a rebellion, but the text of the edicts, which include in the same condemnation native soothsayers and magicians, indicate that, whatever may have been the immediate occasion, the persecution, like many that followed, was animated by hostility to heterodoxy as such. The crisis was brief, and under the favour of the next king the temples and monasteries were rebuilt.

In the following centuries the Chinese histories record many memorials of ministers and other officials protesting against the alien religion as incompatible with genuine Chinese principles of society and government and numerous edicts of rulers intended to restrict its spread; but it is clear that these measures were not very thoroughly or persistently enforced. In 844 A. D., however, the emperor Wu Tsung inflicted on Buddhism a blow from which it never fully recovered. An investigation made by the board of sacrifices early in that year showed that there were then within the empire more than 4,600 Buddhist monasteries and 40,000 or more minor establishments. By imperial decrees the buildings, with a few specified exceptions, were to be destroyed, the bronze images, bells, and metal plates coined into money, the iron statues recast into agricultural implements, those of gold and silver melted and turned in to the auditors of the treasury. The extensive lands of the monasteries were sequestrated by the state; the 260,500 monks and nuns were ordered to return to the secular life; the convent serfs, to the number of 150,000, were similarly registered. These edicts embraced not only the Buddhists but the Nestorian Christians (Ta-ts'in) and the Mu-hu (Magians, Zoroastrians?) to the number of 3,000; the foreigners among these were to be sent back to their native country. A decree of the preceding year (843) had put both the Mo-ni (probably Manichæans) and the Buddhists among the Uigurs under the ban.

The indictment of Buddhism in these various memorials and decrees is substantially the same. It is a foreign religion of which nothing was known in the good old days;

since its introduction, in the time of the Han dynasty, evils and disorders of many kinds have afflicted the empire, and have been at their worst under the rulers who favoured the foreign faith. Its doctrines are heretical; that is, at variance with the teaching of the national religion and ethics as these are embodied in the Confucian literature, and are nonsense besides; the tales it gives out for veritable history are absurd fabrications; it promotes many superstitions, such as the worship of idols and the veneration of relics; it withdraws men and women from useful—and taxable—labours to a life of idleness; by playing on the superstitions of the masses, especially their fears of the hereafter, it persuades them to impoverish themselves to support these lazy drones and to provide means for the building and furnishing of the costly temples and pagodas; ever widening areas of the richest land are withdrawn from taxation by donations to the monasteries; the celibate ecclesiastics breed neither tillers of the soil nor soldiers for the king's armies; and, worst of all, it teaches sons to neglect their parents, neither serving them while living nor ministering to them when dead, and leaving no descendants to perpetuate the ancestral worship—religion, in a word, consists in not caring for anybody but yourself. From the point of view of religion, of morals, or of economics, Buddhism is a pernicious evil which must be extirpated.

Succeeding emperors somewhat mitigated the stringency of Wu Tsung's measures, allowing the rebuilding of the destroyed monasteries, not so much out of favour to Buddhism as from regard to the influence of the buildings on the natural and spiritual climate (Feng-shui); but the confiscated lands and goods were not restored. The legislation of later dynasties imposed onerous restrictions on Buddhism, limiting the number of monasteries, confining the right of ordination to a few of them, requiring a government licence to enter the order, and establishing a registration of ecclesiastical persons. Under one such law, in 955 A. D., 3,336 religious houses were demolished because they could not produce an imperial charter; 2,694 were left standing. The number of registered monks and nuns was returned at 61,200.

Under the Mongol rule of Kublai Khan and his successors (1280–1368), Buddhism was freed from external restraints, and the number of monasteries rapidly increased, while the foreign priests, chiefly from Tibet, who came in the wake of the Mongols, did something to revive Chinese Buddhism from the low estate into which it had sunk in the preceding centuries. The restoration of native supremacy under the Ming dynasty (1368–1644) was accompanied by a national reaction, in which Buddhism had to pay the penalty for Mongol favour. The first of the line, T'ai Tsu, though he had himself been a Buddhist monk, was hardly seated on the throne when he renewed the restrictive laws, and in the following years made them more and more stringent. The same policy was followed by his successors, one of whom decreed that ordinations should only be held once in three years, and that only a limited number of persons in any department or district might receive consecration; another, in the fifteenth century, allowed ordination to be administered only once in ten years. Severe penalties were prescribed for violations or evasions of the law. The later Ming emperors treated all heretical sects with great severity; Buddhism and Lamaism were subjected with the rest to a persecution which in 1566 provoked a formidable rebellion.

The Manchu chiefs who profited by these internal dissensions to make themselves masters of the northern provinces and eventually (in 1644) of the empire were not more favourably disposed toward Buddhism. The statutes of that dynasty, agreeing substantially with the Ming code, made the building or rebuilding of monasteries and the admission of members to the order very difficult. As a result, the number who have actually received the tonsure is comparatively small. The much larger class of so-called Buddhist priests, who, though unconsecrated, constitute a kind of secular clergy, wearing a distinctive dress and performing religious rites, particularly for the benefit of the souls of the dead, live among the people, marry, and possess property, eat meat and fish, and are consequently, from the point of view of the Buddhist discipline, mere laymen. They exert all the greater influence, however, through their intimate association with their neighbours, and to them the amalgamation of Buddhist ideas and practices with the old religion of the Chinese people is largely due.

In its antipathy to the sects, the government has repeatedly taken measures to restrict or reduce the number of this irregular clergy by forbidding them to take pupils, or more than a single pupil, and requiring them to register and obtain certificates from the authorities. More radical edicts were issued in the eighteenth century, by which they were to be compelled either to procure ordination, if the government would grant them leave, and retire to the monasteries, or to abandon their clerical pretensions altogether; but this law was soon relaxed.

In its prosperous times Chinese Buddhism was divided into many sects, representing various Indian schools or native offshoots from them. In the decadence of Buddhism under the Manchu dynasty the distinctions between the schools have been mainly obliterated; regular Buddhism in modern China is the result of a fusion of the various Mahayanist sects, in which the Vinaya and Dhyana elements are dominant; while the secular clergy, if they may be so called, who attend funerals and read sutras for the souls of the dead represent the Pure Land school, with its Western Paradise to be gained by calling on the name of Amitabha, and this doctrine has also, more than any other, influenced the salvationist sects.

To avoid repetition the history and distinctive tenets of various schools of Chinese Buddhism are reserved for discussion in a later chapter on Buddhism in Japan.[1] Here we shall confine ourselves to a brief survey of the present state of Buddhism in China.

[1] See below, pp. 119 f., 122 f., 125 ff.

Mahayana Buddhism is a universal religion in the largest meaning of the name; its aim is the salvation not merely of mankind, but of all sentient beings. The chief agents in this great salvation are the Buddhas; the goal of the Mahayanist is therefore Buddhahood. The monasteries are institutions in which men are in training for this high mission, and at the same time endeavouring to promote the spiritual and temporal welfare of others by pious exercises. The methods employed to attain this end are manifold, and adapted to the varied capacities or predilections of the seekers. The mendicant friar of the early days of Buddhism has, however, disappeared, and the eremite ascetic in his solitary cell or cave is rare. The monks live in their simple fashion from the revenues of the monastery, from pious donations, or from collections made under the direction of the abbot.

Members are received into the order and advanced to the successive degrees of postulant, novice, monk, saint, and Bodhisattva, or Buddha-candidate, by a series of ordinations which were formerly separated by considerable intervals of time, but are now completed within a few days. The earlier steps in the candidate's progress correspond to the old Buddhist rule, and are therefore found in all branches of the church; the last is distinctively Mahayanist. The novices bind themselves to observe the Buddhist decalogue; the monks promise obedience to the discipline of the order as set forth in the Pratimoksha. The Vinaya in Four Chapters, originally the recension of the school of Dharmagupta, is now universally accepted in China, though it is, in fact, little studied. At the final stage, the aspirants vow that they will conform their lives in all respects to the fifty-eight precepts for Bodhisattvas contained in the Sutra called "Brahma's Net." This, as the higher law, is the actual guide of the Chinese monks in the path of Buddhahood. No Sanskrit text of this sutra is known, and no reference to it has been discovered in China before the eighth century.

The elementary commandments which are the foundation of Buddhist ethics are here interpreted in the broadest sense and extended to the remotest contingencies. Thus, the prohibition of taking life is made not only to include eating flesh, but trading in animals, keeping cats and dogs, borrowing or buying and selling weapons, entering a military camp or even looking at soldiers, or serving as an ambassador, since diplomacy often leads to war. It is as grave a sin to rob a man of his good name as to rob him of his property. And it is one of the greatest sins to be directly or indirectly the occasion to sin to another. To the comprehensive principle, Do no harm to any being, is joined its positive counterpart, Do good to all beings. Not to kill, but to save life; not to hold slaves, but to ransom men from bondage, is the duty of the benevolent man; so far from eating the flesh of animals, he would, like Buddha in the Jatakas, give his own body to feed the wild beasts. Higher still is the obligation to minister to men's spiritual welfare, to instruct them in the truth, to guide them and further them in the way of salvation. There are other means besides propaganda of promoting the good of all sentient beings. In early Buddhism the cultivation of universal benevolence was part of the self-culture of the monk, and methodical exercises were devised to attain this state of mind. Mahayana Buddhism attributes to thought and wish efficacy to realise their objects—mental concentration is a creative force. Fixing the undivided mind on supreme blessedness attains it. To yearn with all one's soul for the salvation of others is the means of bringing them into the way of salvation and helping them on to its goal. The potency of the will to save is not confined to human beings; when the monk sees an animal he should say, "You are a living being; may the saving intelligence awake in you!" To neglect so efficacious a means of doing good is a grave dereliction of duty and a great hindrance to a man's own progress in the religious life.

Every monastery has a hall where at stated times sermons

are preached by the abbot or by the preaching brothers. Being drawn from the Sutras, these discourses are constructively Buddha's own sermons, and all the Buddhas and Buddha-aspirants, saints, and deities in the universe are supposed to assemble reverently to hear the holy word. It is a serious fault for a monk to absent himself from such an august gathering; he ought rather to betake himself eagerly to any place where he hears that preaching is to be held. Preaching and the reading of the sacred texts are more than means of enlightening hearers in the knowledge of the truth; the holy virtue that is in them drives away demons and averts all sorts of calamities, whence the officials, in seasons of drought or plague, command the monks to set the "wheel of the law" revolving. On such occasions special altars are set up, offerings made, and an elaborate ritual is gone through day after day. The recitation of the appropriate sutras—particularly the Sutra of Amitabha, the Buddha who presides over the Western Paradise—has power to deliver the dead from his past and advance his soul to the rank of Bodhisattva, and, as has already been noted, all classes of Chinese cause such masses to be said for their departed kinsmen.

The larger monasteries have, further, their "meditation halls," where in profound silence the brethren may immerse themselves in contemplation, or in the mental vacuity which is the opening of the mind to transcendental wisdom. Some of the brethren devote themselves assiduously to this way of blessedness; certain seasons of the year are appointed when it is commended to all to engage in this sort of retreat. The Buddhist semimonthly confession is still observed,[1] and, in addition, each day begins with an act of penitence at matins. The Sutra of Brahma's Net, in fact, lays great stress on penitence as a means of removing the sins which, unless removed, are an insuperable obstacle to salvation. Penitence consists in a man's fixing his mind on the evil that he has done so as to be

[1] See India, pp. 299 f.

fully conscious of it, at the same time experiencing sorrow and cherishing the hope that it may be wiped away. Here also the efficacy of thought and wish to accomplish their own fulfilment is implied; it is not a god who remits the sin of the penitent, but penitence itself that rids him of it.

Buddhist temples are, properly speaking, halls of worship in the monasteries. They have the same general arrangement in all parts of the empire, though they vary greatly in size and splendour. Fierce-looking genii guard the entrance; the tutelary divinities of the four quarters stand on the corresponding sides of the fore hall; in the sanctuary, facing the entrance, are the images of the Triratna, viz., the Buddha, the Law, and the Order, represented as seated human figures; or of three Buddhas, usually Amitabha, Sakyamuni, and Maitreya, the Buddha of the next age, restorer of the law—a Messianic figure. Many other images of Buddhas, Bodhisattvas, or saints, are distributed about the temple or in side chapels. Kuan-yin, the goddess of mercy, who has changed sex since leaving India as Avalokiteçvara, has a place of honour in almost every temple. In these temples flowers and incense are offered, and sometimes cakes and the like; bloody sacrifices and offerings of flesh involving the taking of life are contrary to the whole spirit of the religion.

Under the favour of the Mongol emperors the Tibetan form of Buddhism which Western scholars distinguish as Lamaism made great progress in China. Kublai Khan took the most powerful of the Tibetan ecclesiastics, the abbot of the La-skya monastery, as his religious guide, and conferred upon him the title of tributary sovereign of Tibet. The reformed Lamaism of the fifteenth century also spread to China, and has maintained itself there under the native Chinese Ming dynasty, some of whose rulers treated it with special favour, and under their Manchu successors, so that both the old red Lamas and their more recent yellow brothers are represented.

CHAPTER VI

JAPAN

THE NATIVE RELIGION, SHINTO

Sources—Character—Gods and Myths—Temples—Priesthood—Ritual
—Festivals—Purifications and Expiations—Morals—Apotropaic
Deities—The Dead—Worship of Ancestors—Domestic Religion—
Revival of Pure Shinto.

THE indigenous religion of Japan is called Shinto, "the way of the (national) gods." The name is Chinese, and was given to the old religion in the sixth century to distinguish it from the new and foreign Butsudo, or "way of the Buddha"; "Kami no michi" is a Japanese purist equivalent of "Shinto," and of later invention.

The historical period of Japan, according to native tradition, opens with the emperor Jimmu Tenno, 660 B. C.;[1] behind that date lies a mythical antiquity, "the age of the gods." To our way of looking at things mythical antiquity lasted much longer, and although in the following ages historical persons and events stand out here and there from a background of legend, authentic history does not begin much before the sixth century A. D. Buddhism came in from Korea about the middle of the sixth century with all the prestige of a high and ancient civilisation, and having this advantage in addition to its intrinsic superiority and the zeal of its missionary monks, it is not strange that it spread rapidly, especially among the upper classes. Its complete triumph was won, however, by an astute compromise; the gods of old Japan were identified with Buddhist saints, or

[1] So the official chronology promulgated in 1872.

declared incarnations of Buddha for the enlightenment of the forefathers. In return the adherents of the old faith had only to recognise the fuller revelation which the missionaries brought. In this way arose in the eighth and ninth centuries what was called the "Twofold Way of the Gods" (Ryobu Shinto), in which Shinto was fused with Buddhism. Buddhist idols and relics found their way into Shinto temples, and in the domestic religion of the people the rites of the two religions were observed without any thought of their diverse origin. For many centuries Shinto existed almost exclusively in this mixed form; only a few temples, like those at Ise, successfully resisted the intrusion of the foreign cult. The combination was, however, a mechanical mixture rather than a fusion, and when the religious reformers of the eighteenth and nineteenth centuries addressed themselves to the restoration of Pure Shinto they had less difficulty in recognising and eliminating the properly Buddhistic elements in the mixture than in clearing their own minds of the preconceptions of Confucian philosophy. Pure Shinto was easier to restore on paper than to revive in practice; the tradition and custom of a thousand years cannot be put out of the world by antiquarian researches, even with the concurrence of a revived national consciousness. To the present day there are among the people few who are exclusive Buddhists or exclusive Shintoists; the greater part seek their welfare by both ways—it is impossible to have too many patrons and helpers among the powers above.

The most important source for knowledge of primitive Shinto is the Yengishiki, which contains a minute description of the traditional ritual as practised in the ninth century A. D., incorporating a body of liturgical texts recited by the priests at the festivals of the court and in other religious ceremonies. These were probably reduced to writing in their present form when the Yengishiki was compiled,[1] but the prayers themselves are indubitably centuries older, having been transmitted from generation to generation in the

[1] It was promulgated in 927 A. D.

priestly families or guilds with little or no change; Chinese influence has not infected them. The Shinto mythology is principally contained in two works: the first book of the Kojiki, or History of Antiquity, collected from the mouths of various narrators and published in 712 A. D., and the first two books of the Nihongi, Japanese Annals, in Chinese, completed in 720; with these may be named the Idzumo Fudoki, an official description of the province drawn up in the eighth century, which includes numerous local myths, especially such as are connected with temples or holy places.

The religion which lies before us in these sources is that of a people upon the plane of primitive civilisation, with many survivals of ruder times, especially in the myths. The further development of civilisation was largely imitative or assimilative. Chinese models of administration, Chinese law, Chinese philosophy and ethics, Chinese art, Chinese literary forms, however accommodated to the national genius, are the dominant factors; and with them belongs Buddhism as the religion of the superior culture. In consequence, the native religion did not keep step with the progress of Japanese civilisation, but survived in a state of arrested development.

The Shinto deities are chiefly gods of nature and natural forces. At the head of the pantheon is the sun goddess; by her side, but of minor importance, stand a moon god and an uncertain star god; otherwise heaven and the heavenly bodies are of no considerable moment in the religion. Gods of storm, rain, and thunder, of the sea, rivers, or waters in general, of the earth and its productive powers, a goddess of food-crops, gods of mountains, trees, a god of fire—in short, the usual constituents of a natural polytheism—have a place in worship as well as in the mythology. Besides these are gods who were once men—rulers, heroes, or men eminent in various arts or pursuits. As has been observed in another connection, what we call the deification of human beings involves, from the point of view of the religions in which it occurs, no translation to another category of being. It is peculiarly easy in Japan because the language employs the

same word, *kami* (literally, "high, exalted," in both physical
and figurative senses), for the "superiors" whom we should
call gods (*cf.* Latin *superi*), and for human superiors, living
or dead. It does not appear, however, that deities of human
origin were as common or as important in primitive Shinto
as in later times, and probably the development of this side
of the religion as well as of ancestor worship, with which it
is closely connected, was stimulated by Chinese influence.
The name *kami* is not restricted to the powers who are habitually beneficent; malignant beings which are universally
feared, such as the fire demon which so often devoured the
flimsy towns, were also *kami*.

The nature-deities are personal gods, to whom not merely
human intelligence, passions, and actions are attributed, but
human forms. The sun goddess was, indeed, the visible orb
in the sky, but at the same time the woman who hid in a
cave or with her maidens wove garments in the hall of the
palace. These gods not only manifest themselves in the
operations of nature, but are present at the shrines where
offerings and prayers are made to them, and one god has
often many shrines. Yet it is evidently neither the orb of
the sun nor the sun goddess in human form who inhabits the
shrine at Ise; it is her *mitama*, men said, a kind of spiritual
presence not unlike the *skekinah* of the Jews, and this is frequently associated with some holy object (*shintai*), for example, the mirror of the sun goddess.

It will be seen from this preliminary outline that the religion of the ancient Japanese was in essentials like that of
peoples on similar planes of culture in all parts of the world.
It is worthy of note that, unlike the religion of China and of
other Mongol peoples, the highest deity is not heaven but
the sun. Other striking differences from the Chinese religion are due to different stages or circumstances of development. The sun goddess is not the personified moral order
of the world, the guardian and vindicator of that order in
the relations of men, like Heaven in China; the Japanese
had not arrived at the conception of such an order. Again

the gods of Shinto do not, as in China, form an organised polytheism with ranks and functions corresponding to the constitution of the empire; in the old Japan there was no such political organisation to serve as a model for a hierarchy of gods, nor has the Japanese mind the same exorbitant fondness for system. On the other hand, Shinto has a luxuriant mythology, while in the state religion of China, whether by original defect or through later expurgation, this element is almost wholly lacking.

The myths collected in the Kojiki and the Nihongi exhibit many variants, in part expressly noted as such in the text, representing divergent traditions of professional reciters or of local priesthoods. Critical examination discloses the more important fact that the common stock itself is the result of a fusion of myths from three distinct regions; namely, the province of Idzumo, where the invaders, coming probably from Korea, first established themselves; the island of Kiushiu, the first seat of the tribes which eventually gained the supremacy over the whole land; and the province of Yamato, where the same tribes later had the centre of their power. In particular, the subjugation of the older colonists in Idzumo by the later comers from Kiushiu is reflected in the myths in the banishment of Susa no wo, and still more plainly in the abdication by his son Ohonamochi in favour of the "heavenly grandchild" Ninigi, from whom the Mikados are descended, and in the slaying of the rebellious spirits and deities of Idzumo by the two gods who were sent down to prepare the way for Ninigi.

In both the Kojiki and the Nihongi the history of the divine age is introduced by a mythical cosmogony. The description of chaos and the formation of heaven and earth by gravity which precedes this in the Nihongi is clearly a piece of Chinese wisdom, and of interest only as showing that at the beginning of the eighth century Chinese speculation about Yang and Yin had already gained currency in Japan. The first five generations of gods, as often in similar schemes, have no place in religion; they serve only to provide the first gods who do anything with a pedigree of respectable length. The real cosmogonic deities are Izanagi and Izanami. This pair descended from the floating bridge of heaven upon an island which came into existence in the ocean *ad hoc*, where, coming together, they procreated the islands of Japan and a complete outfit of deities, gods of earth, water, plains, mountains, trees, the goddess of food, and the god of fire. The birth of the fire god cost the life of his mother, who died and went down to the underworld, the land of Yomi. Thither Izanagi followed her; but having, against her warning, by the light of a torch looked upon her in her loathsome corruption, he was forced to flee, pursued by the "hideous females" of Yomi and by Izanami herself. By the hardest, he escaped to the upper air and barred the exit from Hades against his irate spouse. The various things which he threw away in his flight turned to gods, as did the water with which he purified himself from the pollution contracted in his visit to the land of the dead. His part being now ended, Izanagi retired to an island where he dwelt in solitude and silence.

The next chapter of the mythical history deals with the sun goddess, Hirume ("sun female"), or Ama-terasu no Oho-kami ("heaven-shining great deity"), and her boisterous brother, Susa no wo. According to one version of the story, the sun goddess sprung from the water with which Izanagi washed his left eye after his return from Hades, while that with which he washed his right eye became the moon god, and from the washing of his nose arose Susa no wo. It is surmised with much plausibility, however, that this account is an adaptation of the Chinese myth of P'an Ku. The simpler, and probably the older, myth includes all three gods among the children born to Izanagi and Izanami. To the sun goddess was given the "plain of high heaven" to rule; to the moon the night; to Susa no wo in the original partition the sea was allotted, but he begged for and obtained the empire of the dead.

Before descending to the nether world, Susa no wo paid a visit to his sister in heaven. By crunching jewels, swords, and suchlike, and blowing out the fragments, each magically produced a number of children, to whom in later times various noble families traced their lineage. Susa no wo then proceeded to justify the popular etymology of his name, "violent man," by breaking down the divisions in his sister's rice fields and sowing them over, letting loose in them the piebald colt of heaven, defiling with ordure the hall where she was celebrating the feast of first-fruits, and, worst of all, flaying a piebald colt of heaven, beginning at the tail, and throwing the carcass through a hole in the roof into the room where the goddess was weaving garments for the deities. Outraged by this misconduct, the sun goddess shut herself up in the rock cave of heaven and left the celestial and terrestrial world in darkness. The gods resorted to various devices to draw the indignant goddess from her hiding-place; at last, moved by curiosity to know the cause of the inextinguishable laughter of the gods—which was in fact evoked by the not over-decent dance of Ame no Uzume—she opened the door half-way, whereupon the god Stronghand seized her and kept her from retreating to the cave again.[1]

By sentence of a council of gods, Susa no wo's beard was cut off, his finger-nails and toe-nails were pulled out, and he was heavily fined and banished. On the way to his own realm, he visited first Korea, and then Idzumo, where, like another Perseus, he slew a dragon and rescued a distressed maiden.

The great god of the province of Idzumo was Susa no wo's son Ohonamochi, of whom the myth tells many things, among them a visit to the nether realm of Susa no wo, whose daughter saves him from her father's machinations and finally elopes with him. Susa no wo, having vainly chased the runaway couple to the entrance of Hades, calls after them his paternal benediction, bidding Ohonamochi pursue and destroy his eighty bad brothers, and with his wife reign over the land—all which came to pass.

[1] The myth probably plays upon ancient rites used in time of a solar eclipse.

The gods of heaven did not look with favour on the rule
of Susa no wo's son, and sent down in succession several
messengers to prepare the world for the coming of Ninigi, a
grandson of the sun goddess, to assume the dominion. The
first did not return, but at length two of them came to
Ohonamochi's residence in Idzumo and induced him to resign the conduct of earthly affairs to the "august grandchild,"
while he confined himself to divine affairs. Ohonamochi
accordingly abdicated and withdrew from earth. The am-
bassadors of heaven then went on a circuit of pacification,
and exterminated all the spirits and deities who refused allegiance to the new sovereign. After this Ninigi, having received from Ama-terasu a commission to rule the world and
a promise of eternal duration for his dynasty, descended to
earth, attended by the progenitors of the five hereditary corporations, and alighted—not in Idzumo, as the previous
course of the story would lead us to expect—but on a mountain in the island of Kiushiu. From Kiushiu, in a later age,
Jimmu Tenno, the first human emperor, set forth to the
conquest of central Japan, and established his capital in
Yamato, according to the mythical chronology, as we have
seen, in 660 B. C.

In the earliest times the gods did not dwell in houses built
by men's hands; the place of worship was merely a *temenos*,
the sacred precincts being enclosed by a stone wall. According to tradition the first temples were erected about the
beginning of the Christian era; in the following centuries they
were multiplied so that the Yengishiki (927 A. D.) enumer-
ates more than three thousand officially recognised shrines,
of which seven hundred and thirty-seven received appropriations from the central government. Even the most famous
Shinto temples are of no great size, and the architecture is
simple, resembling, it is said, that of the old Japanese house.
Those at Ise, which, though periodically renewed, have probably preserved the primitive form, are built of the white
cedar wood, unpainted, with a thatch of rushes. The characteristic features are the gable timbers crossed and con-

tinued beyond the apex, and the cigar-shaped beams laid on the ridge at right angles to it, both originally structural, but now only decorative motives. The interior has two rooms: an open prayer-hall in front, for the worshippers, and a sanctuary containing the symbol of the deity, which only priests may enter. In the court stand a laver for ceremonial ablutions and a stage for religious dances and pantomimes at the festivals. The greater temples have several courts, enclosing numerous buildings for different auxiliary uses, among them frequently a hall for the deposit of votive offerings, or pictures and figurines as surrogates for such offerings. Before the entrance is the *torii*, a kind of portal, standing free, and in its original simple form consisting of two round uprights of natural wood, with a round cross-beam resting on them and projecting at both ends. Some old temples have, however, red torii, and some temples themselves are painted red, notably all the temples of Inari.

The emblem or symbol of the deity (*shintai*, "form of the god," or *mitama-shiro*, "representative of the spirit") is in Ise a metallic mirror which the sun goddess gave, with a sword and a jewel, to Ninigi when he was about to descend to earth; it is preserved, carefully enveloped and enshrined from all eyes, in the sanctuary. In other temples also a mirror is the most common representative of the god; at Atsuta it was the sword found by Susa no wo in the great serpent's tail. On the altar table and elsewhere in the temple stand *gohei*, upright wands from the top of which hangs paper in several thicknesses cut zigzag, a conventionalised substitute for the bast cloth in ancient times offered to the gods on the bough of a tree. At the entrance of the prayer-hall hangs a gong which the worshipper strikes with a rope's end to attract the attention of the god to his petition, and by it a contribution-box into which he drops his mites.

In many places more than one deity is worshipped, either in the same temple or, as at Ise, where the food goddess shares the honours with the sun goddess, in separate shrines. The old sources frequently do not give the name of the god

worshipped even at the greater temples. This is a not uncommon phenomenon in religions, and it is unnecessary to
call in the supposed "impersonal habit" of the Japanese
mind to account for it; the god is sufficiently designated by
the name of the place.

The priests did not form a sacerdotal caste or class set
apart from other men by personal sacredness; they were not
hindered by their calling from ordinary occupations; and, on
the other hand, secular officials took part in religious ceremonies in the regular course of their duties. The cultus, on
which the welfare of the state in no small part depended,
was supported and regulated by the government through
a department of religion. It may be conjectured that in
this, as in other features of administration, Chinese influence
led to a more formal organisation, but not to radical changes
in the relation of the state to religion. The priesthood of
the several shrines was in general hereditary in certain families, and there were two families or guilds which had special
functions and prerogatives in the worship at court: the
Nakatomi, who recited the liturgy (*norito*) at the festivals
and on other solemn occasions, and the Imbe, who prepared
the offerings according to the rules of ceremonial purity.
Besides these there was a corporation of Urabe, or diviners,
whose business it was to answer by means of their art questions propounded to them by the emperor or the officials.
The oldest method seems to have been by interpreting the
cracks which appeared in the shoulder-blade of a sheep when
it was held over a fire; the use of the tortoise-shell was introduced from China. Urabe were also distributed through
the provinces.

At the greater temples there were numerous priests of
different ranks and offices. The chief priest at Ise bore the
highest title; next in honour stood the chief priests of Atsuta,
Kashima, Usa, and Aso. The temples of lower rank had
priests of corresponding standing; the vast majority of the
little shrines had no priest permanently attached to them.
The priests wear a distinctive dress only when engaged in

religious functions; then they put on a loose robe with wide sleeves, confined at the waist by a girdle, and a black mitre bound on by a broad white fillet—a survival of an old form of court dress.

The daily ritual is simple, consisting in the offering of food and drink morning and evening. At Ise the offerings to the two deities there worshipped, the sun goddess and the food goddess, are to-day four cups of rice whisky (*sake*), sixteen saucers of rice and four of salt, besides fish, birds, fruits, seaweed, and vegetables.

Much more elaborate, naturally, are the ceremonies at the various festivals, which differ in number and importance at the different temples; at some places there is but one in the year, at others they occur with greater frequency. The description of such an offering at Ise may serve for illustration. As a preliminary, rites of purification are performed in a spot set off for the purpose before the temple; a special deity of purification is invoked, and the place, the offerings, and the worshippers are cleansed from all accidental defilement. The presiding priest then opens the sanctuary, the other priests arrange themselves in a broken line between the hall where the offerings are in readiness and the altar, and pass from one to another the stands on which the offerings are set out until they are put down on the small tables of different height arranged like a flight of steps in the sanctuary. The offerings consist of silk (in ancient times bark cloth); food, as in the daily offering but in greater variety; a branch of the sacred Sakaki-tree, to which are attached a mirror, sword, and jewel; and a large *gohei*. The presentation is accompanied by the music of pipes and drums. When it is concluded, the chief priest recites the liturgy. This is followed by two dances on a permanent stage in the temple court, one executed by men, the other by a dozen girls twelve or thirteen years old who carry in their hands branches of the Sakaki-tree. Finally, the offerings of food are removed and consumed by the priests. In olden times these offerings to the gods included the flesh of the wild animals which the people themselves eat, such as the deer, wild boar, and hare; when, under Buddhist influence, men abandoned a flesh diet, the gods had to give it up too. The food of the gods is commonly presented uncooked, but at Ise it is cooked over a pure fire and with minute precautions against contamination by the hands or the breath of the cooks, as the emperor's food also is prepared.

A regulation of the eighth century divided the festivals observed by the state according to their importance into three classes. In the greatest of all, standing alone in the first rank, is the Daijowe, celebrated by each new emperor in the eleventh month of the year of his accession, or, if that did not give time for the prolonged preparations, a year later. The emperor with his own hand offered to the gods as the first-fruits of his reign the newly harvested rice and fresh-brewed beer. The grain must be grown on two pieces of land selected by divination, and every step of the operations, from the designation of the fields on, was conducted in accordance with the minutely prescribed ritual. For the offering itself new buildings were erected with many ceremonies in a suburb of the capital; in them, on a carpet of reed mats, was laid a large cushion, the "deity seat." Emperor and people prepared themselves for the great occasion by avoiding for a month, and still more strictly for three days preceding the festival, various sources of uncleanness. The recitation of the liturgy, an address of congratulation and benediction to the emperor by members of an ancient noble family of Idzumo, was accompanied by a present of jewels of different colours. The ceremonies, which are in substance an elaboration of the annual festival of first-fruits, served as the solemn religious inauguration of the new reign.

The festivals of the second class were observed annually, and were all connected with agriculture. At the first the gods were implored to protect the growing crops against injury by wind or rain and to give abundant increase; in the autumn several harvest festivals were celebrated with offerings of first-fruits at the temples—for example, to the two goddesses in Ise—and at court. In one of the latter the emperor offered new rice to all the gods and partook of it himself.

The prayers for harvest in the second month, when the rice is sown, take in part the form of a vow of the emperor to make large offerings to the gods of the harvest if they give large crops this year. The greater part of the liturgy for this occasion has, however, nothing particular to do with the harvest or the harvest gods, but is addressed to several other classes of deities, and seems to have been originally composed for the half-yearly (in early times, monthly) festivals of a general character.

Among the minor festivals are those in which the god of waters is invoked to avert destroying floods of rain; the wind gods, that storms may not rage; the fire god, that conflagrations may not break out; for protection against pestilence; for the long life of the emperor; to drive away evil spirits, and the like.

Besides festivals and offerings such as those thus far described, by which the favour and protection of the gods were sought or gratitude expressed for blessings already received, piacular offerings and rites of purification have a prominent place in the old Japanese religion. Individuals who had incurred guilt by some offence had to make expiatory offerings; those who had contracted uncleanness, for instance, from a dead body, purified themselves by ablution. But inasmuch as the guilt or defilement of the individual might infect the whole community, a general purification of the land and people was also necessary. In earlier times such rites seem to have been occasional, being ordered when there was special reason; but from the beginning of the eighth century they were performed at the close of each half-year.[1] The ritual of these days, the so-called Great Purification (Oho-harahe), is of peculiar interest for the insight it gives into the religious and moral conceptions of ancient Shinto.

To the thinking of the natural man, all the world over, defilement, disease, and guilt, with no sharp lines of demarca-

[1] Like the semiannual days of atonement in Ezekiel.

tion, are contagious evils, physically transmissible and physically removable; they may be transferred to an animal or a
human scapegoat, or to some inanimate object, and sent
away bodily. On a higher religious plane the gods are invoked to take away these evils, and offerings, propitiatory
or expiatory, are made to induce them to do so; but the old
physical means of disposing of sin as a substance are often
conserved—the higher conception does not supplant the
lower, but is superimposed upon it. The ceremonies of the
Jewish Day of Atonement represent such a fusion of diverse
notions and rites, and so does the ritual of the Shinto days
of atonement. The offerings of food are propitiatory, and
the priest declares that the gods, hearing the potent words of
the liturgy, will remove both physical and moral uncleanness; but the "purification offerings" proper are sent off in
a boat and cast into the depths of the sea.

The catalogue of offences distinguishes between heavenly
misdeeds—so-called because they are like those perpetrated
by Susa no wo in the myth[1]—and earthly misdeeds; but it
makes no distinction between crimes against person or property, skin diseases, and calamities such as being struck by
lightning.

Now of the various faults and transgressions to be committed by the
celestial race destined more and more to people this land of his peaceful
rule, some are of heaven, to wit, the breaking down of divisions between
rice-fields, filling up of irrigation channels, removing water-pipes, sowing seed over again, planting skewers, flaying alive, flaying backwards.
These are distinguished as heavenly offences. Earthly offences which
will be committed are the cutting of living bodies, the cutting of dead
bodies; leprosy, kokumi [a disease]; incest of a man with his mother or
daughter, with his mother-in-law or step-daughter, bestiality; calamities from creeping things, from the high gods and from high birds,
killing animals, bewitchments.

So persistent are the primitive notions that in relatively
modern times they have given rise to a new custom quite in
the ancient spirit. A few days before the semiannual Oho-

[1] See above, pp. 98 f.

harahe, a man or woman who wishes to be purified procures
from the temple a small piece of white paper cut rudely in
the shape of a shirt. On this he writes his name, sex, the
year and month of his birth, rubs the paper over his whole
body, and breathes into it, thus transferring to it his sins or
ailments, and brings it back to the temple, where the collection is deposited on a black table during the purification
ceremony, and at the end is sent off in a boat and thrown
into the water.

It is a commonplace with writers on Shinto that it has no
ethics. The enthusiasts of "Pure Shinto" made a virtue
out of this defect: moral precepts and ethical systems are
made necessary only by depravity; the Chinese needed them,
but the ancient Japanese were good by pure nature, and
therefore did not have to talk about goodness. Western students have commented on the absence of moral teaching in a
less favourable sense, but have been equally positive about
the fact. It is doubtless true that Shinto had no ethical doctrine to be compared with Confucianism or Buddhism;
equally true that we should look in vain in the Kojiki and
Nihongi or in the ritual books for either moral instruction or
moralising reflections on history. Nevertheless, the ancient
Japanese had a customary morality corresponding to their
plane of culture, and that to this morality religion gave its
effective sanction the Great Purification itself is sufficient
proof. The function of religion in the stage in which Shinto
was in the age which produced its oldest literary monuments
never goes beyond such a sanction. Here, as in other things,
the early introduction of the standards of a higher civilisation forestalled the development which would doubtless have
taken place if Japan had gone its independent way.

To ward off ills caused by demons, especially the demons
of disease, the ancient Japanese sought the protection of a
particular group of gods, the Sahe no Kami, or "preventive
deities" (ἀλεξίκακοι), who are invoked in an old liturgical
text to defend the worshippers against the "hostile and savage beings of the root country," such as the "hags of Hades"

who pursued Izanagi. These deities were represented by phalli, often of gigantic size, which were set up along highways and especially at cross-roads to bar the passage against malignant beings who sought to pass. In the liturgy referred to, one of these gods is called "No Thoroughfare" (Kunado, or Funado), the name of the staff which Izanagi threw down to prevent his pursuing spouse from breaking out from Hades into the world above; two others are the prince and princess of the eight cross-roads. They had no temples, and were worshipped at the end of the sixth and twelfth months—the time of the semiannual lustration—and on occasion at other times, for example, on the outbreak of a pestilence. The phallic form of the end post of a balustrade or a bridge has a similar meaning; it keeps evil influence from passing. The apotropaic virtue of this symbol— a virtue which it has in many other countries, notably among the ancient Greeks—is due to the association of virility with manly strength, power to overcome invisible foes as well as visible, and to protect those in need of help. Standing as they did on the roadside and at cross-roads, these gods became the protectors of the wayfarers; travellers prayed to them before setting out on a journey and made a little offering of hemp leaves and rice to each one they passed. These gods had nothing to do, so far as the evidence shows, with fertility or the reproductive functions;[1] no peculiar rites were observed in their worship, and however objectionable to the taste of a more refined age, the cult was in no sense immoral or conducive to immorality. In modern times, out of regard to the prejudices of Europeans who connected obscene notions with them, they have been generally removed

[1] In a kind of Japanese Lupercalia described by a writer of the Middle Ages, the boys in the imperial palace used on the first full moon of the year to go about striking the younger women with the pot-sticks used in stirring the gruel made for the festival. This was believed to promote fertility. The festival is said to have been for the Sahe no Kami; but the association of this magical performance with these deities is perhaps secondary, induced by their phallic form. Phallic shrines in brothels have probably, as in Greece, an origin independent of the wayside gods.

from the roads, remaining only in out-of-the-way corners of the empire.

The ancient Japanese buried their dead; and this custom only slowly gave way under Buddhist influence to burning, which became universal in the course of the ninth century; from the eighth to the seventeenth centuries even the bodies of the emperors were burned. In the modern revival of Shinto the effort was made to return in this respect also to the old way; but the masses of the people continue to burn their dead with Buddhist rites. The tombs of the rulers and nobles were megalithic vaults covered by great mounds of earth, in which food, utensils, arms, and ornaments were deposited—evidence, if evidence were needed, that the Japanese entertained the universal belief in the survival of the dead under conditions and with needs similar to those of this life. The Nihongi narrates that in the year 2 B.C.,[1] at the funeral of a brother of the emperor, his personal attendants were "all buried alive, upright, in the precinct of the tomb," and that the Mikado was so affected by their sufferings that when, in the following year, the empress died, he forbade a repetition of the barbarous custom, ordaining that in future clay images of men, horses, and other objects should be set up in the tumuli instead of living creatures.[2] The common people were merely interred in some piece of waste land at a distance from the habitations of men, and the provision for their needs was correspondingly simple—a little rice and water.

The story of Izanagi's descent to Hades shows that by the side of this primitive belief in a continued existence in the tomb was the notion of an abode of the dead in the depths of the earth or beneath the sea, a place of darkness and loathsome corruption, imagined like the interior of some great tomb filled with decaying bodies. There are the "ugly hags of Hades," perhaps a kind of ghoul. To this "root country, the bottom country," as the remotest end of the world whence

[1] The reader need hardly be reminded that the chronology is not historical.

[2] Similar substitution in China, p. 76; cf. Egypt, pp. 157 f., 173.

there is no return, the sins and uncleanness of the people are sent off in the great ritual of purification. A different conception seems to be implied in the myths which make Susa no wo the ruler of the nether world: the land that Ohonamochi visits is a counterpart of this earth, with trees and moors and a great palace of the god; it does not appear, however, that the dead go thither. There is no notion of retribution beyond this life; Buddhism, with its whole system of heavens and of hells, left neither need nor room for a development which might otherwise, perhaps, have taken place in Shinto.

The cult of the dead had no such prominence in the old Japanese religion as in China. It may be assumed from the world-wide prevalence of the custom that food was from time to time set out at the tombs; such pious provision for the wants of the departed, however, even when conjoined with the fear that the neglected dead may work mischief to the living, is not to be confounded with offerings to the forefathers for protection and prosperity, the motive which alone makes them in the proper sense religious.

Before the sixth century there is no evidence of the worship of even the ancestors of the Mikado; in the Kojiki and the Nihongi (eighth century) references to such worship are rare. By the time of the Yengishiki (tenth century) the ritual of worship to deceased emperors was prescribed, and offerings like those to the gods were periodically made to them; but among the ancient liturgical texts (norito) there is none that belongs to this cult, and it is significant that the care of the imperial tombs was not assigned to the ministry of religion. The inference can hardly be avoided that the religious worship of the imperial ancestors is not an original feature of Japanese religion, but a result of Chinese influence. It is to be observed also that, though assimilated to the worship of the nature deities, the imperial ancestors never actually take their place among them as they do in China, where they rank immediately after Heaven, the Supreme Emperor, himself, taking precedence of all other gods. A few emperors have become in their individual capacity great gods; the most conspicuous instance being the Mikado Ojin, son of the militant empress Jingo, who under the name Hachiman has become the god of war; but precisely in this case foreign influence—Chinese, Buddhist—is peculiarly plain; it was as Hachiman Dai-bosatsu that he was worshipped by mediæval warriors. Since the restoration, in 1868, increased honour is paid to the deceased Mikados. Four annual services now have a place in the calendar of court observances, viz., the anniversary of the death of the last emperor; the commemoration of the death of Jimmu Tenno, the first emperor; and two, in the spring and autumn respectively, in memory of all the imperial ancestors.

The living emperor, who claims direct descent in unbroken line from the sun goddess, is called the "Heavenly Grandchild"; in decrees he may describe himself as "manifest deity" (cf. ἐπιφανής); the heir apparent is entitled "August Child of the Sun." These magniloquent titles, which have many parallels in other countries, do not prove that the Mikado was believed to have divine powers, but that he was entitled to divine reverence; religious worship was, in fact, not paid to him any more than to the emperor of China, who, as the designated Son of Heaven, had actually a higher place in the religion of the state than the Mikado in Japan.

The homage paid by the masses of the people to the ancestors of their own family resembles at a distance the religious veneration of the Chinese, of which it is obviously an imitation. In most modern households the ancestral tablets bearing the posthumous Buddha-names of the deceased stand on the Buddha-shelf (Butsu-dan); only the strictest sort of reformed Shintoists put similar, but plain, unpainted tablets, bearing the real name, on a shelf by themselves; never on the same shelf with the gods, and, if possible, not in the same room. At stated times food is offered to them, and prayers recited. The worship of the Uji-gami (literally, "surname gods"), or reputed progenitors of the clan, is not true ancestor worship; many of these first forefathers—originally, it seems, all of them—are gods belonging to the pantheon of religion or mythology; others are probably merely imaginary figures. With time they have become no more than the tutelary deities of a man's birthplace, at whose shrine infants are presented soon after birth, as in Christian countries at the parish church.[1] The common people in ancient times had no Uji-gami; they had no surnames, and made no pretence of divine parentage.

The prevailing notion that Shinto was, like the old Chinese religion, from the beginning a fusion of nature worship and ancestor worship can appeal to the authority of many modern Japanese students, including some of the Shinto reformers. A learned jurist, Hozumi, has shown how it underlies the laws of marriage and succession and of adoption; inasmuch, however, as the earliest Japanese codes are framed on Chinese models, this does not prove that ancestor worship in the proper sense was a constitutive factor of primitive Japanese society as it is in China, and there are many indications that it was not.

The domestic rites of Shinto are simple: in a corner of one of the rooms—usually the living-room—of the house is a shelf on which stand tablets or strips of paper inscribed with the names of the gods peculiarly venerated, especially the sun goddess and other deities of Ise, and the tutelary god of the owner's calling, or one or more small, unpainted wooden shrines for the habitation of the gods; images, introduced in the Middle Ages by imitation of Buddhist statues, are also not infrequently found on this "god-shelf." It is hardly to be doubted that the tablets and the shrines are borrowed from the Chinese. To the furniture of the shelf belong, further, two jars for rice whisky (*sake*), a pair of vases to hold flowers or a twig of Sakaki, and a miniature lamp, lighted, except in very poor households, every evening. The *sake* and the flowers or twigs are renewed on the first, fifteenth, and twenty-eighth of each month. On New Year's

[1] Compare also the registration of children in the phratry at the Athenian Apaturia.

the shelf is adorned also with the sacred straw-rope, and cakes of peculiar form are offered to the gods. Worshippers bring home pieces of the *gohei* from the temple and place them on the shelf, in the belief that the spirit of the deities has taken lodgment in it.

Besides visits to near-by temples, either to present to the deity a private petition or to participate in a festival, pilgrimages are made to distant shrines; for instance, to Ise, or to the Kasuga temple at Nara, or to Fujiyama. Like pilgrims to "ferne halwes" in countries nearer home, the Japanese combine the pleasures of a grand excursion with the profit of a visit to the sacred places. The worship at these places was not of a sort to damp the spirits of the visitors by gloomy solemnity; Buddhism took the dark side of life and the dark prospects of the hereafter for its province, and left to Shinto the more joyous aspects of existence. So it has retained through all the centuries something of the spirit of happy childhood.

It has been observed above that for a thousand years Shinto hardly existed except in combination with Buddhism. With the re-establishment of peace and order under the strong rule of the first Tokugawa Shoguns came a revival of the national consciousness, one manifestation of which was a zealous study of the national history and an endeavour to promote Japanese literature and learning, which had long been neglected for Chinese studies. From one thing these students of antiquity went to another, till they convinced themselves of the vast superiority of the native Japanese character and culture to all foreign peoples, particularly the Chinese; the golden age of Japan was before the influx of Chinese ideas and customs, which have been in every sphere a cause of declension and corruption. Of the scholars who thus endeavoured to dispel the illusion of their countrymen that China was the fountain of wisdom and culture, the greatest were Mabuchi (1697–1769 A. D.), Motoöri (1730–1801), and Hirata (1776–1843), and these are also the chief names in the revival of Pure Shinto. The first two contented themselves with showing from the ancient books what the native religion was, and how much better it was in its original purity than all foreign religions and philosophies. It alone was in truth the "Way of the Gods" (Kami no michi), established by Izanagi and Izanami, delivered by them to the sun goddess, and by her to the people over whom her descendants rule. That men have been turned aside from it to Buddhism and Chinese philosophy is the work of demons ("spirits of crookedness").[1] Motoöri has no thought of a reformation by which the ancient religion, freed from all alien admixture, should be established as the religion of the present time; for according to his deterministic theory the actual religion is what it is by the will of the gods, and it is not for men to be wiser than the gods.

Hirata was of a different temper. His ideal was the restoration of Pure Shinto as the religion of rulers and people, to the exclusion of both Buddhism and Confucianism; and he composed, among other works, forms of prayer suitable for the worship of reformed Shintoists. Despite Hirata's antipathy for all things Chinese, he could not divest himself of his education. He was too much of a thinker to be able to do without philosophy in his theology; and his ethics, in particular, are based on the worship of ancestors and the filial piety which this veneration cultivates, quite after the Confucian model. Hirata's efforts for a revival of Pure Shinto in practice had not much more immediate effect than the antiquarian restoration of his predecessors; but the writings of these scholars, with their enthusiasm for native Japanese culture literature and religion, their highly idealised pictures of the good old days, and the prominence they gave to the divine origin and right of the Mikado, contributed not a little to the movement which resulted in the political restoration of 1868.

[1] There is a noticeable dualistic strain in these authors.

CHAPTER VII

JAPAN

BUDDHISM

Introduction—Influence of China—Compromise with Shinto—Spread among the People—Monasteries and Their Feuds—Conflicts with the State—Tenets of the Sects: Shingon, Tendai, Zen—Pure Land Sects: Jodo, Shin—Salvation by Faith—Relation to Christianity —Common Characteristics—Popular Buddhism—Confucianism in Japan.

IN 552 A. D. the ruler of the little kingdom of Pekché, in the south-western corner of the Korean peninsula, being hard pressed by more powerful neighbours and desiring to secure Japanese support, sent to the emperor, with other presents, an image of Shaka Butsu[1] in gold and copper, several flags and umbrellas, and a number of volumes of Sutras. In an accompanying letter, he commended the Buddhist religion as the most profitable of all faiths.

A division of counsels arose over the question whether the new god should be worshipped or not: the chief minister, Soga, was in favour of following the fashion of all the western neighbours; other no less influential voices gave warning against provoking the anger of the native deities, the gods of heaven and earth, of the land and grain, by giving them a rival. It was thereupon decided that Soga might set up the worship himself in his own house and see what happened. A pestilence which shortly ensued was interpreted by the opponents of the foreign religion as a confirmation of their warning; Soga's temple was burned and the image thrown

[1] The Buddha Sakyamuni. Buddhism had been introduced into northern Korea in 372 A. D. and into Pekché in 384, where it at once became the court religion.

into a canal. A second attempt to introduce Buddhism, in 577 A. D., had a like ending.

In the conflicts over the succession which followed the death of the emperor Bidatsu (586 B. C.), however, the leaders of the opposition lost their lives, and the house of Soga, which from the beginning had been favourably disposed to Buddhism, became all-powerful. Under the empress Suiko Tenno (593–628 A. D.), whom the Soga raised to the throne, with the prince Shotoku Taishi as heir apparent and virtual regent, Buddhism became the religion of the court, and the nobility made haste to follow the fashion. Shotoku was a man of high character and of remarkable learning, not only in Buddhist doctrine but in Chinese literature, and he tried to instil into the governing class some of those lofty notions of official obligation and responsibility which he found in Confucius and Mencius. In the second of the seven articles of his instructions for officials he strongly commends Buddhism: "Zealously venerate the three jewels (the Triratna). The three jewels are the Buddha, the Law, and the Order. These are the last refuge of the four classes of beings and the ultimate principles of all lands. What age, what men should not honour these laws? There are but few men who are wholly bad; men can be instructed and so brought to follow the laws. How can they be rightly controlled except by refuge in the three jewels?" His example and influence doubtless did as much to further the spread of Buddhism as his formal commendation. In an enumeration taken shortly after his death (621 A. D.) 46 temples were reported, with 816 priests and 569 nuns.

In 607 Shotoku despatched a company of students, monks and laymen, to Loh-yang, then the capital of China, where they remained for many years, devoting themselves not only to the abstrusities of scholastic Buddhism, but to the classic ethical and political philosophy, and to Chinese methods of government. A few years after their arrival in China the Sui dynasty was overthrown (619) and the T'ang succeeded it. The second emperor of this line, T'ai Tsung (627–650), brought China to the very highest pitch of its power. His dominions extended to Persia and the Caspian Sea and to the confines of India, and under him China was "the most powerful, the most enlightened, the most progressive, and the best governed empire, not only in Asia, but on the face of the globe." He remodelled the university and other educational institutions, instituted the system of examinations which have ever since been the way into the service of the state, and undertook a new codification of the laws of the empire. The last of the Japanese students sent over by Shotoku returned to their native country in 640, having lived for a dozen years at the capital of this great monarch.

They had not been long at home when they had opportunity to put their knowledge to use: the great reforms of 645 were largely directed by them. These reforms consisted essentially in a reorganisation of the whole Japanese system of government on the Chinese model. In the place of a clan system, which is often, though not quite accurately, called feudal, was erected a strongly centralised government, with eight ministerial departments, whose functions were minutely defined, and a hierarchy of officials; provision was made for the registration of the people in census lists and laws were enacted regulating the division of land, taxes, and the like. The successive codes from 662 on are framed in the same spirit; the definitive code of 702, the Taiho-ryo, was based throughout on the contemporary Chinese code, T'ang-ling, and was promulgated in the Chinese language.

In short, Japan appropriated Chinese civilisation in the seventh century with more avidity and with less discrimination and independence than it manifested toward Occidental civilisation in the nineteenth century—naturally, inasmuch as in the former period there was no old and high national culture to withstand the foreign way. Schools for the study of Chinese were established by the emperor Tenchi (668–671), with foreign and native teachers, and later a university, in which instruction was given in the *quadrivium*, history, the Chinese classics, law, and mathematics. Buddhism seemed to be an integral part of the new civilisation—to be, in fact, its religious side. Confucianism as a moral and political philosophy was of undisputed authority in its own sphere; but the Chinese official cultus, being specifically a state religion, was not exportable.

The reforming emperor, Kotoku (645–654), "honoured the religion of Buddha and despised the way of the gods" (Shinto). The second of his successors, Temmu, in 674, ordered that every house in his kindgom should have an altar for the worship of Buddha. The progress that Buddhism made in this period may be judged by the fact that in the code of 702 it was found necessary to forbid the gift or sale of lands to the temples and to prohibit monks and nuns from owning real estate individually—so rapidly were the saints inheriting the earth. This legislation proved, however, to be of as little effect as similar statutes of mortmain in Christian countries.

Down to the end of the eighth century Buddhism, like the Chinese learning with which it was so intimately associated, flourished chiefly at court and in official circles; the masses remained ignorantly loyal to the faith of their fathers. A virulent epidemic of smallpox, which, starting in Kiushiu, reached the capital in 735, set all classes to propitiating the offended powers—whoever they were—or to invoking the protection of the friendly gods against the demons. The Buddhist priests did their part as experts in such business, and the emperor promised to erect a colossal statue of Buddha for deliverance from the plague. The common people resorted to the old gods for help, and as the pestilence continued to rage the thoughts of other classes also turned to them. Perhaps, as at the very introduction of Buddhism, it was feared that the deities of Japan resented the intrusion of the foreign cult. At least they must not be neglected.

Gyogi, a patriarch of the Hosso sect of Buddhists, was accordingly sent to the temple of the sun goddess at Ise to present to her a relic of Buddha and to inquire how she looked upon the emperor's project of a great image of Buddha. He returned with a favourable oracle, and the following night the emperor dreamed that the goddess herself appeared to him and said, "The Sun is Biroshana," the highest deity of the national religion, Ama-terasu, thus declaring herself to be identical with Vairocana, who in some sects occupies a similar exalted station among the transcendental Buddhas. An extension of this doctrine made it easy to identify every aboriginal god with some Buddha or Buddhist saint, and served as the theological basis for the syncretism of Ryobu Shinto.[1]

The colossal Daibutsu of Nara was not successfully cast till 749; but in 737 the emperor had ordered the construction of a large monastery in each of the provinces, and later required each local government to erect a seven-storied pagoda. Under such favour it was not long before Buddhist monks began to play an ambitious rôle in state affairs. One of them, Dokyo, the spiritual adviser and favourite of the empress Shotoku Tenno (765–769), not content with being chancellor of the empire and ruling it through his mistress, formed the audacious plan of seating himself on the throne of the descendants of the sun goddess. The warning was not lost, and in the succeeding period, under strong rulers like Kwammu (782–805), the ecclesiastics were kept in their place.

The older Buddhist sects, of which there were six before this time, had planted their principal establishments at Nara, the first permanent capital of the empire (710–784); at the new capital, Heian (Kyoto), built by Kwammu in 794, two others, more recently introduced from China, took the lead, and soon left their older rivals far behind. One of these, the Tendai, propagated in Japan in the first years of the ninth century by Saicho, better known under his posthumous name, Dengyo Daishi, covered with its monasteries Mount Hiyeizan northeast of Kyoto, which at a later time sheltered thirty or forty thousand monks. Kukai (Kobo Daishi) returned in 806 from a long residence in China, bringing with him the

[1] See above, pp. 93 f.

doctrines of the Yogacarya school, and founded the Shingon sect, whose principal seat was the monastery of Koya, south of the capital. The Tendai was much the more numerous and influential of the two, and from it most of the later Japanese sects sprang or split off.

The fusion of Buddhism and Shinto for which a formula had been found by Gyogi was greatly promoted by Kobo, who taught that in ancient times the Buddhas had appeared in Japan as Kami to bless the people of the land. The Butsu and Hotoke (Buddhas and Saints), to whose worship the people were now invited, were, under other names and in fuller revelation of their nature and attributes, the same beneficent beings they had always worshipped. In consequence of this benevolent assimilation, Buddhist images were set up in Shinto fanes and native Kami, rebaptised, were worshipped in Buddhist temples. The barriers being thus thrown down, Buddhism made rapid progress among the common people. Many things contributed to this success: its gods, so much more human than the vague Shinto Kami—gods not only habitually well disposed to men, but the very embodiment of an infinite compassion—the splendid cultus, which all the arts conspired to make beautiful and impressive; the voluminous scriptures, enveloped in the mystery of a strange tongue; the repute of its priesthood for learning and holiness; the higher morality they preached; the power they had over this world by their supernatural attainments or arts; and their possession of the secrets of the other world and the assurance they offered of a blessed hereafter—all this had its full effect now that Buddhism came not as a foreign rival of the native faith but as Shinto itself unfolded; the common man was Shintoist and Buddhist at once, unconscious of the duality. One great field, however, Buddhism had to itself, namely, death and the future life, for here Shinto had nothing to say: heavens and hells, with all the fears and hopes that they excite, were beyond its primitive horizon.

The emperors, without ever renouncing their place as chief priests of the native religion or suffering its rites to fall into complete desuetude, were in their personal faith Buddhists. Several of them in the succeeding centuries laid aside their state and assumed the monk's tonsure to find peace from a world of trouble in the seclusion of the cloister, or to pull the strings of government from behind the scenes.[1] Monasteries and temples multiplied and grew rich, thousands entered the order from worldly motives, many of the monks were ignorant and lazy, some were vicious—a parallel to the contemporary history of Christian monasticism.

The religious establishments were frequently at strife with one another, and settled their controversies over points of doctrine or more worldly issues by force and arms. Before the end of the tenth century the abbot of Hiyeizan had organised a regular body of mercenary soldiers in the service of the monastery, and so illustrious and menacing an example was promptly followed by other powerful ecclesiastics. The monasteries were turned into fortresses, fitted to defy not only the assaults of their rivals in religion but the authority of the state. By the close of the eleventh century any one of the great monastic foundations could put into the field a force of several thousand men—hireling bravos, retainers from the wide estates of the church, novices, and tonsured monks.

Private wars were frequent. The two chief Tendai monasteries, Hiyeizan and its daughter Miidera, on the shores of Lake Biwa, were always at enmity. The occasions of their quarrels were rivalry for places of power, the nomination of abbots in dependent establishments, rights of precedence, the conduct of court ceremonies. In 1082 the army of Hiyeizan took Miidera, stripped its shrines of their treasures, and burnt it to the ground. The same thing happened again forty years afterward and once again in the latter part of the century; while Hiyeizan was at least once burned by Miidera. The other sects and minor monasteries had their own smaller broils. In fact, there was hardly a decade in that anarchic period when such struggles were not going on among the bellicose saints. They sometimes undertook to

[1] Beginning with Shirakawa's retirement in 1086, there was a succession of cloistered emperors, who down to 1156 were generally the real rulers of Japan.

intimidate the secular rulers, as when in 1039, three thousand Hiyeizan monks, complaining of the regent's distribution of ecclesiastical preferment, marched into Kyoto and besieged him in his palace.   Over and over again the capital was thrown into a panic by an invasion of turbulent monks.   In the civil wars of the period between the Taira and the Minamoto, the armies of the church took an active part, and on more than one field proved themselves as hard fighters and as ruthless victors as the doughtiest knights.

As in Europe from the eleventh to the thirteenth century the growing worldliness of the older monastic orders led to the establishment of numerous new orders all aiming at a restoration of faith and morals, so in Japan the rise of four new Buddhist sects in the end of the twelfth and the beginning of the thirteenth centuries shows that, however far the orders had declined from their primitive virtue, the recuperative power of the religion was by no means exhausted. The parallel can, unfortunately, be carried a step farther: in Buddhist Japan as in Christian Europe the reforming orders soon succumbed more or less completely to the influence of environment and example and followed in the footsteps of their predecessors.

One of these, the Zen (Sanskrit *Dhyana*), or Contemplative, sect, was founded by Eisai, a monk from Hiyeizan, who went to China to study about 1168, and after a second visit in 1187 erected a Zen shrine at Hakata, whence he removed in 1202 to Kyoto.   A typhoon which devastated the capital three years later was interpreted by the monks of the older orders as a judgment on the city for harbouring this heresy, and the emperor expelled the heresiarch.   Eisai thereupon betook himself to Kamakura, where he won to the new doctrine the powerful Hojo family, and where the famous "Five Temples" were for long the chief seats of the sect. Besides this older Rinzai branch of the Zen-shu, another school, the Soto, was introduced in 1223 by Dogen, and a third, the Obaku, about 1650.   "Contemplation" is not the way of salvation that would be expected to commend itself most to the belligerent gentry whose hands were more wonted to the sword than the beads; but the paradox is fact, the Zen variety of Buddhism was especially favoured by the military class. After all, this is not so strange, for in the contemplative scheme of salvation as interpreted by this sect neither learning nor retirement from the world was necessary; the great thing was to discover the essential Buddha in man's own heart.

The Jodo sect, founded in 1175 by Genku, and the Shin, an offshoot from it, founded by his disciple Shinran about 1224, are of a different type from all the rest. Salvation is in them not achieved by man's own striving in the "Holy Way," but is bestowed by the grace of Amida Buddha on those who call upon him in faith. This way of admission to the "Pure Land" soon became very popular. Emperors patronised it, and in the first zeal of its evangelisation it won multitudes of the common people, who had hitherto been only superficially influenced by Buddhism. This strange doctrine not only aroused vigorous opposition from the side of the older sects, but provoked Nichiren to found (1252 A. D.) a new one, more reactionary and intolerant than all the rest, which bears the founder's name, and has perpetuated to this day his intransigeant spirit.

The success of the new sects brought them large endowments, and with wealth came the lust of the flesh and the pride of life. Their abbots were great feudal lords, some of them having whole provinces for their feoffs; one of them could even dream of making himself master of all Japan. Like their older rivals, they fortified their monasteries, and often took the field in secular as well as ecclesiastical commotions. In the turbulent time from the middle of the fourteenth to the middle of the sixteenth century the monks were a formidable evil. Not the smallest part of the great task of Nobunaga and his coadjutors and successors in restoring order and authority in Japan was the crushing of the church militant. To his soldiers, hesitating from religious scruples, Nobunaga said: "If I do not destroy them now, this trouble will be everlasting. Moreover, these priests violate their vows; they eat fish and stinking vegetables, keep concubines, and never unroll the sacred books. How can they be vigilant against evil or maintain the right? Surround their dens and burn them, and suffer none within them to live." His orders were carried out: the three thousand monastic buildings that studded Mount Hiyeizan were destroyed and thousands of monks perished. The Monto monastery at Osaka, under its abbot, Kennio, proved more difficult. Repeated assaults on it were repulsed with great loss, and Nobunaga with sixty thousand men had to sit down to a regular siege. It was more than four years from the investment to the surrender; and at the end the monks set fire to the monastery as they evacuated it, and left the captor only a heap of smoking ruins. A year before Nobunaga had decided a dispute between the Jodo and the Nichiren by decapitating the leading disputants of the latter sect and deporting many more to desert islands.

The Jesuit missionaries who witnessed these events wrote home: "This man seems to have been chosen by God to open and prepare the way for our holy faith, without knowing what he was doing." They underestimated the intelligence of the Japanese leaders if they dreamed that they were going to allow foreign ecclesiastics to build up a power which was bound to be more dangerous to the state than the native bonzes. Hideyoshi's edict of expulsion was issued in 1587, the first of a series of progressively drastic measures against Christianity which succeeded within half a century in virtually extirpating it.

In the suppression of the intruding faith Buddhism was a useful instrument, and the Tokugawa shoguns made good use of it. To escape the severe laws against Christianity, every man had to prove that his name was inscribed in the parish register of a Buddhist temple. The rulers themselves were attached to the Jodo branch of the "Pure Land" school, and this sect with its daughter, the Shin-shu, took the lead among the sects, while the Zen declined from the importance it had enjoyed in the preceding period.

But if the Tokugawa rulers patronised the church, they also put it under the supervision and control of the state. Iyemitsu prescribed the conditions—including an examination—on which priests might be ordained, the period of study before one might set up for a preacher or found a temple, the way in which intestine disputes in a sect were to be decided, and the like. Notwithstanding the favoured situation of the church—or because of it—the Buddhist clergy of this period cannot be given a very good name for either learning or virtue. Monks who strictly observed the rule of the order were few; the great mass was lazy and ignorant, if nothing worse; simony was rife. The priesthood throve on the superstitions of the people; they had magical powers for all purposes, and above all, the destiny of the dead was in their hands. The better educated among the military class held them in contempt, and found more edification in the Neoconfucian philosophy of the Sing-li school. The intellectual and moral decay of Buddhism also turned the minds of Mabuchi and his successors to the revival of Pure Shinto.[1]

It has been remarked in an earlier chapter that in the decadence of Buddhism in China the numerous schools and sects which once flourished there have run together into one composite type, in which the doctrines and methods of the Dhyana, or Contemplative, school predominate, though no other variety of Mahayanist salvation is excluded. In Japan, on the contrary, the great schools which were introduced from China in the ninth and following centuries have not only maintained their separate individuality but kept up their sectarian controversies, and the books of the old sects which have long been extinct continue to be studied as part of the history of Buddhist doctrine. Consequently, while libraries of Chinese monasteries commonly contain only such works as are regarded as of actual importance, in Japan the greater part of the voluminous canon of northern Buddhism has been preserved, together with a multitude of commentaries, treatises, and controversial writings by Chinese and

[1] See above, pp. 94, 113 *f*.

Japanese authors. The canonical literature is mainly in Chinese translation; but some copies of Sanskrit originals have also been recovered. In the modern revival of Buddhist learning in Japan, native scholars have turned with new zeal to the study of this literature and have done much to make it known to Western students.

A history of Buddhist schools or sects does not fall within the scope of the present survey; it must suffice to give a brief account of some of the more typical varieties. Of the so-called "old sects" which flourished in the Nara period (710–784) the most influential was the Hosso, or Dharma-lakshana. The fundamental text-book of this school was the Yogacarya-bhumi of Asanga, an Indian monk who lived in the fifth century of our era. In contrast to the Madhya-mika of Nagarjuna, represented by the contemporary San-ron school, Asanga postulates the reality of individual personality and of the external world, approximating thus to the Sankhya philosophy.[1] In this sect the worship of Gautama Buddha (Sakyamuni) was pushed into the background by that of Maitreya, the future Buddha, who was supposed to have revealed its *shastras*. The great apostle of Asanga's doctrine in China was the famous traveller Hiuen Tsang, who brought its scriptures from India; it was introduced into Japan shortly after 653 A. D., and through another channel fifty years later. It was a patriarch of this sect, as will be remembered, who happily discovered the identity of Shinto and Buddhism in the "two-fold way of the gods." Like the rest of the "old sects," the Hosso was supplanted or absorbed in the Middle Ages by more popular successors.

The Shingon sect was introduced from China, as has already been noted, in 806 A. D., by Kukai (Kobo). Its name, "The True Word," does not refer to the speculative system, but to its possession of the efficacious word (*mantras*, magical formulas). In China it is called "the secret doctrine of Yoga," Yoga being here the magical side of religion. The first patriarch of the sect in China was Vajrabodhi (719 A. D.).

[1] See below, pp. 307 *f.*

The Shingon doctrines have been not inaptly described as a Buddhist gnosticism. They distinguish an exoteric and an esoteric teaching; by way of the latter it is possible even in this earthly body composed of the six elements to attain the absolute knowledge which is Nirvana, or, in other words, to become Buddha. The supreme being in this system, the Dharmakaya, is Vairocana, one of the Dhyani (Contemplative) Buddhas of the Mahayana. He is the great sun, around whom are grouped four other Dhyani Buddhas; each of these Buddhas has as satellites a group of Bodhisattvas; these in turn have their satellites, and so on *in infinitum*. To the four Buddhas who surround Vairocana belong Shaka (Sakyamuni)—who thus occupies a wholly subordinate place in the system—and Amida, of whom there will be much to say later. Cabalistic diagrams illustrate the constitution of this "diamond world," or ideal world, as well as that of the "matrix," in which Vairocana is the centre and source from which the phenomenal world is evolved, the first emanations being eight Buddhas who form the petals of a lotus.[1] To attain the supreme enlightenment it is necessary to ascend step by step ten rounds of a ladder of thought, which, originally corresponding to different classes of beings, was adapted by Kobo to the various sects, the highest, the stage of mystic enlightenment in which man recognises for the first time the source of his own thought and while still in the body becomes Buddha, being attained only by followers of the Shingon. The practical methods of achieving the great end are an adaptation and development of the Indian Yoga, as on its speculative side the doctrine returns to a pantheistic type of Brahmanism.

The belief that mental operations are efficient causes of phenomena—in other words, that a man who has acquired the method can bring about desired results merely by thinking them—though not peculiar to this school, is peculiarly

---

[1] Amida is the only one of the four Buddhas of the diamond world who reappears in the matrix system.

prominent in it. This power can be exerted for the benefit of the dead as well as the living: the Yoga school is credited with the invention of the masses for the dead so generally used in China and Japan, in which the priest *thinks* that the gates of hell open, the souls throng forth from their prison, the food of the gods rains upon them, and the Buddhas descend to deliver them—thus by the power of thought really saving souls. The efficacy of thought is fortified by the recitation of magical formulas (*dhāranis* or *mantras*), by magical figures made with the fingers or hands (*mudras*), and by passes with a magic wand supposed to represent the thunderbolt (*vajra*), actually a small bell with a handle. In its temple service the Shingon is the ritualistic high church of Buddhism, a supernatural virtue being attributed to the performance of the liturgy as in all "high" churches.

The Tendai sect (Chinese T'ien-t'ai) received its name from the group of mountains in the modern Chinese province of Cheh-kiang among which its founder, Chi K'ai (died 597 A. D.), lived in retirement. Chi K'ai had been taught in the Dhyana school, but, not finding himself satisfied with their doctrines, withdrew and developed in his mountain solitudes a more comprehensive system of his own.

The Tendai takes for its fundamental scripture the Saddharma Pundarika, together with the Nirvana Sutra and the Mahaprajnaparamita-çastra. The Saddharma Pundarika, purporting to contain the supreme doctrine of Buddha, endeavours to transcend the distinction of the three "Vehicles" (for disciples, for Pratyeka Buddhas, and for Bodhisattvas respectively). There is in reality but *one* all-comprehending "Buddha Vehicle"; the lower teachings and motives are only an accommodation to the incapacity of men in lower stages of religious development. Men have to be lured like children to their own salvation by the offer of goods which they comprehend and desire; these are not the true good— Nirvana, for example, as the saint (Arhat) conceives it, is not the true Nirvana—yet the teaching is no untruth, for the good which Buddha purposes to bestow on them is infinitely better than his promise. The lesser vehicles are, therefore, not rejected; but they are ranked with the beggarly elements. The Mahayana schools accordingly distinguish in the life of Buddha certain periods, in which he successively revealed the completer and profounder truth. According to Chi K'ai, Buddha at first proclaimed the fulness of the truth; but finding men unable to bear it, he taught for twelve years the doctrines comprised in the "three collections" which are the Bible of the Hinayanists; then for eight years he set forth the ideal of the Bodhisattva, in contrast to the selfish aim of the Arhat; in the two and twenty years following he expounded the metaphysics of universal unreality; finally, in the last eight years of his life he disclosed the sublime truth which is the theme of the Saddharma Pundarika, namely, that all beings are capable of becoming supreme Buddhas, because they are all partakers of the Buddha nature.

The Tendai doctrine is broad in another aspect: there is no one exclusive way of attaining salvation. "The true method is found neither in book-learning, nor external practice, nor ecstatic contemplation; neither in the exercise of reason nor the reveries of fancy; but there is a middle condition, a system which includes all and rejects none, to which all others gravitate, and in which alone the soul can be satisfied." [1]

According to the Saddharma Pundarika, Sakyamuni, whom we call the historical Buddha, was only one of the innumerable incarnations or manifestations of an eternal Buddha; his passing away is only a deceptive appearance, a "device" of his to lead men to obey his words. His knowledge embraces the remotest past and the remotest future. In his own words: "I am the father of the world, the self-existent,[2] the healer, the protector of all creatures." "What reason should I have to continually manifest myself? When men become unbelieving, unwise, ignorant, careless, fond of

[1] This comprehensive synthesis claims the authority of Nagarjuna.
[2] Buddha thus puts himself in the place of Brahman, the All-Father, the Self-Existent.

sensual pleasures, and from thoughtlessness run into misfortune, then I, who know the course of the world, declare, 'I am so and so.'" The words recall the speech of Krishna in the Bhagavad-Gita, "Whenever righteousness languishes and unrighteousness prevails, then I create myself; for the deliverance of the good and the destruction of the evil, I arise in every age of the world to re-establish righteousness." It is plain that to this type of Buddhism not only the Brahmanic philosophy of the Absolute but the theistic conceptions of Hinduism have contributed.

The identity of the Buddha Sakyamuni with the Buddha of original enlightenment, and consequently his eternity, is the great revelation of the Saddharma Pundarika; faith in it and joyful acceptance of it outweigh all the merit that a man could heap up by the practice of all the Buddhist virtues and perfections through countless ages.

The Tendai metaphysics pass for the most profound among the Buddhist sects; fortunately we are not required to fathom them. The system is defined as a pantheistic realism; the Bhutatathata[1] is the essence of all things, immanent in nature and in thought—a conception in which some modern Buddhists discover a resemblance to Spinoza's "substance."

The Dhyana school was introduced into China from India by the patriarch Bodhidharma in 527 A. D. The older branch of the Zen school (Rinzai) was imported into Japan, as we have seen, in 1168, the younger (Soto) in 1223. The distinctive peculiarity of this school is that the supreme truth cannot be expressed in words nor communicated by teaching, but only by a kind of thought-transference. Study and the practice of devotion are therefore little esteemed. It is by immersing one's thought in his own original nature that he makes the great discovery, the successive steps of which are described. Part of this discovery is that the nature of his own thought is in origin pure; therefore it is not necessary to expel the passions and to seek intelligence. The final stage is the absolute illumination which is equivalent

[1] The Absolute; see below, pp. 308 f.

to becoming Buddha. The Soto does not, like the Rinzai, make contemplation the beginning and end of the matter, but regards study also as a means, and its priests have, in fact, been distinguished for learning. The effect of the highest wisdom, says one of the most valued sutras of the school, is that we see that all the elements of phenomenal existence are empty, vain, and unreal. "Form does not differ from space nor space from form; all things surrounding us are stripped of their qualities, so that in this highest stage of enlightenment there can be no longer birth or death, defilement or purity, addition or destruction. There is, thus, no such thing as ignorance, and therefore none of the miseries that result from it. If there is no misery, decay, or death, there is no such thing as wisdom, and no such thing as attaining to happiness or rest." This unutterable void is, however, not the void of non-being, but the abyss of absolute being, of which we can think only in negations.

Of peculiar interest are the two "Pure Land" sects, the Jodo and the Shin, which are one of the most significant developments of Buddhism. All the other divisions of Buddhism, ancient or modern, whether of the Hinayana or the Mahayana branch, however widely they differ in their conception of the nature of the goal or the method of attaining to it, are at one in this, that in some fashion or other man must arrive at the goal by following the way laid down by Buddha, and are therefore classed together as sects of the Holy Way, in contrast to the sects of the Pure Land. This classification has a good ground, for while all other forms of Buddhism are schemes of salvation by self-discipline or by the achievement of transcendental knowledge—in either case man's own work—in the Jodo and Shin-shu salvation is by grace through faith.

These sects are in the wider sense Mahayanist; they base their doctrine on the two Sukhavati Sutras, which describe the Land of Bliss, the Western Paradise of Amitabha Buddha, and on the so-called Meditation on Buddha Amitayus. In the two sutras first named the mendicant Dharmakara describes what sort of a Buddha country his shall be when he is Buddha. If all may not be to his wish, then he desires not to obtain supreme enlightenment. Among the other conditions is this, that those who have directed their thought to be born in his Buddha country, and for this purpose have brought their stock of merit to maturity, shall have their wish fulfilled, even those who have only ten times repeated the thought.[1] In the Shórter Sutra it is taught that beings are not born in that Buddha country as a reward and result of good works performed in this present life; but whoever shall hear the name of the blessed Amitayus and keep it in mind one, two, three, four, five, six, or seven nights, when he comes to die, Amitayus and a host of Bodhisattvas shall stand before him, and he shall be reborn in the Land of Bliss, the Buddha country of Amitayus. The Meditation ends with a similar doctrine. This Buddha country of Amitabha, or Amitayus, in the West is described with a wealth of sensuous imagination; it is a veritable paradise in which no beautiful and pleasant thing is lacking, nor is the moral perfection of its inhabitants less dwelt upon. But the best is that there, free from all the hindrances that make attainment on earth so infinitely difficult, they go on to the perfect knowledge which is Buddhahood.

Genku (Honen Shonin), who in 1175 founded the Japanese Jodo sect, was born in 1133. As a mere boy he entered the order in the Tendai monastery on Hiyeizan, but soon withdrew from it and gave himself for years in seclusion to the study of the sacred books and the writings of former sages. The paths of salvation laid down in those books, Mahayana as well as Hinayana, seemed to him impracticable. In older times—the first fifteen hundred years of the faith—men of stronger intellect and more heroic will were able, walking by their own strength in the Holy Way, to attain in this life

[1] "If I arrive at Buddhahood, I will not take to myself complete enlightenment (*i. e.*, become Buddha) unless all living beings in the universe who sincerely believe in me and desire to be born in my land shall be born there, though but ten times they direct their devotion to me."

wisdom and deliverance; but in these "last days of the religion," and for such as we, this attainment is impossible.   The
doctrine is too hard for our understanding and the way too
hard for our strength.   One day, as he was re-reading Zendo's comment on the Meditation on Amitayus, his attention fastened on the passage, "Above all, with whole and undivided heart keep the name of Amitayus in remembrance."
In a flash of illumination the meaning became clear to him:
Not by works of the law nor by superhuman wisdom is salvation to be achieved in this world; it is secured for us by
the grace of Amitabha, who has promised that whosoever
calls upon his name shall be born again in the Pure Land, and
there, in Amitabha's paradise, be made perfect.   At once he
abandoned all the religious exercises he had practised for
years, and did nothing but repeat innumerable times daily:
"*Namu Amida Butsu!*" ("Hail Amida Buddha!"), which is
the symbol of the sect.

In his own words: "The Pure Land teaching bids us, letting this world go, hasten to be born in the Happy Land.
This is made possible by the solemn promise of Amida Buddha; and the choice does not depend on whether we are good
or bad.   No, the only question is whether a man has faith
in this promise of Buddha or not.   Therefore Doshaku[1] said,
'There is no other way in which we can really walk except
this one which the Holy Way doctrine shows us.'"

Shinran, the greatest of Honen's disciples, developed the
doctrine further in some directions, and the result was a
division.   The conservative side, which presently split into
several branches, kept the name Jodo, while Shinran and his
followers called themselves Jodo Shin-shu, the "True Pure
Land Sect," commonly abridged to Shin-shu.   The Shin-shu
agrees with the parent sect in making a new birth in the
Western Paradise the immediate aim of religious endeavour,
and in grounding its hope upon the gracious purpose of Amida
to make all men sharers of the salvation which he wrought

[1] Tao-cho, one of the Chinese teachers of the Pure Land doctrine
(d. 628 A. D.).

out for them. But while some Amidaists in Japan as well as in China made the accumulation of a stock of merit indispensable to salvation, and others thought the endless invocation of the name all-sufficient, Shinran made faith, in a more spiritual sense, the sole condition: renouncing every thought of saving himself by his own effort, man must put all his trust in the promise of Amida.

In a modern exposition of the doctrine we read: "When we examine our own heart, it is far from being pure and true; on the contrary, it is wicked, foul, false, and hypocritical. How can we then extirpate all our passions and achieve Nirvana by our own strength? How attain the three states of heart?[1] Recognising, therefore, the complete impotence of our own power, we must put our trust alone in the help of another's power offered us in the original resolve of Amida. When we do so we enter into Buddha's knowledge and are filled with his great compassion, as the water of a river becomes salt when it flows into the sea. For this reason the doctrine is called "Faith in the Higher Power."

The invocation of the name of Amida is not a means of obtaining the great salvation, but an expression of gratitude for salvation already received by faith. Gratitude is also the motive for observing his law; it is not enough to confess him with the lips, the thoughts and deeds of believers should be in conformity with his good will; but this conformity will follow naturally from keeping the mercies of Amida ever before the mind.

The Jodo, while recognising Amida as the only hope of man's salvation, allowed resort to other Buddhas such as Kwannon, the goddess of mercy, for temporal benefits, and even admitted the statues of these deities to its temples. The Shin-shu forbids worship of any being except Amida. It teaches, further, that prayers should not be made to ob-

---

[1] *I. e.*, sincere, believing, desiring to be born in the Pure Land, as expressed in Amida's vow. These are all summed up, it is explained, in the one word "faith," or "whole heart."

tain earthly goods or to avert earthly ills; what befalls man
in this life is determined by former deeds, and it is in vain
to invoke the aid of the gods to alter this destiny.   Prayer
to Amida should be only for what concerns man's eternal
welfare, and that not as petition, but as grateful acknowl-
edgment of his mercy.   On the same principle the use of
amulets, charms, and all magic rites are excluded.

Inasmuch as neither learning, nor contemplation, nor religious exercises are necessary, or even profitable, nothing is
gained by withdrawal from the world; salvation is as easy
for the householder as for the monk, and the members of the
sect are encouraged to remain in their own vocations.   Its
priests are in reality not so much an order of monks seeking
to become saints or future Buddhas by ways not open to
laymen as a ministry to whom is committed the conduct of
worship and the religious instruction of the church; they
marry and live among their fellows, wear secular garb when
not engaged in religious functions, and are not even bound
to abstain from eating meat.

The Shin-shu grew rapidly in numbers and power in the
first centuries of its existence, and is to-day the most numerous and vigorous of all the Japanese sects.   Since a metaphysical system forms no part of its plan of salvation, it
has not the same difficulty as some of the others in accommodating itself to modern science and philosophy, while the
freedom of its priests fits them better to be leaders of a progressive movement.   In the modern revival of Buddhism in
Japan they have taken a conspicuous part.

As a system of salvation by grace through faith, the Pure
Land sects have an obvious resemblance to Christianity,
which appears the more striking in contrast to what we may
call the orthodox Buddhism of the Holy Way.   The virtual
monotheism, especially of the Shin-shu; the emphasis on
man's inability to achieve salvation by his own powers, his
dependence on the power of another; the infinite compassion of Amida, who before innumerable ages provided this
way by which even the weakest and the most ignorant and

the greatest sinners may be saved; faith in Amida's gracious purpose to save all as the essence of religion; gratitude as the spring at once of piety and morality—such are the salient points of comparison. To not a few students it has seemed that a teaching so widely at variance, not only with primitive Indian Buddhism but with its later developments, and so closely akin to Christianity,[1] not in certain isolated features but in a whole complex of fundamental ideas, can only be explained by Christian influence.

The age of the Pure Land sects excludes the possibility of contact with Christianity in Japan. When the Jesuit missionaries arrived, in 1549, they found these sects, already three centuries old, among the most flourishing of all; Father Cabral describes their doctrine of salvation by faith alone as a sort of Buddhist Lutheranism. The attempt has been made, however, by more than one scholar to show that this doctrine might have been derived from the Nestorian Christians in China. It is noted that Zendo (Shan-tao), from whose writings Genku got his inspiration, lived about the middle of the seventh century at the capital, Ch'ang-an (modern Si-an-fu), where the Nestorian missionaries had established themselves in 635. The coincidence is certainly interesting; but more than one reason must deter the historian from attaching any further significance to it. The way of salvation which Zendo set forth did not originate with him; he found it, we are told, in the Amitayurdhyani Sutra, and was further instructed in it by teachers who stood in a scholastic succession that went back more than a century in China. The Sukhavati Sutras, in which the gist of the doctrine is contained, had been translated into Chinese centuries earlier, the oldest version of the Longer Sutra before the end of the second century of our era. Açvagosha's Awakening of Faith in the Mahayana, commonly ascribed to the first century of our era, commends this way of salvation, quoting from "the Sutra" a passage substantially embodying the teaching of the existing Sukhavati texts.

[1] More accurately to certain types of Protestantism.

Moreover, no form of Christianity which penetrated to the East in those centuries taught a doctrine of salvation by faith in God's gracious purpose of salvation for all mankind. To the church, Nestorian or Catholic, saving faith meant the acceptance of a body of doctrines, especially about the Trinity and the Person of Christ; in the centre of its teaching and its cultus stood, not the universal love of God, but the incarnation and the death of Christ; the benefits of his salvation were not appropriated immediately by faith, but communicated by the sacraments as administered by the church. In short, the doctrine of salvation by faith alone cannot have been borrowed from any branch of the Christian church because the church acknowledged no such doctrine.

On the other hand, the example of India shows how religions of salvation by faith may grow up by the side of systems of salvation by works and by transcendental knowledge, and in the end supersede them. The Sukhavati Sutras and the sects which base their doctrines upon them represent a development in Buddhism corresponding to the contemporary development of Hinduism and probably not independent of it. It is to be observed, further, that the conception of salvation in the Pure Land sects is thoroughly Buddhistic: the evil from which man is to be saved is not sin and its penalty, but the round of rebirth, and the positive goal is the supreme knowledge which makes man a Buddha.

The last of the great divisions of Japanese Buddhism, the Nichiren, represents a violent reaction against the Pure Land sects. Its founder, whose name it bears, was born in 1222; he was as a boy a student in a Shingon temple and later in the principal monastery of the Tendai at Hiyeizan. An incident that occurred on his way thither had a marked influence on his career: in a village which he passed through he saw some children dragging about a plaything, an image of Buddha (Shaka). When he remonstrated at this profanation he was told that since Shinran had taught that Amida was the only Buddha to worship they had no further use for the others. From that moment he resolved to become a reformer. As the basis of his system he too, like Dengyo the founder of the Tendai, took the Saddharma Pundarika, but he developed its teachings in an altogether different way. When he appeared as a preacher of reform his plain speaking and his often violent denunciation of abuses made a deep impression among the people, but provoked the enmity of the monks, who got him banished. On his return he made himself so obnoxious by his pugnacious methods of evangelisation that he was condemned to death, but was saved by a miracle. After another term of banishment he seems to have become more temperate; at least he spent his last years quietly teaching those who resorted to him to learn. He left his spirit to the sect as well as his name; in all its history it has been reactionary, intolerant, and violent. Its differences with the Shin-shu were fought out on more than one bloody battle-field.

Widely as the sects differ among themselves, and violent as the contentions among them have been at times, they nevertheless represent essentially the same type of Buddhism. They all acknowledge the same canon of scripture, though out of the immense bulk of this canon (6,771 volumes) each principal sect makes certain sutras peculiarly its own. They all start from the same fundamental assumptions, some of which are a part of primitive Buddhism, while others are specifically Mahayanist.

The round of rebirths in which man's destiny in general and in particular is determined by the deeds of a former existence, and salvation in its negative aspect as escape from this "wheel," of course underlies all; that the world is evil through and through, and life miserable are corner-stones of the creed and lend their sombre colour to the literature of certain periods. But the Indian pessimism which such utterances originally voice is wholly alien to the Japanese temperament, and, as in the Great Vehicle schools generally, the positive aspect of salvation, both in the popular and the philosophical conception of it—the bliss of the Western Paradise, the blessedness of the Buddha state—predominates.

The belief that the goal can be reached only by renouncing the world and submitting to the discipline for monks is rejected only by the Pure Land sects; the discipline itself also is substantially the same in all schools.

All accept, further, the same cosmology, with its succession of innumerable worlds in time and its array of Buddha worlds in all the corners of n-dimensional space. For them, as for all Mahayanists, Nirvana is not surcease of sorrow through the suppression of its cause, desire; still less is it extinction, but the highest positive good, the possession of the supreme knowledge, that is, a transcendental knowledge of the Absolute, the Bhutatathata. The Japanese schools are all, in their peculiar fashion, pantheistic; their Absolute is immanent not transcendent. Inasmuch as this Buddha nature is in all, all are potentially Buddha—not, of course, what we call the historical Buddha, but the eternal Buddha of whom all the Buddhas of all worlds are manifestations, the Dharmakaya. It is egoism, which as self-consciousness and self-love isolates us mentally and morally, that hinders the realisation of Buddhahood. The knowledge of the Absolute is therefore the knowledge of man's own true nature in its identity with the Absolute. The chief differences among the sects lie in the choice of methods by which the goal is to be reached; their distinctive teachings are principally concerned with vindicating the method and explaining its application.

To the masses these abstruse doctrines and scholastic controversies signify little or nothing; at most they can comprehend that the Pure Land sects give the layman a better chance than the Holy Way. For them Buddhism is not a pantheism, but a polytheism, of whose multitudinous gods they may obtain protection from the tangible evils of this life and the satisfaction of their worldly desires, and by the efficacy of whose funeral rites they may escape the evils of the hereafter.

The pantheon of Japanese Buddhism is very comprehensive; it includes popular gods from India and from every country which it passed through on the long road to Japan, a host of native Kami, besides many Buddhas and saints out of its own history and mythology. Among these Sakyamuni occupies a somewhat inconspicuous place, though images of him, alone or with groups of his disciples, are not infrequent. The imaginary—or, if you please, ideal—Buddha Amitabha (Amida) is a much greater figure in Japanese Buddhism, and not solely through the influence of the Pure Land sects; there are few temples in which a statue of Amida is not found either as the principal or a subordinate figure. The goddess of mercy, Kwannon, is a hardly less conspicuous figure. Binzuru, the divine healer, is also a very popular deity; his idols are polished by the hands of suppliants who believe that they can get rid of all sorts of ailments by rubbing the images of the god. One of the commonest idols is Fudo, represented as enveloped in flames with a sword in his right hand and a rope in his left; this terrifying figure destroys or binds evil-doers. The king of hell, Emma-sama, before whom all souls must stand in judgment, is also frequently represented, a warning to men to think upon their ways. A friendlier figure is Jizo, the special protector of children, whose statues are often almost buried under heaps of pebbles, a vicarious service for the little souls in hell whom an old hag compels to heap up pebbles on the river bank. The seven gods of good fortune are peculiarly venerated, and have a place on the Buddha-shelf in many homes: foremost among them the god of riches, oftentimes the god of abundant food, the gods who give comfort, long life, wisdom, the valiant protector from dangers, and the goddess of beauty.

The Buddhist temples are much more splendid affairs than the Shinto shrines, and the worship in them far more imposing. The gorgeous vestments of the priests, the solemn intonation of the service, the clouds of incense in the dimly lighted sanctuary, have reminded many observers of the services in a Christian cathedral. Such services are held in the great temples every day, and with augmented splendour on the high days of the calendar. Many of the temples, however, are hardly used for worship at all. The laity do not participate in these rites even as a worshipping congregation, but go singly to the temples to offer their petitions and drop an offering into the contribution-box, or buy from the priests amulets and talismans, holy water, ashes, and the like, for protection against disease and other ills.

In all Japanese homes, except those of adherents of the most reactionary Shinto sects, there is a Buddha-shelf, on which stand little shrines, often richly ornamented in lacquer, for Buddhist gods; the tablets bearing the posthumous names of the deceased members of the family stand on the same shelf; offerings of food and incense are made before them. The funeral rites are conducted, as has already been observed, by Buddhist priests; there are minor differences in the practice of the several sects. They are in part at the house, where a soul tablet bearing the posthumous or Buddha name of the deceased is set up, lights are kept burning, food and incense offered, partly in the temple, where prayers are recited and a kind of eulogy pronounced. The body is then removed to the burning-place.

From the 13th to the 15th of July an All-Souls feast is kept, at which time it is believed that the souls are permitted to return to their kindred and be entertained by them. A staging of bamboo canes is erected in one of the rooms of the house, on which food and lanterns are placed for the spirits, and a Buddhist priest reads a mass before them. On the first evening fires of hemp leaves are lighted before the entrance of the house, and incense strewed on the coals, as an invitation to the spirits. At the end of the three days the food that has been set out for the spirits is wrapped up in mats and thrown into a river. Dances of a peculiar kind are a conspicuous feature of the celebration, which is evidently an old Japanese custom; the Buddhist elements are adscititious. At this season the graves are decorated, and frequent visits are paid by the kinsfolk. For those who have no relatives living a mass is said in all the temples for "the hungry devils."

In the political restoration of 1868 Shinto was at first proclaimed the religion of the state, and the ministry to which it was committed took precedence of all others. Buddhism was no longer recognised by the government; the payments for the support of its temples were cut off, the temples of the mixed cult (Ryobu Shinto) were purged of Buddhist images and emblems, and as far as possible Shinto simplicity was restored; for a while even the burning of the dead was forbidden. This excess of zeal soon passed, and in the next stage both Shinto and Buddhist priests, in the quality of religious teachers, were put under the supervision of a ministry of religion, which was later reduced to a mere bureau for Shinto-Buddhist temples. The constitution of 1889 acknowledges no state religion, and guarantees complete religious liberty. Shinto continues to be, however, the religion of the imperial house and of the court; and on high festivals the emperor himself officiates in the ceremonies for himself and his people. Thus Shinto enjoys the prestige, though not the legal status, of a national religion.

The history of religion in Japan would not be complete without at least a few words about the influence of Confucianism. This influence was chiefly in the field of ethics. Shinto, as we have seen, gave its sanction to the ancient customs, including the customary morality, but it had no moral teaching of its own; Buddhism brought its own double standard of morality, for monks and for laymen, the latter not unaffected by Chinese notions, but it made no attempt to systematise or rationalise ethics. The Japanese had some acquaintance with Confucian teaching before the advent of Buddhism, and in the period of active communication with China, especially in the ninth century, when the zeal for Chinese learning and literature was at its height and the study of the Chinese classics was regularly pursued in the higher schools, this influence was greatly increased. Even Buddhist sects recast their teaching in the mould of the Five Relations. The feudal period created its own chivalric ideals; loyalty to the feudal superior became the supreme virtue, and was pushed to romantic excesses in which all other ethical ideals were overridden.

With the restoration of unity and order under the Tokugawa shoguns there began a new epoch of Chinese influence. The Neoconfucianism of Chu Hi was fostered by the state, even to the extent of punishing such as had the audacity to criticise or attack the school which the government had declared orthodox. This philosophy spread especially among the Samurai, and led many to turn away from Buddhism as a superstition unworthy of thinking men. Japanese exponents of Chu Hi's philosophy, such as Muro Kyuso, developed not only its ethics but its religious possibilities, so that it answered spiritual needs as well as offered elevated moral principles. More decidedly religious, with a mystical turn, is the contemporary philosophy of Nakae Toju, better known as the Wise Man of Omi, which likewise had a large influence in the eighteenth century.

CHAPTER VIII

EGYPT

THE RELIGION OF THE OLD KINGDOM

The Nomes and Their Gods—Divine Beasts—The Old Kingdom—
Celestial Deities, Temples, Priests, Worship—Tombs—Conservation of the Body—Souls—Abodes of the Dead—Heaven and
the Nether World—Morals and Magic.

EGYPT and Babylonia are the oldest seats of civilisation.
The investigations of Eduard Meyer have led him to believe
that the Egyptian calendar was established in the year
4241 B. C., on the basis of observations that must have
taken centuries to accumulate. Whether this precise date
be confirmed or not, there is no doubt that the accession of
Menes, the first king in Manetho's catalogue of dynasties,
falls before 3000 B. C.,[1] and that the kingdom of all Egypt
which he founded was preceded by the two kingdoms of
Upper and of Lower Egypt through a period so long that
the dualism was indelibly impressed on the institutions of
the country. The rulers before Menes, who were for Manetho semi-mythical (νέκυες, ἥρωες), turn out to be real men
of flesh and blood; and before them the stage of culture at
which the Egyptians had arrived in the age of its first monuments demands for its development centuries which we have
no means of counting.

[1] Meyer, 3315; Sethe, 3360; Breasted, 3400. The dates of the great
epochs of Egyptian history, according to Breasted, History of Egypt,
are as follows: (Old Kingdom) Fourth Dynasty, 2900–2750 B. C.;
Fifth Dynasty, 2750–2625; (Middle Kingdom) Twelfth Dynasty,
2000–1788; (New Empire) Eighteenth Dynasty, 1580–1350; Nineteenth Dynasty, 1350–1205; Twenty-second Dynasty, 945–745; (Saite
Restoration) Twenty-sixth Dynasty, 663–525.

The earliest burials show that many centuries before the dawn of Egyptian history the valley of the Nile, from the Delta to Nubia, was occupied by the same race which inhabited it in later times, and which, notwithstanding subsequent admixture of foreign blood, maintained its characteristics essentially unaltered to the last. The conditions of tillage in the valley, with its long narrow strip of arable land watered and fertilised by the inundation, not only constrained the earliest inhabitants to settle in towns, but to undertake common works for the regulation and distribution of the water, and in this necessity of co-operative labour under directive authority we may see, as under similar conditions in Babylonia and in the valley of the Yellow River in China, one great reason why these regions were the predestined cradles of civilisation. Egypt possessed other advantages in being by its situation and configuration comparatively secure against attacks from without, and of having in the river the means of easy communication not only between neighbouring towns, but throughout its whole length from the first cataract to the sea; conditions which, even before the establishment of any political unity, tended to a certain equalisation of progress. The observation of Herodotus that Egypt is the gift of the Nile is true in a larger meaning than was in his mind.

The towns, each possessing its belt of tillage within the reach of the overflow, its pasture-land on higher ground, and perhaps its unreclaimed marshes, were the oldest political units. If they had been originally clan settlements, every trace of this origin had long disappeared; they were, at the beginning of our knowledge, communities held together, not by real or imaginary ties of kinship, but by common social and economic interests. When Egypt was united under one sovereign, the old city-states lost their independence, but not their political existence; in the centralised rule of the Old Kingdom they preserved as administrative divisions much of their former importance; in the decadence of the monarchy they regained a large measure of autonomy as hereditary feudal counties; upon its fall they reverted to independence. Reduced for a time to the status of provinces under the Empire, as its power declined they again recovered themselves; down to Ptolemaic and Roman times these earliest political centres, called by the Greeks "nomes," survived all the vicissitudes of native rule and foreign conquest.

Each of these primitive city-states had its own god, who presided over all its interests. He made its husbandry fruitful and gave the increase of its flocks and herds; his standard was carried before his people when they went out to war. His house—primitively a wattle-and-daub hut, like the habitations of men—stood in the middle of the town, with a pair of tall masts before it, a rude fence marking off the sacred precincts. The political head of the community, by whatever name we should call him, was by virtue of his headship the chief minister of the god, though the ordinary services were doubtless performed by other hands. The gods of the several nomes were alike in character and operations; each was the god of his city, and its people were his people. What distinguished one from another was his relation to a particular community: "He of Edfu," "She of Nekheb," suffices for a designation, and some of the gods never got any other. Besides these gods, who concerned themselves with the public interest of the community, there were many functional deities, who had for their province single specific moments or spheres of life, existing, so to speak, only in and for these activities, like the gods who are catalogued in the Roman Indigitamenta. In a corresponding way there were demons for every kind of mischief.

The gods of several different cities often bear the same name: Horus, for instance, is the god of three nomes in Upper and of two in Lower Egypt (and, with distinguishing titles, of two or three more), Hathor is the goddess of five in Upper Egypt and of one in Lower. In some cases this may be the result of migration, the colonists naturally worshipping the god of the old home, or of political causes; but it is probable that in most cases the name of a more famous deity, especially of one connected with the great powers of nature, has been assumed by the originally nameless god of the place—a thing to which the religion of Greece, for example, offers many parallels, and of which the subsequent identification of all the local gods of Egypt with Re, the sun, is a further development.

A feature of the Egyptian religion which struck the first Greek observers as characteristic was the intimate relation of the gods with animals. Many of the Greek gods also were associated with certain animals, but in the age in which the Greeks became acquainted with Egypt these animals were little more than conventional attributes—the eagle of Zeus, the owl of Athene, the dove of Aphrodite—while in Egypt, on the contrary, there was in that period a distinct recrudescence of animal worship. The irrationality of this worship, especially in a people of immemorial civilisation and a great reputation for wisdom, made the Greeks think that it must have some mysterious profundity, an impression which the Egyptian priests probably fostered. Modern writers, especially in the days when symbolism was a great word with them, have sometimes deluded themselves in the same way.

There can be no doubt that in early Egypt the animal was the manifest god; Khnum of Elephantine was a ram, Hathor a cow, Nekhhebt a vulture, Bast a cat, Horus a falcon, Anubis a jackal, Sebek a crocodile, Thoth an ibis, and so on. Both domestic animals and beasts and birds of prey are found in the list, which, indeed, fairly comprehends the fauna of Egypt. By exception, one or two gods appear only in human form. What determined the selection of the particular species of animal in different places can seldom be discovered. A crocodile is a suitable god for the Fayum district, and the connection of the falcon with a god of the sun has many analogies; but in most cases the association is beyond guessing. Divine powers may also be embodied in trees or lodge in them; and an originally anonymous

"Sycamore-tree-deity" may be succeeded by a "Hathor of the Sycamore," quite like Artemis Kedreatis or Karyatis.

Various theories of the origin of Egyptian animal worship have been proposed. De Brosses included it in his voluminous "fetishism"; in recent years it has become fashionable to call it "totemism." A label, however, even if rightly applied, is not an explanation, and in this case the propriety of the label is more than questionable: there is no evidence that the Egyptians of the Hare Nome, for instance, regarded themselves as descended from a divine hare ancestor, nor is there any trace of the distinctive social organisation nor of the divine sacrifice which have been commonly regarded as characteristics of totemism. Succession in the female line, which persisted in the great houses, is doubtless the survival of a primitive form of the family, but has no necessary relation to totemism. And even if proof were forthcoming that the forefathers of the prehistoric Egyptians were totemists of strict observance according to modern doctrine, the question how they came to worship animals as their divine progenitors would be as far from an answer as ever.

The motives which have led savages in all the ends of the earth to worship animals are various but not mysterious; the only thing that is peculiar in Egypt is the perpetuation of this worship as a common pattern for religion to the latest times. This is itself only a phase of the general conservatism of Egyptian cult, in which, as in other respects, the Egyptians like the Chinese paid the penalty of early—we might almost say prematurely—attaining a very high stage of civilisation; in the centuries of decadence which followed the Old Kingdom men looked back to the golden age and fixed the habit. Partly for this reason, partly from temperamental causes, the Egyptians of later ages could learn but not forget—the most fatal of all disqualifications for progress.

If we could get a glimpse of the history, say in the beginning of the fourth millennium B. C., we should probably find that some of the city-states, favoured by situation and by stronger or wiser rulers, had outgrown their neighbours and made them tributary, to be, in the vicissitudes of dominion, subjected by their former subjects or by a more powerful city; and that, ambition growing with might, larger kingdoms were formed, or many cities brought under the hegemony or rule of one, as happened in Babylonia. We know at least that the union of all Egypt in one kingdom was preceded by the two kingdoms of Upper and Lower Egypt, corresponding to the natural divisions of the land, the former including the long narrow valley of the Nile, and the latter the Delta. Evidence of more than one kind indicates that at the beginning these kingdoms contended for the supremacy under the banners of different deities: the god of the rulers of the Delta was Horus, of the kings of Upper Egypt, Set. The hostility of these brothers is an old and persistent trait of the mythology, the origin of which appears to be political rather than natural. The union of the two kingdoms finds expression in the coupling of the two gods; a title of the queen is "She who beholds Horus-Set," *i. e.*, the king. At a later stage in the history the kingdoms are "the two kingdoms of the worshippers of Horus," from which we may infer that a dynasty from the Delta had established itself on the throne of Upper Egypt. As the god of the kings in the south as well as the north, Horus became the first national god in Egypt, and it is probably in consequence of this that he became the god of several cities in Upper Egypt—perhaps of cities which were at one time or another the residence of the kings.

The union of the two kingdoms under one sceptre was accomplished in the thirty-fourth century B. C. Menes, who stands at the head of Manetho's catalogue, may not have been the first who ruled over all Egypt, but he was the founder of the first dynasty that perpetuated itself upon the throne. The kingdom of Menes and his successors was a dual monarchy. The king wore the two crowns of Upper and Lower Egypt, and adopted the insignia and titles of both kings; the administration was throughout twofold,

with distinct treasuries, for example. In the separate kingdoms the autonomy of the nomes had evidently been lost;
the united kingdom is not organised on a feudal basis, but
as an absolute monarchy with a thoroughly centralised administration, as in ancient China. This centralisation did
not, however, invade the sphere of religion. The kings
might worship Horus as the god of the royal house—and
in this sense of the state—and promote his worship in the
capital and the court, but in the cities the old gods continued to be the gods of the people. Horus did not even
take a place beside them. The local priesthoods were independent; the priesthood of Horus had no primacy or supervision over them, and there was no such thing as a ministry
of religion.

The king was not a plain mortal like his subjects, but was
himself Horus in human form, an incarnation of the deity,
and he bore a name expressive of the fact. He ruled, therefore, by divine right and was addressed with titles of divinity, but there is no indication that religious worship in any
form was paid to the living ruler.

The union of all Egypt under a strong rule was followed
by a great advance in civilisation. The vast resources of
wealth and labour at the command of the king were lavishly
expended in the building and adorning of palaces and temples which have long since perished, and of imperishable
tombs, and the high officials of the state emulated the royal
example. The capital was established, for obvious reasons,
near the old frontier between the two kingdoms, and there,
in the vicinity of Memphis, the kings of succeeding dynasties built their "eternal houses," the pyramids. Only a few
years ago it was the universal opinion that the culmination
of Egyptian art was reached under the Twelfth Dynasty
(from about 2000 B. C.); recent discoveries have shown that
nearly a thousand years earlier, in the age of the pyramid-
builders, particularly under the Fourth Dynasty, a perfection had been attained which was never afterward surpassed. In this age the Egyptian religion, also, already ap-

pears in the forms which were perpetuated without essential change to the end.

It has been already observed that the gods were first of all the gods of cities or districts which they protected and on whose inhabitants they bestowed "life, health, strength, victory, and prosperity." However strange the beast or bird in which the deity is embodied, he is inwardly not beast but man, with human character and motives; his relation to his worshippers is similar to that of a beneficent ruler to his people. Even the myths—such fragments as survive—are not animal myths, but doings of manlike beings. The powers of nature were also great gods, especially the sun and moon and the sky. The Nile, too, was a beneficent deity, but less eminent than the dependence of Egypt on the river for its very existence might lead us to expect.[1] These powers, however, bestow their blessings on all alike. They do not favour one locality above another, and for that reason they were not in the beginning the gods of any particular communities. In actual religion, therefore, of which worship is the measure, they were subordinate figures.

Under the first dynasties, however, and in all probability in the earlier kingdoms of the Horus worshippers, Horus, the falcon god, was the sky (the sun is the eye of Horus) or —and this view prevailed—the sun itself; and then, naturally, his old enemy, Set, became the power of darkness. It is not unlikely that the political consolidation of the kingdom favoured this development; the god of the king and the state is not a local deity of some obscure nome who has risen to his high place by conquest, but a universal god. But the solar religion which eventually prevailed in Egypt had a different origin. At On (Heliopolis), only a few miles from Memphis, the god of the nome was Atum, whose sacred animal was apparently a bull (Mnevis). The worship of

---

[1] In some places in the pyramid texts Osiris seems to be a Nile-god; but nothing in the myth or cult indicates that he was originally the divine stream.

the sun (Re) assumed at this place, for reasons which are beyond our conjecture, a far greater prominence than elsewhere; he had a priesthood of his own and a temple of peculiar type. The priests of Re at Heliopolis were the first religious thinkers in Egypt, and their theology, as we shall see, made its way in the course of time to general acceptance. The fundamental doctrine of this theology was that the sun (Re, the visible sun in the sky) is the greatest of all gods.

With the Fifth Dynasty (2750 B. C.) the solar religion of Heliopolis became the religion of the state. A legend of the Middle Kingdom related that the founders of this dynasty were three sons of the god Re, born at a single birth by the wife of a priest of Re, at Sadkhu, not far below Memphis. It is possible that in this legend may be preserved the memory that the founder of the new dynasty was a priest of Re. These kings are the first to assume, in addition to the Horus name, a throne title containing the name of Re. The temples of this dynasty, of which that at Abu Gurab has been most completely excavated, were constructed on an altogether singular plan. They consisted of a large open court, at the farther end of which, upon a basis in the form of a truncated pyramid, stood an obelisk with a pyramidal apex, the seat of the god, upon which, later inscriptions say, "the soul of the god rested when it came out of heaven" as upon its body. The obelisk, therefore, took the place of the cultus image in the sanctuary of other temples. In front of the obelisk stood the great altar of the god; the whole worship was thus carried on under the open sky. At Abu Gurab the covered passage which leads out on to the basis of the obelisk was decorated both on the inner and outer sides, and in one series of these pictures the seasons of the year are represented as bringing offerings to the king, exhibiting thus the occupations and products of each season, a motive unique in Egyptian temple decoration.

Another characteristic feature of these temples was that on either side, on a brick foundation, was set a ship, representing the two barges in which the sun god sailed through the sky in the day and the night respectively. The temple was richly endowed, and its services maintained by a body of priests of five different ranks. Each of the earlier kings of the dynasty built a new temple of the same type, of which the same priesthood assumed charge. The temples bear such names as "Favourite Abode of Re," "Satisfaction of Re." Although temples of this style were no longer built after the Fifth Dynasty, the religion of Re had, through the zeal of the Heliopolitan priests and of the kings of this period, gained a pre-eminence which it never afterward lost. In the same age we find the first of those identifications of the old local deity with the sun god which was destined in the end to embrace almost every Egyptian deity; Atum-Re of Heliopolis was the natural beginning.

The course of the sun through the heavens and the way in which he goes back again at night to his daily starting-point are things which had exercised primitive fancy among the Egyptians as in other countries. Sometimes they imagined him as a falcon (Horus, later identified with Re) winging his way across the sky; sometimes as a dung-beetle (*Scarabæus Ægyptiorum*) rolling the solar globe, from which, by combination of associations, they thought the new sun was to be born; sometimes he was a calf, self-begotten, born each day of the cow-goddess of the sky, Hathor. The commonest representation, however, made him traverse his course along the belly or on the back of the sky-cow in a boat such as the king used in making a progress on the Nile. At evening he exchanged the boat of day for another, in which during the night he returned to the east either by a subterranean river or by a circuit which passed through the dark north quarter. The sky, as we have seen, was imagined as an immense cow, whose four legs were planted at the corners of the earth and who is usually upheld besides by a number of deities. The name of this goddess, Hathor, "House of Horus," is appropriate to the sky; the notion of the celestial cow has parallels elsewhere. The identification with earthly cow-goddesses, in particular with the nameless local deity of Dendera, is in all probability secondary.

The moon likewise traversed the sky in a boat, whence his name Khonsu, "the sailor." But it was early connected also with the ibis-headed god Thoth, a deity who enjoyed a great reputation for wisdom and was esteemed to be the inventor of letters and patron of literature, and the great authority in medicine, astronomy, and other sciences. Since this character is in no way suggested by the ibis head, nor by the dog-headed baboon, in which form also Thoth appears, the most probable conjecture is that the priests of Thoth had at an early time distinguished themselves in learning and science, and that the god appropriated their reputation.[1] The association with the moon, who as a measurer of time may easily be imagined to have astronomical knowledge, possibly came about in this way.

Among the stars Sirius was especially honoured as a goddess, Sothis, who was early identified with Isis. The place thus given to Sirius is explained not alone by the splendour of the star, but by its fundamental importance in the Egyptian calendar. Various constellations, notably Orion, have a place in the myths, but do not seem to have been of any corresponding significance in religion. The circumpolar stars which never sink below the horizon were called the "imperishable ones," and were sometimes imagined to be the abodes of the blessed dead.

Except the peculiar temples of Re from the Fifth Dynasty described above, no temples of the gods dating from the Old Kingdom are preserved. Many of them doubtless fell into decay during the period of eclipse which followed the brilliant dawn of the Egyptian kingdom, while such as survived were replaced by larger and more splendid structures in the time of the Middle Kingdom, as the latter, in turn, almost everywhere had to make room for the immense temples of the Theban Empire. The ruins of pyramid temples of the Old Kingdom, of which enough remains to show their

[1] The case of Ea in Babylonia is similar.

plan and construction, make it probable that the temples of the gods did not differ in their essential features from those of later times, as, indeed, we should infer from the conservatism of the Egyptians in all such matters. We should imagine them, therefore, as consisting of a dark cella, within which, screened from vulgar gaze, was the image of the god; before the cella a larger hypostyle hall, and in front of the latter the principal altar. The whole temple stood in the midst of a walled court, around which lay rooms for the use of the priests and storehouses for utensils and materials for worship.

The image in the cella was of moderate dimensions, and generally made of wood or with a wooden core. From an inventory of the temple at Dendera we learn that the principal image of Hathor was somewhat above four feet tall; the deities associated with her in worship were only a cubit in height. It was thus possible to carry the images about in the festal processions. The image stood in a shrine, frequently cut out of a single block of stone, closed by metal doors. Every morning the shrine was opened by a priest, who, after smoking out the demons by burning incense, performed the god's toilet and set food and flowers before him, accompanying the several stages of a circumstantial ritual with the recitation of the proper formulas. The specimens of these which have survived attach to the acts of the cultus an occult mythical symbolism. Thus when the priest draws the bolt which fastens the door of the shrine he says: "The finger of Set is withdrawn from the eye of Horus which is excellent (*bis*). I loosen the leather behind the god. O god, N. N., take thy two feathers and thy white crown out of thy Horus eye, the right eye out of the right eye, the left eye out of the left eye. Thy beauty belongs to thee, O god, N. N.; thou naked one, clothe thyself," and so on through the like dreary profundities. The whole liturgy is magical, not devotional.

Among the priests one class, the Kherheb, had for their special business to learn and recite these sacred texts in the daily service and on festivals; their second title, "scribes of the divine books," shows that their wisdom was already incorporated in a literature which probably had much the same character as the Indian Brahmanas, if we imagine the latter with the poetic quotations from the Vedas and the nascent philosophical ideas eliminated. Besides these ministers of the word there was another order called the "Pure Ones" (Ueb), indicated in the hieroglyphs by a kneeling man over whom a jar of water is pouring itself. In sacrificial scenes one of these priests inspects the blood of the victims and pronounces it clean, and it may be that they included among their functions the practical application of the rules of clean and unclean. They were divided into four classes, each of which served for a quarter of the year, and during this term had their living from the table of the god. The permanent establishment of the temples, even in the Middle Kingdom, was apparently not very numerous. A temple of Anubis endowed by Sesostris II had a high priest and a chief Kherheb. Nine other priests took regular turns there: a superintendent of classes, a temple scribe, an ordinary Kherheb, and so forth, besides eight minor officials. The enormous multiplication of the clergy came in the days of the Empire.

The kings not only built or rebuilt many temples, but provided for their support by gifts and endowments. In the New Empire all worship was in theory offered by the king; hence in sacrificial scenes he always takes the leading part, and this tendency, which belongs to the logic of a state religion,[1] doubtless began much earlier, at least in the capital.

In addition to the daily presentation of food to the god in his private apartment, individuals brought their gifts to the great altar in the court, and at the festivals sacrifices were made on a much larger scale. The food, after being set out on the table of the god, was consumed by the priests or distributed among the worshipping people, and was

[1] Compare the imperial cultus in China, above, pp. 7 f.

doubtless believed to have acquired by the god's partaking of it a divine—or, as we should say, a magical—property, by virtue of which it conveyed all sorts of benefits besides the stilling of hunger.

The festivals, of which every god had his own calendar, were celebrated not only with multiplied offerings and more elaborate ceremonials, but by religious processions, in which the image of the god, in his ark (frequently in the form of a boat), was carried on the shoulders of priests through the streets of the city; sometimes he paid a visit of state to the temple of another god in a neighbouring place. Hymns in honour of the god were chanted to the accompaniment of the sistrum—a kind of rattle—and castanets, often in the hands of women; later a harp is included among the temple properties. The dates of the festivals often had some connection with the myth of the god, and it is probable that the celebration itself frequently included an acting out of the myth by the priests or the people, whether symbolically or with such violent realism as appears in the descriptions given by Greek travellers.

In the oldest graves, dating probably from the fifth millennium before the Christian era, the body is merely laid in a shallow pit in the sand beyond the overflow of the Nile, and with it vessels of pottery or stone containing food and water, household utensils, weapons and implements of the chase, and toilet articles, especially a slate palette for triturating the malachite face-paint. Small clay models of boats and of houses are sometimes found, and pottery or stone figurines representing wife and servants—usually without feet, presumably to keep them from running away. The contents of these graves thus give ample evidence that the earliest Egyptians shared the universal belief that the dead survive, in a different mode of existence, indeed, but with the same needs as in this life.

With the progress of civilisation, more permanent and secure habitations are provided for the dead. The nobles and high officials of the Old Kingdom are buried deep beneath the earth, a vertical shaft being sunk through the overlying sand and gravel to the native rock below, in which a chamber is excavated to receive the body. On the surface a rectangular structure with sloping sides is erected over the shaft, which passes up through it—an architectural evolution from the heap of stones earlier reared to protect the body from wild beasts and grave-robbers. On one side of this structure—as a rule on the east—is a false portal with no opening, through which the spirit is imagined to be able to pass at will; before it stands the stone table, or shelf, on which food and drink were laid from time to time for the use of the dead. The burial-chamber was furnished for all the needs of man, and when the body had been laid to rest in it, the shaft was blocked up with stone and the opening covered. In later forms of these so-called "mastaba" tombs accessible chambers are made in the structure, and the blind door with the table for offerings in front of it then takes its place at the inner end of a kind of mortuary chapel. The tombs of high officials often contain a large number of chambers; that of a prime minister of a king of the Sixth Dynasty has no fewer than thirty-one—a complete establishment. The walls of the chambers are often, as in the tomb just mentioned, covered with paintings representing the herding of cattle and tilling the soil, harvest and vintage, butchering and hunting, artisans and boatmen at their work, musicians playing and ballet-girls dancing. The primitive motive for these pictures is the same that led to the depositing of pottery models and figurines in the tombs, they magically take the place of the real things; but art has got far beyond the purely utilitarian end and depicts these scenes with an obvious delight in the representation itself. Portrait statues of the dead, commonly in stone, were also placed in an inner chamber of the tomb, a custom which greatly promoted the development of the sculptor's art. The motive was, however, not memorial; the image of the man was another body in which the soul might have an imperishable habitation. The early kings were buried in similar tombs; in one of them, at Abydos, not only the king found his last resting-place, but in small chambers about him his wives, his guard, and even his dwarfs and his dogs were laid.

The royal pyramids differ only in form, not in purpose, from the mastabas. Access to the burial-chamber was made as difficult as possible by blind passages and formidable obstructions in the true one, precautions which proved ineffective to thwart the robbers, who, attracted by the wealth of buried treasure, have everywhere anticipated the modern archæologists. The pyramids enclose no mortuary chapels, in lieu of which a temple dedicated to the king was erected before his pyramid. Here a regular cultus was maintained, and offerings of food, drink, clothing, perfumes, and ointments were made in great variety and lavish profusion. In some cases a raised way led from this temple to a landing on the bank of the river, where it terminated in another temple.

The conservation of the body was a matter of momentous concern, and the embalmer's art was perfected to accomplish it. The viscera having been removed, the body was steeped in natron and asphalt, and when sufficiently impregnated with these preservatives was wound, with various aromatics, in endless coils of bandages, and laid in a sarcophagus. Fashions changed in mummies and coffins as in other things; but the object always was not merely to prevent decay, but to keep as far as possible the form of the man as he had been in life. At the burial, the priests went through the motions of opening the eyes, ears, mouth, and nose of the mummy, reciting meanwhile potent spells to restore to the dead man the use of his senses. In the pyramid ritual the assurance is given that the king's heart (the seat of intelligence) has not been taken from him, or, if it has, that a god will put it back in his body. The priest presents food and drink in which are magical virtues, and bids the king stand upon his feet and partake of this imperishable bread and beer. Yet the dead in their tombs were dependent for their well-being on the continued care of the living, and, lest posterity or piety should fail, endowments were created to provide in perpetuity for the maintenance of the tomb and the offerings to the manes of the founder.

As among numerous other peoples, the soul was associated with the breath which leaves the body in the last expiration, and it is frequently pictured as a human-headed bird hovering over the mummy, or perching in a tree near by, curiously surveying its own funeral. The name *ba* properly belongs to the departed soul, like ψυχή in Homer; in the living man the Egyptians spoke of the mind (heart, inwards), the Homeric φρένες, κραδίη. Another word, *ka*, is commonly understood to mean "soul," specifically the body-soul, or ghostly double of a man; but it seems rather to correspond to the Roman *genius*, a spirit companion and guardian from birth to death and in the other life.

By the side of the primitive belief that the dead inhabit the tombs and lead there an existence as closely resembling their former life as the dead can be like the living, we find in the age of the pyramid-builders various notions of an abode of the dead remote from the dwellings of men. The vaguest notion of this kind is expressed in the phrase, "those whose places are hidden"; they are gone to "the undiscovered country, from whose bourn no traveller returns."

More frequently the land of the departed is in the west; the dead are called "The People of the West," and the ruler of that realm, "First (or Chief) of the People of the West" (Khent Amenti), who was early identified with Anubis, the jackal god of desert cemeteries, guardian and guide of the dead, who in turn was superseded by Osiris. This land of the dead may have been imagined as an oasis in the western desert over which the sun went down.

Others imagined the dead dwelling in the "Field of Rushes" (Earu), the scenery of which seems to have been suggested by that of parts of the Delta. It was intersected by canals, which were opened at the time of inundation. The inhabitants tilled the soil just as in this world, but the land was of marvellous fertility and wheat grew higher than a man's head. To reach these islands of the blest a river must be crossed. The ferryman, whose name is "Facing Backward," because he stands in the stern of the boat punting it across the channel, will not take everybody for a passenger, but only him of whom it is attested that he has done no evil, one who is "righteous before heaven and earth and the island." The "Field of Rushes" amid the watercourses, like the oasis in the western desert, was doubtless originally a region of mythical terrestrial geography; but in the pyramid texts, as part of the solarisation of the royal hereafter, the boatman is the ferryman of Re, the sun god, and the islands of the blest have been transplanted to the sky.

In several pyramid tombs of kings of the Fifth and Sixth Dynasties (between, say, 2625 and 2475 B. C.) the walls of the galleries and chambers are covered with hieroglyphic texts, having chiefly to do with the post-mortem fortunes of the king. An analysis of these texts finds among them a ritual for burial and for offerings at the tomb, magical formulas of various purport, an ancient ritual of worship, hymns, fragments of myth, and prayers on behalf of the dead king.

The texts brought together in these inscriptions are diverse in age and origin as well as in contents. All the imaginations the Egyptians had entertained of a happy hereafter are represented in them side by side or confusedly mingled. The characteristic conception, however, is that the dead king ascends to the eastern sky and joins the rising sun: "This king Pepi lives as lives he (*sc.* the sun god) who has entered the west of the sky, when he rises in the east of the sky." He reaches this destination, now in the boat of Re's ferryman, now by taking the wings of a bird, now he mounts up by a ladder. The gods salute him as "an imperishable glorious being," and he is conducted to Re, the sun-god: "O Re-Atum! thy son comes to thee, Unis comes to thee. Lift him up to thee, enfold thou him in thine embrace. He is thy bodily son forever." Taking his place in

the barge of Re, he sails with him across the sky, himself
a great god. A remarkable poem in the pyramid of Unis
pictures him as devouring the gods, small and great, thus
appropriating the magical power and knowledge of them all.[1]

This future is the prerogative of royalty; it is as the
"bodily son" of Re that the portals of the firmament are
thrown open to the king. Only at a much later time did
common mortals presume to seek passage for themselves in
the solar barge, and then for a different voyage.[2]

Another conception of the hereafter, which has a considerable place in the pyramid texts and was destined in time to
outgrow all others, is connected with Osiris, who was originally, it seems, the god of Busiris, in the Delta, but early
made his way up the Nile, and had his most famous seat
at Abydos. Osiris was murdered by Set; but by the piety
of his son Horus his dismembered body was pieced together and restored to life, he was vindicated in judgment
of the charges his enemy brought against him, and became
king of the realms of the dead in the west, or of the nether
world whose entrance was in the west—such, in brief outline, is the oldest form of the myth. In other versions, as
we shall see, the tragic story is told with more detail, the
pathetic part of Isis is enlarged, and Anubis, in his professional character, makes the mummy,[3] but the essential features remain unchanged.

Like corresponding myths among other peoples, the history of the god who was dead and is alive again opened a
door of hope for men. The means by which Osiris was restored to life must be equally potent for others; if then the
body is mummied in the same fashion, if the same rites are
performed, the same words recited at each stage in process,
the dead man will be made to live again, not, indeed, the life
of the world, but such a life as Osiris himself leads in the
world over which he reigns. In the pyramid texts, the king

---

[1] Perhaps the cannibal image was suggested by disappearance of the
stars before the rising sun.
[2] See below, pp. 194 *ff.*　　　　　　　　　[3] See below, pp. 191 *ff.*

is assimilated to Osiris, he receives his heart and limbs back as Osiris did: "As he (Osiris) lives, this king lives; as he dies not, this king dies not; as he perishes not, this king perishes not." The texts go further than this to an outright identification of the king with Osiris: the body, flesh, and bones of Osiris are those of the king. Osiris, his father, makes over his throne to the king, who thus becomes the sovereign of the dead. Like the ascent to the heaven of Re, the Osiris future was originally for royalty only—the dead king became the king of the dead; the common man could as little aspire to be god of the dead as to be a sun-god in the sky. But the chief thing in the myth, after all, was not that Osiris reigned among the dead, but that he lived again, and in this men of humbler rank might be like him. In a later age they even appropriated the identification, and every dead man was "Osiris so-and-so."

The two representations of the other life, the solar and the Osirian, are not only evolved from wholly diverse—one might say antipodal—premises, but were developed by the priesthood of two distinct religions, and doubtless spread from different centres. There are passages in the pyramid texts which show that the compilers of that miscellany were aware that the conceptions are not only diverse but incompatible. In the dedication of a pyramid it was adjured not to admit Osiris and his allied gods when they come "with an evil coming." To a king, now become a star in the sky, it is said: "Thou lookest down upon Osiris commanding the glorious dead. There thou standest, being far from him; for thou art not of them (the dead), thou belongest not among them." The sun-god "has freed king Teti from Kherti, he has not given him to Osiris." The Egyptians were, however, too much concerned to accumulate all possible plans of salvation to be balked by contradictions, and they overcame the antipathy of heaven for hades by transplanting Osiris and his realm to the sky. In one place the ascent of Osiris to heaven is described: "The sky thunders, earth trembles for fear of thee, Osiris, when thou ascendest

. . . he goes to the sky among his brethren, the gods." He is even called "Lord of the Sky." The dead king may, therefore, become a celestial Osiris.

The harmony of Re and Osiris is more formally established. Thus, when the king has mounted to heaven by the ladder which Re and Horus provide for him, "The gate of heaven will be open to thee, and the great bolts will be drawn back for thee. Re takes thee by the hand and leads thee into the sanctuary of heaven and sets thee upon the throne of Osiris, upon this thy throne, in order that thou mayest rule over the illuminated. Thou sittest like Osiris, with thy sceptre in thy hand, giving command to the living . . . the servants of the god stand behind thee, the nobles of the god stand before thee and cry: Come, thou god! come, thou possessor of the throne of Osiris. . . . Thy son (i. e., the reigning king) sits upon thy throne, provided with thy form. He does what thou didst use to do before; he is the first of the living, according to the command of Re. He cultivates barley, he cultivates spelt, and gives thee thereof (in funerary offerings).[1] Thou causest thy house behind thee to prosper and guardest thy children from harm."

It has been noted above that the ferryman "Facing Backwards" is sometimes said to require a clean bill of moral health before he will allow passengers to embark for the islands of the blest. Inscriptions in royal and noble tombs of the Old Kingdom frequently contain eulogies of the character of their occupants. Thus a nomarch of the twenty-seventh century B. C.:

"I gave bread to all the hungry of the Horn-snake Mountain;[2] I clothed him who was naked therein. I filled its shores with large cattle, and its lowlands with small cattle. I oppressed no man in possession of his property so that he complained of me to the god of my city; I spake and told what was good. No one ever feared because of one stronger

[1] One of the great blessings of being an Osiris is to enjoy a filial piety like that of Horus.
[2] The domain of the deceased nomarch.

than he, so that he complained to the god. . . . I was a benefactor to the district in the folds of the cattle, in the settlements of the fowlers. . . . I speak no lie, for I was one beloved of his father, praised of his mother, excellent in his character to his brother, and amiable to [his sister]."

It was believed, moreover, that uprightness and goodness commended man to the gods. In a tomb of the twenty-sixth century we read: "I never spoke evil of any one to his superior; I desired that it might be well with me in the presence of the great god." But the general tenor of the texts shows that the chief reliance was on the efficacy of forms of words, which, whether they take the shape of petition or of command and threat, were conceived to be of themselves potent to secure the desired end—to constrain the boatman to ferry the king over the river, the gates of the sky to open, the sun-god to take the king into his barge, and all the rest. Magical means of salvation were greatly multiplied in the composite eschatology of the decadence, but the character of the system was magical from the first. The Osirian salvation from the power of death, for example, is nothing but one of the commonest types of magical deliverance through the performance of rites and the repetition of words by which in the myth a god was delivered from the same evil.[1] The moral element in the doctrine is adventitious, and always subordinate.

Abydos was the centre from which the Osirian theology was disseminated, and the elaboration, if not the origination of it, may probably be attributed to the priesthood of that city. According to a common form of the myth, the head of Osiris had been found and buried there. The tomb of the god was shown in the necropolis,[2] and became, as a recent

---

[1] This association explains the fact that most of the Egyptian myths that have come down to us have been preserved only in the context of a magical ceremony. The same thing is true of many Babylonian myths.

[2] Excavation has shown that it was really the tomb of an ancient Thinite king who had been dead and forgotten for many centuries before his burial-place was usurped for Osiris.

writer has said, the holy sepulchre of Egypt, to which thousands made pilgrimage. At the festivals, scenes from the myth were acted out by the priests and people in a kind of passion-play, and such a representation, more impressive than any teaching in words, must have contributed greatly to spread the faith and give it convincing power. Inasmuch as it behoved those who hoped for a new life like that of Osiris to conform in all things to the example of the god, it was deemed of great advantage to be buried near him, and for many centuries bodies were brought from all parts of Egypt to be laid in the necropolis of Abydos. High officials and nomarchs whose tombs were actually in the royal cemetery at the capital or in the principal towns of their nomes, were sometimes transported to Abydos and back before being finally laid to rest; and multitudes who for other reasons could not be buried in the holy city caused at least a stela bearing their names to be set up in its necropolis that they might thus be in company with the god.

CHAPTER IX

EGYPT

THE MIDDLE KINGDOM AND THE EMPIRE

The Rise of Thebes—The Sun as Supreme God—Local Gods—Identifications—Enneads and Triads—The Dead—Judgment before Osiris—Moral Ideas—The Empire—Amon-Re the National God—Power of the Priesthood—Attempt to Establish Solar Monotheism—Reaction—The Nineteenth Dynasty—Mythology—Theban Tombs and Texts—The Book of the Dead—Amulets—The Saite Restoration—Foreign Rule.

UNDER the Sixth Dynasty the power of the kings declined; the governors of the districts became virtually hereditary rulers and more and more independent of the central authority. The result was that the Old Kingdom disintegrated, and Egypt, after a thousand years of union under a strong government, reverted to the conditions which prevailed before the rise of the kingdom. From the following centuries royal monuments are lacking, but numerous tombs of nomarchs and local notables show something of what was going on. Toward the end of these dim centuries Thebes first appears on the stage of history. Hitherto it had been an insignificant provincial town; the chief city of the canton was Hermonthis. But beginning about 2150 B. C. the Intefs and Mentuhoteps, Manetho's Eleventh Dynasty, laid the foundations of its greatness. The Twelfth Dynasty, also of Theban origin, reunited Egypt under a strong rule, and not only extended their dominion in Nubia beyond the utmost limits of the Old Kingdom, but carried their victorious arms far into Syria. This recovery of power and prosperity was attended by a brilliant renaissance of art. In

many ways these two centuries of the Middle Kingdom are
the culmination of Egyptian civilisation.

The monuments of the Middle Kingdom show that in the
intervening period religion had continued to develop in the
direction in which it was moving when the Old Kingdom fell
into decadence. The Heliopolitan solar religion which had
been adopted by the state in the Fifth Dynasty had not gone
under with the state; its doctrines had, on the contrary,
gained wider acceptance. Re is now a universal god, self-
originated, the author and ruler of the world; a god, as every
one must see, not alone of higher attributes and greater
power than the tutelary and functional deities, but of a
different kind. His supremacy is due to his nature, not to
political circumstances such as might raise the god of one
city to a monarchy among the gods corresponding to the
rule of a dynasty from that city among men. The way had
been prepared for Re by Horus, and in fact Re makes himself
heir of the sun-god of the earlier dynasties as Re-Harakhte,
that is, "Re, the Horus of the two Horizons"; but Horus
had been primarily the god of the kings, while Re was a
god of priests.

The exaltation of one god, especially of a great power of
nature such as Re, to the supreme place in the pantheon is
a step toward monotheism; we shall see how, in the New
Empire, Ikhnaton tried to go the rest of the way and make
an exclusive solar monotheism the religion of Egypt.[1] But,
with the exception of his unsuccessful attempt, the solar religion was not exclusive; the theologians were content to
let the other gods remain as ministers and helpers of Re, or
as names or forms of the sun-god—an accommodation of
theoretical monotheism to practical polytheism which has
been found convenient in other countries—in the theistic
religions of India, for example. This pantheistic doctrine
remained, however, a piece of priestly wisdom in the possession of "them who know," and had no discoverable consequence in actual religion even for them.

[1] See below, pp. 181 ff.

The increased political importance of the provincial cities, which after the fall of the Old Kingdom became independent states, gave a correspondingly increased importance to their gods. The rulers of the cantons erected new temples to the deities under whose banners they fought with one another or against their nominal overlords; the same conditions which had developed the independent city religions in prehistoric Egypt now gave them new vitality. Under these circumstances the effect of the higher theology was not that the local god was subordinated to Re, much less superseded by him, but that Re was identified with the local god, who thus appropriated the universal attributes and powers of Re. The incongruity of many of these identifications did not hinder them when once they were in fashion; the crocodile-god of the Fayum has as little trouble in becoming a sun-crocodile, Sebek-Re, as the ram of Thebes in becoming Amon-Re, or the ithyphallic idol of Min in being similarly promoted. Practically, therefore, the whole gain of the higher theology accrued to the lower religion, making it equally acceptable to the few who were indoctrinated in the priestly wisdom and to the many to whom the god of their fathers was good enough without any speculative improvements. In the end almost every Egyptian god who had a public cult was hyphenated with Re. Osiris, notwithstanding an inextricable confusion with Re in magical mystifications from the pyramid texts to the Book of the Dead, is hardly identified out and out with Re; besides him, Ptah, the old god of Memphis, and Thoth, the moon-god and vizier of Re, are almost the sole gods who in the end escape the combination.

From the Heliopolitan priests came also a theogony which put the god of their city, Atum, at the beginning of all things, and derived from him, through two intermediate generations, the gods of the Osirian circle as it appeared in the Delta. This Ennead, which had almost as great success as the doctrine of Re, is thus constructed:

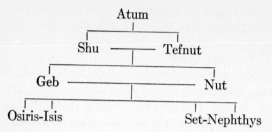

The scheme, which is already found in the pyramid texts, combines disparate elements. The first and the last generations are gods in religion as well as in myth, the two intervening pairs are cosmogonic figures. Geb and Nut are earth and sky, divine, doubtless, but having in early times no cult. Shu and Tefnut may have been local deities somewhere in the Delta (they are sometimes represented as lion-headed), but in this connection are conceived as gods of the air or of atmospheric space; Shu supports the sky, whether the latter is imaged as the celestial cow or in human form.

The question how the sky is held aloft, or how it was ever raised up from the earth, is one which much exercised primitive speculation. In a well-known Maori myth, heaven and earth, man and woman, lay for ages locked in close embrace, until the offspring of their union, finding the quarters too close, after much debate and with mighty effort, thrust their parents apart, and lifted their father, the sky, into his present place. In Egypt, by an accident of grammatical gender, sky (Nut) was feminine and earth (Geb) masculine. In the representations of this myth, which are common in the monuments, Geb is depicted as a prostrate giant, on whose body, to leave no doubt of the significance of the figure, grass is often growing, while astride over Geb's form stands Shu, upholding with his two arms the body of Nut (often decorated with stars), whose inordinately long arms and legs dangle down to the horizon, giving her some resemblance to the vault of heaven with its four supporting columns. The rôle of Shu in this myth obviously belongs, as in the

New Zealand parallel, to a child of the pair; and from this it is to be inferred that the myth is independent of the genealogical scheme which now inconsequently makes Shu the father of Geb and Nut.

In a late magical papyrus, which notwithstanding its date bears intrinsic marks of antique conception, the place of Atum in the Heliopolitan scheme is taken by Nun, the primeval watery chaos out of which in certain other myths Re emerges, and it is at least a plausible surmise that Atum in the Heliopolitan Ennead was elevated by his priests to the position originally occupied in the cosmogony by chaos. Furthermore, inasmuch as the obvious motive of the cosmogonic theogony is to provide a proper ancestry for Osiris and his group, the conjecture is not remote that the system originated, not in Heliopolis, where there was no particular reason for interest in the Osirian gods, but at some other centre of the Delta—perhaps Busiris—where the origin of these gods was a matter of concern to their worshippers.

In the form which it assumed at Heliopolis the Ennead was adopted and imitated all over Egypt. But in this instance also the obstinacy of the local religions asserted itself; each city in accepting the Nine Gods made a place for its own god in the group, sometimes replacing one of the minor figures, often usurping the supreme position of Atum. Upon the model of the Great Ennead, a second group of Nine, the Lesser Ennead, was also fashioned by the priests of Heliopolis. Only one rival system managed to maintain itself. At Hermopolis Magna we find Thoth, the god of the district, in his character of creator, accompanied by four gods and a corresponding number of goddesses, sometimes represented as four frog-headed men and four women with serpents' heads, sometimes as eight baboons dancing around Thoth, the principal baboon. The goddesses in this scheme are plainly supernumerary, introduced in imitation of the Heliopolitan Nine: the original scheme at Hermopolis knew but five, Thoth himself, and the deities of the four corners of the earth, or rather of the supports of heaven at the four corners of the earth.

Besides these artificial constructions of theologians and their imitators, the gods form natural family groups. In the commonest type, the chief god of a canton has a wife and a son, who are associated with him in worship as subordinate figures. The spouse is often a goddess whose seat was in another town in the district or in the capital of a neighbouring nome, and the son is borrowed in a similar way. Thus, Amon of Thebes makes Montu (who, as the god of the older capital, Hermonthis, had been the god of the canton while Amon was still a local nobody), his son, thus emphasising Amon's newly established superiority; Amon's consort is Mut, a vulture goddess, who was by that sign identified with Nekhebt, the goddess of the original capital of Upper Egypt, Eleithyiapolis. Another name is Amont, a deity created by the simple device of adding a feminine ending to Amon. In his character of sun-god, Amon-Re, however, took the moon god, Khonsu, as his son, and Montu was thus supplanted. If the cantonal deity was a goddess, she took a husband from among the neighbouring gods, but in her own temple kept him in a position of masculine subordination. An unnecessary deal of nonsense has been written about these groups of three gods, on which the question-begging name "Egyptian Trinities" has been bestowed. They have not even a mythological significance, much less a metaphysical.

The greater independence of the provincial cities was evidently accompanied by greater prosperity. Whereas under the Old Kingdom the wealth of all Egypt was drawn off to the capital, the residence of the court and the high officials, where even the governors of distant corners of the kingdom were buried, now the cities in the provinces themselves grew rich from agriculture and trade. One of the results of these political and economic changes was the rise of a well-to-do middle class, who, after the manner of middle classes in all the world, conformed as far as they could to the customs and fashions of the nobility. Accordingly, we now find tombs not only of the lords and lordlings of the district, but of prosperous tradesmen and artisans; and since the tombs even of the rich were now much less luxurious than in the days of the Old Kingdom, even people of moderate means could provide themselves with respectable burial-places. The rulers of the nomes, indeed, perpetuated the old style of tombs with numerous chambers, on the walls of which the possessions of the deceased were represented; but the common form was a small brick pyramid, before which, in the place of the old false door, is a stela inscribed with the name of the occupant, and often bearing a relief showing him surrounded by his family at the funeral feast.

In the burial-chamber are usually models of houses and granaries, and clay figures of servants kneading bricks, carrying sacks of grain, grinding meal, baking bread, brewing beer, and preparing dinner; also models of boats and their crews. Similar figures and scenes painted on the wooden coffin may take the place of the pottery figurines. All this makes it evident that the old beliefs about the continued existence of the dead in the tomb and their needs persisted. As a substitute for an offering of real bread and beer, haunches of beef, and roast geese, stone imitations of these viands cut in low relief on the surface of the table of offerings are common. By a form of words they were supposed to be transsubstantiated into digestible food, or provisions corresponding to those thus represented were conveyed by Anubis or Osiris to the deceased. By this device the danger that through the neglect of his descendants or the dying out of the family the dead man might be left without sustenance was averted. It was only necessary that the passer-by should recite the formula to procure for the dead man "a thousand loaves, a thousand jars of beer, a thousand roast geese," and to this pious service the inscription summons all who read it "as they love life and hate death."

The assistance of the gods is hardly necessary to enable

the occupant of the tomb to eat what is set before him on his own table; their offices are required to make the offerings at the tomb of use to the dead in the underworld. Thus the old customs were made to fit into another circle of ideas and serve a second purpose. The instance is characteristic of the propensity of the Egyptians to put new patches on the old garment, oblivious of the ensuing rents.

The beliefs about the abodes and destinies of souls became more confused also through the appropriation by ordinary mortals of hopes and prospects which were originally confined to the king. In the texts which were now written on the inside of coffins, passages borrowed from the inscriptions in the pyramids appear side by side with new pieces of similar intent but of more general application, the beginnings of the heterogeneous aggregation to which the name Book of the Dead is given. Among these are many for the protection of the dead on his perilous way to the other world, on which he is beset by many fearful and monstrous enemies against whom he can defend himself only by the use of magical formulas or rites. One of the most effective means is to identify himself with some god, especially one of the great gods of light, who has safely passed through the same perils. The god of the city also is frequently invoked to protect his faithful worshipper.

At the same time moral conditions of future blessedness become more prominent. Many inscriptions, particularly on the tombs of the nobles or officials, proclaim their uprightness, justice, humanity, and goodness toward those under their authority or dependent upon them. The conception of a formal judgment of the dead is completely developed. In the old myth of Osiris his implacable enemy Set, pursuing him even beyond the tomb, brings grave charges against him, of which the god Thoth vindicates him.[1] After this example every man now desires to be justified as Osiris was, and to hear the favourable sen-

---

[1] Originally Thoth seems to have appeared as the advocate of Osiris before the tribunal of the gods of Heliopolis, or before Re.

tence which declares him "true of speech." In the Book of the Dead[1] the judgment scene is not only described in words, but is often portrayed in an accompanying picture. The trial takes place before Osiris, the king of the dead. The deceased is led by Anubis into a great hall, around the sides of which are seated the forty-two associate justices of this great court.[2] In the presence of this august court the man protests his innocence of sins against gods and men. To determine whether his protestation of innocence is true or not, his heart, witness of all his words and deeds, is weighed by Anubis in a balance against an ostrich-feather, the symbol of Maat, the goddess of right and truth, while Thoth, with tablet and stylus, as clerk of the court, records the issue. Thereupon Horus conducts the justified man into the inner shrine, where Osiris, with sceptre and scourge in his hands, is seated upon his throne. What would happen if the trial resulted unfavourably is impressively suggested by a monster with the body of a hippopotamus and the head and jaws of a crocodile which squats beside the scales with open mouth. The name of this monster is "Devouress." She "lives on the entrails of the great on the day of the great reckoning."

The protestation of innocence, in one form, runs thus:

Hail to thee, great god, lord of truth. I have come to thee, my lord, and am led hither to see thy beauty. I know thy name; I know the names of the forty-two gods who are with thee in the hall of truth, who live on evil-doers and devour their blood on the day of reckoning of character before Wennofre (Osiris). Behold, I come to thee; I bring to thee righteousness and I expel for thee sin. I have committed no sin against people. . . . I have not done evil in the place of truth. I knew no wrong. I did no evil thing. . . . I did not do what the god abominates. I did not report evil of a servant to his master. I allowed no one to hunger. I caused no one to weep. I did no murder. I did not command to murder. I caused no man misery. I did not diminish the food in the temples. I did not decrease the offerings of

[1] Chapter 125 of the Theban recension.
[2] The number forty-two corresponded to the number of the nomes in the age when these texts were given their present form.

the gods. I did not take away the food-offerings of the dead. I did not commit adultery. I did not pollute myself in the pure precinct of my city god. I did not diminish the grain measure. I did not diminish the span. I did not diminish the land measure. I did not load the weight of the balances. I did not deflect the index of the scales. I did not take milk from the mouth of the child. I did not drive the cattle away from their pasturage. I did not snare the fowl of the gods. I did not catch the fish in their pools. I did not hold back the water in its time. I did not dam up the running water. I did not quench the fire in its time. I did not withhold the herds of the temple endowments. I did not interfere with the god in his payments. I am purified four times; I am as pure as the great Phœnix is pure which is in Heracleopolis. . . .

There arises no evil thing against me in this land, in the hall of truth, because I know the names of these gods who are therein, the followers of the great god.[1]

In another version of the protestation, which is found as a doublet in the completer recensions of the Book of the Dead, the sins are with some difficulty made to count forty-two, and the names of the forty-two assessors which the dead man professes to know are enumerated. Among them are such terrifying compounds as "Bone-Breaker from Heracleopolis," "Fiery-Eyes from Letopolis," "White-Teeth from the Hidden Land," "Devourer of Bowels," "Blood-Eater." It is no less necessary to be able to recite these names correctly than to be free from sin; and lest the unfortunate should forget them, or be unable to connect them with their several owners, the likenesses of the infernal judges are commonly depicted in the copies of the Book of the Dead which were laid in the coffin, distinctly labelled with their names.

These professions of rectitude exemplify the moral side of Egyptian religion. As is natural, in view of the religious character of the judgment, offences against the gods, especially trespass upon their rights of property, and wrongs done to men, are not discriminated. Among the latter are murder, theft, oppression, adultery, lying, fraud, false witness, slander, abusive speech, and tale-bearing. Like the second

[1] Translation by Breasted, Religion in Ancient Egypt, pp. 299 f.

table of the Mosaic Decalogue, these are elementary things, against which even savage society reacts in self-defence, and by no means indicate a particularly advanced morality. Nor is it a mark of signal progress that the customary morals of the community are put under the sanction of religion— that also is common among peoples on a much lower level of civilisation. What is noteworthy is the extension of the divine sanction of morals over the future life; for this is by no means so inevitable as it might appear to us. Nothing of the kind seems to have taken place in the religion of Babylonia and Assyria, nor in that of China; and in Israel, notwithstanding the strongly ethical character of the religion and the large development of the idea of divine retribution, the belief that men's lot after death is determined by their conduct in this life came very late and not without foreign stimulus.

While the conceptions of what awaits man after death thus took more definite shape in the Osirian doctrine—and perhaps in natural reaction from them—sceptical voices begin to be heard.[1] From that world about which priests profess to know so much no traveller has returned; the famous kings and sages of olden time are dead and gone, only their names remain; we are following them to the grave; let us make the most of our brief span on earth, denying ourselves no pleasure it affords. Such is the refrain of the Song of the Harper at the Feast, one of the best-known poems of the Middle Kingdom. What gives it more significance is the fact that it is not the utterance of a solitary pessimist, but of a court poet, enlivening the guests at the banquet with the Egyptian version of "let us eat and drink, for to-morrow we die."

Several interesting writings from the time of the Middle Kingdom exhibit the moral principles of members of the ruling class or throw light on the moral conditions of the age.

---

[1] So, in the Old Testament, much confident talk about the accuracy of divine retribution and the new doctrine of immortality provoked the author of Ecclesiastes to give voice to his disbelief.

The Wisdom of Ptahhotep is in the form of instructions delivered by an aged vizier to his son and designated successor. The instructions are chiefly counsels for the deportment of a minister in official and private relations. He should be upright, just, true, discreet, moderate, knowing how to assert his own dignity without arrogance; warning is given against avarice and the pride of possessions; vices are to be shunned, but the wise man will not deny himself the enjoyment of life nor make it bitter with vain regrets. If the son will follow this wholesome advice and the example of his father, it will go well with him. In an Instruction for a Minister, purporting to be delivered by a king to a vizier at his installation, the vizier is enjoined to deal justly and impartially with all, not favouring his own kin nor showing respect of persons to princes and counsellors. A story with an evident moral, called The Peasants' Appeal, tells how a poor man who had been unjustly treated by underlings, and even by the high steward, gets redress from the Pharaoh himself.

Other texts are filled with loud complaints of the degeneracy of the age—"righteousness is cast out, iniquity is in the midst of the council hall"; society is thoroughly corrupt. A very interesting papyrus, The Prophecies of an Egyptian Sage, paints in even darker colours the universal demoralisation and disorders of the age, aggravated as they were by foreign invasion. The only imaginable remedy for these ills is a wise and good king, and the author depicts such an ideal ruler, "the shepherd of all the people, who has no evil in his heart," in a strain in which a resemblance has been seen to the Messianic prophecies of the Old Testament, though the Egyptian parallel has no distinctly predictive element.

The two glorious centuries of the Twelfth Dynasty were followed by a decline more swift and a fall more deep than those of the Old Kingdom. The long lists of ephemeral rulers which are the sum of our knowledge of this dark age show only that legitimate and orderly succession was the exception; pretenders and usurpers mounted the throne, only to be supplanted by fresh conspiracies and revolutions. Reduced to impotence by these internal disorders, the unhappy country could present no effective opposition to the foreign invasion which was not long in coming. The Hyksos kings, at the head of hordes of Asiatics, poured into the Delta, and in a few years reduced to subjection not only Lower Egypt, but the whole valley of the Nile to a point south of Thebes. In the early stages of the invasion the cities and temples, particularly in the Delta, doubtless suffered many outrages at the hands of the conquerors, but the later kings of the line were at least superficially Egyptianised; they adopted the old royal titles and gave themselves Re names like their native predecessors. Their principal god was identified—whether by themselves or by their subjects—with the old Egyptian god Set, who, as the foe of Horus and Osiris, seemed the natural god of the barbarian enemies of Egypt, and temples to this god were erected by Hyksos kings at Tanis and at Avaris, their great fortified camp on the eastern frontier.

Who these invaders were is an unsolved problem. It is certain, however, that they entered Egypt from the side of Syria, and when they were driven out they made a strong stand at Sharuhen, in the south of what was afterward the territory of Judah. It is probable that Kadesh, the objective of several of the campaigns of Thothmes III, was in his time the centre of their power. These facts, as well as the names of some of the kings, support the testimony of Manetho that the invaders, or at least the dominant element among them, were Semites.

The duration of their supremacy in Egypt, notwithstanding the large figures given by Manetho, can hardly have exceeded a century or two, and in the latter part of this time their hold on Upper Egypt must have become less firm. At Thebes a family of local dynasts ruled the city, probably at first as vassals of the Hyksos, and gradually extended their power over Upper Egypt, being reckoned by Manetho as the Seventeenth Dynasty of Egyptian kings. About 1580 Ahmose I, the founder of the Eighteenth Dynasty, after a severe struggle, captured the last stronghold of Hyksos at Avaris and expelled them finally from Egypt. He followed them into Syria, and took Sharuhen after a siege of six years. At the other extremity of Egypt he recovered from the Nubians the territory between the first and second cataracts, and thus re-established the kingdom within its old limits.

The empire which Ahmose I founded was extended by his successors, the Amenhoteps and Thutmoses, far into Nubia on the one side, while on the other it included all Syria to the Euphrates and the Amanus. These conquests brought to Egypt, as the booty of war and as tribute, enormous riches and great multitudes of captives; commercial expeditions, especially to Punt (southern Arabia), contributed to the growing wealth and luxury. In little more than a century Egypt, which had been reduced by internal disorder and foreign invasion to complete impotence, reached the highest pitch of its greatness. The state was an absolute monarchy with a strongly centralised administration; the princes and counts who in the break-up of the Middle Kingdom and the turbulent times that followed had made themselves virtually independent lordlings were deprived of all power; the landed nobility disappeared, and a great part of the land was now crown domain. The long wars of liberation and conquest gave the monarchy a military character unlike anything the temperamentally unwarlike Egyptians had ever known; the introduction of the horse and the prominent part the chariot force now played in the battle, the employment of numbers of foreign mercenaries, created a professional army which overshadowed the old national levies.

Nowhere is the new order of things more noticeable than in religion. The capital of the empire was Thebes; under the banner of the Theban Amon-Re the kings drove out the Hyksos and conquered Syria; to him they erected temples in their Asiatic provinces. As the god of the Egyptians in their wars against foreigners in every quarter and of every colour, Amon became the national god in quite a different sense from that in which the Heliopolitan theology had made Re a national god; as Amon-Re he was supreme by a double title.

Out of the spoils of war and the revenues of the state the kings of the Eighteenth Dynasty built him temples of size and splendour hitherto unheard of, and enriched them by enormous gifts and endowments. A large part of the captives of war were dedicated as slaves of the god; great estates with all their serfs were settled upon the temples. The priesthood now for the first time became a numerous and powerful class. The chief priest of Amon was the head of the state religion, with authority over all the other priesthoods, and these great ecclesiastics sometimes filled high offices in the state. Amenhotep III had one chief priest of Amon for treasurer and another for vizier. Before the sun of Amon all the other gods began to pale; only Ptah of Memphis and Re of Heliopolis, who shared with him in smaller measure the favour of the kings, retained something of their old prestige.

This was the situation when Amenhotep IV (1375–58 B. C.) made his revolutionary attempt to dethrone the mighty Amon and establish the worship of Aton as the sole religion of the state. The change meant much more than a monarch's capricious preference for one cult above another, such as Elagabalus's devotion to the sun-god of Emesa; it was a serious effort to introduce a higher monotheism. It has been noted above that the Heliopolitan priesthood had exalted Re as creator and ruler of the world to a place far above all the gods, but that they had compromised the monotheistic principle of their own theology by recognising the many deities as the One under other names, so that the practical result of the acceptance of the doctrine had been to confer on every god the attributes and power of Re. Yet the conception of the unity of god, in vaguely panthe-

istic form, was firmly fixed in the religious philosophy of the
Egyptians. The priests of Memphis called this god Ptah;
at Heliopolis he was, as of old, Re; at Thebes, Amon—in
truth he is "the god of innumerable names."

Among these names is one which, though ancient, had
never gained wide currency—Aton, the solar orb, or disc,
visible in the sky. As the divine sun, he is closely akin to
Re, but he had not, like Re, been fused with terrestrial gods
of various beastly shapes nor represented in human form,
and by its freedom from such associations his name was a
fit symbol for God in a purer solar monotheism. Where this
movement began is not certainly known; there is some reason to think that it was at Heliopolis, where Amenhotep
IV built a temple to Aton. The fact that Amenhotep III
named a pleasure barge in his artificial lake "Aton gleams"
and had a company of Aton in his body-guard shows that
the god—and presumably the doctrine—was known in
Thebes before the reformation.

In the early part of his reign, Amenhotep IV began the
erection of a stately temple to Aton in Thebes, between the
temples of Karnak and Luxor, on grounds which his father
had laid out as a garden of Amon. Thebes, Amon's city,
had to hear itself officially renamed "City of the Brightness of Aton," and the quarter in which Amon's great temples
lay "Brightness of Aton the Great." The proud and powerful priesthood of Amon is not likely to have looked with
complacency on this exaltation of the upstart god, and still
less on the diversion of the streams of treasure they had
been wont to see pour into their coffers. But there was
worse to follow. Not long after the completion of the
temple of Aton, the king ousted the priesthoods from the
temples throughout the land, suppressing the public worship
and effacing the names of the gods wherever they occurred
in inscriptions; the very word "gods" was treated in the
same way. Amon was pursued with peculiar vindictive-
ness not only in the temples, but in the cemeteries. The
monuments of the king's ancestors, and even those of his

own father, were mutilated to destroy the obnoxious word.[1] The king's own name was the same as his father's, Amenhotep, "Amon rests"; he changed it to Ikhnaton, "Spirit of Aton."

But, after all, Thebes was Amon's city. The silent temples on whose walls the king's forefathers were worshipping Amon or conquering an empire in his might, the obelisks commemorating their jubilees, their tombs across the valley, all proclaimed him; every brutal scar on a historic monument cried out his name. There must have been other things to make Thebes an unpleasant residence for the iconoclastic king. An obsequious court might change its religion at the royal pleasure, but the people must have seen with sullen discontent, if not with open protest, the sacrilegious outrages perpetrated on the gods and the temples; and the priests were there to fan the flame.

It is easy to imagine, therefore, why Amenhotep formed the plan of removing the capital from Thebes. Nearly three hundred miles farther north, on an unoccupied site, he founded a new city, Akhetaton, "Horizon of Aton." Three temples of Aton were erected there, besides magnificent palaces and government buildings. The court and officials built them residences in the new capital, a flourishing city sprang into existence as by magic, and tombs were hewn in the eastern cliff for the kings and the nobles—a city of the dead. Ikhnaton also ordered temples of Aton to be built not only at Heliopolis, but in remoter parts of his empire, in upper Nubia and in Syria.

The great temple of Aton differed from the ordinary type of Egyptian temples chiefly in having no cella for the image of the god. Instead of this there were behind the hypostyle hall two large halls or courts, surrounded by small chambers and having an altar in the middle. In these the more solemn rites of worship took place, while the great

[1] The mutilation of the name of Amon was not an exhibition of impotent hatred; it was, according to ancient notions, the destruction of the bearer of the name.

altar in the fore court received the common sacrifices, which consisted, as in other temples, of the flesh of bullocks, geese, and the like, in great quantities.

In various scenes Aton is represented by a disc from which long rays issue, each ending in a hand; in one of these the common symbol of life, the Ankh, is held out to the king.

The teaching of the new religion, which Ikhnaton professes to have received by revelation from his father Re, is best learned from the great hymn to Aton, which is notable not only for its nobility of conception, but for its poetic beauty.[1]

What is remarkable in this hymn is not its recognition of one god as creator and ruler—the hymns to Amon do the same, and in very similar phrase; it is, in fact, not so much in what it says as in what it does not say that it differs most widely from even the highest utterances of the orthodox Egyptian religion. There are no references to the ancient solar myths, such as the combat of the sun with the dragon monster, to his voyage in his morning and evening barks, to his ancient and magical names. Not the fabulous adventures of an anthropomorphic sun god, but the beneficent works of the divine sun, move the poet's admiration and gratitude. The realism of the art which Ikhnaton fostered is a product of the same disposition to see things as they are. Besides this expurgation of the mythical and conventional, there is a strikingly universal strain in the hymn. The Syrians and the Ethiopians are not only creatures of God, but are subjects of his providential care; men's speech and their colour are diverse as God has appointed. Of the theological chauvinism which makes a national god out of a universal one there is no trace.

Even more significant is the disappearance from the tombs of the whole Osirian eschatology, mythical and magical, and, indeed, of all those fantastic notions of the hereafter which had so much exercised the Egyptians through

[1] Translations of it are given in Breasted, History of Egypt, pp. 371 ff.; Religion in Ancient Egypt, pp. 324 ff.

all their history. The deceased prays to the sun to grant the certainty of beholding him, and to refresh him with the breath of the north wind; the scarab bears a prayer to Aton, and the pyramid amulet is inscribed with his name and symbol.

All this seems to many scholars so strange that they think it necessary to look abroad for the source of these ideas. A favourite theory with them has been that the religion of Aton was introduced from Syria. It seemed for a time to be made out that the queen mother, Tiy, who had great influence over her son, and Nefertiti, his wife, were Syrian princesses; the name Aton suggested to etymologists by sound the Canaanite Adon. These combinations have proved to be mistaken; the discovery of the tomb of Tiy showed that she was a native Egyptian, a woman of the people. But the fatal objection to the theory, before as after these discoveries, is that there is no trace of such a solar monotheism in Syria. On the other hand, it was the logical end of Egyptian theological thinking and of Amenophis's own career. In his first years he built temples to the sun-god Re-Harakhte at Thebes, Memphis, Heliopolis, and other cities. When Aton first appears it is under the title, "Harakhte who triumphs in the horizon in his name 'Splendour who is Aton' " (the disc of the sun). What is really strange is not the monotheism, but the exclusive turn Amenophis gave it and his determination to make it the sole religion in his dominions.

Whatever the actuating motives may have been, the sincerity of the king's conviction can as little be questioned as the logical consistency of his action. He made, at a cost greater than he could foresee, the attempt to reform the religion of his country by putting into effect its highest conceptions, and by rejecting the incongruous survivals of its barbarous beginnings which choked these ideas and rendered them unfruitful. We cannot but be reminded of the like attempt of Josiah to make monotheism the religion of Judah in reality as well as in prophetic doctrine by casting out all foreign gods and destroying the high places. The event, too, was not dissimilar: no sooner was the strong hand of the royal reformer withdrawn than his reforms were engulfed in a flood-tide of reaction.

While Amenhotep was building temples and arranging ceremonies and composing hymns in honour of Aton, the Asiatic provinces of the empire, the conquests of his great forefathers, were slipping from his grasp. The letters and despatches from Syria found in the archives of the new capital (called the El-Amarna letters, from the modern name of the place) contain urgent appeals to the Pharaoh to come to the rescue of his hard-pressed governors and loyal vassals, but these appeals remained unheeded. It is evident from the records of Harmheb's reign that internal affairs had also suffered from the same preoccupation. An absolute ruler cannot give his whole mind to religion without neglecting more vital concerns of the state. We hear of no serious disorders, however, so long as he lived, though the sequel shows that disaffection must have been wide-spread.

Amenophis IV died about 1358, after a reign of seventeen years or more. He had no son, and was succeeded by the husband of his eldest daughter, who was soon followed by another son-in-law, Tutenkhaton ("Living Image of Aton"). The turn things were taking is shown by the fact that Tutenkhaton transferred the capital back to Thebes, and not only permitted the resumption of the worship of Amon, but restored the temples and himself conducted the great festival of the god at Karnak and Luxor; it was not long before he changed his own name to Tutenkhamon. The reaction was in full swing. The name of Amon was restored in the inscriptions which Amenophis had mutilated. Tutenkhamon's successor, Eye, who seems to have had no better title to the throne than that he was the husband of Amenophis's nurse, was the last of the heretic kings. After a brief period of anarchy, Harmheb, the commander-in-chief of the army, with the support of the military and the priesthood of Amon, proclaimed himself king. When he had re-established order with a hard hand, his first concern was to restore the temples throughout the land, replace the images according to the old pattern, furnish the shrines with the vessels of silver and gold for use in worship, provide them with priests, assign them the materials for offerings, and endow them with lands and cattle. The work of restoring the names of the gods in the mutilated inscriptions was completed; every mark of Amenophis's iconoclastic fury was as far as possible effaced. The temples of Aton at Thebes were razed, and the stones used to build two pylons for Amon. At the abandoned capital, Akhetaton, the temples and tombs were ruined; everywhere the name of the Ikhnaton was obliterated, and when it was necessary in legal proceedings to cite enactments or documents of his reign, he was referred to as "that criminal of Akhetaton." Amon-Re was avenged. His priests in their hymns exulted over the fallen foe of the god: "Woe to him who injures thee! Thy city endures, but the city of him who injures thee has perished. Shame upon him who commits sacrilege against thee in any land. . . . The sun of him who knew thee not has set; but he who knows thee, he shines; the sanctuary of him who injured thee lies in darkness, and the whole earth is in light."

The reform that fails always leaves things worse than they were; and especially a reform put through by force provokes a more violent reaction, which is carried by its own momentum farther than its first leaders foresee or desire. So it was with Amenophis's reforms. From the time when the old religion was triumphantly reinstated, its face was turned backward, and the only visible progress it made for a thousand years was in reviving ancient superstitions and inventing new ones.

The kings of the Nineteenth Dynasty who followed Harmheb endeavoured to reconquer the Asiatic provinces which had been lost under Amenophis IV and in the disorders that followed his death. Seti and Rameses II had little difficulty in recovering Palestine and southern Syria, but

the new Hittite power which had arisen in the north barred
their way in that direction. After a series of campaigns
extending over some fifteen years, which, notwithstanding
the boasts of conquest in the inscriptions, do not seem to
have permanently advanced the Egyptian frontier much
beyond Beirut and the southern end of the Bika', a treaty
of alliance was contracted between the two states. These
wars, like those of the great kings of the Eighteenth Dynasty, were conducted under the banner of Amon-Re as
the national god, and again, as in the earlier conquests, a
great part of the spoils was bestowed on his temples. Rameses II removed the residence from Thebes to Tanis, in
the Delta, for its greater convenience as a base for his Syrian
enterprises, but the city of Amon was not neglected; to say
nothing of other buildings, such as the enlargement of the
Luxor temples, the great hall of columns at Karnak surpasses
all that his predecessors had done. Nor were the other
gods forgotten; everywhere Rameses enlarged, rebuilt, or
beautified their temples, so that there are few temples remaining in Egypt on which his name does not appear.

Great additions were also made to the wealth of the
temples by occasional gifts and by endowments. It was the
theory of the state religion that the temples were royal
sanctuaries where the king worshipped the god; in the
scenes on the temple walls depicting religious rites the king
is always the central figure. The successors of Rameses
continued to lavish treasure upon the temples, and as their
possessions were exempt from taxation they became enormously rich. From the figures given in the Harris Papyrus
it appears that under one of the later kings of the dynasty
three-quarters of a million acres, nearly one-seventh of all
the land of Egypt, was church property, and the temples
held among them 107,000 slaves, besides enormous herds
of cattle. By far the greater part of these riches belonged
to three gods, Amon of Thebes, Ptah of Memphis, and Re
of Heliopolis; Amon alone held 583,000 acres of land and
420,000 cattle, large and small. The office of high priest

of Amon, the head of all the priesthoods of the land, had now become hereditary. He maintained a body of troops, and altogether wielded a power which even the strongest king could not with impunity defy. Under the Twentieth Dynasty the Theban high priest, Hrihor, who had long been the real ruler of Egypt, boldly set aside the fiction of ruling for the Ramessid king and seated himself upon the throne (about 1090).

The more completely the worship in the temples became the business of the rulers and the priests, in which the people had no part except as spectators, the more the common man turned to gods who had no place in the state cult—such figures as the bandy-legged dwarf, Bes, or the she-hippopotamus Thoueris, to Onuris and Nefertem, and the wise Imhotep. Many foreign gods also appear in this age; soldiers and captives introduced the Syrian deities Baal and Resheph, Anat and Astarte.

There is no doubt that the Egyptians had a large store of myths about both the local deities and the great nature gods; the liturgies are larded with allusions to such stories. Among the few specimens that have been preserved, chiefly in texts from the time of the Empire or later, the most interesting are that which tells how Isis learned the secret name of Re, and the myth of the destruction of mankind. Isis was an adept in the magical arts, but her most potent spell was the hidden name of Re, and this is how she got the secret from him: Re was drooling with age, his slaver trickled to the ground; Isis kneaded earth with it and made a viper, which she laid in the path where Re went out to walk; the viper smote Re as he passed attended by a train of gods, and he cried out in pain. To the concerned inquiry of his companions he at length replies: "I am a prince and son of a prince, the divine offspring of a god; I am a great one and the son of a great one. My father and my mother told me my name, and it has remained hidden in my body since my birth, that no magician might gain magical power over me. I went abroad to behold what I had made, and passed through the two lands (Upper and Lower Egypt) that I had created. Then something stung me, I know not what. Fire it is not, water it is not; my heart is burning, my body shivers, and all my limbs tremble."

All the gods are summoned, and among them comes Isis, with well-feigned solicitude. "What is it? what is it, divine father? A reptile has hurt thee, one of thy children has lifted up its head against thee. It shall yield to a potent charm; I will overthrow it by powerful magic." Re repeats the story, and Isis rejoins: "Tell me thy name, O divine father, for the man's life is saved who is called by his (true, but secret) name." Re recites a string of mouth-filling titles such as abound in the ritual, concluding: "I am Khepre in the morning and Re at noon and Atum in the evening"—an old priestly formula—but it did no good. "That is not thy name," Isis says; "tell me thy true name, that the poison may leave thee." At last Re yields, and by its magical virtue she restores him to health.

This is what may be called a professional myth; the enchanter who has learned from Isis to heal ailments by the magic power of names explains how Isis came to know the greatest of all.

The myth of the destruction of men belongs to a different class, of which the widely distributed deluge myths are the best known.[1] Re has grown old and feeble, and his authority is despised; men conspire against him, as might happen to a Pharaoh who had outlived himself. Re summons the gods to a council, and on the advice of Nun sends the fierce lion-headed goddess Sekhmet to pursue men into the mountain fastnesses whither they have fled and destroy them. The goddess descends to earth, and executes her mission with such good-will that the whole valley swims with blood, and Re, fearing that the human race will be exterminated, repents of his command. It was not so easy to call off the lioness who had tasted blood, but Re found a way. A mixture of

[1] Egypt, where the inundation is the greatest of blessings, has, of course, no flood myth.

beer with the juice of (narcotic?) fruit and human blood
was prepared—seven thousand jars full—and poured out
in the early dawn upon the fields. Sekhmet, sallying forth
to resume her work of slaughter, found these pools of blood
as she thought and drank till she was too far gone to recognise men any more; so the remnant was saved. But Re
was weary of the thankless task of ruling the world, and,
after appointing Thoth his viceroy on earth, retired to rest
on the back of the sky-cow in the heavens.

The myth of Osiris is known to us most fully through
Plutarch, but innumerable allusions in texts from all ages
show that the story is very old. The actors are the four
deities who constitute the last generation of the Heliopolitan Ennead, Osiris and Isis, Set and Nephthys. Osiris was
a wise and good king, who taught the Egyptians agriculture
and gave them laws—the founder of Egyptian civilisation.
His brother Set plotted his destruction, and accomplished it
by an ingenious trick. At a feast he produced a beautiful
and richly decorated chest which he had had made exactly
to the measures of Osiris, offering to present it to any one
whom it should fit; one after another tried it, until at last
Osiris laid himself in it.[1] Thereupon Set and his accomplices
clapped on the cover, fastened it securely, and threw the
chest into the Tanitic arm of the Nile. Isis fled to a retreat
in the marshes, where she gave birth to a son, Horus. Leaving
him there, Isis set forth in quest of Osiris's body, and found
it at last at Byblos, in Phœnicia, whither the current had
borne the coffin. She brought it back to Egypt and concealed
it; but while she was gone to Buto to see her son Horus,
Set, hunting by moonlight, discovered the coffin, and vented
his hatred on the dead body by rending it limb from limb
and scattering the members far and wide. Isis sought
them out, and buried them wherever she found them—
the backbone, for example, at Buto, the head at Abydos—
and each of these places became a seat of Osiris worship.

[1] This feature of the story has thus far not been found in native
Egyptian sources.

When Horus grew up he took it upon him to avenge his father, and engaged in a fierce conflict with his uncle, in which he had one eye torn out and Set was emasculated. Finally Thoth parted the combatants and healed their wounds. Set had to own himself beaten, and Horus ascended the throne of his ancestor, Geb, and ruled on earth, while his father Osiris became king of the dead.

From the time when Rameses II removed his capital to Tanis, in the Delta, Thebes was never again permanently the residence of the kings; but it was still the religious capital, and there the rulers were buried. The kings of the Eighteenth Dynasty cut their tombs in the face of the cliffs in a narrow lateral valley. Long galleries, here and there opening out into chambers, were drifted far into the solid rock; at the farther end was the "golden house," in which the stone sarcophagus laid. The walls of the galleries and chambers were covered with religious texts, pictorially illustrated, dealing with the other world, and the same texts were also painted on coffins. The longest of these is Amduat, the "Book of Him Who is in the Under-World," which has for its subject the nocturnal voyage of the sun, from his setting behind the mountains in the west to his reappearance in the east. In this voyage he passes through twelve regions, or districts (corresponding to the twelve hours of the night), which lie strung out along the course of a river on which the god in his barge passes from town to town, ordering their affairs and bestowing feoffs on his companions, just as the Pharaoh did when he made a royal progress on the Nile. The regions of the other world are peopled with gods and demons, and with the dead; over each a deity presides. Numerous gods accompany the sun in his barge or convoy him on his way. At the end of the journey the boat is dragged through a serpent six hundred yards long, and when he emerges from the jaws of the serpent the sun is the beetle Khepre, the god of the morning sun. Then the sun god seats himself in his morning barge and ascends the sky.

The composite origin of this picture of the other world is obvious. The regions traversed in the fourth and fifth hours are the gloomy realm of Sokar, the old Memphite god of the dead, which has a character altogether its own. The country is a sandy desert, full of reptiles; there is no water for Re's boat, and he continues his journey on the back of a long serpent or serpent-shaped sledge drawn by four gods. It is so dark that he cannot see the inhabitants of the land, but at length he emerges through a narrow passage or tunnel, "the road by which the body of Sokar entered," *i. e.*, through the mound of sand in which Sokar is buried. Evidently a piece of the local eschatology of Memphis is here preserved. The following regions, from the sixth hour on, are lands of Osiris, but of an Osiris who is not so far removed from Sokar; the inhabitants are called "those who are upon their sands," as in Sokar's realm. All these are dead, gods as well as men. Re sees the mounds of sand under which are buried not only the bodies of Shu and Tefnut, but of Atum, Re, and Khepre; he sees also the house of Osiris, in which are the mummies of kings of Upper and Lower Egypt, as well as of private persons well provided with offerings. In another place vengeance is taken on the enemies of Osiris, who lie beheaded or bound before the "flesh" (the dead body) of the god. In the eleventh hour there are fiery furnaces in which the enemies of Osiris are consumed, soul, shadow, and head, under the direction of goddesses in full armour, belching flames, and there are other like tortures—it is a corner of hell. Another Osirian realm is traversed in the third hour, where Osiris and his companions live. But not even here is there anything like the Fields of Earu, the paradise where Osiris rules over the blessed dead, nor is there anywhere an allusion to the Osirian judgment. The sun is the overlord in the world of night and the dead; Osiris is but a feudal vassal of his. One feature of properly solar mythology—besides the night voyage itself—is embodied, the encounter with the dragon Apophis, "whose place is in heaven," that is, according to the common view, the demon of storm; more likely the eclipse dragon.

The texts and illustrations have, as the texts do not fail to emphasise, a magical value; what particular benefit is to be gained by knowing this or that name or formula or accurately copying such and such a scene is explained at every turn. For example, "he possesses food in the underworld, and is satisfied with the gifts of the followers of Osiris, while his kindred upon earth also make gifts to him," or "he is a passenger in the barge of Re in heaven and in earth." "But he who does not know these things" cannot escape Apophis.

A work of similar nature is the Book of Portals. The sun in his night journey through the twelve regions has to pass fortifications like those of Egyptian cities. These formidable gates, each guarded by a great serpent, open, however, when the god pronounces the potent word. The picture of the lower world in this book is more in accord with the common Osirian doctrine, including the judgment.

The tombs of the Theban kings were both by their form and their situation ill-adapted to the maintenance of the cult of the dead, and mortuary temples were accordingly built on the western bank of the river at Thebes. In the tombs of persons of lower rank the decorations and inscriptions had hitherto been chiefly concerned with provision for the material needs of the dead—the thousand loaves of bread and the thousand jars of beer. Now texts and illustrations from the Book of the Dead and similar compilations become common, and the walls are decorated with representations of the daily life or the public career of the occupant. The funeral and the funeral feast are frequently depicted, and while the old beliefs and customs have not been outgrown, human relations and sentiments find here freer expression.

That the dead man might be forearmed against the many and varied perils of the tomb and the other world, he was provided with a library of magical texts, so that whatever happened he might know what to do and say. The surest defence against all evils was to identify himself with some god and overcome by his divine magic. Such texts were now written on papyrus rolls and deposited in the coffin. A certain selection and grouping of them became customary, and grew eventually into what we call the Book of the Dead; but it was only in the Saite time that this collection assumed what may be called a canonical form, in one hundred and sixty-five "chapters," and even then copies differ widely in completeness. They were fabricated commercially, like the other funerary necessities, blanks being left for the insertion of the man's name in the proper places—for example, in the verdict of acquittal before the judgment seat of Osiris. In these writings notions of every age and origin are jumbled together, and the whole is enveloped in an impenetrable veil of mystification; for what might by any chance be intelligible is ineffective in magic.

Besides the Book of the Dead and kindred texts, amulets of many varieties were deposited in the coffin or the tomb; the symbols of Osiris and Isis were frequently placed in the dead man's hand, models of the crowns of Upper and Lower Egypt, crowns and sceptres in the form worn by deities, eyes, hearts, a head-rest, a level and square, a staircase, and many more, the particular use of which is unknown, were laid, each in its proper place. At a later time we hear that one hundred and four amulets were necessary to protect the body as completely as that of Osiris himself. The tombs of this period are equipped with furniture and ornaments, but the older devices for supplying the dead with an unfailing abundance of food have fallen into disuse. The viscera are now enclosed in four jars with the heads of the four sons of Horus for covers, and these gods are trusted not to let the inwards suffer from hunger.

Of conceptions of the life after death, the abode in the Fields of Earu continues to be the most popular. The notion, however, that the dead might be called out by Osiris to work in his fields as in the *corvée* of the king was not altogether pleasing to the great of this world, unaccustomed to such labours on earth. They therefore provided themselves with numbers of little mummy figures of labourers in glazed pottery or stone, with hoes and baskets, to do the work for them. The inscription makes the purpose plain: "O thou Answerer (Ushebti), when I am called, when I am required to do any kind of work which is done in the other world . . . and am required at any time to cultivate the fields, to irrigate the banks, to convey sand from the east to the west, thou shalt say, Here am I." In every sphere magic prevails; all good fortune can be secured, all perils averted by its potent aid. The moral element in religion, which promised to convert the future life into a sphere of just retribution for the deeds done in this, is nullified by amulets and spells. On the breast of the dead, over the place of the heart, was laid a scarab, a symbol of the new-born sun god, with the inscription: "O heart that I have from my mother! O heart that belongs to my spirit! Do not appear against me as a witness, do not oppose me before the judges, do not contradict me before him who governs the balance; thou art my spirit that is in my body . . . do not suffer our name to shrink . . . tell no lie against me before the god!" Wherever the doctrine of retribution has been taken seriously, men have addressed themselves to find some escape from its rigour, and they have frequently fallen upon ways which we call magical; but it probably never occurred to any other people to effect this end by vitiating the testimony of conscience itself at the bar of God.

The collapse of the empire under the Twenty-first Dynasty was followed by three centuries under Libyan and Nubian dynasties, at the close of which came the Assyrian conquest of Lower Egypt. With the loosening of the Assyrian hold on its western provinces in the conflicts which preluded the fall of Nineveh, a vigorous line of Saite kings once more reunited Egypt for a century and a quarter under native rule, and endeavoured to revive the great traditions of ancient times. Nowhere is this effort more conspicuous than in religion; and what gives the Saite restoration its distinctive character is that it did not take the New Empire for its model, but the Old Kingdom, the golden age of Egypt's far-off youth. The researches of the priests in the monumental inscriptions and the long-neglected manuscripts in temple libraries brought to light things forgotten or unheeded for centuries, and to their antiquarian souls precious in proportion to their antiquity and obscurity. Nor did these discoveries remain the proud possession of the learned; they were brought out for every-day use, and titles and names of the pyramid age were worn by the courtiers and priests of Psammetichus; ancient cults and rites were repristinated; complete catalogues of the gods with their epithets were drawn up and inscribed on temple walls. It is no wonder that the Greeks, whose nearer acquaintance with the land began in this period, thought that the Egyptians were the most religious of mankind, however they appraised such excess of religiousness.

The worship of animals, installed as living gods in the temples, was cultivated in this age and subsequently in Greek and Roman times more zealously than ever before. At Memphis the bull Apis was regarded as the body of the god Ptah, whose spirit resided in the beast, or as a son of Ptah, or of Re, or of Osiris—varying attempts to connect the worship of the beast with the religion of the gods. The bull was black, with certain distinctive white markings; when one died there was universal mourning until a successor, recognised by these marks, was discovered, whereupon all Egypt rejoiced in the assurance of divine favour. He received all the veneration due to a god manifest in the flesh, and when he died was buried with the pomp and circumstance of a Pharaoh. In the Apis cemetery (Serapeum) have been found the tombs of over sixty of these divine beasts, ranging from the time of Amenophis III (about 1400 B. C.) to that of Ptolemy Alexander I (died 88 B. C.). The carcases were embalmed in the most costly manner; for one that died in 547 B. C. Amasis provided a sarcophagus of red granite "such as never has been made of stone by any king or at any time." It was hewn out of a single block thirteen feet long and nearly ten feet high. The bull Mnevis at Heliopolis and the bull Bacis at Hermonthis, both as "the living body of Re," received similar honours. The ram at Mendes was hardly less famous. Both at Memphis and at Lake Moeris, according to Herodotus, a tame crocodile was adorned with jewels in his ears and bracelets on his paws, and daily received rations of bread and a number of victims; when he died he was embalmed and buried in a holy place.

The sacredness of the whole species to which the living god belonged was now carried to the absurdity of its logical conclusion; not only were these animals protected while alive, so that to kill one even by accident was a grave or even a capital crime, but when they died a natural death they were often carefully mummied and transported to the cemetery of their kind, cats, e. g., to Bubastis, falcons to Buto, ibises to Hermopolis. Such cemeteries have been found in many places in Egypt; at Beni Hasan cats were buried in such enormous numbers that sacrilegious modern enterprise has turned them to practical use for fertilisers. Each region had its own sacred animals, which might be unconsidered or even detested in an adjoining district, and violent collision between the people of neighbouring towns sometimes resulted from this localisation of holiness.

The priests were subject to many and minute rules of ceremonial purity in shaving, bathing, dress, and diet; they were attached in great numbers to the several temples, from which they had their whole living. The Greeks give interesting accounts of popular religious festivals, at which scenes from the myths were acted out, and the participants threw themselves so thoroughly into the spirit of the thing that the controversies of the gods resulted in many broken heads among their devoted followers.

As in the religion of the gods, so also in the religion of the dead, the Egyptians of the Saite period gave themselves great pains to gather up everything that had come down from antiquity and to restore texts which had been for centuries disused. The Book of the Dead was continuously enlarged, until a papyrus roll seventy feet long was necessary to transcribe it. The voyage of the sun by night as it was depicted in the Book of the Other World and the Book of Portals in the tombs of the Theban kings, and even the earliest funerary texts from the pyramids of the Fifth and Sixth Dynasties, were brought into use again, and original additions made to this funerary literature, such as the Lamentation of Isis and Nephthys over Osiris, the Lamentation for Sokar, the Conquest of Apophis, and the Book of Breathings. The tombs of wealthy private citizens exceed in size at least those of all their predecessors; the coffins were frequently wrought in the hardest stone. Ushebtis were provided by hundreds —sometimes one for every day in the year—and amulets in great variety.

The Persian conquerors did not always treat the religion of their Egyptian subjects with respect; Cambyses is reported to have killed the Apis bull with his own hand, and a similar story is told of Artaxerxes Ochus. But the wiser rulers among them adopted a more conciliatory policy. The Ptolemies followed in this respect the example of Alexander, who made an expedition to the famous oracle of Amon in the oasis to get himself recognised as the son of the god, and reverently offered sacrifice to the gods of Memphis. His successors sedulously cultivated the fiction of legitimacy, and supported the old Egyptian religion as the religion of the state. Early in the Ptolemaic period a new era of temple-building began which continued well down into Roman times. Among these structures are some of the greatest now remaining in Egypt. The kings and queens took part in the Egyptian festivals, as though they had been descendants of the great Pharaohs. The priests of Mendes celebrate in a memorial inscription that their ram was the first sacred animal visited by Ptolemy Philadelphus after his accession to the throne. He fulfilled all the ceremonies of a royal visitation as they are described in the books, and returned to his residence full of joy for what he had done for "the Fathers, the rams of Mendes." When

Queen Arsinoe died, her statue was carried in procession with the sacred ram, and she received the honorary title: "She who is beloved by the ram, Arsinoe Philadelphus." Later in the reign of the king a new sacred ram was discovered which fulfilled all the requirements of the ancient writings, and the king honoured this "king of the animals of Egypt" with a great feast.

The introduction of Greek deities, which had begun long before, made no impression on the Egyptian religion beyond perhaps the creation of some sadly mixed types of gods and goddesses for domestic use. One foreign god, however, had the distinction of being taken over bodily into the Egyptian religion. When the second Ptolemy, in consequence of a dream, imported Sarapis, the Hades of Sinope, the priests at once discovered that, notwithstanding his very un-Egyptian exterior, Sarapis was nothing else than Osar-Hapi, Osiris-Apis; and when he began his somewhat successful career in the Roman world it was as a genuine Egyptian deity.

Isis, who in early times was celebrated in the mythology as the faithful wife of Osiris and mother of Horus, but enjoyed, as it appears, no conspicuous honour in religion, became of much greater importance in the Greek and Roman period. Among the foreign cults which, in the form of mysteries, spread widely in the Roman Empire that of Isis was one of the most popular.[1]

Early Christianity in Egypt was almost exclusively Greek, and made slow progress among the native population. The edict of Theodosius closed the temples, and put a legal end to the public worship of the gods, but even after the valley of the Nile had been for centuries nominally Christian, the old burial customs in considerable part survived, and with them doubtless the fundamental beliefs which had given birth to them.

[1] See below, pp. 584 ff.

CHAPTER X

BABYLONIA AND ASSYRIA

THE conditions under which at a very remote time civilisation developed in Babylonia were in many ways similar
to those in Egypt. The lower course of the Euphrates and
the Tigris, like the valley of the Nile, has an alluvial soil of
inexhaustible fertility, and with its spontaneous products
invited early settlement by the promise of easy living. As
the population multiplied under the favourable natural conditions, or poured in from the surrounding regions to share
them, it became necessary to regulate the waters, to reclaim
the marshes by building dikes, to dig canals and extend the
expanse of irrigation. The construction and maintenance
of these works demanded the united and organised labours
of the community, and thus conduced to the establishment
and consolidation of political order.

In other respects Babylonia was very differently situated from Egypt. While Egypt was by its position protected from the invasion of powerful neighbours, and even
isolated from the great main currents of history, so that its
civilisation was essentially homogeneous and developed its

characteristic type almost unaffected from without, Babylonia was exposed on one side to the incursions of the desert tribes and on another to the attacks of the Elamites and other habitants of the mountain country east of the valley, while to the north it lay open without a natural barrier to invading armies or to the influx of migrating nations set in motion by the great upheavals of population in Syria and Asia Minor. From a very early time two widely different races disputed with each other the supremacy or peacefully mingled; and when the older Semitic population of the north got the upper hand, it was to be submerged in turn by fresh waves of migration or conquest. But this situation, which repeatedly subjected Babylonia to alien dominion, early incited its rulers to enterprises of foreign conquest in the east and the north. In the third millennium B. C. Babylonian armies seem to have pushed their way to the shores of the Mediterranean. Commerce, with its peaceful penetration, reached even farther than arms and with more durable results. Thus Babylonian civilisation and religion were both more influenced from without and exerted a far wider influence in the ancient world than those of Egypt.

The inhabitants of southern Babylonia at the earliest time of which we have any knowledge called their country Sumer, and in consequence we call them Sumerians. The ethnographical and linguistic relations of the Sumerians are still an unsolved problem; they cannot, with our present light, be certainly connected with any other stock. There is some reason to think that they had descended into the river plain from the high lands to the east; among their gods such names as "ruler of the mountains" are not infrequent, and that for the worship of Enlil—and eventually of many other gods—an artificial mountain was erected in the midst of the plain seems to point in the same direction. It is probable that the Sumerians were not the only, nor perhaps the earliest, inhabitants of this country. Semitic nomads from the Arabian peninsula had doubtless roamed

there ages before the beginnings of history, and the oldest
records of the Sumerians themselves seem to show traces
of Semitic mixture. But there is no reason to doubt that
the earliest civilisation was the creation of the Sumerians.
The first centres of culture were in the south near the
head of the Persian Gulf. Ur and Eridu were near the
ancient mouth of the river; somewhat farther up the river
lay Uruk, and east of it, on another branch of the stream,
Larsa; while still farther to the north, on the main canal
of the Euphrates, was Nippur; and approximately in the
latitude of the later Babylon, Kutha. The northernmost
seats of this ancient civilisation were in the vicinity of the
modern Bagdad—Opis, Kish, Agade, and Sippar.

In Babylonia, as in Egypt, the city with the territory about
it was the primitive state. Each had its own god, who was
before all things the protector and patron of the city. Around
him were grouped many other deities of various character
and origin, some of whom had shrines of their own, while
others found a place in the temple of the chief god, constituting his family or court. The rulers, as the civil heads
of the community, were also its religious heads, the chief
priests of the god, and the commonest title of these rulers,
patesi, is derived from these religious functions. The French
excavations at Lagash (the modern Tello) give us a glimpse
of the pantheon of one such community in the twenty-fifth
century B. C.

The chief deity of the rulers of Lagash was Ningirsu,
"the lord of Girsu," one of the quarters of the city—perhaps
the original settlement. By his side was the goddess Bau,
his consort, and around him a number of gods who served
him in various ways. One had charge of his flock of goats,
another of the asses which drew his chariot; there is a third
to look after the fish-ponds, and another who is responsible
for the irrigation canals and the grain fields; there is an
armourer, in whose keeping are the weapons of the god; his
musical instruments are in the care of another. A divine
vizier receives the petitions of the people and lays them be-

fore Ningirsu; there is a superintendent of the god's harem, and other gods with other functions, like the officials of the king's court. The great goddess Gatumdug also had a shrine in the principal temple, while the goddesses Nina and Innina presided each over her own quarter of the city. Many other gods and temples are named in the inscriptions, but it would serve no purpose to catalogue them here.

Wars were frequent among these cities. One of them subdued its neighbours and ruled over them till they grew strong enough in turn to throw off the yoke and establish themselves in power. In this way the gods of one city found a place in the pantheon of others; and to such political vicissitudes the multiplication and distribution of gods is doubtless in part to be ascribed. In time the foundation of larger states brought the god of the ruler to temporary precedence among the gods, but raised none to permanent sovereignty. Some of the gods were very early—if not from the beginning—identified with heavenly bodies: the tutelary deity of Ur (Nannar), for example, was the moon; Utu, or Babbar, of Larsa, was the sun; the great goddess of Uruk was the planet Venus; but it does not appear that the religion of these cities differed in any material way from that of their neighbours, nor did the fact that the gods were thus visible in the heavenly bodies hinder their being worshipped in their temples in idols of human form like the others.

The gods who stand at the head of the pantheon owe their prominence, however, neither to the political fortunes of the cities whose patrons they were nor to their connection with the heavenly bodies, but, so far as we can judge, to the fact that their temples and priesthoods had a leading part in the development of religion. Thus, Ea of Eridu had through the whole history the highest reputation for wisdom; it was he who knew, as no other did, the rites and the potent charms by which evils of every kind could be averted, the wiles of malevolent demons thwarted, the favour of offended deities recovered, diseases cured, uncleanness purified; and by putting all his wisdom at the service of those who sought his help he proved himself not only the wise god but the friend of mankind. The most probable explanation of Ea's "wisdom" is that the priests of Eridu had at a remote time distinguished themselves in the invention and employment of the arts and texts which for ever after remained classical in their sphere.

An even higher rank belonged to Enlil (or, with assimilation, Ellil) of Nippur, who was plainly the head of the old Sumerian pantheon. Great gods, such as Sin of Ur and Ningirsu of Lagash, are called his sons; he is the king of the lands, the father of the gods. Kings of the cities which succeeded one another in dominion claimed to rule *jure divino* because Enlil had raised them to power; they rebuilt or restored his temple at Nippur, or deposited there votive objects bearing their names. This temple, Ekur, the "Mountain House," was the most famous of Babylonian sanctuaries; many gods of other cities had shrines in it. Inasmuch as Nippur, so far as we know, never had any corresponding political hegemony, the most probable explanation of this acknowledged religious precedence is that Nippur was the oldest settlement of the Sumerians in Babylonia, where they first réared the artificial high place for the worship of the deity of their native mountains.

With these two is associated as third Anu, who was in high honour at Uruk, where he was the father of Nana (Ishtar), but he is not known to have been the patron deity of any city. He is in mythology the sky god, and if this was his original character it would account at once for his exalted place in the pantheon as the head of the divine commonwealth, the father of the gods, and for the fact that he has no corresponding prominence in religion.

In very ancient inscriptions these three are named together; Anu, Enlil, and Ea constitute the original divine triad. Among them the rule of the universe is partitioned: Anu presides in heaven, Enlil in the earth with the circumambient air, and Ea in the waters—the subterranean ocean as well as the ocean which surrounds the earth—an association probably suggested by the situation of his city, Eridu, at the head of the Persian Gulf. The supremacy of this triad over the local gods is universally acknowledged; around them chiefly the common mythology and religion of the Sumerians centres.

In the north of Babylonia, in the region which, from the name of its principal city, Agade, is called Akkad, the Semitic element in the population was evidently much more numerous and compact than in the south. The Akkadians, as we may call this first stratum of Semitic stock in Babylonia, appropriated much from the civilisation of the Sumerians, and developed and improved it in accordance with their own genius. Their growing power is evinced by the rule of Semitic kings in Kish whose power extended to southern Babylonia. Here, about 2500 B. C., Sargon founded the kingdom of Akkad, and in a series of campaigns subjected all Sumer (southern Babylonia), waged successful war against Elam, and in later expeditions not only extended his empire to the upper valley of the Tigris, but subjugated the Amorites in northwestern Syria, advancing to the Mediterranean seaboard. His son, Naram-Sin, maintained and even extended the dominion of his father; a stela of his, commemorating a victory, has been discovered near Diarbekr; he not only subdued the warlike tribes in the Zagros mountains, but conquered a considerable part of eastern Arabia (Magan), and assumed the title "King of the Four Quarters." This first great Semitic empire was, however, very short-lived; of the successors of Naram-Sin nothing is known beyond a list of names. Upon its ruins arose again Sumerian states, and then, under kings of Ur in the far south, an extensive Sumerian empire, the kingdom of Sumer and Akkad, which lasted for about three centuries.

The First Dynasty of Ur was succeeded by dynasties from Isin and Larsa, whose latter days witnessed the decay and dissolution of the kingdom. The Elamites took advantage of its weakness to invade and subjugate the land, the Assyrians made themselves independent, and a new Semitic kingdom arose in northern Babylonia, which in turn expelled the Elamites and brought the whole country under its sway.

The rulers of this kingdom, the First Dynasty of Babylon, did not spring from the old Semitic population of the region, but were newcomers from Syria. The Amorites, whose principal seat was the region of the Lebanon and eastward toward the Euphrates, seem in the last century of the kingdom of Sumer and Akkad to have found their way in increasing numbers into Babylonia as traders, settlers, or perhaps as mercenaries, and contributed to the steady infiltration of Semitic elements into the Sumerian body politic which had long been in progress. Now, however, it would appear that they came as invaders, and somewhere about 2060 B. C. one of their chiefs made himself king in Babylon. His successors established the kingdom on a firm basis, and the sixth of the line, Hammurabi (1958–16), conquered the whole of Babylonia, driving out the Elamites. Assyria and at least a part of Mesopotamia were included in his empire, and he assumed, after the ancient fashion, the titles not only of king of Sumer and Akkad, but of the four quarters of the earth. The greatness of Hammurabi appears even more conspicuously in the organisation and administration of his kingdom than in the wars by which it was established and enlarged. The code of laws discovered a few years ago at Susa and his correspondence with administrative and judicial subordinates, as well as the records of his efforts to increase the prosperity of the land by building canals and irrigation works, show how many-sided and far-reaching were his activities for the welfare of his people. The zeal which he manifested in rebuilding and enriching the temples of the gods had the same motive: the fortunes of the nation in peace and war depended on their favour.

The religion of the older Semitic inhabitants of Babylonia did not differ essentially from that of their Sumerian neighbours, from whom they doubtless borrowed much. The gods whom they particularly affected were Sin, Shamash, and Ishtar, who often appear together as the second triad. The

Sumerian sun and moon gods they recognised as their own Shamash and Sin under other names; the goddesses they called indiscriminately Ishtar, and the one name thus covered most diverse characters. The Amorites worshipped a god Amurru, who like Assur bore the same name as his people; but they were particularly devoted to Adad, whose title Ramman ("the thunderer") and attributes indicate that he was a god of storm as well as of battle. He is often joined in a triad with Sin and Shamash, displacing Ishtar, or is added as a fourth in the group. The new masters of the land behaved very differently from the Hyksos conquerors of Egypt; from the beginning they appeared as the patrons and protectors of the native gods, and rapidly assimilated the old Babylonian culture and religion.

The fact that the new dynasty made Babylon their residence greatly increased the importance of that city, which hitherto had played no conspicuous part in history, and with Hammurabi it became the capital of a wide empire. In this elevation Marduk, the god of the city, shared, and from being an insignificant local deity he became the greatest of the gods, just as Amon rose to the foremost rank among the gods of Egypt when Thebes became the capital of the New Empire. The prestige thus politically achieved did not, however, content the priests, and they added a theological legitimation. As Amon, the ram of Thebes, was identified with Re, the great sun-god, so for Marduk of Babylon the titles, myths, and functions of the venerable Enlil of Nippur were appropriated. Marduk was also discovered to be the son of Ea, and that wisest of gods made over to him all his wisdom. Combining the attributes of the two most renowned deities of the old religion, Marduk was from this time on the head of the Babylonian pantheon. The religious texts which have come down to us from the library of Assurbanipal show clearly that they were in great part recast to adapt them to the supremacy of Marduk. It is not to be imagined that these politico-theological inventions made outright any great change in the religion of the people,

who worshipped as their fathers had done from time immemorial at the temples of their own cities, or that the priesthoods of Nippur and Eridu allowed Enlil and Ea to be thrust
into the background in their own sanctuaries by the new
doctrine of Babylon; but in the end neither the conservatism
of the people nor the opposition of the priests could prevent
Enlil, the Bel of Nippur, from being overshadowed by Marduk, the Bel of Babylon. Nabu, the god of Borsippa, opposite Babylon, who in earlier times had been of greater
fame than Marduk, had to be content with the honour of
being Marduk's dear son and prophet.

The Babylonians had an extensive mythology, which
early received at the hands of the priests a literary form.
Two or three mythological poems of considerable length
have been preserved, besides fragmentary remains of a
number of others. Of the former the combat of Bel (Marduk) with the monster Tiamat, entitled, from its first words,
"*Enuma elish,*" and often called by modern scholars the
Cosmogonic Epic, is from a religious point of view the most
important. The Assyrian copy which we have was made
in the middle of the seventh century B. C. for the library
of Assurbanipal at Nineveh, but it is certain, on internal
grounds, that the poem in its present form dates from the
times of the Semitic kingdom of Babylon, say the twentieth
century B. C. It was written on seven tablets, of which
the third and fourth are nearly entire, while larger and
smaller parts of the others have also been recovered. The
missing portions of the earlier tablets can in the main be
supplied, thanks to the repetition of their contents in those
better preserved. The loss of the last tablets is more serious, because—until further discoveries—it leaves the conclusion, which apparently dealt with the establishment of
the present order in heaven and earth (creation), to arbitrary conjecture.

The origin of all things was the primeval watery chaos,
represented by the pair Apsu and Tiamat, whose "waters
were mingled together." With them the cosmogonic the-

ogony begins. The next generation are Lahmu and Lahamu, then Anshar and Kishar, the Above and Below of the as yet unordered universe; to them were born, after a long time, Anu and Ea, and probably—the name is not preserved— Bel (originally Enlil). Apsu and Tiamat see their peace threatened by these gods, and with Mummu, their son, plot to destroy them and their new-fangled ways. As their allies in the coming war they create a host of monsters. Tiamat appoints to the chief command Kingu, one of the gods on her side, and hangs upon his breast the tablets of destiny, saying, "Thy order shall not be in vain, and the word of thy mouth shall be established." Ea learns what is brewing and brings word to Anshar, who thereupon de-spatches Anu to restore order; but Anu turns back in dismay, and Ea himself has no better success. Then Marduk steps forth as the champion of the gods, and promises to over-come Tiamat on condition that the gods formally confer on him the supreme power. A council is accordingly held, and after a feast at which they drink till their courage is high the assembled gods solemnly bestow on Marduk the sovereignty over the whole world, and give him the emblems of royalty—the sceptre, throne, and ring. Marduk then arms himself for the fray, and with the thunderbolt in his hand, his mighty weapon, mounts his four-horse chariot and rides out to meet the foe.[1] At the sight of him Kingu is palsied with fear, but Tiamat is of better mettle and stands her ground. Marduk throws his net over her, and as she opens her mouth wide, the winds he let loose strangle her. Marduk kills her with his spear and triumphantly bestrides her body. Her allies try to save themselves by flight, but are caught and destroyed. From Kingu the victor takes the tablets of destiny and lays them on his own breast. Then he returns to Tiamat, and, after savagely mutilating her dead body amid the rejoicing of the gods, finally splits her in halves, "like a flat fish," and of one half makes the

[1] The steeds which drew Marduk's *quadriga* should probably be im-agined as mythical beasts rather than horses.

firmament to restrain the waters of the celestial ocean, and of the other half the earth as a lid above the subterranean ocean.[1] Over against the Deep he sets the dwelling of Ea; he founds Eshara, and causes Anu, Bel, and Ea to occupy their several provinces.

With this the fourth tablet ends. The fifth begins by telling how Marduk made the stations for the great gods, fixed the stars and the constellations, ordered the astronomical calendar, and delivered to the moon god the laws he must observe in the several phases of the moon. Here the text breaks off. From the opening of the next tablet it may be inferred that the fourth closed with a complaint of the gods that there was no one to worship them. Marduk thereupon resolves to create man, and communicates his plan to Ea:

> "Blood will I take and bone will I [fashion],
> I will fashion man, that man may . . .
> I will create man, who shall inhabit [the earth],
> That the services of the gods may be established,
> And that their shrines [may be built]." [2]

This apparently corresponds to the account of the creation of man given by Berossos: Bel commanded one of the gods to cut off his (Bel's) head, knead earth with the flowing blood, and fashion men and animals which could stand the air. Probably, therefore, the first line quoted above from the tablet should be rendered "*my* blood will I take." [3] In the immediate sequel the badly mutilated text lets us see only that Bel announced to Ea some further plan about the gods, to which Ea replies in a long speech. In the last lines of the tablet the gods are again assembled to honour their avenger; and the seventh tablet, if it be correctly identified, contains the homage of the gods to Marduk,

---

[1] So Berossos.

[2] King, Seven Tablets of Creation, p. 86.

[3] This singular way of making man has an exact parallel in a Maori myth. The New Zealand poet adds the obvious significance—man is part divine, part earthy.

consisting principally of a recital of his fifty names, or honorary titles, with their significance.

It will be seen from this summary that in the parts of the poem still extant there is no account of the creation of the world nor of the production of plants and animals; while for the creation of man an eminently hieratic motive is given, namely, that there may be somebody to worship the gods and build their temples. It is indeed not improbable that the missing portions of the later tablets may have referred to the creation of plants and animals, but in any case this is not the main subject or purpose of the poem, and it is only misleading to call it the "Epic of Creation."

It is plain that Marduk was not the original hero in the great conflict between the gods of the cosmic order and the monstrous powers of the primeval chaos, and the usurpation of this rôle by Marduk has introduced numerous inconsistencies and even contradictions into the tenor of the myth. There can be little doubt that in its older form the conqueror of Tiamat was Enlil, while various indications in the earlier part of the poem point to a previous victory of Ea over Apsu. The poem in its present form thus represents a combination of myths from different religious centres and different periods in the history of the Babylonian religion, to which final literary shape was given by the priesthood of Babylon somewhere about the age of Hammurabi. The motive of the recension is the legitimation of Marduk: the gods have solemnly acknowledged him as supreme; they hymn his praises as an example to men.

In view of the composite character of the poem the possibility must be admitted that the conflict of Bel with Tiamat originally had a different significance, but the interpretations which find in it the victory of light over darkness or summer over winter are, like the corresponding interpretations of the flood myth, anything but convincing. They proceed from the assumption that Marduk was from the beginning a sun god, specifically a god of the early morning sun or of the sun in the spring of the year, and sometimes display extraordinary ignorance of the climate of Babylonia. The question is without significance for the history of religion.

Outside the poem *"Enuma elish"* there are various allusions to creation—the creation of the domestic and wild animals by the gods in their assembly; the ordinances of the moon and the sun established by the three great gods Anu, Bel, and Ea; the creation of all things by the river which the great gods dug out. The most interesting of them is one in which creation is ascribed to Marduk with the co-operation of the goddess Aruru:

"Marduk laid a reed upon the face of the waters;
  He formed dust and poured it out beside the reed.
  That he might cause the gods to dwell in the habitation of their hearts' desire,
  He formed mankind.
  The goddess Aruru together with him created the seed of mankind;
  The beasts of the field and the living creatures in the field he formed.
  He created the Tigris and the Euphrates, and he set them in their place;
  Their names he declared in goodly fashion.
  The grass, the rush of the marsh, the reed, and the forest he created,
  The green herb of the field he created,
  The lands, the marshes, and the swamps;
  The wild cow and her young, the wild calf; the ewe and her young, the lamb of the fold;
  Plantations and forests,
  The he-goat and the mountain-goat . . ."

In the sequel the fragmentary text narrates how Marduk built the cities and the great temples of Babylon. The whole text, it may be observed, is only the preamble to an incantation.

A poem in twelve books, or tablets, tells at considerable length the adventures of the hero Gilgamesh. Notwithstanding many longer or shorter gaps in the text, the progress of the story can in general be followed, and parts of it are in good preservation. Gilgamesh is ruler of Uruk.

The people of the city, groaning under his tyranny (?), be-
seech the goddess Aruru to make an adversary for him; she
creates Eabani, a wild man who makes his abode with the
beasts of the field. By the seduction of a holy harlot
Eabani is brought to Uruk, where he makes friends with
Gilgamesh. Gilgamesh and Eabani undertake an expedition
to the sacred cedar forest, the abode of the gods, the holy
place of the goddess Irnini, and—as must be supplied—
overcome and slay Humbaba, whom Bel has made guardian
of the tallest cedar of all. Ishtar, the goddess of Uruk,
offers herself to the returning hero, whose prowess has
captivated her, but he spurns her advances, throwing up
to her the lamentable fate of her whole catalogue of lovers,
beginning with the youthful Tammuz: "Me, too, thou
lovest, and wilt serve me like them." The insulted goddess
lays the *iniuria spretæ formæ* before her father Anu, who at
her importunity creates a mighty bull to avenge her, but
the two friends, after a desperate fight, slay the bull. Ishtar, from the walls of Uruk, curses the slayer, to which
Eabani replies by flinging a quarter of the bull at her head,
with the words: "If I could only lay hands on you and serve
you in the same way!" The victors, having washed their
hands in the Euphrates, enter Uruk in triumph amid the
acclaim of the multitude. The following tablet, of which
very little remains, told how Eabani was stricken by disease and died—the working of Ishtar's curse. The ninth
tablet shows us Gilgamesh, inconsolable for the loss of
his other self and fearing a like fate, wandering alone over
plain and mountain in search of the abode of his deified ancestor Utnapishtim. Through a pass guarded by scorpion-
men he enters the land of darkness, a rugged region thick
with perils, beyond which he arrives at a paradise whose
trees bear precious stones. With the aid of an ancient
mariner who had been with Utnapishtim through the great
flood, he is ferried over the waters of death to the shore,
where he finds the far-sought forefather. In answer to
Gilgamesh's questions, Utnapishtim tells the story of the

deluge, which thus forms an episode in the poem (Tablet XI).

Various means are employed to confer "life" (immortality) on Gilgamesh; Utnapishtim's wife prepares him magical food, and he purifies himself in a sacred bathing-place. Utnapishtim tells him also of a plant with the promising name, "The Grey-Haired Man Renews His Youth," growing on the bottom of the sea. Gilgamesh dives with a stone to the depths and gathers the plant, but at the next landing-place, as he is washing himself in a fountain, a serpent snatches the life-giving plant away. Bitterly lamenting his loss, Gilgamesh pursues his way afoot to Uruk. The fragments of the last tablet show that Ea accedes to the desire of Gilgamesh to see his friend Eabani once more, and causes Nergal, the god of the nether world, to let Eabani's ghost rise "like a vapour from the earth, and make known to his brother Gilgamesh the law of the earth," *i. e.*, of the abode of the dead. Eabani's disclosure of the secrets of his prison-house is lost, but the lack may be in part supplied from the last lines of the tablet and from Eabani's dream in the second tablet.

The poem brings together myths and legends of diverse origin, to which it gives unity by a plot which, if we understand it, is not devoid of ingenuity. The main action of the poem centres about Uruk; the hero is a ruler of that city, and its amorous goddess is the author of his undoing. The expedition against Humbaba, also, the motive of which in the fragmentary state of the text cannot be made out, may very well belong to the legends of Uruk; the name Humbaba sounds Elamite, and the divine cedar forest was perhaps imagined to lie in the mountains east of Babylonia. The gods who appear in the poem, besides Ishtar, are Anu and Ea; it was Bel who installed Humbaba as keeper of the great cedar.

Many scholars since Rawlinson have interpreted the story as a solar myth, or at least imagine that it had its origin in a solar myth: Gilgamesh was, they think, an ancient sun god, and his adventures reflect the course of the sun through the twelve signs of the zodiac; the friendship of Gilgamesh and Eabani points to the sign of the Twins; the fact that the flood story is on the eleventh tablet is significant, for the eleventh sign of the zodiac is Aquarius.[1] The slaying of the bull is a favourite subject on seals; Gilgamesh is commonly represented as a man with shaggy hair and beard, while Eabani has the head, arms, and breast of a man, with the lower body and legs of a bull. It was formerly the fashion to see in the hero of this exploit the prototype of the Biblical Nimrod, who was "a mighty hunter before the Lord." George Smith thought that the name (written Gish-tu-bar) might be read Nimrod, and though this conjecture has long since been laid away and the name Gilgamesh established on good evidence, the title "Nimrod Epic" still clings to the poem.

The story of the great flood, as told by Utnapishtim to Gilgamesh, fills, as we have seen, a large part of the eleventh tablet of the poem, but there is no doubt that it was originally an independent myth. In the present form there are slight discrepancies in detail which point to different versions, but it is not necessary to dwell upon them here.

In a council of the gods it was determined, at the instance of Enlil—who sometimes appears as the sole promoter of the catastrophe—to destroy the city of Shurippak on the Euphrates by a flood.[2] Ea, ever the friendly god, warned Utnapishtim to build a ship in which to save himself; if his townsmen asked why he was doing it, he should say Enlil was angry with him and he might no longer abide in their city, which was on Enlil's earth, he must fare forth upon the sea, Ea's domain. The dimensions of the ship and details of the construction follow. When it was completed, he put on board all his possessions, his family and household, cattle and beasts of the field, and various craftsmen. The handling of the vessel was intrusted to the

[1] We have no proof that the zodiac was laid out into twelve signs earlier than the Persian period.

[2] In the sequel all mankind seem to be involved in the ruin.

shipmaster, Puzur-Bel. Then came a great storm; Adad thundered, the torches of the Anunnaki were lighted up; Nabu and Marduk and Nergal did their part. The mounting waters overwhelmed the earth, men perished, the gods themselves in terror fled aloft to the heaven of Anu and cowered like dogs; the mistress of the gods loudly lamented that she had given her consent to the destruction of the race which she had created; the heavenly gods wept with her.

Six days and nights the tempest raged; on the seventh, when it ceased, Utnapishtim looked out and saw that the world was one great sea, and all mankind was turned to clay. At length the waters subsided, and the ship grounded on Mount Nisir. After a week Utnapishtim sent out a dove, but it found no resting-place and returned to the ship; a swallow did the same; then he released a raven, which did not come back. Knowing by this sign that the waters were abated, Utnapishtim disembarked and offered sacrifice and incense to the gods on the summit of the mountain. The gods, smelling the sweet odour, gathered like flies to the sacrifice, among them the mistress of the gods. When Enlil saw the ship, he was wroth that any men had escaped destruction. Ea reproached him for having caused the destruction: the guilty should suffer for their sins; Enlil might send wild beasts or famine or pestilence among men, but should not involve good and bad in one common ruin by a flood. Ea also defends himself against the charge of betraying the secrets of the gods. At last Enlil was appeased; bringing Utnapishtim and his wife out of the ship, he made them kneel before him, and decreed that henceforth they should be no more men but gods, and dwell afar at the mouth of the rivers. Thus they came to be in the distant abode where Gilgamesh found them.

With the main features of this story we were already acquainted through Berossos, though he seems to have had before him a recension somewhat different from that which is incorporated in the epic. Several fragmentary tablets have also been discovered, containing, as it appears, variants of the myth, in one of which the flood seems to have been preceded by other judgments, such as years of drought.

Numerous other myths are more or less completely known. One of these tells of the flight of Etana to heaven on the back of an eagle and his fatal fall—a story which, like the adventures of Gilgamesh, was transferred to Alexander the Great. Another is the story of Adapa, who on the advice of Ea refused to eat the food set before him by Anu, a myth of a not uncommon type explaining the failure to attain immortality; the same motive occurs in Gilgamesh's loss of the plant which makes the grey-head young and in the expulsion of Adam and Eve from the garden in which the tree of life grew.

The only building material in Babylonia was loam brick, ordinarily sun-dried; the scarcity of fuel made burnt brick so costly that they were used only for a veneer, and rarely even for that purpose. The heavy rainfall at certain seasons of the year made necessary great attention to conductors and drains for carrying off the water. Structures for any reason neglected speedily washed into a shapeless heap of earth. Such mounds, often of vast size, are all that remain of the Babylonian temples; only patient excavation reveals anything of their plan, and even after much labour of this kind our knowledge is in many respects incomplete. The characteristic feature of the Babylonian temple is the staged tower, or pyramid, of solid masonry, which rose within the temple precincts. A ramp led up to the summit, on which, according to Herodotus, stood a small shrine. The "Mountain House" at Nippur was probably the oldest of these towers, which belonged primarily to the worship of Enlil. About the tower was a complex of buildings and courts covering an extensive area and in some cases occupying an entire quarter of the city. Before the temple proper, in which the image of the god was housed, lay one or more courts surrounded by rooms for the vessels used in worship and the treasures of the god, the storage of materials for the offerings and the revenues of the temple in agricultural products, and for the use of the priests. Other buildings served as record offices, where legal instruments of every kind were deposited. Schools, also, were connected with the temples in which youths were taught to read and write the complicated script, and more advanced students pursued the higher branches of priestly learning, the liturgies and incantations, the arts of divination, the myths of the gods, the history of the temple, and the like. Probably young men destined to an official career also got their education in the temple schools.

The great temples were endowed with extensive lands, and had large revenues from them as well as from the priests' fees and from pious donations. Their capital was often put out to loan at the customary high rates of interest. In addition to their other functions, the temples thus, as frequently in antiquity, did a banking business.

Of the ranks of the hierarchy little is known. A "great priest" is frequently mentioned, probably the chief priest of a particular temple. The multiplicity of titles—some thirty titles of priests have been collected, besides twenty of priestesses—may in part be due to specialisation of functions, but it is probable that many of them are names for the same classes at different places and times. That the priesthood early attained much power—and abused it—is evident from the record of Urukagina's reforms at Lagash in the twenty-ninth century.

The priesthood was divided into several classes with distinct functions; one class had to do particularly with the offerings; another intoned hymns or wailed lamentations; a third knew the rites and incantations by which evil spirits, especially the demons of disease, were exorcised and malicious magic thwarted, as well as the manifold purifications and piacula that went with them; while a fourth was expert in divination and the interpretation of omens and portents. All these, except perhaps the sacrificial priests, possessed their own collections of texts, and the last two, at least, had a highly elaborated traditional art to master. There were also multitudes of attendants and servants of inferior rank down to the temple slaves. Women dedicated to the service of the gods were attached to the temples, whether as a kind of vestals (called, in the legislation of Hammurabi, "Sister of the God") or as consecrated harlots ("holy women"). The latter were associated with the worship of Ishtar at Uruk and elsewhere, so that another name for them is Ishtaritu; whether they were exclusively connected with her cult is doubtful.

The animal sacrifices included bullocks, sheep and goats, fish, and several kinds of birds; among the bloodless offerings are named grain, dates, figs, wine, oil, milk, honey, and incense of sweet-smelling woods. The worshipper is often represented with a lamb or kid in his arms, doubtless the commonest victim. The rituals sometimes make a difference between the offerings to be made by the well-to-do and by the poor. It appears that in private sacrifices the god received only a part of the victim; the right hind leg is occasionally named. Regular offerings of food were set before the gods daily; royal inscriptions record the provision made or renewed by the kings for such stated sacrifices. These offerings were not consumed by fire on the altar, but placed on the table of the god, and subsequently, we may assume, eaten by the priests. The burning of an offering seems to occur only in connection with magical or piacular rites. Libations of water have a large place in the ritual. In the incantation texts frequent mention is made of loaves of bread (twelve or a multiple of twelve) set out before the god.

Festivals were celebrated at fixed times in the year; each temple doubtless had its own sacred calendar. In the inscriptions of Gudea, king of Lagash, there is repeated mention, for example, of a New-Year's festival of the goddess Bau, and of the "wedding gifts" which the king made on that occasion, as though a ἱερὸς γάμος, the marriage of the goddess with Ningirsu the tutelary deity of the city, was celebrated on that occasion. A divine marriage seems to have been part of the New-Year's festival at Nippur also. The New-Year's festival at Babylon at the beginning of the month Nisan (March-April) was observed with great pomp; the god Nabu of Borsippa was carried in procession to visit his father Marduk, and when he returned Marduk escorted him on his way. On the eighth and eleventh days of the month was a great assembly of the gods, in whose presence Marduk, seated on his throne, decreed the fates of mankind for the coming year. The festival of Tammuz, to which we shall return in another connection, was a midsummer festival. It lies in the nature of our sources that we hear much less about the calendar festivals than about those which were appointed by the rulers on the occasion of the building or restoration of a temple or in celebration of their victories. At such times, besides multiplied sacrifices, images of the gods were dedicated, and offerings of gold, silver, precious stones, and votive objects of various kinds were presented; many such, bearing the inscription of the royal donors, have been preserved.

The Babylonians perpetuated and systematised in a higher stage of culture the universal belief of savages that misfortunes of every kind, especially disease and death, are caused by evil spirits, either out of spontaneous malevolence or instigated by human enemies. The primitive defence against them is apotropaic magic, which by words and gestures averts their onsets or expels them from the body of their victim. This early developed into a mysterious art, which was often transmitted from one generation to another in the families of its adepts. An essential part of it was the diagnosis: it was necessary to recognise the particular mischief-maker in each case, for knowledge of his secret name gave the magician power over him, and the treatment by which a headache devil was exorcised would not expel the toothache worm. Often the demon is detected and driven away by a more powerful spirit which is under the control of the practitioner, as in what is called shamanism. Upon a higher stage, the gods, as the patrons and protectors of the community, are invoked to defend its members against their malignant foes, and the ordinary forms of religious appeal are combined with the methods of magical self-defence. With a more advanced conception of both the power and the character of the gods, it comes to be thought, at least by those who have made this advance, that the demons have power to harm men only when permitted to do so by the gods, and that the gods give their license only when a man has offended them by his misdeeds. Thus the propitiation of the offended god by confession and contrition may come to have a prominent place in ceremonies which bear the indelible impress of magical origin; hymns in praise of the gods appear in similar contexts, and myths telling how a god escaped some peril or attained some good are combined with incantations which enable the user to do the same.

In Babylonia all this formed a recognised part of the public religion, and was the special province of a class of priests who from their functions bear the title Ashipu, or incantation priest. Magical performances are joined with sacrifices and purifications, prayers with exorcisms, all together forming a great body of temple ritual. It is not probable that the official magic of the priests wholly supplanted unofficial practice among the common people; but of such quacks—from the regular point of view—we learn as little as we should of herb-doctors and bone-setters in orthodox medical treatises. Of the practitioners of the black art, on the other hand, of wizards and witches who use their diabolical art to injure and destroy honest folk, there is much to say in the incantation texts; their procedure is described, and is imitated to turn their malice back upon them and entangle them in their own snares. Making an image of the victim, containing, if possible, some particle of himself, or at least identified with him by the name, and burning or melting it, sticking pins in it, shooting arrows into it, drowning it in water, are universal forms of sympathetic magic well known to Babylonian witches, as are also magic knots by which the victim is bound fast in evil, potions and poisonous herbs, or plants to which, on magical principles, harmful properties were attributed.

The Ashipu priest had his library of rituals and incantations for all cases; his only embarrassment can have been to select the efficacious text for the particular occasion. Numerous series of such texts have been more or less completely preserved: one is entitled "Evil Demons," another "Headache," a third "Fevers"; one whole series is devoted to a she-demon named Labartu; two others are "Burning" series, because the consumption by fire of magical figures with the proper charms is in some of the tablets the climax of the performance. The texts of these incantations have been preserved chiefly in Assyrian copies. It is intrinsically probable that the collections grew larger with time in the effort to provide for every contingency; the forms in high repute for efficacy at one temple would be borrowed by the priests of another, and adapted by introducing their own gods into the catalogues. It is possible in some cases to recognise such changes. There is no reason to think, however, that their character was materially altered.

The most famous source of this particular kind of wisdom was Eridu, with its wise and benevolent god, Ea. In many instances in our copies Marduk lays a case before Ea, who makes the stereotyped reply that his son Marduk knows all that he knows, but after this perfunctory preamble Ea reveals the rites and charms that will be effective in the circumstances. We shall hardly err if we see in the somewhat otiose introduction of Marduk an adaptation of the incantations of Ea by the priests of Babylon after that city had become a great political and religious centre, just as the part of Marduk in the combat with Tiamat is a usurpation of the rôle of Enlil.

The texts in which a long array of deities, including not only the great gods of the pantheon, but many obscure or otherwise unknown figures, are invoked to thwart the wiles of the adversary or undo the mischief he has wrought, and the fact that in many cases the ritual is principally occupied with offerings and incense to these gods, show how the resources of religion are added to those of both primitive and sophisticated magic; but, as in similar circumstances elsewhere, religion in taking magic into its service itself descends to the plane of magic. Of greater interest are the incantations in which the possibility is reckoned with that the misfortunes of the sufferer may have been occasioned by some misdeed. Thus, in the second tablet of the Shurpu series, the priest recites a catalogue of offences against gods and men, inquiring whether his client has been guilty of any of them:[1]

Has he offended his god or goddess?[2] . . . Did he put discord between father and son, mother and daughter, mother-in-law and daughter-in-law, brother and brother, friend and friend, comrade and comrade? Is it that he did not free a captive, release one in bonds, let a prisoner see the light of day? . . . Is it a sin against a god, a transgression against a goddess? Has he offended a god, contemned a goddess? Is it a sin against his own god, a fault against his own goddess? Violence toward his lord, hatred of his elder brother? Has he scorned father and mother, insulted his elder sister, given in little and withheld in great matters, to Nay said Yea, to Yea, Nay, spoken basely or wickedly, used false weights, taken false money, refused good money, deprived a lawful son of his inheritance and set in the inheritance one who had no right, marked out false boundaries or failed to mark right ones, displaced the landmarks? Has he occupied his neighbour's house, approached his neighbour's wife, shed his neighbour's blood, robbed his neighbour of his garment? Has he kept a man under his power, driven an honest man out of his family, broken up a united clan, resisted a superior? Was he upright with his mouth and false at heart, with his mouth full of Yea, his heart full of Nay? Is it because of unrighteousness which he devised to destroy and ruin upright men, to rob and permit robbery and busy himself with evil? Is his mouth vile, his lips rebellious? . . . Has he meddled with magic and witchcraft? Is it on account of gross injustice that he has done, the many

[1] Zimmern, Beiträge zur Kenntniss der Babylonischen Religion, I. The heathenish repetitions on which so much depends in incantations and liturgies are here retrenched.

[2] That is, the god and goddess who were his special patrons and protectors. These patrons were not an inferior class of deities, but were taken from among the great gods.

sins that he has committed? . . . Is it because of aught wherein he has despised his god and his goddess? Has he promised with heart and mouth but not kept his word, contemned the name of his god with a gift, vowed something but kept it back, given something but consumed it himself? Did he withhold an offering he was bound to make, incensing his god and his goddess? Did he rise up in an assembly and utter mischief? Loosed be all wherewith he is banned!

It will be observed that there is no question here of penitence or reparation; the important thing is not to overlook any possible reason why the man may have fallen under the ban; and in the sequel, where gods and goddesses in scores are invoked, it is not to forgive, but to "loose" by their superior magic the ban which is upon him. Ea, and after him Marduk, is often called "the arch-magician of the gods."

The belief that the gods themselves inflict evils on men for their misdeeds is, of course, not foreign to the Babylonian religion, and there are litanies in which a suppliant in deep distress through personal or public calamity implores the gods to turn their anger and restore the transgressor to favour. The recitation of these lamentations seems to have been the business of a special class of priests; some of them have been published under the title "Babylonial Penitential Psalms." Perhaps the most interesting of them begins:

May the anger of my lord's heart be appeased! May the god whom I know not be appeased; the goddess whom I know not be appeased! Known and unknown god be appeased; known and unknown goddess be appeased! May the heart of my god be appeased; the heart of my goddess be appeased! Known and unknown god and goddess be appeased! May the god who is angry with me be appeased!

The sin that I have committed I know not. The misdeeds that I have committed I know not. A gracious name may my god—my goddess, known and unknown god, known and unknown goddess—name! Pure food I have not eaten; clear water I have not drunk. The suffering sent by my god, unnoted it was my food; the misery sent by my goddess, unnoted it trod me down. O lord, my sins are many, great are my misdeeds. My god, my sins are many, great are my misdeeds. My goddess, my sins are many, great are my misdeeds. Known and unknown god, my sins are many, great are my misdeeds. Known and unknown goddess, my sins are many, great are my misdeeds. The sin that I committed I know not; the misdeed that I committed I know not. The suffering that was my food, I understand it not; the misery that trod me down, I understand it not. The lord in the anger of his heart looked upon me. The god in the wrath of his heart visited me. The goddess was angry with me and brought me to grief. Known or unknown god has brought me into straits; known or unknown goddess has brought me to woe. I sought for help but none took me by the hand; I wept but no one came to my side. I cry aloud but no one hears me. In anguish I lie on the ground and look not up. To my compassionate god I turn, I sigh aloud. I kiss the feet of my goddess. . . . To known and unknown god I sigh aloud; to known and unknown goddess I sigh aloud. O lord—goddess, known and unknown god, known and unknown goddess—look upon me, accept my prayer! When at length, oh my god—goddess, etc.—will thy wrath be appeased? Mankind is perverse and knows nothing. Men, so many as they are, what do they know? Whether they do good or ill, they know nothing at all. O lord, thy servant, cast me not down. In the miry waters take me by the hand. The sin that I have committed change to favour. The misdeed I have done, let the wind bear it away! Rend in twain my wickedness like a garment!

My god—goddess, known and unknown god, known and unknown goddess—my sins are seven times seven. Forgive my sins! Forgive my sins! I will bow humbly before thee. May thy heart like the heart of a mother be glad; like the heart of a father to whom a child is born, may thy heart be glad!

The suppliant knows from the evils that have come upon him that he must have offended some deity, he knows not whom—by some fault, he knows not what—and pleads for forgiveness and restoration.

As the Ashipu priests were the legitimate magicians, adept in all the arts of frustrating the wiles of demons and witches, so their colleagues, the diviners, were learned in all methods of discovering the mysterious meaning of strange happenings, the outcome of public and private undertakings, the lucky and unlucky days for inaugurating them, and the like.

In this domain the Babylonians were pre-eminent. Out of the crude procedures of savage sorcerers they gradually developed a whole group of pseudosciences. The interpreters of dreams systematised their art in manuals of oneiromancy. Omens and portents were classified and their significance noted. A text dealing with monstrosities, for example, begins, "If a woman bears a child with lion's ears, there will be a mighty king in the land; if the child's right ear is lacking, the prince will come to old age; if the left is lacking, there will be distress in the land and its territory will be diminished," and so through defects or deformities of the various members of the body from head to foot.

The exegetes of dreams and prodigies formed an inferior class of diviners; above them, in the very foremost rank of the priesthood, were the Baru, or "seers," who had the art of taking omens, and were thus able to answer inquiries of every kind. One method much employed by them was to drop oil into a basin of water, or water into a basin of oil, and observe its forms and movements. Another way was by examining the liver of a sheep or goat. The liver is a very variable organ, and every variation in the dimensions of the lobes, the markings on them, the size and position of the gall-bladder and ducts or the great blood-vessels, had a meaning which the priest by his art could read off as if it were an oracle written on a tablet. Models of the liver mapped off geometrically in regions, with catch-words inscribed on them, have been preserved, besides many texts telling just what is to happen in case this or that peculiarity exists. Divination by the liver is very common; the head-hunters of Borneo to-day learn from the liver of a pig whether it is a good time for an expedition; but the Babylonians made a science of it, which in later times the Greeks and Etruscans learned from them.

Unusual astronomical and meteorological phenomena are everywhere regarded as ominous. The Babylonian priests reduced these signs also to a system. They could tell what a lunar eclipse, for example, portended according to the month in which it occurred, and what the king should do or avoid in order to avert the unfavourable omens. Certain conspicuous constellations took in their imagination the form of animals or of the strange composite monsters which were associated with particular gods; the mythical beast of Ea, half goat, half fish, was discovered in the sky in the constellation which we call Capricorn. On the so-called boundary stones of the Kassite times and later, these creatures are represented in varying order and number, and in one, at least, the names of the gods to whom they belong, or whom they represent, as a kind of coat of arms, accompany them. A few of the most brilliant of the fixed stars were also named. In course of time a much more elaborate system of astral divination was worked out, and the observations and records made for this purpose were the foundations of Babylonian astronomy.

It has been noted that the incantation priests derive their wisdom from Ea. The diviners are a hereditary class who trace their descent from Enmeduranki (Εὐεδώραχος, *Edoranchus*), the seventh in Berossos's catalogue of antediluvian kings, but the gods who initiated him in these arts, the gods whose names occur regularly in the divination texts, are Shamash and Adad, and many of the classical oracles purport to be from the age of Sargon. The frequent interpretation of omens as referring to Akkad and Amurru points to the same period. We may, therefore, with some confidence infer that the systematic elaboration of the science of divination was Semitic rather than Sumerian.

A striking difference between Egypt and Babylonia is the paucity in the latter, through all periods, of material from the tombs. The "eternal houses" of the dead in Egypt, with their inscriptions and decorations and the funerary texts written on the walls or deposited in the coffins, reveal to us in much detail the life of this world as well as the notions of the other world. To all this there is no counterpart in Babylonia. The fact itself is significant; the hereafter never occupied the imagination of the Babylonians as it did that of the Egyptians, and their notions about it never got beyond a very primitive stage.

In the old Babylonian cities the dead seem ordinarily to have been buried beneath the houses in which they had lived, sometimes in pottery coffins or great jars, sometimes simply wrapped in reed mats. A water-jar and drinking-cup, ornaments, tools, and weapons, were deposited with the body. If, as it is natural to suppose, food and drink were offered to the dead after the interment, it must have been in the house itself, and no trace of the custom is to be looked for. From an inscription in which Urukagina records his reforms it appears that priests officiated at funerals, and that they demanded extortionate fees for their services— seven jars of wine or beer, four hundred and twenty loaves of bread, a hundred and twenty measures of corn, a garment, a kid, a bed, and a seat. These exactions were sharply re-trenched by the king, though, according to our notions, the compensation was still ample. Wherein the services of the priests consisted does not appear, and, singularly enough, in the voluminous ritual literature burial offices seem not to have turned up.

From literary sources we learn that the Babylonians imagined the nether world as a vast cavern in the heart of the earth, into which the light of day never penetrates; its inhabitants sit in darkness, their food is dust and mud. A vivid description of this gloomy abode is given in a poem which tells how the goddess Ishtar went down into it to recover—if the obscure lines at the end are rightly under-stood—her lost lover, the youthful Tammuz. She takes her way to the "land whence is no return" by the "road on which there is no turning back," to the dismal house which they who enter never leave. Arrived at the portal, she imperiously orders the gate-keeper to open to her, threaten-ing, if he refuse, to batter down the door and bring up the dead, outnumbering the living. The porter announces the visitor to Ereshkigal, the queen of Hades, who falls into a rage at the intrusion, but orders that she be admitted and treated "according to the ancient laws." Through seven gates in as many concentric walls of the infernal city Ishtar is conducted; at the outer gate her crown is taken from her head, and at each succeeding passage some ornament or piece of apparel, till at the last her girdle is stripped off, and she stands stark naked before the mistress of hell, who commands Namtar, the demon of plague, to shut her up and inflict on her sixty diseases. The disappearance of Ishtar from the earth threatens to be the end of the race of men and the beasts of the field, for with her departure all procreation ceases. The gods take counsel to avert this disaster, and send a messenger, who after a rough reception persuades Ereshkigal to release her divine prisoner. Namtar is ordered to sprinkle Ishtar with the "water of life," and take her back by the way she came; at each gate she is invested again with the apparel she had been despoiled of, and so returns to the world above. The last verses, as has been said, speak of Tammuz, who is to be washed with pure water, anointed with choice oil, and clad in a red robe; further there is mention of music and of mourning-men and mourning-women, but in what sense is not clear.

In the second tablet of the epic of Gilgamesh, in a dream of Eabani which he repeats to Gilgamesh, there is a description of the underworld which agrees, in part even in phraseology, with that in the Descent of Ishtar to Hades. Here also the inhabitants of that world sit in darkness with dust for their food and without hope of escape. Among them Eabani sees some who had ruled as kings on earth, and priests of various classes, besides mythical figures such as Etana and the god Gira. Above them Ereshkigal, the queen of Hades, sits enthroned, while the goddess Belit-seri who serves her as scribe kneels before her and reads. In this vision Nergal also appears as a god of the nether world. In the last tablet of the same poem the fate of the dead is again the theme: "He who met death by the sword—sawest thou this? Yea, I saw it!—in his chamber he rests, drinks pure water. He who was slain in the battle—sawest thou this? Yea, I saw it!—his father and mother lift up his head and his wife. . . . He whose body was cast out upon the field—sawest thou this? Yea, I saw it!—his ghost has upon earth no rest. He whose ghost has none to care for him—

sawest thou this?   Yea, I saw it!—remnants of the pot, scraps of food, what is cast out into the street, must he eat." The lines just quoted show that for the Babylonians as for many other peoples there was one fate worse than to go to the dismal abode of the dead, the realm of Ereshkigal; namely, to wander upon earth as the restless ghost of the unburied dead and feed upon offal with the neglected spirits.

In the Descent of Ishtar to the lower world we recognise without question a poetical version of an old vegetation myth; the disappearance of the goddess from earth is the death of nature, which revives at her return.   Her youthful lover Tammuz, for whom, as Gilgamesh taunts her, she has ordained mourning year by year, is originally a vegetation demon.   The mourning for Tammuz is mentioned in the myth of Adapa, who sees him, however, not in Hades, but at the door of the celestial palace of Anu.   The fourth month of the Babylonian year, corresponding roughly to July, has its name Tammuz from the mourning for the god, and several hymns sung at this season have been preserved.   There is no indication, however, that at the time when these myths and hymns took shape the Babylonians were conscious of the primitive significance of the story or the rites; and if the myth in its complete form told of the restoration of Tammuz to life or his return to earth, as is made likely by the transition from mourning to rejoicing in the hymns, it is certain that it did not suggest to the Babylonians, as the myth of Osiris did to the Egyptians, the conception of a new life of blessedness for the dead, though it has been thought, with some probability, that the myth was rehearsed in an incantation for the recovery of persons who were mortally ill.

Beyond this dismal outlook neither the Assyrians nor the Babylonians of later times appear ever to have advanced. Of a judgment of the dead or of any deliverance from the gloomy world below there is no suggestion.   Even the association of dead kings with the gods in the worship of the

temples does not seem to be connected with the notion of
the immortality of the deified ruler.

About a hundred miles north of Babylon the alluvial
plain between the two rivers ends; the limit may be roughly
defined by a line running from the Tigris below Samarra to
Hit on the Euphrates. This is the natural boundary of
Babylonia, and seems to have been also at most times its
political boundary. With a small increase of elevation the
character of the country completely changes. The Mesopotamian plain is for the most part pure desert; only on the
banks of the Euphrates and Chaboras and along the Tigris
are narrow strips of arable land, in which here and there
towns early sprang up. Between the Tigris and the mountains which form its eastern line is a region of larger extent
watered by the streams which fall into the Tigris. This
territory was occupied by Semitic tribes, some of which even
penetrated into the mountains and subdued the native peoples whom they found there.

Between the Little and Great Zab, on the west of the
Tigris, lay the city Assur, the first capital of the Assyrians.
Further north, opposite the modern Mosul, was Nineveh,
also a very early foundation. Between the two, at the
mouth of the Great Zab, was Calah, and nearly east of
Nineveh, at the foot of the mountains, Arbela. The earliest ruler of Assur of whom we have historical notice is
Ilusuma, who was engaged in a war with Sumuabu, founder
of the kingdom of Babylon (ca. 2060 B. C.). Under the
great kings of the First Dynasty the Assyrians were vassals
of Babylon, but in the decline of Babylonian power under
the Kassite kings Assyria regained its independence. The
ups and downs of its history in the following centuries it
is unnecessary to recount here. When it was strong enough
it extended its rule to the mountains of Armenia and over
all northern Mesopotamia. Early kings not only carried
their victorious arms far into the heart of Asia Minor, but
established colonies there which long maintained themselves. In the first half of the thirteenth century an As-

syrian king conquered Babylon, though his possession of it
did not last long, and the struggle between these two powers,
in which sometimes the one was the aggressor and sometimes
the other, continued intermittently through the following
period, until from the latter part of the eighth century for
more than a hundred years Babylonia was completely overshadowed by Assyria. In 689, in punishment for repeated
revolts, Sennacherib totally destroyed the city of Babylon;
but the city was soon rebuilt.

The Assyrian civilisation shows at every point the influence of Babylonia. The system of writing was learned from
the Babylonians; the art has the same origin, though
northern influences also are clearly manifest in it; in religion
Babylonian gods have a large place; and the ritual and the
arts of divination are those which had been developed by
the Babylonian priesthoods. The common impression, however, that the Assyrians took their whole civilisation, as it
were, ready-made, from Babylonia appears to be an exaggeration; it would perhaps in the present state of our knowledge be more accurate to say that the Assyrians, like the
Semitic Babylonians, were largely indebted to the Sumerian
culture, and shared with them considerable elements derived
from the civilisation of western Syria and Asia Minor—
Amorite and, later, Hittite.

The Sumerian kingdoms which at one time and another
embraced the greater part of Babylonia had been formed
by the supremacy of one city over its rivals; they never
succeeded in welding the people together into a Sumerian
nation. Still less did the Semitic empires of Akkad or of
Babylon accomplish this. The Assyrians, however, appear
from the beginning as a national unity. The change of the
capital from Assur to Calah or Nineveh does not signify
the hegemony of one city over others, but the removal of the
royal residence from one city to another. Consequently
the religion has a national character which distinguishes it
from that of Babylonia, and this character was undoubtedly
strengthened by the continual wars which the Assyrians

waged either in aggression or defence against other peoples. Assur thus became the god of the Assyrian hosts; in his standard, the winged sun, he went before them in the march and the battle and bestowed upon them victory over their enemies. Inasmuch as the inscriptions of Assyrian kings are largely occupied with their campaigns, Assur appears oftenest in this character. But for the Assyrians themselves he was, as the national god, the giver of all blessings in peace as in war. Late Assyrian scribes sometimes write the name of Assur in such a way as to identify him with the Babylonian Anshar, who in the Combat of Bel and Tiamat figures as one of a former generation of gods, the ruler of the upper world, and modern scholars have sometimes allowed themselves to be misled by this cuneiform pun; but it is in the highest degree improbable that these militant Semites picked out for their national god a figure who among the Sumerians themselves belonged only to the cosmogonic myth, and had, so far we know, no place at all in the religion.

Next in importance to Assur stand the goddesses, whom, after the manner of the Semites generally, the Assyrians named Ishtar, distinguishing them when necessary by the name of the cities over which they presided—the Ishtar of Arbela, for instance, and the Ishtar of Nineveh. As the tutelary deities of cities, the Ishtars of Assyria, like the city goddesses of Syria and Asia Minor, or like the Greek Athene, are their defenders against the assaults of enemies, their champions in the fray, and in conformity with the prevailing temper of the Assyrians are warlike goddesses. Assurbanipal, on the eve of a battle with the Elamites, appealed to the Ishtar of Arbela, who for his encouragement appeared to him in a dream: "On the left and right of her hung quivers; in her hand she held a bow, and a sharp sword did she draw to wage the battle."

Adad, a west Syrian god who comes into prominence with the First Dynasty of Babylon, had a high place in the Assyrian pantheon. He is a god of storm and of the storm of war; his attributes are the three-forked thunderbolt and the axe, his sacred beast is a bull. He fights in the armies of the Assyrians, and shares with Assur the sacrifices which victorious kings offer on the battle-field.

The sun (Utu, Babbar) was the city-god of Larsa in southern Babylonia and of Sippar in the north; the Semites naturally named him by their own word for sun, Shamash. As has happened to sky-gods and sun-gods among other peoples, the all-seeing sun became in a peculiar sense the guardian of right and justice; he receives the title "judge." At Sippar his two daughters bear the significant names Kettu and Mesharu, which we may render Justice and Equity. On the stela on which Hammurabi's code of laws is inscribed the king is represented standing before Shamash, evidently as the god of justice, though it is not otherwise intimated in the text that the law is a revelation from him. The Assyrian kings, especially the later ones, emphasise the moral attributes of Shamash even more strongly than their predecessors. As their enemies are of course in the wrong, Shamash becomes also the vindicator of the right by punishing the foe.

Among the hymns to the gods—most of them would be more accurately entitled incantations—which seldom display either poetic afflatus or religious feeling, some of the hymns to Shamash are favourably distinguished. The splendour of the sun-god, illumining heaven, earth, and sea, and his vision of all the ways of men, are sung in verses that sometimes rise out of the commonplace. To Shamash the wayfarer, the hunter, the herdsman, and he who is set upon by robbers, cry for help, and not in vain; the friendly god watches over and protects them. He is the vindicator of right. Himself the incorruptible judge, he punishes the judges who take bribes and pervert justice, and rewards those who cannot be bought and have a care for the oppressed.

"The offspring of those who deal unjustly will not prosper.
What their mouth utters in thy presence thou wilt undo,

What issues from their mouth thou wilt annul.
Thou hearest their transgressions, the plan of the wicked thou re-
    jectest.
All, whoever they be, are in thy care;
Thou undertakest their suit, those in bonds thou dost release;
Thou hearest, O Shamash, supplication, prayer, and invocation."

We have observed that in the divination books of the
Baru priests the gods whose names incessantly recur are
Shamash and Adad. The all-seeing god is appropriately the
revealer of hidden things; the use of divination to determine
guilt or innocence, moreover, stands in intimate relation to
his office as judge. For the association of Adad with Shamash there is, however, no obvious explanation in the character
or other functions of Adad; the robe of the soothsayer fits
the tempestuous warrior ill. It may be surmised that Adad
got into the formula as the tribal or national god of the people among whom the divination texts were compiled or recast. It may be added that the inscriptions make no reference to Adad's oracular talents.

The moon-god, Sin, was the chief deity of Harran in
Mesopotamia as he was, under the Sumerian name Nannar,
in Ur. At Harran he was the head of a divine family; his
queen is called Ningal (Nikkal), he has a daughter Ishtar
(the planet Venus), with the title "princess," and a son,
Nusku. In Assyria itself the worship of Sin seems never
to have attained great proportions, though several kings
bear names compounded with his name, and in the order
of the triad he regularly precedes Shamash—a survival,
probably, of an older stage of Semitic religion.

Of the old Sumerian gods Anu was perhaps the first to be
honoured in Assyria with a local cult, a fact the more noteworthy inasmuch as in Babylonia itself his religious importance was by no means commensurate with his rank in the
pantheon. He is the king and father of the gods. At the
city Assur a double temple for Anu and "his gallant son
Adad," erected about the end of the twelfth century B. C.,
has recently been excavated. A temple on the same site

about a thousand years earlier was dedicated to Adad alone, without any mention of Anu. The great triad, Anu, Bel, Ea, is often invoked. The Assyrian kings who ruled over Babylonia are at pains to give a religious legitimation to their rule. They have been chosen by the gods to rule over the land of Bel; to "take the hand of Bel" belongs to the ceremony of investiture. When Shalmaneser II makes an expedition into Babylonia to put down a revolt, he declares that he did it by Marduk's command. On the other hand, they give Marduk the next place after Assur when they list several gods together. To secure the favour of the Babylonian gods they restore their temples and offer sacrifice in them. In all this we may see not only a wise policy, but true reverence for the ancient seats of religion and sources of priestly wisdom; but this homage to the Babylonian gods in Babylonia did not give them any corresponding increment of importance in Assyria; the kings built no temples for Marduk in their own land.

A god designated by the signs "Nin-ib"—what he was really called is unknown—was especially honoured by some of the Assyrian kings. He was, as might be supposed, an invincible warrior, whose strength and prowess are lauded in swollen phrases; like his admirers, he was also a mighty hunter. His great temple was in Calah. Nergal, the god of Kutha in northern Babylonia, whom we have already met as a god of the realms of the dead, was also worshipped in Assyria as a god of war and the chase—a character, indeed, which all gods and goddesses took among that bellicose folk.

The Assyrian temples, to judge from the few examples of which anything is known, were of the same general type as those of Babylonia; the characteristic temple tower stood beside them also. The ritual, the arts of incantation and divination, were taken over from the Babylonians, as has been already said. The kings entitle themselves in religious inscriptions priests of Assur, and stand at the head of the state religion. Many reliefs from their palaces represent acts of worship in which the king participates, and from them our knowledge of the apparatus of the cult is chiefly derived; it is, however, more frequently sacrifice or divination in the camp or the field than worship in the temples that appears in these reliefs.

The latter half of the eighth and the first half of the seventh centuries were the climax of Assyrian greatness; the rule of the Assyrian kings at its widest extent reached from Babylonia to Egypt, but it was never a stable and well-ordered empire, and was maintained only by incessant wars which in the end exhausted the race as the Napoleonic wars exhausted France. A new upheaval in those Asiatic steppes which so often in history have poured out the scourges of God set in motion the Scythian hordes, who overran the weakened countries of western Asia; a new power arose in Media; the dynasts of the "Sea Country" on the shores of the Persian Gulf, whose independent spirit the Assyrians had never been able to subdue, made themselves masters of Babylon and allied themselves with the Medes against Assyria. In 606 Nineveh fell, and with that catastrophe the nation which but a generation before had seemed invincible disappears from history in a way that has hardly a parallel.

The Neobabylonian, or Chaldean, kingdom which arose upon its ruins had a national character which the old Babylonian states lacked; Marduk was the national god in the same way that Assur had been in Assyria. The exaltation of national consciousness expressed itself in a religious revival or restoration; not only were the great temples of Marduk in Babylon and of Nabu at Borsippa rebuilt with unprecedented splendour, but throughout all the land the gods, great and small, were honoured in similar fashion. Nebuchadnezzar, whom with our mind on the Old Testament we think of chiefly as a conqueror, records in his inscriptions not his successes in war, but his piety in building and renewing temples. The last of the kings, Nabonnedos, was digging up long-buried corner-stones of ancient temples and rejoicing over them with archæological enthusiasm while the Persians were knocking the empire to pieces about his head. The signature of the period is artificial repristination, very like that which the Saite Dynasty was busy with in Egypt about the same time.

The Persian conquest (538 B. C.) put an end to Babylonian nationality. Cyrus treated the religion of the country with statesmanlike respect; he attributes his victory to Marduk, who had bidden him visit on Nabonnedos the god's displeasure at some of his religious innovations; he orders the images of the gods which that king had collected in Babylon to be restored to their own temples. But though the Persian kings and the Greeks after them did something for Marduk and Nabu, the great gods of the capital, the religion was no longer the religion of the state, and under new political and economic conditions and in contact with an alien civilisation it slowly but steadily declined.

While the gods thus sank into provincial obscurity, the arts of the Babylonian magicians and diviners were celebrated in all lands, and the adepts found new and lucrative fields for their practice in the West. Hoary antiquity, mystifying hocus-pocus, and elaborate pretence of method conspired to give these Chaldeans, or "mathematicians," or whatever else they were called, a great vogue. Divination from astronomical phenomena, in particular, was an imposing pseudoscience, which formed the basis of astrology. Reasons have been given above[1] for the opinion that this method of divination was developed by the Semitic Babylonians, rather than by the Sumerians. It is known to us chiefly through the reports of Assyrian court astrologers and still later sources, but bears clearly enough the impress of its Babylonian origin. Signs were taken not only from the moon and the sun, but from the planets, their heliacal rising, brightness, positions relatively to one another, to the moon, and to certain stars or constellations, their presence within a ring around the moon, and the like. The planet Venus was from the earliest times the star of Ishtar (and her Su-

[1] See p. 228.

merian doubles of various names); the astrologers connected the other planets with the greater gods of the Babylonian pantheon, but with which gods they were severally associated, and whether at all periods the same gods, is still subject to controversy. For the Assyrian and Neobabylonian period it seems to be fairly made out that Jupiter was assigned to Marduk, Mercury to Nabu, Mars to Nergal, and Saturn to "Nin-ib." An examination of the texts does not show any dominant correspondence between the sphere or character of the deity and the prognostications drawn from the behaviour of his planet; Mars is generally a baleful star, but for that there are other possible explanations besides association with Nergal. The omens of Jupiter have no such specific reference to the fortunes of the king and the nation as might be expected of Marduk's planet; Venus gives substantially the same omens. In general, the planets have no such distinctive and significant characters as in European astrology, in which they determine the fortune of individuals.

It has been asserted that the Babylonian astrology was based on the theory of an exact correspondence between celestial phenomena and terrestrial events: the world is in all respects the counterpart of the heavens, and there is a complete and necessitated parallelism between what goes on above and below. This theory of the universe, it is affirmed, underlies the Babylonian religion and gives it its peculiar character; from Babylonia it passed to the West, and dominated Greek as well as Hebrew thought. In short, the conception of the universe which prevailed in all our world down to the epoch of modern science is at bottom the Babylonian "Weltanschauung." The Babylonian theory itself, according to this doctrine, rests upon an observation and interpretation of astronomical phenomena which in very remote times led to extraordinary results. Not only was the track of the planets early mapped off into the twelve signs of the zodiac, but the precession of the equinoxes was known to the Babylonian star-gazers thousands of years before our era.

It has been proved, on the contrary, that the Babylonian

astronomers at the height of their art, down to the second century B. C., were ignorant of the precession of the equinoxes, and that, though some zodiacal constellations appear on "boundary stones" from Kassite times, there is no trace of the equal division of the ecliptic into twelve parts till the Neobabylonian or Persian period. Anything like a scientific astronomy, as distinguished from observations for purposes of divination, begins only in the last millennium before our era, and reaches its highest point only after the fall of Babylon—in fact, in the Greek and Arsacidan time.

Divination by the stars was practised by the Babylonians and Assyrians to learn what was going to befall kings and peoples; they do not seem to have imagined that the private fortunes of individuals were determined by the heavenly bodies, and therefore to be read in the sky. The development of this side of astrology, with its elaborate methods of forecasting the whole life of a man by the position of the stars at the hour of his birth (genethlialogy), is of later date, and, however much they may have learned from the "Chaldeans," the Greeks were its inventors.

The religion of Assyria, as we have seen, was closely akin to that of its neighbours in northern Babylonia, from which it borrowed largely. The extension of Assyrian dominion over a great part of Syria introduced the worship of Assyrian-Babylonian gods. In the eastern part of this area, which was for centuries really a part of Assyria, the influence of Assyrian civilisation and religion was most profound and durable. The worship of the Babylonian Bel and Nabu at Edessa, for example, flourished until Christian times. Even in this region, however, the native elements greatly preponderated in the local religions; and farther west Assyrian-Babylonian influence is, speaking generally, sporadic and superficial, while there is a larger admixture from Asia Minor. On the seaboard, finally, the most diverse civilisations in successive ages left their mark—Syrian, Hittite, Phœnician, Cypriote, Egyptian—but it is hardly at all affected, directly or indirectly, by Babylonian culture.

Not only has the influence of the Babylonian religion been enormously exaggerated, but wholly erroneous notions are entertained about the religion itself. So far from being the religious initiators of humanity, the Babylonians remained to the end on a relatively low plane of religious development—compared with the ancient Chinese, for example. They were great in demonology and divination, but showed no capacity for religious ideas. The "latent" monotheism which some Assyriologists attribute to them comes to no more than such banal litanies as

> "Ninib is the Marduk of might,
> Nergal is the Marduk of fight,
> Zamama is the Marduk of battle,
> Enlil is the Marduk of rule and dominion,
> Nabu is the Marduk of superintendence(?),
> Sin is the Marduk of nocturnal light,
> Shamash is the Marduk of decisions,
> Adad is the Marduk of rain," etc.

That is to say—putting the utmost possible into the words—the many gods are names of Marduk in various functions and operations. Such utterances may signify much or little. When we read in the Veda,

> "Men call it Indra, Mitra, Agni, Varuna,
> Or heavenly Garutman with glorious pinions.
> By many names the poets name what is but One;
> They name it Agni, Yama, Mataríçvan,"

we recognise the dawning of a philosophical conception of unity, out of which the monism of the Upanishads will spring. We understand the pantheistic self-laudation of Isis in Apuleius. But the Babylonian text before us conceals no such subtleties; what it says is that Marduk is the whole pantheon, and that, not as a piece of speculation, but as a liturgical glorification of Marduk. Even such purely verbal unifications of the godhead are late and infrequent.

CHAPTER XI

INDIA

THE RELIGION OF THE VEDA

The Aryans in India—The Hymns of the Rig-Veda—Vedic Deities
—Indra, Varuna, and Mitra—Nature Gods—Agni and Soma—
Nymphs and Elves—Demons—Worship: Priests, Sacrifice, Expia-
tions—Magic in the Atharva-Veda—The Dead and Their Abodes—
The Beginnings of Speculation—The Philosophy of the Upanishads
—Brahman-Atman—Rebirth and Deliverance—Dualistic Philoso-
phy—Practical Means of Salvation.

THE peninsula of India was occupied in early times by
peoples of several ethnic and linguistic stocks, the most numerous, if not the oldest, being the Dravidians, who now
form the characteristic population of the Deccan, but once
extended farther to the north into the Panjab and the Gan-
getic plain. In the north and east of the latter region there
were also Mongoloid tribes, akin to the peoples of Nepal and
the Tibetan plateau, which in time mingled with the Dravidians. In the second millennium before the Christian era,
or perhaps in the third, Aryan tribes began to enter India
from the northwest. The movement was a migration in several successive waves, rather than an invasion, and doubtless continued for several centuries. As the Aryans pressed
southward and eastward they subjugated and enslaved the
older dark-skinned natives or forced them back before them.

The Aryan division of the Indo-European family, before
the migration, was settled north of the Hindu-Kush. One
branch, the forefathers of the Aryo-Indians, moving southward, made their way into the valley of the Indus, perhaps
by the river gorges of the Kabul, and thence into the Panjab,

while the branch which we know as Iranian remained in their old homes or moved westward as far as Media and Persia. Before the division the two branches of the race spoke closely related dialects of the same language, and had substantially the same primitive religion; through centuries of separation, and in widely different surroundings, they diverged ever more widely in character, and the development of religion, especially, took wholly different directions.

The Aryan invaders of India were, like their Iranian kinsmen, a hardy and vigorous race, and the climate of the region which they first occupied was by no means so enervating as that of the Ganges plain. They were already beyond the stage of pure nomads; they lived in unwalled villages, with forts on high ground in which they could take refuge from attack. At the head of the several tribes were chiefs or kings, "protectors of the people," their leaders in war. The principal wealth of the people was in its herds of cattle, for which the region offered wide pasture lands. Horses, which were highly prized, were used to draw chariots, while the ordinary draught animals were oxen and asses; flocks of sheep and goats were also kept. Barley was cultivated; rice seems not to have been known.

The herds were the chief support of the people—milk fresh from the cow or made into a mush with meal, curdled milk, butter. Meat was an infrequent addition to their diet, domestic animals being rarely slaughtered except in sacrifice or on festive occasions such as weddings. Intoxicating drinks were prepared from the juice of the soma plant mixed with milk or from grain, and inordinate indulgence in them was not infrequent. Trade was by barter, the standard unit of value being the cow; ornaments of gold and silver and precious stones were also used in exchange. The people were fond of sport, especially of chariot-racing and of the chase, and much addicted to gambling. The social distinctions natural to such a society existed, but there were no castes, nor was there a priesthood with exclusive prerogatives. The position of woman was freer and more honourable than in later times. Wars with the natives and between different Aryan tribes or confederacies were frequent; the motive was often cattle-lifting, if we may judge from the fact that one of the words for battle means literally, "seeking of cows."

The earliest knowledge of this people and its ways, its civilisation and religion, is derived from the Rig-Veda. Veda (from the root which appears in "wit" and Greek οἶδα) means "knowledge," pre-eminently religious knowledge, and is applied in later times to the whole sacred literature regarded as revealed. The Rig-Veda is a collection of poems in ten books, comprising in all somewhat over one thousand pieces. Most of them are hymns of praise and prayer addressed to particular gods or groups of gods. Books II–VII, called the "family books," are collections belonging to different families of priests whose eponymous ancestor is supposed to be a famous poet of ancient times. The seventh book, for example, is the hymn book of the Vashisthas; the third, that of Viçvamitra and his family, and so on. It is not improbable that these families originally belonged to different Aryan tribes or clans. Speaking generally, the oldest hymns are found in the family books, while books I and X contain the latest. In each book the hymns are primarily arranged by the gods to whom they are addressed; those to Agni first, next those to Indra, then hymns to all the gods.

The hymns of the Rig-Veda are far from being, as was thought in the first enthusiasm of discovery, primitive poetry, or the spontaneous expression of primitive and unsophisticated religion. Many of them were composed by priestly poets for princely patrons, to be recited or sung on sacrificial occasions; not a few are uninspired and artificial productions, in set forms, full of stereotyped phrases and the imitation of imitations. The effort to be original without originality results in far-fetched figures and laborious obscurity. As belief in the god-compelling power of the word grew, a peculiar potency was attributed to cryptic epithets and enigmatic allusions; actual riddles are not infre-

quent. For reciting the hymns, and especially for composing new ones for great occasions, the poets expected liberal
remuneration; they laud generous patrons and often express
with unblushing frankness their desire for many cows. There
is little of deep human emotion in these hymns and little
genuine religious fervour. Yet there are among them some
of real poetic power and of elevated religious sentiment, and
in the later books several which display philosophic insight.
Even in dull hymns the sublime phenomena of nature occasionally evoke flashes of genuine poetry. The poets sometimes ascribe the thoughts embodied in their verses to divine
inspiration; priestly theory in later times attributed the whole
sacred literature to revelation in the most literal sense.

In the age of the great heresies, Jainism and Buddhism,
the Rig-Veda collection and the prose liturgical texts (Brahmanas) dependent upon it had long enjoyed this supreme
authority, and through the possession of the divine "knowledge" the Brahman priesthood had acquired its great spiritual power. The Brahmanas not only breathe a different
religious atmosphere, but have a different geographical horizon; they were composed in the valley of the Ganges. For
these great changes several centuries must be allowed, and
since the heresies of the sixth century had precursors a good
way further back the round estimate of 1000 B. C. for the
lower limit of the Vedic age seems rather too low than too
high. How ancient the oldest hymns in the collection are
we have no means of judging. The thing of importance is
that all the hymns reflect Indian surroundings and conditions, and are therefore subsequent to the invasion and the
settlement in the Panjab, and apparently separated from
it by a considerable interval of time, since not even in the
earliest hymns is there any memory of the migration.

The picture of the Vedic religion which the Rig-Veda
gives is in several respects incomplete. In hymns addressed
to the gods we naturally find rather allusions to the myths
than detailed narrations. A hymn like Rig-Veda, I, 32, the
glorification of Indra's victory over the dragon Vritra and

the liberation of the imprisoned waters, is a rare exception. So also of the forms of worship: most of the hymns were composed to accompany sacrifices, but they give no description of the rites. Here the Brahmanas, which not only prescribe the ceremonies with the minutest circumstantiality, but explain the allusions in the hymns or rehearse the myths in connection with ritual, often furnish a clew, though their age and character demand critical caution in the use of their statements. On the other hand, we learn from the hymns the character of the gods to whom they are dedicated, the things which they are desired and expected to do for their worshippers, the conditions of their favour, and the feelings with which men approached them—matters of much greater significance in religion than the tales about the doings of the gods or the externals of the ritual.

Among the gods of the Rig-Veda we find neither tribal nor local deities. It is not improbable that in particular tribes or regions the worship of certain gods was especially favoured, or that in the course of time, with changing conditions, one god had to cede the pre-eminence to another, but the indications of this are few and uncertain. If the pantheon of the Rig-Veda is in any degree the product of a fusion of the religions of different Aryan tribes, that stage of the development lies far back of the age which produced the hymns—in them it is the pantheon of the Aryan people. The gods are in the main the great powers of nature which affect human welfare or the objects and phenomena in which these powers are manifested—the bright sky, the enlivening sun, the rosy dawn, the storm which brings the longed-for rain. These gods the Aryans had worshipped in their old seats, and these had accompanied them in their migration to new homes, while the divinities who were attached to certain places were necessarily left behind.

Of course, as in all such cases, it was not the natural object or phenomenon as such that was worshipped, but a power actuated by a will and prompted by motives such as determine human conduct, and conceived, after the analogies of

primitive physiological psychology, as a spirit. Even when
his name seems to identify him with a natural object, as, for
example, Surya, the sun, the god is thus in his inner nature
like man, and the myths give him also human form, and
describe solar phenomena as human doings. The inseparable association of the deity with an object in nature puts
restraint, however, on the growth of myth, which cannot in
such cases get much beyond extended metaphor, and upon
the religious development, since gods grow great by being
appealed to in all sorts of need, while the functions of such
"transparent" gods are limited by their very obviousness.
It is the gods whose nature and function are not expressed in
the mere utterance of their names who become more completely anthropomorphic, and in corresponding degree their
original physical nature recedes into the background, till in
the end it may be wholly lost from view, while the human
character of the god grows more distinctly individual.

The Vedic deities do not attain the concrete and plastic
personality of the Greek gods. The difference is due principally to the Homeric epics, in which the gods play their
parts right manfully in a heroic but eminently human
action, while the Vedic poets are concerned with the gods
only as protectors and benefactors of their worshippers. In
this capacity their functions are not sharply delimited; as in
all other religions which have reached this stage, the same
blessings are sought from gods of the most diverse origin
without regard to their ultimate physical associations; the
same laudatory and descriptive epithets are applied to them.
The appropriation by imitative poets of fine passages in
praise of one god to adorn a hymn to another has done much
to blur the outlines of even the most distinct figures in the
pantheon.

A native classification of the Vedic gods by one of the most
esteemed authorities divides them, according to the sphere
in which their activities are chiefly manifest, into gods of the
sky, gods of the atmosphere (that is, of the space between sky
and earth), and gods of the earth; but this distinction does

not imply a difference either of rank or of religious importance.

The first place among the gods of the Vedic age belongs
indisputably to Indra; not far from a fourth of the hymns
in the Rig-Veda are dedicated to him, and in perhaps fifty
more his praises are incidentally sung. He leads the Aryans
in war, and gives his people the victory over the dark-skinned
natives and the demons they worship. He is a gigantic
figure, with tawny hair and beard, who rides into battle on
a chariot drawn by tawny steeds, and wielding his peculiar
weapon, the thunderbolt. The great exploit of Indra is the
slaying of the dragon Vritra, which had shut up the waters.
Fortified in body and soul by deep draughts of soma, Indra,
with his train of Maruts, sallies forth to the encounter, and
in fierce combat smites the monster with his thunderbolt,
and lets out the pent-up waters.[1]

Indra is classed among the gods of the air, and the Vritra
myth is clearly meteorological. Yet if we call Indra a storm-
god, it must be noted that even in this myth he is not so
much the power in or behind stupendous physical phenomena as the beneficent deity who delivers men in their need
by breaking the sore drought and letting the clouds pour
down the reviving rain and the rivers stream with water.
And it is as the heroic destroyer of the enemy, not as the
mighty god of tempest, that he becomes the national god of
the Aryans in their wars with their foes, human and demonic.
He has a heroic capacity for food and drink, devouring the
flesh of bulls by the hundred, and draining whole tubs of
soma, by which he waxes valiant in fight and renews his
strength for such great tasks as upholding earth and sky.
In a hymn of the tenth book (119) he describes his expan-
sive sensations and emotions when he is full of this intoxicating beverage. He has also a martial weakness for the
fair and gives his wife Indrani too good ground for jealousy.

[1] Rig-Veda, I, 32. There are very many references to the myth in the
other hymns. Another myth tells of the release of the cows imprisoned
by the Panis.

Indra is often lauded as the greatest of gods, "no being in heaven or earth has ever equalled him." He is sometimes called "the universal monarch," a title more frequently bestowed on Varuna; but this does not import a sovereignty over the other gods like that of the Homeric Zeus. The Vedic pantheon is not, like the Olympic, a divine state with a supreme ruler upon its throne; every god is the greatest when the hymn is addressed to him.

A god of a wholly different type is Varuna.[1] There are no ancient myths which might give a clew to his origin, and the oldest interpreters were evidently as much in the dark about it as we are; later associations and explanations are valid, so far as they are valid at all, only for the age that produced them. Varuna had already in the Vedic period become so completely an anthropomorphic god that his relation to physical nature, if any consciousness of it survived, was no longer of any significance. Varuna is king of gods and men, universal monarch; titles of sovereignty are oftener bestowed on him than on any other god; it is in some sense his proper attribute. He established heaven and earth, and keeps them apart by his law; he makes the sun to shine in the heaven, and appointed for him his broad highway; by his ordinance the bright moon and the stars move through the night; the wind which resounds through space is his breath. He gives to nature its law, and upholds it by his law. He is also the upholder of the moral law: from his seat in the highest heaven he, "the all-seeing," the "far-seeing," beholds all that is done upon earth; his "spies," like those of an earthly ruler, take note of men's deeds and report them to the god. He punishes wrong-doing, and to him, before all others, prayers for the forgiveness of sin are addressed. The hymns to Varuna have a moral elevation rarely attained elsewhere in the Rig-Veda; indeed, they stand in this respect so apart that one eminent scholar has been led to conjecture that the religion of Varuna was not an Aryan development, but was

[1] "The one (Indra) slays the foe in battle, the other (Varuna) evermore protects the ordinances."

adopted from a Semitic people. This hypothesis is for more than one reason untenable; but it suggests that if we knew the history we should find that the religion had taken shape under different conditions from that of Indra or Rudra, and perhaps among different tribes. There are, in fact, some indications, in the Vedas as well as in the Avesta, of a rivalry between two types of Indo-Iranian religion, or at least two religious tendencies. If, as seems probable, Ahura Mazda, the "Wise Lord" of the Zoroastrian Gathas, is the same god whom we meet in the Vedas as Varuna, the outcome of the rivalry among the Iranians was the opposite of that in India.[1]

With Varuna another god of similar character, Mitra, is often joined in the dedication of hymns and otherwise. Mitra is identical with the Iranian Mithra, who is a solar deity, and in the Veda itself his attributes are at least suitable to an original sun-god or god of light; but, as in the case of Varuna, the physical character has been put completely in the background by the moral. In view of the constant coupling of Mitra and Varuna—an association so close that only one hymn is addressed to Mitra alone—it may with some probability be surmised that Varuna was primitively the divine sky, though the etymological relation to οὐρανός is questionable. In the Brahmanas Varuna is especially connected with the night, and indeed traces of this view appear in the Rig-Veda. Varuna and Mitra are members of a group of deities to which the collective name Adityas, or sons of Aditi, is given, and who are repeatedly invoked as a class; the most important of them after the two already named, to judge by the frequency with which he is mentioned in the Rig-Veda, is Aryaman.

Closely associated with Varuna is Rita, Order. The word corresponds to the Avestan Asha, which is similarly connected with Ahura. In the Veda, Rita represents the order of nature, the social order, and the order of the ritual, which are, indeed, from the Indian point of view not distinct, but aspects of one universal order; the movements of the heavenly

[1] See below, pp. 367 f.

bodies, the regular round of the seasons, were in some way correlated with the orderly performance of sacrifices. This order is usually the ordinance of Varuna; occasionally, however, it seems to have an existence and right of its own, but is not distinctly personified.

The bright sky, Dyaus, is also a god. The word is the same as the Greek Zeus, but the god occupies no corresponding position in the Vedic religion. No hymn is addressed to him alone; he is most frequently associated with the divine earth, Prithivi, as the universal parents ("father heaven," "mother earth").[1] Several gods are called his children, oftenest Ushas, the Dawn, also the Açvins, Surya, the sun, and others.

Ushas (*cf.* Ἡώς Aurora) is the rosy Dawn, a beautiful maiden in festal attire, nothing loath to display her charms, who comes to meet her lover or husband, the sun. The personification is transparent; but the treatment is more poetical than that of any other Vedic divinity. With the dawn appear also the Açvins, the twin horsemen, who are among the most prominent figures in the Rig-Veda after Indra, Agni, and Soma. They are glorious youths, children of Dyaus (Heaven), brothers of Ushas, husbands of Sūryā (sun as female, or the daughter of the sun), who mounts their swift car and accompanies them in their course. What natural object or phenomenon they originally represented is uncertain. The oldest native commentators made different guesses, and recent investigators have offered others. The association with the dawn and the sun suggest the morning star; but why did the poets see the morning star double? Here again the question what the Açvins were in nature is for the mythologer; what they were in religion is not in the least obscure—they are gracious deities who hasten to succour men in distress or perils on land or water by their wonderful interventions. Especially are they divine healers, who restore sight to the blind and cure the sick and wounded. Many miracles are reported of them, all works of mercy and

[1] The phrases occur but rarely in the Rig-Veda.

beneficence. The parallel to the Greek Dioskouroi can hardly be fortuitous.

Surya is the sun which we see in the sky; he traverses the way prepared for him by Varuna in a car drawn by swift steeds, or flies across the sky like a great red bird; or he is the eye of Mitra and Varuna, or of Agni. He sees all the good and bad deeds of men. He rouses men, and stirs them up to perform their tasks; and drives away sickness, disease, and every evil dream—the malign powers that do their mischief at night.

Savitar, "the one that arouses, impels," seems to have been originally an epithet of the sun, which being often used by itself became the name of a distinct deity. As the name designates a many-sided activity, not a concrete object, Savitar had greater freedom of development than Surya. It is perhaps not without significance that most of the hymns to Savitar are in the family books, while those to Surya are chiefly in the first and tenth.

Somewhat like the relation of Savitar to Surya is that of Vayu to Vata. Both are wind-gods; but Vata is more the physical phenomenon, while Vayu is more the personification of the wind power; hence Vayu is a comrade of Indra, while Vata is associated with Parjanya, the rain-god.

The Maruts, to whom more than thirty hymns are dedicated, are also probably wind or storm gods. They are sons of Rudra, but the allies of Indra, and their numerous troop follows and aids him in his dragon-slaying exploits. They come in roaring winds, rending trees and making forests bow before them in fear; they cover the eye of the sun with rain, and cause the mountain streams to pour down water.

A deity who is of only secondary importance in the Rig-Veda, but was destined in later times to supplant the greatest of them, is Vishnu. He appears repeatedly in company with Indra, and is in some hymns his ally in the combat with Vritra. Of Vishnu's deeds that which most impressed the poets was his "three strides," which are mentioned at least a dozen times; the epithets wide-going, wide-striding, refer to the same thing. But what the three strides were is nowhere explained. The commonest opinion makes them the progress of a sun-god across the sky; greater probability attaches to the view that they traverse the three divisions of the universe. If Vishnu was originally a sun-god, the solar features have almost entirely disappeared.

A curious figure is Pushan, a kind of Pan in the Vedic Olympus. Instead of a golden chariot with golden steeds, he drives a little cart drawn by goats; the chief of his diet is porridge, and—whether it be cause or consequence—he is toothless. Notwithstanding this drollery, Pushan is a deserving and respected deity, he possesses all wealth and bestows it liberally on his worshippers. He protects cattle, keeps them from falling into a pit, and brings them safely home. He knows the paths, guides men on them, and guards wayfarers from harm by wild beasts and robbers. He thus becomes, like Hermes, the guide of the dead, who conducts the souls by the distant paths of the fathers.

Tvashtar is the divine artificer, the most skilful of craftsmen; he forged the thunderbolt of Indra and made the cup for the gods to drink from. He fashions the embryo in the womb and all forms of beast and man; presides over generation, bestows offspring. He is called universal father, for he produced the whole world.

One of the greatest gods in the Rig-Veda is Agni, to whom at least two hundred hymns are dedicated—more than to any god except Indra. Agni (*ignis*) is fire in all its forms in heaven and earth, but it is as the hearth fire in the household ritual and the three fires of the greater sacrificial ceremonies that he has his primary religious importance. Offerings of butter are made to him, and sacrifices to the other gods are committed to him which he conveys in his mounting flames and smoke to their seats on high, with the praises and prayers of the worshippers. As sacrifice propitiates the gods and removes guilt, and as fire purifies and expels evil influences, Agni is a god who takes away sin and restores the sinner to favour. In this way the moral side of Agni's character is more developed than that of any other god save Varuna. Agni is the priest of the gods, and in a special sense the god of the priests; he knows all the rites and accurately performs them. He is also a seer, possessed of all knowledge, and begetter of wisdom in men. He is the friend and kinsman of men, a guest in every house; he watches over his worshippers and protects them, driving away demons and averting hostile magic; he delivers from all perils, and bestows prosperity, offspring, domestic welfare.

A favourite theme of the poets is the births of Agni. He is begotten on earth daily when the fire is kindled with the two fire-sticks, and must, therefore, lie hidden in the wood. The waters—terrestrial as well as celestial—also are the abode and origin of Agni. In the lightning which breaks from the streaming cloud he is born; from heaven he descends to earth in the lightning stroke. Finally, Agni is the sun, the great fire in heaven. The three abodes of Agni, in heaven, among men, in the waters, his three stations, three bodies, threefold light, are even in the Rig-Veda subject of mystical speculation, or, more accurately, of mystifying obscurities.

Soma, the libation to the gods, the preparation and offering of which is the main feature of the ritual with which the Rig-Veda is connected, is also one of the most important deities. One whole book, the ninth, comprising one hundred and fourteen hymns, is exclusively devoted to him. The drink of the gods, by which they are moved to grant the requests of their worshippers, is itself a divine power, and like all other divine powers is personified. The belief in its efficacy with the gods passes easily into the notion of power over the other gods, and the way is thus opened to the foremost ranks of the pantheon.[1] The drink gives to the gods strength and courage, as we have seen in the myth of Indra and the dragon; it is the draught of immortality for gods and men. Its worshippers exclaim: "We have drunk the soma, we have become immortal, we have come to the light, we have found

[1] The deification of means by which good things are procured is very common, especially sacrificial or sacramental means.

the gods; what can enmity do to us now, and what the malice of mortal, O Immortal?" It is, therefore, a potent medicine; Soma heals whatever is sick, making the blind to see and the lame to walk. It is also a remedy for moral ills; it dispels sin from the heart, destroys falsehood, and promotes truth. As the draught gives wisdom to men, Soma is a wise seer, who knows the races of the gods and with intelligence surveys the creatures.

Soma, being the inspirer of Indra's valour, is himself a great warrior, most heroic of heroes, fiercest of the terrible, ever victorious; he conquers for his worshippers cows, chariots, horses, gold, heaven, water, a thousand boons. As sacrifice sustains the order of nature, Soma causes the sun to rise or the dawns to shine; he generated the two worlds, created heaven and earth, and so on. There are in fact no limits to the potency of this divine draught. The soma plant grew upon the mountains, but terrestrial mountains and the cloud heights of heaven are not easily discriminated in the turgid rhetoric of the priestly poets.[1] From the highest heaven the eagle brought down the soma—perhaps not the plant but the streaming rain.

The use of a drink derived from the intoxicating juices of a plant mixed with water, milk, or honey, and the offering of libations to the gods, goes back to Indo-Iranian antiquity; the Haoma of the Avesta is identical not only in name but in use.[2] In post-Vedic times Soma is identified with the moon, by what association of ideas—whether the colour of the milky mixture or the shape of the moon, which is compared to a bowl drained by the gods each month, or both combined—is uncertain.

The gods of the Rig-Veda are friendly powers; man confides in their good-will and rejoices in their presence. The one exception is Rudra, a great but terrible deity, destructive as a wild beast, the ruddy bull of heaven. The hymns addressed to him are filled with deprecation of his deadly

[1] Indeed, the word *parvata* means both 'mountain' and 'cloud.'
[2] See below, pp. 388 *ff*.

wrath; he is implored not to slay his worshippers, their parents, children, men, cattle, or horses; to avert his great malevolence and his terrible bolt; to keep from them his cow-slaying, man-slaying missile. In the Atharva-Veda and the Brahmanas he is still more terrible in aspect and deed; even the gods are afraid of his arrows lest he should destroy them, and when the other gods attained heaven Rudra remained behind. Under the euphemistic name Çiva he became one of the greatest gods of Hinduism. Yet, on the other hand, he is peculiarly a god of healing, the best of physicians, who has a thousand remedies by virtue of which his worshipper hopes to live a hundred winters. He is, as has already been said, the father of the Maruts, and is commonly thought to have been originally a storm-god. Others see him rather a god of forests and jungle, a kind of Indian wild huntsman.

The divine waters had an important place in the religion of the Indo-Iranians before the separation, and maintained it in both branches of the race; even the name "Child of Waters," Apam Napat, has been preserved in the Avesta as well as in the Veda. In the latter the rivers of the Panjab, on which the prosperity of the people was largely dependent, are gods, foremost among them the Sarasvati. The Ganges, pre-eminently the holy river of India in the following ages, is named only in one of the latest hymns.

Mention must be made also of certain gods whose names show the beginnings of priestly speculation or theological reflection, such as Brihaspati, the praying priest among the gods, the "lord of prayer," i. e., the deified religious formula; Viçvakarman, "the all-creating"; Prajapati, "the lord of creatures," of whom more will be said in another connection.

Goddesses in their own right have only a minor place in the Vedic religion; Ushas, the Dawn, is the only one to whom many hymns are addressed, and next to her in this respect stands Sarasvati. There is one hymn to Night, the sister of Dawn. Other goddesses are Vac, deified Speech, and certain personifications of Plenty. The wives of the gods, such as

Indrani (the feminine of Indra), are figures—and not very prominent figures—of myth rather than of religion.

The gods whose praises are celebrated in the Rig-Veda thus vary widely in nature and in religious importance; by the side of the gods, old and new, who make up the popular pantheon and are chiefly worshipped, are found gods who owe their importance to the ritual or theological interests of the priesthood, and gods who are favourite figures with the poets, without having been, so far as we can see, of corresponding prominence in worship.

Besides the gods who have been named, there are several classes of superhuman beings who belong not merely to the realm of mythological fancy, but at least, in some secondary way, to religion. Among these are the Ribhus, to whom about a dozen hymns are dedicated, and who are frequently invited to the sacrifice. They are skilled artificers, who rival and outdo Tvashtar in fashioning the drinking-vessels of the gods; they made also a wonderful car for the Açvins; they made a cow that gave nectar for milk, and the like. The Apsarases were, the name implies, originally water-nymphs, but are not restricted to the aquatic sphere. They are beloved by the Gandharva (or the Gandharvas), whose abode is on high, and who appears as the guardian of the soma; but Apsarases sometimes bestow their favours on mortals, as in the story of Urvaçi and Puraravas.

Many mythical heroes, priests, and seers of olden times—Manu, the man who first offered sacrifice, Bhrigus and Angirases, Kutsa, the hero who fought by Indra's side against Çushna, Atharvans, the Seven Seers, and others—are mentioned in the hymns; some apparently forming an intermediate class between gods and men, others men who by association with the gods become participants in their mythical deeds. It does not appear, however, that they were actually worshipped with the gods.

The powers at work in the world are not all friendly and beneficent. There are multitudes of demons and evil spirits who, out of their own malignity or moved thereto by malicious magic, work manifold harm to men in their person and property. Of these hostile powers there are several classes. In the Atharva-Veda and later the Asuras are demons who are mythical antagonists of the gods and enemies of men. In the Rig-Veda the name usually designates the gods, or a group of gods of which Varuna is the chief, as in the Avesta Ahura is the highest god; seldom, and almost solely in the tenth book, they are opposed to the gods and are combated by them: Indra is invoked to scatter the godless Asuras; Agni promises to make a hymn by which the gods shall vanquish the Asuras. The name Dasas or Dasyus, originally the godless dark-skinned natives of India, was probably extended to the gods they worshipped, equally the adversaries of the Aryan invaders. Perhaps the reputation which inferior races often possess for superiority in magic contributed to the belief that their deities were evil demons. Several of these Dasas are named individually in the Vedic mythology—Namuci, Çambara, Çushna, and others; they appear chiefly as antagonists of the gods, and are therefore transported, with the scene of combat, into the air; it is not necessary to suppose that they were by nature "atmospheric demons."

The demons who most trouble men are the Rakshases (occasionally called Yatu, persecutory magician). They have, or assume at will, the form of beasts or ill-omened birds such as owls or vultures; or they are, as more commonly in the Atharva-Veda, manlike, two-headed, four-eyed, with feet turned backward, and the like. They lurk about the habitations of men, especially at night and in the dark of the moon; they invade man through all the orifices of the body, consume his flesh, suck out his marrow, drink his blood, confuse his speech, make him mad. They drain the milk of his cows and devour the flesh of his horses. They come not singly but by families and troops—Fever with his brother Wasting, his sister Cough, his cousin Rash. They frequent the place of sacrifice to defile the gifts and disturb the liturgy; to the offerings to the manes they throng in the likeness of ancestral spirits. Marriage, pregnancy, childbirth are beset by demonic perils; they swarm about the dying and haunt the house of death. The Piçacas, in particular, are ghoulish devils. For defence against these malignant powers men have recourse to counter-magic or invoke the protection of the gods; Agni, especially, is besought to drive them away or burn them up.

Since the gods are—with the exception of Rudra—friendly and helpful powers, worship has prevailingly the character of propitiation. Offerings are made to them of things which men prize, and are accompanied by the recitation or chanting of hymns in their honour and prayers for their favour. These actions are believed to please the gods, and thus to gain or maintain or recover their good-will. The forms of worship are known in detail only from the Brahmanas, ritual treatises which represent a later age and exhibit a high degree of priestly elaboration, and from the more recent manuals called sutras; the allusions in the hymns show, however, that the characteristic features of the Brahmanic cultus came down from Vedic times.

There were no temples nor precincts permanently consecrated to worship. When sacrifice was to be made, a place was set off and prepared for the occasion and the gods invited to the feast; after the ceremony was over and the gods had taken their departure, it was no longer holy ground. The spot marked off for sacrifice was not consecrated to a particular god, but to a group of gods or to all the gods. We may recognise in these features a survival from the nomadic state: the tribe worshipped its gods—chiefly the great powers of nature—wherever its encampments happened to be. Another peculiarity of the religion which is also doubtless of ancient origin is that there are no sacrifices by and for the people as a whole, or for the smaller social groups—tribe, clan, village—as such; all offerings are made by individuals. The sacrifices of the king before setting out to battle or foray, or upon other occasions of public interest, are, indeed, for the benefit of his people, but in form they are private sacrifices, like all others.

The proper conduct of sacrifice demands the assistance of

priests who are expert in the ritual and know the proper in-vocations, and can recite the ancient hymns of praise and prayer or compose new ones. Kings and other great persons had a priestly adviser, Purohita, a kind of private chaplain, who often held his place for life and had much influence with his princely patron. In the greater sacrifices a considerable number of priests was employed, each of whom had his own particular function. In a verse of the Rig-Veda (II, 1, 2) seven classes are named. The most important of them are the Hotar, who recites the hymns, and the Adhvaryu, the officiating priest, who, himself or with the assistance of others, attends to the sacrificial fire, strews the grass for the gods to sit on, arranges and purifies the utensils, prepares and offers the cakes, presses, filters, and offers the soma. Besides these, the Udgatar, or singing priest, who is not named in the list cited, is a conspicuous figure in the de-veloped liturgy; he accompanies certain stages of the cere-mony with his hymns set to fixed melodies. Over all these stands, in the later ritual, the Brahman, a master of ceremonies learned in all three Vedas, who keeps an eye on the whole performance, and promptly intervenes to correct or remedy any error or omission.[1]

For the household rites which every Aryan observes the fire on the domestic hearth suffices, and the head of the house in person or a Brahman for him officiates. Princes and wealthy men, as well as Brahmans, offer greater sacrifices with an elaborate and complicated ritual, for which three fires are necessary. One of these is lighted from the hearth, and is called the householder's fire; the second, situated toward the east, is the sacrificial fire, to which the offerings are actually committed; the third, or southern, fire serves for rites of aversion, to ward off the evil influences of the manes and other spirits.

The fixed times of sacrifice are the new moon, the full

[1] The prose formulas which the Adhvaryu pronounces at each turn in his performance constitute the Yajur-Veda; the songs of the Udgatar the Sama-Veda. The texts of the Hotar form the Rig-Veda.

moon, and the beginning of the three seasons of the year; further, the solstices, particularly the winter solstice, and the feasts of first-fruits. The material of the offerings includes various species of food: milk, butter, grains, meal, cakes of different kinds, and domestic animals—neat cattle, sheep, and goats. The commonest victim was a goat; the horse sacrifice, the most costly of all, was offered only by kings on great occasions. The colour and sex of the victims are related in many cases to the deities to whom they are offered, and in other respects the choice is subject to various rules; many physical defects render an animal unfit for sacrifice. The victim was "quieted" by strangling or suffocation, without shedding blood, and, if possible, without allowing it to make a sound, the priests and worshippers turning their backs upon the scene. The caul (great omentum) was first removed and broiled on a spit; then various parts of the animal, beginning with the heart, were boiled and offered to the gods. Other parts were eaten by the priests, and what was left was divided between the priests and the giver of the sacrifice. The blood and offal from the carcass was given to the demons (Rakshases).

The soma offering holds beyond comparison the highest place among the Vedic sacrifices; with it the Rig-Veda is especially associated. This pre-eminence is perhaps to be attributed in some degree to the partiality of the priests, though the importance of soma even in Indo-Iranian times is unquestioned. In the form which it has in the ritual books, this offering must have been restricted to the very rich. The soma offering has no fixed season, though spring is named as an auspicious time for it. The libation is made to a whole catalogue of gods in a fixed order at the three "pressings" (morning, midday, and evening); but principally to Indra, who not only shares at morning and evening with the other gods, but has the midday pressing for himself alone. The gods who participate in the morning pressing are Indra and Vayu, Mitra and Varuna, the Açvins, Sarasvati, "the All-gods." In the evening, according to the ritual of the younger Vedas, the Adityas, Savitar, the All-gods, Agni, and Indra.

The preparations for the offering lasted through many days, and called into requisition the services of numerous priests and attendants. On the day of sacrifice the rites began in the early morning; the priests were busy with the preparation and offering of cakes and the libation of milk, the sacrifice of eleven he-goats to different gods, the expressing of the juice from the stalks of the soma plant, filtering the liquid, mixing it with water, milk, or honey, decanting it from one vessel to another, pouring out libations to the gods, drinking the priests' share, all with manifold and minutely regulated forms and motions; the singing priests intoned their chants as the soma dripped through the sieve, to the responses of the officiating priest, with his solemn "Om." The gods and their wives, above all, Indra, who has come with his chariot and pair of tawny steeds, are seated invisible on the mat of grass spread for them. So it goes on morning, noon, and night.

Before and during a sacrifice certain preparations were obligatory, including fasting, abstinence from cohabitation, sleeping on the ground, bathing, shaving, fresh garments, and the like. The duration and severity of the restrictions varied with the solemnity of the occasion; at the great soma offering the fasting was, at least in the theory of the ritual books, protracted to emaciation. At the close of the ceremonies another bath was prescribed. The purifications keep away the malign demonic influences from the holy place, and remove from the worshippers the hardly less dangerous contagion of holiness; the fasting, as in many savage religions, predisposes to abnormal psychical states, which are attributed to spirits and in higher religions become communion with the gods and revelation from them. The rites of worship are attended at every turn by words and acts to repel the demons that frequent the place of sacrifice and try to nullify it; water and fire and the potent formula are the means chiefly employed.

The notions of the operation and effect of sacrifice which appear in the Veda are sufficiently simple. Man wants the protection and help of the gods, the gifts which they can bestow—health, good fortune, children, cows. He believes that they are approachable in the same way as the great of this earth and amenable to the same motives. They enjoy hearing their own praises sung, their power and goodness magnified, their assistance asked; they are pleased with the gifts men bring them, especially with ample provision of food and of the divine drink, soma. Like generous men, they will not fail to make a liberal return for the good things they accept. This is commonly taken for granted, or more or less delicately hinted in the praise of the god's goodness; but it is not seldom more frankly outspoken: "Give me; I give to thee." "Drink, strengthen thyself; thine are the pressed draughts of soma, O Indra, now as heretofore. As thou hast drunk the old, so drink to-day, thou blessed one, the new. . . . Bring on! None shall hinder thee. We know thee, the owner of treasures. Indra, lord of the tawny steeds, grant us thy greatest gift." "Enjoy the soma, satisfy thy desire with it; then turn thy mind to give treasures." Gifts to the gods are accompanied, therefore, by petitions for their gifts—petitions common and general, or specific of particular needs. The sacrifices which are made to avert the displeasure of the gods and recover their favour do not differ either in ritual or conception from those which take their gracious disposition for granted; only the petition takes a different form, as in many hymns to Varuna beseeching him to forgive the sin and loose its bonds, removing the guilt and the punishment.

This is the prevailing notion of sacrifice in the Rig-Veda; but beside it is the belief that the rites are potent of themselves to ward off evils proceeding from human or demonic ill-wishers. The belief in the effectiveness of sacrifice to propitiate the gods and procure their blessings tends everywhere to become a faith in the unfailing efficacy of the rites and formulas themselves, when duly employed, to secure the desired good; and in the hands of the Brahman priesthood sacrifice becomes a veritable power over the gods, which logically ends by exalting the possessors of this power to the rank of human gods who constrain the gods of nature, and takes the cultus back again completely into the sphere of sacerdotal magic out of which the rise of anthropomorphic deities incompletely extricated it. Of this portentous regression the beginnings, or at least the premises, can be discerned in the Rig-Veda; the consequent development comes later.

Besides sacrifices and offerings, expiations have a large place in most religions. These rites are much more persistently connected with magical conceptions and customs than sacrifices proper. We can trace in them several stages of development. Most ancient expiatory rites are in form a purification; that is, they are means employed to remove an evil which is imagined as an invisible and highly contagious substance, adhering to the person affected by it, a disease, for instance, a ceremonial defilement, or the anger of the gods. All of these may be removed by the use of water or fire, or of blood, which has always been regarded as possessing extraordinary potency in this sphere. In other cases, the evil, whether disease or pollution or guilt, is magically transferred to an enemy, personal or tribal, or laid upon an animal, which is then sent away, carrying away with it the mischief with which it is laden. Such rites are commonly called, from the ceremonies of the Jewish Day of Atonement, "scapegoat" rites. Of course any sort of an animal, or a human being, as in the Thargelia at Athens, may be so used, or an inanimate object, as among the Malay peoples, who ship the smallpox off to sea in a boat.[1]

With the development of the higher religion such evils come to be attributed, though not consistently, to a deity who has been offended in some way by men, and inflicts, directly or through the instrumentality of demons, the evil consequences of his displeasure upon men. This change in

[1] See also above, pp. 106 f.

the conception of the source or cause of the evil does not, however, involve any change in the notion of the nature of the evil; the old rites of expiation and purification are still efficacious, but they take their place in the religion of the gods, with the result that the notions of disease, uncleanness, guilt, sin, and punishment are still more hopelessly confused.

The Rig-Veda, being a collection of hymns to the gods, gives us only occasional and incidental glimpses of the under side of religion, which is the proper sphere of magic. The Atharva-Veda, on the other hand, is a collection of magical charms, as indeed its name imports. The collection as such is later than that of the Rig-Veda, and contains many younger hymns, but the bulk of the magical verses themselves, in substance, if not always in their actual form—some of them have been subjected to Brahmanic manipulation—are of great antiquity. The charms accompanied magical ceremonies, and are often intelligible only when we know, *e. g.*, from the Kauçika Sutra, the nature of the rites.

Diseases and ailments of all sorts are the work of demons, or, with less distinct personification, are produced by a foreign disease-substance, a kind of fluid or ether, which gets into a man and undoes him. Remedies, often chosen on the principles of magical homœopathy from all the kingdoms of nature, exhibited *secundum artem*, and the efficacious charm pronounced over the sufferer, expel the mischief or the mischief-maker. Other formulas are potent against the whole genus of Rakshases or Piçacas, or thwart the machinations of sorcerers and turn their devices back on their own heads. There are charms to harmonise family discords, to avert jealousy, and the like; to procure a good husband, male offspring, and a thousand other ends of human desires. The magic of self-defence is not, however, the only kind; by its side are rites and charms to inflict manifold injury on a man's enemies, to constrain unwilling love, to destroy a dreaded rival. The gods are sometimes invoked to launch their curses against the object of man's hate. The large place such black magic has in the Atharva-Veda is probably the principal reason why, in its Brahmanised form, it was not put on the same footing in the canon with the three Vedas (Rik, Sama, Yajus); but this lack of canonical recognition did not detract from its reputation for efficacy nor restrict its use.

The oldest belief of the Indians, like that of most other peoples, was that the dead continued to exist in a ghostly state. They still had need of food and drink, and came back from time to time to their former homes to receive the provision which their surviving kinsfolk made for them; if their wants were not supplied, they might avenge the neglect. Ghosts are an uncanny folk whom the living do not like to have about; hence, at stated seasons, especially at the new moon, a meal is prepared for them, consisting chiefly of boiled rice. The "fathers," from their "ancient pathways," are formally invited to this feast. Water is poured into little grass-lined trenches for their ablutions; then a portion of the rice is put into the trenches, designating by name the ancestors—father, grandfather, and great-grandfather—for whom each portion is meant, and they are bidden to fall to; other offerings, of oil, perfume, and the like, follow. When this ceremony is completed, the offerer expresses in set form his veneration of the "fathers," and his wishes, for example (looking at the house): "Homage to you, O fathers; give us a house, ye fathers!" (looking at the balls of rice): "May we have, ye fathers, wherewith to offer you!" Pieces of cloth or tufts of wool are then presented in a similar way. In conclusion, the fathers are dismissed, with a polite request not to present themselves again until the next moon.

The primitive notions which are implied in this ritual have even in the Rig-Veda made room for other conceptions, according to which the blessed dead have their abode in the heaven of light where Yama (the first man to die, ruler over the realm of the dead) dwells. "Where pleasures and bliss, where enjoyment and gratification, where all wishes are attained, there let me be immortal!" (Rig-Veda, IX, 113, 7 *ff*.). In this shining home the souls enjoy the offerings which their pious kinsmen make to them. It would be a mistake to think that this heavenly happiness was the lot of all the dead. Like the Greek Elysium or the Islands of the Blest, like the Egyptian Fields of Earu, the heaven of Yama was doubtless originally the abode of "the death-defying heroes" and of generous princes who make great offerings to the gods and liberal donations to the priests; the godly, "who by ascesis have attained to the sun"; those who have done good.

The opposite fate of the bad is seldom, yet unmistakably, intimated in the Rig-Veda: "Indra and Soma, hurl the evil-doer into the prison, into fathomless darkness, whence none shall come out again! So shall your stern might constrain them"; "Beneath the earth shall all they dwell who by day and night contrive deceit against us." "Those who roam like brotherless maidens, who lead an evil life like wives that deceive their husbands, who are wicked, faithless, false— such have prepared for themselves that deep place." The Atharva-Veda and later texts, Brahmanic and heretical, de-pict in lurid colours the horrors of hell and develop more strictly the notion of retribution. Of the transmigration of souls which fills so large a place in the following ages, the Rig-Veda knows nothing.

The centuries following the age of the Vedic hymns may be described as the Brahmanic period. In it the great body of ritual works which are called Brahmanas was elaborated and attained fixed form in the tradition of the several Vedic schools, and by the exclusive knowledge of the complicated ceremonies and the efficacious formulas on the correctness of which men's welfare here and hereafter depended, the Brahman priesthood, now become a caste in the strictest sense of the word, raised itself to a superhuman rank. This enormous power was achieved without worldly means; the priests had no hierarchy, no ecclesiastical organisation, no temples under their control.

The Brahmanas are primarily minute prescriptions for the performance of religious rites; but to these are attached ex-planations of the origin and significance of the ceremonies as a whole or of particular details in them—interpretations sometimes mythological or legendary, sometimes symbolical. This commentary on the liturgy, if we may call it so, finds not infrequent occasion for theological or philosophical digressions, the starting-point of which is usually the cosmogonic problem. These subjects are the chief themes of the so-called Forest Books (Aranyakas) and the Upanishads, which are appended externally to the Brahmanas.

In several hymns in the Rig-Veda which by various marks are recognised as among the latest in the collection, and in similar compositions in the Atharva-Veda, the unity of the godhead is taught. It is not one of the great gods of the Vedic religion and mythology who is thus exalted to a supreme place, but sometimes one, sometimes another, of a class of deities who owed their importance to the favour of priestly circles, such as Brihaspati or Brahmanaspati, or are abstract creations of priestly poets like Viçvakarman or Prajapati. Brihaspati or Brahmanaspati, the Prayer Lord, is a transparent personification of prayer. "Prayer" must not, however, be understood in this connection as the humble, spontaneous petition of the worshippers, but as the potent word of the priest which even in the Rig-Veda "strengthens" the gods, who are dependent on it as they are on offering, and in the Brahmanic age both enables and constrains the gods.

By this logic Brihaspati becomes the greatest god; the deeds of Indra and of Varuna are attributed to him directly. He is called the father of the gods; before there were any gods he brought out of non-being all that is. The origin of the world is ascribed in the Rig-Veda to Viçvakarman also, the Maker of All (Rig-Veda, X, 81 and 82), and to Prajapati, the Creator (X, 121); in the Brahmanas usually to Prajapati. He brings it into existence, not by fiat out of nothing, nor by shaping formless matter, but produces it out of himself. Repeatedly it is said that Prajapati was this universe in the beginning, alone; he desired, "I will reproduce myself, I will become many"; by fervid ascetic exercises, with utmost effort, he brought forth the three worlds—the earth, the atmosphere, the heaven; brooding over these, there arose the three great lights, Agni, Vayu, and Aditya, and from them the three Vedas; or he produced the creatures by means of a sacrifice or other ritual performances. There are many different representations of the order of creation; but the sacerdotal conceit that the cosmogony itself was effected by the magical power of religious ceremonies runs through them all. Prajapati is not only the author of the universe, but he upholds and rules it; he is not only in the gods but in men. It is said: "Of this Prajapati, half was mortal, half immortal; with the mortal part of him he feared death." The demons (Asuras) are also his creatures, and he assigned to them darkness and black magic.

Other cosmogonic myths in the Brahmanas put at the beginning of all things a chaos of waters, on which Prajapati breathes like the wind; or the waters produce a golden egg, from which Prajapati emerges; or he appears alone on a lotus-leaf, amid the waters—a material principle is before the creative god. More metaphysical are the cosmogonies which put being or non-being at the beginning and make the creator himself the outcome of a kind of evolution.

The cosmogonic hymn (Rig-Veda, X, 129) goes a step further back, to a time when there was neither being nor non-being. It names no god, only "that One" beside which was naught else. The whence and the how of cosmogony are an inscrutable mystery. The gods, who themselves came into being only after this world, know naught of it. Only he who brought the creation into being—whether he made it, or did not make it—he knows, or does he himself not know? The poet does not venture to decide whether the world was made, or whether the One, the ground and cause of the universe, is a conscious agent. A still different conception of the origin of all things is set forth in the hymn of the Purusha (Rig-Veda, X, 90). Man, as the microcosm, has often been set over against the universe-macrocosm; here, on the contrary, the universe is imagined as the infinite man.

It is, however, not the varying forms these speculations take that here concern us, but the fact that in many, and to our feeling often grotesque, forms the poets and thinkers of this period are struggling to express mythologically, theologically, or metaphysically, after their ability, the idea that at the origin of all things, before heaven and air and earth, above the whole pantheon of nature deities, there is one ground of being—one god, some would say, and call him creator; to others it is the nameless One. The antecedents of monotheism, pantheism, monism lie crossed and tangled in these early ventures at the riddle of the universe.

In the progress of time a scheme of life was laid out to which in theory every Aryan, that is, every member of the three upper castes, should conform. In this scheme life was divided into four stages: The life of the student, in which the boy attached himself to a teacher and learned the Vedas; the life of the householder, in which, after the completion of his studies, the man married, reared children, and fulfilled his duty in offering to the gods; the life of the hermit, when, as age approached, abandoning his home for the forest, he no longer actually performed most of the sacrifices, but gave himself instead to reflection on the mystical significance of the ritual; and, finally, the life of the ascetic, who no longer concerned himself about offerings and sacrifice even in thought, but devoted himself to meditation on the highest themes—the relation of the soul to the principle of the universe. It is for our purpose not essential to inquire how generally or how strictly this systematisation was followed; hermits and mendicant ascetics were many, and for them the external observances of religion chiefly or wholly fell away, their place being taken by meditation and speculation.

The subjects with which they occupied themselves and the substance of their thinking lie before us in the Forest Books (Aranyakas) and the Upanishads, of which the former are in theory the studies of the hermits, the latter of the ascetics (Sannyasins). The line between the two is not, however, a sharp one; Upanishads are embedded in Aranyakas and the

title Upanishad sometimes covers an Aranyaka. The name
Upanishad (literally, "session") means secret or esoteric
teaching, mystery; and the Upanishads contain, along with
profound philosophical ideas, mystical speculations and mysterious rites. The older Upanishads are in prose, and usually
in the form of a dialogue in which one who possesses the
higher knowledge explains to an inquirer the nature of this
knowledge and the way to attain it. It is noteworthy that
the possessors of this knowledge are much more often laymen than priests; and it has been inferred, not without probability, that the Upanishad philosophy originated and was
earliest cultivated, not among the Brahmans, but in the
other castes, especially among the nobility (Kshatriyas), and
was only subsequently adopted by the priesthood.

When we speak of the philosophy of the Upanishads, it
must not be imagined that they contain anything resembling
a system, nor even that they consistently develop certain
fundamental conceptions. They represent the teachings of
different thinkers or schools through a period of several centuries; they go straight at the ultimate problems of metaphysics—the nature of reality, the relation of appearance
and reality and of the many to the one. The thinkers came
to these questions from the mythological cosmogonic speculations of their predecessors; their thinking, like that of the
earliest Greek philosophers, is often half-mythical; they express themselves in mythical or ritualistic terms. Without
being conscious of it, the same teacher sets forth views that
seem to us to be inconsistent or even irreconcilable. The
phrase, philosophy of the Upanishads, can therefore signify
only certain prevailing ways of envisaging the problems and
a certain general type of solution.

The Upanishads find the ground of the universe, the one
reality, in a principle which is oftenest called Brahman. The
name has ritual associations; it is connected with the god
Brahmanaspati, or Brihaspati, who, we have seen, at one
stage in the priestly cosmogonic speculations or in certain
priestly circles was the creator of the world. Other thinkers,

more philosophically minded, put in the place of the cosmogonic deity who somehow produced or evolved a world out of
his own substance a first principle, the self-existent Brahman
(neuter). Thus, in the Çatapatha-Brahmana (XI, 2, 3), in
obvious correction of the cosmogonic myth of Prajapati:[1]
"Brahman, verily, was in the beginning this world. It created the gods and assigned them the rule over these worlds—
Agni over this earth, Vayu over the atmosphere, Surya over
the heaven, and higher gods than these over the higher
worlds. As these worlds here (earth, air, heaven) and these
gods are manifest, so also are those (higher) worlds manifest
and their gods whom it set over them. Itself (the Brahman),
however, retired to the half beyond" (*i. e.*, beyond the sphere
of empirical reality).

This "self-existent Brahman," the one reality, is called
also, with a name of psychological origin, the Atman. The
word denotes the "self," sometimes in an empirical sense, the
individual man; then, in a higher sense, his true self, in distinction not only from the body but from the inner organs of
sense and cognition, which also are non-ego—in a word, the
ideal self, the essential being. In this highest sense the word
is used of the Brahman, which is the ideal principle of the
universe.

The great mystery of the Upanishads is that the Atman
in man is identical with the Atman in the universe, the
Brahman. The soul of man is not a particle, an emanation,
of the universal principle, but *is* that principle, whole and
single. Thus in the Chandogya-Upanishad (III, 14):

"Verily the universe is Brahman. Let him whose soul is at peace
worship it, as that which he fain would know.

"Of knowledge, verily, is a man constituted. As is his knowledge
in this world, so, when he hath gone hence, doth he become. After
knowledge, then, let him strive.

" Whose substance is spirit, whose body is life, whose form is light,
whose purpose is truth, whose essence is infinity—the all-working, all-
wishing, all-smelling, all-tasting one, that embraceth the universe, that
is silent, untroubled—

[1] See above, pp. 269 *f.*

" That is my spirit within my heart, smaller than a grain of rice or a barley-corn, or a grain of mustard-seed; smaller than a grain of millet, or even than a husked grain of millet.

" This my spirit within my heart is greater than the earth, greater than the sky, greater than the heavens, greater than all worlds.

" The all-working, all-wishing, all-smelling, all-tasting one, that embraceth the universe, that is silent, untroubled—that is my spirit within my heart; that is Brahman.   Thereunto, when I go hence, shall I attain.   Who knoweth this, he, in sooth, hath no more doubts.

" Thus spake Çandilya, Çandilya." [1]

"The Brahman, the power which presents itself to us embodied in all beings, which brings into existence all worlds, supports and maintains them, and again reabsorbs them into itself, this eternal, infinite, divine power, is identical with the Atman, with what, after stripping off all that is external, we find in ourselves as our inmost and true being, our real self, the soul." [2]   For this identity of Brahman and Atman the pregnant formula is found in the "great word," *tat tvam asi*, "That art Thou." [3]

Men had long thought of the highest blessedness as an endless life hereafter in the abode and company of the gods. For this external conception of blessedness the Upanishads substitute oneness with God in the fullest meaning of the word, not a union to be realised after death, but a present and eternal reality.   This is the new doctrine of salvation which makes an epoch in the history of philosophy and religion in India.

In its purest form the "identity of Brahman-Atman," to use their own phrase for it, is consistent idealistic monism. But the innate realism of the human mind, the necessity of clothing abstract thought in figurative or traditional language, the difficulty of the cosmical problem from this standpoint, and the inheritance of earlier speculations upon it, combine to give to the enunciation of the teaching in many passages either a theistic or a pantheistic turn which

[1] Translated by C. R. Lanman.

[2] Deussen, Allgemeine Geschichte der Philosophie, I, 2 (1899), 37.

[3] Chandogya-Upanishad, VI, 8, 7 *f*.

in the later Upanishads, under the influence of the rising religious movement of Hinduism, predominates. This development, as well as the systematisation of the Upanishad philosophy in the Vedanta school, will engage us later.

In the Upanishads appears for the first time the doctrine of the transmigration of souls, which thenceforward fills so great a place in the religions of India. Belief in the reembodiment of human souls in men or animals is wide-spread among savages, and was doubtless nothing new in India. What is characteristic in the Upanishads is that man's character and lot in this life is determined by his deeds in a former existence, and that what he now does in like manner determines what he shall be in a future existence. An inquirer asks Yajnavalkya, When after death a man's bodily organism is dissolved into the elements, what becomes of the man? "Take me by the hand, my dear Artabhaga; we must talk about this by ourselves, not here in the assembly. So they went out and conversed with each other, and what they spoke of was works, and what they praised was works. Verily by good works a man becomes good, evil by evil." The meaning is clear in another utterance of Yajnavalkya: "According as a man acts and behaves, so he is born; he who does good is born as a good man, he who does evil is born as a bad man; by holy works he becomes holy, wicked by wicked. Therefore, it is said: Man is wholly made up of desire; as his desire is so is his insight; as his insight, so are his deeds (*karman*); according to his deeds so is his destiny."

The predetermination of character and destiny appears in these passages as an esoteric teaching, a mystery not to be discussed in public. It is improbable that the origin of the popular belief is to be traced to these philosophical circles. The emphasis in the vulgar doctrine of transmigration is not on the moral predisposition that a man inherits from his own character in a former existence, but on a retribution in kind which his deeds have incurred, a species of automatic *talio*, by which, for example, a greedy man may return as a pig, and the like. The caste, sex, condition, and fortune of every man is determined by his former deeds under an inexorable law of cause and effect. Speaking anthropomorphically, we may call this sequence retributive; in reality it is not reward or punishment dealt out by divine justice, but the inflexible causal nexus of the universe itself; yet the quality in men's deeds which prescribes their issues is fundamentally moral.

The doctrine of the transmigration of souls is harmonised with the older belief in heaven and hell by making heaven and hell only temporary states of retribution between successive embodiments of the soul; this combination is found in the Upanishads, in the lesson of the Five Fires,[1] just as the corresponding conceptions are combined by Plato in the tenth book of the Republic.

The prevalence of this belief in an endless series of lives upon each one of which man entered laden with the deeds of his previous life gave to the problem of salvation in India a new meaning and a new urgency: How can man escape this eternally revolving wheel of birth and death? Men seek in philosophy a *saving* knowledge; they demand of religion henceforth, not that it shall satisfy them with life, but that it shall save them from endless lives.

The Upanishads have the secret of salvation in the oneness of Brahman-Atman. For him who has attained this knowledge the illusion of separate individuality is dissolved with all its consequences. He is free from all desire—what can he wish who is all?—his former deeds are consumed like rushes in the fire; deeds done after the achievement of knowledge adhere to him no more than water to the lotos-leaf.

"He who is without desire, free from desire, his desire attained, whose desire is set on Self (Atman), his vital breath does not pass out, but Brahman is he, and in Brahman is he absorbed. As the verse says:

> "'When all the passion is at rest
> That lurks within the heart of man,
> Then is the mortal no more mortal,
> But here and now attaineth Brahman.'

[1] Brihadaranyaka-Upanishad, VI, 2; Chandogya-Upanishad, V, 3–10.

As a serpent's skin, dead and cast off, lies on an ant-hill, so lies this body then; but the bodiless, the immortal, the life is pure Brahman, is pure light." [1]

The idealistic monism of the Upanishads is not the only solution of the problem of the universe which Indian thinkers propounded in those centuries. Both Jainism and Buddhism are indebted to a philosophy which, at variance with the Upanishads, maintained the objective reality of the phenomenal world, ascribing to forces inherent in the primary substance underlying this world not only the eternal flux of nature but our own thoughts and feelings, and, on the other hand, by definition excluded the soul, or ego, from this sphere of changeful activity. Such a philosophy is known to us later in the Sankhya system, and there is good reason to believe that its fundamental doctrines antedate the rise of the great heresies.

The system is dualistic. On the one side is the primary substance, Prakriti, eternally active and productive, the source and seat of all change; and, on the other side, a vast number of individual souls (Purusha), simple, eternal, unchangeable. Each of these souls, so long as it has not attained deliverance, is enswathed in a subtle body, which in turn produces in each successive existence the coarse material body. This bondage, and with it all the misery of existence, is the consequence of a rooted error by which the soul imagines itself to be affected by the changes in the Prakriti; it is broken for ever when man becomes aware that the soul is but a passive spectator of the play in which it deemed itself actor and sufferer—the saving knowledge is the knowledge, not of identity, as in the Vedanta, but of absolute diversity.

This system is atheistic: the popular gods are only souls, like others, which in the round of rebirths are for the time being in the *Deva* state; for a supreme god (*Içvara*, lord) the system has no use nor place. The evolution and involution of worlds is caused by the disturbance or re-establishment of

[1] Brihadaranyaka-Upanishad, IV, 4, 6.

equilibrium among the three constituents, or components, of the primary substance. The conception of existence is much more pessimistic than in the Upanishads. Life is nothing but pain and sorrow, and endless other lives will be the same. In consequence, this philosophy is more conscious of its mission to save men from the eternal misery of existence, and impresses on those who have found the great salvation to bring others into the way.

The attainment of union with the Brahman or the severance of the true self from all that is not self was sought, not alone by profound reflection, crowned in a supreme moment by intuitive certainty, but by the use of various means believed to conduce to the desired end or to produce states favourable to its achievement. Among these means ascetic self-mortification has a large place. It is a common belief that privations and inflictions which produce abnormal psychical states bring supernatural knowledge and supernatural powers; they have been employed in many higher religions for the attainment of an ecstatic experience the character of which is predetermined by expectation. Ascetism has had another significance where pessimistic conceptions of life have obtained. If existence is itself an evil, then the extinction of desire, which is the bond of attachment to existence, is the logical remedy. This is peculiarly true where desire (the will to be) is the cause of rebirth, or where desire as the motive of action is the ultimate cause of the burden of deeds which man carries from one life to another.

There are other methods of inducing trance states, of which sitting immobile in certain postures, the management of breathing, and certain exercises for the suspension of sensation and the suppression of mental activity are the most important. At a later time these methods are systematised in the Yoga, but in essentials the method is very old; it had a place in Buddhism from the beginning.

CHAPTER XII

INDIA

THE GREAT HERESIES

Ascetic Orders—The Origin of the Jains—The Way of Salvation—The
Order—Buddhism—The Life of Buddha—The Saving Truths—The
Mendicant Brotherhood—Buddha's Last Days—Primitive Bud-
dhist Doctrine—Rebirth Not Transmigration—The Eightfold Path
—The Goal, Nirvana—The Order and Its Rule—History of Bud-
dhism in India—Councils and Schisms—The Higher Goal of the
Mahayana—Metaphysics—Influence of Popular Religions—Deca-
dence and Extinction in India—Buddhism in Other Lands.

In the sixth century there were great numbers of men who,
leaving their homes and sundering all social ties, lived as
hermits or mendicants, devoting themselves to the quest of
salvation in various ways. It was universally assumed that
sacrifices to the gods, moral integrity, goodness to fellow-
men, did not lead to the goal; for good works were still
works, and all voluntary deeds entailed their appropriate
consequences in another life, keeping the doer thus bound
fast in the endless chain. Only the sovereign knowledge
which enabled a man to say, "This is not my deed, this is
not I," brought liberation.

The seekers of salvation were perhaps at the beginning
solitary ascetics, as many have been in more modern times;
but in the sixth century we find them gathering in companies
about men whose teaching and example gave promise that by
following them others might reach the goal, and more or
less loosely organised in orders or brotherhoods having their
own rule, professing and propagating a specific doctrine or
method, superior to all others, if not the *only* way of de-

liverance. Though our first evidence about these orders or sects comes from Buddhist and Jain sources, there is good reason to think that the movement began a century, perhaps even two centuries, earlier.

Two of these sects attained historical importance, the Jains and the Buddhists. The former still survives in India, beyond whose bounds it never spread, numbering, by the most recent census, about 1,300,000 adherents; Buddhism, long since extinct in the peninsula of India, was carried by missionary effort to the countries beyond, and remains the religion not only of Farther India, but of a great part of eastern Asia.

The historical Jain sect, by their original name, the Nirgranthas (Nigganthas), those who are loosed from bonds, "the emancipated," was founded in the latter part of the sixth century B. C. by Vardhamana, an older contemporary of Buddha. According to the Jain books,[1] however, this was not the beginning of the religion, but a revival or restoration; and many European scholars are inclined to regard Parçva, the next preceding Jina in the series of twenty-four, who is said to have lived two hundred and fifty years earlier, as a historical person.

Vardhamana,[2] more commonly called Mahavira, "the great hero," and Jina, "the victorious" (whence his followers have the name Jainas), was the son of a petty prince or baron in Magadha. When he was thirty years old, he left his home and became an ascetic. After twelve years of self-mortification, he achieved the end of his quest. Thereupon he began to proclaim the truths which Parçva and the Jinas before him had taught, and gained many converts, who in part became members of the mendicant order, in part continued to live in the world under a rule for laymen. The resemblance of this account to the story of Buddha is suffi-

[1] The Jain scriptures consist of forty-five Agamas, of which the eleven Angas are the oldest, and appear to contain in substance the teaching of Mahavira. Translations by H. Jacobi, "Jaina Sutras," in Sacred Books of the East, XXII and XLV.

[2] In Buddhist books usually called by his family name, Nataputta.

ciently explained by the fact that the two sects arose in the same age and region and under identical conditions, without supposing that one has served as a pattern for the other.

Jainism is anti-Brahmanic, rejecting the Vedas and the authority of the priests. It is an atheistic, dualistic system, but differs radically from the Sankhya philosophy in lodging activity, not in the primary world-substance, but in the individual souls. These souls by their activity produce works (karman, the deed with its entail, good or bad), and are thereby enthralled in bodiliness and pass from existence to existence in the round of retributive rebirths, sinking by evil deeds to lower forms of life or rising by good to the state of the gods, but not even so escaping their fate. There is no deliverance but in making an end of karman once for all and altogether.

This was the universal belief of the time; what is distinctive is the way by which the karma is to be got rid of. To this three things are necessary, namely, right faith, right knowledge, right living—the so-called Three Jewels. The right faith is that the Jina (Victor) has overcome the world, has found the way of salvation, and is a refuge to believers; the right knowledge is the knowledge of the metaphysics and psychology of the religion as taught by the founder— what the world is, and what the soul, and how the soul can emerge victorious from the struggle; right living means living, according to the precepts of the founder, in such a way as to stop the production of karma by suppressing its cause. This cause, in the Jain analysis, is the activity of the soul; the remedy, accordingly, is to check the impulses to action by control of the senses. The effect of deeds done in former existences or in the present life before conversion must be annulled by self-mortification. As death approaches, a Jain may extinguish the last remains of karma by starving himself. In the value which it puts on asceticism, Jainism is in the main current of the times, and stands much closer to Brahmanism than does Buddhism.

The goal of these endeavours is Nirvana, a state of the

soul in which it is free from the entail of deeds (karma) and from bodiliness. The soul itself is indestructible, and the great deliverance does not, apparently, imply a cessation of consciousness.

The Jain community consists of ascetics (monks and nuns), and the laity (men and women), who take the fundamental vows in a mitigated interpretation, but—in contrast to the Buddhist "adherents"—are reckoned as members of the church. This peculiarity of organisation is probably one of the reasons why the Jains have maintained themselves while other sects which were nothing but ascetic brotherhoods disappeared.

The primitive atheism of the sect did not satisfy the religious needs of the masses, and the veneration of the founder grew in the course of time into a worship. Temples—perhaps the earliest temples built in India—were erected to him, with images, festivals, offerings of flowers and incense—a complete cultus. The earlier Jinas took their place by his side, and along with them in later times Çasanadevis, female powers who execute the will of the Jinas like the Çaktis of Hinduism.

A split in the church occurred about the third century B. C., and divided the Jain ascetics into two branches, the Digambaras, or "sky-clad," with whom nakedness is essential to holiness, and the Çvetambaras, or "white-robed," who entertained the milder opinion that garments, provided they are sufficiently simple, are not an obstacle to salvation. Other issues, concerning, for instance, the canonicity of parts of the scriptures, as well as dogmatic differences, also divide the two parties.

The Jain ascetics early ceased to be homeless beggars and took up their abode in monasteries. In later centuries philology and science—especially astronomy—as well as literature, were cultivated in these monasteries; in the development of Indian architecture and sculpture the Jains took a leading part.

Injury to anything that has life, that is, anything in

which there is a soul, is naturally a grave sin in a religion which takes transmigration seriously, but none of the Indian sects have carried precautions against this offence as far as the Jains. They cannot till the soil on account of earthworms; they cannot even walk abroad in the rainy season without a broom of twigs, gently sweeping the path before them to remove insects; they must drink water through a cloth strainer, and many like things.

Jainism was and remained distinctively, even exaggeratedly, Indian. By its side, in the same age and on the same soil, Buddhism arose, the first of the universal religions, a gospel of salvation, which, propagated by missionary effort, by the preaching of the Great Truths, transcended the bounds of language and race, and spread to remote lands and peoples.

The founder of this religion, Siddhartha—to call him by his personal name—was born, according to the most probable computation, about 560 B. C., and died about 480. His father was a noble landed proprietor of the Çakya clan, which occupied a district, a few thousand square miles in area, between the Nepalese foot-hills of the Himalayas and the middle course of the river Rapti, with the Rohini as its eastern limit—territory now mainly belonging to Nepal, but extending across the border into British India. His bringing-up was probably like that of young men of his class, his education more in manly sports and the arts of the chase and war than in what the priests or the wandering sophists of the age could teach. He married, and had one son, Rahula, who became in due time a member of the order.

Immediately after the birth of this son, at the age of twenty-nine, Siddhartha abandoned his home, wife, and child, and wandered forth, like thousands of others in his day, in search of salvation. Legend has surrounded the great renunciation with a halo of poetry—not without its own psychological verisimilitude—the ominous sights of old age, disease, and death, and of an ascetic, the last look at his sleeping wife and child, the night ride with his faithful charioteer, the steed that dies of a broken heart at the loss of his master. He first put himself under the guidance of two adepts in the art of cultivating trance states, but, becoming convinced that this was not the way, turned to self-mortification with such zeal that five other ascetics followed him about in expectation of his immediate enlightenment; he pushed his fasting at length to such extremes that he brought himself to the verge of death, but without result. This way also having proved to lead nowhither, he desisted from such austerities, whereupon his companions lost faith in him and left him.

At last, seven years after he began his quest, as he was seated in meditation beneath a tree, the hour of illumination came, and he saw through the causes of the world-misery; in that moment he became the Buddha, the Enlightened. Mara (Death), who saw his empire threatened and had already tried to frighten him from his purpose, now endeavoured, by the aid of his three daughters, Desire, Discontent, and Lust, to seduce the Buddha; but their allurements were wasted on one who had done away with love, hate, and illusion. A greater temptation was the thought that the truth was too profound for the common apprehension; it would be lost labour to preach it to men who could not understand and would not accept it; was it not better to enter forthwith into Nirvana, carrying the secret with him? This suggestion, too, he resolutely put aside, and set about proclaiming his good tidings. The two Yoga teachers were dead, but he sought out the five mendicants who had been the witnesses of his austerities in the forests of Uruvela. They met him with prejudice as one who had turned back from the hardships of the "great effort," but when he set forth his discovery they gladly embraced the saving doctrine.

The discourse the Buddha held with the five ascetics, sometimes called the Sermon at Benares, contains the fundamentals of the faith: The seeker of salvation should be warned equally against the two extremes of self-indulgence and self-mortification; both are unworthy and unprofitable.

There is a middle way, following which man arrives at peace of mind, knowledge, enlightenment, Nirvana. This way, the so-called Eightfold Path, comprises right belief, right resolution, right speech, right conduct, right means of subsistence, right effort, right meditation, right absorption.[1]

This is the sovereign remedy for the misery of existence. Buddha, as a healer of the soul, habitually sums up his doctrine under four heads corresponding to the formula in which the task of the physician is defined by Indian medical authorities (the nature of the disease, its ætiology, the removal of the cause, the remedy). These are the "four great certainties," the universality of suffering, the universal cause of suffering, the removal of the cause, the means by which this may be achieved, namely, the Buddhist regimen as prescribed in the Eightfold Path. The first step in this path, right belief, is the conviction that Buddha has traced misery to its cause and found the infallible remedy.

The first of the four certainties, the universality of suffering, was the self-evident truth which set men to seeking salvation in manifold ways. To the mendicants it needed no demonstration: "Birth is suffering, age is suffering, illness is suffering, death is suffering; contact with what we dislike is suffering, separation from what we like is suffering, failure to attain what we crave is suffering—in brief, all that makes bodily existence is suffering."

The question of the cause of this universal human ailment, and particularly the cause of its continuance from existence to existence, had long exercised Indian thinkers. Buddha finds it in the craving (literally, "thirst") which leads from rebirth to rebirth, accompanied by sensuous pleasure and desire, plucking pleasures here and there—the craving of lust, the craving for being, the craving for well-being. The solution is not new: in passages of the Upanishads, some of which have already been quoted, "desire" is the root from which springs the deed with its dire entail, freedom from desire puts an end to it all; but Buddha was the first to

[1] For the definition of these terms, see below, p. 295.

make it a corner-stone. The ætiology of the disease being thus understood, it is self-evident that a radical cure can only be wrought by the extirpation of the cause, the extinction of this fatal craving, through the wholesome regimen of the Eightfold Path.

The news that Buddha had discovered the sure way of deliverance drew to him inquirers, and converts rapidly multiplied. Many of these were men of his own social class or of the well-to-do middle class, but there were some Brahmans among them. Indian asceticism, in its Brahmanic forms as well as in the heretical sects, has always been beyond caste distinctions, and in like manner Buddha's way of salvation was for all mankind. It is, however, a complete misunderstanding to conceive that Buddhism was a revolt against the system of caste, which, indeed, was in that age and region only in an undeveloped stage. Buddha's attack on the Brahmans is directed against the false conceit that Vedic learning and ritual observances could save a man —a delusion which not only kept them out of the kingdom, but made them oppose his work as the Pharisees opposed Jesus. On the other hand, very few of the lowest classes are found in the following of Buddha. It is a common observation that it is not the people whose life seems to us most intolerable that are most discontented with life; despair is a child of the imagination, and pessimism has always been a disease of the well-to-do or at least the comfortably-off, and peculiarly virulent when it attacks youth. So it evidently was in India in Buddha's time.

Some of the converts came over from other sects or from among the solitary ascetics, but there were many also who had not previously assumed the mendicant life. According to the fashion of the time, Buddha gave to his disciples a simple rule of life; the yellow robe, the shaven head, and the begging bowl were probably from the beginning the badge of the monk. Ere long the disciples were commissioned to receive new adherents upon the triple confession: "I take refuge in the Buddha, I take refuge in the Doctrine, I take refuge in the Order." The instructions which Buddha is said to have given to his apostles are an interesting testimony to the missionary spirit of primitive Buddhism: "Go forth, disciples, and wander, to the salvation and joy of much people, out of compassion for the world, to the blessing, salvation, and joy of gods and men. Go not two together on the same way. Preach, disciples, the doctrine which is salutary in its beginning, its course, and its consummation, in the spirit and in the letter; proclaim the pure way of holiness. I am going to preach the truth in Uruvela."

As the rainy season approached, the mendicants gathered in the vicinity of a town, in groves or parks, often put at their disposal by rich patrons; simple huts sheltered them from the weather, their single meal was got by gathering alms from door to door. The rest of the day was spent in listening to the teaching of the Master or repeating his words on former occasions, in conversation about the great lessons, or in solitary meditation. Three months each year, from the middle of June to the middle of September, passed thus, and the formation of the fixed tradition which was eventually gathered up in the sutras may be traced to this custom. When the rains were over, the brethren dispersed in different directions, carrying with them everywhere the message of suffering, its cause, the extirpation of the cause, the remedy. Buddha himself, with a more or less numerous following, including the inner circle of disciples whose names are more constantly associated with his own, wandered from season to season in different parts of a somewhat extensive district, in Kosala and Magadha (modern Oudh and Bihar). In this fixed round forty-five years went by with little to distinguish one year from another. Tradition usually connects particular discourses and conversations or institutions of Buddha with certain persons and occasions, often with places, but only at the beginning and end of his ministry is there anything like an order of time.

Besides the members of the order, who alone belong in the proper sense to the religious community, Buddha had many friends and supporters among the laity, both men and women, who listened gladly to his teaching and observed the first five commandments of the Buddhist decalogue. They daily filled the monks' alms-bowls, and often invited numbers of the brethren to a meal. Wealthier patrons bestowed on the order for their retreat groves and parks, such as the garden at Jetavana presented by a rich merchant, Anathapindika, or the mango grove at Vesali, the gift of the courtesan Ambapali; the simple huts in which the brethren lodged were later replaced by more permanent monasteries. The order boasted princely patrons in King Bimbisara of Magadha and King Pasenadi of Kosala. Such adherents, or "reverers" (of Buddha) as they are called, living in the world, could not expect to attain saintship in this life, but might hope, in virtue of their faith and good deeds, to be reborn with a predisposition thereto.

The new doctrine encountered opposition from various sides. In the eyes of the Brahmans it was a heresy, because it rejected the Vedas and the Vedic sacrifices, the Vedanta and the Yoga; but the Brahmans had no ecclesiastical organisation and no secular arm at their command; their influence with the classes to which Buddha appealed seems to have been small. In the controversies with them the Buddhists are almost always the aggressors. A much more serious hindrance was the rivalry of other heretical sects. Buddhist tradition preserves the name of six such bodies, the most vigorous of which were the Ajivikas, the followers of Gosala,[1] and the Nigganthas (Jains) with their head Nataputta. Each of them professed to possess the saving truth and the rule of life which alone led to deliverance, and disputes about doctrine and practice inevitably followed when the contentious representatives of the different salvations crossed one another's paths on their beggars' errand.

Both Buddhists and Jains display a peculiar animosity toward Gosala, whom they accuse of grounding a practical

[1] See the article, "Ajivikas," by Hoernle, in Encyclopædia of Religion and Ethics, I, 259–268.

libertinism on a theoretical fatalism.   Charges of loose living
are, however, favourite arguments in sectarian controversy,
and Buddhists and Jains exchange them, along with less
concrete polemics.   The Buddhist "middle way," with its
rejection of self-mortification, seemed to thorough-paced
ascetics mere pampering of the flesh, and is a favourite butt
for Jain jibes.   In the temper of the times this feature of
Buddhism was to many unprejudiced by sectarian jealousy
a suspicious thing.

In the Buddhist community itself voices were early raised
in favour of a stricter rule, more in accord with the reigning
fashion; the first serious dissension in the order is said to
have been over such a proposal.   Devadatta, a cousin of
Buddha, who cherished an ambition to succeed him, having
failed to persuade Buddha to resign the headship of the order
to him, put certain monks up to ask the master to prescribe
a severer discipline for all members of the congregation, and
this also being refused, drew five hundred monks away with
him in an abortive schism, the forerunner of graver ones to
come.

The Suttas give a sufficiently clear notion of the method
and form of Buddha's teaching.   To men of the world who
came to hear him he set forth first the secular virtues, the
great evils that follow ill-doing in this life and beyond, the
great blessings that reward well-doing.[1]   Only when he finds
by their response that there is in them an understanding or
receptive mind does he expound the higher lessons of suffering, its cause and cure, the gospel of redemption.   In this
there is no distinction of exoteric and esoteric, but only the
tact of a wise teacher who finds his hearers where they are
and leads them on to his ground as they are able to follow.
Buddha often tries to clear the minds of inquirers of false
notions and to bring them to see the truth by skilfully directed questions, and refutes opponents by entangling them
in their own answers, in a fashion sometimes called Socratic.
But the reader of the Suttas who is led by this inapposite

[1] See, e. g., Maha-parinibbana-Sutta, I, 23 f., Maha-vagga, V, 1.

comparison to look for something of the genius of Socrates, the freshness, the humour, the unconventional in thought and expression, will be disappointed. The clatter of the dialectical machinery, the numerical schemes, the tedious repetitions *totidem verbis* of the self-evident or the not-at-all-evident, make the impression of a dreary scholasticism rather than of creative originality. There is no doubt that much of this is only the clumsy mnemonic apparatus by which the words of the master were preserved from generation to generation; but that Buddha's own thinking and teaching ran in the scholastic mould created by the Indian sophists before him is equally unquestionable—how else should he have convinced his contemporaries?

The story of the last months of Buddha's life is more detailed than that of any other period of his career; as the end approaches we can follow him almost from day to day. It is natural that the doings and sayings of these days should have been indelibly impressed on the memory of his companions, often repeated to others, and earliest crystallised in a fixed tradition.

During the last rainy season he was seriously ill, and though he recovered it was evident that the end could not be far off. Ananda, the most intimate of his disciples, expressed his anxiety lest the Blessed One should pass away without leaving final instructions for the guidance of the order. Buddha replied that he had nothing to add to what he had taught for so many years. As to the order, he had never regarded himself as its head, or the order as dependent upon him. Its members must be a light and a refuge to themselves, seeking no refuge besides themselves, but holding fast to the truth as lamp and refuge;[1] such mendicants shall reach the highest goal—but they must be anxious to learn!

[1] The Pali word, *dipa*, means both 'lamp' and 'island.' The last words of Buddha may therefore be translated:

"Therefore, Ananda, with yourselves for islands [of safe retreat from the overwhelming floods of desires and lusts] live ye, with yourselves for refuges, with none else for refuges; with the Teachings for an island, with the Teachings for a refuge, with naught else for a refuge." Such

After the end of the rains, Buddha went to Vesali, and thence by slow stages toward Kusinara. On various occasions, in conversation with individuals, or in larger companies, as in the assembly of the monks at Vesali, Buddha repeated the fundamentals of the faith. At a meal to which he was invited with his followers by Cunda, the son of a smith, Buddha ate some dried boar's flesh, which in his enfeebled state brought on a fatal illness. In his last hours he is said to have asked the monks whether there were any doubts or difficulties in their minds about the teaching that he could clear up. His last words to the beloved disciple Ananda were: "Perhaps you may think that the word has lost its master, we have no master any more. You must not think that, Ananda. The doctrine and the discipline which I have taught you and proclaimed, that is your master when I am gone." And to the disciples: "Now, O disciples, I say to you, Dissolution is the nature of all composite things. With heedfulness work ye out!" (sc. all that ye have to do).[1] Then he passed through the successive stages of contemplation and ecstasy, and entered into Nirvana. At sunrise the nobles of Kusinara, paying him such honours as befit a universal ruler, burned his body before the gate of their city.

Buddhism, like all the religions and religious philosophies which flourished in that age, is a way of salvation, and it has in common with all of them certain fundamental assumptions. Foremost among these is the conviction that salva-

is the import of the metaphor according to the greatest of all the commentators, Buddhaghosa. It amounts, says he, to this: "Stand on your own feet," that is, "With all heedfulness (see next note, below), work out your own salvation, and in reliance on no one but yourselves and naught else than the Teachings." (I am indebted for this note, as well as for the following one, to the kindness of my colleague, Professor Charles R. Lanman.)

[1] So the commentator Buddhaghosa supplies the object. The Western reader is tempted to say "your salvation," nor would the meaning be essentially different. The really important thing is the "heedfulness," and in that one word, Buddhaghosa adds, the Exalted One, lying on his bed of death, sums up all his teachings of five-and-forty years.

tion must be achieved by each man for himself. No god can deliver him. The Vedic gods have no powers or functions beyond the sphere of natural good; they are themselves not exempt from the cycle of rebirth,[1] and themselves stand in need of salvation. A second point of agreement is the nature of the evil from which man is to be saved—the bondage to the ills of corporeal existence and the endless repetition of these ills in the infinite series of rebirths in which man enters every new existence laden with the consequences of former deeds.

There is, however, one fundamental difference between Buddha's conception of the problem of salvation and that of the contemporary systems. They all assumed that there is a soul, an ego, which passes, with its load of deeds, from one existence to another to receive its just recompense of rewards; their starting-point was the common notion of transmigration. The Upanishads might deny that the soul was in reality an individual soul and declare individuality a fatal illusion; but so long as the illusion lasted the soul went its separate way from life to life. To the Sankhya and the Jains individual, imperishable souls were one-half of their dualistic universe. Buddha, however, denied that there is any such thing as either common opinion or the technical speech of philosophers called soul.

The ground of this denial is made abundantly plain: if there be an ego, a personal soul, permanence must be its characteristic mark. So his opponents also conceived it, and found the true ego in the unchanging One or in the unchanging psychic monads. But these are alike figments of speculation; in all our experience there is no simple unity, whether it be All or Atom, and no permanence. Our observation of the world reveals only a perpetual flux; our consciousness attests only the stream of ever-shifting sensa-

---

[1] If sects were already in existence which hoped for salvation through the grace of a supreme lord (Içvara), as seems probable, their teachings made no impression in the regions or circles with which we are here concerned.

tions, emotions, conceptions. We know only becoming; of unchanging being behind or beneath it there is no sign. The empirical individual is a transient combination of five components (*skandhas*), viz., bodiliness, sensation, perception, predispositions, consciousness. At death this complex is resolved into its elements. But all composite things are impermanent, and "what is impermanent is suffering, what is suffering is not I; what is not I is not mine, it is not I, it is not myself." That there is no ego, no soul, we should say, is thus a fundamental tenet of primitive Buddhism; it is equally an error to say that the soul is an entity different from the body and to say that soul and body are identical, and the error is not theoretical merely, it is a hindrance to the religious life.

But though Buddha does not admit the transmigration of souls in the common understanding, for the reason that there is no permanent entity called soul to migrate, he holds no less firmly to the belief in the round of rebirths and the dependence of each existence on preceding existences. A favourite illustration is that of one lamp kindled from another; neither the second lamp nor its flame is the same as the first, but without the former the latter would not be alight. To the question, What passes from one life to another? the answer is, karma and nothing but karma. This does not mean that the deed of one man is saddled on another; it is a heresy to hold that he who experiences the fruit of a deed is different from the one who performed the deed, and equally heretical to assert that he is the same. Where the existence of an ego is denied, the question of identity has no meaning.

The problem which obviously arises here is, How does a new existence depend on a former one, and how is it determined by it? This is, if I mistake not, the question which the formula of "dependent origination" is proposed to solve. On (1) ignorance depends (2) the diathesis; on this (3) (potential) intelligence and consciousness; on this (4) individuation; on this (5) the six spheres of sense (including the intellectual sense); on these (6) contact (with their re-

spective stimuli in the sensible and intelligible world); hence
follow in order (7) feeling; (8) craving; (9) cleaving (to the
world and life); then the new series, (10) beginning of existence (the formation of the embryo), (11) birth, (12) old
age and death with all their train of sorrows—the so-called
Twelve Causes. The formula has been very diversely interpreted by Buddhists as well as by Occidental scholars.
The point that concerns us here is that all that a man does
in ignorance of the truth produces a certain complex of predispositions—we might say, a form of character with its
accordant destiny—and this diathesis realises itself in another life which is thus determined by that former life.[1]

However obscure this theory of the chain by which one
existence is linked to another, there is no question that there
is but one way to break this sequence, namely, to put an
end of the production of karma. It is not action itself
that does the mischief, the mere functioning of the physical
and psychical mechanism, but the motivation, the craving
for what men in their ignorance call the good things of this
life, the blind clinging to life itself as a good, the desire for
another life, the will to be. Stop that, and the deeds done
without self-regarding motive or purpose have no consequence
in them, their karma is barren. The karma left over from
a former existence or accumulated in the present life before
the attainment of this state must exhaust itself before the
complete deliverance comes, as a potter's wheel keeps on
revolving for a time by the force of the impulse given it,
but if it receive no new impulse gradually comes to rest, or
as the lamp that is not freshly fed with oil burns till the oil
in it is consumed and then goes out. For such there is no
rebirth.

The method by which this blessed end is achieved is the

[1] Tradition makes this Buddha's great discovery, following immediately on the recognition of the Four Certainties, and Buddhists of all
schools have so regarded it. Some European scholars see in it an illogi-
cal attempt to couple the genuine Buddhist doctrine that desire is
the root of misery with the common Indian philosophy which made
nescience (*avidyā*) the origin of all evil.

religious life as outlined in the Eightfold Path. The first step in this path is right belief; that is, belief in the four fundamental principles as enunciated by Buddha; then follow right resolution, the resolve to renounce all sensual pleasures, to have malice toward none, and to harm no living creature; right speech, abstaining from backbiting, harsh language, falsehood, and frivolous talk; right conduct, not destroying life, not taking what is not given one, not being guilty of unchastity; right means of subsistence, giving up a wrong occupation and getting one's livelihood in a proper way; right effort, the strenuous endeavour to overcome all faults and evil qualities, to attain, preserve, and cultivate all good qualities. These six paths are ways of moral self-discipline, and might be comprehended under one head. The next, right reflection, might be called the intellectual discipline, a higher ascesis by which man rids himself of lust and grief. The highest stage is the mystical discipline, right absorption, or concentration, a series of trances through which man rises to the bliss which is as far beyond happiness as beyond misery, reaches the intuition of higher and higher ranges of truth, and passes into ecstasies that lie beyond consciousness.

These trances are self-induced hypnotic states, for the attainment of which common Indian methods are employed, attentive management of breathing, staring at a reflecting surface, and the like. It is only the content of the experience, determined by suggestion, that is specifically Buddhist. For right reflection, or contemplation, also, there are certain defined exercises which are followed under corresponding physical conditions. The higher attainments in this sphere bring with them various supernatural powers: their possessors transcend the limitations of material bodies and of mortal mind; they can pass at will through walls, fly through the air cross-legged like a winged bird, and perform similar magical feats; they are able to recall their experiences in previous states of existence, and have unbounded insight and wisdom. It is the common belief that saints and ascetics, who are beings of a higher order than every-day humanity, must be endowed with superhuman knowledge and miraculous—that is, magical—powers. Such powers are constantly attributed to Buddha, not only decoratively in the later poetical biographies, but quite as a matter of course in very prosaic Suttas. It belongs, indeed, to the very definition of a Buddha to be omniscient, and when he knows by his omniscience that something is going wrong in a distant place, he transports himself thither on the wings of the wind.

The progress toward perfection has several stages, and may extend through more than one lifetime. The highest is that of the saint (Arhat), in whom all causes of moral infection are exhausted, all evil propensities rejected; he has fulfilled his task, laid down his burden, removed all bonds, obtained the four kinds of transcendent faculties; he is no more subject to rebirth. The supreme goal is Nirvana. The word means, literally, "blowing out," as of a lamp, extinction. There is a sense in which it may be reached in this life. To a Brahman ascetic who asked what Nirvana is, Sariputta answers: "The cessation of desire, hate, mental confusion, O friend, is called Nirvana." As in the Brahmanic philosophy a man who has attained the saving knowledge is "delivered in this life" (*jīvanmukta*), so the Buddhist saint may be said to have gained Nirvana. "They who by steadfast mind have become exempt from evil desire, and well-trained in the teachings of Gautama, are in the enjoyment of Nirvana. Their old karma is exhausted, no new karma is being produced; their hearts are free from the longing after a future life; the cause of their existence being destroyed, and no new longing springing up within them, they, the wise, are extinguished like this lamp." But the full fruition is entered on only at death.

Does the saint continue to exist after death or does he not exist? This question Buddha declined to answer. Like the question whether the world is infinite and eternal or the opposite, it is of no concern to man to know; for whether the world is eternal or not, whether the saint exists after

death or does not exist, or both or neither, the evils of life
and the necessity of salvation remain the same. His mission is not to gratify men's curiosity about irrelevant matters,
but to show the way by which man, in the present life, ex-
tinguishes birth, old age, death, sorrow, lamentation, misery,
grief, and despair, and from this calling he will not let himself be diverted.

The logical implication of his teaching is perfectly clear:
there is no soul; the empirical individual, a composite of the
five *skandhas*, ceases to be when this combination is dissolved at death; all that goes over from one life to another
is the karma, the predispositions which originate another
existence. But when the saint attains Nirvana, the residuum
of karma has been consumed, and there is nothing left to
continue existence in any form.[1] Men do not always go to
the end of their own logic, and annihilationists, or at least
men who craved annihilation, passed for heretics. All that
we can say with entire certainty about the early Buddhist
conception of Nirvana is that it meant a peaceful end un-
haunted by the fear of rebirth. This blessed assurance fills
the saints with the joy of salvation; the strife is over, the
victory won; henceforth there remains peace, perfect peace,
endless peace.

The only way to become a saint is to follow to the end the
Eightfold Path, and this is possible only for such as, severing
all the ties which bind men to this world, live the religious
life according to the Buddhist rule. From the beginning
the confession of faith ran: "I take refuge in the Buddha,
I take refuge in the Doctrine, I take refuge in the Order."
The order was open to all men, without distinction of rank
or caste; excluded *a limine* were only criminals such as
murderers and robbers, persons afflicted with certain bodily
defects or diseases, and persons who were not *sui juris*—
slaves, soldiers, minors. The candidate, by a formal renunciation of the world, entered upon a novitiate, a period

[1] *Cf.* the Maha-parinibbana-Sutta, V, 21: "The utter passing away
which leaves nothing whatever to remain behind."

of instruction in which also the constancy of his resolution was tested. For converts from other sects a term of probation was appointed. Admission to membership in the order was by the act of a chapter consisting ordinarily of at least ten monks. The Senior, who presided, satisfied himself by inquiry that there was no impediment to the ordination and that the candidate had been properly instructed and was provided with the requisite garments and almsbowl. If the chapter consented to the ordination, the Senior exhorted the new monk to avoid the four deadly sins and to restrict his belongings to the four necessities.

At the beginning converts were brought to Buddha himself, subsequently they were admitted by his disciples on their missionary journeys; the rule and form of ordination by a chapter is a later regulation. The ritual was further elaborated in the course of time, and somewhat differently in different branches of the church, but its essential features remain the same. So also in early days the renunciation and ordination were frequently continuous without the interposition of a protracted novitiate. The monk was free to leave the order if he chose.

Buddha originally founded an order for men only, and, according to the tradition it was only after long hesitation and with grave apprehension that he established a sisterhood. But, pressed with the question whether women were incapable of attaining salvation in his way, he yielded to the importunity of a noble lady of his own clan and her spokesman Ananda that women might be permitted to exchange the shelter of the home for the houseless life. The order of nuns is subject to certain special regulations, and is in all things dependent on the brotherhood. Even so, Buddha is reported to have warned Ananda that the admission of women would have disastrous consequences for religion—the good doctrine will not endure more than half as long as it would otherwise have done; he compares the mischief they will do to mildew in a rice field or rust on sugarcane. Early Buddhist texts abound in reflections and stories about the falseness of women—a favourite subject of monk-ish jibes in all lands. "How shall we behave toward a woman?" Ananda asks. "Avoid the sight of her, Ananda!" is Buddha's reply. "But if we do see her, Sir, what shall we do then?" "Not speak to her, Ananda." "And if she speaks to us, Sir, what then?" "Then be wary, Ananda."

The Ten Commandments, the fundamental law for Bud-dhist monks, prohibit: (1) the destruction of life, (2) theft, (3) unchastity, (4) falsehood, (5) the use of intoxicating drinks, (6) eating at forbidden hours, (7) frequenting worldly amusements or spectacles, (8) using perfumes and ornaments, (9) sleeping on a raised couch, (10) receiving gifts of money. The first five of these are binding on lay adherents also, but for them the definition of the offences is less strict. These commandments are not materially different from the cor-responding precepts of the Brahmans and of other heretical sects like the Jains.

A much more detailed code of discipline is contained in the Patimokkha, the form of fortnightly self-examination and confession for monks. At the head stand the four deadly sins which signify defeat in the war of the spirit, namely, unchastity, theft, destruction of life, pretence of supernatural powers; these *ipso facto* cut the sinner off from the brotherhood. Then follow in long catalogue offences which require formal action by the order: the illegitimate acquisition of various objects, punished by forfeiture; ac-tions which require penance; such as should be spontane-ously confessed; and breaches of decorum in alms-getting, teaching, and so on. Many of these regulations have to do with the dwellings of the monks, their rugs, beds, vest-ments; others concern the peace and order of the community and the intercourse of its members with others, especially conduct toward women, whether nuns or outsiders. In ad-dition to these there is a body of rules, part of which are in theory for all members of the order, though not all gen-erally observed, while others are specifically for those who live, not like the most as cœnobites in communities, but as eremites after the fashion of the Brahman recluses; namely, living solitary in the forest, lodging at the foot of a great tree, under the open sky, in a burning-ground, spreading a mat where one happens to be, never lying down.

The order was a democratic brotherhood; there was no central authority and no local organisation. In the stated or occasional assemblies of the monks it was customary for the senior in date of ordination to preside, but this precedence carried no authority.

It is plain that in primitive Buddhism there was no place for any form of worship, whether in outward act or spiritual adoration; for there was no being to whom man owed homage for benefits bestowed, none whose help he could invoke to save him from his sad estate. The only liturgical acts are the recitation (later, reading) of the words of Buddha, which corresponds in a fashion to preaching, and the self-examination and confession, the fortnightly assembly for which was undoubtedly instituted by Buddha himself. On the fourteenth or fifteenth day of each half-month (full moon and new moon) the monks in a neighbourhood gathered at some central point for this service. In time the boundaries of the parishes were fixed and halls designated for the meeting. The senior, or in case he be ignorant, a learned and competent monk of later ordination, after exhorting the brethren not to dissemble their shortcomings, recites the several categories of offences; at the end of each he thrice bids every monk who is conscious of having transgressed one of these precepts to confess his fault. Silence is taken to signify a clean conscience. When the recitation has been concluded in this manner, the assembly dissolves. These gatherings also brought laymen together to hear the doctrine, and gave occasion for sermons. Other sects had the custom of reciting their doctrine weekly before congregations of the people, and Buddha is said to have been led by their example to establish the ceremony just described.

The general character of Buddhist morals has been already indicated. They are, it is to be remembered, primarily the morals of an ascetic order, precepts and counsels of perfection for men who have renounced the world. But they represent in this form the Buddhist ideal, and could not fail to exert a great influence on householders also. There is little specifically Buddhist in them; many of the principles and precepts recur in Brahmanic sources and among the other anti-Brahmanic sects. Yet the Buddhist teaching has a distinctive note; nowhere else is gentleness in act and speech so exalted. Noteworthy, too, is the condemnation of soothsaying, sorcery, magic, and practising on popular superstitions.

Of the history of Buddhism in its first two centuries very little is known. It is clear that in that time it had grown strong in the region of northeastern India where it had its origin, but it does not seem to have spread much beyond those limits. The period of rapid expansion began after the middle of the third century B. C. The Maurya Dynasty, founded by Candragupta (321 B. C.), had built up an empire which took in all northern India as far as Kabul and extended over a considerable part of the Deccan. The third king of this line, Açoka, became a convert to Buddhism, and under his patronage it made progress in all parts of his wide dominion.[1] The new missionary impulse carried it even beyond these boundaries to Ceylon, where it is said to have been preached by a son of the king himself; in the same age it reached Cashmere.

The two centuries and more between the death of Buddha and the conversion of Açoka had not left the order wholly unchanged. Apart from dissensions, chiefly about points of discipline, to which we shall return later, the order had been endowed with many monasteries, in which its members chiefly resided. Reverence for the master made his birth-

---

[1] In the inscriptions from the earlier part of Açoka's reign he does not figure as the patron of Buddhism exclusively, though he showed especial favour to it—the more as years went on. But in his latest monuments he boasts of an increase of zeal which showed itself in doing away with the gods who had till then been worshipped in India.

place, the tree under which he attained enlightenment, the scene of his first preaching, the place where he died, holy spots to which pilgrims resorted; an early Sutta promises that those who die on such a pilgrimage shall be reborn in the happy realms of heaven. Relics of Buddha, also, were held in veneration; the same Sutta tells how, after the burning of his body, the bones were divided among eight clans or individuals who claimed a right in them, and mounds were erected over them. Princes reared monuments (*stupas*) over relics of the Blessed One, and flowers were laid before them or lights kept burning. This modest beginning of a cult originated with lay adherents; the monks at first took no part in it. Their reverence was not, however, less real or profound. Legend surrounded Buddha's birth and enlightenment with miracles significant of the fact that the whole universe, gods, devils, and inanimate nature, were not merely spectators, but impassioned actors in the drama of salvation; he descended from the Tusita heaven to become incarnate in the womb of Maya; his knowledge was omniscience, his word was infallible; and already in the transcendentalist school it was held that he was, not alone in supreme moments of insight but at all times, superior to the conditions and limitations of human existence; a docetic theory of his humanity was developed. If he was not conceived as a god, it was not that he was less than a god, but more.

Under the Greek-Indian kings, the greatest of whom was Menander (ca. 100 B. C.), Buddhism gained ground in the northwest. Their empire was succeeded by that of Indo-Scythian kings, of whom Kanishka,[1] in the early second century after Christ, became a Buddhist, and did perhaps as much in his time for the expansion of Buddhism to the north beyond the confines of India as Açoka had done three centuries earlier for its success in India. Its great conquests in Bactria date from this time; its first introduction into China falls somewhat earlier in the same century.

[1] It seems to be well established that the rulers of this dynasty were Tartars.

In the absence of any central regulative authority, differences early appeared in minor points of practice, such as the proper observance of the fortnightly confession, for the settlement of which appeal is made in the Vinaya books to a decision of Buddha in a particular case. More serious dissensions arose about the discipline for monks. There were some, even in Buddha's lifetime, who desired a stricter rule, more nearly conformed to that of other ascetic communities; others found the rule too strict, and wished especially to see the prohibition of receiving money relaxed. With the multiplication of collections of the traditional teachings of the master and the appearance in some of them of a sectarian tendency, the question of canonicity inevitably came up. Nor was it long before differences of opinion concerning the person of the Buddha emerged, foreshadowing the great philosophical and theological controversies that were later to rend the Buddhist church.

The effort was made to settle these differences by councils. About these councils the northern and southern branches of the church give conflicting accounts, and the historical facts can hardly be determined from them. That a council held immediately after Buddha's death definitively fixed the doctrine and discipline as they are contained in the first two divisions of the triple canon is equally irreconcilable with the canon and the subsequent history.

A century later a council was held at Vesali. Both traditions agree that ten points in which some monks departed from the discipline in the direction of an easier life were condemned as pernicious innovations.[1] The consequence, according to the southern version, was that the dissatisfied monks seceded and held a "great council" of their own, thus starting the first real schism in the church. According to northern tradition, on the contrary, it was the "great coun-

---

[1] The first in the list is preserving in a receptacle of horn a remainder of salt to use at some future time when they happened not to have been given any salt.

cil" that condemned the ten lax practices. All the accounts
indicate, however, that the real divergence of the monks
of the great council from the rest was not in points of
discipline but of doctrine and of canon. Another council is
said to have been convened by Açoka about 240 B. C., at
Pataliputra (the modern Patna), where false doctrines were
condemned and the true faith re-established. From the fact
that this council is recognised only in the southern church it
may be inferred that only the conservatives took part in it,
the partisans of the great council and other progressives
remaining aloof, or more probably not being summoned.[1]
On the other hand, the council held in the second century
of our era, in the reign of Kanishka, at Jalandhara, is acknowledged only by the northern branch of the church. It
is said to have endeavoured to put an end to long-standing
dissensions by recognising all the eighteen sects as preserving the true doctrine, and to have completed and revised the
canon of scripture.

The first great doctrinal controversy in Buddhism was
about the nature of Buddha. The school of the great
council (Mahasanghikas) maintained that Buddha's nature
was transcendent, free from all the imperfections of corporeal existence, and his life absolutely spotless; his every
word had a deep spiritual sense which each hearer interprets to his own edification, and all his teaching was perfect.
The body of the Buddha is above all limitations, his power is
unlimited; he needs no rest nor sleep; his knowledge is immediate and intuitive. The conservatives, while exalting
Buddha above common humanity, would not admit that he
was exempt from all the limitations of mankind.

These were but the first steps in a path which led to a
radical transformation of Buddhism, comparable to that
which out of the religion of Jesus made Catholic Christianity.
The Catholic Buddhism gave itself the name Mahayana,
"the great vehicle," that is, the comprehensive scheme of

[1] More sceptical critics doubt whether the whole story is not a
southern fiction.

salvation; with a derogatory comparison they called the old-fashioned religion Hinayana, "the little vehicle," a scheme of individual salvation.

The most striking departure from primitive Buddhism is, in fact, indicated in these terms. The goal which Buddhism, like the other redemptive religions of India, proposed was strictly individualistic: each man for himself strove, by mastering the Four Certainties and by following the Eight-fold Path, to put an end to rebirth by extinguishing its cause; one who has attained this end, and will at death pass finally into Nirvana, is an Arhat, a saint. The saint, or one who is on the way to saintship, may try to bring his fellow men to salvation by proclaiming to them the truth as Buddha taught it and leading them to enter on the path, but this missionary effort is the sum of his contribution to their deliverance. The end which the Mahayana sets before its adherents is a loftier one—not to become a saint and enter upon Nirvana, but to become in some future existence a universal Buddha, a saviour of all beings. Sakyamuni was not the first Buddha; from age to age in the past, when the truths of salvation had been forgotten among men, a Buddha appeared to set the wheel of the law revolving again; in the future, too, the good religion would fall into decadence, and another Buddha would come to restore it. The name of this next Buddha was known; he will be called Maitreya.

There were many stories of Buddha's former existences, as man or beast, illustrating chiefly his self-sacrificing disposition. In all these lives through thousands of years he had been cultivating in himself the perfect virtues which a Buddha must possess; namely, generosity, morality, renunciation, wisdom, perseverance, long suffering, truthfulness, firmness of purpose, charity, and equanimity, as well as the other high qualities which are conditions of attainment. Those who embrace the higher Buddhism of the Mahayana propose to themselves to imitate their great exemplar in this, and endeavour to become not an Arhat, or saint, but a

Bodhisattva (literally, "one whose essence is intelligence"),[1] that is, one who has qualified himself to be a Buddha. The salient characteristic of a Bodhisattva is compassion, an active sympathy with suffering beings in distinction from the saint's ideal of dispassionateness. The best evidence of this compassion is that he will not enter into Nirvana as he might, but voluntarily remains in the round of birth and death till the age comes when he shall appear as a saviour.

This shifting of the religious ideal from the salvation of the individual to the salvation of the world is not, however, the only radical departure of Mahayana Buddhism from the primitive type. Buddha steadfastly declined to be drawn into philosophy: whether the world be finite or infinite, eternal or non-eternal, whether one who has attained Nirvana exists after death or does not exist—however such questions may be answered, or whether they be left unanswered, the necessity of salvation remains the same and the way the same. But agnosticism, though it cloak itself with the mantle of religious earnestness, is not a permanent resting-place for thoughtful minds. The defenders of Buddhism, in controversy with rival religions and religious philosophies, were constrained to face problems which the founder blinked; men of philosophic training came over to Buddhism, bringing their habits of thought and their metaphysical impedimenta with them. The result was the same as in Christianity: when it converted philosophers they converted it into a philosophy. The analogy might be carried farther, for the metaphysical principles in the two cases have a notable similarity, and the problem how to fit an historical person into the rigid frame of an absolutist system is the same in Mahayana Buddhism and in Catholic theology.

The outstanding names which Buddhist tradition con-

---

[1] The Pali *satta* is the phonetic reflex not only of Sanskrit *sakta*, "attached to," but also of *sattva*, "essence." The original meaning of *bodhi-satta* was probably "one set on (the attainment of the transcendent) illumination." But the other interpretation, "one of whom the essence is illumination," is so apt and so obvious that it naturally became the accepted one. [C. R. L.]

nects with this development are Açvaghosha, Nagarjuna, and the brothers Asanga and Vasubandhu. If the author of the Awakening of Faith in the Mahayana be the same Açvaghosha who composed the Buddhacarita—in view of the frequency of the name, a doubtful assumption—he was a contemporary of Kanishka in the second century after Christ; Nagarjuna probably lived in the second or third, Asanga in the fifth. The Madhyamika school, of which Nagarjuna is the recognised founder, are metaphysical nihilists in the literal sense. There is no death, no birth, no destruction, no persistence, no oneness, no manyness, no coming, no departing. These denials are not limited to phenomena; the very dilemma, existence or non-existence—for Buddhist logic a tetralemma: existence or non-existence, or both existence and non-existence or neither existence nor non-existence—is false. The transcendental truth is beyond even the category of being: it is the void, the silence which is neither affirmation nor negation. "The truth," says another author of the school, "does not lie in the domain of intelligence, for intelligence moves in the order of the relative and of error." Quite logically, the radical Madhyamika disclaims having any theory of its own to sustain; it occupies itself in a *reductio ad absurdum* of all conceivable theories. Yet if from the critical point of view appearance has no relation to reality, from an empirical point of view appearance is real, it exists and evolves under immutable laws. The effect is as illusory as the cause, and the nexus as illusory as both, but so long as we are in the bondage of illusion, they exist *for us*. When they are recognised for what they are, and illusion is dispelled, there remains—the void.

The Yogacara of Asanga is usually defined as a dogmatic idealism, which denies the reality of the external world but affirms the reality of thought. The very illusion that the phenomenal world is, supposes the reality of the thought in which the illusion exists. A different opinion has been recently expressed by Anesaki, according to whom Asanga admitted both the reality of the external world and of individual personality, resembling in this the Sankhya philosophy.[1]

The ontology of the Mahayana posits an absolute, which transcends knowing and being.[2] Nothing can be affirmed of it, not even that it is; for existence and non-existence are relative terms, one of which supposes the other. No significant name can be given to it, but since some term is necessary it is called "the empty," i. e., void of definable content, as we speak of "the absolute," i. e., free from all relations; another term is Bhutatathata, "that which is such as it is," i. e., cannot be compared to anything else. The phenomenal world is a manifestation of the absolute in seeming finiteness, manifoldness, and changefulness. This seeming arises from ignorance, and the ignorance is not subjective merely—the inborn realism of the human mind—but is potentially in the absolute; being a pure negation, it is held to be not incompatible with the monistic premises.[3] The absolute in itself is above consciousness, which implies individuation (personality); the principle of individuation is ignorance. Confronted with the question how the unconscious absolute through ignorance comes to consciousness, the unconditioned becomes the conditioned, there is nothing for it but to say, "spontaneously," that is, not with reason and purpose. Corresponding to these two aspects of the absolute are two forms of knowledge, transcendental and relative, the knowledge of the unconditioned and of the conditioned.[4] So long as we remain in ignorance, the world as it is for us, and we ourselves with our self-consciousness,

[1] See the article, "Asanga," in Encyclopædia of Religion and Ethics.

[2] In attempting to present the general features of Mahayana doctrine I have principally followed Suzuki, "Outlines of Mahayana Buddhism," 1907. It is not perhaps superfluous to say that the Mahayana has far too many faces to be a good subject for a composite photograph.

[3] For southern Buddhism, on the contrary, avidyā is subjective, and Buddhaghosa is at pains to prove that it is positive.

[4] The same distinction is made in the Vedanta philosophy, to which, indeed, the whole system is closely related.

have a relative reality; when once ignorance is overcome the illusory reality vanishes, and there remains only the absolute that is what it is.

As the Vedanta has not only its transcendent Brahman without attributes, but its Brahman with attributes, personal god and object of religious devotion,[1] so Mahayana Buddhism has beside its ontological absolute the conception of a supreme being endowed with all perfections. Intelligence, will, and, above all, love, are not mere attributes but the essence of this being. The commonest, and apparently the oldest, name for this being is Dharmakaya, often translated "Body of the Law" (i. e., religion). The protean senses of Dharma make every interpretation uncertain; or rather make it certain that those who used the name found in it different meanings. Suzuki renders, "System of Reality," which has a very modern philosophical sound. Dharmakaya, the ground of being, the one true reality, is not somewhere, but everywhere in the universe; the finite and fragmentary consciousness of individuals is a partial manifestation of the universal intelligence. Man may say: "The Dharmakaya is incorporate in me"—in a pantheistic sense, however, rather than in the consciousness of absolute identity as in the pure Vedanta.

In an eminent sense the Buddhas are manifestations or incarnations of the Dharmakaya;[2] in a later time even the word *avatāra* is used, as of the incarnations of Vishnu, and doubtless under the influence of Vishnuite notions. The motive of the incarnation is love: the compassion which fills the heart of the Bodhisattva for the suffering of beings who in their ignorance think thoughts, cherish desires, do deeds, whose consequences they must suffer from existence to existence, is in God an infinite compassion, and moves him to seek the salvation of all. Sakyamuni, whom we call the historical Buddha, was such a manifestation of the Dharmakaya. After his entrance into Nirvana he did not cease

[1] See below, pp. 317 *f.*
[2] Incarnation in a docetic sense.

to be Buddha; the love and devotion of those who through him had found salvation has its transcendental expression in an eternal Buddhahood. Even in his earthly life, his "transformation body" (*nirmānakāya*, a magical docetic body), he was above the limitations of humanity; after he voluntarily submitted (in seeming) to death, he continues to be Buddha in the "blissful body" (*sambhogakāya*). Thus three states are distinguished: Buddha as Dharmakaya, Buddha on earth as Sakyamuni, and the exalted Buddha. This doctrine of the three states or forms (literally, "bodies," *trikāya*) has a striking resemblance to the distinction of Christian theology —the eternal Logos, the Logos incarnate in Jesus, the exalted Christ. It has an even closer parallel in the Vishnuite doctrine of Avataras, especially as exemplified in the Krishna incarnation. There is no reason to think that there is a historical connection between the Christian and Indian conceptions; they are entirely explicable as independent—and indeed inevitable—solutions of an identical problem.

There are several other systems at the head of which is a primitive or eternal Buddha from which all proceed; the most interesting of these is the theistic Buddhism of Nepal, with its Adibuddha (original Buddha); but limits forbid the discussion of them here.[1]

In its religious aspects Mahayana Buddhism reflects the contemporary trend of religion in India, as on its metaphysical side it shows the influence of the great absolutist systems of Indian philosophy. The theistic current—always with a pantheistic tendency—can be followed from Vedic times down to modern Hinduism, and compels concessions even from the absolutists. Sects which found the essence of religion in devotion to a gracious god are at least as old as Buddhism itself, and in the centuries in which the Mahayana was taking shape the religions of Çiva and of Vishnu-Krishna were rapidly gaining ground in India at the expense of Buddhism itself.

[1] See the article, "Adibuddha," by de la Vallée Poussin, in the Encyclopædia of Religion and Ethics. On the system of Amitabha and the Western Paradise (Sukhavati), see above, pp. 131 *ff.*

The influence of Indian religion is manifest in less favourable ways. The old notion of a succession of Buddhas was enlarged to make room not only for innumerable Buddha aspirants (Bodhisattvas), but for many past manifestations of the eternal Buddha, and among these manifestations the gods of the Indian pantheon without difficulty found recognition, while others figure as champions and protectors of the faith. As Buddhism spread in northern lands, it made room in a similar way for the native deities, much as Christianity and Islam did under the names of angels or saints. The cultus underwent a corresponding transformation. Stately temples arose, adorned with many images, and elaborate forms of worship were developed, with a paraphernalia of vestments, bells, and incense, which seemed to a good Catholic traveller in the last century a travesty of Christian rites. The veneration of Buddha and the saints which prevails in the south is in the northern church replaced by adoration of transcendent Buddhas and Bodhisattvas, among whom Amitabha, Avalokiteçvara, and Maitreya occupy the first place after the Triratna itself, that is, the Buddha, the Teaching, and the Order, personified. This worship is, in theory, for the masses, a religion for this world; while the monks train themselves for Bodhisathood by study and spiritual exercises.

The fifth and sixth centuries after Christ were the most flourishing period in the history of Indian Buddhism. The Chinese pilgrim, Fah-hien, at the beginning of this period found monasteries at every stage of his long journey. The Mahayanists were numerous, though speaking generally in the minority; their stronghold was in the northwest, but there were many in the old holy land; only in the south they never seem to have had much success. By the time of Hiuen Tsang, in the seventh century, the proportion had changed; the Mahayana was plainly in the ascendant. So far as the statistics of the two travellers can be trusted, the number of monasteries had materially increased in the interval between Fah-hien's visit and that of his successor. In some regions the church had lost ground, in others it had gained; but, taking India over, there was little external indication that Buddhism was declining either in numbers or in influence. From the eighth century, however, the decadence was rapid, and by the thirteenth or fourteenth it was extinct in India proper from the Himalayas to Cape Comorin, surviving only in Nepal on the north and in Ceylon on the south.

The complete disappearance of Buddhism in the land of its origin, where for centuries its monks had been numbered by scores or hundreds of thousands, is something unexampled in the history of religions, and the causes of it are not at once obvious. Buddhism did not always enjoy the favour of rulers, and sometimes suffered from their active disfavour; but its persecutions—to give them a larger name than they deserve—were local and temporary. In general, the Indian kings, of whatever persuasion they might be personally, were tolerant, and often generous to other kinds of religion in their states. The Arab conquest of Sind in 711 was no doubt a severe blow, for that was a region in which Buddhism was especially strong; but it was not till nearly five hundred years later that the Moslems subdued the east of Hindustan. In the invasion of Magadha (ca. 1200 A. D.) monasteries are said to have been destroyed and many monks killed; others took refuge in the south or beyond the confines of India altogether. There is, however, no reason to think that the Moslems singled out the Buddhists for worse treatment than other Hindu religions.

The accounts of an uprising of Brahman orthodoxy, inflamed by Çankara, and of an exterminating persecution in the eighth century, though repeated by Vedantins as well as Buddhists, deserve no credence. Çankara exhibits no particular animosity against Buddhism; he combats all departures from the Vedic authority with impartial strenuousness. External causes are thus insufficient to explain the extinction of Buddhism. Nor do the internal causes appear much more adequate. The long controversy between the great salvation and the little salvation cannot but have weakened the church; the order itself had doubtless lost much of its early zeal; its well-endowed monasteries may have sheltered multitudes of indolent and ignorant monks; it is certain that the contamination with Hindu—especially Çivaite—superstitions was extensive; but neither corruption nor contention is ordinarily fatal.

Unquestionably the chief cause of the decline of Buddhism was the rise of newer types of religion more attractive to the mass of men. It was an inherent weakness of Buddhism that it was a way of salvation for such only as, renouncing the world, gave themselves exclusively to the task; for others there was no more than the lame consolation that in another existence they too might become monks. In the age when it arose, its competitors, Brahmanic and heretical alike, were at one with it in this; indeed, no small part of the early success of Buddhism may be ascribed to the fact that its "middle way" was a more practicable way for many than the rigorous asceticism or the metaphysical subtleties of other schools. But in the intervening centuries religions had grown up which held out the promise of salvation to pious householders as well as beggar saints. They were religions whose essential features the common man could understand, while the philosopher could make them as profound as he needed. Their living and loving gods answered the longing of the soul for an object of devotion, and rewarded men's devotion not only with the good things of this life but with deliverance from the fear of after lives. These religions were, moreover, in the main line of Indian development; they made no radical break with the gods of the fathers and the rites with which all life was interwoven. In short, it was the growth of the religions which were comprehended under the name Hinduism that undid Buddhism by depriving the order of both recruits and supporters.

The permanent conquests of Buddhism were on missionary ground. It was introduced into China in the first century of our era, was carried thence to Korea in the fourth, and reached Japan in the sixth; it had spread in Afghanistan and far into what we now call Turkestan in the first centuries after Christ; in later times it made great progress among the Mongols, contesting the field with Christianity and Islam. From large regions once possessed by it in central Asia it was ousted by the triumphs of Mohammedan arms and by the conversion to Islam of Mongol Khans. Buddhism spread to Burmah in the fifth century and to Siam in the seventh, and in these countries has continued to flourish to the present day. The Buddhism of the south, in Ceylon, Burmah, and Siam, has departed much less widely from the primitive type than that of the north. In becoming the religion of whole peoples—a church, rather than an order of mendicant friars—and of peoples on lower levels of civilisation, it has taken up much from the native religions which it superseded; it has its luxuriant Buddha legend and its arid scholasticism; it has had its share of sectarian controversies about dogma and discipline, and not only in its commentaries and systematic treatises but in the canon itself there is doubtless much that Buddha never dreamed of; but it has not adopted an absolutist metaphysics with a transcendental mysticism or gnosis, nor, on the other hand, has it been so deeply infected by Hindu polytheism and magic as the northern branches of the church. The discipline also has kept closer to the original model.

In Tibet, where Buddhism was introduced about 650, there was developed in the ninth century, by a fusion of degraded Buddhism with native superstitions and magic, a religion, called from the title of its highest ecclesiastical dignitary, Lamaism. This patriarch, the Grand Lama, is the incarnation of a Bodhisattva. The Tibetans possess translations of many Buddhist works, besides a great many specifically Lamaist books, so that their canon is of enormous bulk. A reformation early in the fifteenth century divided the Lamaists into two sects, distinguished outwardly by the colour of their garments—red, the unreformed, and yellow, the reformed body.

CHAPTER XIII

INDIA

THE PHILOSOPHICAL SYSTEMS

Relation to the Veda—The Vedanta—Idealistic Monism of Çankara
—Metaphysics: Brahman as the Absolute—Theology: Brahman
as Personal God—The Higher and the Lower Knowledge—The
Theistic Vedanta of Ramanuja—The Pluralistic Realism of the
Sankhya—The Yoga—Its Practical Methods—Other Orthodox
Philosophies—Atheistic Materialism.

In the centuries during which the great heresies were flourishing in India, and partly in opposition to them, the Brahmanic philosophies were systematised—the monistic conception of the Upanishads, as the Vedanta; the dualistic view
of the universe with which Jainism and Buddhism have closer
affinity, as the Sankhya. The Brahma-Sutras of Badarayana as expounded by Çankara in the eighth century of
our era present the Vedanta in the form which has been most
widely accepted in India; the oldest extant text of the rival
system is the Sankhya-Karika.

The Vedanta professes to be based, not on speculation
but on revelation; it is the teaching of the Veda, specifically
of the Upanishads, to which it refers as irrefragable authority.
The Upanishads, however, proceeding from many individual
thinkers or schools of thought, naturally contain numerous
inconsistencies, not to say contradictions. These inconsistencies were most keenly felt at the vital point, the nature
of the Brahman. On the one hand Brahman is, ontologically,
absolute being; on the other hand, Brahman is pantheistically
conceived as the ground of being, the soul of the universe, or
theistically as a personal god, the supreme Lord.

The metaphysics of the Vedanta develops the first of these conceptions, the higher doctrine of the Upanishads. Brahman is the sole reality, without attributes, distinctions, or determinations; of it nothing more can be said than *neti, neti*—it is not anything that you can say of it—pure being. This one reality is not material but spiritual, it is absolute intelligence; intelligence is not an attribute of Brahman, which would be irreconcilable with its simple unity, but its essence. Its unknowableness lies in the fact that it is universal subject without object; and for the same reason consciousness, which implies the duality of subject and object, cannot be predicated of it. The true self of man (*ātman*) is identical with the universal Brahman (*paramātman*, the supreme self)—"That art Thou!" The world of appearance owes its seeming existence to illusion (*māyā*), as when our senses are deceived by the art of a conjurer. The illusion is objectively conceived; Brahman is the great magician who projects it. Man's individual consciousness is an illusion of the same kind. The essence of the illusion is man's failure to distinguish the true self from the faculties of mind and sense, the principle of life, the subtle body, and the substratum of moral character, which seem to make him a person distinct from other persons and things, an individual ego.

Yet although the phenomenal world and the empirical ego are in a metaphysical sense non-existent, a kind of reality is allowed to them, as the experiences of a dream are real experiences though no reality corresponds to them;[1] but when nescience (*avidyā*) is overcome, the semblance of reality vanishes as the dream-reality when one awakes. So long as the state of nescience subsists, the round of death and birth continues; the only salvation is the knowledge that the phenomenal world and the individual soul have no true existence, the knowledge of the identity of Brahman-Atman. Therewith the thrall of deed is free, the round of death

---

[1] Çankara distinguishes the unreality of our waking world from that of dreams: the latter is not co-ordinated in time, space, and causality.

and birth is ended—"it cometh not again." He is "saved in this life" (*jīvanmukta*); and when the residue of former deed is exhausted, the substrata of existence are dissolved into the elements, and the soul is finally and for ever Brahman.

Salvation cannot be gained by the works of the law nor by the striving for moral perfection; knowledge alone saves. This knowledge is the opposite of all empirical knowledge in that in it the distinction of subject and object vanishes. It is not a doctrine that can be taught and accepted, even on the authority of scripture, nor can it be reached by any effort of thought. It is an experience that comes like the new birth in the Gospel of John to him that is born of the Spirit. There are, indeed, means which help put a man in the frame to attain this knowledge, but it is not the effect of these means, for the Atman is superior to the category of cause and effect.

There are, however, as has already been observed, numerous passages in the Upanishads in which Brahman appears, not as attributeless being, but as the source of all light, the life from which all beings spring, the principle of order in the universe, or as a personal god, the supreme Lord. The latter conception, relatively infrequent in the Upanishads, has a great place in the systematic Vedanta. Brahman is the creator of the world—its material as well as its efficient cause—and the ruler of the world; the lot of the soul in the round of rebirth is appointed by him in accordance with the deeds of a former life; it is by his grace that the saving knowledge comes to men. When the Upanishads thus endow Brahman with various perfections, it is —so Çankara interprets—as an object of adoration, and by way of accommodation to the limitations of men's understanding.[1] This lower knowledge of the Brahman "with at-

[1] Çankara's distinction of the two Brahmans is more explicitly anticipated in the Upanishads: "There are two manifestations of Brahman, the one personal, the other impersonal; the personal is unreal, the impersonal is real." (Maitri-Upanishad, VI, 3; *cf.* Brihadaranyaka-Upanishad, II, 3, 1.)

tributes" has its reward. The soul that has attained it takes at death the way of the gods to heavenly bliss, and progresses by stages toward true knowledge and final deliverance; it is vastly better off than those who, with no knowledge of Brahman at all, seek their good by the way of works, the old Vedic sacrifices and observances, and fare when life is over by the "way of the fathers" to the reward of their offerings in the moon; while those who have neither knowledge nor good works atone for their misdeeds in hell, thence to return to earth as beasts or as men of castes reckoned lower than beasts.

The lower, theological, knowledge cannot, however, bring salvation; for at bottom it is not knowledge but ignorance which ascribes attributes and personality to Brahman, and sets him, as creator and ruler, over against a world of finite reality, and, above all, conceives him as another and a stranger to the soul itself.

A radically different system, also in the form of a commentary on the Vedanta-Sutras of Badarayana,[1] was expounded by Ramanuja (*ca.* 1100). The author belonged to the Bhagavatas, or Pancaratras, an ancient—probably pre-Buddhistic—sect which developed the pantheistic-theistic ideas in the Upanishads into a philosophical theology. In the evolution of Hinduism the Bhagavatas identified their supreme lord with Vishnu, and contributed not a little, it may be surmised, to the higher teachings of Vishnuism. Ramanuja rejects Çankara's distinctions of a higher and a lower Brahman and the corresponding discrimination of higher and lower knowledge. Brahman is the one reality, but so far from being a metaphysical absolute, devoid of all attributes, he is endowed with all perfections; intelligence is not his essence, but his highest attribute. Brahman is all-embracing, all-pervading, all-powerful, all-knowing, all-merciful, the opposite and the enemy of all that is evil. The external world of our experience and individual souls are

[1] It is now generally admitted that Ramanuja is closer to the sense of the sutras than Çankara.

not the baseless fabric of a troubled dream, but constitute the body of the Lord, of which he is the inner ruler. The unity of Brahman is therefore not a simplicity that excludes all distinctions, but a systematic unity which embraces them all. The passages in the Upanishads which seem to contradict this view—the teachings on which the absolutist Vedanta of Çankara is based—refer, according to Ramanuja, to the periods of world-involution, when matter and souls subsist in Brahman in a germinal state; matter being "unevolved," and without those qualities by which it is empirically known, and the intelligence of disembodied souls being in a state of contraction, or non-manifestation. When this period, which we may call a resting-stage, is over, the world is created again by the will of God; the "unevolved" matter evolves and assumes the qualities with which we are familiar; the intelligence of souls expands; they are united to material bodies according to their deserts in former existences, and the round of death and birth begins again.

From this endless cycle there is no deliverance by the works of the law; but he who by the study of the Upanishads, by thinking on God and by love to him, seeks the knowledge of Brahman is aided by the grace of the Lord to attain it, and at death such a soul passes by the several stations on the way of the gods to the world of Brahman, and there abides for ever in bliss, sharing all the attributes of Brahman except only his cosmogonic functions.

The dualistic philosophy was earlier systematised than the monistic doctrine. For a long time, it seems, regarded as heretical because of its divergence from the main tendencies of Brahmanic thought, it was later counted as one of the orthodox systems, which means that it gained currency among the Brahmans and was fortified with proof-texts from the Upanishads; and not only the epic but the law-books plainly show that in the early centuries of our era it was widely accepted. The essential features of the Sankhya system have been briefly set forth above.[1] It is a pluralistic

[1] See p. 277.

realism, recognising on the one side an eternal universal matter, on the other eternal individual souls.

The primary substance is a subtle matter, not perceptible by the keenest sense; its existence is proved by the necessity of positing an ultimate uncaused cause, or, more exactly, a producer that is not a product. This substance is one, infinite, and eternal. It is composed of three constituents, the upsetting of whose equilibrium—occasioned by the proximity of souls, as iron is drawn to a magnet without the magnet's doing anything to draw it—is the cause of the evolution of worlds, and whose presence in varying proportion gives their character to all things. The soul is eternal and unchangeable; it is in its essence spiritual, pure intelligence; no attributes or qualities can be ascribed to it; it is a kind of monad absolute. Not only perception and sensation, but all psychical processes and experiences, including the self-consciousness which refers these phenomena to an ego, are not affections or activities of the soul, but functions of a psychical mechanism, the origin and construction of which are minutely described. This mechanism, which belongs wholly to the realm of the material (*prakriti*), is not an organ or instrument of the soul, nor does it produce impressions on the soul; nor, finally, is there a psychophysical parallelism between the two. The soul is entirely unaffected by what thus goes on about it.

In the "evolved," or actual, state of the universe the absolute soul is always associated with a psychical mechanism, and with an ethereal body composed of subtle material elements which in turn produce the common matter of which bodies consist. The source and substance of the misery of life, the ground of the endless succession of rebirths, is that the soul confounds itself, the true self, with the empirical self thus constituted, mistakenly imagining that it is actor or sufferer in the tragedy of existence, as though a crystal on which the image of a red hibiscus flower falls should deem that it was itself red. The salvation of the soul is the knowledge of itself as metaphysical, not as empirical ego. This dissociation makes an end at once of suffering and of the doing which is the germ of future suffering: "It is not I, it is not mine." When the residuum of deeds done in the time of ignorance is exhausted, the gross body dissolves into the earthly elements; the ethereal body, the psychical mechanism, the individuating principle which manifests itself in self-consciousness, and the emanated intelligence, return into the "unevolved" state of the primal substance out of which they sprang; and the soul remains for ever the absolute monad soul it really is, subject without object, pure spiritual intelligence without consciousness, as in the bliss of an eternal dreamless sleep.

This emancipation cannot be achieved by works; the Vedic offerings and ceremonies have not even a pædagogic use, nor do they lead to a lower and temporary blessedness in the heavens of the gods, as in the Vedanta; the whole "work branch" of the Brahmanic religion is rejected. Deeds of humanity and charity do not further a man in the way of salvation; for deeds, good as well as bad, must bear their appropriate fruit in another embodiment. Only philosophy conducts to the goal. The guidance of a teacher who has attained salvation in this life is of great use, but the knowledge itself is an intuition, not a tradition nor a conclusion of reason.

Whereas the Brahmanic Vedanta restricts salvation to the three high castes, whose members alone can fulfil the condition of Veda study, the Sankhya, like the great heresies, excludes no class or condition of men; the Çudra can achieve emancipation as well as the Brahman.

The system is highly intellectualistic; it undertakes to solve the problem of life by purely rational means. But it was far too profound and abstruse for the ordinary mind, and many who accepted it in theory sought a shorter and surer road to the saving intuition of the soul's true nature, and found it in the teaching and practice of Yoga. The name and thing are far older than the philosophical systems; in the later Upanishads it appears as a means of realising the unity of the soul with the universal soul, Brahman, and the essential features of the Yoga method already appear in these texts; but the systematised Yoga of Patanjali (second century B. C.)[1] attaches itself to the Sankhya, and accordingly presents itself as a means of realising the isolation of the soul from all that is not self, the whole realm of material reality. It is an interesting evidence of the rising tide of Hindu theism that the Yoga Sutras, while adopting the atheistic metaphysics of the Sankhya, introduce, illogically and superfluously, an otiose personal god. This god is not employed to account for the origin of matter and souls, nor for their association; he neither requites men's deeds nor delivers them from the inexorable natural law of retribution; nor, finally, is salvation a return to him and union with him; he is at most a paradigm of a blissful soul untouched by the evils of ignorance, egoism, love, hate, and attachment to life, or by deeds and their consequences.

The essence of the Yoga, as defined in the sutras, is the suppression of the intellectual functions (the psychical apparatus and all its operations belonging, it will be remembered, to the sphere of the non-ego—Prakriti); only so is the emancipation of the ego to be achieved. The method has eight stages. The first two, the observance of five prohibitions and five commandments, are not essentially different from the moral and ascetic discipline of other Indian ways of salvation. To these succeed the cultivation of postures and the regulation of breathing—in later hand-books of the Hatha-Yoga thirty-two salutary postures are enumerated and illustrated, and breathing exercises practicable only in the mythical anatomy of the Hindus. The retraction of the senses follows, compared to a tortoise drawing his head and limbs back into his shell. So far the external stages. The higher discipline comprises the binding of the thoughts, concentrated meditation, and absorption. By the last a trance is meant, in which the absolute isolation of

[1] If Patanjali be identified with the grammarian. A recent critic dates the Yoga Sutras in the fifth century A. D.

CHAPTER XIV

INDIA

HINDUISM

The Emergence of the Popular Religions—Their Character—Salvation by Divine Grace—Variety of Types—Vishnu and His Incarnations—Krishna—The Bhagavad-Gita—Rama—Vishnuite Sects—Ramanujas—Controversies Over the Doctrines of Grace—Madhvas—Vallabhas—Çaitanyas—Çiva—Çivaite Sects—Gods of Çiva's Circle—Goddesses—Worship of the Çaktis—The Triad: Brahma, Vishnu, and Çiva—Hindu Temples, Idols, Priests—Pilgrimages—Domestic Religion—The Dead and the Hereafter—The Influence of Mohammedanism in India—The Sikhs—The Brahma-Samaj and Other Theistic Reforming Sects.

OUR attention has thus far been fixed almost exclusively on the philosophies of later Vedic and post-Vedic times, which all present themselves as a way of salvation by knowledge, and on the great heresies, Jainism and Buddhism, which—notwithstanding Buddha's antipathy to metaphysics—are also essentially philosophies of salvation. Wide and deep as these movements were, they appealed by their very nature to limited circles; even when the ideas filtered into the popular mind in various dilution and confusion, they did not disturb, much less supplant, the inherited religions.

In the same centuries great changes were, however, taking place, from other causes, in these religions. The old Vedic deities were not displaced, but Indra and his peers had to yield the precedence to gods who in the hymns are but figures of secondary rank, Vishnu and Çiva. How these religions got started on their career toward supremacy is unknown. Megasthenes, who visited India about 300 B. C.

as commissioner of Seleucus Nicator to Sandracottus (Candragupta), reports that Dionysos (Çiva) was worshipped in the hills, while the worship of Herakles (Krishna) prevailed in the Ganges valley, where he was said to have founded, among other cities, Palimbothra (Patna), the capital of Sandracottus's kingdom. In the religious and didactic parts of the national epic, the Mahabharata, the growth of which extends through several centuries before and after the Christian era, Vishnu is the dominant figure, but poets of the rival faith who have contributed to it exalt Çiva to the highest place; the Ramayana, which was composed perhaps in the second or third century B. C., has for its subject one of the incarnations of Vishnu; the Puranas, the oldest of which are probably of at least equal antiquity, are the proper holy scriptures of these younger religions, for which they have the same importance as the Vedas for Brahmanism. In the following centuries the worship of Vishnu and of Çiva spread over all India, not so much supplanting the popular religions that were there before them as absorbing them; and to the present day, in their innumerable branches and subdivisions, they divide between them the two hundred millions of the population who are entered as Hindus in the religious census.

It is characteristic of these religions that each of them has a supreme personal god of much more concrete individuality than the deities of the old Vedic pantheon. We have remarked in later hymns of the Rig-Veda a monotheistic tendency which made Prajapati or Brihaspati-Brahmanaspati the author of the universe; but this priority in cosmogonic speculation does not carry with it the effective sovereignty in the actual world of nature and history which alone leads to religious monotheism. The sectarian religions in time made themselves heirs of this tendency in Brahmanism, along with others, but they did not spring from it.

The monotheism of these religions is not of the exclusive type represented by Judaism and Mohammedanism: the other gods are subordinated to the one supreme God, or identified with him. From this it may be inferred with considerable probability that the supreme gods were originally the chief gods of certain tribes, or groups of tribes, comparatively little affected by Brahmanism, which in these centuries emerged into political prominence. Their victories in war or their success in founding states brought their gods into corresponding prominence, somewhat as the Aryan invasion of India many centuries before had made Indra the greatest of the gods in the Rig-Veda.

One of these gods, called by his worshippers "the great god" (Mahadeva) or "the propitious" (Çiva), was perhaps from the beginning identical with the Vedic Rudra, whose wild and cruel character he has maintained in bloody sacrifices and orgiastic revels. The other is identified with Vishnu, a Vedic deity highly honoured in the hymns, where already some of the exploits of Indra are ascribed to him.[1] Vishnu is a much more civilised god than Çiva, as becomes the god of more civilised tribes or regions. Both religions exhibit their unbrahmanical origin and character in having temples, images or material symbols of the deity, and a temple priesthood (not necessarily of the Brahman caste)— all at variance with the old Vedic tradition and the Brahman law.[2]

By the time when they first make their entrance into literature, however, they had already been drawn into the main current of Indian theological development. The cosmogonic myths and speculations are appropriated for the sectarian gods; sectarian Upanishads echo the pantheistic note; and in the epic the ideas of the Vedanta and the Sankhya-Yoga jostle one another. In revenge, the firmer theism of the new religions compels concessions both from the absolutism of the Vedanta and the atheism of the Sankhya; the theistic Vedanta and the deistic Yoga are witnesses to the power of the idea of a personal god in Vish-

[1] See above, pp. 253 f.
[2] The law-books forbid Brahmans to serve as priests of the non-Vedic religions.

nuism and Çivaism. The Brahman priesthood, following
the movements of the times, made of the vaguely personal
Brahman of some Upanishads a god more after the type of
the new religions. The whole religious history of India
from that time on is the result of the confluence of these
two streams.

In another more important respect the sectarian religions
fell into line with the previous development: they were
doubtless in the beginning natural religions; they may have
come into prominence as tribal religions; but from our first
knowledge of them they offer not only the good gifts of God
in this life, but salvation from the round of retributive rebirths—something which the Brahmanic religion (as distinct
from the philosophies) had never undertaken to do. But
they make the great salvation depend primarily, not on
works—that good works as well as evil involved a man in
the consequences of works, that is, in the round of rebirth,
was then axiomatic—not on knowledge of the absolute
Brahman-Atman or of the transcendental monad Ego, and
not on the suppression of the activity of the soul or the extinction of the will to be by the circumstantial methods of
Jain or Buddhist monks, but on devotion to a saving god.

Hitherto it had been universally assumed that man must
achieve his own salvation by works or by knowledge; the
new religions proclaimed salvation the gracious gift of God
to men who seek it of him in faith and love. It is possible
that this solution of the problem of salvation which had tormented India for centuries did not originate in either Vishnuism or Çivaism, but was adopted from a sect which worshipped its divine Saviour under some other name; but,
wherever the doctrine came from, it was these religions whose
essentially theistic character gave it meaning and power.
This was a way of salvation for the masses of men, a way
they could comprehend, and by which they might hope to
attain deliverance. The spread of the new religions, not
only among the less advanced peoples of the peninsula, but
in regions and classes in which Brahmanism, on the one hand,

and Buddhism, on the other, had had the greatest influence, is thus explained. But, conversely, the influx of seekers of salvation by other methods brought all these methods over into the sectarian religions; in particular, asceticism of both the Sannyasin and the Yogin types.

In the course of their expansion both religions have incorporated a multitude of local and aboriginal gods and cults, which are in theory regarded as manifestations or forms of the one supreme God, but for the uninstructed worshipper remain the venerable gods they were for his forefathers before this benevolent assimilation. Vishnuism and Çivaism are thus actually vast amorphous conglomerates of the most heterogeneous elements; monotheistic in essence, multifarious and grotesque polytheisms in semblance, with pantheism for a harmonising principle. In addition to the great number of popular religions of wider or narrower vogue which have been taken up into the two great branches of Hinduism, hundreds of sects, founded by individual teachers, have sprung up, flourished, split, fused, fallen into decay, and died out in the centuries, and the same process is still going on. Hinduism is therefore a protean phenomenon; every attempt to describe it must confine itself to certain salient features, but in so doing runs the risk of making an impression of simplicity and unity which is widely remote from the truth.

On the Vishnuite side, Vishnu is not so much worshipped in his own person as some of his incarnations (*avatāras*, descents), foremost among which are Krishna and Rama. The doctrine of incarnation is specifically Vishnuite: "Every time that religion is in danger and that iniquity triumphs," says the god in the Bhagavad-Gita, "I issue forth. For the defence of the good and the suppression of the wicked, for the establishment of justice, I manifest myself from age to age." A complete Avatara is not a mere self-manifestation of God in a human form, nor the production of an intermediate being, but a real incarnation of the supreme God in a human being, who is at the same time truly God and truly man;

and this union of two natures is not dissolved by death, but continues to eternity. The importance of this theory is obvious: it gave men gods who were truly and completely human, who contended and suffered in men's behalf; gods who could be touched with the feeling of our infirmities, because they were tried in all points as we are; gods whom men could not only revere across the awful distance between finite and infinite, but love, as they loved their fellows, and be assured of God's responsive love. On the other hand, the theory made it possible to transform all the native religions of India into orthodox Vishnuism by merely declaring the old gods incarnations of Vishnu; even animal worship created no difficulty, for Vishnu had repeatedly been embodied in an animal.

The Krishna incarnation is, perhaps, the oldest, and was possibly the starting-point of the whole theory; in any case it is religiously the most important. The legend of Krishna is in brief outline this: He was of the race of the Yadavas and was born at Mathura (on the Jamna between Delhi and Agra), his father was Vasudeva, his mother Devaka. King Kamsa, his uncle, had been informed by an oracle that the eighth son of this pair would kill him, and to avert this fate put his nephews out of the world as fast as they came into it. Krishna's parents therefore secretly conveyed him to the other side of the river, where, in company with an older brother, Balarama, who had been saved in a miraculous way, he was brought up by a herdsman and his wife. The brothers spent their youth in the forest, fighting dragons and demons and making love to the cow-girls of the region. The bad uncle heard reports of the exploits of the young herdsmen, and, suspecting the truth, summoned them to court, to his own undoing; Krishna became king of the Yadavas. After many victories over human and demonic enemies, he took part, as the charioteer of Arjuna, in the internecine war between the Kauravas and the Pandavas which is the central theme of the Mahabharata. Many years after, strife broke out over a trivial matter among the Yadavas and they slew one another to the last man. Krishna himself was soon after accidentally killed by the arrow of a hunter which wounded him in the heel, his only vulnerable point.

Krishna's participation in the great eighteen days' battle gives occasion for the introduction into the epic of the Bhagavad-Gita, to which we shall return below; the sacred legend of Krishna is really the story of his infancy and youth in the forests of Vrindavana, and the scenes of his adventures there are the holy places of the Krishna cult. It must be admitted that the legend is not particularly edifying; in it Krishna is a very human, not to say all-too-human, hero; but religious devotion is capable of extracting nourishment from strange sources. What is fairly clear is that in the oldest epic Krishna was a chieftain of the Yadavas, a herdsman tribe, not an incarnate god; and even in the story of the infancy he does not wear his godhead all the time.

How this hero came to be Vishnu in the flesh can only be conjectured. An hypothesis for which a good deal can be said is that the real Krishna was not only a warrior but a religious reformer, who taught his people to worship God under the name Bhagavata, "the Adorable." After his death he became himself an object of religious veneration, was regarded as an incarnation of the Adorable.[1] The identification with Vishnu, a Vedic deity, would be a contribution of the Brahmans, who thus threw the mantle of orthodoxy over a popular religion and, so to speak, asserted their right over it. Brahmanic theology is the source also of the sectarian doctrine that makes Krishna the Paramatman, or Supreme Soul, one, eternal, without qualities, exempt from the cosmic illusion (Maya), conferring upon him thus the attributes of Brahman.

In all the voluminous sacred literature of India no book has exerted so profound and universal an influence on the religious thought and life of Hinduism in all its branches as

[1] See Grierson, "Bhakti-marga," Encyclopædia of Religion and Ethics, II, 540 *f.*

the Bhagavad-Gita. It is current in hundreds of editions, many of which are issued by societies or individuals at small price or for free distribution, as the New Testament is circulated among us. When it first became known in Europe through translations it excited much enthusiasm; Wilhelm von Humboldt declared it the most beautiful—nay, perhaps the only truly philosophical—poem in the literature of the world. In theosophical circles it has been still more extravagantly lauded as the gospel of the only true faith. The Western reader who takes up the book without preconceptions and tries to understand it and the secret of its power finds it, with all its elevation of sentiment and poetic beauty of expression, repetitious, confused, and self-contradictory—a complex of conflicting ideas standing in unmediated juxtaposition. This very fact is one source of its wide-spread influence: every kind of opinion finds itself in the poem—the orthodox Brahman his offerings and their fruits; the Vedantist his All-One; the Sankhyan his Matter and Spirit; the Yogin his practical method; the theist his personal God—by whatever way man prefers to seek salvation he will find that way enounced and commended in the Gita: works, knowledge, faith, and various combinations of these; inactive reflection and unflinching action in the way of duty.

In explanation of these inconsistencies it has been maintained that the Bhagavad-Gita, like the epic in which it is embedded, represents a transitional philosophy in which, as yet not thought out to their consequences nor conscious of their discord, the ideas lay side by side which afterward were developed in the great Indian systems. To most students, however, it appears more probable that the phenomenon is to be ascribed to additions to the original poem and interpolations by various hands rather than to the confused mind of the author. And this view is confirmed by the fact that many of the passages whose content is at variance with the main tenor of the teaching interrupt the continuity or disturb by repetition the progress of the thought. Leaving aside the first arguments of Krishna, with which he urges

Arjuna to plunge into the battle and fearlessly slay or be slain—a discourse which has no inner connection with what follows—there are two easily distinguishable elements which are foreign to the dominant conception of the poem, the one Vedantic pantheism, the other the Brahman commendation of the "way of works." What remains, and what we have reason to believe to be in substance the original poem, is purely theistic.

In this Vishnu-Krishna is the supreme personal God. The human soul is eternally personal. Its highest good is to abide for ever in a godlike existence in the presence of God. This great salvation is attained by love of God and devotion to him, from which alone springs the saving knowledge of God. Not only knowledge but morality has its root in love of God. "That worshipper of mine who cherishes no hate against any being, but is full only of friendliness and compassion, who is free from self-seeking and from the illusion of self, to whom sorrow and joy are the same, always patient and content, given to meditation, self-controlled, resolute, with heart and mind set on me, and loves me— he is dear to me. He before whom none are disquieted, and who is disquieted before none, free from elation and vexation, fear and disquiet—he also is dear to me. He who is unconcerned about the things of this world, who is pure, impartial, untroubled, undertaking nothing from self-interest, —he is dear to me." The gist of all the moral teaching of the Gita is contained in what the commentators call the quintessential verse: "He who does all his works for my sake, who is wholly devoted to me, who loves me, who is free from attachment to earthly things, and without hate to any being, he, O son of Pandu, enters into me."

The conception of the universe which everywhere underlies the original poem is pluralistic, but while in the scholastic Sankhya matter is eternal and instinct with all the forces of evolution, thus leaving no room for a divine author either of primeval matter or of the existing cosmic order, in the Bhagavad-Gita, as in the sectarian theisms, the supreme

God is creator as well as saviour. The Yoga teaching has also a large place in the poem, but its technical methods are not so prominent as the motive and end of its discipline—to learn to act in this world as necessity or duty demands without by action entangling one's self in the world through the attachment of desire, or, to express it in terms more familiar to us, to do a man's duty in this world for God's sake, in utter disregard of the consequences to himself, either in this life or in another.

Second in importance only to Krishna is the incarnation of Vishnu as Rama, and here also the same problem arises: Rama was clearly an epic hero before he was Vishnu incarnate, and the motive of the transformation is no more obvious in his case than in that of Krishna. The story of Rama in the epic Ramayana may be epitomised as follows:

Rama was the favourite son of a king of Ayodhya (Oudh), and his designated successor. The king had long before promised the mother of another son to fulfil for her one wish; she demands the throne for her son and the banishment of Rama for fourteen years. Accompanied by Sita, his devoted wife, and by a brother, Lakshmana, Rama dutifully wanders forth. The father dies of a broken heart; the brother, Bharata, summoned from a distant land to assume the government, scorning to take advantage of his mother's intrigue, follows Rama and tries in vain to persuade him to take the throne which is rightfully his; but he, as a filial son, holds himself bound by his father's decree, and concedes only that Bharata may rule as his vicegerent during the exile. In the forest whither they have retired, Rama and Lakshmana wage war on demonic monsters; Rama's prowess captivates a she-demon, and she makes frank advances to him; repulsed by both brothers, and enraged by the insult, she appeals to her brother, the demon Ravana, a ten-headed monster whose power alarms the very gods, further inciting him by describing the marvellous beauty of Sita. While the brothers are abroad in the forest, Ravana seizes

Sita and flies with her through the air to his kingdom in remote Ceylon. Having learned what has become of her, the brothers enter into alliance with the king of the monkeys. Hanumat, the shrewdest of the monkey tribe and at the same time the champion broad-jumper, clears the straits at a single leap, discovers Sita, assures her that deliverance is at hand, and returns to Rama. A bridge of rocks, which can still be seen, is thrown across the straits; the monkey host besieges the capital of Ravana, and after many battles, with varying fortunes, the climax comes in a single combat between Rama and Ravana, in which with the aid of the gods Rama is victorious. The purity of Sita is proved by a kind of ordeal by fire, and the reunited pair return under escort of the whole tribe of monkeys to Oudh, where Rama, the years of exile being at an end, is enthroned as king amid universal rejoicing. The seventh book, obviously a later addition to the poem, relates how Rama allows his mind to be poisoned by suspicion of Sita and banishes her. Despite the assurance of the great ascetic Valmiki, he insists on purgation by oath. At this ceremony all the gods assist. Sita invokes the goddess Earth, as she has been ever faithful to her husband in thought and word and deed, to open her bosom to receive her, and, her honour thus vindicated, sinks into the earth, whence—as her own name Sita ("furrow") tells—she came.

In all the proper action of the poem, richly embellished as it is with supernatural incident, there is no sign of the incarnate god; in the first book, however, the gods, harassed by the demon Ravana, persuade Vishnu to be born on earth to destroy the monster, and he chooses to be born as the son of the good king of Kosala. By virtue of the religious appropriation and transformation of the legend, the Rama-yana has become a favourite and influential source of moral instruction and edification. Rama is the type of the filial son, Sita of the faithful wife, Lakshmana of the devoted brother. Rama is also everywhere accorded a high place among Vishnuite deities, though the sectarians who are devoted specifically to Rama above all others are not as numerous as the adherents of many other cults.

The number of the "descents" of Vishnu is reckoned all the way from ten to infinity; many of these are, however, partial incarnations, in which the god does not descend in his full divine nature, and many are poetical figures without further religious significance. The founders of sects, in their lifetime or after their death, have often been recognised by their followers as incarnations of Vishnu, and this theory is occasionally extended to hostile or heretical sects—for example, the Lord became embodied in Buddha in order to lead his enemies astray to their undoing.[1] When Vishnu descends to earth and becomes incarnate as a man, his wife, Çri or Lakshmi, usually descends at the same time and becomes a woman; thus the favourite wife of Krishna, Radha, is an incarnation of Lakshmi, as is also Sita, the wife of Rama.

The Vishnuites are divided into many sects, distinguished partly by theological or philosophical doctrines, partly by external peculiarities. One of the most important of these branches of Vishnuism are the Ramanujas, who claim as their founder that Ramanuja whom we have already met as a commentator on the Vedanta-Sutras. He taught, as we have seen, that there are three principles, the Supreme Being, individual souls, and "non-soul" (the material universe), which have an eternal and distinct existence. In the periodical involutions of the universe, human souls are latent in God, but without losing their separate identity. God is manifest on earth in images, in partial and in complete incarnations, in the all-pervading spirit, and in the spirit within man ruling the human soul. Only when man recognises and adores the god enshrined in his heart, the spirit that guides his own spirit, does Vishnu take him to himself in his own heaven, where, free from fear of rebirth, he enjoys for ever the blessedness of God's presence, of likeness

---

[1] There is a sect, however, which worships Buddha as an incarnation of Vishnu, in the character of a teacher of religion.

to God, of oneness with God; absorbed in God, yet without losing personal consciousness.

Controversies in the thirteenth century divided the Ramanujas into two branches between which there was acute controversy. The northern school maintains that the female counterpart of Vishnu is, like him, infinite and uncreated, and that through worship addressed to her salvation may be attained; the southerners hold that, though divine, she is a created and finite being, a minister or mediator, not an author of salvation.

The sharpest conflict, however, was over the doctrines of grace. The principle that salvation is the gift of God, attained neither by works nor knowledge, but through faith and devotion to God (*bhakti*), raised in India the questions which have divided Christian theologians: Is faith a free act of man, or is it infused by God? Is God's grace alone operative in salvation and man purely passive, or does man co-operate with God? The southern school were the Augustinians or Calvinists of Vishnuism, adherents, in their own phrase, of the "cat-hold theory," namely, that a man has no more part in his own salvation than the helpless kitten which its mother seizes by the nape of the neck and lugs out of danger. The northern branch were synergists; theirs was the "monkey doctrine"—man is like the baby monkey, which, when its mother takes it up to carry it to a place of safety, hangs on with all the strength of its little arms. These doctrinal differences are now matters of historical orthodoxy rather than of present-day concern; but the two parties still stand obstinately apart, wearing their sectarian mark on their forehead—one foot of Vishnu or both feet. Each branch has a head, who claims to be the successor of the founder in an unbroken line; like a Christian bishop, he makes periodical visitations of the communities of his sect in different districts, in which the boys at the age of seven or upward, and the girls after marriage, are confirmed by being stamped on the breast and arms with the discus and conch-shell emblems of Vishnu.

Next in importance to the Ramanujas are the Madhvas, who are almost confined to the south. The founder, whose name they bear, is said to have lived in the thirteenth century, and was peculiarly zealous in opposing the monism of Çankara. The Supreme Lord, he argued, is different from the human soul, because he is the object of its obedience; a subject who obeys a king differs from the king, and this distinct individuality is eternal. The elements of the material universe existed from eternity in God; they were ordered and arranged by his power and will, but not created *ex nihilo;* having once emanated from God, however, the world abides for ever a distinct entity, though not, as with Ramanuja, an independent principle. The worship of Vishnu is threefold: branding with the symbols of the god; giving children one of his names or titles; and venerating him in word, by truth, kindness, friendliness, and study of the Veda; in deed by alms-giving and by saving and protecting living things; and in thought by sympathy, zeal, and faith.

A third sect are the followers of Vallabha, who flourished in the early sixteenth century and embodied his teachings in a commentary on the Bhagavata-Purana. He drew the antiascetic consequence of a doctrine of salvation by grace, namely, that God is not pleased by self-mortification; the satisfaction of natural appetites and the enjoyment of the good things of this life are not evil in themselves and are no hindrance to salvation. His successors carried the principle to extremes; they assumed the title Maharaja (great king), and lived in luxury and often, unless their reputation grossly maligns them, in degrading sensuality. The sect especially affects the worship of Krishna the child; the images in their temples represent him as a boy under twelve years old. The loves of Krishna and the cow-girls are allegorically interpreted of the yearning of the soul for union with God. The heads of the sect, the so-called Maharajas, are regarded as Krishna's representatives, or even as his embodiments, and are adored as earthly gods with incense and offerings; the water in which such a holy man has washed his feet is drunk, the very dust he has trodden upon is eaten, as being charged with a miraculous virtue exuding from the divine man; complete self-surrender to the service of these gods of clay, even in the gratification of their grossest passions, is promised a heavenly reward. The Gosains, or teachers, of this sect are usually married, well-dressed, and well-fed; to put body, mind, and property at the disposal of the teacher is a fundamental article of religion for their followers.

The founder of another Vishnuite sect, Caitanya, was born in 1485 in Bengal, where its adherents are still most numerous. He drew another inference from the doctrine of salvation by grace, namely, that "the mercy of God regards neither tribe nor family"; all believers are equal before God without regard to distinction of caste.[1] Devout faith in Krishna is the only way of salvation, as is taught in the Bhagavata-Purana.

Of this devotion there are, according to Caitanya, five stages or degrees: calm contemplation of the godhead, the attitude of a slave to his master, personal friendship, filial affection, and, highest of all, self-surrendering love, like that of a maiden for her lover. Various bodily exercises are prescribed for inducing ecstasies in which the soul loses itself in God. The founder of the sect passes for an incarnation of Krishna and his two chief disciples for partial embodiments of the same deity; their successors to the present time, like the *gurus*, or teachers, of other sects, exercise great authority and are accorded little less than divine honours. The endless repetition of Krishna's names, particularly of the name Hari, takes a man to Vishnu's heaven, just as in the Jodo sect of Japanese Buddhists the repetition of the name of Amida Buddha secures entrance to the Western Paradise.

[1] In actual fact, this indiscriminateness does not extend beyond the sphere of religious observances; socially the ordinary caste lines are observed.

In all Hindu sects the names of the deity are of much importance; Vishnu has a round thousand, Çiva's catalogue exceeds this by eight. Many of them are the commonplaces with which men of all tongues and creeds glorify God—all-seeing, all-knowing, all-powerful; or by which theologians define him—infinite, self-existent, all-pervading, and the like; among the more notable titles of Vishnu are the holy, or the holiest, the true, the pure spirit, the way, the truth, the life, the healer, the world's medicine.

Çiva has no incarnations like Vishnu; but the various gods who are identified with him are said to be "forms" of Çiva. He is, like his prototype the Vedic Rudra, a destructive deity, and is described as a grotesquely horrible monster, in imagery drawn in part from the Hundred-Rudra litany in the Yajur-Veda. In becoming the supreme god of one of the great branches of Hinduism he has not lost this character; but other sides of his nature have acquired greater prominence, while the merely malevolent traits have been passed over to his female worse half. He is the author of life as well as its destroyer, and personifies the reproductive forces of nature, for which reason the bull and the phallus (*lingam*) are his common symbols. The orgiastic features of his cult which led Megasthenes to identify him with Dionysos, his fondness for hunting, drinking, and dancing, are but one side—doubtless the older side—of his complex character. On the other he is the ascetic god, who sits naked, with matted hair and body besmeared with ashes, under the Pipal-tree, and as the "Great Yogin," by self-mortification and age-long meditation, has attained supernatural knowledge and power. Again, he is the divine philosopher and sage, and is represented as a Brahman skilled in the Vedas; Panini's grammar is a revelation from Çiva. In fact, the learned Brahmans seem inclined to acknowledge Çiva as Lord rather than Vishnu, but stand aloof, for the most part, from sectarian Çivaism.

Çivaism has not been so prolific in divisions over doctrinal questions as the rival faith, and of sects which existed in the Middle Ages the greater part have lost their separate identity. The most numerous in the south to-day are the Lingayits (so called from wearing the *lingam* as an amulet); they reject the authority of the Vedas and of the Brahmans, recognise no caste distinctions, and bury their dead instead of burning them. There are also many species of Çivaite ascetics, commonly called Yogins, distinguished more by external peculiarities than by beliefs; they are generally filthy beggars and often otherwise vile.

The theological affinities of Çivaism were originally with the pluralism of the Sankhya-Yoga system rather than with Vedantic monism; but the theistic modification of the Vedanta was equally compatible with their religious conceptions, and doctrines closely similar to those of the Ramanujas are attributed to Çivaite teachers. An idealistic Çivaism, wholly Vedantic, was developed in Cashmere between the ninth and eleventh centuries by Somananda and Abhinavagupta: God is the only substance, objects are his ideas; and as he is identical with ourselves, these objects are really in us. What we think we see outside of us we see within. The individual ego perceives, or rather reperceives, in itself, as in a mirror, the ideas of the transcendental Ego, and cognition is only a recognition. By inner contemplation, and enlightened by the grace which it has received through faith in Çiva, the soul overcomes the illusion (Maya) which is the source of all diversity, and attains the consciousness of self in God. This system is Çivaite only in the sense that the name Çiva is given to the theistic-pantheistic deity.

Of the gods grouped about Çiva in the sectarian pantheon the most important are Ganeça and Skanda. The former, represented with an elephant's head, symbolical of his shrewdness, is, as his name imports, the lord of troops (that is, the troops of good and bad demons that form the train of Çiva), who can restrain them from harassing men or leave them free hand to work their malign will. By thwarting their wiles he gives success to men's plans, and so becomes the bestower of prosperity. Skanda is the general who leads the hosts of good demons in the conflict with the powers of evil, and thus, as the marshal of the divine allies, is the war-god in the epic, supplanting Indra, with whom he is identified. To Çiva's company belongs also Kubera, the god of riches.

The goddesses play a far larger part in Çivaism than in the Vedic religion or in Vishnuism. They are, in theory, one, the consort of Çiva, worshipped under many names and attributes: Devi, the goddess; Gauri, the bright one; Sati, the faithful wife; Parvati, the daughter of the mountains; Durga, the unapproachable; Kali, the black one; Bhairavi, the terrible; Karala, the horrible. The last names indicate the predominating character of the goddesses, to whom the unfriendly features of Çiva's nature have in large measure been handed over. They are worshipped as deities in their own right, and bloody sacrifices and cruel rites belong specifically to their cults. Another large class of female deities are the "Mothers," local tutelary divinities, of which each village has its own, or functional divinities with highly specialised spheres of activity—one causes cholera, another averts it; one keeps away mad dogs, another sends smallpox, and so on. They are often propitiated with the blood of fowls or goats.

A feature original in Çivaism, though not confined to it,[1] is the worship of female deities as active powers (*çakti*) of the supreme God. The god himself abides, as philosophers say he should, in bliss untroubled by the administration of a universe; while his "energies" in female personification— like the δυνάμεις of Philo's system—are the efficient causes of all that comes to pass in the world. As a matter of course, these productive energies are identified with Çiva's consort, Mahadevi, "the great goddess," who is at the same time the great illusion (Mahamaya) of the Vedantist or the primal substance (Prakriti) of the Sankhyan. Besides the public cultus, which, except for the offering of bloody sac-

[1] Tantric Buddhism has its Taras, who are the Çaktis of Çiva under another name.

rifices to Durga or Kali, conforms to the common Hindu type, there are sects (Çaktas of the left hand) whose worship of the powers takes the form of mysteries. These sects have scriptures of their own (Tantras), which chiefly purport to be revelations from Çiva, in the form of dialogue with his wife, Durga. Like the Puranas, they are supposed to deal with five subjects—the creation and destruction of the world, the worship of the gods, the attainment of supernatural powers, union with the Supreme Being. The last two, particularly the supernatural powers, are the chief objects of pursuit, and consequently the magical element is prominent in the Tantras.

These Çaktas are strictly secret societies, and in such ill repute that no one with a shadow of respectability would admit connection with them; in their own circle they call themselves "the perfect," and speak of outsiders as "beasts." The members are initiated by a teacher, who communicates to them certain texts or mystic syllables; the utmost precautions are taken to conceal the teachings and practices of the sect. The mysteries are celebrated by a circle of men and women seated promiscuously, without regard to caste or kinship. In one of their texts Çiva says to his wife: "All men have my form and all women thy form; any one who recognises any distinction of caste in the mystic circle has a foolish soul." The performances consist of drinking various kinds of wine and strong drinks, eating of meat, of fish, and of parched grain, and finally of copulation. The only salvation, according to one of their Tantras, is that which results from spirituous liquors, meat, and cohabitation with women. These orgies are magical-mystical rites; each pair is for the hour Çiva and Devi, and through the texts which detail these abominations runs a vein not only of moral reflection but of religious exaltation.[1]

The rivalry of the religions of Vishnu and Çiva has sometimes led to violent collisions, but in the present they live

[1] Whether these mysteries are actually celebrated nowadays is doubtful; at all events they must be infrequent.

in the main peaceably side by side, with some degree of mutual recognition. The worshipper of Vishnu is content to regard Çiva as a minister of the Most High or as a divine prophet and *doctor doctorum*, and the Çivaite is similarly accommodating. The two are even coupled and adored as one god under the name Hari-Hara, to whom numerous temples are dedicated, particularly in the south. Elsewhere the shrines of the two gods are often close beside each other, sometimes within the same sacred precincts.

Beside Vishnu and Çiva stands Brahma,[1] the All-Father —the personal god whom theistic religion made out of the metaphysical absolute, Brahman (neuter)—and forms with them a triad (*trimūrti*). In what may be called the orthodox, that is, the Brahmanical, form of this triad, Brahman, the Absolute, manifests himself in three persons of equal rank—Brahma, the creator, Vishnu, the preserver, and Çiva, the destroyer. Kalidasa sings:

> "In those Three Persons the one God was shown—
> Each first in place, each last—not one alone;
> Of Çiva, Vishnu, Brahma, each may be
> First, second, third, among the Blessed Three."

The three persons are connected in the Puranic doctrine with the three qualities, or constituents, of the Sankhya. When activity prevails, the supreme being is Brahma, the creator; when goodness, Vishnu, the preserver; when apathy, Çiva, the destroyer. This theory naturally did not satisfy the sectaries who worshipped either Vishnu or Çiva as in reality the one God, and they modified it to conform to their own premises, usually identifying their Lord outright with the Supreme Being and subordinating the two other members of the triad. Inasmuch, moreover, as the religions of Vishnu and Çiva felt themselves more closely akin to each other than to the Brahman theology, Brahma usually gets the last place in the sectarian triad, which is Vishnu, Çiva,

[1] Only a very few temples are dedicated to Brahma, and he has no exclusive worshippers.

Brahma; or Çiva, Vishnu, Brahma. In none of its forms is this triad very old; the three-headed figure on the island of Elephanta, near Bombay, formerly interpreted as a Trimurti but now regarded rather as a representation of Çiva, is probably not older than the tenth century of our era. Nor has the formula ever had any considerable religious significance: it is a method of reconciling the claims of rival monotheistic religions with one another and with a traditional philosophy. Groups of three gods, or the classification of gods in three groups, may have suggested the idea, if any suggestion was needed. The origin of the formula is thus sufficiently accounted for from native premises, without the supposition that the Christian Trinity—the resemblance to which is wholly superficial—stood model for the Hindu Trimurti, though such a supposition is exposed to no chronological objection: Christianity had long been established in India before the Trimurti is heard of.

The old Vedic religion had, as we have seen, no temples or other permanent places of religious worship; the spot chosen for sacrifice was consecrated for the occasion and was sacred only for the duration of the ceremonies. Hinduism, however, in both its great branches, has innumerable temples, some of them of imposing size and splendour, others modest village shrines. In contrast again to the older religion, both have material representations of the gods. The commonest emblem of Çiva is the phallus (*lingam*), ordinarily accompanied by the corresponding female organ (*yoni*), together symbolising the productive powers of nature. Contrary to a prevailing impression, neither the conventional form of these objects nor the cultus has any obscene suggestion. The other gods are usually represented by idols, many of which are to our taste grotesquely hideous—a human body with an elephant's head; tricephalous monsters; heads with a third eye in the middle of the forehead; human trunks with supernumerary arms and legs, and the like. It should be remembered, however, that all this ugliness is symbolical; the supernatural powers of the deity are intended to be expressed by these unnatural forms. The Hindu gods are less beautiful than the purely anthropomorphic gods of Greek art, because of the effort to make them more manifestly divine. Besides the idols set up for worship in the temples, great numbers are made to serve as ex-votos or to be tutelary genii of the household. As in other countries, these objects become holy only after a priest, with appropriate rites, has invited the god to lodge in them.

The larger temples have a numerous personnel of priests and attendants of various degrees and functions; many support also a band of musicians and a troop of dancing-girls for the delectation of gods and men. The priests who minister to the idols have to wake them up in the morning, bathe them, paint their faces, dress them, burn incense and wave lights before them, present them flowers, drinking water, and cooked food (chiefly rice), which is afterward consumed by the priests or distributed among the worshippers. The usual tendance of Çiva's symbol consists in pouring water on the standing stone and laying bilva leaves upon it; but in some places it is treated like the idols. There is no public cultus other than this; even when multitudes assemble in the temple, each comes about his personal concern.

To places of high repute for holiness pilgrims come from great distances, and at high festivals vast numbers congregate from all quarters. Among the holy cities of India, Benares takes the foremost place; every pious Hindu aspires to make at least one pilgrimage thither, and it is common belief that those who die within the encircling road, whatever crimes they may have been guilty of, go straight to Çiva's heaven; even Christians and Moslems share this blessing. To bathe here in the sacred Ganges or in one of the holy tanks is to be cleansed of every sin. There are upward of fifteen hundred temples in the city to a population of some two hundred thousand. Many other places draw vast numbers of pilgrims, such, for example, as the shrine of Vishnu at Jagannath in Orissa. A pilgrimage by which the highest merit is acquired is to go afoot from Benares, carry-

ing a jar of the holy Ganges water to pour on the *lingam* in
the temple of Rameçvara, on an island in the extreme south,
a journey of nearly twelve hundred miles. Many rivers
besides the Ganges are holy, not because they are sacred to
a deity, but because their waters are pervaded by the divine
essence, and have therefore the power to remove all sin and
bestow the immortality of the gods. Allahabad, where the
Ganges and the Jamna meet and the Sarasvati is believed to
join its waters by underground channels with theirs, is triply
holy. In the south the Godavari, Narbada, Kistna, and
Kaveri have the like power.

As in the ancient law-books, the whole domestic life of
the modern Hindu is inwoven with religion, from the auspicious naming of the child, through the boy's investiture
with the sacred cord of the twice-born (if he belong to one of
the castes which are capable of this second birth), and his
marriage, to the burning of his dead body. Similarly in his
daily life, from the cleansing of his teeth and the morning
bath—his first business on rising, and very important religious purifications—to the last waking moment, there are
prescriptions and observances innumerable, especially for
the Brahmans, whose obligations are proportioned to their
privileges. These acts are accompanied by the proper formulas of devotion, some of them ancient Vedic prayers and
invocations, others found in the Tantras of the sectarian
religions.

In almost every house is a shrine where the inmates or
their representative perform religious worship each morning. The shrine contains images of the gods, or, in the
south more commonly, five stones supposed to be instinct
with the divine essence; the black Çalagrama of Vishnu, the
white stone of Çiva, the red of Ganeça, a bit of ore for Devi,
and a piece of crystal representing the sun, differently grouped
on a metal plate according to the precedence the worshipper
chooses to give to one or other of them. To these, orthodox
Brahmans add the ancient Vaiçvadeva ceremony with its
offering of cooked food to Agni, the divine fire, and to all the

gods, spirits, and living beings. The domestic meal itself is surrounded by religious forms.

Burning of the dead has been for many centuries general, except in the case of young children and great saints. If it is possible, the body is borne, even before death, to the banks of a holy river; otherwise various precautions are taken to keep the messengers of hell at bay, such as surrounding the bed with a ring of cow dung, or putting a sacred stone and plant by its side; or a cow may be brought, that the dying man may seize her tail and thus be transported across the waters of death. The burning takes place on an open pyre; when the body is partly consumed, the top of the skull is cracked by a blow with a club to make sure that the soul has an open exit. The bones are subsequently collected in an urn and deposited in the ground, from which they are again removed after a few days to be thrown into the Ganges or some other sacred waters. Offerings of balls of rice and clarified butter are made in connection with the cremation and the bone-gathering. Offering and ceremonies for the benefit of the dead (*çrāddha*) should be held within a month after his decease, followed by a feast on the next day for the Brahmans. In a simpler form the Çraddha should be repeated monthly for a year, and thereafter on each anniversary of the death. The daily religious observances of every householder include an offering of water to the ancestors generally, which, unlike the homage to the gods, cannot be deputed to another person.

The prevailing beliefs about the state of the dead have undergone considerable change in the course of centuries and under the influence of the theistic religions. Salvation means in these religions an immortality of conscious blessedness in the heaven of Vishnu or Krishna or of Çiva, and all faith and observance exist to insure immediate entrance on this state. Over against these heavens stands a whole array of hells, commonly counted twenty-one or twenty-eight. Yama, once the ruler of the blessed dead, has become the infernal judge and executioner; his two messengers bind the soul of the dead man and hurry him before Yama's judgment seat; there he is confronted by the recorder with his book, in which all the man's deeds, good and bad, are set down. The account of merit and demerit is balanced up to the last moment, including on the credit side his religious devotion and observances—the latter taken at an extravagant valuation compared with moral derelictions. The rites performed by his relatives after his death are also imputed to him as merit.

On the thirteenth day, the soul having in the meantime grown a kind of intermediate body, the minions of Yama conduct it either to heaven or hell. The road to the latter is eighty-six thousand leagues long, and the hardships the hapless sinner encounters upon it are a foretaste of the torments to which he is being hurried. Plunged at last into the particular hell to which he has been adjudged, he may find himself in a *bolgia* full of heated caldrons, or of red-hot irons, or in a lake of blood or stinking mire, or be driven through a jungle where the leaves of the plants are sharp knives, or a plain paved with iron spikes; there is a hell of pincers with which the flesh is torn from the bones, and many more. These hells are not places of eternal punishment; the doctrine of rebirth, the transmigration of souls, maintains its place, and serves its old use in explaining the inequalities of earthly fortune; but it no longer casts its pall of terror over all life as it did for the age of the great heresies, partly, perhaps, because the more vivid imagination of hell has superseded it, but chiefly because man no longer faces the problem of saving himself from the succession of rebirths, under the inexorable law of the deed that cannot be undone, without help from god or man; the gods of Hinduism are saviours of those who put their trust in them, and that confidence stills the fear of rebirth as well as of death.

The pessimism, too, which lies at the root of the Sankhya philosophy and the great heretical religions, Jainism and Buddhism, was, at least in its acute despair of the world, a passing phase of Indian thought; on large parts of the people it doubtless never had much influence, even when theoretically accepted. The pantheistic or semi-theistic Vedantism which in latter times suffused all Indian religions with a gentle mysticism was at bottom optimistic, and the superimposition of the Yoga on the atheistic Sankhya lightened the gloom of even that ultra-pessimistic system. What is called Hindu pessimism to-day is rather a tranquil resignation to the evils of this degenerate age (the Kaliyuga) than a metaphysical doctrine of despair.

The early Moslem invasions of India had no lasting results, but in the latter part of the tenth century, under Mahmud of Ghazni, the Mohammedan power was firmly established, and under various dynasties and with many vicissitudes maintained itself and extended its domain not only over Hindustan, but from the fourteenth century in the Deccan also. At the time of Baber's invasion (1525) the greater part of the peninsula was under Moslem rule, and in the northwest Moslems formed a considerable element of the population. Contact with the austerer monotheism of Islam led to efforts to reform the native religions by ridding them of their polytheistic and idolatrous features, or to form an eclectic theism in which Moslems and Hindus could unite. The great emperor Akbar (reigned 1556–1605) addressed himself with much zeal to the latter task, but his synthetic religion died with him.

Much more lasting were the results of a reforming movement inaugurated by Kabir a century or more earlier, whose followers, under the name Kabirpanthis (those who follow the path of Kabir) are still numerous and influential. He is said to have been a disciple of Ramananda, the founder of a Vishnuite sect (a subdivision of the Ramanujas) in the fourteenth century. Kabir rejected the Hindu scriptures and the distinctions of caste and creed; all who love God and do good are brothers, by whatever name they call God, and whether they be Hindus or Moslems. Idolatry and superstitious rites are unsparingly condemned; the temple should be, like the mosque, a house of prayer. He commends

unworldliness and the contemplative life, but puts above it
moral integrity, which may be possessed by the man in the
world as well as by the recluse. Broad as these teachings
are, the followers of Kabir are at bottom a Hindu sect; the
authority which they deny to Brahmans or Pandits they
ascribe in the fullest measure to the Guru, or spiritual guide,
of the sect, to whom the disciple is to submit in everything.
Man's welfare depends on his choice of a guide: "When the
master is blind, what is to become of the scholar? When
the blind leads the blind, both will fall into the well." [1]

It is, however, not so much through the sect which bears
his name as through the Sikhs, who ultimately derive from
him, that Kabir has exerted a great and lasting power in
India. Nanak, the first Guru (teacher) of the Sikhs (disciples) was professedly a follower of Kabir, to whose utterances he frequently appealed. He was born in 1469, near
Lahore, in a region predominantly Moslem, and in the spirit
of his predecessor he endeavoured to transform the Vishnuism of his countrymen into a simple theism divested of idolatry and superstition, a religion in which all believers in
one God could unite, without distinction of race or caste.
The theology of this religion was, however, of the Hindu,
specifically Vishnuite, type. God is the supreme Lord; he
may be called Brahma, or Govinda (an epithet of Krishna),
or Ram, or by other titles, but the name preferred by Nanak
is Hari (Vishnu). Works and ceremonies are meritorious;
but the only deliverance from the round of rebirths is the
saving grace of God, which is bestowed on those who call
upon his name (Hari), in a formula (*mantra*) which can be
communicated only by a teacher who stands in the apostolic
succession, and which he bestows only on those in whom he
recognises the marks of election. The positive aspect of
salvation is reabsorption in the absolute, in which the separate individuality of the soul is merged, or rather the illusion of its individuality is dissolved.

[1] It may be noted that there are Moslem as well as Hindu precedents
for this unqualified dependence on the spiritual guide.

For two or three generations after Nanak's death (1538) the Sikhs were merely a reforming sect, but as they grew in numbers the unlimited authority exercised by their religious heads (Gurus) tended to consolidate them more firmly than is the wont of Hindu sects. Contrary to the old ascetic ideal in all its modifications, Nanak bade his disciples seek salvation, not by withdrawing from the world, but while living in it as householders and pursuing their ordinary occupations, and this contributed not a little to the growing strength of the sect; its teachers soon had large worldly resources at their command. The fourth in the succession from Nanak was able to build the famous lake temple at Amritsar, which became the centre of the Sikh community. He also made the leadership hereditary in his own line, a step which did much to make the Gurus princes as well as pontiffs.

His son, Arjun, compiled the Granth (Book, Bible) of the Sikhs, gathering up the utterances of his predecessors back to Nanak and Kabir, and adding many of his own; to show that the teachings were not novel he introduced also numerous verses of older saints (Bhagats). The earlier heads of the religion had been supported by voluntary offerings; Arjun established a system of fixed contributions, collected by his deputies in the several districts, and surrounded himself with a considerable retinue. Under him the numbers of the Sikhs increased more rapidly in the Panjab, and this fact, together with the secular state assumed by the Guru, attracted the notice of the Mohammedan government at Lahore. The reports about Arjun's death are conflicting; intrinsically the most probable account is that he was arrested for offering prayers in behalf of the emperor's rebellious son. His successors surrounded themselves with armed bands, whom they led to battle, now in the service of the emperors, now against them, now in partisan forays on their own account.

The religious community rapidly became a veritable church militant, recruited largely from the warlike Jats of the Panjab. The emperor Aurangzeb undertook to crush them; the ninth Guru, Teg Bahadur, fell into his power and died in prison at Delhi in 1675. His son, Govind Singh, completed the transformation of the church into a fanatical host, and laid the foundations of a nation. He organised an inner circle, the Khalsa, whose members were admitted by a sacramental initiation, and received individually the surname Singh ("lion"); they were always to wear steel upon their persons; to these companions of the sword God himself was the "All-Iron One"; they were never to return the salutation of a Hindu, and to kill every Moslem at sight. Govind Singh composed a new Granth, fitter to inspire soldiers to heroic deeds than, like the old Granth, to guide saints to Nirvana. He had the worse of the unequal struggle with Aurangzeb, and was fain at last to give it up and take service under his lifelong foe; he died in 1708 by the hand of a Pathan assassin. Before his death he declared that the succession of Gurus was closed; henceforth the Granth should be the only teacher.

The long and bitter strife with the Moslems had the natural effect of making the Sikhs more complacent toward Hinduism; Govind Singh himself paid homage to Durga, the savage consort of Çiva; Banda, who became the leader of the army, undertook to prohibit the eating of meat and the drinking of spirituous liquors, but these innovations did not survive him. As in Hinduism itself, the pantheistic god of the thinkers becomes the personal god of the masses; and probably the conception of Hari entertained by the ordinary Sikh does not differ much from that of a Vishnuite. But the simplicity of worship has been maintained. Amritsar is their one holy place; in their temples are no images nor offerings; the services consist in reciting and singing texts from the sacred book and the distribution of a sacramental cake made of butter, flour, and sugar. The religious observances with which Hinduism surrounds life and death are all forbidden in the Granth, as well as worship in the Hindu temples. Truthfulness and kindness to the poor are espe-

cially emphasised; falsehood, fraud, theft, slander, and for-
nication are deadly sins.

Numerous sects and schisms have at different times arisen
among the Sikhs, some of which have been formally cut off
from the church, while others are recognised as within its
pale. The oldest, the Udasis ("indifferent," *i. e.*, to the
world) have for their founder a son of Nanak; they are
ascetics, and observe numerous Hindu customs, such as the
Çraddha. Of the others it is sufficient to mention the Akalis
(worshippers of the Timeless), said to have been founded by
Govind Singh; they were the zealots of Sikhism, fanatically
resisting all innovations, and a constant cause of apprehension to the Sikh rulers. Since the end of the Sikh nation
as a political power, they have lost their importance.

Another theistic sect, which arose in the seventeenth
century, are the Dadupanthis, whose founder, like Nanak,
traced his spiritual lineage through Kabir to the Ramananda
branch of the Vishnuites. Their religious principles are in
many ways similar to those of the Sikhs, but they have never
played a part on the political stage. They have no temples
nor images, and wear no sectarian mark on their foreheads;
their worship consists chiefly in adoration of God under the
name Rama and the invocation of the sacred name itself.
Unlike the Sikhs, they do not eat flesh, and otherwise strictly
observe the principle of "non-injury." The founder did
not demand that the seekers of salvation should abandon
their families or their ordinary occupations; but those who,
like himself, have this vocation may do so. Besides ascetics
and householders, there were formerly many adherents of
this sect who took service as soldiers under the Hindu
princes; the Rajah of Jaypur is said at one time to have had
ten thousand of them in his army. The extracts from their
sacred books which have been published make a highly favourable impression. The stiffening up of Hindu theism by
contact with Mohammedanism is very plain; there is even
a certain strain of determinism in the sayings attributed to
Dadu. It does not appear that the veneration for the Guru,

or teacher, and the slavish submission of mind and body to his authority ran to such extravagant lengths as among the Sikhs and in many other reforming sects. There were several other reform movements of the same general character in the seventeenth and eighteenth centuries which cannot here be more particularly described.

The theistic reformers of the nineteenth century felt the influence of Protestant Christianity as well as of Islam. The first of these was Rammohun Roy (1774–1833), a Bengali Brahman, the founder of the Brahma-Samaj (Theistic Society), organised in 1830. The object of the association, as expressed in the deed of trust, was the worship of the one eternal, unsearchable, and immutable Being, the author and preserver of the universe; the promotion of piety, morality, and charity, and the strengthening of the bonds of union among men of all religious classes and creeds. Images and sacrifices were excluded. The ritual consisted of readings from the Veda and Upanishads, an address, and the singing of hymns. Upon this simple platform and in this spiritual worship it was thought theists of all opinions could unite. The movement thus inaugurated has grown, but its adherents have repeatedly split upon social, ritual, and theological issues, so that there are now three Samajes. After the founder, the most conspicuous names in the history are those of Debendra Nath Tagore and Keshab Chandra Sen (died 1884). The members of the societies have been chiefly drawn from the educated classes, and their influence through the press and by public speech has been greater than their numbers, but they can hardly be said to have made any visible impression on the masses.

A reforming movement of a more distinctly Hindu type is represented by the Arya-Samaj, whose founder was Swami Dayanand Sarasvati (1824–83). Like Rammohun Roy, his watchword was, "back to the Veda," but whereas the Brahma-Samaj early gave up the infallibility of the Vedas, for Dayanand they are the sole revelation, the fountainhead not only of religion but of science for all mankind. The hymns of the Rig-Veda, as interpreted by Dayanand, foreshadow the most recent inventions—steam-engines, for example. The theology of the Aryas is essentially that of the Sankhya-Yoga.

Apart from these organised bodies, of which it is impossible to speak here at greater length, it is evident from many signs that a spirit of revival is at work in Hinduism, in part at least a concomitant of the rising race-consciousness. Those who are animated by this spirit recognise that revival involves reform; but while the reformers of the last century avowed, sometimes in sensational utterances, their admiration for Christianity, or at least for Christ, and regarded the Christianisation of India as its manifest destiny, the face of the present-day revival is not turned to the West: India has much to learn from Europe and America in material things, but nothing in religion, is the prevailing attitude. Many, indeed, go farther: India is to be teacher of the Western nations in the higher doctrine and practice of religion and in the true goal and method of human life.

CHAPTER XV

ZOROASTRIANISM

ORIGIN AND HISTORY

The Iranians—Their Religion—The Zoroastrian Scriptures—The Prophet Zoroaster—His Message—The Mazdæan Confession—Character of the Religion — The Achæmenian Kings — Readmission of Popular Deities—Mithra and Anahita—Worship of the Amesha Spentas—Macedonian and Arsacidan Rulers—The Sassanian Revival—The Moslem Conquest—The Modern Parsis.

THE ancestors of the Aryo-Indians and of the Iranians before their migrations lived side by side on the high plateau north of the Hindu Kush. Thence the former made their way into the valleys of Kabul and the Indus and southward to the Panjab, while the latter spread from their old seats westward into Media and Persia. The age of these movements is not certainly known. In the fifteenth century B. C. rulers of Mitanni, on the upper Euphrates and eastward, bear Iranian names, and names of the same origin appear about the same time in the Amarna despatches among the invaders of Palestine. At Boghaz Keui in Asia Minor, a Hittite capital, the names of Aryan gods, Mitra and Varuna, Indra and Nasatya, have been found in Mitannian documents dating from the beginning of the fourteenth century. The mass of the population in these countries was, however, plainly not Aryan. Beyond this fragmentary evidence of the presence of Aryans in the West in the great upheaval of nations between the fifteenth century and the thirteenth, the Iranians first appear on the stage of history in the ninth century, when the Assyrian king Shalmaneser made a campaign in Media (836 B. C.). His successors were frequently at war in the same regions, but evidently with petty princes and rulers of cities, not with a united Median kingdom. Such a kingdom, indeed, can hardly have arisen before the second half of the seventh century.

Though it suffered greatly from the Scythian inroads, Media reaped the benefit of the more severe blow which the barbarians inflicted on Assyria, and in 606 Cyaxares took and destroyed Nineveh and made an end of the Assyrian Empire. In the following years he extended his sway over Asia Minor as far as the Halys, and to the east over a large part of the Iranian lands. In 553 the Persian Cyrus, a vassal king reigning at Anshan in Susiana, revolted against his Median overlord, Astyages, and made himself king in his room, the supremacy of the Persians succeeding to that of the Medes. In 546 Sardes fell, and in the next few years Caria, Lycia, and the Greek cities on the coast were subdued; Babylon was taken in 538, and its empire passed to the Persians; Egypt was conquered by Cambyses in 525. Shaken to its foundations by the revolts which followed the death of Cambyses and the usurpation of the false Smerdis, the Persian power was re-established more firmly than ever by Darius Hystaspis. It surpassed the empires that preceded it not more in the extent of its dominion than in the strongly centralised organisation which gave it a stability none of them had known.

The inscriptions of Darius display him as a zealous worshipper of Ahura Mazda, the Wise Lord,[1] the supreme god of the Zoroastrian faith, to whom he attributes his victories over enemies and rebels. That similar testimony is not borne by the inscriptions of Cyrus may be explained by their limited extent and different character.

The religion of the early Iranians was closely akin to that of the Vedic Indians. One of the greatest of the Iranian gods is Mithra, the Vedic Mitra; other Indo-Iranian gods are Zoroastrian devils, like Indra and Nasatya (Naonhaithya); the myth of the dragon-slayer appears among both peoples,

[1] Literally, "the Lord Wisdom."

as do the first man, Yama (Iranian Yima), first to die and ruler in the realm of the dead, and the conception of the order of the world, natural, ritual, moral (Vedic *Rita*, Avestan *Asha*). The preparation and offering of a drink made from the expressed juice of a plant has the same central place in both religions under the same name, *Soma, Haoma;* the priests who kindle and tend the sacred fire bear the same title, Persian *Athravan*, Indian *Atharvan*. These agreements are all the more conclusive because Zoroastrianism did its best to efface every vestige of Iranian heathenism.

Apart from the changes thus purposely wrought, there are fundamental differences in the temper and spirit of the two religions that must be attributed to other causes, among which climatic environment and the conditions of livelihood were doubtless peculiarly potent. In India, from the Brahmanic period when speculative thinking sets in, the prevailing trend is toward monism, now metaphysical, now pantheistic. Even more universally the world is denied as unreal or renounced as evil through and through. Salvation, the end of all philosophy as well as of religion, is escape from the endless chain of bodily existences upon each of which man enters laden with the deeds of previous lives, a deliverance achieved by overcoming the ignorance or the blind desire which holds man bound on the wheel of rebirth. Abnegation of the world, withdrawal from society, repression of the body, meditation, methodical cultivation of trance-states are the means by which transcendental knowledge may be attained and desire extirpated in all the orthodoxies and heresies of India. It is not strange that a people who thought so ill of the world should never have played a part in the history of the world, nor have developed a national consciousness in any other form than antipathy to their foreign masters.

For the Iranians, in vastly less favoured lands, where man had to wring a meagre living from an unkindly nature, subject to violent extremes of cold and heat, perpetually on his defence against the predatory hordes of the steppes and the desert, life was an unceasing conflict with hostile powers, visible and invisible; watchfulness, courage, energy, were the virtues on which existence depended. In contrast to the metaphysical turn of the Hindu mind, the Iranian genius was eminently practical; hard reasonableness marks its thinking, adaptability distinguishes its action. The race had not only the qualities needed to conquer an empire, but the higher qualities that are required to organise and govern one, in a degree matched only by the Romans, whom in other respects also they much resemble. All these traits are reflected in their religion. It, too, is a conflict with innumerable evil powers; but the Iranians do not for that reason despair of the world, for the good is mightier than the evil, and shall prevail. Man's salvation is not to flee from the world, but to combat evil wherever he finds it and do a man's part to overcome it. This strenuous and militant type was not first impressed upon the religion by the Zoroastrian reform; it is rather a characteristic of the popular religion which is impressed upon the higher faith.

Zoroastrianism is the result of a prophetic reformation of the old Iranian religion which may be compared in various ways to the work of the Israelite prophets, and its sacred scriptures, containing prophetic utterances, liturgy and ceremonial, hymns, cosmogony, and the like, have many points of resemblance to the Old Testament. The comprehensive name of the scriptures is Avesta. Besides the canonical writings, there are many works of later date and in another language which are of value for the history of the religion in Sassanian and Moslem times.

The Avesta, as we have it, is only a part of a much larger collection made, according to a credible tradition, under the first Sassanian king (226–240 A. D.), and extant, it seems, even in the ninth century of our era. According to the Parsi tradition this collection consisted of twenty-one books, of which only one, the Vendidad, has been preserved substantially in the original form, though perhaps not complete. The rest of our Avesta is made up of the remains of other books combined and arranged for liturgical purposes, not without some later additions. As now in our hands, the Avesta consists of five parts: the Yasna, a liturgy recited by the priests at the offering to all the deities, with the Vispered, a supplement used on certain occasions; the Vendidad, dealing chiefly with the rules of clean and unclean, and with purifications and expiations, all from the point of view indicated by its title, "Antidemonic Law," since the unclean is the sphere of evil spirits; the Yashts are hymns of various age and poetic merit in honour of particular divinities;[1] finally, the Khordah Avesta is a collection of prayers for the private use of the laity as well as the priests. Inserted in the Yasna (chapters 28–54) are the Gathas, metrical texts in a different dialect from the rest, the oldest and most sacred part of the Avesta, in the form of utterances of Zoroaster himself or revelations of God to him.

Credible tradition has not much to tell us about Zoroaster. Concerning the age in which he lived there is wide diversity. The Greeks put him 5,000 years before the Trojan war or 6,000 years before Plato, probably in consequence of some misunderstanding of the Zoroastrian theory of the ages of the world. The Bundahish (ninth century A. D.),[2] offers a seemingly exact date for the beginning of the prophet's ministry, namely, 258 years before Alexander the Great, from which, with certain corrections, it has been reckoned that Zoroaster was born in 660 B. C. The Bundahish gives, however, the list of kings on which the 258 years was computed, with the duration of their reigns, beginning with Vishtasp, the patron of Zoroaster, and ending with the last Darius (Codomannus) and Alexander. The succession does not correspond even remotely with the Achæmenian line; it gives two successive reigns of 90 (or, as West corrects the figures, 120) and 112 years respectively. Under these circumstances it is hazardous to assume that the total is a trustworthy tradition, while the particulars are inexplicable. The fact, already noted, that Darius Hystaspis was a Maz-

---

[1] See below, pp. 374 f.

[2] The Bundahish derives much of its material from books of the Avesta that have since been lost.

dæan proves that the religion had taken root in leading circles in Persia by the sixth century B. C., and as it certainly did not originate there, we should be inclined to allow a somewhat longer time for the propagation and acceptance of the faith than the century which the Bundahish gives us. There are other considerations that may be urged for an earlier date, but there is no conclusive evidence one way or the other.[1]

Tradition, though not with unanimous voice, points to Bactria, in far eastern Iran, as the scene of the first triumphs of the new faith. Vishtasp (Hystaspes),[2] Zoroaster's royal convert and patron, came of a line native in Seistan; with this the horizon of the Gathas seems to agree. About Zoroaster's birthplace there is no agreement; the vicinity of Lake Urmia in Aderbeijan (Atropatene) and Rai (Ragæ) in northeastern Media are rival claimants, while some Greek authors made him a Bactrian. To reconcile these conflicting representations it may be supposed that he was a native of Media, who, being, like other prophets, without honour in his own country, migrated to Bactria and there found better success, and this hypothesis is entertained by some scholars who have made a special study of the subject.[3] However that may be, it seems probable that the doctrine spread westward into Media and Persia from eastern Iran.

From the Gathas we learn that much of the success of the new faith was due to the support of Vishtasp, who seems in some passages to have stood model for a portrait of the ideal king. Zoroaster had other allies in high places in the wise counsellor Jamaspa and his brother Frashaoshtra; he married Hvovi, a daughter of the latter, and gave his own daughter by another marriage to the former. One of the first believers was his cousin, Maidyoi-maonha, and others of his

---

[1] It has been inferred from the name Mazdaka twice occurring in Assyrian inscriptions in lists of Median petty kings, that there were worshippers of Mazda in Media as early as the eighth century.

[2] It is perhaps not superfluous to remark that this Hystaspes is not the father of Darius.

[3] See especially A. V. W. Jackson, Zoroaster, pp. 182 ff.

family are known by name. A Turanian convert, Fryana, receives a high encomium from the prophet for his piety and generosity. The progress of the new faith was doubtless slow, and when it began to overcome indifference it was confronted by opposition. Zoroaster's most persistent adversaries, as might be supposed, were the priests of the popular religion he attacked. He not infrequently confides to God his discouragement, and sometimes gives utterance to the questioning of his soul: If the Lord has really given him this mission and message, why is it that men do not recognise the truth? His kindred and patrons cast him off; he knows not whither to turn, to what land to flee.

The allusions in the Gathas are from their nature obscure,[1] but they have the intrinsic marks of verity—not least in the fact that they do not attempt to explain themselves. No serious student any longer doubts that Zoroaster was an historical person. Legend early made itself busy with him; some of its inventions were known already to the Greeks. The Vendidad tells of Zoroaster's temptation, at the instigation of Ahriman, by Buiti, the demon of idolatry, and "insidious perdition," that is, misbelief. His miraculous birth and miraculous works were narrated in lost books of the Avesta, and are retold with further embellishment in mediæval writings. The wars between the believing king Vishtasp and the Turanian Arjasp, as wars of religion, fill a large space in this literature and in the Persian epic. The biography in the Zerdusht Nameh is wholly legendary. According to these stories, Zoroaster died at the age of seventy-seven—murdered by a priest, or sorcerer, of the old religion, some tell; slain with the priests in the fire temple by Arjasp's Turanians at the storming of Balkh, as the Shah Nameh narrates it.

In the Gathas, Zoroaster declares that Ahura Mazda, the Wise Lord, has revealed to him the word which he proclaims to men, and he tells at length of his calling to this ministry.

[1] The critic may consider how it would be with the allusions in the Koran without the concomitant tradition.

It is his mission to teach men to obey Ahura Mazda and strive after the Right (Asha), through which they shall obtain the good things of this world and the other; none but he thus teaches the law of the Lord. His message is a way of salvation from destruction revealed by Ahura Mazda, who knows. He sets before men life and death, and every one must choose between them. Even a Turanian who obeys the truth can be saved. In the day of the great affair (the judgment), each will receive the reward of the teaching he has followed. The truth may now be hard to discern from falsehood, but one day Ahura Mazda will establish the faith by visible proof.

What the true religion demands of men is that they should decide for Ahura Mazda, choosing the way of truth and goodness. Man must give himself to Asha, Vohu Mano, and Ahura Mazda; he must follow the Lord, be like him, and teach others to be like him; and must labour for the renewal of the world; one of the most effective means to this end is the faithful teaching of the true religion. The teaching of the evil (the old religion) is to be scrupulously shunned.

The characteristic conception of the Gathas, indelibly impressed on the whole subsequent development of the religion, is the antagonism of good and evil, in all the senses of those words—of true religion and false, of right and wrong in thought and word and deed, of help and harm. This cleavage runs through nature as well as humanity, and divides the world of spirits. So it has been since the Good Spirit declared his irreconcilable hostility to the Evil Spirit and all his ways and works. The Daevas (the gods of the popular religion) chose to ally themselves with the Evil Mind, and strive to mislead and destroy men; the wicked follow them. The primary duty of religion is, therefore, to combat and overthrow the false religion which worships demons instead of God.

The ruling principle in dealing with fellow men is to do good to the good and harm to the evil, for the evil are the foes of the Lord and his good world, the allies of the evil spirit and the Daevas; to do good to them would therefore be treasonably to give aid and comfort to the enemy in the great conflict. The evil are, first of all, those who reject the true religion and its distinctive morals and customs. Gifts to the bad are a sin; but to support the poor who live in holiness and good thought is a virtue. The same rule extends to the brute creation. The useful animals, especially cattle and dogs, are to be kindly treated, well fed and cared for; cruelty and neglect are grave sins, wanton killing of cattle—under which head the animal sacrifices of the Daeva-worshippers fall—a crime. On the other hand, we shall see that the destruction of beasts of prey and noxious vermin is in later books a highly meritorious work.

So also the tilling of the soil, the reclamation of waste land by rooting out weeds and thorns and extending irrigation to make grain and fruits grow, is a part of practical religion; it is in fact the conquest of a piece of the enemy's country for the Lord. No religion has set so high a value on agricultural labour as the service of God. The enemies of the Lord are the predatory Turanians who raid the settlements and carry off the husbandman's cattle; believers are bound not to harry Mazdæan villages. The conflict of religions is a struggle of agricultural civilisation against nomadic barbarism, a situation which throws an instructive light on the beginnings of Zoroastrianism. From the first, Mazdaism was thus directly a civilising force.

The Gathas give other glimpses of the conditions of the time. The prophet denounces unjust judges, the corrupt rulers who for gain put power into the hands of the wicked, the tyrannical and oppressive princes, and those who oppose the true religion—for a misbeliever cannot be a good king—the false teachers, deniers, and deceivers. He paints with affection the character of the good prince. The good king is he who practises the good in thought and word and deed, according to the teaching of the prophet—"He, O Ahura, is the being who best embodies thee." He is generous, and nourishes the virtuous poor. Blessed of Ahura, above all, is the prince who adopts the Mazdæan faith and makes it prevail. Like the Israelite prophets with their ideal king of the golden age to come, and like Plato with his royal philosopher, Zoroaster sets his hope of the triumph of the good world on a good sovereign.

The Gathas cannot be thought to contain anything like the full presentation of Zoroaster's teaching; in them he speaks, for example, in a standing phrase of good thoughts, words, deeds, but seldom defines what is good. The observances of religion, prayer, adoration, offering, are referred to, but nowhere prescribed. The sacred fire is a gift of Ahura Mazda; the Lord himself appeared to the prophet when he made the sacred offering on Ahura's fire; but of the Haoma offering, which has so large a place in the Persian worship, there is no mention. Zoroaster speaks as a prophet, not as a law-giver or a liturgist. A comparison of the Gathas with the rest of the Yasna, in which they are embedded, makes this all the clearer.

The character of the religion is well illustrated by the old Zoroastrian confession of faith (Yasna, XII):

I repudiate the Daevas. I confess myself a worshipper of Mazda, a Zarathushtrian, as an enemy of the Daevas, a prophet of the Lord, praising and worshipping the Immortal Holy Ones (Amesha Spentas). To the Wise Lord I promise all good; to him, the good, beneficent, righteous, glorious, venerable, I vow all the best; to him from whom is the cow, the law, the (celestial) luminaries, with whose luminaries (heavenly) blessedness is conjoined. I choose the holy, good Armaiti (Humble Devotion), she shall be mine. I abjure theft and cattle-stealing, plundering and devastating the villages of Mazda-worshippers.

It is my duty to grant to the inmates of the house freedom of movement and residence,[1] and to the cattle with which they live on earth. With due reverence I vow this to Asha (Righteousness) by the consecrated water: I will henceforth not plunder nor lay waste the villages of Mazda-worshippers, nor assail their persons and lives. I renounce fellowship with the wicked, lawless, evil-doing Daevas, the most deceitful, corrupt, and wicked of all, and with adherents of the Daevas, with sorcerers and those who follow them, with every bad man, who-

---

[1] Abolition of slavery?

ever he may be, in thoughts and words and deeds and deportment, as I hereby renounce fellowship with the mischievous heretic.

As the Wise Lord, in all his communings with Zarathushtra instructed him, as he in all his communings with the Wise Lord renounced fellowship with the Daevas, so I also, as a worshipper of the Lord and follower of Zarathushtra, renounce the fellowship of the Daevas, as Zarathushtra, the representative of the true faith, renounced them.

Of the faith of the waters, the plants, the useful cow, the faith of the Wise Lord who created the cow and the upright man, the faith of Zarathushtra, of King Vishtaspa, of Frashaoshtra and Jamaspa, the faith of all the messengers of salvation and their helpers and of every right believer—in this faith and in this promise I am a worshipper of Mazda. I confess myself a Mazda-worshipper, a Zarathushtrian, by vow and confession. I promise well-thought thought, well-spoken word, well-done deed. I pledge myself to the religion of the Mazda-worshippers, which makes an end of strife and lays down weapons and promotes kindred marriage, which is the highest, best, most beautiful of those that are or shall be, the religion of faith in Ahura, the religion of Zarathushtra. To the Wise Lord I promise all good. This is the profession of the Mazdæan religion.

The antecedents of this teaching are unknown. The title Ahura, which becomes in Mazdaism the name of the supreme God, is the same word as Asura, which in the Vedas is the name of a group, or class, of deities among whom Varuna and Mitra are the foremost. Of all the Vedic gods, Varuna is the one whose character most nearly approaches that of Ahura Mazda, so that some scholars have been led to think that Zoroaster's Wise Lord is an Iranian Varuna, with moral attributes much farther developed than the Indian, and raised to a supremacy which allows no other gods beside him. Ahura (or the good spirit which is identified with Ahura) is clad with the solid firmament as with a vestment,[1] like a god of heaven. The Iranian Mithra, ignored in the Gathas, could not be kept in the background, and in the religion of later times became the first of the gods. He is closely assimilated in character to Ahura, being, as a god of light, the god of truth and good faith. The Daevas are the gods of the popular religion and of the tribes who did not embrace

[1] Yasna, XXX, 5.

the Zoroastrian reform. The word is in India the prevailing name for the gods (*deva*), while *asura* came in later times to be applied to demons. Among the arch-devils of the later Avesta are Indra, Sauru, and Naonhaithya, the Indian Indra, Çarva (Rudra), and Nasatya (a title of the Açvins). It is a tempting conjecture that the ancestors of the Iranian tribes among which Mazdaism arose were more intimately connected with the Aryo-Indian tribes whose greatest god was Varuna than with the Indra-worshippers who in the invasion and conquest gained for themselves and their gods the leading place; but the conjecture that a religious conflict between the Mazda-worshippers and those who adhered to the old nature religion preceded the separation of the Indian and Iranian branches of the race and was one of its causes has not found general acceptance.

At most, these relations only reveal the background of the Mazdaism, not the origin of the religion itself. That the latter is not the evolution of a natural polytheism is obvious. It is the work of a prophetic reformer who combats the religion of his people; its gods are his devils and its priests their servants. The teaching of the Gathas is, as distinctly as that of the Upanishads, the outcome of reflection; much more distinctly it bears the stamp of an individual thinker. It may very well be that the problems which engaged Zoroaster were not raised by him for the first time, but, however many others may have thought about these questions, he thought them through.

The monotheism of the Gathas is much more advanced than that of the loftiest Vedic hymns to Varuna; Ahura Mazda[1] has no partner nor rival. He is the creator of the world and all that therein is. He knows all that men do; his eyes behold their secret deeds as well as those done in open day; he knows all that is and is to be. He requites men for their deeds in this world and the other. The existence of the beings whom the people worship as gods is not denied, but they are false gods, demons, who, deceived, made

[1] No other god is even named in the Gathas.

choice of the evil spirit as their lord, and in turn delude men into following them. A similar conception is common in Judaism, and is expressed by Paul, "The sacrifices which the heathen offer, they offer to demons and not to gods." [1]

Zoroaster sees everywhere in the moral world good and evil arrayed over against each other: there are men whose head and heart are right, who strive to be good and do good, and there are others whose aims and conduct are just the opposite, and so it has always been. This difference is not accidental; every man has the character he has chosen. The types of these contrasted characters are two primal spirits, antagonists from the beginning of history, the good, or beneficent, spirit—or, as it might not improperly be rendered, the Holy Spirit—and the evil, or baleful, spirit. The good spirit sometimes seems to be Ahura Mazda himself, as the spirit in the Old Testament is sometimes distinct from Jehovah, sometimes identified with him; the evil spirit, the evil mind, is akin to the demon Lie. [2] The principles of good and evil are thus personalised, but the evil spirit is a much less concrete and dramatic figure than the Ahriman of later writings, who is not only a deceiver, but creator and ruler of the bad half of the world. The question of the origin of moral evil is followed back to the "primal" evil spirit; where he came from is left as a problem for later centuries.

By the side of Ahura Mazda, ministers who do his will, are the "Immortal Beneficent Ones," the Amesha Spentas, [3] Vohu Mano, Good Mind (intelligence, purpose, disposition), Asha, Right (as conformity to the moral order), Khshathra, Sovereignty (the Kingdom of God), Armaiti, Devotion (humble piety), Haurvatat and Ameretat, Welfare and Immortality; with these six the genius of obedience, Sraosha, is sometimes joined. These are attributes of God, ideals of human character in the likeness of God, and spiri-

[1] I Cor. 10, 20.

[2] The Lie (Druj) is the name for evil comprehensively and for the evil spirit; hell is "the world of the Lie."

[3] The name Amesha Spenta is not found in the Gathas themselves, but occurs in a prose text of approximately the same age.

tual blessings which God bestows on those who strive after
them in the way of his appointment; they are not abstract
ideas, but personified qualities, or spirits and genii of qualities. Among them Vohu Mano and Asha naturally hold
the highest place. Here also penetrating and constructive
thought is apparent. Asha (Arta, in Persian proper names;
Vedic, Rita), Order, is indeed an Aryan conception and
name, which in the Vedas sometimes appears as the will or
law of Varuna, sometimes as an independent principle; but
in the Gathas it is raised to a higher ethical plane as the law
of righteousness in every relation. The other figures and
the part they play are characteristically Mazdæan.

The religion of the Gathas is an ethical religion, not as that
term may be applied to the higher nature religions of civilised peoples—the Greeks, for example—which make the
gods the guardians of customary law or vindicators of an
ideal righteousness, but in the sense that the nature and will
of God are wholly moral. The human virtues are the divine
attributes—the fact tells more than the direct moral injunc-
tions of the new religion. This explains the silence of the
Gathas about worship. It is only by allusions that we learn
that the cult of the sacred fire, the element of light and purity,
belonged to primitive Mazdaism as it did to the older Aryan
religion and to later Zoroastrianism. In all this we are
reminded again of the ethical monotheism of the Hebrew
prophets. There is, however, one noteworthy difference.
In Israel ethical philosophy moves within the limits of a national religion: it is the national god who becomes in the
hands of the prophets a righteous god, and consequently,
down to the fall of the nation, the religious subject is the
people, the retribution is national and historical. Zoroastrianism addressed itself in the beginning to individuals,
bidding every man choose between truth and falsehood,
good and evil; the retribution is individual, not collective,
whether it be on the day of the great affair or after death.
By converting kings and people, it became the national religion of the Iranian people and the Achæmenian kings.

God's righteous rule involves the idea of retribution. He rewards faith and good works in this life, but, on the other hand, the good may be harried and persecuted by the bad. Zoroaster's mind is on the imminent crisis, when by the ordeal of molten metal God shall discern between the righteous and the wicked, between believers and unbelievers, or on the separation at the judgment bridge. This bridge, of which Zoroaster speaks as though it was a familiar notion, may have been a piece of popular eschatology—it has an interesting parallel among some North American Indians—and the glimpses of heaven and hell have nothing distinctive about them, but the standard is new in its moral rigorousness, and, above all, in that a man's religious confession is a decisive factor.

The conception of revelation, also, is characteristic. The Vedic Rishis were inspired poets; the gods put in their mouths the hymns they sang to the god's honour at the sacrifices; but Zoroaster's revelation is prophetic: what comes to him is not how the gods elect to be praised or worshipped, but what God will have man believe and how he will have him live. What Ahura Mazda thus makes known to him the prophet proclaims to his fellow men.

Nothing is known of the way in which Zoroastrianism spread through the Iranian lands. We may surmise that the efforts of its adherents were directed, like the prophet's own, to the conversion of princes who should support the good religion and cause it to prevail over the Daevas and their worshippers. Like every other religion which is conceived as the only true and saving faith—like Christianity and Mohammedanism, for example—Mazdaism is in principle intolerant; in the Gathas believers are exhorted to chastise the misbelievers with the sword, and it is not improbable that forcible suppression of heathen worship at home and wars with heathen neighbours were from the beginning effective means of establishing the kingdom of God and expanding its dominion—so much of truth there may be in the legends of the wars of the faith, however little of historical fact they may embody. How generally Zoroastrianism was the religion of the Iranian peoples before the rise of the Persian empire, there is no means of determining; only about Media have we testimony that it was the dominant, if not the exclusive, religion of the country, whose priests, the Magi, were a powerful hereditary class.

In becoming the religion of rulers and people, Zoroastrianism took up again many features of the older religion which the founder had rejected or ignored, and its distinctive teachings were reshaped in forms more easily apprehended by the vulgar mind. Darius in his inscriptions names no god but Ahura Mazda, though he speaks generally of the clan-gods, or genii of the clans—a conception not alien to the fundamental ideas of Mazdaism—and of "the other deities." Artaxerxes Mnemon (404–362 B. C.), however, names Mithra and Anahita by the side of Ahura Mazda, and Berossos reports that this king first set up images of the goddess Anahita, not only in his capitals, Babylon, Susa, Ecbatana, but at Damascus and Sardes, from which it may be inferred that he was especially devoted to her worship. Darius Ochus prays: "May Ahura Mazda and Mithra protect me and this land." That the inscriptions make no mention of the evil principle is not evidence of unorthodoxy;[1] the inscriptions of Christian kings, it has been pertinently remarked, do not abound in references to the devil, however sincerely their authors may have believed that he was the instigator of rebellion.

The Achæmenian kings were buried in tombs, a mode of disposing of the dead abhorrent to the sacred law of the Vendidad, but seemingly not condemned in the Gathas. Herodotus affirms of his own observation that the exposure of the dead was practised by the Magi, but adds: "the Persians envelop the body in wax and bury it in the earth," and Strabo makes the same distinction: the Magians alone leave the bodies to the birds of prey. The exposure of the

[1] In the inscriptions of Darius Hystaspis, the Druj (Lie) appears to be, as in the Gathas, the comprehensive word for evil.

dead on raised platforms is not infrequent among wandering tribes,[1] and has of itself nothing to do with a fear of polluting the earth, which might seem to be equally well attained by coating the body in wax. We can only infer that the former was no prescription of primitive Zoroastrianism, but a custom—doubtless very old—of a particular region or tribe which in Sassanian times succeeded in being made law.

In the Indian Vedas Mitra is the constant comrade of Varuna, so closely associated with him, indeed, that there are hardly any hymns to Mitra alone. It is possible that the worship of this god was more prominent among the western Iranians than in either India or in Bactria.[2] In character he is much like Ahura Mazda, but, as becomes a god of the old mythology, he is a more heroic figure. A champion of truth and right, a god who gives victory to the good cause, it is not strange that as a popular god he outshone his theological superior.[3] His worship spread widely in the subject lands, especially in Armenia and Cappadocia, and he appeared to many Greek observers to be the chief god of the Persians. Anahita Ardvisura was a goddess of the waters, especially of the fructifying waters of heaven which pour down into the mythical lake Vourukasha and are thence distributed to the seven regions of the earth. She supplies the unfailing sources which revive vegetation and the herds; she creates in men and women the powers of reproduction, gives mothers easy childbirth and abundant milk. In the hymn to her praise (Yasht V) the goddess is described as a fair and buxom maiden in rich attire, with a golden crown, perhaps as she was represented in art. As a goddess of fertility she resembled a whole class of West Asiatic goddesses, and was in many places assimilated to them or identified with them, sometimes borrowing features of their cults —in Armenia, for example, religious prostitution—but there

---

[1] Examples are found in America as well as among the Mongols.

[2] A Mithradates is named among the assassins of Xerxes.

[3] One of the longest of the hymns in the Avesta (Yasht XIX) is devoted to the praises of Mithra.

is no sufficient ground for the opinion that the goddess herself was borrowed from the Semites. A male counterpart of Anahita Ardvisura is Apam Napat, the Water Child, an old Aryan deity of frequent occurrence in the Veda.

The religion of the Persians seemed to Greek observers a pure nature worship. They had no temples or images—as Herodotus opines, because they did not, like the Greeks, conceive the gods to be of the same nature as men. They offer sacrifice, he tells us, on mountain tops to Zeus, by which name is to be understood the whole circle of heaven; they sacrifice also to the sun and the moon and the earth, to fire and water and the winds. The Avesta contains hymns to the sun and the moon and to the star Sirius (Tishtrya); of the divine fire and the sacredness of water and air there will be more to say in another connection.

By the side of these nature powers the Immortal Beneficent Ones become personal deities and receive divine worship. In Strabo's time Vohu Mano ("Ωμανος) had fire temples in Cappadocia, and images that were carried in procession. Ahura Mazda is the father and creator of them all; he brought them into being that they might be his ministers, and what he does in the world is mainly done through their instrumentality. Each of them presides over a province of nature: Vohu Mano over the useful animals, Asha Vahishta over fire, Khshathra Vairya over the metals; Spenta Armaiti is the goddess of earth, Haurvatat and Ameretat are the genii of waters and plants respectively. In the ecclesiastical calendar of later times each of these Amshaspands is regent of a certain month of the year and of a certain day of the month. All these divinities (Yazatas, modern Persian Izads) are subordinate to Ahura Mazda; the theology is so far forth consistently monotheistic. But they receive individually and collectively the same kind of worship as the supreme God, and from the practical side the religion may be described as a monarchical polytheism with a somewhat numerous and varied pantheon.

The great Yashts betray a consciousness of the inconsistency, or perhaps we should say the innovation, by making Ahura Mazda himself commend or prescribe the worship of the other divinities. The Mithra hymn begins: "Ahura Mazda said to Spitama Zarathushtra, When I created Mithra with wide pastures, I created him, O Spitama, as worthy of sacrifice and worship as I, Ahura Mazda, myself am." The hymn to Anahita opens similarly:[1] "Ahura Mazda said to Spitama Zarathushtra, Worship, O Spitama Zarathushtra, my Ardvi, rich in blessings, pure, copious, wholesome, foe of demons, believing in Ahura, to whom the bodily world owes sacrifice and praise." To Anahita Ahura Mazda himself first made the Haoma offering, and prayed that Zarathushtra might accept his religion, which prayer she granted. Yet she also is produced by the word of Ahura Mazda.

The ethical dualism of the Gathas, if it may be so called, hardened in time into a theological dualism, in which an evil being of supernatural power stands over against Ahura Mazda. Aristotle and Hermippus had heard that according to the Magi there are two principles, a good divinity ($\delta\alpha\iota\mu\omega\nu$) and an evil divinity, the former called Zeus, or Oromasdes, the latter Hades, or Areimanios. To Ahriman the later Zoroastrian writings attribute the creation of all evil things, and he has his ministers, with the Evil Mind as Grand Vizier, each standing over against one of the Beneficent Ones. The eschatology also underwent a change. The great crisis which the prophet expected in his time did not come, and to later generations it did not seem imminent. The result was that the judgment of the individual at death became a separate act. The general judgment of Zoroaster's original conception was postponed to the end of the age, and to appear at that final assize the dead of all generations were brought to life again in the resurrection. This doctrine also was known to the Greeks before Alexander: Theopompus reports that the Magi teach that men will come to life again and be immortal in a spiritual state in which they neither need food nor cast a shadow.

[1] See also Tishtrya Yasht (LII).

The Macedonian conquest signified much more than the overthrow of the Persian empire; it was the invasion of the East by Western civilisation. Greek colonies were founded wherever the armies penetrated, and many of them became flourishing cities and centres of more or less exotic Greek culture. The division of Alexander's empire left the greater part of its territory under Macedonian or Greek rule. A Greek Bactrian kingdom which arose about the middle of the third century comprised the old East Iranian lands and reached into India; on the west it bordered on the Seleucid empire. Parthia, however, under the native Arsacidan dynasty, succeeded a little later in conquering its independence (247 B. C.), and Mithradates (174–136 B. C.) united in his kingdom a large part of the Iranian lands, while the Greek Bactrian kingdom went down (139 B. C.) under an invasion of nomad tribes from the great Scythian steppes. From the middle of the first century B. C., the Arsacidans were repeatedly involved in wars with Rome. Trajan cherished the ambition of reclaiming for Western civilisation the empire of Alexander, but by the destruction of Seleucia in 164 A. D. the Romans themselves dealt a blow to Greek influence in the East which the Parthians had been unable to inflict. Meanwhile the Parthian kings, who in earlier times had proudly put "Philhellene" on their coins, showed themselves more and more averse to foreign culture; a national, or perhaps we should rather say an Oriental, reaction set in in the first century of our era, the knowledge of Greek declined, and from the beginning of the third century Western learning was accessible only in Aramaic translations.

The history of the religion during these centuries is very obscure. It is probable that it suffered in the beginning from the withdrawal of the state support it had enjoyed under the Achæmenians, and in the period of "acute Hellenisation," which apparently lasted for some generations, the would-be cultivated classes may have been as indifferent Zoroastrians as the upper classes in Jerusalem were indifferent Jews. The Parthian kings do not seem to have been distinguished for religious zeal, and the perpetual internal disorders of the kingdom and frequent changes of the ruling family were unfavourable conditions. The reaction of which we have spoken may have had its religious side; mediæval Persian tradition, which there is no reason for discrediting, records that a Parthian king, Valkash, caused all that could be recovered of the Avesta from manuscripts and the memory of men to be collected and copied. It is uncertain whether Vologeses I (contemporary of Nero) or the third of the name (148–191 A. D.) is meant.

In Persia proper several series of coins show that native lines ruled over smaller or larger regions as vassals of Greek or Parthian kings or virtually their own masters. Early in the third century one of the Persian petty kings, who bore the historic name Artaxerxes (Ardashir I, acceded 212 A. D.), subdued the other kinglets in the vicinity of Persepolis (Istakhr), and, when called to account by his Parthian overlord, beat him in a series of battles, the Persian Sassanian rule succeeding the Parthian much as, seven centuries and a half before, the Persian Achæmenian succeeded the Mede. The vassal states were subdued and incorporated in the kingdom, and Ardashir assumed the title, King of Kings of the Iranians, becoming thus the founder of the Sassanian empire (224–650 A. D.). In Persia, on one side of the turbulent main current of history, Zoroastrianism had been preserved in greater purity than in regions where it was in contact with other religions, and it had evidently a stronger hold on both rulers and people. The rise of the Sassanian kingdom was both a national Persian restoration and a revival of the religion of the glorious Achæmenian times as a national religion. Ardashir includes "Mazdayasnian" (Mazda-worshipper) among his royal titles; at his order the priest Tansar prepared an authoritative canon and text of the Avestan scriptures. What we possess is, as has been already remarked, the remains of this Sassanian Avesta.

It is characteristic of the early Sassanian kings that Ardashir and Shapur I, during their occupation of Armenia, destroyed the images even of the Iranian gods and turned the temples into fire shrines; and there is a remarkable statement that Ardashir wished to suppress the venerable sacred fires in other centres, leaving only that in the capital—a singular parallel, if it be historical, to Josiah's reformation in Jerusalem. The inherent intolerance of Zoroastrian orthodoxy appeared in another way when Christianity, with its exclusive claims and its active propaganda, began to push into Sassanian territory. Political considerations also had a good deal to do with the treatment of Christians, especially after the Roman Empire became Christian. Severe persecutions of the Christians occurred repeatedly; strict laws were made against heresy, and apostasy from the Zoroastrian faith was punished with death. The priesthood was an organised and powerful body, whose head had his seat at Rai, in Media, and was the first person in the state after the king.

The hundred years of wars between Rome and Persia, which began in 527 and were waged with great energy by Chosroes II (Parvez, 590–628), weakened both the decadent empires. The Arabs wrested Syria from the Romans in 636 and Egypt in 639. By the battle of Kadesiya in 637 and that of Nehavend a few years later, the Persian empire passed into the hands of the Moslems. In a short time the armies of the Caliphs had subdued even the remotest East Iranian lands. Of the decline of Mazdaism under Mohammedan rule little is known. Doubtless many Zoroastrians embraced Islam, as multitudes of Christians did, to escape the disabilities or the oppressions to which they were subject. But systematic efforts to force them to change their religion were not made by the early Caliphs, the Zoroastrians being reckoned with Jews and Christians as "people who have scriptures," and therefore, according to the Koran, to be left undisturbed on condition of paying a head tax; only later were the Zoroastrians excluded from this protection. The extensive literary activity of the Parsi priests in original works as well as in Pahlavi translations and synopses of Avestan books, which lasted at least through the ninth century, shows that the religion still possessed some vitality, and even after that time less significant works were written in modern Persian. The number of Zoroastrians in Persia, however, steadily declined, especially, it may be surmised, after the more fanatical and intolerant Shiites came into power. Two hundred years ago they were estimated at one hundred thousand; to-day they cannot count much more than ten thousand souls, chiefly in Yezd and Kerman.

In the early centuries of Islam, Persian Zoroastrians established themselves in India; the descendants of these emigrants, now numbering about ninety thousand, chiefly in the Bombay Presidency, are very prosperous. They have always adhered pretty faithfully to the practice of their law, but in the decadence of the religion in Persia, on whose authorities they were dependent in matters of learning, the Indian community also suffered. Their sacred scriptures, which they could read only in translations twice or thrice removed from the original, became with every generation less understood. The interest of European scholars in these scriptures awakened that of the Parsis themselves, and in the last half century a revival of learning, and a revival of religion by a return to its sources, have been in progress among them.

CHAPTER XVI

ZOROASTRIANISM

ZOROASTRIAN THEOLOGY

Ahura Mazda—His Attributes—Creation—Ahriman and His Creatures
—The Ages of the World—The Call and Temptation of Zoroaster
—Conflict of Good and Evil—Worship—Uncleanness and Purifications—Ethics—Legalism—The Hereafter—The Judgment of Souls
—Heaven and Hell—The Visions of Arda Viraf—Resurrection and
the Last Judgment—Messianic Expectations—Character of Zoroastrian Dualism.

In the foregoing pages the endeavour has been made to
outline the fundamental ideas of Zoroastrianism as they are
set forth in the Gathas and to indicate, so far as the sources
permit, the directions of subsequent development. It remains to describe the religion as it appears in the Sassanian
Avesta and in later Pahlavi writings. This more complete
survey will show that, through all its development and the
manifold vicissitudes of its fortunes, Zoroastrianism has preserved its original character substantially unchanged.

Ahura Mazda is the supreme God; he is "the creator,
Ahura Mazda, resplendent and glorious, the greatest, best,
most beautiful of beings, the most constant, wisest, most
perfect of form, supreme in righteousness, knowing to do
good, giving joy at his good pleasure; who created us, formed
us, and sustains us; who is the most beneficent spirit"
(Yasna, I). He is the "omniscient Lord, the most beneficent
spirit, the creator of the material worlds, the righteous one"
(Vendidad, II, 1). There are representations of Ahura Mazda
in relief from both the Achæmenian and Sassanian times, as
God the Father is represented without scruple in Christian
art, but there were no images in his worship.

Ahura Mazda is absolutely good, and therefore cannot be the author of any kind of evil, natural or moral. All the evil in the world is the work of a power hostile to God and his good creation. The Persians preferred to admit, for the present order of things, a limitation of God's power, rather than to leave room for doubt of his perfect goodness. The first chapter of the Vendidad tells how Ahura Mazda created in order the several Iranian countries with their various excellences, and how for each Angra Mainyu created corresponding plagues—the killing cold of winter, intemperate heat; serpents, locusts, ants; rapine and lust, foreign oppression; unnatural vice, magic and witchcraft, the interment of the dead, and the eating of carrion; pride, doubt, disbelief. Evil spirits and demons, men of devilish character—who are, in fact, demons on earth as well as after death—beasts of prey and noxious vermin, all belong to Angra Mainyu, and the ninety-nine thousand nine hundred and ninety-nine diseases the flesh is heir to are his invention.

The first of Ahura Mazda's creations was Vohu Mano, "Good Mind" (both good intelligence and good moral sense), in consultation with whom he produced all his other creatures, just as in the Old Testament (Prov. 8) Wisdom is the first creation of Jehovah, and stood beside him as masterbuilder when God established the heavens and the earth.[1]

What is said of Vohu Mano in the Gathas is sometimes strikingly similar to what Philo says about the Logos. Darmesteter was led by this resemblance, among other things, to think that the Gathas (which he regarded, not as the oldest part of the Avesta, but as comparatively recent) were directly influenced by Jewish Alexandrian philosophy.[2] The conception in the Gathas is, however, vastly simpler than Philo's. Ahura Mazda is no transcendental absolute, but a living god, and his Good Mind is not a metaphysical link between unchanging being and the manifold and changing

[1] With these verses in Prov. 8, compare especially Gatha 1.

[2] This radical theory has made no converts. All Avestan scholars are agreed that the Gathas are the oldest part of the Avesta.

world of becoming, but an hypostasis of the intelligence and goodness with which God created the world. Vohu Mano is in this world the special guardian of the faithful; Good Mind is in a way embodied in them, so that when one of them has contracted uncleanness and is purified by the peculiar disinfectants prescribed in the "antidemonic law," it is said that the Vohu Mano (i. e., the man) is purified. He is also, as has already been noted, the guardian of the flocks and herds, with which the religion is hardly less concerned than with human beings. He receives the righteous at the gates of paradise; and the significant name of the state of the blessed is "the blessings of the Good Mind," as hell is the abode of the Evil (or the worst) Mind.

The Bundahish (ninth century A. D.) describes the creation of the world, doubtless following substantially the lost Avestan books. The first of Ahura Mazda's "mundane creatures" was the sky, from which Vohu Mano produced the cosmic light and the good religion of the Mazdæans—true religion was pre-existent, like the Torah in Judaism. Then followed the Amesha Spentas, Asha, and the rest. "Of Ahura Mazda's creatures the first was the sky, the second water, the third dry land, the fourth plants, the fifth animals, the sixth mankind." The work of creation filled just a year (365 days), and the six acts correspond to the six divisions of the year, each ending with a festival of the religious calendar. The similarity of this scheme to the six days of creation in Genesis was early remarked, and some have thought it probable that the Persian cosmology was borrowed from the Jews. There is no external difficulty in such a supposition, for even the lost Avestan book on which the Bundahish depends was probably not as old as Genesis. On the other hand, the number and order of the creative acts are perfectly natural, we might almost say, inevitable—sky, sea, land; plants, animals, man—while the several acts of creation fit into the six days of Genesis so awkwardly that many Old Testament critics regard the latter as superimposed on the original cosmologic scheme. Aside from this, one great difference remains: in Genesis the sun and moon and other celestial luminaries are introduced after the plants, as the first of the animal creation, a point of view in itself quite in accord with ancient notions, but perhaps inspired here by Jewish antipathy to the worship of the heavenly bodies. In view of these facts the conjecture that the Persian Genesis is dependent on the Hebrew Scriptures is superfluous.[1]

The Bundahish tells much in detail about the creation of the luminaries and the constellations; the different regions of the earth, with their mountains, rivers, and lakes; the families and species of animals, real and fabulous; the origin of mankind, and the races of men distributed over the earth. The three great races are called Airya, Tura, and Sairya (the Aryan Iranians, their hereditary Turanian foes, and the peoples of the eastern Roman Empire).[2]

If God made mankind, the question must arise, How comes it then that there are wicked men? The answer of the Bundahish is that in the minds of the first pair an evil thought arose, namely, that it was the evil spirit that had created the water, earth, plants, and animals; from this they went on to sins of act, until at last they became worshippers of the Daevas, just as in the Gathas we read that the Daevas themselves chose not rightly between the two primal spirits, but were deluded into choosing the Evil Mind. Reflection has gone a step further, to the question how God could have permitted this. According to the Bundahish, Ahura Mazda bade the guardian genii of men (*fravashis*) say whether is better, that men should contend on earth against the fiend and overcome at last, the fiend perishing, or should always be protected against the destroyer. Christian theologians have reasoned similarly about the fall of Adam and Eve.

The Bundahish has much to tell of Ahriman's evil creatures

[1] The contrary theory, that the Jewish cosmology was derived from the Persians, is, on chronological grounds, not worth considering.

[2] *Cf.* Dinkart, VIII, 13, 9, and 15, from the lost Citradat Nask. Here, again, the three groups in Genesis, Shem, Ham (Canaan), and Japhet will suggest themselves, or the three Greek stocks, Æolians, Ionians, Dorians.

with which he filled the world, and of the varied mischief they wrought. First of his creatures was Akem Mano, Evil Mind, the counterpart and antagonist of Vohu Mano, the Good Mind. For each of the other Amesha Spentas also he makes a particular deadly foe, but in the others there is no such obvious correspondence; they are, as has already been mentioned, ancient deities, Indra, Sauru, Naonhaithya, Tauru, Zairi—the catalogue is not so constant as that of the good powers. Occasionally Taromaiti, Arrogance, appears as the enemy of Armaiti, Humble Piety.

The Greeks in the fourth century B. C. were acquainted with the fact that the Magi divided the history of the world into periods of three thousand years, of which the present age of conflict is one. This scheme appears in full in the Bundahish, and there is evidence in the older Avesta that it is an early, if not a primitive, feature of Zoroastrian doctrine. The cycle is 12,000 years. At the beginning Ahura Mazda produced his spiritual creation, and his creatures remained for three thousand years with intangible bodies, free from corruption. The second period of three thousand years is the period of material creation. In the third, Angra Mainyu breaks into the creation of God and causes the greatest distress; this is the age of human history prior to the revelation of the true religion. At the beginning of the fourth period (Anno Mundi 9000) Zoroaster appears; at its close will be the last judgment. Theopompus, if he is completely reported, seems to have said nothing of the age of the spiritual, or ideal, creation; according to him good and evil prevailed each for three thousand years, then for three thousand—the present—they contended and destroyed each other's works; at the end of this period Hades would succumb and the age of perfect blessedness would begin. It would be incautious on this ground to infer that the first period is a later addition to the scheme: the 12,000 years are plainly a great world-year, and Theopompus is concerned only with the idea of the conflict.

The ideal creation has a striking resemblance to Platonic

theories. Philo sets forth how God, "when he made up his mind to form this visible world, first produced the intelligible world as its type, in order that, employing a bodiless (immaterial) and most godlike pattern, he might fabricate this bodily world." But the parallel is less significant than striking, for the spiritual world of Ahura Mazda is not the ideal type of the material creation: it is simply the beginning, before the intrusion of the devil, when things were in that perfect state in which they will be at the end when he has been finally banished. The material creation is made necessary by the invasion of the enemy; the battle with him must be waged and the victory won in a real world, with carnal weapons as well as spiritual. Plausible as the hypothesis of Greek influence at first seems to be, closer examination does not sustain it.

According to the Vendidad, Ahura Mazda revealed the true religion in the beginning to Yima, son of Vivanhant, and invited him to proclaim it to men. Yima, however, excused himself: the task was beyond his powers. He accepted the humbler charge, to multiply the creatures, care for them, and rule over them. "In my realm there shall be neither cold wind nor hot wind, nor disease nor death." Ahura Mazda bestowed on him the regalia, a seal and sword. The good creatures multiplied so that thrice the earth had to be enlarged to make room for them. But at the end of this golden age of nine hundred years God announced to Yima the approach of a terrible winter, a kind of ice age, and bade him make a great shelter in which to keep alive choice specimens of plants and animals and human beings, two of every species, to perpetuate their kind and repeople the earth. This myth of the ice age destroying plant and animal life, and of the preservation of a remnant in the Var of Yima, is the Iranian parallel to the wide-spread flood myth, of which the Babylonian and Jewish forms are the most familiar. The arid Iranian lands were no climate for a flood; but of winter, "the worst of plagues, the creation of the demons," they had experience enough.

Long ages elapsed after Yima's "gran rifiuto" before God
again designated a prophet of the true religion. The second
of the Gathas (Yasna, XXIX) represents the "soul of the
kine" complaining to Ahura of the cruel wrongs it suffered
at the hands of brutal men, and Zoroaster is commissioned to
be its deliverer by converting men to the law which makes
them merciful to beasts. The Vendidad tells how Angra
Mainyu, foreseeing the discomfiture he and his creatures
were to suffer at Zoroaster's hands, sent demon emissaries to
kill him,[1] but Zoroaster routed them by reciting the confession of faith, Ahuna Vairya, not to speak of rocks as big as
houses that he had ready to pelt the devils with, defiantly
declaring his purpose to destroy the fiend's creation. Angra
Mainyu begs him not to destroy his creation, and tempts
him by promising him that if he will abjure the good law
of Mazda he shall have dominion as wide and long as that
of the mythical Vadhaghana, "master of the countries."[2]
Zoroaster rejects the offer, and declares that he will put the
devils to flight with the apparatus of worship and the holy
words. Thereupon the whole host, with cries of terror,
precipitately flee down to the world of darkness.[3]

The world is a great battle-field, on which beneficent powers
ceaselessly contend with baleful forces, light with darkness,
the vivifying waters with drought and barrenness, the genial
warmth with icy winter; the useful animals are beset by
beasts of prey, the industrious peasant and herdsman by
the marauding nomads; the civilised Iranians have ever
to defend themselves against the wild Turanians. Religion
teaches men to see in all this the age-long struggle of Ahura
Mazda and Angra Mainyu, the good God and the demon of
destruction, each with his hosts of allies. It teaches, too,
that man is not a passive spectator of this war of gods and

[1] For the age of this myth it is significant that the name of the demon
of idolatry is Buiti, if, as has been conjectured, Buiti is Buddha. The
most idolatrous religion in Asia was northern Buddhism.

[2] *Cf.* Matt. 4, 8–11.

[3] This attack and rout of the demons is apparently in the infancy of
Zoroaster, not at the beginning of his ministry.

demons on whose issue his fortunes and his very existence depend, but a combatant in the thick of the fight. Every man is by his own choice arrayed under the one banner or the other, contending for the triumph of the good world or the bad. The whole conflict is moral: the strife of the productive and the destructive agencies in nature is not the play of physical forces guided by blind laws or blinder chance, but the warring of benevolent and malevolent wills. Men, animated by Good Mind or by Evil Mind, battle for the truth and right and goodness or for falsehood and wrong; and their contending is not alone with flesh and blood, but with the "world-rulers of this darkness, the spirit hosts of wickedness in the heavenly places." [1] This conception of life as a war with the demons gives its peculiar colour to the religion, morals, and customs. In many particulars these resemble the lower religions in which self-defence against evil spirits is the principal feature; but the central theistic and ethical ideas give them a different significance.

The individual believer does not engage in this warfare fighting for his own hand, but as a member of an army. Of the organisation of the Zoroastrian state church we have little information. From the Avesta it appears that in Sassanian times the religious heads of the several towns, districts, and provinces constituted an ecclesiastical hierarchy, at the summit of which, the head of the church in the whole empire, stood the Zarathushtrotema, Zoroaster's vicar on earth, whose seat was at Rai, in Media, the system thus corresponding to the political organisation as did that of the Christian church in the Roman Empire. The ancient name of the priests, the only name in the Avesta,[2] was Athravan, "fire priests." The Greeks call the Zoroastrian clergy "Magi," which according to Herodotus was the name of a Median tribe; and the Parsis use the same name, the modern Mobed being from *Magupat*, "Head Magian." The priesthood was probably

---

[1] *Cf.* Ephes. 6, 10 *ff.*, and with it Minokhired, c. 43 (Sacred Books of the East, XXIV, 84).

[2] An exception in Yasna, LXV, 7.

from very early times hereditary in certain families, as it is now.

In heroic antiquity the Yashts tell of sacrifices of "a thousand stallions, a thousand bulls, ten thousand sheep," but in the Zoroastrian religion worship consists essentially in the tending of the sacred fire and the offering of Haoma. The Avestan ritual which we have in the Yasna is the liturgy of the Haoma offering on ordinary and extraordinary occasions. Considerable parts of a lost book of the Sassanian Avesta, the Instructions for the Priests, have been preserved in the Nirangistan. The rubrics in modern copies of the Yasna and the traditional ritual of the Parsis doubtless perpetuate the important features of the ceremonies as they were in Sassanian times. Early reliefs and coins show the king standing before a fire altar under the open sky; the Magi, like the modern Mobeds, had portable altars for service in the houses; but there were also, from Achæmenian times on, fire shrines, in which the sacred fire was kept burning on an altar, or, as at present, in a vase filled with ashes. Strabo tells how the priests in Cappadocia went daily into these shrines and sang for an hour before the fire, holding a bundle of twigs, and wearing a head-dress which covered their mouths. The shrine was constructed so as to keep the sunlight from falling on the fire and dimming or extinguishing it, according to a wide-spread belief. The fire is guarded from every kind of pollution; it is fed with scrupulously selected wood—modern Parsis in Bombay use sandalwood—the priest wears a thick veil over his nose and mouth, that his breath may not fall on the fire;[1] his hands are encased in long gauntlets, and the wood is handled with tongs. This service is performed five times a day, at the canonical hours.

No other ceremonies take place in this inmost shrine; the preparation and offering of the Haoma is done in other rooms in the temple. The similarity of these rites to those of the

[1] A similar precaution is used by Shinto priests in Japan and by cooks in the Mikado's kitchen.

Brahman Soma offering shows how tenaciously they have been perpetuated from a time before the forefathers of the Indian and Iranian peoples separated. The twigs of the sacred plant are pounded in a mortar, the expressed juice is mixed with milk and holy water and strained. The draught thus obtained concentrates in itself all the virtues of plants, animals, and the waters; it is drunk sacramentally by the priests in the course of the service, and is administered to the dying as a φάρμακον ἀθανασίας. The "green Haoma" of this world is a type of the "white Haoma" of the *gaoko-rena*-tree from which is obtained the draught of immortality. Besides the Haoma, the offering comprises small cakes peculiarly marked, with butter or fat to represent animal sacrifice; these also are eaten by the officiating priest in the course of the service.

In former times eight priests took part in the rite: the Zaotar recited the Gathas as the Hotar recites the Vedic hymns in the Brahmanic ritual; another pressed the Haoma, a third mixed it with milk, others tended the fire on the small altar and waited in different capacities on the principal ministers, while a master of ceremonies (corresponding to the Brahman) had general oversight of the whole. At present these various functions are concentrated in the hands of two priests, the Zot (Zaotar), who performs the essential parts of the sacrifice as well as the recitation of the sacred text, and the Raspi, who (theoretically representing the three absent priests) assists him and makes the responses. The celebrant must be in the superlative stage of ritual holiness which is acquired by the great nine days' purification—the Barashnum ceremony—with cow's urine, the antiseptic for demonic infection; and every stage of the ceremony itself is marked by washings and sprinkling with holy water. The principal service is addressed to Ahura Mazda and all the holy divinities of the celestial world; to Zarathushtra and all the holy divinities of this terrestrial world; to the Yazatas who preside in turn over the thirty days of the month, beginning with Ahura Mazda and the six Amesha Spentas, and including the genii of gods and of the pious dead. The central part of the liturgy is the recitation of the Gathas.

The whole cultus is a singularly arid ritualism consonant with the practical genius of the race. The exact performance of the rite and the exact recitation of the long texts in a dead language is the essential thing; so done, it is sure to be efficacious. It not only procures blessings from the gods, but reinforces the gods and gives them power to overcome hostile influences and work for good. This is the plain lesson of the Tishtar Yasht, where Tishtrya (Sirius), the rain star, is worsted by the drought demon Apaosha until Ahura Mazda himself offers a sacrifice dedicated to Tishtrya by name; then the demon is ignominiously put to flight and the blessed rain descends. Here, as in many other religions, primitive notions of the magical efficacy of the cultus which seem for a time to be overcome in the development of the idea of the supreme power and goodness of God and the ethical nature of religion come back and intrench themselves impregnably in the ritual. God can be worked for man's advantage by offering, praise, and prayer; or, as theological reflection less bluntly puts it, God has appointed these means of moving him to bestow his favours and protection.

A large part of practical religion consists in the observance of the rules of clean and unclean and in the purifications necessary to repair witting or unwitting infractions of them. Uncleanness in the religious sense is a demonic contagion. The demons and all their ways and works are unclean, and persons and things that get into the infected neighbourhood catch the contagion and may communicate it to others. The sphere in which the presence and agency of demons is most clearly seen is death, and here the greatest precautions must be taken. When death is near, a priest is called in; the dying man recites after him his confession of sin, and the priest puts into his mouth some drops of Haoma as a last sacrament. The demon of death is imagined to wear the form of a carrion fly; to drive him away, a dog is brought into the chamber when the body is laid out—if possible a dog with "four eyes," that is, with spots of light colour above the eyes, or a white dog with yellow ears—for the "glance of the dog" is a terror to demons.[1] Fire is then brought into the room and fed with sweet-smelling wood, the odour of which kills the demons wherever the wind carries it.[2] A priest, sitting at least three yards from the dead, recites Avestan texts until the funeral procession sets out.

This must take place by daylight, and should not be in rainy weather. The body is carried on an iron bier, by bearers whose business it is and who take professional precautions against infection, to the place where it is to be exposed. In ancient times this might be a dry and barren spot far from the abode of men; but special structures for the purpose, the Dakhmas (now called in India "towers of silence"), are mentioned in the Avesta. The motive of this singular mode of disposing of the dead is to prevent the defiling of the elements; it is from a Zoroastrian point of view a mortal sin to burn a body, to inhume it, or to cast it into the water. The modern Dakhma is so constructed that the rain which may fall on the bodies is rapidly carried off into a catch-basin and thence through filters into cisterns beneath. Prayers for the dead are recited while vultures make quick work of the bodies thus exposed; the bones (which when dry are no longer unclean) are from time to time cast into the central pit.[3] Religious services for the benefit of the deceased are kept up for three days, partly in the house, partly in the fire temple, directed especially to Sraosha, the psychopompos, and are observed with especial diligence on the fourth day, on which the soul confronts the judgment at the Cinvat bridge; during this time the mourners are required to fast from flesh.

[1] This performance is repeated at intervals so long as the body remains in the house.

[2] This seems to be the original motive for the use of incense in the worship of the gods.

[3] The Dakhmas are represented in the Avesta as the favourite haunts of demons who smite men with all manner of diseases.

For those who have contracted uncleanness by contact with a dead body from which the devil has not been driven away by beasts or birds of prey, and who are therefore themselves possessed by the demon Nasu (νέκυς), a special purification is prescribed in the Vendidad. The active disinfectant is cow's urine applied by aspersion, whereby the demon is driven successively from one lodging-place to another, from head to foot, till at last he escapes from the left great toe and rushes away, buzzing wildly, to the regions of the north where the devils are at home. For greater assurance, this is gone through five times more. Then the man rubs himself down with dry earth, and finally washes in water at three depressions in the ground, at the first once, at the second twice, at the third three times. These purifications are repeated at intervals of three days, during which the man must remain in quarantine, and only at the end of the ninth day may he approach the fire or water or earth, or cattle or the faithful. If the demon had been expelled by dogs or birds of prey, washing of the body with cow's urine and water thirty times repeated suffices. A field in which the dead body of a dog is found lying must remain fallow for a year. To throw out on the ground any part of the body of a man or the carcass of a dog of the size of a joint of the little finger or larger is punishable by stripes in proportion, up to a thousand blows of the horsewhip. The ground in which a body has been buried is unclean for fifty years. Running or standing water in which a body is found is unclean; how far, and what to do about it, are subjects of long-drawn-out casuistry. A large part of the Vendidad is taken up with these matters. By a singular yet strictly logical theory the body of an evil beast, creature of Ahriman, or of an idolater or heretic, is not unclean; the devil who was in him while he was alive has now gone off with his soul, leaving the body pure. Eating the flesh of a dead man or dog is a prodigious and inexpiable sin.

Next to death the most redoubtable uncleanness is that of a menstruous woman. She is shut up in an isolated apartment, remote from fire and water, from the bunch of sacred twigs, and from believers, and receives her meagre allowance of food in a metal vessel; whoever brings this food must keep at least nine feet away from the woman. If menstruation is prolonged, it is because the demons have brought this scourge upon her; the cow's-urine panacea is prescribed again, and revenge is taken on the demons by killing some hundreds of Ahrimanian insects such as ants. Needless to say, commerce with a woman in such a state is a deadly sin: it is as bad, the Vendidad declares, as if a man roasted the flesh of his own son and let the fat run into the fire. Childbirth is similarly unclean, and any one who touches the mother catches the uncleanness. The rigid quarantine lasts forty days and is followed by a similar purification. Much graver is the case of a woman who has had a still-born child or a miscarriage. She is shut up in absolute seclusion for three days, without food or drink; then the Dakhma within her is disinfected by a draught of cow's urine and ashes, after which small rations of boiled milk, or gruel made in milk, or wine without water are allowed; only in peril of death may she be given water, and this profanation of the pure element must be penally expiated. We are familiar with the same notions and with similar, if less rigorous, religious regulations in the Jewish laws, but in these the association of uncleanness with demonic influence is not so obvious.

Diseases were brought into the world by the malice of Angra Mainyu; some of them, like leprosy, are in a peculiar degree unclean, and demand the seclusion of the victim from the company of men and the proximity of the pure fire and water and the apparatus of worship. Some can be cured by the knife, others by healing plants which Ahura Mazda created as specifics for the demonic maladies; but the final resort is to the beneficent divine word, the incantation in the Avesta itself, above all, the potent formula Airyama Ishyo (Yasna, LIV), the prayer to Airyama, who puts to flight diseases, death, pain, and fever, every disease and every death, all the Yatus and all the Pairikas and all the evil Jainis.[1]

The ethics of Zoroastrianism bear the distinct impress of its fundamental religious conceptions. The good life is an unceasing conflict against evil within and without. Virtue, like purity, is a defeat of the demons. Morals have therefore a strenuous and militant quality. There is no place for saints who flee from the world; the saint is he who overcomes the evil in the world. Character lies not in overt act alone, but in the inner springs of conduct; "good thoughts, good words, good deeds," is the ever-recurring formula.

Among the virtues of the Mazdayasnian, truth has the foremost place: the devil is a liar, and the father of lies. In the Gathas, as we have seen, the Lie (Druj) is the comprehensive name for the demon host and its head, and the world of the Lie is hell. It may well be that the false religion of the Daevas is here chiefly in mind, but in later times, when this phase of the conflict was past, the words bore a more general sense. The Greeks expatiate upon the value the Persians set on truth and the stress laid on this virtue in the education of well-born youths. They abhor falsehood above everything, Herodotus says, and next to that, making debts, for that leads to lying and fraud. A special form of this virtue is good faith in keeping promises and agreements. Mithra is the guardian and vindicator of oaths and covenants; the man who breaks his solemn word is a "Mithra-liar," and incurs the honest god's deadly wrath. "The miscreant who lies to Mithra brings death on a whole country, he harms the good world as much as a hundred malefactors could do. Never break an agreement, O Spitama, neither one that you make with a wicked man nor with an upright man of your own religion; for an agreement holds with both wicked and upright." [2] Perjury is as bad as a hundred heresies—an extraordinary triumph of ethics over orthodoxy!

Justice and equity—righteousness in the widest sense in

[1] Names of classes of demons. See Vendidad, XX.
[2] Mithra Yasht, 1.

dealing with fellow men—has its ideal and presiding genius in Asha, personified Right. The unjust judge is denounced in the Gathas; it is related of Cambyses that he flayed a corrupt judge, and, for an effective reminder, covered with his skin the chair on which his son was seated to succeed him.[1] Justice, next to truth, was inculcated in the education of princes and noble youth.

What we should regard as moral offences in the relations of the sexes fall chiefly, from the Zoroastrian point of view, into the class of impurity, which, however, we do well to remember, is not merely physiological but moral. Pæderasty and bestiality, unnatural vices, are crimes punished by death; the offender caught *flagrante delicto* may be killed on the spot by any man without trial. They are also mortal sins for which there is no repentance or expiation; hell is the inevitable punishment in the other world. Such a sinner is wholly demonic in this life, and hereafter becomes one of the invisible demons. The prostitute is a dire affliction of gods and men, a human fiend, whose look dries up the waters and withers the plants; such creatures should be killed sooner than vipers or wolves. Abortion is treated as homicide.

Since all barren land belongs to the devil, reclamation of such land by irrigation or by the draining of marshes is a meritorious work; he who makes two blades of grass grow where one grew before is not only a benefactor of his kind but a faithful servant of God.

Who most makes glad the earth? He who plants the most grain, grass, and fruit trees, who brings water to a field where there is none and draws it off where there is too much. . . . How is the Mazdæan religion nourished? By zealously sowing grain. He who sows grain sows good; he makes the religion of Mazda progress, he nourishes the religion of Mazda as much as a hundred men's feet could do, a thousand women's breasts, ten thousand formulas of the liturgy. When grain was created the devils jumped, when it grew they lost heart, when the joints appeared they wept, when the ear was formed they fled away. In the house where grain perishes the demons abide, but when grain comes up in abundance it is like hot iron in their mouths.[2]

[1] Herodotus, V, 25; *cf.* VII, 194. [2] Vendidad, III, 23 *ff.*

When the cock, before daybreak, calls men to arise and say their morning prayers, the long-armed Bushyansta, the lazy devil, assails them: "Sleep on, poor man! it is not time yet," but he who at cock-crowing first gets up will be the first in paradise. Compassion and benevolence are also strongly commended in the Avesta; in the Ahuna Vairya, one of the most sacred formulas of the religion, which we may call an ethical confession of faith, charity is declared to be the foundation of the Kingdom of God. Ahura Mazda appointed Zarathushtra "a shepherd to the poor."

Morals are in the later Avesta part of a sacred law, and that law includes in the same categories and under the same sanctions much that is not intrinsically moral at all, or to which religion gives fictitious moral values. This is one of the universal evils of nomistic religions: ritual correctness, ceremonial purity, sacerdotal casuistry are raised to the dignity of moral obligations, with the effect of confusing the fundamental difference between them. The dog, especially the shepherd dog, is a very useful animal in a pastoral society, and it is not strange that killing or maltreating him should be a grave offence against the law; but the penalties in this world and the next which the Vendidad attaches to these offences make a dog's life more sacred than a man's. The hedgehog is a great destroyer of the creatures of the evil spirit; a man who kills one shall abide in hell for nine generations unless he expiates his offence on earth by thousands of stripes with the horsewhip. Still more sacred is the otter, probably because it is supposed to destroy noxious water vermin; a whole chapter is devoted to the expiation of the enormous crime of killing one, beginning with ten thousand strokes of the horsewhip. If nothing is more important in morals than a just sense of proportion, not much can be said for the Vendidad. It is fair to observe, however, that such extravagances have the air of priestly fantasias, like some of the incredible programmes of sacrifice in the Brahmanas, rather than of serious chapters of legislation.

The legal spirit appears also in the system of penances by

which offences are expiated. The commonest of these penances is horse-whipping, and the scale runs from five stripes up to ten thousand. The flagellation was doubtless supposed to drive out the demons, a frequent motive of this pious exercise. A large class of more serious sins are expiated by two hundred stripes; so, for example, if a man give another a blow of which he dies, for the first offence the penalty is ninety stripes, for the second, two hundred. Wilful murder is rated at eight hundred; nocturnal emission[1] (*i. e.*, intercourse with a succubus) at two thousand. The scale runs into such high numbers that the beating must either have been symbolical or commuted for a fine paid to the priests.

Other penances were the providing of materials for worship—a thousand loads of choice wood for the sacred fire, a thousand bundles of twigs (Baresman), a thousand libations of Haoma, for example. Works useful to the community, especially the digging of irrigation canals and the construction of bridges, are also prescribed in expiation of sins. The killing of noxious or demonic animals is another mode— serpents, tortoises, frogs, ants, worms, and the like, by thousands. Here, again, the priests probably had, at least in later times, a tariff of commutation for money, but a system in which every offence has its fixed price, whether in stripes or in fines, cannot be regarded as favourable to morality. Not all sins, however, can be thus compounded for: there are inexpiable sins, such as the inhumation of the body of a man or a dog by a Zoroastrian who knows that it is forbidden by his religion, the polluting of water or fire by putting a dead body into the pure elements, eating the flesh of a dead man or dog, unnatural vice, and so on. It is to be noted that if a heathen who has committed a deadly sin embraces the Mazdæan faith, repenting of his fault and purposing never to sin thus again, the religion removes all his former sins, however heinous, precisely like Christian baptism. As in all religions which derive their authority from a prophetic revelation and have formulated the content of revelation in

[1] *Cf.* Lev. 15, 16; 22, 4.

dogma, apostasy and heresy are the greatest of sins, for they are the rejection or perversion of the truth of God.

The hereafter loomed large in Zoroastrianism from the outset. The approaching crisis, the great judgment day when all the powers of evil (the Lie, Druj) shall be delivered into the hands of Righteousness (Asha), their whole army beaten down and shattered, when the ordeal of molten metal divides between the servants of God and the worshippers of the demons, is one of the ruling ideas in the Gathas. The prophet knows but two kinds of men, those who are for him and those who are against him, on the side of truth and right or opposed to them, allies of God or of the devil. To these contradictory characters correspond their diverse destinies. The Zoroastrian heaven and hell are not conceived of primarily as spheres of retribution, but as the places of God and of the devil, and every man, as he has chosen to serve the one or the other, goes to his own place; it is this that gives them their distinctive character. On the other hand, as the line of moral cleavage is run through the natural world, and even the kingdoms of plants and animals are divided between Ahura Mazda and Angra Mainyu, the very hardening of the dualism made the final and complete triumph of good over evil in every sphere a more vital article of faith. As has already been observed, these two aspects of the doctrine, the individual retribution and the ultimate annihilation of all evil, are in the Gathas embraced in one great act of judgment. Time introduced perspective into the Persian eschatology as it did into that of the early Christians. The soul goes to its reward or punishment immediately at death; when the appointed time is fulfilled and the end of the age is come, the body will be raised from the dead and the last judgment will be held.

After death—so runs the simplest story in the Hadokht Yasht—the soul of the righteous lingers three days and nights near the head of the body, reciting the hymn that begins, "Good comes to him who does good to another; may Mazda, the Almighty, give him his gifts," in bliss as great as the whole world of the living contains. At daybreak on the fourth day a perfumed breeze comes wafted to him as it were from the south, and with it comes to him a beautiful maiden, who, at his question, declares herself his own religion, fair with his virtues and pious observances. Through the three forecourts of good thoughts, good words, good deeds, the soul passes into the endless light, into the company of the good and the presence of Ahura Mazda. Other texts add more details. Sraosha and other good angels conduct the soul to the Cinvat bridge, protecting it from the assaults of demons by the way. There Mithra, Sraosha, and Rashnu sit in judgment. Rashnu weighs a man's merits and demerits in the true balance, which does not deviate from justice by a hair's breadth and shows no partiality, but deals alike with the mightiest monarch and the meanest of mankind. Religion goes into the scale, it is needless to say, as well as morality; the good Zoroastrian profession of faith and the penitent confession of sins weigh heavily on the side of salvation, and the funeral mass which the friends of the departed cause to be celebrated is another good work put to his credit. Then he must make essay of the bridge itself, which stretches from the peak of Mount Daitya to the summit of the Elburz, spanning the abyss of hell. For the good it is nine spear-lengths, or even a parasang, wide, and he passes with ease to the heavenly mansions on the other side; the wicked finds it narrow as a razor-blade, and pitches headlong into the gulf below.

Beyond the bridge, the soul which has happily crossed it comes first to the limbo where those in whom good works and evil were evenly balanced abide till the day of the resurrection, suffering no other pain than the climatic changes of heat and cold. Then follow the three regions of good thoughts, good words, and good deeds, that is, according to the Persian notion of the celestial spheres, the sphere of the stars, of the moon, and of the sun, respectively. The older writings do not seem to have any permanent occupants of these regions; they are successive forecourts of the highest heaven. In the journey of Arda Viraf, however, he sees in them souls who on earth "made no prayers, recited no Gathas, contracted no consanguineous marriages," but through other good works came thither; in the highest are such as "in the world exercised good sovereignity, rulership, and chieftainship," as if they were limbos for good heathen.

The "infinite light," or "light eternal," is the abode of Ahura Mazda with the archangels and the spirits of the just. When the soul arrives there, the pious dead throng around the newcomer inquiring, "How art thou come from the material world to the world of spirit, from the perishing world to that which perishes not?" but Ahura Mazda bids them not recall to the spirit the distressful journey, and commands that angels' food, butter made in the height of spring, be set before the traveller,[1] and that he be given a richly adorned throne. "Forever and everlasting they remain in all glory with the angels of the spiritual existences eternally."

Very different is the lot of the wicked. His soul lingers about the body in great perturbation for three days, murmuring the words of the Gatha, "To what land shall I turn, O Ahura Mazda, whither direct my prayer?" and suffering all of distress that the world holds. The fourth morning, a cold blast, as out of the demonic north, smites him, laden with foul stench. A demon lassoes the soul with his evil noose and drags him to the bridge, where Rashnu with his balances detects all his wickedness. His evil ways confront him embodied in a hideous witch, whose ugliness is the expression of his character. Hell has its vestibules, evil thoughts, evil words, evil deeds, through which the damned sinner arrives in the "infinite darkness," where the wicked dead surround him, the demons mock him, and Angra Mainyu bids bring him loathsome and poisonous food. "And until the resurrection he must be in hell in much misery and torments of many kinds."

The book of Arda Viraf narrates how that pious man's soul was conducted by Sraosha through heaven and hell and

[1] The spiritual world is, therefore, not without its creature comforts.

safely reinstalled in his body to tell the tale, an Iranian parallel to Plato's Er the Pamphylian, Enoch, the Apocalypse of Peter, and the mediæval Christian vision literature, and a rude forerunner of Dante. The Persian author's imagination does not succeed in giving much variety to heaven: golden thrones, fine carpets, rich cushions, gorgeous raiment, fragrant perfumes, and over all the glorious light, exhaust his resources. Hell is, as usual, much more vividly depicted. Its darkness is so dense that, though the souls are crowded thick together, each imagines himself alone, and when three days have passed he thinks the nine thousand years must be over and the hour of release at hand. Further on his way through the Zoroastrian inferno, the voyager sees men and women subjected to all manner of ingenious tortures, often retaliatory, as when the man who talked at the dinner-table and said no grace over meat, but greedily devoured his water and vegetables, is tormented by hunger and thirst, crying ever, "I shall die"; or the tradesman who gave short measure, and watered his wine and put dust in his grain, and sold his adulterated foodstuffs at high prices, has to spend the millenniums of his sojourn in hell measuring dust and ashes in a bushel and getting nothing else to eat; or, again, a woman is condemned to lick a hot stove with her tongue because she answered back snappishly to her husband. The catalogue of sins is long and repetitious, and the writer's ingenuity in devising tortures runs out before he is through. Last of all, Arda Viraf sees the fiend himself, who taunts the sufferers: "Why did ye ever eat the bread of Ahura Mazda and do my work, and thought not of your own creator but did my will?" Returning then to heaven, he is dismissed by Ahura Mazda with a parting injunction: "Say to the Mazdayasnians, 'There is only one way of piety, the way of the primitive religion; the other ways are no ways. Take ye that one way which is piety, and turn not from it in prosperity nor in adversity . . . and practise good thoughts and good words and good deeds . . . and keep the proper law, but abstain from the improper. And know ye this, that cattle are dust, and gold and silver are dust, and the body of man is dust; he alone mingles not with the dust who in the world praises righteousness and performs duties and good works.' "

The bliss of souls in heaven and their torments in hell are not the final state of mankind. When the appointed time comes, Shaoshyant, the Saviour, will appear, and the dead will be raised, beginning with Gayomard, the archetypal man, and Mashya and Mashoi, the first pair of human beings. All, righteous and wicked, will rise in the places where they died, the bones being demanded back from the earth, the blood from the water, the hair from the plants, and the life from the fire, to which they have respectively been delivered, so that the body is reconstituted of its original materials.[1] The risen dead will be assembled in one place and will know one another; the deeds of all will be manifest, so that the wicked man will be as conspicuous as a white sheep among black ones.[2] The wicked will reproach his pious friend for not turning him from the evil of his ways. Then the righteous and the wicked will be separated, the former going to heaven, while the latter are cast into hell, there to be punished in the body for three days, certain monsters of iniquity being subjected to exemplary sufferings. When this is over, the fire will melt the metal in the mountains till it flows like a river, and in its stream all are made pure. To the righteous it will be like walking in warm milk, to the wicked it will be molten metal. Father and son, brother and friend, will inquire: "Where hast thou been these many years, and what was the judgment on thy soul? Wast thou of the righteous or the wicked?" All men become of one speech, and loudly praise Ahura Mazda and the archangels. Shaoshyant then sacrifices the ox Hadhayos, and of his fat and of the white Haoma is prepared the ambrosia (*Hush*) which is given to all men, the food of immortality. Adults are restored as men and women of forty; children as youths of fifteen. Each man has his own wife and knows his own offspring;

[1] This is Christian doctrine also. *Cf*. Athenagoras, De resurrectione, cc. 3 *ff*.
[2] Black being the more common colour in a mixed flock.

the life is like that of this world, but there is no begetting of children.

Finally, Ahura Mazda seizes the Evil Spirit, and each of the archangelic Amesha Spentas lays hold of his antagonist among the arch-fiends, Sraosha grappling with Aeshma. The devil, Ahriman, flees back into gloom and darkness by the passage by which he first invaded the upper world; hell itself is purified by the molten metal, and is reclaimed for the enlargement of the world. Thus by God's will the restitution of all things is accomplished, and the world is immortal for ever and aye. The mountains, which were created by the evil one, are levelled, even the summit which served as abutment for the Cinvat bridge; the earth becomes an even plain, never again buried in ice.

The Zoroastrian dogmatic chronology[1] counts twelve thousand years from the beginning of the spiritual creation to the renovation of the world, in four ages of three millenniums each. The revelation to Zoroaster and the founding of the true religion fall at the beginning of the last age, the appearance of Shaoshyant at its close. As in the preceding age each millennium has its salient figure, so the millenniums which lie between Zoroaster's appearance and the end are to have their heroes, bearing the significant names Increaser of Good and Increaser of Prayer, in the Bundahish, Hushedar and Hushedar-mah, who restore the good religion and deliver its oppressed people. Both these and the final deliverer, Shoshans (Shaoshyant), are sons of Zoroaster, conceived in a miraculous way of his seed.

These Messianic expectations, which are found in the Fravardin Yasht as well as in the Bundahish, are worked up in a remarkable apocalypse, the so-called Bahman Yasht, in which are revealed to Zoroaster the successive periods of history (four or seven) down to the close of his millennium, the iron age when the myriad demons with dishevelled hair of the race of Aeshma (Wrath) invade Iran from the east, and leather-belted Turks and Arabs and Christians make a reign of terror. In this dark time, Hushedar will be born,

[1] See above, p. 384.

and, with gods and heroes on his side, will destroy the heathen hordes and their demon allies in a veritable Armageddon.

Zoroastrianism is frequently described as a dualism. To the Gathas, as we have seen, the term is in any strict sense inapplicable; and for the religion of Achæmenian times it is not without significance that Aristotle,[1] though acquainted with the two principles, the good and the evil *daimones*, Oromasdes and Areimanios, yet in the Metaphysics classes the Magi with philosophers like Empedocles and Anaxagoras who made the supremely good the first principle and ground of being. The name dualism might seem more appropriate to the doctrine of later writings, such as the Bundahish, which make Ahriman the creator, not only of the demons, but of all that is bad in the natural world, from the wandering planets to the noisome insects. To Moslem controversialists, for whom creation was one of the chief attributes of deity, a creative devil was plainly an evil god; but this is only the logic of opponents, not Zoroastrian teaching or fair implication from it. The Bundahish itself contrasts in the strongest way the omniscience of Ahura Mazda with the limitations of the evil spirit's knowledge either of the present or of the future. It was through ignorance of the event that he accepted the conditions of the nine thousand years' conflict proposed by Ahura Mazda. He has no power to destroy the creatures of God or permanently to deprive God of them by drawing them to his side. However in the present age evil may seem to prevail, the outcome is certain: the works of the devil shall be destroyed, and he himself shall be for ever banished from the universe; the earth will be renewed, and hell itself purged by fire; men whom the evil spirit has seduced from their allegiance to God, after receiving the just retribution of their evil deeds, will be purified and restored to the eternal life of holiness, and all evil will be for ever done away. The triumph of God is in this respect more complete than in Christianity, which leaves hell, with

[1] According to Diogenes Laertius.

the devil and his angels and the wicked in torment for ever, an unconquered realm of evil.

The "dualism" of Zoroastrianism, as has been said above, is an attempt to account for the evil of the present world, physical as well as moral, upon the premises of an ethical theism which cannot admit that God is the author of any kind of evil. But because God is almighty as well as perfectly good, it can as little admit that evil, even in hell, is a permanent factor in the universe. The Zoroastrian theologians were concerned with the solution of the ethical problem rather than with the remoter problems which their solution raised. The evil spirit appears on the scene like a *diabolus ex machina;* whether he was eternal they do not seem to have asked, nor would they probably have been much disturbed if their logic had carried them to that conclusion, for since they did not define God metaphysically as the infinite and the eternal, but as the good, an eternal devil would not thereby become God. Acquaintance with Greek philosophy or Christian polemics ultimately raised this question, however, and a school of Zoroastrian thinkers posited as the unitary first principle, Space or Time, from which were separated a good god and an evil demon.[1] The one undivided nature being thus divided, these form the dual system of higher powers, one headed by Ormazd, the other by Ahriman. Theodore of Mopsuestia reports that Zervan (Time), whom he calls also Tyche, was the origin of all things, and that, in the act of making a libation to produce Ormazd, by some error in the rite, he produced both Ormazd and Satan. Shahrastani, in his History of Doctrines, describes a sect of Zervanites who held that Ahriman was born of a doubt in the mind of the great Zervan. This theory seems to be controverted in the Selections of Zad Sparam, I, 24, where it is declared that Ahura Mazda produced the "creature Zervan" (Time). There is no reason to think that the Zervanite metaphysics ever had any religious significance.

[1] Damascius, ed. Kopp, p. 384.

CHAPTER XVII

THE GREEKS

RELIGION IN EARLY GREECE

The Ægæan Civilisation—The Hellenic Migrations—Prehellenic and
Greek Religion—The Land—The Gods—Zeus—Artemis—Apollo
—Hermes—Athena—Aphrodite—Hera—Hephaistos—Ares—Other
Gods—The Dead in Early Greece—Homer—Influence of the Epics
on Religion—Hesiod—Cosmogony and Theogony.

THE civilisation which is historically associated with the
name of the Greeks was preceded in the peninsula, on the con-
fronting coasts of Asia Minor, and on the islands, by a high
civilisation of a distinct type and of great antiquity. The
surprising wealth of this civilisation and the advanced stage
of its artistic development were first revealed by Schliemann's
discoveries at Mycenæ, and this, combined with the leading
part which Agamemnon has in the Homeric poems as the
head of the Greeks in the expedition against Troy, made the
name Mycenæan seem an appropriate designation for the
civilisation and its products. More recent excavations in
other quarters have shown that the so-called Mycenæan civilisation not only embraced a wider area in the eastern Mediterranean basin than was imagined, but that it spread, not
from the peninsula to the islands, but from the islands to the
continental Greece. Later writers, therefore, prefer the more
comprehensive and non-committal term "Ægæan."

The discoveries in Crete since 1893 have made it year by
year more apparent that the characteristic Ægæan art had
its origin and highest development on that island. Egyptian
objects found in the palaces of Crete and Cretan wares or
representations of them in Egyptian tombs securely establish

certain fundamental synchronisms, and make it possible to assign dates to the principal epochs in Cretan art and architecture. The last of the three great periods into which this history is divided by archæologists—a period on the whole of decadence—was contemporary with the Eighteenth and Nineteenth Egyptian Dynasties, that is, say about 1600–1200 B. C.; the preceding period, the culmination of the civilisation, includes the time of the Twelfth and Thirteenth Dynasties, so that its prime falls, at the latest, about 2000 B. C. Behind this lies the long period of evolution (Minoan I, of Evans); while beneath this stratum at Cnossus lies the debris of neolithic occupation to the depth in places of twenty feet, showing that the site had been continuously inhabited for many centuries. Disregarding this, the beginnings of Cretan civilisation as represented by Minoan I are probably as old as the pyramid age in Egypt or the Sumerian civilisation of southern Babylonia. Commerce with Egypt was early established; Egyptian decorative motives may be recognised in Cretan art at several stages, but they are developed in accordance with the native genius and tradition, never slavishly imitated. On the other hand, there is no trace of Babylonian influence. The Cretans were early in possession of a hieroglyphic writing whose symbols have no connection with the Egyptian characters; this was superseded toward the end of the second great period (contemporary with the Thirteenth Egyptian Dynasty) by a linear script, of which two distinct, but not necessarily independent, types are recognised.

From Crete this civilisation spread to the Cyclades, and to Greece, where its monuments have been discovered at many centres from Laconia to Thessaly, to western Asia Minor, and to Cyprus, where it found a cognate indigenous civilisation already considerably advanced, and whence, in turn, the products of Ægæan art or domestic imitations of them reached seaboard Syria and Phœnicia. In Cyprus, too, the Mesopotamian and the Ægæan cultures met, and this contact and fusion gives their peculiar character to the Cypriote remains. The Mycenæan age in continental Greece, the age of the tombs in the acropolis of Mycenæ and at Tiryns, is contemporary in general with the last period of the Minoan civilisation in Crete.

At what time peoples of Hellenic stock established themselves in Greece it is impossible to determine; tradition preserves no memory of the movement. It is certain, however, that they came in from the north, and probable that they were pushed farther and farther southward by following waves of migration of Indo-Germanic tribes from the Balkans and the Danube valley, of whom the Thracians and Illyrians were the descendants. Whether the tombs, the citadels, and palaces at Mycenæ and Tiryns and Argos were built by Greeks or by the older population, the remains cannot tell us; that the civilisation which they represent is prehellenic there can be no doubt. The first Hellenic migration was followed, apparently after a considerable interval, by a second invasion of Greek tribes from the northwest, to which, unlike the former, many traditions bear witness. They did not displace their predecessors, but pushed through into the Peloponnesus, where in historical times they formed the bulk of the population, and thence to the Cyclades, Crete, and southeastern Asia Minor. This Dorian movement probably took place not later than the twelfth century; the Achæan migration must have preceded it by some centuries.

The discoveries in Crete enable us to form some notion of its religion. There were no temples; but altars have been found in the palace courts, and in one place at least what seems to be a temenos, or consecrated enclosure. Certain small chambers in the palaces at Cnossus and Phæstus apparently served as a cella or chapel. The Dictæan cave and the cave on Mount Ida, both of which are connected in Greek myths with the birth of Zeus, were probably places of worship from the remotest times. Buildings decorated with religious symbols are frequently figured on gems or in frescos, and have been interpreted as representations of shrines, but it is possible that they are meant rather for the façade of a palace.

Among the symbols to which religious significance attaches are a conventionalised pair of bull's horns, which have been called, somewhat awkwardly, "horns of consecration," and the *bipennis*, or double-bitted axe, which occurs with such great frequency as to be a characteristic feature of the Minoan art. Sacred trees are often figured; and there is no reason to doubt that the Cretans, like the Greeks of historic times, worshipped sacred stones, whether rude or shaped by human hands, though it is very doubtful whether all the pillars and table legs in which the English explorers recognise what they call "bætyls" were really objects of religious veneration.

Small idols in rough semblance, or at least suggestion, of the human form are found even in neolithic strata which antedate the rise of the Minoan civilisation, and persist without much improvement to the latest times. They are probably for the most part amulets or votive offerings; rude little idols were found in the palace chapel at Cnossus also. Works of a much more advanced art are the faience figurines handling serpents, which are thought to be the great Cretan goddess and her acolytes. The imprint of a seal found at Cnossus shows a goddess standing on a rocky peak, with lionesses rampant on either side. She wears a flounced robe; in her left hand she brandishes a sceptre or spear, while her dishevelled hair streams wildly. A worshipper stands before her on the ground in a posture of adoration; behind her is the front of an edifice decorated with horns. Another seal impression exhibits a goddess in long robe and peaked cap striding, spear or staff in hand, by the side of a lion. Various acts of worship are depicted—adoration, libation, offering. Scenes from a sacrifice are painted in elaborate detail on a sarcophagus from Hagia Triada on the southern side of the island.

In the centres of the Mycenæan civilisation in Greece little has been found that throws light on the gods or religious rites. The tombs, however, at Mycenæ and elsewhere reveal beliefs about the existence after death which are common to all mankind, while in their forms a connection with

Crete may be clearly traced. They are of various types: pit and shaft graves, structural tombs with domed roof, or let into the hillside and entered by a long gallery, like the so-called Treasury of Atreus at Mycenæ. Whatever the fashion of their abode, the dead were supplied with such things as belonged to their estate on earth—arms, ornaments, vessels in precious materials or of ingenious art, figurines— in short, the familiar funeral furniture. Food and drink were provided at the time of burial and subsequently. Human bones have been found in situations which make it probable that men were killed at some funerals in order that they might accompany and serve their dead lord, a custom of which reminiscences are preserved in the epic.

That the religion of the Greek invaders was influenced in many ways by that of the more advanced civilisation of which they made themselves heirs cannot well be questioned. In view of the pre-eminence of a great goddess in the religion of Crete and the cognate religions of Asia Minor, it is natural to surmise that certain Greek religions which exhibit the same characteristics were taken over from the older inhabitants; and confirmation of this conjecture in a particular instance is given by the excavations on the site of the Argive Heræum, which show that a goddess had been worshipped there from immemorial times. With our present knowledge it is not possible to define or demonstrate the influence of the Mycenæan religion on that of the Greeks; but it is important to keep in mind the fact that Greek civilisation and religion was not purely an evolution of what the Greeks brought with them into the land, but appropriated and assimilated much that they found there.

In the first enthusiasm of the comparative study of Indo-Germanic languages and mythology, it was thought that the Vedas had much light to shed on the religions of the European branch of the race, which was then generally believed to have migrated westward from a common centre in high Asia, whence the ancestors of the Aryo-Indians struck off southward. Scholars made bold to reconstruct the primitive

Indo-Germanic religion as well as the primitive Indo-Germanic speech. More cautious philology, broader knowledge of the history of religions, sounder principles in the interpretation of myths, have left little of these combinatory hypotheses, which their authors often mistook for scientific results; and the residuum is of small significance for religion. A sky god was worshipped by many of the Indo-Germanic peoples, and the name Dyaus, Zeus, Juppiter, Ziu, is common to the Vedic Indians, Greeks, Romans, and Teutons; but it is only among the Greeks and Romans that he becomes the head of the pantheon as the sky god of the Mongols is in China. The connection of the name Varuna with Ouranos is doubtful, and beyond this etymological identity—if it be one—the two deities have not the smallest resemblance. Ushas-Eos-Aurora, the rosy dawn, is a figure of mythological poetry rather than religion; Surya-Helios-Sol is the divine sun, but sun-worship is not distinctively, nor even pre-eminently, Indo-European. The Açvins, the twin horsemen, helpers of men in distress on land or sea, are doubtless identical with the Dioskouroi; the case is unique, and significant in its solitariness. The myth of Hercules and Cacus is a counterpart to that of Indra and the Panis, and other bits of myth and folklore may, with more or less plausibility, be connected. But when the largest allowance is made, it remains true that to an understanding of the religion of the Greeks the Vedas have no considerable contribution to make.

The physical features of the area in which the Ægæan and Hellenic civilisations were evolved and flourished present the strongest contrast to Egypt and Babylonia. The valley of the Nile and the alluvial plain of the Euphrates and Tigris are unbroken by any natural divisions; the same climate, the same productions, the same cultivation, prevail through their whole extent. They were predestined by their very configuration not only to become the cradles of civilisation, but to be early united, more or less firmly, in powerful kingdoms, and to develop a uniformity of culture that has something of the monotony of the landscape, and a uniformity in the type of the *plante humaine* which is unfavourable to further evolution.

The Balkan peninsula, on the other hand, is intersected in all directions by mountains which cut it up into valleys and small plains, so that Greece has not inaptly been called "a land in compartments." On three sides it is surrounded by the sea, whose gulfs and bays penetrate deep into the peninsula and, with the sounds between the mainland and the adjacent islands, make many good roads and harbours. The islands of the archipelago lie like stepping-stones across the Ægæan to the coasts of Asia Minor, where the features of Greece itself are repeated on a larger scale. Diversity of elevation, climate, soil, production, occupation, is as characteristic of the Greek lands as uniformity is of Egypt or Babylonia. Political history was preformed in nature: the city-state, the *polis*, was free to live its own life within its little territory, yet in close communication with its neighbours and open seaward to the larger world; forming confederations with others, acknowledging the hegemony of a more powerful city, but never, at least until Macedonian and Roman times, losing its individuality in the mass of a great empire. To this were added differences of stock, speech, and culture, such as distinguished the Dorians from the Æolians and Ionians, or the Bœotians from the people of Attica. Everything thus tended to the variety, idiosyncrasy, originality, in cities and individuals, which is the condition of collective progress. All this is reflected in the Greek religions, and constitutes one of the great charms, and also one of the chief difficulties, of a study of them.

The Greeks never produced a sacerdotal literature such as the Indian Vedas, they had no universal priesthood like the Brahmans. There were hymns in honour of the gods, of which some of the Homeric Hymns may be taken as examples, and formulas of prayer for special occasions, such as the Athenian prayer for rain; the ritual of the greater sanctuaries, particularly at the festivals, was elaborate and splendid, and there were manifold expiations for public and private use.

It is doubtful, however, whether much of this was ever committed to writing, and certain that it was never compiled and systematised even for single temples. The knowledge we have of these things comes through incidental quotations and descriptions in secular literature and from representations of acts of worship and festival scenes in art. About the myths, which from Homer on were the favourite subjects of poets and artists, we are more abundantly informed, though it is necessary to remember that they have not only been selected and embellished with æsthetic rather than religious intent, but have not infrequently been expurgated or changed in deference to a more refined taste or a more sensitive morality. For the very important question of the local distribution of deities and cults, besides literary testimonies and handbooks for travellers such as Pausanias, the inscriptions furnish the most valuable evidence, to which additions are yearly being made by research and excavation.

The relations of the Greek dialects show that the invaders or the successive waves of invasion were of different tribes, and it is a natural surmise that certain gods were peculiarly favoured by one tribe, others by another, but the attempts to prove this in particular cases—for example, that Apollo was originally a Dorian divinity—have not been permanently convincing. In the age from which our earliest evidence comes, the greater gods are gods of all the Greeks, and though their relative prominence varied much in different regions or cities, these preferences do not coincide at all with the dialect boundaries which may be taken in general as indicating the settlement or migration of different groups of tribes.[1]

The greatest god in all branches of the Hellenic stock was Zeus, and his pre-eminence undoubtedly dates from the remotest antiquity. He is not only a god of the Greeks universally, but stands in close particular relation to the smaller

---

[1] It would be unwarranted to infer that this state of things existed before the immigration; the amalgamation may have taken place largely in the course of the movement itself, and on Greek soil, though no sufficient evidence of the fact remains.

political and social groups.   One of his oldest titles is Her-
keios, the "Zeus of the Fort," the protector of the village
stronghold or the fortified dwelling, whose altar stood in the
courtyard of the Homeric castle, as it stood later on the
Acropolis in Athens and other cities and in the court of private houses. As Polieus he is later the guardian of the city-
state.   Several tribes or political communities regarded him
as their divine forefather (Patrōios). At Athens, where Apollo
took that place, Zeus was the god of every phratry; from the
altar of Zeus Phratrios the votes of the members were brought
when a father presented his child at the chapel for enrolment
in the phratry (curia). As Genethlios, Zeus blessed marriage; as Ktesios he watched over domestic storerooms. It
is probable that in such cases Zeus has usurped the office of
the functional deities whose names became his titles in these
specific aspects; but this only makes the fact more significant:
it was not beneath the majesty of Zeus to be in religion an
every-day god and serve very common uses.

Zeus, as has been observed above, is an ancient Indo-Germanic sky god, whose name corresponds to the Vedic Dyaus.
His original nature may be discerned in Greek religion in the
worship on many mountain summits, as well as in his association with cloud and rain, with storm and lightning, and in
the fact that omens and portents in the sky are particularly
"Zeus-signs" (διοσημία).   But it does not appear that the
Greeks knew that the word Zeus meant "sky"; for them
Zeus was a completely anthropomorphic deity who reigned
in the heaven and controlled meteorological phenomena, not
a personification of the heaven and its phenomena; myths
that seem to us transparently to deal with the fructification
of the earth by the sky do not seem to have been so understood by the Greeks until the sophists interpreted them in
the way of their rationalism and the Stoics developed their
"physical" theory of mythology with mixed scientific and
apologetic intent.

The worship of Zeus was carried with the Greeks in all
their migrations; it cannot—like the religion of Hera, for

example—be traced to any particular centres of diffusion.
A famous ancient seat of Zeus was at Dodona in Epirus, in a
region inhabited in historical times by a non-Hellenic people.
Achilles addresses his prayer:[1]

> "King Zeus, god of Dodona, Pelasgian, dwelling in far lands,
>   Guarding the wintry Dodona, while ever around thee the Selloi,
>   Oracle prophets, unwashen of foot, lie prone on the bare earth."

The sanctuary stood in an oak grove; to the copious
springs of water the god probably owes the title by which
he was invoked in the local cult, Naïos. Zeus was here
associated with Dionē, whose name marks her as the feminine counterpart of Zeus, presumably the oldest of his part-
ners. The oracle of Dodona was the only one in which the
response came direct from Zeus, and if in later times it had
to take second place to the Pythia of Apollo at Delphi, no
other oracle could vie with it in credit. The oldest mode of
divination seems to have been the interpretation of the voices
of the wind in the tops of the oak-trees.[2] Pausanias has preserved a prayer of the priestesses of Dodona, doubtless from
a comparatively late time: "Zeus was, Zeus is, Zeus will be,
O great Zeus! Earth sends forth fruits, wherefore proclaim
the name of mother Earth!"

It is probable that Zeus and Dionē succeeded at Dodona
an older pair of powers whose presence was recognised in
the springs and who may already have been resorted to for
omens. The same thing repeated itself in many other places;
the Greek immigrants identified their own chief god with
the greater powers whom their predecessors called by different local names, taking over the peculiar rites with which
the *numen loci* was worshipped, and borrowing or inventing
myths that explained the strange features of the worship.
This is strikingly illustrated by some of the Arcadian cults
of Zeus. Thus, Zeus Lykaios was worshipped on the summit
of Mount Lykaion in southwestern Arcadia; in the inviolable

---

[1] Iliad, XVI, 233 *ff.*   [2] Odyssey, XIV, 327; XIX, 296.

precincts (*abaton*) stood an altar of earth and two eagles facing the east. The myth ran that the founder, Lykaon, had inaugurated the altar by the sacrifice of a child, whereupon he was changed into a wolf and fled; only after nine years of this expiatory lycanthropy was he restored to human form and society. It seems clear that the old deity of the mountain, whose name as well as the myth connects him with the wolf, was worshipped with human sacrifice, and has taken the name of Zeus in exchange for his savage cult. Human sacrifices were offered to Zeus at other Arcadian shrines—Mount Ithome is particularly named. They were not confined, however, to the wilds of Arcadia, but were connected with Zeus Laphystios in both Thessaly (Phthiotis) and Bœotia, in whose worship they survived to classical times.

The Cretan Zeus, again, whose birth is the theme of a singularly savage myth, and whose tomb was shown at more than one place in the island, whom the Greeks themselves treated almost as a distinct deity, represents a fusion of a native god and his myth with the Greek Zeus. Thus, while Zeus was the universal name for the greatest of the Greek gods, and while the titles under which he was invoked often convey his universal functions, in cultus and myth there were many and diverse Zeuses. The same thing is true, as we shall have frequent occasion to observe, of all the other gods whose worship was widely distributed.

It has been observed that Zeus was the protector of political and social groups from the state to the household. He also took under his especial cognisance moral relations among men. As Xenios he watches over and vindicates the obligations of hospitality, fundamental among which is the sacredness of the guest's person; as Horkios he presides over oath-taking and visits the breach of faith with condign punishment; as Hikesios he is the refuge of the suppliant, the man-slayer seeking asylum, the persecuted fleeing from his oppressor. "Man needs must dread the jealousy of Zeus, the suppliant's god; this is the profoundest fear among mortals." The god marks and avenges the wrongs which man is unable to detect or punish. These conceptions, which have a large development in the historical period, are found already in Homer, and doubtless existed, at least in germ, in a much earlier age.

No worship is more wide-spread among all branches of the Greek race in the home land and in the dispersion than that of Artemis, and no figure among the gods exhibits more varied and seemingly conflicting features, a circumstance due in part to the influence of civilisation, which in some regions had tamed her more completely than in others, but in much larger measure to the fact that she supplanted all manner of wild goddesses, Hellenic and barbarian. The notion that the primitive Artemis was the moon, though generally entertained by the Greeks from the rise of the Stoic exegesis on and adopted by many moderns, is supported by no early evidence, and is, indeed, irreconcilable with the facts. The Greek Artemis was a deity of wild nature in both the plant and animal kingdoms; she is associated with lakes and rivers and the lush vegetation of marshes; she haunts the thickets and roams free through the mountain forests. Wild animals belong to her domain, beasts of prey, such as the lion, wolf, panther, the wild boar, and the bear, also the stag, deer, and hare; the quail is her favourite among birds. "Huntress" is one of her commonest titles, and her exploits in the chase a frequent theme of poetry and art. But all life is her sphere; boys and girls in the flower of youth are under her care, and she gives to mothers easy childbirth. When the tribes of hunters come to till the soil and tempt the sea, Artemis makes the crops grow for the husbandman, protects and guides the wayfarer on his road, and gives a safe and prosperous voyage to mariners. The goddess not only protects life, but takes it; her far-shot shafts bring death, particularly to women; under various titles, such as the "Indomitable," she becomes a dispenser of death.

That primitive ceremonies like the bear dance of the little girls at Brauron, or such savage rites as the flogging of the Spartan youths before Artemis Orthia, should have place in her worship is not surprising,[1] and stories of human sacrifice cluster about the Tauric Artemis and the Brauronian Artemis Tauropolos, who, on the strength of their names, were early connected. In more civilised times the semblance only remained; the knife was drawn over the victim's throat so as to break the skin and bring a few drops of blood. Numerous myths plainly indicate that, though this athletic bachelor-maid never bowed her neck to the yoke of matrimony, a virginal character was not uniformly ascribed to her. But from Homer on she is not only unwed but unwooed—of unsullied chastity herself, she mercilessly punishes lapses among her nymphs;[2] and finally, in the Hippolytus of Euripides, she becomes the exponent of an ideal of chastity as a higher state. The association of Artemis with Apollo is not primitive, though it is as old as Homer. In the oldest cults of Artemis, Apollo is not recognised, nor does Artemis appear in the earliest legends of Delphi. How Artemis came to be made the sister of Apollo it is idle to conjecture; all that can safely be said is that the worship of the twin offspring of Leto, wherever it arose, spread from Delos.

The savage origin of the Greek Artemis appears in the fact that the wild goddesses of the barbarians were one after another identified with her—the Thracian Bendis, the Cappadocian Ma, the Cretan Dictynna and Britomartis; sometimes, as in the case of the Crimean goddess and the many-breasted deity of Ephesus, the fusion is so complete that the proper name is unknown. The Italian Diana, originally a goddess who aided women in childbirth (like Juno Lucina) and in other perils of their sex, and a healer of diseases, was early identified with Artemis, who had the same functions, and in consequence of this identification Diana became a goddess of the chase and, like Artemis in the later Greek conception, a moon goddess.

Apollo also is a god who unites the most varied char-

---

[1] They are probably survivals of savage initiations.

[2] The frail nymphs are sometimes substitutes for Artemis herself in older versions.

acters. He is a shepherd and a shepherds' god, and in Thessaly, and particularly in the Peloponnesus, where very primitive cults subsisted to late times, he supplanted, or, more exactly, absorbed various gods, who, as their names (preserved as 'ἐπικλήσεις of Apollo) show, were protectors of the flocks or functional deities of pastoral life. Myths told how Apollo himself had served as shepherd to Admetos and Laomedon, and how Hermes lifted his herds of cattle. His skill in music, his love for fair maids and youths, which gave so many subjects to idyllic poets, are traits of the shepherd god. Where agriculture was more important in the life of the people than flocks and herds, Apollo was a god of the fields and crops, giving increase to the husbandman's labours and protecting the grain against rust and insect plagues, taking over the occupation of various functional divinities. For seafaring communities he was the patron of navigation, guiding the ships across the sea and home again; the dolphin is his sacred animal (Apollo Delphinios). In this character he had shrines on many headlands and mountains that served as landmarks for mariners. In the age of Greek expansion overseas, Apollo, in his double capacity of oracular deity and god of navigation, naturally became the god of colonisation.

It is as the god of revelation that his influence in the development of Greek religion is greatest. At Delphi, the seat of his most famous oracle, he supplanted an older oracular numen, slaying the dragon guardian of the spot (Python). This sacrilegious blood guilt demanded expiation; only at the end of nine years of wandering and servitude was he purged of the stain. This phase of the myth is associated with the fact that the religious expiation of blood guilt and the consequent restriction of the ancient law of blood vengeance was an institution of the Delphic oracle. With the oracular god's knowledge is probably to be connected his prominence as the god of oaths, covenants, and treaties: he sees and punishes broken faith, even if the wrong be done in secret. Of the many other characters of Apollo it must suffice to mention only that he is the patron of young men, and is himself commonly represented in art as a beautiful youth in the fresh vigour of manhood; he naturally presides over manly sports and gymnastic exercises, and is a helper and defender in fight. Among the Ionians he is Patrōios, the god from whom the stock claims descent. The Delian myth made him a son of Zeus and Leto and twin brother of Artemis.

Hermes was another shepherd god, and the myth brings him into close connection with Apollo. His first exploit—while still an infant in the cradle—was to steal Apollo's cattle with the art of a master-thief; he was the inventor of the lyre, which he ceded to his brother, and of the pan-pipe. He was so swift of foot that he became the messenger of the gods and the patron of heralds on earth. As god of flocks and herds when these were the chief of men's possessions, he was the god of wealth. He is also guardian of the ways, he knows the paths and guides travellers on them; later he conducts the soul on its last journey. Night is his time, and he dispenses sleep and dreams. He is the patron of thieves, traders, and orators; the god of the market-place and its gatherings for trade. The name Hermes is apparently derived from *herma*, a stone-heap, or cairn, or the upright stone out of which the classic Herm was developed, a square stone pillar with human head.

Poseidon was a god of waters, originally, as the name implies, of sweet waters—springs, and streams, and lakes; some of his most primitive cults are inland, in Thessaly, and in Arcadia, where he is the husband of Demeter. He is the god of horsemen; in the myth of his rivalry with Athena he creates the horse. Chiefly, however, he is god of the sea, and in this character he was generally worshipped throughout the Greek world. It should be observed, however, that while in mythology Poseidon is lord of the sea as Zeus is lord of earth and sky, in religion men prayed for favourable winds, prosperous voyages, and safe returns, to many other gods as well—to Zeus, Apollo, Aphrodite, Athena, or the Dioskouroi.

Athena was from early times one of the greatest of the gods; in Homer she is second only to Zeus. She has no fixed association with any sphere or phenomena of nature, her sphere is civilisation. She is, before all, the protectress of Greek cities (Athena Polias). In this character she is a warrior maiden, and is figured fully armed with helmet, spear, and shield, wearing the Gorgon's head upon a collar or breast-plate. She is not, however, an embodiment of blind battle fury and brute force, like the barbarian Ares, but wins the victory by superior mind and skill in the art of war. Of all the deities, she is wisest in the council. As the god of civilised communities she is versed in the arts of peace also. She is said to have invented the plough and taught men to yoke oxen and to break horses. In the Attic myth, she won in the competition with Poseidon for precedence in the religion of Athens by producing the olive-tree, a greater boon to men than Poseidon's horse. It was, how-ever, in the arts that her inventive genius and skill gave her the palm. Weaving and embroidering, women's arts, were naturally under her patronage; but the goldsmith, the pot-ter, and homelier craftsmen like the shoemaker, were her pupils. Athena Ergane, the Industrial Athena, was not the least honourable of her many titles, especially when Athens became a manufacturing city. In this character she is associated with Hephaistos, the divine artificer, and even wears the title Hephaistia.

The worship of Aphrodite was widely distributed in Greece from Thessaly to the Peloponnesus, in the islands, and on the coast of Asia Minor. She is associated with the gentler aspects of nature as Artemis with its wild side; her season is the spring with its genial moisture and fragrant breezes, its fresh verdure and blooming flowers; calm seas and gentle winds and propitious voyages are also her sphere. Above all, she is the goddess of fertility in the animal kingdom, and among men the goddess of love in the widest sense of the word. Herself imagined as the fairest of her sex, she bestows on her favourites beauty and irresistible charm; the Graces are drawn into her train, Eros (Desire) is her son, and Peitho (Persuasion) is her daughter. Aphrodite is invoked alike in marriage and to abet the consummation of illicit unions; with the restrictions which the *mores* of the community put upon the gratification of desire she is not concerned. She is in this as unmoral as nature itself, but not immoral.[1] There is no evidence that in ordinary Greek cults her worship was any less pure or decorous than that of other deities. Her statues were fully draped; the nude goddess appears in Greek art only in the age of Praxiteles, and the Hellenistic and Roman works which realistically portray the physical perfections of the Phrynes of the time have no more to do with Greek religion than a fleshy Flemish Magdalen by Rubens with Christianity.

There were centres, however, where sanctified prostitution belonged to the religion of Aphrodite. Cyprus is the most important of these, but we find the same cult in other places, notably in Cythera, at Eryx in Sicily, and at Corinth. Many scholars are inclined to regard Aphrodite as a foreign, more specifically a Semitic, deity (Astarte),[2] appropriated and imperfectly assimilated by the Greeks. The connection of the Cyprian goddess with Syrian cults such as those at Byblos and Aphaka is unquestionable. In religion, as in art, Cyprus is a place where two currents meet. The whole problem assumes a new aspect in view of the recent revelation of the Cretan-Ægæan civilisation. Nor is the question of origins of vital concern for the history of Greek religion. From the epic age, at least, Aphrodite is as Greek as any deity in the pantheon; the recognition that certain cults are foreign no more conflicts with this than does the same phenomenon in the case of other gods. Still less does the fact that the Greeks, on the ground of similarity of functions, identified with Aphrodite numerous foreign goddesses. The association of Aphrodite with the planet Venus is not attested before the fourth century.

[1] The fact that *hetairai* and prostitutes were particularly assiduous in the worship of Aphrodite does not prove the contrary.

[2] Some punsters in etymology would even derive the name Aphrodite from Ashtoreth.

Hera was, probably even in prehellenic times, the great goddess of Argos; in Homer she names Argos, Mycenæ, and Sparta as the cities dearest to her. After Argos, Samos was in historical times the most important seat of her worship, and the local myth made it the scene of her birth. As the chief deity of these places, she was not only "defender of the city," but presided over husbandry and industry. The cow was sacred to her, and in religious processions her car was drawn by oxen; a standing epithet in Homer is βοῶπις (literally, "cow-faced"), poetically understood as having large and beautiful eyes like a cow. In other places agricultural rites are not a prominent part of her cult—an argument against the theory of some scholars that she was primitively an earth goddess.

Hera was worshipped throughout the Hellenic world as the spouse of Zeus, having, perhaps as a result of migration, superseded his older consort, Diōne. In consequence, Hera was worshipped by the side of Zeus in many temples. The sacred marriage, which was acted out in varying forms in different places, annually celebrated their nuptials. Since Zeus was a sky god, this is interpreted as the marriage of heaven and earth, the fertilisation of the earth by the sky, but neither the rites with which we are acquainted nor the myths that grew about them sustain this theory; they seem rather to reflect the customs of human marriage, over which, as has been said, Hera presided. As the married goddess—the only one in whom this character is emphasised—Hera was the goddess of matrimony and of wedded women. Sacrifices to Zeus and Hera, as the divinities who bless the consummation of marriage (Teleios, Teleia), were part of the wedding service. Women in childbed were also under Hera's protection; she took over the occupation and even the title of the functional deity of childbirth, Eileithyia, and her kindly interest is extended to all the interests of woman's life.

Hephaistos is the skilled artificer among the gods and the patron deity of craftsmen, especially of smiths, armourers, and cunning workers in gold and silver. The most important local seat of his worship was the island of Lemnos, where he alighted, according to Homer, when Zeus threw him out of heaven for intervening on his mother's behalf in a domestic jar between his parents. In Lemnos, Aphrodite also was especially worshipped, and through this local conjunction Aphrodite became the wife of Hephaistos,[1] while in other places she was the wife of Ares. Hephaistos is, further, the god of fire; not the fire of the hearth or the altar, but of the fire in the forge, the fire used in the arts. In Lemnos, and later in Sicily and other volcanic regions, he had his smithy under the mountain, and when columns of smoke rose from the crater men knew that he was at work. At Athens, which was early a manufacturing city, Hephaistos was the patron of the lower town, and was closely associated in worship with the city goddess, Athena.

Ares is a warrior god, whose home was among the fierce Thracian barbarians, and his barbarian origin clings to him. He loves the fight for fighting's sake; strong and brave and skilled in arms, he rushes into the fray in a frenzy, with a troop of kindred spirits at his heels whose significant names are Battle and Strife, Fear and Terror. He represents the brute side of war, and it is brute strength and courage, the rage of battle, with which he fills the warriors who invoke him. But he is a fickle god, in whose constancy it is folly to trust, and his somewhat scanty wit is no match for the mind of Athene. Victory in war is bestowed by the gods of the city, or by Zeus the sovereign, not by Ares. In his quality of god of the fray, he was, however, universally worshipped. In Thebes he was married to Aphrodite, and in the later system of the twelve gods Ares and Aphrodite are regularly joined.

Demeter, whose name was even in antiquity explained by *Gē mētēr*, "Mother Earth,"[2] was a goddess of the fertile soil and of tillage. Like other earth deities she was connected

---

[1] So in the Odyssey.

[2] Cicero, Natura Deorum, II, 67. The Etymologicum Magnum gives, among others, the etymology, "Barley Mother," from a Cretan dialect form δηαί for ζειαί.

with the nether world, the abode of the buried dead; she is the mother of Persephone, the queen of Hades, or of the maiden (Korē) whom Pluto carries off to his gloomy realm. On the other hand, as the deity of settled communities of husbandmen, she is Thesmophoros, the goddess to whom the ordinances of family life and society are attributed. Many local deities of similar functions were identified with Demeter or absorbed by her, the more easily that they seem often to have had no proper names but to have been addressed only as "mistresses, ladies, august holy ones," and the like— titles which Demeter and her daughter assumed. In the epic, which deals with the aristocracy of the gods, Demeter is seldom mentioned; but one of the longest of the Homeric Hymns belongs to her and recites the myth of Korē. The great importance of the worship of Demeter in the religion of Greece in historical times will engage our attention later, as will also the religion of Dionysos, which in Homer is still a wild foreign cult.

Besides these gods, who were worshipped throughout the whole Hellenic world, there were many other deities, some of them conspicuous and universal, such as the Sun (Helios) and the Earth (Gē, Gaia), some localised in mountains and rocks, in lakes and streams and springs of water, in forests and glades, or in single trees; and innumerable powers which were recognised in particular operations of nature or functions of life. We have had occasion repeatedly to observe in the foregoing pages how the favoured gods grew great by appropriating the functions and the local cults of the older numina, whose names then became specific titles by which the gods were invoked in worship (ἐπικλήσεις), a process which was greatly facilitated by the fact that the names of gods such as Artemis, Apollo, Aphrodite, suggested no meaning—they were true proper names—while the names of the local and functional deities were generally intelligible and in the form of adjectives. Yet in spite of the absorption of the smaller gods by the greater, many of the former remained distinct figures in religion. The preservation of their individuality was helped by the myths which the poetical imagination of the Greeks wove about them, often drawing them into the train of one of the greater gods as attendants or companions —Artemis and her nymphs, for example—but thus most effectively keeping them separate personalities.

The Greeks shared the belief of all mankind that the dead exist after death, and though notions about the mode of this existence were not always the same, they never ceased to cherish them. The tombs at Mycenæ and elsewhere were furnished with treasures and weapons, and give abundant evidence that offerings were made both at the entombment and afterward. The description of the burial of Patroklos in Homer is a vivid picture of the funeral rites of a fallen chieftain: twelve Trojan youths were slain at the pyre, besides horses and dogs, to accompany their master, and many cattle and sheep.

The furnishing of the tomb with articles of use and luxury was discontinued in later times; Attic tombs of the sixth and fifth centuries scarcely contain anything but vases (*lekythoi*). Offerings to the dead were made at the tomb on the thirtieth of each month and on the birthday of the deceased; probably also on the anniversary of his death. The blood of the victims was conducted into the ground by shafts or pipes, the carcass was burned. In a still later period animal sacrifices were disused; libations of milk and honey or of wine (generally unmixed) sufficed. The form of the offerings was similar to that to the chthonic deities, and the same terms are used.

An intermediate place between the tendance of the dead and the worship of the gods was occupied by the veneration of heroes. A hero, in this sense, is a man who after his death has been promoted to a higher rank of existence than the common dead. Legendary founders of cities, and eventually the eponymous ancestors of families, were honoured in this way, as were also many more historical persons who had deserved well of their country. The canonisation sometimes took place immediately after death. Frequently, however, a hero was not recognised as such till long after his time; in such cases confirmation of the discovery was usually sought from an oracle. The cult attached to the tomb; the bones of heroes who had died in foreign lands were brought home like sacred relics. If they could not be recovered, a cenotaph was erected. The hero was a local saint; the benefits he bestowed were confined to his neighbourhood or at least to his native land, though of course strangers might seek his aid there. The rites were generally conformed to those of the underworld powers, but some heroes attained still higher honours and were worshipped like gods.

The centuries which lie between the Mycenæan period and the dawn of Greek history are the epic age. In them the memorable exploits of the later Mycenæan times, especially the expedition to Troy and the wars against Thebes, were celebrated by many poets. Doubtless the earliest efforts were of modest compass, but the volume grew with the art of the singers; new figures, incidents, episodes were introduced, till there came to be a considerable body of epic story, more or less loosely strung on a traditional narrative thread. Of such materials the poets of the Iliad and Odyssey constructed their great works, not as mere compilers and arrangers, but as creators, whose genius is not less admirable that they did not create out of nothing. The oldest parts of the Iliad carry us back into the neighbourhood of 1000 B. C., and in them the epic art appears in its full perfection; it can hardly be questioned that generations of singers had wrought in this field before Homer; and it is not improbable that if we could trace them to their origin, we should find that the legends in part grew up on the borders of the Mycenæan age itself. The culmination of epic poetry falls between the tenth century and the middle of the eighth; after that it declined, though there are passages in the Odyssey which were probably introduced in the seventh or even in the sixth century.

In many countries the oldest literature that has survived is religious in character; the Rig-Veda, for example, is a collection of hymns to the gods for use in religious worship, the Gathas of the Avesta are the utterances of the Iranian prophet. The Greek epic, on the contrary, is purely secular poetry. The gods play a large part in it, but it is not at all the part which religion assigns them. The epic is, moreover, aristocratic poetry, composed and sung for the delectation of princes and nobles by the recital of the heroic deeds and adventures of their kind in olden time, or of their own forefathers. It was created and transmitted by professional bards, skilled in poetry as a fine art, with well-established, if not explicitly formulated, rules not merely of diction and metre but of structure. The fact that the Homeric poems were meant for the ears of the cultivated upper classes, together with the detachment from the soil which is to be spoken of further on, explains the small place which ghosts and spectres, bogeys and demons, occupy in the poems, compared with that which they had in the popular religion and superstition of classical times. The allusions suffice, however, to show that these uncanny beliefs existed, though they are for the most part ignored. It is necessary to emphasise this point: the impression of the religion of the epic age gained from the Homeric poems alone is in this respect as one-sided as that which is got from the Rig-Veda if the Atharvan is left out of consideration.

There are other things that must be kept in mind in using Homer as a source for the religion of the times. One of these is that the gods as well as the human heroes of the epic are drawn from widely separated regions and branches of the race; whatever may be true of the literary unity of the Iliad, its material is highly composite. The gods are not the religious pantheon of the Greeks, but a collection of the principal Greek deities, brought together, not by religion, but by the war against Troy, exactly like the chiefs of the people. The gods, too, are away from their homes and the seats of their worship: Apollo's shrine, at which the Greeks make expiation in the first book of the Iliad, is not a Greek but a Trojan sanctuary. Consequently worship is reduced to prayers and occasional sacrifices, chiefly for divination or expiation; the ordinary cultus, with its offerings and festivals, and the innumerable observances by which religion is inwoven with the whole life of man, are necessarily absent; it was impossible to imagine them detached from the localities where they belonged and the occasions in the lives of the people—the seasons and operations of agriculture, for example—with which they were associated.

For the same reason, the properly religious myths of the gods come into the poems only incidentally, and only, so to speak, the least religious of them. To the myths that were closely connected with places and forms of worship there are in general only allusions; and for those which dealt with the part of the gods in making the earth yield her increase and multiplying the flocks, or as guardians and patrons of the occupations of peace, there is no place at all. The gods, in fact, are not about their proper business; they are playing a part in an heroic action right manfully, and the story of their doings, whatever mythical elements may be disguised in it, is mainly poetical fiction embellishing heroic legend. It is plain, therefore, that we may learn a vast deal about Greek religion in the epic age from the Homeric poems, but they do not give a picture of religion as it really was in any age or place.

The influence of the epics on the subsequent development of Greek religion was very great. Originally composed as an entertainment of nobles, they became, with the upcoming of the people, popular literature, and were recited at festivals and holidays to assembled multitudes. Later still they were taught and explained to youth, and became the foundation of education. And since the inspiration of the poets was a serious belief, what they told about the gods possessed an authority that was not to be lightly challenged. The epics created a universal Hellenic religion. The Olympian gods may originally have been deities associated in local religion with the Thessalian Mount Olympus, but when this group, with Zeus at its head, was made the highest circle of gods, other divinities were raised to the same rank. Hera, for example, whose chief seats were at Argos and Samos, as the spouse of Zeus, follows him to Olympus—all the more easily that Olympus itself was now not the earthly mountain but the celestial city of the gods. In the relation of the gods to one another—a subject about which at different centres there were widely diverse notions, depending on their importance in local worship and myth, or upon historical circumstances—the epics introduced a certain tendency to uniformity, though they did not establish a standard of orthodoxy. The provinces and functions of the gods, in like manner, were more distinctly defined by the poets—Poseidon, the sea-king, Hermes, the messenger of the gods, Apollo, the inspirer of prophecy and poetry, and the like. Such familiar characterisations of the Greek gods are in fact derived from the poets; the gods of religion were much more complex figures.

More than this, the epics gave to the gods a salient individuality, not such as attaches to the powers of a primitive mythology through connection with particular phenomena of nature, nor that of departmental and functional deities who are defined by their specific operations, but an individuality of character. Hera, Athena, and Aphrodite, for example, are as sharply and consistently discriminated as Agamemnon, Achilles, and Odysseus. They are also distinctly imagined: we learn not only how they feel and act, but how they look; the classical types of the gods in art were created, as the Greeks themselves recognised, by the poets.

The epics also enabled men to conceive how the many gods, with their different characters and functions, their conflicting wishes and purposes, could consist with the unity of the divine government of the world. The Olympian state, like the Mycenæan kingdoms which doubtless served as models for it, is a monarchy, with a factious aristocracy who often try to circumvent the sovereign and carry through their designs without his consent, but, when he chooses to assert himself, are powerless to escape his knowledge or resist his will.

The poets know the old myth of Zeus's birth, and how he supplanted his father. A like fate may one day overtake him; but in the age that now is, he alone is supreme over gods and men and nature; his will is law and destiny. Sometimes, however, there rises, behind and above Zeus, the vague and but faintly personified power of fate (Μοῖρα, Αἶσα), or of the moral and social order (Θέμις, Δίκη), something like the Vedic Rita and the Avestan Asha.

The most important influence of the epics on religion was that they made the gods completely human. They are, indeed, superior to men in beauty and strength, in knowledge and in magical arts; they have a different fluid in their veins and subsist on other food, but they are, after all, beings of the same kind and of like character. The necessities of the epic action carry the anthropomorphic tendency of religion to its farthest limit. In becoming entirely human the gods become morally responsible; if they behave altogether like men their actions will be judged by the same standards; and as the moral ideals of the community advance the gods will be expected to be models of uprightness and goodness. This consequence was only slowly realised; doubtless the lordlings to whom the lay of Demodokos was sung laughed with as little scruple as the gods themselves at the embarrassment of Ares and Aphrodite entangled, *flagrante delicto*, in Hephaistos's net. When it was realised, however, it tended to purify and ennoble the conception of the gods; while, on the other hand, the immoral and irrational myths and tales to which a certain religious authority attached, gave ground, as will appear in the sequel, for a trenchant attack on religion in the name of reason and virtue.

Great as the influence of the epic was, it must not be overlooked that on the most important side of Greek religion the poetic theology had little effect. In worship, the deities to whom men offered prayer and sacrifice were those whom their forefathers had worshipped on that spot from time immemorial. Even when one of the Olympians superseded, in name, the divinity of the place, the old conception often remained essentially unchanged, and the ritual was even more conservative. What the worshippers were concerned with was not the feats of prowess displayed by the gods on the Trojan plain, but what they did for the community or the individual who invoked them at their altars. The local myths, inseparably bound to festal rites or secular expiations, had far more significance for religion than the common poetical mythology. Many gods who in religion were of the first consequence, especially the whole circle of chthonic deities—gods of the soil and of the subterranean abodes of the dead—are hardly named in the epics. The gods of the peasantry, rustic as their worshippers, would be as little at home among the Olympian aristocrats as the latter in the simple shrines of their country cousins. In the great social revolutions of the subsequent centuries these gods and cults came into prominence; they give a distinctive character to the later religion of Greece.

In a well-known passage Herodotus couples Homer and Hesiod as the authors of Greek theology: it was they who composed the genealogies of the gods, and gave them their standing epithets, and assigned to them their offices and vocations, and described their appearance. The Theogony of Hesiod is, however, a work of wholly different character from the Homeric epics, and the product of another age. Hesiod is fully aware of this difference. The Muses who called him as he pastured his flocks at the foot of Mount Helicon and sent him to reveal to men the truth concerning the gods say:

"We know many a fable to tell, with semblance of true words;
    We know also the truth to relate, when that is our purpose."

The poet takes his mission seriously; he aims not to entertain but to instruct. He undertakes not merely to set in order the genealogies of the gods of the present age of the world—this occupies, in fact, less than a hundred lines toward the end of the poem, and is chiefly a catalogue of the multitudinous consorts and progeny of Zeus. It is rather to the history of the gods before the dynasty of Zeus, and to the conflicts by which his empire was established, that Hesiod devotes himself, and, farther back, to the earliest divine generations and the origin of the gods. The theogony here becomes cosmogony, and presents the oldest extant Greek speculations on the beginning of things, speculations not only closely akin to the Orphic cosmogonies but anticipating the problems of the Ionian natural philosophy.

First Chaos (the yawning void) came into being; next the broad-bosomed Earth, the firm foundation of all things, and murky Tartarus (the cavernous interior of the earth); then Love. From Chaos sprung Erebos and Night; from Night were born Aither (the circumambient light) and Day. Earth produced the starry Heaven, which covers it completely, the mountains, haunts of the nymphs, and the barren sea. Thus far the cosmogony. With the marriage of Heaven and Earth (Ouranos and Gē) the theogony begins. From this union spring the Titans, the youngest and greatest of whom was Kronos, father of the Cyclopes and the hundred-armed monsters whom Ouranos imprisons in the deep recesses of Earth to her great discomfort. At her instance, Kronos emasculates his father; from the blood that drips upon the earth spring later the Erinyes and the giants, from the froth of the abscinded member cast into the sea, the "foam-born" goddess, Aphrodite. Then follow the offspring of the Titans, a motley brood. Of Kronos and Rhea are born Hestia, Demeter, Hera, Hades, Poseidon, and, last of all, Zeus. Fearing that his children may deal with him as unfilially as he had dealt by his father, Kronos devours his progeny, new born; from this fate Zeus is saved by the ruse of Rhea, who substitutes for the infant a stone wrapped in swaddling-clothes; the young god is brought up in concealment in Crete. When he is grown, the struggle for the empire of the world begins. Zeus is aided by his brothers, whom Kronos has been constrained to disgorge, and by the Cyclopes and the Hekatoncheires, whom Zeus has released from their prison-house within the earth. The Titans are vanquished, and imprisoned in Hades under guard of the hundred-armed monsters. Zeus is acknowledged by the gods as sovereign.

The Hesiodic Theogony is an attempt to reduce to order a body of traditional material of diverse origin. Allusions in the epics show that much of this material was in circulation long before Hesiod's time, and in other things he seems to have followed the authority of Homer. There are traces also of different myths of the origin of the world of perhaps equal antiquity, in one of which the cosmic egg figured as it does in India and in Egypt.

Hesiod's story of the birth of Zeus is derived from Cretan myths: his mother Rhea is the Cretan goddess; the cave where she brought into the world her greatest son was shown on Mount Dicte, or, if you preferred, on Mount Ida; the Kouretes, whose clanging arms drowned his cries, were Cretan sword-dancers—in short, the infancy of Zeus belonged to Crete.

To scholars whose notions of early Greek religion were drawn solely from the epic, the savage features of the Cretan myths seemed singularly un-Greek, and they easily convinced themselves that the Kronos who devoured his own offspring was a Phœnician god and that the non-Hellenic element in Cretan religion was of Semitic origin. According to Philo of Byblos, the sacrifice of children, which was so striking a characteristic of the Phœnician religion, was inaugurated by a god whom he calls Kronos, who sacrificed his only son. There is, however, no real parallel between the two myths: one is a cultus myth, giving divine precedent and authority for a peculiar type of human sacrifice, the other is an example of a common folk-lore motive, the putting out of the way of an infant which is destined, if it grows up, to supplant the ruler (commonly a kinsman). To connect these myths is a very naïve procedure even for comparative mythology. It is unnecessary to dwell on this, however, for in the light of our present knowledge of Cretan civilisation the theory of early Phœnician influence must be abandoned altogether.

The scene of the Titanomachy is Thessaly; the Titans descend to the encounter from Mount Othrys, the gods from Mount Olympus. The war between the gods of the present order and the monstrous powers who ruled the world before them was clearly, in its original conception, a cosmic conflict, though in the Hesiodic version Kronos and Iapetos, the protagonists of the Titans, are completely anthropomorphic deities. A Babylonian poem has for its principal subject a like conflict between Bel, as the champion of the gods, and the dragon Tiamat with her allies, the monstrous brood of chaos.[1] The motives of the two myths are obviously the same, and many scholars are inclined to assume, more or less confidently, that the Greek myth is an echo of the Babylonian.

In the Works, Hesiod paints a sombre picture of the degeneracy of his times. Age by age, from the beginning, the world has grown worse. On the golden age, with which human history began, followed one of silver, and on that the age of bronze; the present is the iron age, and the decadence is still in progress. The heroic age represented in the epic stands in this series between bronze and iron, that is, immediately preceding the author's own day. The present is an evil day: judges take bribes and pervert justice; those who have the might scoff at the protests of their victims as the hawk in the fable does at the cries of the nightingale. The shadows of the actual are deepened by contrast with the picture of the ideal city wherein dwelleth righteousness.

That man has so hard a lot on earth, Hesiod ascribes to the anger of Zeus for the theft of fire by Prometheus. For this fault the gods contrived the maiden Pandora, with her fatal charm and her fatal guile, and sent her to Prometheus's slow-witted brother, Epimetheus, who took her in; whereupon, with feminine curiosity, she lifted the lid off the jar in which all evils were confined and let them loose beyond reclaim.

[1] See above, pp. 209 *ff*.

CHAPTER XVIII

THE GREEKS

FROM THE AGE OF COLONISATION TO THE PELOPONNESIAN WAR

The Age of Expansion—Effect of New Conditions on Religion—
Demeter—Dionysos—Savage Features of Myth and Cult—The
Hope of Immortality—Orphic Mysteries—Cosmogony and The-
ogony—The Other Life—The Eleusinian Mysteries—Salvation—
Other Mysteries and Salvationist Sects—The Ionian Philosophy—
Attacks on the Popular Religion—Parmenides, Empedocles, An-
axagoras—Democritus—The Sophists—Agnosticism—Theories of
the Origin of Religion—Influence of the Sophists—Effect of the
Persian Wars—Greek Worship—Holy Places—Priesthoods—Sac-
rifices—Expiations—Festivals—Oracles

IN Hesiod, as has already been remarked, a very different
spirit breathes from that which inspired the epic poets. This
difference is in part personal: the sturdy Bœotian farmer was
a man of another race and temperament from the bards who
sang at the courts of Ionian princes; his surroundings and
interests were remote from theirs. But besides the individuality of the poet we hear in him the first voice of a new time.
In the eighth century began a period of commercial expansion and colonisation, in which the Ionian cities of Asia
Minor, particularly Miletus, took the lead, closely followed
by those of Eubœa and the Isthmus. All around the eastern
end of the Mediterranean, from Propontis and the Black
Sea to the Cyrenaica, and westward to Sicily and southern
Italy, new Greek settlements were planted and old ones acquired new importance. The maritime cities, with their extensive commerce, outgrew the inland towns; the demand
for export stimulated domestic industries and led to produc-

tion on a commercial scale. The opening of Egypt under Psammetichos, and the rise of a new Lydian dynasty which in the end brought most of Asia Minor this side the Halys under its sway, made new fields for enterprise and adventure; Greek mercenaries and traders penetrated far into these countries. Though the colonies were planted by particular cities, and reproduced the social and political organisation of the old home as they established the worship of the ancestral gods, they drew to themselves immigrants from many places, and, in the presence of races of alien speech and custom, the settlers felt themselves members of one Hellenic people. Commerce had to be protected against pirates, colonies against the aggression of neighbours; thus navies were created, and a new era of Greek politics began.

The effects of these conditions were manifold and far-reaching not only abroad but at home. The landed aristocracy lost its political and social pre-eminence; rich merchants and manufacturers soon thought themselves quite as good as the old nobility with their long pedigrees and their unproductive acres. Household industries were displaced by manufacture; industrial slavery became profitable, and foreign slaves were in demand. The condition of the free peasant was harder with the decline of agriculture, and the country people thronged into the cities in the hope of bettering their fortunes. The freer life of the colonies reacted on the old country. The old social order, in which every man's place and status were fixed, broke down under all these changes; and as in the modern age of colonisation and emigration, individualism was the signature of the time in every sphere of life.

This spirit finds expression in a new form of poetry. The stately hexameter measures of Homer and Hesiod give place to elegiacs and the mordant or familiar iambic; the objective recital of what was done and said in the far-away past of the heroic age, to the subjectivity of the lyric poet, the thought and feeling of the individual and the hour, or to moral reflections and exhortations addressed to his contemporaries.

The institutions which had sufficed for a simpler time were

no longer adequate for the new economic and social conditions; the customary law had no provision for commerce and large industry, the administration of law was ineffective, justice was corrupted or perverted by wealth and influence. The censure of their times by the gnomic poets is strikingly similar to what we read in the Hebrew prophets of the eighth century. The new classes demanded reform in polity and law. First in the colonies, then in Greece itself, men of character and reputation were called on to draft new constitutions and legislation—it is enough to name Zaleucus, Charondas, and the Cretan legists; at Athens, Draco (ca. 624) and Solon (594). It is significant that the Solonian constitution, recognising the existing state of things, accepted the principle of timocracy, in which the citizens were divided into classes on the basis of their possessions—a graduated aristocracy of wealth. The laws aimed to put an end to inveterate evils by reforms in judicial process, and to stay new ones by prohibiting usury, by sumptuary provisions against luxury in dress and retinue, and by punishing idleness and beggary. At home and abroad the spirit of individual enterprise stimulated by a commercial age easily took in practice the form "every man for himself." The traditional ethos of the community was as ill-adapted to this situation as its customary law; the ancient sanctions, both social and religious, were inadequate. Moral aphorisms and cohortations such as we find in Hesiod and the gnomic poets show how grave the evil was in the eyes of serious men, but it can hardly be imagined that they were effective to stay it.

Political and social unrest was universal. A century of class conflict was the consequence, the country people trying to get a foothold in the city, the descendants of immigrants to get equal rights with the old citizens, the new rich to get a hand in the government. The old political order gave way before the rising *demos;* tyrants took advantage of the dissolution and resulting disorder to usurp sole power.

These profound social, economic, and political changes were not without their effect upon religion. It was easy for the colonists to erect altars to the gods of the home land, but they could not transfer to them the sacredness of the ancient holy places at which their fathers had worshipped for centuries, the local myths and the festival rites which attached to them—in a word, the thousand associations by which religion was rooted in its native soil. The peoples on whose shores the Greek settlements were planted had gods whom the newcomers identified with their own, and myths and rites of barbarian origin were engrafted upon the worship of Greek deities.

The country people who poured into the cities brought with them rustic gods and cults, which grew in importance with the increasing numbers and power of the demos. They may sometimes have been favoured by tyrants—who often posed as the champions of the masses against the classes—in preference to the older gods, whose cults were in the hands of certain noble families by hereditary right. Of these deities Demeter was the most prominent. Demeter, as has already been noted, was an old Greek goddess of the soil and the crops; when, incensed with the gods for permitting the abduction of her daughter, she refrains from exercising her divine functions, men plough and sow in vain, humankind is threatened with starvation and the gods with the cessation of offerings. Like other agrarian deities, she is also connected with the abode of the buried dead beneath the earth. In the myth which forms the subject of the Homeric Hymn to Demeter, her daughter Persephone, while gathering flowers with her maiden comrades, is seized by Hades and carried off to his nether realm. The mourning mother, veiling her godhead, serves as a nurse in the household of Keleos, King of Eleusis, and by her abstention brings men and gods to such straits that Zeus intervenes and sends Hermes to bring Persephone back to earth. She has, however, tasted the food of Hades, and must therefore return to live with him a third of the time; but each year, when earth is blooming with fragrant spring flowers, she comes up from the murky gloom, "a great marvel to gods and mortal men."

As a goddess of husbandry Demeter did not supplant the older deities of the state; at Athens the chief agricultural festivals are celebrated in honour of Athena and Apollo, at Argos to Hera; those of Demeter are supplementary, or have their seats in rural demes. Nor did she ever, in her own person, become the mistress of the nether world. Her great importance in the history of Greek religion lies not in her public cults, but in the mysteries to which we shall return presently.

Unlike Demeter, who is a Hellenic deity *minorum gentium* tardily admitted into the company of the Olympians, Dionysos is a foreigner from half-barbarous Thrace. That he also was closely associated with the life of nature, particularly with wild nature, is clear both from myth and from ritual; it was only in Greece, however, that he became specifically the god of the vine. The phallus, which is so conspicuous in Dionysiac ritual, belongs to a wide-spread type of vegetation magic, and the bull is in numerous religions the embodiment of the reproductive forces not only of animal but of plant life.

In the Homeric epics Dionysos is a foreigner: the Iliad (VI, 130 *ff*.), as a warning to men not to contend with the gods, tells the fate of the Thracian hero Lycurgus, who, armed with an ox-goad, chased "the nurses of the raving Dionysos," and so terrified the god himself that he plunged for refuge to the depths of the sea. The savage features of the worship of Dionysos were clearly the first thing that struck the Greeks: the raving god had raving worshippers, especially women votaries, the mænads, who, roaming by night upon the mountains, waving torches, circling in wild dances, crying aloud upon the name of the god, brought on the Bacchic frenzy; living beasts were rent limb from limb, the quivering flesh and dripping blood were fiercely devoured. There are more than suggestions in the myths that human victims were sometimes used in the same way. The god himself receives the significant epithet, "raw-flesh-eater."

That the Greeks were repelled by such savagery is plain;

but that it had for them a singular attraction is no less plain. The irrational and the horrible have, in fact, a fascination of their own, and it has been often noted that the rites of uncivilised peoples, in proportion to their strangeness, seem to more cultivated neighbours to embody a mysterious wisdom or a peculiarly efficacious magic. Other and deeper reasons for the spread of the religion of Dionysos in Greece and for the hold it gained will come under consideration later. That the progress of the new religion was not uncontested appears from numerous myths of the calamities that befell such as opposed the god and his worshippers. Euripides has made one of these the subject of the Bacchæ: Pentheus, King of Thebes, tries to keep the women from joining the wild revels of Dionysos; he is torn to pieces by the mænads, headed by his own mother, who in her madness takes him for a wild animal. Of similar purport are the legends of Minyas at Orchomenos, of the Proetidæ at Argos, and others. The point of them all is the terrible vengeance the spurned god takes on his enemies.

The worship of Dionysos seems to have made its way into Greece by more than one route. In Bœotia, Orchomenos and Thebes were ancient centres of the religion; the myth of the god's birth was localised at the latter. It may be inferred from the silence of the Homeric Hymn to the Pythian Apollo that when that poem was composed Dionysos had not yet invaded Delphi; but when he came, with the prestige of popularity already achieved in Bœotia and perhaps in Attica, the priesthood of Apollo seem to have given him a friendly reception, assigning to him the three winter months, and themselves organising the revels of his women votaries on Mount Parnassus. The religion of Dionysos was probably introduced into Athens in the time of the monarchy, and it had been received in some of the country demes before it reached the capital; the Pisistratidæ were especially addicted to his worship. An early and important centre of the religion was Crete; the worship flourished also in the Peloponnesus and in the Greek cities of Asia Minor.

In becoming a Greek god, the wild Thracian deity was tamed and civilised; in the public cults of classical times the savage features of his original worship have pretty much disappeared, or linger only, like the savage rites of the older Hellenic religions, in obscure corners. If one of his great festivals at Athens, the Lenaia, still bears in its name the memory of the "wild women," the wildness had been conventionalised. In Attica, where Dionysos in his character of god of the vine takes his place by the side of Demeter the goddess of the grain crops, the broaching of the jars of last year's wine at the Anthesteria in February is a feast in his honour, but that the vintage is not his great festival is one of the many things which show that his vinous character is secondary. The Attic festivals of Dionysos fall in the winter and spring (December to March). The torches at the Lenaia, the phallic procession and songs, particularly at the rural Dionysia, characterise them as Bacchic; but in other features they took the common type of Attic celebrations. They are of the greatest importance for the history not only of religion but of literature, for out of the dances and mummery of the Dionysia the Attic drama was evolved.

The religion of Dionysos gave freer room to the emotional element than the worship of the old Hellenic gods. Not that this element was lacking in the latter, but, speaking generally, it was kept within decorous bounds and expressed in dignified and measured forms; elevation rather than excitement was the prevailing mood of the festivals of Apollo or Athena. The Thracian cult of Dionysos had a different character: through it men strove to experience religion by union with the godhead. As they enacted the savage myth, rushing breathless through the mysterious solitudes of the mountains by the light of flaring torches, or rending the victim limb from limb and tearing its palpitating flesh with their teeth, the divine frenzy overcame them, the god himself possessed them. In all ages and in the most diverse religions men have sought thus to feel the divine life throbbing fiercely in their pulses, their senses quickened to perceive the unseen world. Consciousness, overwhelmed by the incoming flood of god-consciousness, swoons, and man is rapt into the fulness of the godhead with its all-comprehending intuition and ineffable beatitude. It is a long way from the mænad to the Neoplatonic philosopher, but both in their own ways sought —and found—the supreme experience of God.

It is altogether likely that the Thracian ritual had at the beginning another and more practical significance. Dionysos was, as we have seen, the power which revealed itself in the life of trees and plants and in the new life which awakes after the wintry death of nature. Midwinter ceremonies to call the god to life again, or, in more primitive apprehension, to put new life and power into him, are common, and the cults which have grown out of what we from our superior standpoint call "vegetation magic" have elsewhere a tragic or an orgiastic character.[1]

In religions of this type the hope of another life for man frequently emerges.[2] He too dies like nature, like the nature god; why may he not live again like him? The conception lies the nearer because the deities of plant life are also often gods of the earth from which the plants spring, and in which seeds, like men, are buried. The Greeks, as has been noted above, thought of the dead as dwelling in the tombs and having the same needs as when they were alive; but they also imagined a common abode of the shades in the recesses of the earth—a dismal, phantom-like existence, from which they shrank with all their healthy love of life. The ancient Thracians seem to have entertained similar notions and to have imagined Hades yet more dismally as a kind of a quagmire; the *borboros*, the slimy mud, which is so characteristic a feature of the Orphic hell, is derived from that source.

Such is by nature the lot of mortals; a blessed immortality belongs to the gods only. For man, then, the only hope of

[1] In climates where it is not icy winter but the burning sun of summer which is the death of nature, the rites of mourning and resuscitation, of course, fall in corresponding seasons.

[2] This is particularly true of the religions of the Mediterranean area and the nearer East.

escape from the gloomy nether world is participation in the divine nature. It is not, however, to the bright Olympians who know naught of struggle and pain and death, but to gods who have shared these experiences, who have triumphed over death and risen to new life, that the hope of immortality attaches itself, for in their victory is the evidence that death can be overcome, and their example shows the way. It was, therefore, not Zeus nor Apollo, but Demeter-Korē and Dionysos to whom men turned for eternal life. The experience of union with Dionysos, the Bacchic enthusiasm, thus acquired a new value; it was the earnest and assurance of immortal blessedness.

The public cults exhibit little or no trace of these ideas, which were brought into Greece by a second wave of Dionysiac religion particularly associated with the name of Orpheus, a Thracian singer, who, after charming with his lyre wild beasts and savage men and even moving the heart of the queen of Hades, was torn to pieces by the mænads, thus, as Proclus significantly says, suffering the like fate as his god. The Orphic gospel had reached Athens in the time of the Pisistratid tyranny; Onomacritus, who lived at the court of Hippias, is said by Aristotle and other Greek authors to have composed—or forged—Orphic scriptures, and modern scholars have attributed to him the interpolation of the torments of exemplary sinners in the Nekyia of the Odyssey. With the literary question we are not here concerned; enough that from the middle of the sixth century on the influence of Orphic doctrine is to be seen on every hand.

As a way of salvation for the individual it spread by a missionary propaganda and gathered its converts into societies not unlike the early Christian churches. There were rites of initiation having the character of purifications, scriptures claiming the authority of revelation, symbols, and sacraments. A rule of life was enjoined which forbade animal sacrifice and the eating of flesh—a natural corollary of the belief in the transmigration of souls—and regulating diet, dress, and conduct to the end of avoiding uncleanness. The organisation of these voluntary societies seems to have been loose, and there is no sign of a central authority nor of a uniform standard of belief or practice; it is altogether probable that there were considerable differences among them in both respects. In some places the orgiastic features of the Dionysiac rites were perpetuated, while elsewhere the enthusiasm took a soberer tone.

Dionysos is not the only god whose name is linked with these mysteries. Sabazios, a deity of the Thracians' Phrygian kinsman is invoked; his votaries in their exaltation become Saboi as those of Dionysos are Bacchoi or Bacchai. Zagreus also, whom some of the ancients connect with Crete, is peculiarly an Orphic divinity. But whatever diversities there were in rite and myth, however barbarian and Hellenic elements are blended, the important fact remains that in the Orphic circles a new kind of religion was introduced in Greece. The old religions concerned themselves with this world only: the gods gave protection and prosperity to the state; on individuals they bestowed health and strength and beauty, welfare and happiness, long life, and the good things of this life richly to enjoy; and that was all men asked of them. So long as the sum of human desire was no more than nature could satisfy, these religions sufficed; but to the aspirations and yearnings of the soul for a supernatural good, for an eternal divine life, and for a foretaste of it now, they had no answer. The Orphic gospel awakened the consciousness of this need and promised its satisfaction. Like other redemptive religions, it addressed itself to the individual; it demanded personal faith, and set forth a plan of salvation; by its purifications the initiate put off the old man which is corrupt; its sacraments and mystic rites made him partaker of the divine nature; myth and ceremony excited the emotions, while theology offered to thinkers a solution of the problems of God, the universe, and man. Taking for itself a sphere unoccupied by the older religions, it did not come into collision with them: it did not undertake to distribute mundane goods; they had nothing to do with the supernal blessedness.

The Orphic literature which has been transmitted to us is in considerable part a product of later centuries, but the substantial antiquity of its ruling ideas is evinced by the allusions to them in the poets from Pindar down, and especially by their influence in the development of philosophy. The Orphic Theogony, of which only fragments are preserved, is closely related to Hesiod's, which in the main lines it follows, transforming it in the spirit of its pantheistic theology. In the beginning—so the rhapsodic theogony ran[1]—were Chaos (Space), Chronos (Time), and Aither (the Primal Matter). Chronos forms the world-egg; cleft by the generative forces in it, the two halves of the shell form the firmament and the earth, while from it emerges Protogonos (the First-Born), called also Phanes (the Manifest) and Erikapaios.[2] Phanes produces Night, the great mother; gods and men and all things in nature spring from him, he is the universal light and life and intelligence. When, in the series of divine generations, the age of Zeus arrives, he swallows Phanes—a way of saying that the supreme deity of the Greek religion is what he is by virtue of the indwelling of the universal godhead. Zeus is for the Orphics another Phanes:

Zeus was first, Zeus of the vivid lightning, last; Zeus the head, Zeus the middle, of Zeus were all things made. Zeus is the support of the earth and of the starry heaven; Zeus is male, Zeus the immortal bride, Zeus the breath of air in all things, Zeus the rush of tireless flame; Zeus is the root of the sea, Zeus is the sun and the moon; Zeus is the king, Zeus the ruler of all things. For, having concealed all beings, he again to the gladsome light brought them forth from his holy heart, working wonders.

Among the children of Zeus the greatest in the Orphic theology is Dionysos, also called Zagreus, son of Zeus by Persephone, whom he has designated to succeed him in the rule of the world. The Titans, striving to recover the dominion for themselves, lure the child into their power, rend

[1] For the present purpose it is unnecessary to consider variant forms.
[2] This all-god is Dionysos in his cosmic aspect.

him in pieces in the form of a bull, which he assumes in the vain effort to escape them, roast and devour him; only his heart is saved by Athena, and lives again in the third Dionysos, the son of Zeus and Semele. Zeus consumes the Titans with fire from heaven and scatters their ashes to all the winds. But through their cannibal feast—a mythical counterpart of the orgiastic rending of the Dionysos-bull—the essence of Dionysos has entered into the Titans themselves, and their wind-borne ashes convey the germ of the divine life into all animate things; the human soul is such a particle of the godhead. There are traces of a version in which man is formed of the ashes of the Titans, and has thus a dual nature, Dionysiac and Titanic, divine and demonic.

At death—such seems to have been the primitive conception of the transmigration—the soul is carried hither and thither by the wind, until it enters into another body.[1] The body is the prison-house of the soul, the tomb in which it is buried (σῶμα-σῆμα); it can attain life and freedom only by deliverance from the body.

The Orphic imagination expatiated on the misery of those who went down to Hades. The marsh, or quagmire, of the Thracian nether world lends a characteristic feature to the Orphic hell: there those who in this world have not been purged of their defilement by the rites of the sect, its initiatory purifications and *katharmata*, wallow in filth, the appropriate destiny of their unclean souls!

The Greeks had already made some progress in infernal geography, as appears from the Odyssey (X, 512 *ff.*); the sectarians appropriated and improved on it. They peopled their underworld with monsters borrowed from folk-lore as well as literature,[2] "serpents and myriad dreadful beasts," the

[1] When it came to be the prevalent belief that the souls of men go at death to the nether world and are re-embodied only after a period of retribution there, it was held that it is only the souls of animals and plants which are breathed out into the air and carried by it into other plants or animals.

[2] See Aristophanes, Frogs, 137 *ff.*, 293 *ff.*, 474 *ff.*—The caricature may accumulate the horrors, but certainly does not invent them.

hideous Empusa; the hundred-headed earth-dragon, Echnida, which rends men's vitals; the Spanish sea-serpent that clutches at their lungs; the Tithrasian Gorgons that tear in pieces their bleeding kidneys with the entrails. In the strongest contrast to this is the bliss of the saved. Aristophanes almost desists from his mocking as he poetically depicts it:

> "And then a breath of flutes envelops thee,
> Thou seest the fairest light, as here above,
> And myrtle groves, and many happy groups
> Of men and women, clapping hands in joy.
> 'And who may these be pray?'
>   'The mystic band.'" [1]

The delights of the Dionysiac Elysium were not always so refined; it is indeed not improbable that Aristophanes is here influenced by Eleusinian conceptions. There are persistent allusions to the banquet at which the garlanded saints spend eternity in drinking: "They seem to think," says Plato, "that an immortality of drunkenness is the highest reward of virtue." Here, as in the "miry pit" of hell, we may with much probability surmise that the Thracian barbarians, who had a name for deep potations, were the authors of the conception; but it should not be forgotten that intoxicants have been widely employed as a means of inducing enthusiasm, and vinous exaltation taken for divine possession. What should eternal bliss be but the perpetuity of this experience of godfulness?

As in other redemptive religions, the saved are the initiated, the members of the mystery-church, who have been purified by its cathartic rites of admission, and through its sacraments have become partakers of the divine nature. On the other hand, as Plato quotes the doctrine, "He who arrives in Hades uninitiated and without having participated in the mysteries lies in filth." Even the most conspicuous virtue does not avail for salvation apart from the church and its means of grace. This is the logical attitude, and was

---

[1] Frogs, 154 *ff.*; see also the hymn of the Mystæ, *ib.*, 448 *ff.*

always maintained. It drew from Diogenes the caustic comment, "Will the robber Pataikon, because he was initiated, fare better after death than Epaminondas?"

The moral sense of the Greeks, the more ethical conception of religion represented particularly by the religion of Apollo and the influence of Delphi, revolted against a doctrine of salvation by initiation and orgy, regardless of character, and this temper could not fail to react on the mysteries themselves. More or less explicitly and emphatically they insist, not merely on a life of ceremonial purity according to the rule of the sect, but on an upright and virtuous life according to common standards of morality as a condition of salvation. "Many carry the sacred wand, but rare are the Bacchoi," became a proverbial saying in their own circle—multitudes take part in the rites, but few receive the spirit. In general, however, in accord with the universal tendency of the redemptive religions, the moral division is made to run on the ecclesiastical line: the initiated are the pure, the holy, the righteous; the uninitiated are the unholy and unrighteous.

Nor is the fate of the lost the same for all. Hades is not merely the foul slough into which all unpurified souls sink, as the Homeric Hades was the gloomy abode of all souls; it becomes a place of retribution where the wicked suffer the penalty of their misdeeds. The contrast is well seen in the Orphic addition at the end of the eleventh book of the Odyssey—the torments of Tityos with vultures tearing at his liver, of Tantalos, consumed by thirst and hunger within reach of plenty; of Sisyphos, with knotted muscles pushing the rock up-hill, which, just as he gains the summit, breaks away and thunders to the foot again. A characteristic group in the painting of Polygnotos at Delphi were the women carrying water in sherds of broken jars; in other representations they are compelled to carry water in a sieve.[1] In the embellish-

---

[1] Originally, perhaps, a popular notion of the fate of the unmarried, then of the uninitiated (double use of τέλος, "consummation"); punishment specifically of the daughters of Danaos who murdered their bridegrooms on the wedding night.

ment of hell with picturesque torments the imagination borrows in part from criminal justice, in part retribution is matched to the offence in poetic justice, the sinner suffering as he has sinned or by the hand of one whom he has wronged. Once started in this way, the inferno became more and more gruesome as each succeeding representation tried to give new thrills of the horror which is a morbid pleasure. When Christianity came, it made itself heir to these hells; the tortures in the Apocalypse of Peter and later writings of the sort are of unmistakable Orphic invention, and the transmission can be followed in unbroken line through the Middle Ages, with variation and increment of horrors from the barbaric imagination of the north.

Upon this doctrine of retribution beneath the earth the transmigration of souls is superimposed, and is itself made retributive.[1] This aspect of the Orphic teaching was apparently particularly cultivated in Pythagorean circles; we shall meet it again in the eschatology of Plato.

The Homeric Hymn to Demeter tells how the goddess bade the people of Eleusis rear her a temple before the city, and how the king fulfilled the command. Before she ascended to Olympus she taught the princes the ritual of her cult, and instituted the hallowed mysteries which may not be divulged. "Blessed is that man, of dwellers on the earth, who has seen these things! But he who dies without initiation and participation in the sacred rites, in the dank gloom below will not have so happy a lot." The mysteries of Eleusis were thus, in origin, a local cult of Demeter the conduct of which was in the hands of certain noble families of the city. Of its character the poet gives no hint, but he says expressly that those who were admitted to the mysteries received the assurance of a blessed life beyond the tomb. The whole content of the Hymn makes it clear, further, that the ground of this assurance was the deliverance of Korē from Hades, which is the gist of the myth. It is another instance of the

[1] The same combination was made in India in the same way. See above, p. 276.

resuscitation of plant life after the winter's death taken as the promise and proof that man, too, may rise to newness of life. To us, the seed of grain falling into the ground in the autumn and dying, coming to life in the spring, flourishing and fruitful, seems but a poetical analogy or a symbol. To primitive apprehension, however, life in plant and animal was one; the overcoming of death was as much a divine wonder in the seed or the tree as in man, and the gods who wrought the one had the secret of the other.[1] It would be quite in accord with these notions if, as some have supposed, the supreme moment in the ritual of Eleusis was the exhibition to the epopts of an ear of wheat.

Eleusis was annexed to Attica, probably in the seventh century, and the mysteries were taken under public control, the chief offices remaining, however, hereditary in the family of the Kerykes and the ancient Eleusinian gens of the Eumolpidai. In contrast to the Orphic mysteries, which always remained sectarian conventicles, the Eleusinian mysteries were a recognised branch of the established religion, though only the initiated were admitted to their secret rites. This privilege, which may once have been restricted to certain Eleusinian clans, was extended not only to all Athenian citizens but to all Greeks without distinction of city or race; women as well as men were eligible, even minors and slaves; only such as were defiled by blood guilt were excluded, as they were, indeed, from the public cults. When Athens became the centre of Greek life, the Eleusinian mysteries became a Panhellenic institution as truly as the Delphian oracle of Apollo. In later times Romans also were admitted.

The first step of one who wished to be initiated into the Eleusinian mysteries was to apply privately to a member of either of the two families in whose charge the celebration of the mysteries was, the Kerykes or the Eumolpidai, who ad-

---

[1] It is not meant that these conceptions were in the minds of the Greeks of the fifth century; to them, and long before them, Demeter and Korē were great personal deities, and the dramatic myth was certainly for them no allegory of the corn-maiden.

mitted him to the first stage by rites which resemble a purification from blood guilt. The next degree was initiation into the Lesser Mysteries, celebrated in Agrai, a suburb of Athens, in February. The Great Mysteries fell in the autumn. The participants gathered in Athens in the middle of Boedromion (September); the observances began with a proclamation by the hierophant warning the unworthy not to profane the mysteries by their presence. On the 16th they went down to the shore and purified themselves by a sea-bath, whence the day bore the name ἅλαδε μύσται, "To the sea, O Mystæ!" The two following days were spent in Athens. On the 19th the great company, dressed in white and escorted by the armed ephebi, set out for Eleusis by the Sacred Street, carrying with them the image of the god Iakchos, and loudly calling on his name.[1] The progress of the procession was slow, not only by reason of its numbers, but because there were numerous halts along the way, which was lined with monuments, hero-shrines, and temples. The arrival at the bridge over the Kephissos was the signal for an outburst of scurrilous abuse, which spared no station nor reputation; every man took the licence of the hour to loose his tongue against such as offended the democratic sense by being leading citizens, or those against whom he had some private grudge, so that "bridging" was common Attic slang for wanton vilification.[2]

The ceremonies at Eleusis lasted two or three days. There were offerings to the gods of the Eleusinian circle and others at the temples, and dances by torchlight out-of-doors; but the properly mystic rites took place in a great oblong hall to which only those who had been previously initiated into the Lesser Mysteries were admitted. On all sides of this hall were rising seats for the spectators, as in a theatre;

[1] Iakchos is identified by Sophocles with Bacchos (Dionysos). His temple was in Athens, and he had no shrine in Eleusis, from which it is inferred that his relation to the mysteries is adventitious and due to Athenian influence. The matter is, however, very obscure.

[2] It is likely that the custom had originally a religious motive, abuse being a familiar apotropaic exercise.

in the middle was a raised platform or stage. The secret of what went on within these walls was so well kept that very little is definitely known about it. One point conclusively established is that the Eleusinian mysteries did not profess to impart an esoteric doctrine concerning the future life. The important thing in them was not what was said, but what was done; not instruction, but impression.[1]

It is probable that scenes from the myth of Demeter were acted or presented in *tableaux vivants*—the rape of Korē, the grief of the mother, the return of the lost daughter from the nether world, the institution of the mysteries. Such representations were not uncommon in the public cults; but here they were surrounded by every circumstance that could quicken imagination, kindle emotion, and give substance to things hoped for, reality to things not seen. This solemn mystery-play was, however, not all. There was a higher degree, that of the ἐπόπτης, which could not be taken under a year after admission to the Greater Mysteries at Eleusis. To those who attained it were displayed the contents of the ark, the nature and significance of which were explained by the hierophant. It may be conjectured that these objects, the sight of which inspired the deepest awe, were things which the goddess was believed herself to have used in inaugurating the mysteries, so that the rite resembled the exhibition of the most venerated relics in a Christian church.[2] This exhibition must have been at a different time from the mystery-play, perhaps on the following night. The attendance was doubtless much less numerous; and it seems probable that the epopts in small groups drew near to the *anaktoron*, or raised platform, on which the shrines containing the sacred objects were placed, while the hierophant displayed and explained them.

---

[1] "The initiated do not learn what they must do, but feel certain emotions and are put in a certain suitable frame of mind."—Aristotle.

[2] For example, the Seamless Robe at Trier or the Sudarium (Veronica) at Rome. It may not be irrelevant to remark that John of Damascus expresses the doctrine of the church when he says that Christ offers the relics to Christians as a means of grace. The legends of the Holy Grail show the mediæval feeling.

Rites of a sacramental character, also, had a place in the Eleusinia. One such rite preceded admission to the spectacle in the great hall; each of the mystæ partook of the *kukeōn*, a kind of gruel which the mourning Demeter, when she broke her nine days' fast, refusing wine, bade the queen, Metaneira, prepare for her of barley-groats, water, and pennyroyal leaves rubbed fine. Other sacramental acts are indicated in the password of the Eleusinian mysteries as reported by Clement of Alexandria: "I fasted, I drank the gruel, I took from the ark, and having tasted,[1] I put it away in the basket, and from the basket into the ark." If the text is rightly restored, the reference would appear to be to some sort of communion bread, or cake.

Whatever obscurity surrounds the rites at Eleusis, there is no concealment of the faith of those who took part in them. From the Homeric Hymn on, the assurance of a blessed immortality is the good which men seek and find in the mysteries; it is this which gave them their persistent attraction not only for the multitudes, but for the noblest souls among the Greeks. Thus Pindar: "Blessed he, who having seen them, passes beneath the hollow earth; he knows the end of life, and knows its god-given origin"; and Sophocles: "O thrice-blessed those mortals, who having beheld these mysteries descend to Hades; to them alone it is given there to live; for the rest all evils are there."

These quotations make it clear, also, that salvation was only for the initiated—as we should say, for members of the church. It does not appear that moral defects, so far as they did not, like blood guilt, involve religious defilement, excluded either from the church or its salvation, whereas the foreigner (the man of non-Greek speech) was not admitted. The sarcasm of Diogenes was as apt to the Eleusinian mysteries as to the Orphic *thiasoi*. But here, too, the moral common sense of the community refused the consequences of ecclesiastical logic; the growing belief in the inexorably just judgment after death also conflicted with it. Thinkers like

---

[1] So the text is emended by Lobeck. The manuscript reading is "having wrought."

Heraclitus ridicule the superstition that physical purifications can purge the soul of moral defilement. Finally, the great thought breaks through at least here and there, "Purity is holy-mindedness."[1]

Branches of the Eleusinian mysteries were established in numerous places, but none of them rivalled the fame of the original. Among other mysteries which flourished in the same age the most notable were those of Samothrace, which according to Herodotus had been adopted by the Greeks from the earlier inhabitants of the island ("Pelasgians"). They attained their great importance, however, in the fourth century, and in the Hellenistic and Roman times stood second only to the Eleusinia, enjoying the peculiar favour of the rulers. The name of the Kabeiroi, who figure in the Samothracian religion, has commonly been interpreted as Phœnician ("the great gods"),[2] and it has accordingly been supposed that the cult was introduced by Phœnician traders, who may early have had a factory on the island. In the age when we know anything about it there seems to be nothing distinctively Semitic in the religion. Demeter was one of the great deities of the island; her daughter Korē was associated with her, and the pair was grouped in divers ways with the two Kabeiroi. At Thebes, where also the Kabeiroi were worshipped, the elder of the two was identified with Dionysos, while in Lemnos he was Hephaistos. The mysteries of Andania in Messenia also enjoyed great repute in this period. The Eleusinian pair was here joined with the two ancient local deities, Apollo Karneios and Hermes Kriophoros.

Ample provision would seem thus to be made for every man to be saved in the fashion that best suited his temperament, from the decorous solemnity of the spectacle at Eleusis to the orgiastic enthusiasm of the Bacchic *thiasoi*. But besides these mystery-churches, voluntary or under state supervi-

---

[1] Quoted by Porphyry through Theophrastus from an inscription at Epidaurus.

[2] The etymology is perfectly good; it can be matched with an equally good Indo-Germanic possibility.

sion, there was a peculiar evangelistic movement, which became prominent in the fourth century, though its beginnings probably lie much farther back. Small bands of men and women went about the country with a donkey-load of stuff—including the ceremonial fawn-skins and the apparatus of initiation, drums and tambourines, their books, and tame snakes—gathering curious hearers and preaching the Orphic salvation, purifying their converts from the sin and uncleanness, and admitting them to the mystic fellowship. Demosthenes taunts his opponent, Æschines, with having, when a young man, acted as acolyte to his mother, who seems to have been a captain in one of these branches of the Salvation Army. When she had an initiation on hand, Æschines read the liturgy and attended to a variety of other arrangements:

In the night time wearing the fawn-skin and mixing the bowl; purifying the candidates, and swabbing them off with mud and bran; then making the man arise from his purification, and bidding him say, "I have escaped evil, I have found a better thing"—priding yourself that nobody ever shouted so loud. . . . By day leading the fine companies marching through the streets, wearing the chaplets of fennel and poplar-leaves, hugging their brown snakes and raising them above their heads, bawling *Euoi saboi!* and dancing to the tune of *Huēs attēs! attēs huēs!* while old women salute you by the titles of Leader, Guide, Ark-bearer, Sieve-bearer, and the like. For such services you were paid with sops and twisted rolls and fresh-baked cakes—who would not count himself a lucky dog to fare so well?

Demosthenes's malicious portrait of his rival may or may not be an accurate description of the doings of the particular band with which Æschines's mother trained, but it gives a vivid picture of the kind of thing his hearers had seen many a time; that was what gave his satire its telling point.

The demand for remedies for the ailments of the soul produced also a multitude of quacks, who peddled infallible purges and panaceas of salvation. Of peculiarly evil note among those who thus preyed on the credulous superstition of the masses were the mendicant devotees of the Phrygian goddess Cybele, the *Mētragyrtai*, whose name describes their vocation—*agyrtēs* is a man who takes up a collection. They dealt in necromancy and magic as well as purifications, and earned for *agyrtēs* its secondary meaning, 'vagabond, impostor.' Others practised according to the Orphic school and called themselves "*Orpheotelestai.*"

The sixth century, in which the orgiastic cults of Dionysos and his congeners were overrunning Greece and religion was taking the nether-worldly turn which has been described above, witnessed also the beginning of philosophy. In the age of colonial and commercial expansion the Ionian cities had taken the lead, and they held the primacy not only in wealth and enterprise but in culture and intellectual life. There the logographers made the first essays in writing prose, and attempted to extract from the epics, the temple legends, and the often fictitious pedigrees of noble families, a history of the cities—particularly of their foundation—set in a chronological scheme, becoming thus precursors of the historians; there Hecatæus of Miletus, as the fruit of his travels and inquiries, composed in the form of a guide-book, The Tour of the World, the first descriptive geography; there, also, Greek philosophy was born.

The Ionian thinkers went straight at the problem of the origin and constitution of the universe. This problem had been prepared for them by theology. The Theogony of Hesiod, as we have seen, was at the same time a cosmogony. Cosmogonic powers such as Chaos, Gaia (Earth), Eros (Love), however invested with mythical personality, are not gods of the popular religion to whom the rôle of world-makers has been assigned, but, in this capacity, creatures of nascent speculation. The first philosophers also often express themselves in mythical language and think in mythical forms—how could they do otherwise? But while the theological cosmogony is only a prelude to the divine genealogies and mythical doings of the gods in heaven and on earth, the end of the philosophers, more or less clearly conceived, was to explain the existence of the world and the phenomena of nature by natural causes.

They seek, therefore, a primordial matter, or world-stuff, not inert and passive, but endowed with an immanent energy which, working in accordance with physical laws, produces all the changes of the phenomenal world. With the exception of Heraclitus, to whom we shall return, the early Ionians seem to have gone their serene way, regardless of the bearing of their speculations on religion, nor does it appear that they were assailed for their opinions. It is clear, however, that if they gave the name of gods to anything in their materialistic universe, they had really no use for them.

A sharp attack upon religion in the name of reason and morals was made by Xenophanes, a native of Colophon, who, driven from home at the age of twenty-five, spent a considerable part of his life in Sicily. Xenophanes found many things wrong in his world—the luxury which his countrymen at home had learned from the Lydians, as well as the Sicilian passion for athletic competitions and the honours and privileges heaped on Olympian winners. His self-esteem, like that of many another professor, is wounded when he sees a man who has won a horse-race more thought of than himself for all his learning. It is all wrong to prefer brawn to brains! He satirises anthropomorphic notions of the gods: Mortals think that the gods are born and have human speech and form. The Ethiopians imagine their gods flat-nosed and black; the Thracians, blue-eyed and red-haired; and if cattle and horses or lions had hands and could draw, horses would draw the gods as horses and cattle as cattle—each kind would make its gods in its own likeness. Worse than this, the poets represent the gods with all the moral weaknesses of men. "Homer and Hesiod ascribe to the gods everything that among men is a shame and a disgrace—theft, adultery, and deceit." And everybody learns about the gods from Homer! Over against the vulgar polytheism Xenophanes sets his own idea of god: "There is one god, greatest among gods and men, not like mortals either in form or in thought."[1] This god "without effort swings the universe by the purpose

[1] Xenophanes rejects mental anthropomorphism as well as physical.

of his mind." "He ever abides in the same place, nor moves at all; it does not beseem him to wander hither and thither." The One of Xenophanes is not, however, a supramundane god, but the universe itself, endued with sense and thought and purpose.

Heraclitus expressly denies that the universe had a beginning or a creator: "This cosmic order, the same for all beings, no god or man made, but it always was and is and will be, ever-living fire, blazing up and dying down in measure." The uniformity of natural law is poetically asserted in another passage: "The sun will not overstep his bounds (literally, measures); for if he does, the Erinyes, the avenging handmaids of justice, will find him out." The pure elemental fire, the first principle, is intelligence. In his oracular style, Heraclitus says of it: "One, the alone wise, is unwilling and yet is willing to be called by the name of Zeus." That is, if you think of god as the vulgar do, it is no god; but if you understand what god is, it is the supreme god.

Man is a microcosm, like the macrocosm compact of earth and water and fire, and the same process of change is continually going on in him. The soul, the conscious and intelligent in man, is of the same nature with the one wisdom of the universe, of which it is indeed a spark; it is, however, not the pure elemental fire, but a dry heat; when this leaves the body, the rest, mere earth and water, is worth only to be cast on the dung heap. It is death to the soul to turn to water; the pleasures that irrigate the soul, like drunkenness which drowns intelligence and consciousness, are evil—"Dry sunlight; wisest and best soul!"[1]

The most highly reputed authorities fare badly at Heraclitus's hands: Homer and Archilochus ought to be turned out of the lists and flogged. Hesiod is most men's teacher, and is credited with knowledge of many things—a man who did not know day nor night! "Varied learning does not

[1] The original of the Baconian "dry light" of reason. A plausible emendation, adopted by many moderns is, "The dry soul is the wisest and best."

teach a man to have sense, or it would have taught Hesiod and Pythagoras, or again Xenophanes and Hecatæus."

Of the popular religion Heraclitus speaks with a keener scorn than Xenophanes: "Men pray to the idols—just as if one were to converse with houses, knowing not what is the nature of gods and heroes!" If a man who had stepped into the mud should wash himself off with mud, every one would take him for mad; to purify a man of blood guilt by blood expiations is no less absurd. The Bacchic mysteries had reached Ionia, and they stirred the honest man's bile; he rails at the "night roamers, magians, bacchants, wild women, mystæ." The initiations are accomplished with unholy rites: "Were it not Dionysos in whose honour they march in procession and sing their obscene song (the phallic hymn), it would be a most scandalous performance. The Dionysos to whom they rave and revel is no other than Hades!"

Parmenides, the founder of the Eleatic school, raised the physical problem of the Ionians into a metaphysical problem, the nature of reality.[1] Starting with the antithesis of being and non-being, he argues that being is, and that its existence is necessary; but non-being is unthinkable and therefore non-existent, for what is must be thinkable. Being is eternal: it cannot have its origin in any other being, for there is no other besides the one; nor can it have arisen out of non-being, for it has been proved that there is no such thing. It does not fall under the category of time; we cannot say of it, "It was," nor "It will be," but only, "It is." Reality is unchangeable, for in all change something that was not becomes something that is, involving the transition from non-being to being, which has been demonstrated to be absurd. In short, all manifoldness, qualitative difference, becoming, change, passing away, are excluded from the idea of reality. This conception of being became classic. Through Plato and Aristotle it passed into theology; the scholastic definitions of God in Christianity and Mohammedanism repeat

[1] Whether Parmenides himself conceived it metaphysically is another question.

this idea of metaphysical perfection, which caused trouble enough when the attempt had to be made to reconcile it with the conception of a living God such as religion requires.

Instead of trying to derive everything from one principle as the Ionians had done, Empedocles took the four elements as he found them—fire, air, water, earth. These elements are eternal and irreducible; they are combined in different groupings and proportions by "friendship," and the combinations are broken up again into their constituents by "strife"—attraction and repulsion, we should say, or affinity and incompatibility. Thus the endless variety of things, arising, changing, dissolving, was accounted for by the four material elements and the two polar forces. In Empedocles's description of the origin of living nature there are curious speculations about evolution and the survival of the fittest. He also elaborated a theory of sense-perception.

The gods of the popular religion, "living long ages through and excelling in honours," spring, like trees, and men and women, beasts, birds, and water-nourished fishes, "all things that are or will be," from the same elements. The Sphere, that is, the universe itself, is god in a higher sense, and Empedocles uses of it language reminiscent of Xenophanes on the One.

Empedocles was a many-sided character—philosopher, democratic politician, and man of science, a preacher of the Orphic-Pythagorean gospel, and an expert in the purification of souls. His extravagant professions are doubtless to blame that he comes down to us as a miracle-monger with a distinct touch of the charlatan. In his religious writings, which bear the significant title Purgations ($\kappa\alpha\theta\alpha\rho\mu\omicron\iota$), the transmigration of souls is a ruling idea. He says of his own metamorphoses: "I was once a youth, a maiden, a plant, a bird, and a mute sea-fish." The slaughter of animals for food or in sacrifice is a deadly sin, for a father may be slaying his own son, a son his father, children their mother. Those who have stained their hands with blood or sworn false oaths are doomed for thrice ten thousand seasons to roam far from the blessed, being born in course of time in every kind of mortal form, exchanging one grievous path of life for another. "For the mighty air chases them to the sea, and the sea spits them out on the land, the earth to the rays of the shining sun, and this tosses them into the whirlwinds of the air; one element receives them from the other, and all hate them. To these I now belong, an exile from God and a wanderer, because I yielded to the impulse of mad strife."

Anaxagoras of Clazomenæ was the last of the Ionian succession. Instead of the four "roots" of Empedocles he assumed that all substances were elementary. These "seeds," or germs, were infinite in number and infinitesimal in magnitude, and were mingled in a primordial matter which had none of the distinguishing qualities of individual things—no colour, for example, because all colours were mixed in it. What gives importance to Anaxagoras in the history of philosophy is not, however, his theory of the constitution of matter, but the fact that, abandoning the monistic hypotheses of his predecessors, he introduces a second principle, Nous (Mind). Starting at one centre, the Nous sets up an ever-extending rotary motion in matter, in consequence of which particles of like nature assemble, separating themselves from the unlike, forming first the ether and the worlds. As the process proceeds the various substances arise, consisting chiefly of the same element and named from this predominance, but containing, nevertheless, larger or smaller portions of all other elements, so that "there is something of everything in everything." The question whether the Nous of Anaxagoras was material or immaterial has been the subject of some unprofitable argument: it was certainly not material in his sense,[1] and there is no reason to suppose that it was immaterial in the Platonic sense; it would probably be nearer the truth to compare his conception with the Stoic Pneuma.

In the Phædo of Plato, Socrates expresses his disappoint-

---

[1] This is the meaning of his definition: "The other things contain a portion of everything, but Nous is infinite and self-determined, and is mingled with nothing, but is alone independent."

ment that Anaxagoras, having introduced mind into the universe, gave it so little to do. The idea that mind ordered the world and was the cause of all things seemed to Socrates a true and fruitful one, but when he got hold of the book he discovered that the author made no use of mind at all, but explained things by physical causes, "airs and ethers and fluids, and many other absurdities." Aristotle's criticism is in the same vein: "Anaxagoras employs mind as a *deus ex machina* to get the world made, and lugs it in when he is at a loss to explain why anything must be as it is, but, for the rest, makes everything rather than mind a cause of what comes to pass." But however incompletely Anaxagoras may have apprehended the scope and consequence of his own idea, the fact remains that he begins an era of dualistic systems in Greek philosophy.

Up to this time philosophy had flourished in the Ionian cities, in southern Italy, and in Sicily; the mother country had taken no part in the movement. Athens was, however, beginning to draw to itself men of note from all parts of the Hellenic world. Among these was Anaxagoras, who made that city his home for some thirty years (ca. 462–432). There he moved in the brilliant Periclean circle, and enjoyed the intimacy of Pericles himself. In the little city he was doubtless a familiar figure; the wits on the street nicknamed him "Nous." As the Peloponnesian war was casting its shadows before, the temper of the masses became ugly; they could not reach Pericles himself, but more than one of his friends had to suffer for his favour. Pheidias was one of these, Anaxagoras another. A certain Diopeithes got a vote passed in 432 B. C. that persons should be prosecuted who did not observe the ordinances of religion or promulgated theories about the heavens. Thereupon Anaxagoras was brought up for his offence against the state religion in teaching that the sun was a red-hot mass of rock.[1] Conflicting

---

[1] And therefore no god. Anaxagoras taught that the sun was a red-hot mass of rock, larger than the Peloponnesus, and that the moon was a cold earth, with hills and valleys, and that it was inhabited.

stories are told about what followed; the only thing certain is that the philosopher left Athens and returned to Asia Minor, where not long after he died at Lampsacus. It was the first exhibition of the religious intolerance of the Athenians which not only Socrates, but Protagoras, Aristotle, Stilpon, and Theophrastus were to experience.

The antipodes of Anaxagoras's dualism of matter and mind was the atomic theory of Democritus, the last word of materialistic monism.[1] Democritus was the most learned and many-sided of the philosophers before Aristotle, a man who had travelled widely, a thinker of notable acumen, a fertile author, and a writer whose style was thought by ancient critics worthy to be compared to Plato. The properties of Being had been convincingly demonstrated by the Eleatics: what truly is must be simple, eternal, and unchangeable. Their mistake was in denying the existence of empty space;[2] the void is as real as body. There is an infinite number of atoms, too minute to be perceived by any sense, qualitatively exactly the same, but differing in shape, position, and arrangement. To these atoms belong the predicates which the Eleatics gave to the universe. The atoms move eternally in the infinite void, but with different rates corresponding to their size and weight. In consequence of collision and composition of motions, rotary movements arise, and worlds are formed. Under purely physical laws, atoms of similar form and weight group and arrange themselves in innumerable ways, constituting thus the elements and bodily objects. Under the same laws these combinations are broken up, things change and decay, worlds are dissolved; only the atoms are unchangeable.

The soul is composed of fine smooth, round atoms, as is also fire; it fills the whole body, but exercises special functions in particular organs. Soul atoms are inhaled from the air and exhaled into it so long as life goes on, the soul being thus

[1] The founder of this system was Leucippus; but his doctrine is sufficiently known only as developed by Democritus.
[2] For the Eleatics empty space was "non-being."

continually renewed.   Gods and demons are beings similar to men but superior to them, inhabiting the air, and manifesting themselves to men sensibly in dreams, "inspiring prophecy, and giving signs."   There is no trace of the hostility to the popular religion which is so strong in Epicurus.   The gods of Democritus have, however, no part in making the world or determining what comes to pass in it; they are composed of an attenuated matter, but they are formed and dissolved like all other bodies.

In the course of these efforts to solve the problem of the universe by speculation, the difficulties had become increasingly apparent, and the question whether knowledge is possible had disturbed the confidence of more than one thinker.   Thus Xenophanes says: "As to certainty, no man ever lived, nor ever will be, who knows about the gods and all the things that I discuss, for even if he should by chance utter the perfect truth, he himself would not know it; illusion is the lot of all." The Eleatics had at last to sum up knowledge in the identical proposition, One is One, and to put the empirical world out of the sphere of knowledge and reality into a limbo of appearance and opinion; while Heraclitus was fain to admit that in his eternal flux things could not be known.   The inquiry into the nature of sense-perception, also, had at least one agreed result, the evidence of the senses is untrustworthy. On the world outside the schools the array of conflicting systems, each annulling the principles of the other, made an impression of futility which bred scepticism.

A concurrent cause of the depreciation of philosophy was the development of higher education under the direction of professional teachers, the so-called sophists.   These undertook to impart general culture, and to prepare their pupils to take part in the social and political life of their times.   Some of them were more particularly rhetoricians, cultivating style and the art of discourse, and training men in forensic or popular eloquence; others, with increasing specialisation, devoted themselves primarily to argumentation.   The practical end was common to them all; theories of the universe, of which a man could make no use in the world, were worthless, even if true. They did not think it necessary to refute them, though Gorgias wrote a book under the expressive title, On the Nonexistent, or on Nature, in which, turning the argument of the Eleatics end for end, he proposed to prove three theorems: *First*, nothing exists; *second*, if anything exists it is unknowable; *third*, if it is knowable, the knowledge is incommunicable.

Without exception the sophists were sceptical about the possibility of knowing the things with which the philosophers occupied themselves. Their scepticism went, however, much further than this. Protagoras of Abdera was the first among Greek thinkers to deal thoroughly with the theory of cognition. His answer to the question, How do we know anything? was that all knowledge is derived from the senses. Inasmuch as both the material organs of sense and the material objects which make an impression upon them are every instant changing, it follows that every sensation is true; but true only for the individual percipient, and for him only in the transient moment. There is no universally valid truth and no knowledge of an objective reality. In a work entitled Truth, he wrote: "Man"—that is, as the context shows, the individual—"is the measure of all things, of the existence of what is and the nonexistence of what is not." His attitude toward religion was agnostic. A book of his, On the Gods, began: "About gods I am unable to affirm either that they exist or that they do not exist, nor what they are like. Many things prevent our knowing; the subject is obscure and life is short." For this heresy he was expelled from Athens, and his books gathered up from their possessors and publicly burned in the market-place.

In these agnostic circles the question of the origin of religion was first raised: if nobody knows anything about the gods, nor even whether there are any, how did men come to worship and fear them? The theory of Prodicus was this: "The sun and moon, rivers and fountains, and in general whatever furthers our life, were deemed gods by the men of old times on account of the profit received from them, as the Egyptians deify the Nile; and on this account bread was worshipped as Demeter, wine as Dionysos, fire as Hephaistos, and, in short, every useful thing." Critias, who was regarded as a typical product of the sophistical education, one of those noble young Athenians whose character their teachers had ruined, in a satyric drama, lets Sisyphos set forth the theory that some shrewd and clever man, seeing that human law and its penalties restrained men only from crimes which their fellows could discover, invented the gods in order that the bad might be afraid to do or say or think evil in secret, and described them as immortal beings who hear and see all that men do and penetrate their very thoughts, having their abode in heaven, whence come the lightnings and thunder that terrify men and the sun and the rain which bless them. The theory has a peculiar fitness, coming from a man who proved one of the most unscrupulous of the Thirty Tyrants.

The charge of corrupting the morals of young men is constantly repeated against the sophists, but the fact that it was made with especial animosity against Socrates must make us cautious about admitting without inquiry this indictment of the class. Some of them were men of unimpeachable probity, and accusations of personal immorality are rarely brought against any of them even by their most hostile critics. The virtue, or excellence, which they professed to cultivate by their scheme of education included morals, and some of them appear to have given particular attention to the subject: Prodicus's apologue of Hercules at the Parting of the Ways is well known. In general, doubtless they presented the conventional morality of the time and its social sanctions, without undertaking to reform or elevate it.

The prevailing sceptical and subjective spirit of their teaching could not fail, however, to appear in their ethics. If the doctrine of Protagoras be accepted, that there is no such thing as universally valid truth, and that everything is true to the individual if it seems so at the moment, the question was bound to be raised, Is there any universal standard of right, or is the individual the only measure of what is right for him? And further, if what seems good to the individual is right for him, what authority has society by law or custom to impose upon him a different rule? In the discussion of the nature of justice in Plato's Republic, Thrasymachus explodes his brutal dictum, "I tell you, justice is simply the advantage of the stronger." The tyrant makes laws in his interest, the democracy in theirs; what is one day lawful and just is to-morrow a crime. Might makes right.

The discussion of a customary or conventional morality always confuses it in attempting to define, and relaxes its obligations by examining them. In the hands of the sophists the discussion did not lead to the firmer establishment of morals on a basis of ethical principles; its results were merely negative. The method of discussion aggravated the mischief: moral questions were made the themes of exercises in disputation; the cultivation and display of the eristic art was the chief thing—the skill with which the disputant maintained his side, not the discovery or defence of the truth. Men are only too easily deluded by their own fallacies, especially when the inclination lies that way, and persuade themselves that evil is good and good evil.[1]

The sophists contributed to the demoralisation of Athenian society in the end of the fifth century, but they have often been made responsible for more than their share; political and economic causes had much more to do with it than the new education.

The vogue of the mysteries, with their new gods and their enthusiastic personal religion, and the dissemination of philosophical doctrines, naturalistic or agnostic, did not have as much effect upon the old religions as might have been expected. The deliverance of Greece from the Persian invaders not only greatly exalted the national consciousness but quickened faith in the national gods who had given their worshippers the victory at Marathon and Salamis, at Platæa

[1] Aristophanes, Clouds, 1019 *ff.*

and Mycale. The temples which had been destroyed by the barbarians were rebuilt with greater magnificence and adorned with the most splendid works of art. Athens, especially, in the meridian of her short century of glory, became a very city of the gods. These temples and sculptures not only expressed religion but ennobled it; Pheidias's statue of Zeus at Olympia was justly thought to have added something to the received religion. Dio Chrysostom says of it: "His power and kingship are displayed by the strength and majesty of the whole image, his fatherly care for men by the mildness and loving-kindness in the face; the solemn austerity of the work marks the god of the city and the law. . . . He seems like one giving and abundantly bestowing blessings." The same sculptor's temple statue of Athena in the Parthenon similarly represented for the whole Hellenic world the ideal of the virgin goddess.

The elements of worship in the Greek religions present little that is distinctive: sacrifice and offering, hymn and prayer, expiation and purification, propitiation of the kindly gods and thanksgiving for their bounty, placation of the dreaded powers of the nether world, riddance of demons and ghosts—these are the components of the cultus, as among other peoples on the same plane of civilisation all over the world. As elsewhere, too, incompatible survivals of primitive rites and superstitions remain to the end by the side of more advanced conceptions. None the less, taken as a whole, the Greek cultus has a physiognomy of its own, very different from the worship of the Vedic Indians or of the old Roman religion, and from the peoples of nearer Asia.

The particularism of Greek politics is reflected in religion. There was much diversity in the cults of different cities and states, not only in the gods who were worshipped, but in the forms of worship. These religions were never subjected to any political centralisation such as might have resulted from the establishment of a national state; nor did any theologically minded priesthood systematise them. The priests and the oracle of the Delphian Apollo exerted a great and beneficent influence upon both religion and morality; but they did nothing toward unity in idea or uniformity in externals.

What is most likely to impress the observer in Greek worship in the classic period are its æsthetic features: in the temples, the statues of the gods, the stately processions, the decorous ritual, we see a people endowed beyond all others with a sense of beauty and an inexhaustible joy in the beautiful worshipping gods who were their ideal of beauty. When we look at the sculptures of the Parthenon, for example, and imagine the Panathenaic procession moving in all its wealth of colour under the vibrant light amid the temples and monuments of Periclean Athens, we cannot conceive that any god was ever honoured with a more glorious worship. The same æsthetic spirit evolved the drama out of rustic masquerades, refined many rude ceremonies, and civilised savage gods. It is another aspect of the same temperament that made the Greeks loath to linger on unpleasant subjects—a disposition which led them in various instances to annex a joyous close to days of expiation and the gloomy services of underworld deities.

It is a serious error, however, to imagine, as many do, that the Greek religions were all sunny and beautiful because this is the side of them that is turned out in literature and grand art; there was always a great deal in them—and not the least sacred part, either—that was ugly, obscene, and barbarous; and it is wholly unwarranted to stamp these features as foreign. Nothing is more genuinely and persistently Greek than some of the grossest of these performances. Nor is it a legitimate inference that the ruder side of the religion is a later degeneration because little of it appears in Homer.[1]

Most of the holy places in Greece were doubtless holy before the advent of the Greeks, who took possession of them as the Israelites appropriated the high places of the Canaanites. The chief sanctuary of the city god was on the acropolis, in the court of the fortress-palace; and deities for one reason or another associated with the chief god were wor-

[1] See above, pp. 428 f.

shipped there by his side. In the city and suburbs other gods had their abodes; and in the open land there were sacred spots—groves, springs or streams of water, mountain tops and headlands—where in some way the divine presence or power had aforetime been manifested. The limits of holiness were marked by boundary stones; the precincts were called a *temenos*. In this area stood an altar for sacrifice, and often some object such as a rude stone or a wooden post, in which the deity was believed to lodge—the seat (ἕδος) of the god. Into this holy place no one might come in a state of un-holiness—that is, of uncleanness from any of its manifold causes—above all, no one defiled by blood guilt or by con-tact with death.

In time temples, that is, houses for the habitation of the deity, were erected in many of these ancient sanctuaries. The house of god is everywhere a later stage; it ordinarily presumes an image which needs to be housed. In historic times the Greeks had reached this stage. The aniconic seats of the gods were succeeded by rude idols, and these in turn by statues wrought with an art which grew more perfect to its culmination in the age of Pheidias; yet a higher sacredness often attached to the old shapeless idol in the adytum. Architecture made parallel progress; nothing is more ex-pressive of the spirit of Greek religion at its best than the temples.

The priests were in some cases hereditary, or even proprie-tary, custodians of the holy place; more frequently they were elected by the community for a limited time or chosen by lot; often the priesthoods, with their emoluments, were sold by the city for a term to the highest bidder. The authority in matters of the cultus was not vested in the priests, but resided in the people; the priests carried out the votes of the assem-bly or the directions of the magistrates. On many impor-tant occasions the civil and military officials themselves had to conduct the festivals or preside at the sacrifices. The duties of the priesthood were not usually of such a nature as to interfere with the incumbent's ordinary occupations or with the holding of public office; only at the festival seasons did they demand his whole time and attention.

Under the priest were inferior ministers who performed the common tasks of the temple; the menial work was chiefly done by slaves. Some temples were in the charge of priestesses, others had both priests and priestesses. The general rule was that priests must be reputable citizens and free from bodily defects or deformities. Divers restrictions were imposed on the priests of certain gods; the priestess of Athena Polias at Athens, for example, was forbidden to touch fresh native cheese, though she might eat what was made no farther away than Salamis; fish was taboo to the priestess of Hera at Argos and the priest of Poseidon at Megara. Continence was prescribed to some during their term of office, and was almost universally required for a limited time before engaging in sacred functions.

For their services in private sacrifices the priests had a right to a toll, the kind and measure of which naturally varied at different temples and at different times; a common tariff seems to have been the hide and a hind leg of the victim; from the bloodless offerings of meal, cakes, wine, honey, and the like, the priests also received a portion. For their services to the public they had appropriations from the city.

The Greek cultus distinguished more sharply than most between offerings made to the gods whose habitat is on earth or in the sky and those who dwell in the recesses of the earth. For the former a raised altar was reared, on which the god's share of the sacrifice was burned; for the latter a low mound, usually of earth or sods, into a hole in the middle of which the blood of the victims was poured and other offerings thrown, and on which the whole carcass was consumed by fire. The latter form was used also in the hero cult and in offerings to the dead. Offerings to the gods of the sea and of rivers were thrown into the water, being thus made over directly to the recipients.

Animal sacrifices fall into two classes: those in which, after the god had had his share and the priest had taken his toll, the flesh was used for food, and those in which no part of the victim might be employed by men in any way, but the whole must be destroyed. To the former category belong the ordinary slaughter of domestic animals for food, offerings accompanying a petition or in the fulfilment of a vow, thank offerings, and the great mass of sacrifices at public festivals, which often served to provide a feast for the whole city; the second class includes offerings to chthonic deities, to heroes and the dead, and all piacular victims. The reason is obvious: offerings to the powers of death and the tomb contract from their proximity a lethal contagion; the piaculum is laden with guilt or misfortune, which is also deadly. Contrariwise, the flesh of animals which have been killed in the precincts of a temple and of which a god has partaken gains —such at least is the primitive notion—a divine virtue which makes it wholesome.

The animals most commonly sacrificed to the gods were those chiefly used for food—sheep, goats, swine, and neat cattle[1]—but many gods had preferences and aversions in the matter of diet: Demeter, for example, preferred swine, while Aphrodite abhorred the beast; to Poseidon bulls were the favourite offering, to Athena cows; but the sex of the victim did not always correspond to that of the deity. That for most purposes the gods accept only physically perfect animals, and in many cults prefer mature ones, it is hardly necessary to say. The colour of the victim was also in numerous instances obligatory. In such matters not all temples of the same god had the same rule. Wild animals were seldom offered, and fish only to a few gods of peculiar tastes. Such victims could not easily be presented living and unmaimed at the altar; it may have been felt also that *feræ naturæ* belong as such to the gods, and cannot therefore be gifts which man brings of his own.

Bread and cakes of various kinds were offered to the gods

---

[1] Sacrifices to the underworld powers frequently require other victims—to Hecate, *e. g.*, a dog at a spot where three ways met, etc. The sacrifice of a white horse to Helios is a foreign rite.

above and below with the same difference of rite as in the sacrifice of animals. Often the oblations, after being laid on the altar as on the table of the god, were removed and eaten by the priests. The offerings to the gods of the underworld, among which a mixture of dough and honey containing poppy seeds was characteristic, were wholly consumed by fire. The cakes were sometimes fashioned in distinctive forms: to Artemis-Selene at Athens cakes shaped like the disc of the full moon and decorated with lights were presented; Apollo is said to have received cakes cut out in the form of a lyre or a bow and arrows.[1] Small images of sacrificial victims, moulded of dough and baked, were very common. Men who were too poor to sacrifice an animal brought its effigy instead, and vegetarian philosophers—the Neopythagoreans, for example—did the same, being thus able to conform to religious custom or obligation without violating their principles against taking life. Honey cakes were used in offerings to the dead; a popular notion was that Cerberus had a sweet tooth and could be appeased by sharing these delicacies with him.

The first-fruits of the grain harvest were dedicated to the gods who gave the increase of the husbandman's labours, and the fruits of trees had a place in worship corresponding to their importance in the diet of the people; cheese also was as much relished by gods as by men. Customs varied with deities and localities. Libations of wine, not only as an accompaniment of sacrifice but independently, were offered to many deities; a dinner or a drinking bout began with such a libation of wine mixed with water in the same proportions in which the feasters drank it. Some gods, however, accepted only non-intoxicating libations of honey mixed with milk or milk and water. The gods of the nether world all refuse wine, and many others were total abstainers at least in particular cults. The Athenians, we are told, made "sober" libations to Helios, Selene, Eos, the muses, the nymphs, and to Aphrodite Ourania. It is not improbable that in some

[1] The testimony in both cases comes from late writers.

of these instances the peculiarity is due to the influence of a foreign cult. When a "sober" libation is made to Dionysos, it may be surmised that it is in his chthonic aspect.

The burning of incense, both in connection with independent libations and as an accompaniment of sacrifice and oblation, came into fashion in the seventh century, and the consumption of fragrant gums, spices, and woods soon attained large proportions. In the temples incense was burned, especially upon a small altar in the interior, before the image of the god.[1]

Purifications and expiations, which among the Greeks as elsewhere constituted a large part of practical religion, do not differ in principle from those of other religions; specialties of form would be a long chapter on which it is impossible to enter here.[2] At the Thargelia, the spring purification of the city of Athens, two human scapegoats called Pharmakoi, after being beaten through the streets with certain plants, doubtless of some magical significance, were "led out," as the phrase is; there can hardly be a doubt that in earlier times they were killed—not as a human sacrifice, as is sometimes said, to gods above or gods below, but to get rid of them and their load of corruption for good and all. In grave emergencies cathartic experts were sometimes summoned from afar; the purification of Athens by Empedocles is a familiar story. Apollo, as the great medicine-man among the gods, is the purifier ($\kappa\alpha\theta\acute{\alpha}\rho\sigma\iota os$),[3] by his arts cleansing the city or the individual from blood guilt and other defilements with their entail of evils.

Each of the Greek cities had its own festival calendar, growing and changing, no doubt, in the course of time. Only that of Athens, from the fifth century, is known with anything approaching completeness. The greater festivals

---

[1] The parallel to Jewish worship will not escape notice. In Jerusalem also the use of costly aromatics to make a sweet smoke before the Lord was in the seventh century a new luxury in the cultus, which Jeremiah protests God does not require.

[2] See above, pp. 105 *ff*., 221 *ff*., 265 *ff*.

[3] The epithet is attached to other gods, *e. g.*, to Zeus.

were celebrated with a splendour of which the descriptions and the representations in art can give but a faint notion. Among them the Panathenaia in July (and more pompously in the third year of each Olympiad), the Eleusinia, of which a description has already been given, the Thesmophoria of Demeter, and the numerous festivals of Dionysos, stand out conspicuously. A bare catalogue would serve no purpose here, while even the briefest description would far outrun our limits. Nor can we do more than remind the reader of the great Panhellenic festivals, the Olympian, Pythian, Isthmian, and Nemean games, with their athletic contests and races, to which participants and spectators thronged from every quarter of the Greek world. The Greek gods loved life and colour, loved manly beauty and strength, skill and courage, as well as the moral manliness—ἀρετή, virtus.

The universal belief that the gods manifest their will or reveal what is to happen by divers signs—meteorological and astronomical phenomena, the flight of birds, dreams, etc.— was shared by the Greeks, and there was an old native art of interpretation practised by diviners (μάντις) and priests. When the gods did not spontaneously offer signs, omens were sought, especially from an inspection of the entrails of the sacrificial victims, in which any abnormality was a bad sign;[1] omens were taken also from the behaviour of the victim, the way the smoke ascended, and many things besides.

Mention has been made in another connection of the oracle of Zeus at Dodona.[2] Of still greater repute in classical times was the oracle of Apollo at Delphi, which was consulted by inquirers from near and far. The answer of the god to the question propounded was given by a priestess, the Pythia, who, seated in the adytum of the temple, on a tripod over a cleft in the earth from which vapour rose, went off into a trance, and muttered half-articulated sounds or disconnected words, which the prophet, standing by, construed secundum artem, and communicated to the inquirer in hexameter verse—of a sort.

[1] See pp. 105 ff. and 221 ff.   [2] Above, p. 265 ff.

CHAPTER XIX

THE GREEKS

POETRY AND PHILOSOPHY

The Higher Religion of Greece—Influence of the Literature—The Poets — Pindar — Æschylus — Sophocles — Euripides — Aristophanes — The Philosophers—Socrates—Plato—Aristotle.

THE higher religion of the Greeks is represented by the poets and the philosophers. It was they, not the priests, who conceived and set forth purer and loftier ideas of the gods and their dealings with men; they who affirmed the essentially moral character of true religion and the nature of true piety; they who, from different sides, advanced toward monotheism.

The priesthoods conserved the traditional forms of religion; but, if they contributed little to progress except the enrichment of liturgy—a sacerdotal predilection in all ages—they were at least no bar to progress. They had no sacred scriptures investing cult, myth, and doctrine with the infallible and unchangeable authority of divine revelation; the sacred legends were rehearsed at the festivals in a traditional form, but in variant forms at different temples; there was no dogma and no ecclesiastical authority. Innovations that seemed detrimental to the religion of the city were prosecuted by the civil authorities under laws passed like any others by the assembly.

Thus the literature which embodies the advancing religious thought of the Greeks is a secular literature in form and freedom, and this is its prime distinction. It may be that the philosophy of the Upanishads originated and was

477

first cultivated among laymen; but it attached itself to an eminently hieratic literature, the Brahmanas; and as soon as it gained any acceptance it was appropriated by the priests and Brahmanised into orthodoxy, as they Brahmanised even the more indigestible dualism of the Sankhya. The metaphysics of Buddhism are borrowed from the Brahmanic systems, and its literature is completely scholastic. These philosophies are thus not only historically the development of particular religions, but have the *character indelebilis* of sacred philosophies. That they have never exerted any considerable influence outside is not due solely to the geographical and historical isolation of the East; a deeper-lying cause is this inveterate religious particularism. And it is, on the other hand, just because the religious thinking of the Greeks was secular that its influence has been unlimited.

Therein lies its great and permanent interest. These thinkers not only restored religion to intellectual respectability; they made of religious philosophy a religion for thinking men. This was their service in their own day, but their influence was vastly greater in after ages. Jewish, Christian, and Moslem theology is built on the foundations laid by the Greek philosophers, and its structural lines mainly follow theirs—it is only necessary to think of Plato and Aristotle in the Middle Ages. Theism, mysticism and theosophy, ethics, and eschatology, in all these theologies have a woof of scripture and tradition, but the warp is Greek. A fuller presentation of the Greek thinkers is therefore in place, not merely as the culmination of Greek religion, but as the foundation of the religions that succeeded it.

The immediate influence of the poets was far greater than that of the philosophers, for they reached, not a small circle of students, but all classes of men. Without deliberate intention of reform, they show what elevation a religion like that of the Greeks was capable of—how noble a conception of God and of the relations between God and man. More than this, while the philosophers before them had sought to reduce to unity the physical order or to penetrate the metaphysical unity of being, Æschylus and Sophocles reveal the unity of the moral order and its essential righteousness. The truths the poets uttered were the more impressive by the form and circumstance of their presentation. The Olympian or Pythian games whose victors are celebrated in Pindar's Odes were not mere athletic contests, they were solemn acts of worship to Zeus or Apollo, surrounded by imposing ceremony, and inspiring reverent awe as well as noble joy. The Attic drama was the crown of the worship of Dionysos, who, beyond any other god, appealed to the soul.

The epinician ode or the tragedy gave no room for didactic theologising or moralising; the poet's task was to exhibit in word or action the ways of God with men. Subject and story were drawn from the wealth of myth and heroic legend, familiar to all his hearers, and sacred to him as well as to them. The poets did not use these myths as the vehicle for lessons they wished to convey, nor the characters as mouth-pieces of their own philosophising and moralising;[1] but they penetrated the hidden causes and underlying laws, the ineluctable concatenation of deed and event, that necessitated the tragic action and its issue.

The mythology had been an offence to many religious spirits; we have heard the outcry against gods who do everything that is disreputable among men, or against the epic poets who told such scandalous stories about them. It was not enough, however, that gods should be respectable and set a good example, they must be righteous, and rule the world in righteousness, nor could right mean one thing among men and another for gods. Some, therefore, rejected the objectionable myths as libels on the gods; others rationalised the myths, as Euripides (after the repentant Stesichoros) does the story of Helen, or gave expurgated versions of them, as Pindar does in the story of Pelops and his ivory shoulder; still others treated the strife and violence as belonging to a bygone age, when the gods of the present order were fighting

---

[1] Euripides does this, and it is one of his most significant departures from the old way.

their way to a supremacy which they now exercise with justice.

In the forty-four extant Odes of Pindar, celebrating athletic victories, there is an inexhaustible wealth of mythical recital and allusion; no small part of his felicity lies in the choice of myths apt to the occasion and the person of the winner and in the ingenuity with which he adapts them to his use. There is piety, too, in his selection; what is not worthy of the gods is not to be told of them. If he introduces such a tale, he makes no scruple of changing it so as to eliminate the offensive features.

Pindar was a member of the old Bœotian nobility, a conservative by tradition and temper. A sincerely pious soul, too, he represents the ancestral religion at its culmination. To a superficial reading it might seem that the Odes stood very close to the epics. The same deities appear in both, with the same functions and attributes; they move before us in the same vivid personality, very real and living gods, as they were in the myth and popular imagination. Upon a more attentive consideration, however, differences appear which evince the progress religion had made between Homer and Pindar. The rejection of crude and immoral stories about the gods is not merely a tribute to a more refined taste, but an avowed religious principle—it is blasphemy to attribute such deeds to gods. The expurgation of the mythology is only the negative consequence of a purer conception of godhead; Pindar's gods are not only powerful and beautiful, but consistently wise and good, and that in a divine manner and degree. Their rule of the world and dealing with mortals is righteous and just. These virtues, which may easily be prosaic in gods as in men, are crowned in Pindar by nobility—the word that best characterises his conception.

The ascription of all divine perfections to every deity obliterates those individual traits which their imperfections—their passion and partisanship and strife—give to the Homeric gods; the distinct figures of the several gods begin to recede before the idea of the godhead. The will of Zeus, in

Homer crossed by the conflicting though unequal wills of other gods, is in Pindar the law of the world. The world is the realm of Zeus; he distributes good and evil, for he is lord of all. Call it Destiny, Justice, or, as it will presently be named, Providence, Zeus personifies the moral order of the world not merely because he is sovereign over gods and men, but because in him is the fulness of the godhead. Once, indeed, in a fragment preserved by Clement, the pantheistic word is spoken out as roundly as by Xenophanes: "What is God? The All."

The Odes contain many prayers invoking the favour and protection of the gods and the blessings they bestow on those with whom they are well pleased. But by the side of these are petitions of a more spiritual character, as when in the eighth Pythian he prays to Apollo that he may always govern his conduct in accordance with the laws of the god and be his obedient servant. To be well-pleasing to the gods, it is before all things necessary that man should recognise the limitations of humanity and keep within his bounds. The warning against self-exaltation is addressed with peculiar point to the fortunate winners in the games—such as the dust of the Olympic course,

> metaque fervidis
> Evitata rotis palmaque nobilis
> Terrarum dominos evehit ad deos.

"Do not strive to become a Zeus," Pindar cautions; let all thoughts, desires, and hopes be befitting a mortal; aspire not beyond thy capacity. Audacity and arrogance the gods do not forgive. To revere the gods, to honour parents, to deal justly and fairly with one's fellows, to be true, generous, kind, and gentle; to shun envy, to forgive injuries, to hate flattery; to be temperate in pleasures, and to bear ill with equanimity—these are the virtues constantly commended.

The state of man after death is commonly pictured in Pindar as it was in the popular religion, a shadowy existence beneath the earth, such as it is described in the original Ne-

kyia of the Odyssey. There are, to be sure, heroes promoted
to the fellowship of the gods, but the common man can
gather no hope from their fortune. "None, by ship or by
land, can find the wonderful way that leads to the feasts of
the Hyperboreans." This is one of man's limitations, to
which he must bow. The brief, vain life of mortals is a
theme that recurs with singular frequency in these triumphal
lyrics: "Creatures of a day, what are we? What are we not?
The dream of a shadow, that is man."

There are other passages, however, in which the new doctrines of the mysteries and the mystical philosophies find expression. In Eleusinian form this hope has already met us
in a fragment of an elegy for an Athenian, presumably an
initiate.[1] In others the Orphic or Pythagorean note is unmistakable.[2] The soul is an impalpable double of the body,
but it is of divine extraction, and therefore immortal. It
dwells in the body in expiation of an "ancient wrong"—a
fallen spirit. At death, forthwith, the helpless souls receive
their retribution, and deeds done in the realm of Zeus are
judged beneath the earth by one who gives sentence by dire
necessity (inexorable law). In the abode of the good the
sun shines by night as brilliant as by day; they are rewarded
with a toilless life, neither vexing the earth with strength of
arm nor the water of the sea for a meagre living, but, in company of the honoured of the gods, such as on earth rejoiced
in faithful oaths spend a tearless age. The others have to
endure ills too horrible to look upon. Those who thrice
have persevered in both states[3] to keep the soul clear of
every wrong pursue the way of Zeus to the court of Kronos.
There sea-breezes blow over the islands of the blest; golden
flowers gleam, some on land from splendid trees, some growing in the water, with wreaths of which they entwine their
arms and crown their heads with garlands.

[1] See above, p. 454.

[2] It has been noted that these are odes for Sicilian victors.

[3] The dwelling of the good described above is not the final state; twice
the soul must be reborn on earth before it may traverse the "way of
Zeus," no more to return.

The notion of transmigration appears more distinctly in a fragment (Frg. 133): The souls whose expiation of the ancient guilt Persephone receives, she sends back at the end of nine years to the upper light, where they are re-embodied as kings, or mighty men of valour, or sages. After this last earthly existence they are released from the round of rebirth, and are honoured among men as heroes, *i. e.*, as superhuman spirits.

Almost contemporary with Pindar is Æschylus, born at Eleusis in 525 B. C., of a noble Attic family. In the prime of his manhood, he fought against the Persians at Marathon and Salamis and Platæa. He died at Gela, in Sicily, in 456, and his tomb bore the epitaph: "Beneath this monument lies Æschylus son of Euphorion, the Athenian, dead in wheat-growing Gela. Of his famous prowess the grove of Marathon can tell, and the thick-haired Mede, who made experience of it." It is a fair surmise that the verses were composed by himself; another would hardly have failed to give him the poet's title to fame.

The great contribution of the Greek poets to religion, as has been remarked above, is the revelation of the unity of the moral order of the world, or, in more theological phrase, the unity of the divine rule in the world, which naturally leads to the exaltation of Zeus to a supremacy of kind rather than merely of degree. Nowhere does this faith in the sovereignty of Zeus find nobler utterance than in Æschylus. He is not merely a god, the greatest of gods, but God. A fragment, the genuineness of which appears incontestable, declares: "Zeus is the ether, Zeus the earth, Zeus the heaven, Zeus is the universe and what is beyond the universe."

It was the general belief that the sins of the fathers were visited upon the children to the third and fourth generation. The tragedy of the house of Atreus, which is the subject of the Orestean trilogy, was a conspicuous example. The whole train of crimes that wrought the ruin of the house was set going by the initial crime, and fulfilled itself with dire necessity. Æschylus exhibits this fatal concatenation of crimes, showing how each followed with grim inevitableness on the other. But they do not, therefore, cease to be crimes which the agent commits in full knowledge and set purpose. There is no mechanical world-necessity that constrains, no judicial madness that blinds. Clytemnestra justifies her deed by the wrongs she had suffered from her lord; she declares herself but the instrument by which the ancient fury of the house, insatiate for blood, has again gratified its craving—it is the vengeance for Atreus's crime. The Chorus refuses the sophistries: This is indeed from Zeus, the cause and doer of all, for naught is decreed for mortals except by Zeus, none of these things but is ordained of God. But neither divine purpose nor demonic nemesis exculpates the murderess; the hereditary avenging spirit is only an accessory. So it is with Orestes: He knows that his mother deserves death; in killing her to avenge the murder of his father he is fulfilling the express command of Apollo, yet he is conscious that neither the justice of her doom nor the divine sanction relieves him of the crime of matricide. The closing scene of the Choephori, in which before Orestes's staring eyes the avenging spirits appear, grey-gowned, gorgon-like, serpents twined in their tresses, blood oozing in gouts from their eyeballs, the "mother's spiteful hounds," is one of the most moving in Greek tragedy.

Nor is retribution limited to this life. The Eumenides threaten Orestes: "I'll cling thee and drag thee down living to pay the penalty of thy mother's murder. Thou shalt see every man who impiously wronged a god or a guest or his loving parents suffering each his just deserts; for Hades is a great judge of men beneath the earth, observing all things with retentive mind." Similarly in the Suppliants: "Not even in Hades's realm after death can a man who has done such things escape the penalty of his profane deed. There, as they say, another Zeus among the shades passes final judgment on men's sins."

The Chorus in the Choephori quotes an ancient saying, δράσαντι παθεῖν, "What a man has done, that shall he suffer."

The words might be made a motto for Æschylus's belief. He does not deny the fatality that forms the very theme of the tragedy, but the sin is in the end man's own act, and for that he suffers, not by sheer fate or blind necessity to expiate the sins of his fathers—so the conscience of the guilty is fain at the last to confess.

Sophocles is less concerned than Æschylus to vindicate the righteousness of the divine rule. "Justice, renowned of old, sits assessor to Zeus by ancient constitution"; sin is punished by suffering. But sin and retribution do not solve the problem of suffering. In the Œdipus Rex the poet shows us a man who, without any fault of his own, does the most horrible deeds and suffers the direst consequences. Nor is this a reversion to the point of view of the legend itself which Æschylus rejects; Sophocles does not represent Œdipus as the heir of the ancestral curse, nor as the victim of chance or fate. He did what any man might have done, with the best counsel and will in the world, but the very means which he took to escape the prediction fulfilled it.

"Sophocles is profoundly impressed with the woes of humanity—woes which may be due to no fault of a man's own. Yet he firmly believes in the goodness and the justice of the gods. He does not fall back on a half-mystic doctrine of nemesis. He leaves the problem unsolved. But he contributes at least one inestimable thought towards its solution. He teaches that suffering is not necessarily an evil. Suffering may educate and ennoble the character, as in the case of Œdipus. It may bring the victory of a cause which the sufferer prizes above life, as in the case of Antigone. Or, even if there can be nothing of comfort or compensation for the individual victim, his suffering may still have been ordained, in the hidden wisdom of just gods, for the good of mankind. . . . He saw the evil and sorrow that are in life as part of a divine scheme, which may, indeed, appoint such discipline for the good of the individual, but which also subordinates the welfare of the individual to the welfare of the race." [1]

In accepting such a statement of the matter, it should be borne in mind that Sophocles was not attempting to solve a problem in theodicy. His interest was in the characters

[1] Jebb, Growth and Influence of Classical Greek Poetry, p. 183.

themselves: not who is responsible for the tragic situation, but how those who are involved in it bear themselves, how their character reveals itself in the action or shapes the issue.

The piety of Sophocles is closer to the traditional type than that of Æschylus. Perhaps for that reason, perhaps because he does not habitually envisage the lot of mortals from the point of view of justice, he is not so strongly disposed to unify the divine rule of the world by exalting Zeus to a godhead apart; the monotheistic-sounding phrases of Æschylus cannot be matched in Sophocles. The other gods, especially Apollo and Athena, are not overshadowed by the head of the pantheon. The conservatism of Sophocles may be recognised also in his references to the nether world, which hardly differ from the Homeric notions. Of reward or punishment there is no word, though he alludes to the peculiar blessedness which the initiates of Eleusis are promised. The assumption of Œdipus in the Œdipus at Colonos is a miracle which throws no light on human destiny.

A man of another spirit, and, although contemporary, a man of another time, was Euripides.[1] It was thought worthy of note that he took no part in public affairs, but lived, by Athenian standards, an unsocial life, liking better to pore over books in his library than to mingle in the busy marts of men. Into the new intellectual life, however, with which Periclean Athens was all astir, he plunged eagerly. Anaxagoras, the last great philosopher of the Ionian school, and Protagoras, called the first of the sophists, were long resident in Athens; other such lights of the new education as Gorgias and Prodicus came and went. By personal association with these men and, doubtless, by the perusal of the writings of others which he gathered in his library, Euripides acquainted

[1] It was a pleasant fancy of the Greeks to make Salamis connect the three great tragic poets: Euripides, it is said, was born on the island and on the day of the great sea-fight; Sophocles, fifteen or sixteen years old, led the boy chorus in the celebration of the victory; Æschylus was a man of thirty-five when he took part in the battle. Euripides and Sophocles died within a few months of each other in 407–6. The extant plays of both poets belong to their later years.

himself with the thought of his times on nature, man, and god. It does not appear from his plays—here our only authority—that he addicted himself to any one school; he had the poet's mobile intelligence rather than the co-ordinating mind. Tradition and dramatic propriety often demanded that his characters should speak and behave with antique piety, nor should we assume that Euripides was so completely sophisticated that he did not himself feel the beauty and power of the faith in which he was brought up. Again, the outbursts of passion against the gods are sometimes inevitable to the character and the situation—as when Bellerophon exclaims: "Does any one say there are really gods in heaven? There are none, there are none!"—and must not be mistaken for the reflective opinion of the poet.

But when all subtractions are made, it remains undeniable that Euripides himself often enough speaks through his characters and in his choruses, and in language that leaves no doubt of his meaning. Sometimes it is the agnosticism of Protagoras, in such expressions as, "the gods, whatever they may be," "Zeus, whoever he may be," whose vagueness is accentuated by analysis, as in Hecuba's prayer: "O thou support of the earth, whose seat is also on the earth, whosoe'er thou art, hard to know by our conjectures, Zeus, whether that mean the inexorable law of nature or human intelligence, thee I address in prayer; for, moving by a noiseless path, thou guidest all mortal destinies according to justice." The audience may well have echoed Menelaus's exclamation, "What a new-fangled prayer!" From the lips of the same Hecuba Euripides lets fall an opinion like that of Critias—the gods and morals are conventions; men believe in them because the law bids so: "We are slaves, and feeble, too, but the gods are strong, and the law which has power over them; for by law we believe in the gods, and distinguish wrong from right in human conduct." Such utterances explain how Aristophanes should have accused Euripides of convincing men that there are no gods. At least, if it pleases the philosophers to call natural law or human reason god, the gods of religion do not recognise themselves under these names.

The attitude of Euripides toward the gods of the popular religion was in truth not the calm suspense of philosophic agnosticism. The unwritten law of the stage constrained him to take his themes from the myths and heroic legends, many of which—and those the most tragic—were morally repugnant to him. He does not hesitate to avow his disbelief, as when he lets Herakles say: "I do not believe that the gods love beds that are not lawful to them, nor have I ever deemed, nor will I be persuaded, that they fasten fetters on other gods' hands, nor that one god is master of another; for a god, if he is truly god, has need of naught. These are blasphemous fictions of epic poets." He does worse than deny: he lets the gods exhibit themselves on his stage in actions and passions that destroy all respect, or work such injustice from behind the scenes that sympathy for the victim turns into indignation against the divine wrong-doer. Such a self-exposure, so long as it followed the familiar myth, doubtless made far less impression on an Athenian audience than it does on the modern reader, and the exaggerated pathos of Euripides tended to fix attention on the sufferer and distract it from the gods. The poet takes pains, therefore, that perfidy, vengefulness, jealousy, cruelty, licentiousness, shall get their right names when gods are the doers. A single example must suffice for many; let it be Amphitryon's frank speech to Zeus in the Herakles:

"O Zeus, in vain I shared my wife with thee, in vain I called thee father of my son; thou hast not proved the friend thou dost pretend to be. Mortal that I am, I am much better than thou, a great god! For I did not betray Herakles's children, but thou understandest how stealthily to find thy way to men's beds, taking possession of others' couches without their consent, but how to save thine own friends thou dost not know. Thou art a stupid god, if not an honest one!"

If we reflect that Euripides kept at this for half a century, not in a schoolroom to pupils who paid for sophistication, but before all Athens in the theatre on a high religious festival and in the religious forms of tragedy, it is not strange that he should be thought to have contributed even more than the sophists to the decay of faith and the decadence of morals; for what they spoke in the ear in closets he proclaimed upon the housetops. Yet he kept within the liberty of the theatre, and does not appear to have been molested by heresy trials, though the pious Æschylus had been driven from Athens by one in the preceding generation, and in Euripides's own circle the process had been invoked against Anaxagoras and Pheidias, while, but a few years after Euripides's death, Socrates fell a victim to malevolent orthodoxy. The *inquisitores hæreticæ pravitatis* in all ages seem to have been blind tools of a tragic irony.

The last year or two of Euripides's life was spent at Pella in Macedonia, at the court of King Archelaus; and there he wrote his last play, the Bacchæ. The Dionysiac religion in the public cult of Greece had long been civilised out of all semblance to its original, and in the Orphic conventicles its mystical communion had degenerated into sacramental magic. In Macedonia, however, it had kept its old character; there Euripides could see genuine mænads in the frenzy of Bacchic possession, not tame Attic citizens' wives in their sober senses playing the wild women. The spectacle seized his imagination, and he yielded himself to the inspiration, the sophist for once forgetting himself in the poet.

The myth of Pentheus, the Thessalian king who set himself against the strange god and his religion of madness, and for his despite done to the god was torn to pieces by the wild women led by his own mother, furnished the theme.[1] Did Euripides, weary of a lifelong rationalism which had nothing to give to the religious soul but reasonable doubts, really surrender himself to enthusiasm? Such things have happened, but all we can say for certain is that the poet threw his soul more unreservedly into his subject than was his wont to do.

[1] Æschylus had made a cognate myth the subject of his Lycurgia, the loss of which cannot be too much regretted.

The fragments of the "Cretans" show, it may be added, that the enthusiasms of other orgiastic cults had interested him before he went to Macedonia.

Aristophanes had a strong dislike for the new education and its professors and for the new generation of poets. His lash fell on Euripides with double vigour as a sinner on both counts. Of the sincerity of his dislike there is no question; but it is taking the comic poet too solemnly to make him a defender of the faith pursuing the neologists with holy zeal, just as it is a mistake to think of him as an aristocrat by conviction and principle because he lampoons Creon, burlesques the sovereign Demos, and exposes the rottenness of that "bulwark of democracy," trial by jury. The calling of the poet in the Old Comedy, for which he had the licence of the state and the authority of religion, was to be the censor of the times, to find fault boldly and roundly with everything he saw amiss in Athens, and to lay the blame where it belonged, on high or low.

Aristophanes did not put tendencies or policies on the stage in abstract or allegorical form; he saw them incorporated in persons, the leading men of his time, and he used his privilege to make them odious, contemptible, above all, ridiculous. To get dark shadows in his picture he had need of light; to show how bad the times were it was necessary to contrast the present degeneracy with the good old days, and nothing, as our own experience confirms, was surer to make an effect in the pit. He was, therefore, a *laudator temporis acti* by his very profession. Add to this, that he had an undisguised personal animosity toward Euripides, and it becomes clear that religious conservatism is not the whole explanation of his attitude. It is, in fact, only in later plays, notably in the Frogs, written after the death of Sophocles and Euripides, that Euripides's theology is a main point of attack, though for a quarter of a century he had been making a butt of him as a poet.

As for the new education, in his first venture on the stage, the lost Daitales (427 B. C.), Aristophanes showed up the modern son, who cut school and learned nothing that a properly brought-up Athenian ought to know, but frequented the courses of the sophists and acquired their art of word-juggling and legal subterfuges, despising work and leading a life of luxury, contrasting him with the manly product of the old-fashioned training—the kind that made the men who fought at Marathon. The Clouds (produced in 423 B. C.) assails the new education from every side—its methods, its eristic, its natural science, its sophistication of morals, its perversion of justice, its subversion of religion, its implicit or explicit atheism. All these sins of the sophists are personified in Socrates.

There is no reason to think that, in presenting Socrates as the sum of all sophistry, Aristophanes was prompted by personal hostility, such as he entertained for Creon and Euripides. The Platonic Symposium brings the two together in the house of the poet Agathon to help him celebrate the success of his tragedy (in 417–6 B. C.), and very good company they make. After all the rest of the guests have gone home or are under the table, the trio keep on passing the bowl around, Socrates meanwhile holding forth to the two poets that the genius of tragedy and comedy are the same, and therefore a tragedian should write comedy also, till first Aristophanes drops out, and then, at dawn of day, Agathon; while the hard-headed senior, after seeing them to bed, takes a cold bath and goes to his daily occupation. Aristophanes's choice is sufficiently explained by the fact that, unlike the migratory professors, Socrates was an Athenian, one of the best-known men in the city, and, perhaps we may add, a figure that the gods seemed to have fashioned on purpose for caricature.

The modern sense of fair play takes offence at the misrepresentation, the more because it suspects that the prejudice created by the Clouds may have had some part in the condemnation of Socrates twenty-five years later. It may be that the Athenian public itself thought the poet had gone too far in making Socrates a "meteorosophist" after the school of Diogenes of Apollonia, for the piece, though one of the poet's best, got only the third prize.[1] But Socrates himself, who had the equanimity to which a sense of humour contributes as much as a good conscience, if he sat in the audience that day, doubtless laughed as consumedly as the next at what he was doing on the stage, not least when, at the end, old Strepsiades set his "idea institute" on fire.

However unscrupulously Aristophanes attached to the name of Socrates a character and teachings most unlike the truth, he could not have taken this name for his arch-sophist if his audience had not put Socrates in that class. Nor could they well have classed him otherwise: like the sophists, he was incredulous about the universes the physicists thought out so neatly; man seemed to him to have enough to do to understand himself. Like them the cultivation of virtue— however that was to be defined—was the principal thing; and, again like them, he believed that virtue could be taught, and he found his mission in this task. He did not, indeed, make his living by teaching; he was odd enough to think that if a man had anything that his fellows would be better for knowing he ought not to keep it back till he had counted his honorarium. But an economic definition of "sophist" as a professor who receives fees for instruction is hardly an adequate characterisation.[2]

Socrates, then, as his contemporaries saw him, was a sophist. That he controverted the teachings of others was what they all did; that, by his subtle dialectic, he tangled them up in the fallacies of their own arguments—or of his— and showed that they did not know what they were talking about, proved only that he was better at that game than the rest. If those who came closer to him felt his greater moral earnestness, that was the character of the man, and, however favourably it distinguished him from some of the tribe, was in no wise inconsistent with the calling nor without example

[1] Ameipsias, in his Konnos, which got the second prize at the same Dionysia, had Socrates for one of his principal characters, a poor beggar who would not flatter, an enthusiast, but a rarely good man.

[2] How Socrates did get his living—when he was not dining out—is uncertain, and still more uncertain is it how Xanthippe subsisted.

among its professors. If we can divest ourselves of the prejudice against the word which we have from Plato, Socrates
was in fact the greatest of the sophists. He would have been
prompt to disclaim being a philosopher in the sense in which
we give the title to Plato and Aristotle, or to his predecessors,
from Thales to Anaxagoras. He was never weary of iterating
that he had no system, no body of doctrine to expound,
physical or metaphysical, political or ethical. The name is,
however, of little consequence; whatever we call him, Socrates makes an era in the history of human thought.

Socrates's starting-point is a scepticism as radical as that
of Protagoras: he rejected not only the conflicting theories
of the physicists, "of whom some conceived of existence as a
unity, others as a plurality; some affirmed perpetual motion,
others perpetual rest; some declared becoming and perishing
to be universal, others altogether denied such things," but
this whole enterprise, their "pursuit of knowledge for its
own sake." No less vain is the search for an absolute truth,
an absolute good, or for a universal standard: man cannot
transcend the limitations of his humanity. What seems to
the individual to be is true for him. Yet, though all opinions
may be equally true, it is plain that when translated into
action they do not all work equally well; some are, from this
practical point of view, better than others, that is, they further the individual in his aims or conduce to the advantage
of the community, which is also his interest. By the consideration of these consequences a man may be led to adopt
better opinions, and in so doing he becomes a wiser man.[1]

The task of the educator is not to impose his truth on
others, but to guide them along this way to make the better
truth their own. This is Socrates's conception of his own
calling. His method is dialectic—the conversational method
of question and answer. He employs it, on the one hand, to
lead the respondent to see not only that his notions are indefinite or inconsistent, but that they will not work; and, on

[1] See H. Jackson, "Socrates," Encyclopædia Britannica, 11th ed.,
XXV, 335.

the other hand, to help him bring to birth the better truth which is embryonic in his mind, and to recognise his own child. This is, in his view, the only sound educational method; and it is in this theory and the application of it that his genius appears most conspicuous.

The end of education is a practical wisdom, a knowledge of the good which results in right action. Knowledge and virtue are inseparable; right conduct without right knowledge is inconceivable, and on the other hand no man does evil knowing it to be evil. More exactly, virtue is knowledge, "knowledge at once of end and of means, irresistibly realising itself in act." The several virtues, such as piety, justice, courage, temperance, are but the one virtue, the good character, manifesting itself in different relations and circumstances, just as wisdom is one, the knowledge of the good. And, consistently with the premises, the good is what is to the advantage of the individual: utility is the measure of conduct and the foundation of moral rule and legal enactment. What Socrates aims at, therefore, is the reformation, or regeneration, of the moral life through education, bringing to man the knowledge of his own true interest. To this he devoted his life, and for this he laid it down.

Socrates faithfully fulfilled all his duties as a citizen in war and peace, but, in deference to the admonition of his inward monitor, abstained from taking an active part in politics. In religion, also, he conformed to the customary observances, sacrificing to the gods and praying to them as others did. He had a special reverence for the oracle of Apollo at Delphi, by which he had been called to his life work. Of his sincerity there is no question. That, with the most truly religious spirits of his age, he thought of the gods as wise and good, and therefore as above the weaknesses and basenesses which the common belief, on the authority of the poets, attributed to them, can as little be questioned. Plato puts into his mouth more than one indignant criticism of the poets who thus malign the gods.

When he prayed, he asked of the gods only to give what is

good, since the gods must know best what gifts are good; and he thought that those who prayed for gold or silver or sovereign power were as foolish as men would be who prayed for a game of dice, or a fight, or something else the outcome of which could not be foreseen. At the end of the Phædrus, the Platonic Socrates prays: "Beloved Pan, and all ye other gods who haunt this place, give me beauty of the inward soul, and may the outward and the inward man be at one." In making his small offerings out of his slender means, he deemed that he was doing no less than those who of their abundance offered many sacrifices; for if the gods were better pleased by large offerings than by small, they would frequently prefer the offerings of the wicked to those of the good, and then life would not be worth living; the gods were best pleased with the homage paid them by the most pious souls. The vulgar notion that in offerings men give to the gods what the gods want, and expect to receive in return the things men desire, would reduce religion to a business transaction.

In the Memorabilia (I, 4), Xenophon reports from his own hearing a conversation of Socrates with a certain Aristodemus, of whom he had heard that he neither sacrificed to the gods nor consulted divination, but ridiculed those who did these things. For the existence of the deity Socrates argues from the evidences of design in nature, and especially in man himself. When Aristodemus objects that he does not see these intelligent and ordering powers, Socrates pleasantly replies that he cannot see his own soul either, so that with equal right it might be argued that his actions were not directed by intelligence. Aristodemus then shifts his ground: the deity must be far too majestic to need his service, and he does not believe that the gods care anything about men. Socrates adduces fresh evidences of the gods' peculiar interest in man; the very upright carriage of man shows this, but above all the soul of man, with its capacity for knowing and serving God; the signs and portents the gods send to peoples and individuals also prove it. As a man's mind within his body directs it as it wills, so we must think that the intelligence immanent in the universe orders the universe as it pleases.   If a man's eye can see things many stadia distant, it ought not to be thought impossible that the eye of God should see all things at once; if a man's mind can think not only of things near by but of things in Egypt or Sicily, it is not incredible that the intelligence of God should care for all at once.

If Socrates had been called on to say how this simple and antique faith was to be reconciled with his sceptical premises, he would probably have fallen back on the pragmatic principle.

"Do you not see," he says to Aristodemus in the conversation quoted above, "that the most venerable and the wisest of human institutions, cities and nations, are the most religious, and that the most prudent ages of human life are the most regardful of the gods."   "As by rendering a service to men you come to know those who are willing to serve you in turn, and by showing a favour those who return favours, and by consulting together you know those who are wise, so by serving the gods you may make experience of them, if they are willing to give you advice concerning things concealed from men; you will know that the deity is of such a nature that it sees all things at once and hears all things, and is every where present, and that its providential care is over all at once.   To me, therefore, it seems that intelligent men will abstain from unholy and unjust and shameful deeds, not only when they are under the eyes of men, but even if they were in solitude, for they would reflect that not one of the things they might do would escape the notice of the gods." [1]

That is, in effect, if knowledge of the gods, like all other knowledge, is unattainable, religion, which rests on the belief that the gods exist and concern themselves about men, when translated into action proves to be the theory that works best; it has the practical verification which is the only verification possible.

That Socrates, of all men, should have been prosecuted for "irreligiousness," is strange, and stranger still that he should have been convicted and put to death upon this charge.

[1] Xenophon, Memorabilia, *l. c.*

The accusation was brought by three members of the popular, or democratic, party, and it has with good reason been suspected that their zeal for orthodoxy was not purely religious. The indictment had two counts: *First*, Socrates does not believe in the gods that the city believes in, but introduces other, new divinities; and, *second*, he corrupts young men. His defence, if Plato's Apology fairly represents its tone, was thoroughly in character, but not of a style to propitiate Athenian jurymen. He was found guilty by a comparatively small majority in the large jury. On the second poll he was condemned to death. He had no regrets. Death, he is convinced, is not an evil, whether it be a dreamless sleep, or, as some say, a migration to another world where all the dead are, and where he may have converse with the heroes and the poets of past ages—whichever it be, one thing is sure, that no evil can befall a good man, either in life or death.

In his ideal scheme of education in the Republic, Plato comes to speak of the harm that is done to children by the tales that they are told in the nursery and the myths they learn in school out of Homer and Hesiod—what Ouranos did and what Kronos did to him. A young man should not be told that in committing unspeakable crimes he is doing nothing outrageous, and that if his father does wrong he may punish him in whatever manner he chooses, for he is only doing what the first and greatest gods did. If we wish the future guardians of the state to regard quarrelsomeness as dishonourable and irreligious, they must not be brought up on stories of how gods fight with gods and plot against them, and the enmities of gods and heroes to their kindred and those of their own families. That Hephaistos fettered his mother Hera, or that Zeus threw Hephaistos out of heaven for trying to save his mother from a beating, that the gods stood laughing about the couch in which Hephaistos surprised Ares and Aphrodite—such myths must be forbidden, whether they are supposed to be allegorical or not, for youth cannot be expected to draw this distinction, and the stories themselves make an indelible impression.

They are to be forbidden, not merely because they are morally injurious, but because they are false. What Hesiod tells of Ouranos and Kronos is the greatest of all lies in high places, and an immoral lie besides. God is in reality perfectly good, and must not be represented otherwise. Being good, he cannot be the author of anything harmful or morally evil, but only of good. God is not, therefore, as men say, the cause of all things in human life, but only of the good things; for the evils, which far outnumber them, some other cause must be sought. That when God desires utterly to ruin a house he plants guilt among men, as Æschylus says, is a doctrine that youth must not be allowed to listen to. The sufferings of Niobe or of the house of Pelops must either not be called the work of God at all, or it must be explained that God did what was just and good, and that the chastisement was of benefit to the sufferers.

The gods are exempt from all human imperfections, their blissful calm is not agitated by emotions, they neither laugh nor weep. They are not subject to change, for the very notion of change implies imperfection. The stories of the deceptive metamorphoses of the gods are doubly distasteful to Plato as involving both change—which must be for the worse —and the intent to deceive. God is no conjurer, either to assume in reality different forms or to delude us with the false appearance of such transformations; he is ever the same, and of all things least likely to depart from his own proper likeness. He is "perfectly simple and true, both in deed and word; he changes not; he deceives not, either by dream or waking vision, by sign or word."

The gods are righteous, and they cannot be prevailed upon to connive at wrong-doing. Men grievously deceive themselves when they imagine that they can propitiate the gods by worship; that by adulation and prayer-spells they can secure impunity in the enjoyment of their fraudulently acquired wealth, or that the gods grant indulgence to those who give them a share of the spoils of injustice. That is to make the gods out inferior to even average men, who would never betray justice for the gifts which are made them by wicked men. Of all impious men he who holds this opinion may most justly be judged the most wicked and impious. The three fundamental propositions on which religion rests are that gods exist, that they concern themselves with men, and that they are inexorable in maintaining righteousness.

In worship, all depends on the moral disposition of the worshipper. Only those can please the gods who are like them, that is, pious, wise, and just. God is good; the man who has not the image of God's goodness in himself has no communion with him.

In making goodness the dominant element in the conception of the godhead, Plato goes a long step beyond those who tried to explain the dealings of God with men from the point of view of justice. A god who is not the author of any kind of evil, and whose inflictions are justified, not by the mere fact that they are deserved, but by the evidence that they are for the good of those upon whom they are laid, stands high above a god who requites with strict justice all the deeds of men. Indeed, it may be said that the ethical conception of God can go no farther than this. Plato, as we have seen, is well aware that in absolving God of all responsibility for evil he has taken upon himself to find "some other cause" for the vast mass of evil in the world. These causes, as they appear in the subsequent development of his philosophy, will engage our attention later. But even if this problem remained insoluble, Plato would stand by his faith in the perfect goodness of God, completely moral. He is the founder of theistic philosophy, or, we may as well say, of philosophical theology; and all the theologies of the Western world, Jewish and Moslem as well as Christian, derive in the end from him.

Socrates had put aside inquiries into the making and the working of the world and speculations on being and becoming, as futile in themselves and fruitless for the great end of right living. In his relentless examination of his own ideas and other men's, his endeavour to attach exact meanings to terms, he recognised the functions of general notions. He confined himself, indeed, to the definition of ethical universals, but that was only his one-sided ethical interest. The method was, as Plato saw, applicable to the whole range of concepts; it was, indeed, the method of all scientific knowledge in distinction from untested opinion. He saw, too, that the universe is a problem, not for science alone, but for theology. Socrates himself, when he got into a discussion with a man who denied the existence of God or of divine providence, employed the argument from design in nature, and explained the orderly structure and operation of the universe by an immanent directing intelligence, like the soul of man in his body.

Plato, therefore, took up again the problems which had engaged thinkers from Thales to Anaxagoras; but he took them up in the light of the new questions the sophists had raised and of the discussions in other schools, notably the Megarians, and with an extended application of the methods of Socrates. "The Ionian natural philosophy in its Heraclitic form, the Eleatic doctrine of Being, the mathematical speculations and the animisms of the Pythagoreans, furnished him important structural materials, but all these ideas are subordinated to the Socratic ruling idea of moral knowledge, and raised to a higher scientific level by the rigour of Socratic method."

Plato's speculative theology is a part of his doctrine of ideas. Behind the world of appearance, in which by sense-perception and representation we are aware of the multitude of objects of diverse kinds, there is the noumenal world, the world of ideas. An idea is the perfect type of a natural kind, of which all the individual members of the kind are imperfect copies; it is eternal and unchangeable; an object, not of sense or imagination, but of rational cognition. To the idea alone belong the predicates applied by the Eleatic school to Being: it alone has true reality. The systematic unity of Being is found in the Idea of the Good, which is at once the cause of existence to all things that exist and of knowledge to all minds that know. It is thus "beyond existence" and "above knowing," since it is that in which both originate and by which they are united to each other as elements of one whole. This is God. The Christian theologian, Origen, and the Neoplatonist philosopher, Plotinus, will repeat the words "beyond knowing and being" in the endeavour to find a formula for the absolute transcendence of God.

Since man can cognise this ideal world, his intelligence, the rational soul, must be in its nature akin to the ideas. At one period Plato explained the general notions, which are antecedent to all experience, by the theory of reminiscence: the soul brought with it into this earthly life the notion, say, of beauty or of justice, which is assumed when we say that an object is beautiful or an action just; the imperfect beauty of the sensible object awakens in the soul the memory of the idea of beauty which in intellectual vision it had seen in the suprasensible world, an indistinct reminiscence which it is the business of dialectic to clear up and define. The pre-existence of the soul opened the door to the Orphic-Pythag-orean mythology of transmigration which figures largely in Plato's eschatology.

The soul not only brings with it vague memories of the ideal world but a native love for it. And just as the memories are called into consciousness by the qualities of sensible objects, so the emotions which physical beauty kindles, and the desire to possess it, may unveil the vision, long obscured by sense, of the ideal beauty and goodness, and arouse in the soul the yearning to mount up again to that world. Love is the master passion: in the soul that is sunk in sense it may be mere brute lust, plunging ever deeper into the mire; in the philosopher it has for its object the ideally beautiful and the good, it is the craving to possess and enjoy for ever the supreme and eternal values. In this passion for eternal good is involved not only the demand of the soul for immortality but its assurance. The origin of the fundamental impulse of the soul is the pledge of its fulfilment.

The conception of an immaterial soul and the correspond-ing conception of an immaterial God have their origin in

Plato.[1] He is also the first to undertake to prove the immortality of the soul, as we understand those words, in distinction from the survival of a ghostly double, or shade. This he does in numerous dialogues from different periods of his life, in different connections and with diverse arguments. The frequency with which he recurs to the subject is an indication of the importance it had in his thinking. It is not possible to analyse these arguments, which are many, and, as may be supposed, not always consistent. Besides that which is derived from the doctrine of ideas, the character of which has been indicated above, mention must be made of one other, drawn from the conception of the soul as the unmoved mover (Phædrus, 245), the resemblance of which to the Aristotelian idea of God as *primum movens* is obvious. Embracing, as they do, the arguments from the universality of the belief in existence after death, from the moral necessity of retribution beyond this life, from the aspirations of the soul, and from its essential nature, the Dialogues of Plato contain explicitly or implicitly pretty much all that has ever been said on the subject, and have been the armoury from which the theologians of revealed religions as well as philosophers of many schools have drawn their weapons.

In his later years Plato felt moved to complete his system of belief by a philosophy of nature, and this, like the pre-Socratic natural philosophies, took the shape of cosmology, an account of the origin of the world. He had never, like the Eleatics, denied to the phenomenal world all reality; he allowed it a kind of reality, but of a lower order than that of the noumenal world. In order to explain its existence, he had now to modify his Eleatic conception of the ideal world, and to ascribe to it not only life and intelligence but transeunt activities. Thus conceived, the Idea of the Good, that is, God, creates the visible world by shaping

[1] It is, perhaps, not superfluous to remind theologians that neither in the Old Testament nor in the New is "spirit" equivalent to "immaterial." -

matter after the pattern of the ideas. Matter itself he did
not create; in a formless state, indefinite and infinite, it always existed, a second eternal principle besides the creator.[1]
This dualism served to explain the imperfections of the phenomenal world: God is perfect, and the ideas are perfect
types, but the matter on which these forms are impressed,
or of which their likeness is fashioned, is not completely
plastic to the creator's purpose; it is an inadequate medium
for the concrete expression of the idea. The imperfection,
the evil, is not, therefore, due to any shortcoming of the
divine wisdom or goodwill, but to the nature of the primordial matter with which God had to work.

The world, being in the image of God, is a living, visible
god, and has a soul, the principle of order and motion, in
which intelligence is, as in man, united with a corporeal element. The peopling of the world began with the creation of
the gods, among whom, in the first rank, stand the heavenly
bodies, which, like the earth, are living beings, visible gods;
after these come the gods of the popular religion. The gods
and the souls of men only were created by the supreme God,
the other classes of creatures in the air, on the earth, and in
the waters, as well as the bodies of living beings, were fashioned by the subordinate gods. Thus philosophical monotheism makes room for religious polytheism, but with reformed gods such as Plato describes in his earlier writings.

With the rational soul are joined two lower elements, one
the seat of the nobler human passions, the other of the animal appetites and lusts which man shares with the brutes;
these form a connecting link between the immaterial soul
and the material body. This association is fraught with
great danger, if reason, instead of asserting and steadfastly
maintaining its supremacy and establishing a harmony, allows itself to be drawn down by unruled passion or base desire. Such souls are re-embodied in lower forms of life, and

---

[1] The material principle of Plato, according to the express testimony
of Aristotle, was identical with space, conceived, of course, as most of
his predecessors conceived it, as a plenum, not as the void.

may sink deeper at every stage; while the soul that has held true to its own higher nature and destiny, and has subdued spirit and body to the ends of the soul, mounts up at death to the star which was its pure abode before it descended to earth. The soul is thus a stranger and a sojourner on earth: its end must be to prove itself worthy to return to its house above. This task is hard, but not beyond the powers of the soul, unless they have been impaired by yielding to evil.

Plato's proposals for the expurgation of mythology extend to the Homeric Hades. Achilles shall not be allowed to say: "I had rather be attached to the soil as the serf of a landless man with a scanty living than be king over all the wasted dead." All the passages that describe the dismal state of the dead, "Cocytus and Styx, ghosts under the earth and sapless shades," must be rejected. These appalling pictures may be useful for another purpose, he significantly adds, but the young men who are to be the defenders of their country are not to hear of them, for no man can be absolutely fearless of death who believes in Hades and its terrors.

When Plato himself pursues "another purpose," he pictures hell in all the colours which the Orphic imagination lent.[1] At death, the soul is conducted by its *daimon* into the presence of the infernal judges, Æacus, Rhadamanthus, and Minos. There, stripped of all disguises and hypocrisies, it stands naked, in all its imperfections and the scars of its sins, the thing it really is. The condemned are led by an opening in the ground on the left hand of the tribunal to the place of their punishment. Those who are not irredeemably bad endure sufferings which are both expiatory and remedial; purified and corrected, they return in due time to earth to inhabit another body. The incurable sinners are cast into hell, where they are tormented without end, their sufferings serving as exemplary warnings to others. In the Vision of Er, some of the damned try to escape; at their

[1] For Plato's eschatology, see Phædrus, 246 *ff.*; Gorgias, 523 *ff.*; Phædo, 109 *ff.*; Republic, X, 613 *ff.*; *cf.* also Timæus, 41 *ff.*; see further, Axiochus, 371, which, though not by Plato, is in the same vein.

approach the mouth of hell gave a great roar, wild, flaming figures seized them, bound them hand and foot, flayed them with scourges, dragged them by the roadside, carding them on teasels like wool, proclaiming to the passers-by their crimes and that they were being taken to be cast into hell.

The great weight of Plato's influence was thus given to the Orphic-Pythagorean eschatology, which, taken out of its sectarian context and embodied in a lofty ethical philosophy, gained a currency among educated men which we can hardly imagine it otherwise attaining. The early Christian visions of hell borrow their gruesome pictures of ingenious tortures chiefly from the same Greek sources, not from Jewish or Persian notions. The eternal torments of the damned in hell was no new Christian doctrine, they had the authority of the greatest of Greek philosophers.

The good leave the judgment seat by a way to the right, to a beautiful and blessed abode, where they enjoy the reward of their virtues till their time comes to return to the life on earth again. Plato lets Socrates, in the hour of his death, thus picture this abode: "Those who have led holy lives are released from this earthly prison, and go to their pure home which is above, and dwell in the purer earth; and those who have duly purified themselves with philosophy live henceforth altogether without body, in mansions fairer far than these, which may not be described, and of which time would fail me to tell." [1]

When the souls of the just and unjust come to return to the earthly life, they choose their own lot in the light of their former experience—sad and laughable and strange is the spectacle of their election! Only philosophic insight and philosophic virtue enables a soul to make a wise choice. This significant variation of the doctrine of transmigration puts the responsibility for man's fortune and character on himself; it is not by chance or necessity or the arbitrary will of the gods that each is what he is, for better or for worse. Yet, in fact, the choice is predetermined.

[1] Jowett's translation.

The philosophy of Plato is a religion for philosophers, a way of salvation. Not only all the idealistic metaphysics of the West, but all its speculative theologies and every ethic which sets for the spirit of man a transcendent goal, have their roots in Plato. For this reason a fuller exposition of his thought has been given.

"*Vidi il maestro di color che sanno*"—thus Dante acclaims Aristotle, whom he finds sitting at the head of the philosophic school, wondered at by all. Aristotle's place in the history of thought could not be better defined than in the simple words, "the master of those who know." He was born in Macedonia, where his father was a physician to the king, and came of the line of Asclepiad physicians who, according to Galen, taught their sons anatomy by dissection. From his father Aristotle probably imbibed the interest in natural science which so strikingly distinguishes him from Plato, and the principles of empirical method. In the catalogue of Aristotle's works, the most numerous titles are writings on natural history. His zoology (Historia Animalium) included the results of investigations for which his royal patron aided by a subsidy; in his school Theophrastus was trained, whose botanical treatises were the most important contributions to that science until late in the Middle Ages, and for some highly interesting regions remained almost to the present time the only source; the scientific men attached to the staff of Alexander's expedition were his pupils; it is plain that he first conceived the idea of organised research which has been so fruitful in modern times. Science did not mean for him mere observation and description, but explanation of processes and causes; and he was the first to inquire into the nature of scientific proof, the induction from particulars to a general principle, or law, and the valid deduction from it. Each science has its own fundamental principles, and above these are the fundamental principles of all science.

Aristotle was for nearly twenty years a member of the Academy in Athens, at first as a student, later also as teacher and investigator. The circle of his interests was widened by the inclusion of ethics and politics, and his attention directed to the problems of metaphysics. He heard Plato's lectures, which in his later years were much occupied with numbers as principles, after Pythagorean precedents, and studied the master's published works.[1] The most recent advances in astronomical science were open to him there in the work of Eudoxos and of Kallippos; the arts of discourse, which Isocrates had raised to a higher plane than the rhetoric of the sophists, were treated with scientific method; he made himself master of the history and literature of philosophy. From Plato he learned much, and he was not lacking in recognition of his indebtedness; but as he came to his intellectual independence, he found himself in disagreement with Plato at fundamental points.

Reality for him resided, not in a suprasensible realm of ideas, whether hypostatised universals or archetypal forms of natural kinds, but in individual things. Science has to do, however, not with individuals as such, but with species. All the members of a species have certain characters in common which, taken together, are distinctive of it. But a species is more than a group of individuals which have these characters in common; it is a permanent kind, and in organic nature perpetuates self from generation to generation. The oak bears an acorn, and the acorn develops into an oak, never into another kind of tree. Besides the matter of which it is made, there is, therefore, in every individual something which determines its kind, and this determining factor is just as much a fact as the existence of the individual. It is, moreover, a fact of a higher order and logically prior. Aristotle calls this the "form" ($\epsilon\tilde{\iota}\delta o\varsigma$), meaning not the outward appearance but the sum of specific determinants by virtue of which a thing is what it is, *e. g.*, a tree. The matter of which the thing is composed possesses only the potentiality of becoming, say, a tree; that it is actually a tree is due to the

[1] All the works of Plato which have come down to us, except the Laws, were written before Aristotle came to him.

"form," the immaterial principle which makes a thing what it is. Individuals come into being and dissolve and pass out of existence, but the type persists—"forms" are eternal.

A problem of a different kind was presented by the heavenly bodies and their movements. Aristotle approaches this from the point of view of contemporary astronomy. A number of concentric spheres rotate around the earth. The cause of their motion is a *primum movens*, itself unmoved, beyond the outermost sphere. This prime mover is immaterial, and it moves, not by an outgoing physical force, but by a spiritual attraction—κινεῖ ὡς ἐρώμενον. It is Mind (Νοῦς); its activity is pure thought, consciously thinking itself. This infinite active mind is God. God is perfect; he has life, continuity of existence, eternity of existence.

Man is a kind of being intermediate between other corporeal existences and God, partaking of the nature of both. He has in common with the plants and animals a nutritive soul, the principle of life; in common with the animals he has also a sensitive, appetitive, motive soul; man alone has an intellective soul. Aristotle distinguishes the passive intellect, which receives from the senses their impressions, and an active intellect in which originate the forms of thought for the interpretation of the sensible impressions. The latter alone can exist apart from the soul and the body; when it so exists, independent of external objects, having no inessential attributes, essentially operant, it is eternal, for it then possesses the attributes of the eternal Mind, God.

Thus Aristotle's system is in the end more completely dualistic than Plato's; his God is more absolutely transcendent. He has no difficulty in admitting the existence of other gods —the heavenly bodies, for example—and there is nothing in his system to exclude such beings. In a lost work, of his earlier years, he explained the origin of the universal belief in gods by two principal causes: *First*, psychical phenomena, such as dreams, enthusiasm, prophecy; and, *second*, the impression made by the heavenly bodies and their regular and harmonious movements. But he did not think that in explaining the belief he had explained away religion. Like his predecessors, he rejects the anthropomorphic mythology; he goes beyond them when he attributes to natural causes the beneficent activities which the multitude ascribe to the gods, "When Zeus rains, it is not in order to make the grain grow, but of necessity," that is, by natural law. Positively, he has little to say about the gods whom the people worshipped; "divine natures are beyond our observation," he says somewhere. Yet he left directions in his will for the erection of a statue to Zeus Sōtēr and one of Athena Sōteira in his native city. The accusation of impiety which drove him from Athens shortly before his death was politically inspired; he was denounced on the charge of deifying his quondam patron, the tyrant Hermias of Assos.

On the lot of man after death which so much interested Plato, Aristotle has nothing to say. The Orphic-Pythagorean eschatology, with its great assize, its bodily torments of the disembodied, and its transmigration of souls, probably seemed to him an objectionable kind of infernal mythology. Personal immortality has no room in his system; the rational soul is eternal, but not as individual soul.

Of Aristotle's ethics it must suffice here to say that he endeavoured to put ethics also on a scientific basis. Abandoning Plato's transcendental goal, he finds the chief end in man's well-being. This well-being lies in the proper functioning of the distinctively human faculties, the attainment of the specifically human excellences. Virtue is not a knowledge which may be imparted, but a habit which must be cultivated. Moral excellence, or virtue, is the steady guidance and control of the appetitive part of the soul by the practical reason; the intellectual excellences are the practical wisdom exercising this control, and speculative wisdom, the proper virtue of the pure intellect. In this activity is the highest human happiness.

CHAPTER XX

THE GREEKS

LATER GREEK PHILOSOPHY

Epicureanism—Stoicism—The Immanence of God—Determinism— Providence—Freedom—Ethics—Attitude toward the Popular Religion—Stoicism as a Religion—Propaganda—Academic Scepticism —Eclecticism—Plutarch—The Neopythagoreans—Dualistic Character of Popular Philosophies—Revelation—Influence of Oriental Religions—Judaism—Neoplatonism—Plotinus—Porphyry—The Closing of the Schools.

THE next turn in Greek philosophy was the attempt to overcome dualism and transcendentalism. Such an attempt was made in the Peripatetic school itself by Straton of Lampsacus, but the scanty notices of his teachings hardly make it possible to say more than this. The atomic materialists, in succession to Democritus, had no inconsiderable following; their doctrine obtained a wider vogue through Epicurus. His religious influence was, however, merely negative. In his mechanical universe the gods were assigned a comfortable lodging in the intrastellar spaces on condition that they should not interfere with things; interest in sublunary affairs could only trouble that undisturbed calm in which they are a pattern of perfect bliss. The worship of the gods is therefore a disinterested æsthetic emotion, induced by the contemplation of their perfect repose, the realised ideal of unconcern. The soul, being material, is perishable. When men understand this, they are emancipated from the fear of death: death itself is no evil, for so long as we are here, death is not, and when death arrives, we are not; and there is no hereafter. Epicurus combated the belief in immortality because it keeps man from making the right use of this life, and because the fear of death—which is at bottom the fear of something after death—is the cause of the gravest moral aberrations. To extirpate the fear of the gods and the fear of the hereafter is the condition not only of a happy life, but of a right one. It is a fine religious zeal that animates Lucretius in his polemic against religion; he would vindicate for man the freedom of his soul. The ethics of Epicureanism are necessarily egoistic and eudemonistic; but the vulgar notion that it made the pleasures of the senses the highest good is false.

The religious importance of Stoicism, on the contrary, is very great, and fuller consideration must therefore be given it. Aristotle, as we have seen, brought the Platonic ideas down to earth: form and matter are not at the poles of the universe apart, but are united in individual objects; formless matter is a mere abstraction, and, conversely, there are in the universe no immaterial forms. This was a long step toward bringing together again the two worlds which Plato had sundered. But above the universe was God, pure form, pure actuality, pure thought, the unmoved prime mover, the final cause of all motion and becoming. The Stoics made the further step that was necessary to arrive at monism: they brought God back from his banishment, they removed the condemnation to inactivity and the disabilities of immateriality, and made him a living God, immanent in every part and particle of the universe. In so doing, they revived the theories of the Ionian naturalists, especially of Heraclitus, to whom they are related in the same way as the Epicureans to Democritus. Like the Epicureans, also, their predominant interest in ethical problems distinguishes them from the older naturalists and reveals their inheritance from Socrates. On this side, the Stoics stand in the tradition of the Cynics, as the Epicureans in that of the Cyrenaic school. Finally, both, as dogmatic philosophies, had to defend themselves at the front door against the scepticism of the contemporary Academy.

Stoicism is an outspoken materialism; not a mechanical materialism, however, like its rival, but a dynamic materialism, akin to the so-called "hylozoism" of the Ionians. The origin of the existing world it explained with Heraclitus by the downward process of the ever-living fire; but—and here the Stoic anthropocentric teleology asserts itself—this world-process is not the law, or necessity, of nature, but the evolution of the one primal substance, which is purposeful intelligence; the multiplicity of the actual universe is the production of intelligent beings; the world was created, or rather evolved, for the sake of men. At the end of its period will come the world-conflagration, the re-involution of the universe into the primal fire—the upward path of Heraclitus.

The cosmos is one, spherical, finite, surrounded by infinite void space. It is a living and intelligent being. Its life and intelligence are God, who pervades it to the smallest particle, like the soul in the human body, and comprehends in one consciousness all that is and comes to pass.[1] This immanent God is not immaterial, like the transcendent godhead of Plato and Aristotle; the Stoic system admits no immaterial reality. God is spirit (πνεῦμα), that is, a form of matter consisting of the two finer elements, fire and vapour. This spirit, everywhere present, but in different degrees of purity and fineness, imparts to all things their distinctive qualities, holds them together, sets them in motion—in short, is, in diverse operations, the one force in the universe.

As there is one force, so there is one universal causal nexus running through the entire cosmos and bringing all things to pass: this is the Stoic Determination (Εἱμαρμένη, Fatum). But the determinism is not mechanical: it is directed by intelligence to the best and wisest ends, and when regarded from this point of view it is Providence. The doctrine of an all-embracing particular Providence raises the problem of

[1] The immanent God, whom some Christian theologians imagine to be a modern discovery, is, when the term is correctly employed, nothing but the Stoic God, as the transcendent God of Christian theology is its inheritance from Neoplatonism.

theodicy: How can evil exist in a world in which God is not merely the cause of all that is or comes to pass, but wills and does all for the best?[1] Cleanthes sought to evade the difficulty by admitting a sphere of fate over which Providence did not extend; but Chrysippus would not put any part of the cosmos thus outside the scope of the divine wisdom and goodness. Much that from our point of view and to our restricted vision appears evil, if looked at with reference to the whole, or from the standpoint of the divine reason, would be seen to be good. In the realisation of good ends in nature, incidental evils may be unavoidable—the so-called "necessary evils." In general, so far as natural evils are concerned, the Stoics stand firm on the principle that, inasmuch as, according to their ethics, the well-being of the wise man is not affected by physical evils, these are not in the proper sense evils at all; they may, indeed, as a discipline of character, be a positive good.

But how can moral evil be included in the world-purpose of God? The Stoic answers, good cannot exist, or even be conceived, without its opposite, evil. A being like man, endowed with intelligence and freedom, has in his organisation both potentialities. The very purpose of creation was to produce such a being, capable of living according to reason and of working freely with God for the realisation of the rational in nature. But the same freedom, which alone gives moral and human value to goodness, makes it possible that man should fail of his destiny and sink to the level of the brutes. Moral evil, therefore, no less truly than good, is part of the plan of God.

The argument assumes the self-determination of man. But where is there room, in the unbroken determinism of the universe, for self-determination—how can fate and free-will coexist? Here we must start with the Stoic anthropology. Man consists of body and soul, the soul being itself a

---

[1] Plato, with his eternal blind matter, imperfectly plastic to the divine idea, did not feel the difficulty with the same force, and for Aristotle, with his denial of particular providence, it did not exist.

subtle, or spiritual, body. The "ruling faculty" in the soul (ἡγεμονικόν), to which belong the higher functions, including not only the operations of the intellect but feeling and will, develops in childhood into a rational soul, which distinguishes man from the animals and relates him to God; it is in fact a particle of God. Reason, so far as man acts as a reasonable being and not on pure impulse like a beast, passes judgment on the actions which present themselves as possible and to which he feels himself prompted, and either assents or dissents to them. In following this judgment of reason, the will becomes a reasonable will. It is in the dominance of reason over impulse that man's freedom lies. Freedom is not, therefore, a native endowment, but a conquest; it is not absolute, but relative. Only in the ideal wise man, whose mind embraces the whole system of truth in which every particular judgment is a matter of demonstrative certainty, is freedom made perfect—a freedom like that of God. "Upon this stage, freedom and necessity are identical. The freedom of will, which man can attain, does not lie in the fact that his volitions and actions have no cause, but that the causes are those which correspond to his character as a rational being."

The chief end of man was defined as "life in accordance with nature," by which is meant at once the true nature of man as rational and the nature of the world as rational, expressed in the universal law. Or, to put it differently, man's task is to achieve the highest possible perfection—to realise so far as in him lies the ideal of human nature. The endeavour and the achievement are progressive; the end is godlike. This is virtue, and this alone is true happiness. Virtue is to be sought only for virtue's sake; the quest is defeated by making it a means to any end. It is the highest good. Other things are good only as they further us in our endeavour to reach this goal; only those are really evil which divert us from it or hinder our pursuit. All else is indifferent. The wise man strives to maintain his independence of things, sufficient unto himself. He strives to suppress the passions, which are false judgments or violent impulses not subject to the control of the informed reason: this state is the Stoic Apathy.

In making virtue, the life according to nature, consist in obedience to the universal law, the Stoics were the first to give to the idea of duty and obligation its full value in Greek ethics; and in conceiving this law as the good, expressing, not the arbitrary will, but the very nature of God, they gave to duty not merely a moral but a deeply religious meaning. In this light, man's moral shortcomings are sin; and to this idea, also, Stoicism gave a far deeper meaning than either religion or philosophy had done before. In some of the later Stoics, particularly, the deep sinfulness of men is dwelt on in a strain that sounds more Christian than Hellenistic. "We are all without counsel or foresight, aimless, complaining, ambitious. Why should I cover over the cancer of society with softer words? We are all wicked, and whatever one reprehends in another, each will find in his own heart. Why do you remark this man's pallor, that man's wasting? It is an epidemic." A man should not flatter himself that he has not done this or that wrong; it is only *not yet done*. "Look at your whole character: even though you have done no evil, you are capable of it."

The Stoics recognise no degrees in virtue: there are only wise and unwise, or, what is the same thing, good and bad. The wise man can do no wrong; and the unwise can do no right, since he does not act with the right insight and from the right motive. The bad and foolish man is wholly bad —he has all the vices, although not all are conspicuous in one individual, or, as Seneca says in the same context, "he has in him all the germs of wickedness." When Augustine affirms that the heathen have no true virtues: "Minus Fabricius quam Catilina punietur, non quia iste bonus, sed quia ille magis malus, et minus impius quam Catilina Fabricius, non veras virtutes habendo, sed a veris virtutibus non plurimum deviando," he is meeting the same objection which was made to the Stoic doctrine, "Quid ergo? Aristides, cui iustitia nomen dedit, iniustus est?" and meeting it in exactly the same way. The total depravity of the unregenerate is matched by the total depravity of the unphilosophical, and it must be admitted that the bishop opens the door of salvation wider than the Stoic. Another parallel to Christianity lies in the fact that the Stoics, who fixed this great gulf between philosopher and fool, would acknowledge no gradual transition. Whatever progress a man might make toward wisdom, the actual attainment which took him out of the one class into the other must be conceived as instantaneous, like that by which the sinner is numbered among the saved. Once attained, wisdom cannot be lost; it is like grace, inamissible.

The fall of the Greek city-states brought of itself the divorce of ethics from politics; the Stoic ethics are strictly individualistic. The lines so sharply drawn between citizen and foreigner, Greek and barbarian, were effaced. Most of the great Stoic teachers themselves were from the Hellenistic East—Zeno, the founder of the school, from Citium in Cyprus, Chrysippus from Soli in Cilicia, Diogenes of Babylon, and ever so many more.[1] Conditions had thus prepared the way for the Stoic cosmopolitanism. But it had a philosophical root: as those who own one law are citizens of one state, so those who live by the universal law are citizens of the world, or, as Epictetus expresses it in religious terms, all men are brethren, for all alike have God for their father. In this society man is not a part of an aggregate (μέρος), but a member (μέλος) of an organism, and the members exist for one another, bound together by an intimate sympathy, "You must live for another, if you would live for yourself." The factitious distinctions between Greek and barbarian, male and female, bond and free, vanish. Eratosthenes censures Aristotle's advice to Alexander to treat Greeks as friends and barbarians as foes: men are really to be divided only by character, which does not run on lines of race. The Stoics

[1] This fact has started a good deal of loose talk about "Oriental" influences in Stoicism.

are the first to recognise that "a man's a man, for a' that."
The founder of the school was so taken with the equality of
the sexes that he proposed in his ideal state to have women
wear men's clothes. The right of women to equal education
is often asserted, and the idea of marriage as a life partner-
ship appears—a definition which is embodied in the Roman
law and has done more than anything else to shape what is
called the Christian idea of marriage.[1]

The Stoics were well aware that an example is more impressive than either principles or precepts. Their ideal of the
wise man is embodied in Socrates, Antisthenes, and Diogenes.
The choice of the last two saints shows that the Cynic life
of self-sufficient asceticism continued to be the highest type
of Stoic virtue; and even in Socrates it was more his indifference to external things that impressed the Stoic imagination
than what seems to us his true greatness. The taking of an
idealised historical person as the type of virtue was of considerable consequence; it gave not only a model for imitation but an inspiring example. Roman Stoics found such
inspiration in Cato. Other philosophical schools made ex-
emplars of their founders or great teachers; Pythagoras and
Apollonius of Tyana are cases in point. The biographies of
these worthies are the more instructive for the ideals of the
school because the writers were unhampered by historical
knowedge or scruples. For the Neopythagoreans they filled
the place which the portrait of Jesus in the Gospels occupied
in Christianity, and served the same end of edification.

To their theoretical ethics, the Stoics subjoined a precep-
tive or parenetic part, in which the general principles were
applied to particular problems of conduct. Of the nature
of these practical handbooks of morals the De Officiis of
Cicero, based upon a work of the Stoic Panætius, gives an
idea. The title itself, On Duties, indicates the point of
view. In any such application questions are bound to arise

[1] At least what Protestants call by this name. The sacramental
mystical conception was as alien to Roman common sense as the modern
romantic notions.

in which there appears to be a conflict of obligations, or between obligations and legitimate interests; justice and humanity, for example, may dictate diametrically opposite treatment of an offender. Or it may be asked: How far does the principle of fair dealing require a man to sacrifice his lawful advantage? A field for casuistry was thus open, and the Stoic moralists cultivated it diligently. The tone of these discussions is generally high, and the decisions often appear to the modern "business" conscience quite Utopian. The principle, "eadem est utilitas unius cuiusque et universorum," no one among us may openly impugn, but when it comes to its consequences it is another matter. We can imagine the derisive comments of practical Christians on the opinion of the honest heathen about taking advantage of exclusive information.

In man's dealings with his fellows in society, two fundamental principles are normative, justice and beneficence, or, as we should say, love. Justice, taken broadly, renders to every man in every respect what is his right; beneficence is unbounded goodwill in the heart and its effectuation in conduct. The good man is gentle, not easily provoked to anger, scorning revenge, prompt to forgive and to help even his enemies, magnanimous, liberal in ministering to others, yet not with a lavish and indiscriminate charity, much less with the corrupting largess, by which "fit deterior, qui accipit, atque ad idem semper expectandum paratior." Every man, bond or free, noble or base-born, has a natural claim on the sympathy and help of his fellow man—"ubicunque homo est, ibi beneficii locus." For we are all members of one body. The love of humanity has never been more nobly, and at the same time sanely, expressed than in the writings of the Stoics. Epictetus, for example, teaches that we should treat all, even slaves, as kinsmen, as brothers, since they are children of the same God.

Stoicism is essentially a religious philosophy. One of the finest expressions of its spirit is the noble Hymn of Cleanthes, which begins:

" Most glorious of immortals, many-named,
All power in heaven and earth is ever thine.
O Zeus, of nature author, and of all
Things ruler, guiding all with changeless law,
All hail!   Yea, thee all mortals should invoke;
For thine offspring are we,[1] we who alone,
Of all the mortal things that live and move
On earth, possess the gift divine of speech.
Thee, therefore, will I hymn unceasingly,
And evermore thy lofty praises sing."

Like their predecessors, the Stoics saw the errors of the popular religion.   But Zeno went farther when he declared images, shrines, temples, prayers, and worship to be of no avail.   A really acceptable prayer, he taught, can only spring from a devout mind: God is best worshipped in the shrine of the heart by the desire to know and obey him. Their pantheism made no difficulty in recognising the sun and moon and other heavenly bodies as gods.   As these are part of the evolved cosmos, however, they came into being with it, and will endure only to the end of the present age.   The souls of the wise and good, in whom the spirit has attained a higher degree of "tonic" energy, survive as "demons," mundane divinities of inferior rank.   The greater gods of the popular religion are identified by the Stoic myth exegesis with the heavenly bodies,[2] or they are names given to the manifestations of the one God in different spheres of nature —in the ether, Zeus; in the air, Hera; in the waters, Poseidon; in the earth, Demeter.

The allegorical interpretation of myths and legends did not, of course, originate with the Stoics.   Long before them it had been employed on Homer and Hesiod to remove the seemingly irrational and immoral features in their stories of the gods by translating them into harmless natural phenomena, or to claim their authority for some favourite philosoph-

[1] Acts 17, 28.
[2] Persæus, an immediate disciple of Zeno, propounded the euhemeristic explanation: the men who taught their fellows to till the soil, build huts, and practise the primitive arts were deified.

ical theory. The Stoics developed the method to perfection, and applied it with a new motive and effect to the whole theology of the Greeks. Their forerunners had allegorised casually, invited by some particular figure or story in the poets. If Theagenes of Rhegium, reputed to have lived before the Persian wars, explained the battle of the gods in the twentieth book of the Iliad as a conflict of the elements— Poseidon water, Apollo fire, Hera air—or made Ares stand for impetuous folly combating wisdom personified in Athena, Leto representing absent-mindedness, and her opponent, Hermes, mindfulness, he was only seeking to find a harmless or an edifying meaning in that peculiarly scandalous fray among the immortals, not saying that Poseidon was nothing but poetry for water, or Athena for wisdom. The Stoics, on the contrary, allegorised systematically: the gods of the popular religion are the elements under various names or in different aspects. In the identifications bad etymologies—or bad puns—play a large part. Zeus is the ether, or the elemental fire, or the cosmos evolved from this original, or the soul of the universe; or, again, he is the Logos, he is law, necessity, fate, intelligence, providence. Athena, also, springing from the head of Zeus, is the ether. Hera is the air; Hades the dense, dark air that is in earth; the sea is Poseidon; Rhea and Demeter are names of the earth; Hephaistos is the earthly fire; Apollo (Phœbus) the bright shining air, or the one fire, or—so the most—the sun; his sister Artemis must then be the moon, and so on, through the catalogue of gods and epic heroes. The theogony and the whole mythology are accordingly interpreted physically. Here was room for the most extravagant ingenuity, and the Stoics showed no lack of it. Their translation of mythology into meteorology often remind us of the school of Max Müller without the added fallacies of the comparative method.

What concerns us here, however, is not the curiosities of their exegesis in particular, but the fact that it sapped the whole popular religion. The travesty on prayer which Aristophanes puts into the mouth of the meteorologising Socrates,

"O mighty king, immeasurable Air, who holdest the earth aloft,
  And resplendent Ether, and ye reverend goddesses, thunder-and-light-
    ning Clouds,
  Arise, appear on high, O Queens, to your thinker!" [1]

was aimed at some precursor of the Stoics, but to the plain
man their ether-Zeus and air-Hera would have seemed to
be equally well hit off by the answer of Socrates to old
Strepsiades, when he offers to swear by the gods, "What sort
of gods will you swear by? The first thing you have to
learn is that gods are not current coin with us."

The Epicureans cast up to the Stoics their rejection of the
popular religion. Yet nothing is more certain than that this
was not their intention. On the contrary, they were sincerely desirous to accommodate their pantheistic monotheism
to the religion of the masses, which they thought useful to
restrain the vulgar from wrong-doing; and, in fact, they
showed that pantheism has, of all philosophies, the least
difficulty in making room for polytheism. They themselves
argued for the existence of gods from the universality of the
belief; they defended the theory and practice of divination;
and their doctrine of demons was a wide back door to superstition. Much less accommodating, as may be seen in
Cicero's Natura Deorum, was the scepticism of the Middle
Academy represented by Arcesilaus and Carneades.

Stoicism is more than a religious philosophy: it was a religion for thinking men, and many of the noblest spirits of
the Hellenistic and Roman world found in it the satisfaction of the deepest needs of the soul. The feeling of absolute dependence, and the independence of the world which
is possible only in that dependence; the conscious oneness of
mind and will with those of the universe; nature and society
a moral order; the chief end of life conformity to the universal law, in which alone man's true freedom and well-being
is found—all this gave to the reason, the emotions, and the
will the satisfaction which the old religion did not offer, and
no one can read the writings, particularly of the later Stoics,

[1] See also Frogs, 888 ff., the prayer of Euripides.

without recognising the deep and sincere piety which breathes in them. Worship, as we have seen, was "the reasonable service" of high thoughts, noble ends, manly endeavour; prayer was not to beg the gods to give this or protect from that, but to grant that we neither dread nor crave any of these things. In a deeper apprehension, prayer is communion with God in the inner man: "Non sunt ad cælum elevandæ manus nec exorandus ædituus, ut nos ad aures simulacri, quasi magis exaudiri possimus, admittat; prope est Deus, tecum est, intus est."

The individual soul, being a part of the evolved cosmos, can endure only to the involution at the next world-conflagration; its immortality is not eternity. Some held, with Cleanthes, that all souls survive to the end of the age; others, with Chrysippus, that only the wise thus survive.[1] The picture of the hereafter of the good man which Seneca draws is not improbably embellished with Platonic colours, but contains nothing at variance with Stoic doctrine. This life is only a prelude to that longer and better life; the body only a brief lodging of the soul, or a prison from which death releases it; the day of death is the birthday of eternity; beyond is the great and eternal peace, undisturbed by fear or care, desire or envy; there the disembodied soul joins the blessed souls, and recognises those who have gone before; on the other hand, the day of death is the day which shall pass judgment on all man's years. The thought of the other life in the splendour of the endless light "permits nothing sordid, low, or cruel to cleave to the soul; it says to us that the gods are witnesses of all things, and bids us make ourselves approved to them, to be prepared to meet them in the hereafter, and to keep eternity before our minds." Heaven is thus not only a consolation in bereavement and a word of courage when death draws near, but a moral power. It is not uninstructive to compare the consolatory epistle of Seneca to Marcia on the death of her son (especially *cc.* 24 *ff.*) with that of Saint Jerome to Marcella on the death of Blæsilla. The advantage is truly not with the monk!

[1] Conditional immortality.

The emphasis which the Stoics laid on virtue as the highest, and indeed the only true, good, and on the duty of doing good to men, naturally prompted them to try to lead their fellows into the way of virtue and happiness. In this, as in so much else, they had the Cynics for precursors. Philosophy, which, in the schools of Plato and Aristotle, had attracted an intellectual élite of speculative and scientific bent, devoted to the pursuit of truth, now went out to seek men in the market-place, proclaiming the worthlessness of all things the world sets such store by and the sole and supreme worth of the self—"What is a man profited if he gain the whole world, and lose his own soul!"—and urging men to save themselves by renouncing the world with its affections and lusts.[1] Only he was truly free, truly virtuous, truly happy, who was above all needs, indifferent to all hardships. The Cynics set the example of this freedom; rejecting all the luxuries and refinements of civilisation, the conventions and even the decencies of society, they went back to the rude simplicity of the natural life—some of them, indeed, went so far back as to scandalise proper souls by the unabashed application of the principle, "naturalia non sunt turpia." The many anecdotes of Diogenes prove that the singular manners of these exponents of the simple life did not fail to make their impression on the imagination of their contemporaries. Their eccentricities of garb and livelihood were not, however, their only title to attention; they were street preachers, trying to convert men from the life of self-indulgence to the life of self-discipline.

The Stoics dropped many of the eccentricities and corrected the extravagances of the doctrine, but they adopted the same means of bringing the truth to the ears of men. Out of the rude give and take of the Cynic street preaching was developed the Stoic diatribe, the moral discourse addressed to a popular audience of hearers or readers. The way in which the authors lashed the vices of their times connects the diatribe with the Roman satire. The philosophic

[1] Instances of conversion, see Oakesmith, Religion of Plutarch, 15, and n. 2.

epistle has, as in Seneca, many of the features of the dia-tribe. Jewish and Christian missionaries followed in the footsteps of the Cynic and Stoic preachers, and the diatribe furnished to both the type of sermon, tract, and epistle. The Stoic philosophers went about making converts, giving coun-sel to perplexed consciences and consolation to those in trouble; they were often charged, also, with the moral and religious education of youth. The high dignity and grave re-sponsibility of this ministry is nobly expounded by Epictetus to a young man who proposes to enter it: It is a divine calling, and he who undertakes it without God incurs the displeasure of God and makes himself a laughing-stock to men; not only must the true Cynic be a man of pure soul and exemplary character, he must be conscious that he is sent from God as a messenger (ἄγγελος) to men, to teach them and to reclaim them from their errors; only a pure conscience and the sense of communion with God can give him power to speak freely to his brethren, children, kinsmen.

Against the current dogmatic philosophies, the heads of the Academy turned the weapons of a sceptical dialectic. In common with the Epicureans, and in part with the same reasoning, they confuted the arguments for the immortality of the soul and for a divine providence, and for the possi-bility of divination; and they disputed the evidences for the existence of God, or of the gods, which Epicureans as well as Stoics alleged. The dialogues of Cicero give us a good notion of the way in which these questions were discussed in polite society by representatives of the several schools in the first century before Christ.

The epistemological scepticism of Arcesilaus and Carne-ades soon lost its rigour even in the Academic school; and the more the conception of philosophy as the guide of life pre-vailed, the more its professors gave prominence to its affirm-ative aspects: for practical purposes man can get on without demonstrative certainties, but not without positive convic-tions. This predominant practical interest, especially among the pragmatic-minded Romans, concurred with the exhaustion of speculative power in all the schools, and with scepticism itself, to incline men to an eclecticism which saw the essential agreements larger than the scholastic differences, and combined the elements of truth and practical worth in various systems without being unduly disturbed by resulting incongruities. The Epicureans maintained their doctrines with greater fidelity, because they were less able than the other schools either to borrow or lend; but Academics, Stoics, and the revived Pythagoreans took their good things where they found them.

The general tendencies of these composite philosophies are ethical and religious; physics and metaphysics were a perfunctory part of the curriculum, but inspired little real interest. The revival of religion which began the first century of the empire reinforced this tendency, and infused into it a strain of mystical piety which grows stronger in the philosophical revival of the following time. One result of this predominant religious interest appears in the more distinctly personal conception of God. We have seen this tendency in the Stoic Seneca, who, without giving up the physical philosophy of his predecessors, lays so much weight on the moral side of God's nature that his conception is little removed from that of a modern theist with strong leanings to immanence. Still more distinctly theistic is the conception of Plutarch (46–120 A. D.), whose writings give a most attractive view of the religion of a cultivated and thoughtful man in the last generation of the first century and the first decades of the second after Christ.

Plutarch called Plato his master, and writes vigorously not only against the Epicureans but against the Stoics; he had an open mind for the good in other schools, especially the revived Pythagorean movement. For him theology is the goal of philosophy. In his own theology he is a monotheist, with a clearly personal and morally lofty idea of God. He rejects the Stoic immanence, because it implicates God in the material universe and makes him subject to change and decay. God is one, eternal, simple, unchangeable, perfectly good; his thought and purpose are the providence that orders all for good and does good to all; he is exalted above the world, abiding in his eternal and unchangeable nature. But he is not exiled from the sublunary sphere, like the Epicurean gods; the denial of God's providential activity in the world is practical atheism. Plutarch's God is not the transcendent Absolute that Neoplatonic metaphysics were presently to make of him, but a personal God. With his Platonic dualism, Plutarch cannot conceive, however, that God is himself active in the material universe; his will in nature and providence is effectuated through the agency of superhuman beings, demons, who thus fulfil a function like that of the angels in later Judaism; revelation also is mediated through them, while some are guardian angels of individual men, guiding them in the right way. The evil in the world, which cannot be attributed to the good God, is the work of other demons—fallen angels, we might say—who are, nevertheless, under the dominion of God, and are punished by him for their ill deeds.

The demons not only serve Plutarch's theology in this way, but they enable him to reconcile his lofty monotheism with his hereditary religion. He was a priest of the Delphian Apollo, and he and his wife were initiated in the mysteries of Dionysos; the sincerity of his religiousness and his reverence for its antique forms of piety are unquestionable. He would see the popular religion purged of its errors and superstitions —superstition, he acutely observes, is worse than atheism— and then he would cultivate it. The heavenly bodies—above all, the sun—which minister to the well-being of mankind, take the first rank among the gods; the inferior gods belong to the class of good demons.

Perhaps the best known of the essays of Plutarch is the dialogue, De Sera Numinis Vindicta, a discussion in theodicy. The belief that there is a righteous Providence in the affairs of men which requites them according to their deserts has to encounter the objection of experience, that not mere every-day sinners, but outrageously wicked men often prosper egregiously, live long, and die unmolested by divine justice. Plutarch's essay, with Seneca's on the cognate difficulty, the evils that often pursue the righteous through life (De Providentia), should be read by all who would see how little these ancient theologians left to be said on the subject. Plutarch, like Plato, has in reserve for those who do not get their dues in this world an exemplary retribution in hell, the imagery of which is much more lurid than Plato's. On the other hand, as he says elsewhere, to thoughtful men the hereafter holds out the pleasing hope of intercourse with the great masters of thought, and the bereaved heart entertains the expectation of meeting in the other world those it has loved and lost.

Reference had been made in more than one place above to the Pythagorean revival; a word more must be said about it here. Pythagoras of Samos is one of the great names of early Greek philosophy, but—*stat magni nominis umbra!*—his teachings are known only by uncertain regress from the systematisation they underwent at the hands of later Pythagoreans, especially of Philolaus (fifth century B. C.). Driven from his home, about 532 B. C. as it seems, he established himself at Croton, in southern Italy, where the rest of his life was mainly spent. While the Ionians were seeking a physical explanation of the universe in a primal matter and its metamorphoses, Pythagoras attacked the problem from the side of mathematics: number and measure (which can be given numerical expression) are the key with which he undertakes to solve the riddle of the universe. He was deeply influenced also by the religious movement of the sixth century, for which we have no better collective name than Orphic. Man's lot in the other world and in the round of rebirth is determined by himself in this life, and he can have no other concern here of comparable urgency with the salvation of his soul. It is the business of philosophy to teach him how; thus Pythagoreanism offers not only a theory of the universe but a way of salvation.

In place of the Bacchic frenzy in which the popular sects

cultivated enthusiasm and gained the assurance of future blessedness, Pythagoras, conformably to his fundamental principles, put the discipline of the soul in measure, order, and harmony. To this end a rule of life was adopted, regulating even garb and diet; the members of the order formed cœnobite communities, which may be compared with the Jewish Essenes or the Christian monks of later times. From purifying their own souls, they were tempted into trying to establish the rule of the saints on this earth. Their political activities were not unnaturally resented, and toward the middle of the fifth century the order was violently suppressed, their houses sacked, and many of the members slain. This persecution scattered the survivors, who carried the doctrines of Pythagoras to less inhospitable lands, especially to Greece itself. Plato, in his later period, was strongly attracted by these theories, as they had been systematised and expounded by Philolaus. In the following century Pythagoreanism as a school became extinct both in Greece and Italy. Pythagorean religious societies, however, perpetuated themselves, and it was doubtless in these circles that the revival of the Pythagorean philosophy in the first century before our era originated.

This restoration could not go back to early written sources, for the teaching of Pythagoras had been orally transmitted as an esoteric tradition; and the continuity of the school tradition itself had for centuries been completely interrupted. Consequently, Neopythagoreanism is in fact an eclectic system, which drew most largely from Platonism, seizing particularly upon the Pythagorean side of Plato's later thinking, but appropriating also Peripatetic and Stoic elements. The fact that the revival sprang from the bosom of societies devoted to the cultivation of personal religion as a way of salvation made it peculiarly open also to the influences of the Oriental mysteries which were abroad in that age, and to the superstitions that they fostered.

The prevailing tendency of the times was dualistic. We have seen how, from the ethical or anthropological side, this

tendency made a wide breach even in the closed monistic system of Stoicism, and it naturally had much freer play in a
philosophy derived from Plato and Pythagoras. In the
main, the thinkers of the day, whether they would be called
Platonists or Pythagoreans, profess, as a modern historian
says, a transcendent, dualistic ontology and metaphysical
doctrine of principles; follow in physics and cosmology—and
in logic, when they go into that subject—the Aristotelian
or Stoic path; return in their anthropology and psychology
to the Pythagorean-Platonic channel, and end with a transcendent, ascetic ethics. They zealously combat materialism,
Stoic as well as Epicurean. Being, in the true sense, is not
to be predicated of matter, which is rather the negation of
being, but of the incorporeal ideas, or numbers. Matter is
the root of all evil, in opposition to God, the principle of
good. God is, as we say, spirit, and to be worshipped only
in spirit—in prayer, which is the communion of the soul with
God, and by a pious and virtuous disposition, not by sacrifice
and liturgy. The human spirit is akin to God; it can realise
its nature and attain its destiny only by subduing the flesh.
The liberation of the soul from the bondage of the flesh is
achieved by an ascetic discipline, by purifications, by abstinence from animal food and sexual intercourse, and by
suppressing the impulses of sense and appetite. Only so can
the soul escape from the round of rebirths and return to its
divine original.

More characteristic than these conceptions, which, in diverse combinations, had long been current, is the place which
the idea of revelation takes in these systems. In the schools
the frequent appeal to the authority of the founders tended
to a principle of authority which made their teaching decisive; the later Platonists, for example, cite Plato as a canon
of truth, even in the act of putting their own ideas into his
words by sophistical interpretation. In none of the schools
was this more natural than to the Pythagoreans, who had
ancient precedent for their deference to the *ipse dixit* of the
master. So far one might see in this only a consequence of

the decline of originality and intellectual independence.   But we must recognise another factor: philosophy had undertaken not only to explain the universe, but to save men's souls; indeed, metaphysics and physics had become subordinate to theology, and theology and anthropology and ethics to the doctrine of salvation.   Scepticism had thoroughly undermined confidence in the ability of reason to know anything for certain beyond the limits of individual experience, if it did not actually invade the field of experience.   On the other hand, the craving for intellectual certitude which scepticism cannot extirpate was reinforced by the demand for religious assurance that the way of salvation in which men are invited to adventure their souls really leads to the goal.   What authority but revelation can give this certitude or this assurance?   The composite Neopythagorean doctrine was—in all good faith, doubtless—ascribed in its totality to Pythagoras; and the truth Pythagoras taught to men he received from a higher source.   In the absence of any authentic old Pythagorean literature, the field was free for apocryphal scriptures under the name of the founder or of his early followers, and a prolific crop of such was produced.   Lives of Pythagoras, in which he was represented as the ideal wise man, inspired teacher, and worker of wonders, were also written; from such sources the extant lives, dating from the third and fourth centuries of our era, are doubtless in considerable part derived.

Inspiration and supernatural powers were not confined to remote times; a Neopythagorean apostle like Apollonius of Tyana, in the first century after Christ, appears in Philostratus's biography[1] as the hero of a religious romance which is an interesting pendant to the Christian Clementines.   The wise man, who had been for the post-Aristotelian schools the ideal type of the philosophical character as exemplified, for instance in Socrates, now becomes the embodiment of all wisdom and virtue in the person of a Pythagoras or a Plato. Not only was the incontestable verity of revelation accorded

[1] Life of Apollonius.   Written about 220 A. D.

to the teachings of these masters, but they themselves were the objects of a religious reverence. Even the Jew, Philo, can speak of the "divine" Plato. Their words carry, in effect, the authority of a supreme personality as well as of inspired scripture.

In the quest for a revelation of the truth by which a man must be saved multitudes in that age turned to Oriental religions. The open cults which had been planted in the centres of commerce and administration by foreign residents attracted many, but it was in the guise of mysteries—a form which strange cults easily assumed—with their secret and esoteric instruction that these religions exercised the greatest influence. Like the Orphic mysteries in an earlier time and their Greek offshoots and rivals, the Oriental mysteries purified men from the defilements of the flesh, expiated their actual and inherited guilt, brought them into communion and mystical union with deity, and gave them the assurance and the earnest of victory over death (or deliverance from the round of rebirth) and of an immortality of divine blessedness. We shall return to this subject in more detail when we come to deal with the religions of the Roman Empire; here we remark only the influence of this whole tendency on the development of religious thought. The philosophies of the time are more and more infected by this strain of mystical religion, and some of the mysteries put on a veneer of philosophy. The affinity of mysticism for magic is also shown in many ways.

Among the Oriental religions which made successful propaganda in the first century before the Christian era and the first century after it, Judaism was not the least important. The ubiquitousness of the race had its part in this; but the chief cause lay in the character of the religion. Its monotheism was of a type to which the popular philosophies all tended; indeed the synagogue, with its gathering for the study of the Law and the Prophets, seemed much more like a school of philosophy than like religious worship or the ritual of a mystery. The possession of these sacred scriptures, descended from an antiquity by the side of which the beginnings of Greek philosophy were modern, and derived from divine revelation, made a doubly profound impression upon an age which turned its eyes to the ancients for wisdom and to heaven for a truth beyond the attainment of reason. The Jewish life, with its multitudinous observances and its meticulous precautions against pollution from unclean men and things, had nothing strange or unreasonable about it when not only religious sects but philosophical schools made diet and dress and rules of intercourse an essential part of their discipline.

On the other side, Jewish thinkers, convinced no less of the inspiration of Greek philosophy than of the Hebrew Bible, and of the unity and consistency of truth in the different forms of its revelation, undertook to show that the truths which Plato sets forth in metaphysical form for the philosophical intellect are revealed in the Pentateuch in concrete example and precept for the apprehension of the common mind. When their deeper meaning is discovered by the allegorical interpretation, they are found to contain the profoundest philosophy.

Philo does much more, however, than in this fashion establish the harmony between Plato and Moses. He is himself a constructive thinker, quite equal to any of his century, and fills a significant place in the history of Greek philosophy among the representatives of the eclectic Platonism of his time and the precursors of Neoplatonism.

The dualistic theism which is the signature of the period we have been considering might suffice for religious needs; it could not permanently satisfy the demands of the intellect, and the last great speculative enterprise of the Greek genius was the effort to overcome it, and to oppose to the materialistic monism of the Stoa an idealistic monism. We should, however, only half understand Neoplatonism if we conceived its problem as purely metaphysical; its abstruse ontology is the foundation of a mystical philosophy of salvation. It was this double aspect which fitted it above all other systems to furnish a philosophical basis for Christian theology, and has enabled it to maintain itself, in its essential features, in the modern European philosophy of religion.

The founder of the school was Ammonius Saccas, of whom little more is known than that he was the teacher of Origen, the father of Christian theology, and of Plotinus, the Neo-platonic philosopher; but to have inspired two such thinkers is a title to enduring fame. The Enneads of Plotinus, edited by his great disciple Porphyry, are the principal extant mon-ument of the system. Plotinus and his followers would have resented the charge of innovation implied in the name *New* Platonism. For them Plato was an absolute and final au-thority; their task was only to expound and defend his doc-trine in its true meaning—that is, in *their* meaning. From Plato and Aristotle they received a transcendent idea of God which Plotinus pushed to its furthest extreme: God is abso-lute Being, of which, as it is in itself, nothing can be predi-cated—not thought nor will nor act. It is only from the point of view of the relation of the world to him that it can be said that he is the infinite One, the Good, or the primal Power.

For Plato the material world is a remote and imper-fect copy of the ideal because it is material; to later Pla-tonists, influenced by their ethical dualism, it is an evil world, and some of them would have an inferior demon or an evil demiurge to make it. That the body was the prison or the tomb of the soul, the senses and appetites of the flesh the root of error and sin, was common doctrine of the ethical and religious philosophies. Between God and the world there was thus a great gulf fixed, metaphysical and moral. Philo had attempted to get across it by his theory of the Logos; some of the Gnostics undertook to span it by a whole myth-ology of emanations; Plotinus, too, in more scientific form, tries a similar way. As the light of the sun, without effort on the sun's part and without subtracting from its substance, for ever streams from that luminary, with diminishing power as it is more remote from its source, until it is lost in the darkness, so from the First Principle, which is the First Cause, proceeds the Intelligence (Νοῦς), from it the World Soul, and from this in turn Primal Matter and the corporeal universe. This procession is not in space and time, for these emerge only in the last stage. Thus all is from God, and God is in all, yet so that his absolute transcendence is not impaired.

The individual souls, which constitute a system of souls in the World Soul, descending into the bodily world, preoccupied with the things of sense and their inferior values, become unmindful of their divine origin, and therewith lose their freedom. From this bondage, which subjects the soul to the round of rebirths, it can be saved only by turning its thought away from the things of sense and upward to Reason (Νοῦς), and through it to the superrational good, to God. This last stage in its reascent can, so long as the soul is in the body, be accomplished only in an ecstasy transcending sense, reason, intuition, and consciousness—a supreme moment in which the soul loses itself in God. But, by conquering its independence of the body and living in contemplation of the things above, the soul may at death by this way enter into eternal blessedness in the bosom of the Absolute. Neoplatonism thus gave the intellectual pattern for European mysticism, as the philosophy of the Upanishads and the Vedanta did for Indian mysticism; in the Moslem Sufis the two streams meet.

The resemblances between Neoplatonism and the Vedanta have led to the surmise that Plotinus was directly or indirectly influenced by the Indian systems, while others speak more vaguely of the infusion of Oriental conceptions in the thinking of the age. From the time of Alexander's expedition on, descriptions of India and its people, of the Brahman priests, and of ascetics of different names and persuasions, were familiar to the Greeks; the similarity of their beliefs about soul and body and their doctrine of transmigration to the Pythagorean teachings had early been noted. The wisdom of the Brahmans was highly lauded; but, so far as we can judge from the notices that have been preserved, the reporters seem to have learned very little about Indian thought, whether Brahman or Buddhist. Doubtless natives of India came and went in great cities such as Alexandria, but whether they colported any intellectual wares is doubtful. How little Clement of Alexandria knew about the Indian philosophers may be seen from the passage in which he writes of the Brahmans, the "Sarmanai" (*çrāmanas*), and the followers of Buddha. Of the first two it is clear that Clement, Origen, and Porphyry derive their meagre information from a passage in Megasthenes, perhaps through Strabo; of the Buddhists Clement has no more to say than that they obey the rules of Buddha and on account of his signal excellence reverence him as a god. Origen, Clement's disciple and Plotinus's fellow student, knows no more. Positive assertions such as that of Numenius, that Pythagoras and Plato only expounded the ancient wisdom of the Brahmans, the Magi, the Egyptians, and the Jews, signify nothing but a desire to vindicate for the doctrines of the Greek philosophers antiquity and universality—they do not imply that the author knew anything more about Indian philosophy than he could have read in a handbook of geography. Porphyry tells us that Plotinus, after long study under Ammonius, had attained such proficiency in philosophy that he was eager to gain acquaintance with that which was studied among the Persians and that which flourished among the Indians. To this end he attached himself to the Persian expedition of the emperor Gordian, being then in his thirty-ninth year. He got no farther than Mesopotamia, however, and after the murder of Gordian was fortunate to escape to Antioch, whence he proceeded to Rome. That he already had any considerable knowledge of Oriental philosophy or subsequently acquired such knowledge is nowhere intimated.

A connection between Neoplatonism and the Indian systems must, therefore, be established solely by internal evidence. Now, a closer analysis and comparison of the system of Plotinus discloses two things: *First*, his system is a summation, or rather synthesis, of the whole movement of Greek metaphysics from the Eleatics down, and there is nothing in it that is not thus adequately accounted for; and, *second*, the characteristic features of this system have no parallel in Indian philosophy. The very problem of his metaphysics has no existence for the Indian thinkers, to whom the world of sense and the individual soul are an illusion. The theory which interposes a descending series of Intelligence, World Soul, and Primal Matter, between the Absolute and a real world has no parallel in any Indian system.

The resemblance lies in the conception of salvation as the soul's realisation of its identity with the Absolute, as in the true doctrine of the Vedanta, or its absorption into the Absolute, as in the popularised Vedantesque notion and in Neoplatonism, and, on the way to this goal, emancipation from the body, reflection, contemplation, and ecstasy. But here, too, Neoplatonism only brings to final and formal expression ideas and tendencies long established in Greek philosophy. If the soul be of divine origin, and its eternal good is union with God, then, when God is an Absolute, beyond knowing and being, the goal can be reached neither by worship nor virtue nor reason, but only by the mystical path in which asceticism is the inevitable first stage, and ecstasy—or, to speak physiologically, self-induced trance-states, the last earthly phase.

Porphyry, one of the most widely and profoundly learned men of antiquity, expounds and defends the teaching of his master; but his own interest lies on the religious rather than on the metaphysical side. Philosophy is for him spiritual cathartic and therapeutic—of what use is all the talk of the philosopher if he does not know how to cure the maladies of the soul? Man is not saved by knowledge, however comprehensive and profound; the intellectual apprehension even of the highest truths of metaphysical theology does not suffice, we must live ourselves into the object of our knowledge.

Though Porphyry repels dualism in his metaphysics, in the practical dualism of his anthropology and ethics he goes as far as any of his contemporaries. The body is not merely a hindrance to the soul in its great enterprise, but is a cause of demonic pollution, for the material is infected by hylic demons. To reach the goal, sense and imagination must be left behind, the pleasures of the body abandoned, the desire for them extirpated. Sexual intercourse, legitimate or illegitimate in law and common morals, is a defilement; he warns against the theatre, horse-races, and dances, with an earnestness that reminds us of the Christian Fathers. Against the use of animal food Porphyry wrote a special tract, which is of double interest to us because the author has made large use of an otherwise lost treatise of Theophrastus. He urges both the wrong that is done to the animals, which are also creatures endowed with reason, and the harm that is done to man by a diet which stimulates the appetites and passions. The sacrifice of animals to the gods falls under the same condemnation.

The bloody sacrifices of the popular religions, and, indeed, the whole cultus, necessarily seemed to him to express a no less false and unworthy idea of the deity than the mythology as commonly understood. His letter to the Egyptian priest Anebo is a volley of questions about the gods, demons, inspiration, divination, astrology, and theurgy, by which the irrationalities and contradictions of the priestly theology are riddled. It is less impious, he writes in another place, not to respect the images of the gods than to entertain such notions of the gods as most men do. The only worship of God consists in the knowledge of God and likeness to God in the inner man. God needs no other being; the wise man needs naught but God. The true temple of God is the soul of the wise man, the wise man is the true priest; God does not demand offerings and long prayers, but a godly life; he cares not for men's words but their deeds.

These are the commonplaces of the higher Greek theology from the fifth century before Christ on; the echo of Plato is distinct, and religious Stoics could talk in the same strain. But, like the other monotheistic philosophies of the age, Neoplatonism had no difficulty in coming to terms with the popular religions. It found much to condemn in the vulgar notions about the gods and in the forms of worship, but it made no attack on polytheism itself. Indeed, its universe in stories was peculiarly adapted to make place above and below for all manner of gods, visible and invisible, and for innumerable demons, good, bad, and indifferent, including the Jewish angels and archangels. The good demons preside over provinces of nature or the occupations of men; they are tutelary genii of cities and countries, and guardian spirits of individuals; through others the will of God is revealed to men, the prayers of men conveyed to God. Evil demons work all manner of mischief, cause earthquakes and plagues and unfruitful seasons, inspire men with false notions and evil lusts, lying in wait for the soul even before its entrance into the earthly life; they appear in visible and tangible forms, beastly or monstrous; they invade the body, especially by way of animal food, and cause physical disorders.

The soul of man can only by degrees ascend to the highest: not only to the Nous and the Soul of the Universe belongs a worship accordant to their nature, but the good demons are to be revered with prayers and bloodless offerings. In a similar way the Catholic church maintains the veneration of angels and saints, distinguishing between λατρεία and δουλεία, that the homage due to God only may not seem to be impaired by being shared with creatures. Iamblichus goes farther, teaching that the help of the gods is necessary to deliver the soul by their intervention from the bondage of destiny—that is, from natural necessity.

Neoplatonism not only thus accommodated itself to the popular religions, Greek and barbarian, but it undertook their defence against the attacks of Christianity. Nor did its adherents confine themselves to repelling assaults: Porphyry was the author of the ablest of all the counter-attacks on Christianity. The philosophical apologetics of paganism come chiefly from this school; from its bosom sprang the last religious revival of the ancient faiths. After the failure of the emperor Julian's attempt to restore paganism, philosophy flourished for a while at Alexandria, where Hypatia fell a victim to the brutal fanaticism of the monks, and then found its last refuge in Athens, until in 529 A. D. Justinian by edict forbade the teaching of philosophy there.

Outwardly the closing of the school at Athens was a small matter—the silencing of a few professors, the dispersing of a small body of students, the confiscation of the endowments; but it impresses the imagination. What thoughts and feelings must have come over Damascius and his fellows as they turned their backs on the scenes where Plato and Aristotle had taught, to seek in Persia the freedom to think like Greeks! The flame of science and philosophy which for nine hundred years had burned, now brighter, now more dimly, was extinguished on its own hearth. Yet here once more the vanquished gave laws to the victors. Philosophy might be suppressed at Athens and die a natural death elsewhere, but Neoplatonism had long since become the orthodox philosophy of the Christian religion, the basis of its dogma and the source of its mysticism.

CHAPTER XXI

THE ROMANS

THE RELIGION OF THE CITY OF ROME

The Sources—The Gods of the Old Roman Calendar—Character of the Religion—Provinces of the Gods—Functional Deities—Legal Theory of the National Religion—The Priesthoods—Offerings and Expiations—Festivals—Augurs and Auspices—Holy Places—Domestic Religion—Di Manes—Introduction of Alien Deities—Greek Gods and Cults—Magna Mater—Differentiations and Gods of Qualities—The Etruscan Art of Divination—Greek Philosophy——Roman Stoicism—Social Demoralisation and the Decadence of Religion.

THE study of the Roman religion is beset by peculiar difficulties. The poets of the Augustan age, through whom we all made our first acquaintance with it, wrote at a time when it had been thoroughly Hellenised: many Greek gods had been given a place in the public cultus; native Italian deities were identified with Greek, and Greek myths appropriated for them; the old forms of worship were enriched with Greek rites. The impression we thus bring from school that the Greek and Roman religions were closely similar, if not substantially the same—an opinion, it may be added, that was universal among the Romans themselves at the beginning of our era—was strengthened by the comparative mythologers of the last generation, prepossessed as they were by the theory of common Indo-European origins and their mistaken notion that the Greeks and Italians formed a closely cognate subdivision of the Indo-Germanic race.

If we turn from the poets and historians to the investigations of antiquarians like Varro, we find that many features of the old Roman religion were hardly less obscure to them

than to us—gods whose names were perpetuated in the calendar, but whose cult had long been extinct; priesthoods
and sodalities whose functions had been forgotten; rites whose
motive and meaning no man knew. We are indebted to these
authors for the preservation of many facts and of some authentic traditions, but their reconstruction of the stages of
development—the origins, the institutions of Numa, the innovations of the Tarquins—is manifestly not based on records
or monuments, but on inference and conjecture, often ingenious and sometimes plausible. The scheme in which they are
framed is the same in which the constitutional and legal history is cast. The results of these learned researches have for
the most part reached us only through extracts in later authors, but their volume is considerable, and their value, apart
from all theories, inestimable. They are confirmed and sup-
plemented by a multitude of inscriptions of diverse character
and age. From these various sources it is possible to form a
picture of the genuine old Roman religion which, however
defective in details, is true at least in its main outlines.

The most important of the monumental sources is the
calendar of public festivals, of which many copies are extant
in more or less complete preservation. These inscriptions
are from the age of Augustus and his next successors, but the
body of the calendar includes only the festivals of the religious
year as the Roman antiquarians believed Numa to have ordered it, and as it remained unchanged through all the centuries of the republic. An alphabetical list of the deities in
whose honour these festivals were celebrated (including a few
which are otherwise attested) enables us to survey this oldest
Roman pantheon: Anna Perenna, Carmenta, Carna, Ceres,
Consus, Diva Angerona, Falacer, Faunus, Flora, (Fons), Furrina, Janus, Juppiter, Larenta, Lares, (? Lemures), Liber,
Mars, Mater Matuta, Neptunus, Ops, Pales, (Palatua),
Pomona, Portunus, Quirinus, (? Robigus), Saturnus, Tellus,
(? Terminus), Vejovis, Vesta, Volcanus, Volturnus.

The catalogue contains many unfamiliar names, though
some of these deities were important enough to have not only

annual festivals but their own priests (*flamines*), *e. g.*, Carmenta, Falacer, Furrina. Of the last Varro could write: "Cuius deæ honos apud antiquos, nam ei sacra annua et flamen attributus: nunc vix nomen notum paucis." In imperial times the site of her deserted sanctuary was appropriated by Oriental gods, beneath the ruins of whose shrines remains of hers have lately been discovered. With her worship the memory of her nature and functions was lost; Cicero could do no better than guess that Furrina was somehow related to the Furiæ. Of Falacer even less was known, though Varro preserves the high-sounding title, "Divus pater Falacer." In some instances the festival survived the god: Palatua, who had once a flamen of her own had disappeared, and of the goddess Pales who seems to have succeeded her all that could be said was that she was the deity of the Parilia. Not less noteworthy than the long array of forgotten deities is the absence of others who in later centuries were counted among the great gods—not only the Greek Apollo, but Italic divinities such as Diana, Venus, and Minerva. The unavoidable inference that when the calendar was formed these gods had not yet been received into the pantheon of the Roman state is confirmed by independent evidence. That Juno's name is also missing is due to the construction of the table; her festivals, falling on the calends of every month, were not specifically noted.

The first place is held by Juppiter, to whom, besides seasonal festivals, the ides of every month are sacred. Next to him comes Mars, with eight or nine festivals in the course of the year; Quirinus, also a god of war, stands by his side. The high rank of Janus in the primitive Roman religion is proved by the fact that his priest, the Rex Sacrorum, takes precedence of all others, and that the sacrificial litanies, no matter to what deity the offering was made, always began with the invocation of Janus; in the hymn of the Salii he is addressed as "good creator" and "the god of gods" (*divom deus*). In the same litanies Vesta always closes the series. The oldest order of precedence was, therefore, Janus, Juppiter, Mars,

Quirinus, Vesta. The Romans sometimes coupled their deities, a god and a goddess, as: Juppiter-Juno, Mars-Nerio, Neptunus-Salacia, Quirinus-Hora, Saturnus-Lua, Consus-Ops.[1] Minor deities appear in the liturgies as the man servants and maid servants of the greater. But these unions of the gods are ritual, not mythological; no theogonies tell of the birth of the gods or recite their genealogies. All the family histories and the *chroniques scandaleuses* in Virgil and Ovid, for example, like the whole *theologica mythica*, are appropriated from the Greeks.

The character of the religion was eminently practical. The gods, whose functions are indicated by their—chiefly transparent—names and by the seasons and rites of their festivals, preside over provinces and operations of nature so far as they concern the interests of men: for the sowing there is Saturnus; for the growth of the grain, Ceres; for the harvest and granary, Consus and Ops; Flora for the blossoming of the fruit-trees, and Pomona for the ripening fruit. The house has Janus at the door and Vesta on the hearth; the Lares preside over the fields, Pales over the pasture, Faunus over the woodland; Fons over springs of water, and Volturnus over the river. Mater Matuta and Carmenta have to do with birth; Larenta, Carna, and Vejovis, with death. Larger is the sphere of Juppiter, who sends rain and sunshine, and gives signs from heaven; he is, above all, the divine ruler and protector of the state in peace and war. These are the gods of a simple culture, when men's living was tilling the soil and tending their flocks; industry was domestic, and trade had not yet found use for a Mercurius. The prominence of the gods of battle, Mars and Quirinus, shows that life was not wholly idyllic; a war with their neighbours was almost as regular a part of the season's business as sowing or reaping.

The Roman gods are the powers which do certain definite things; it is the things they do and the rites appropriate to

---

[1] On these couples, see W. W. Fowler, Religious Experience of the Roman People, pp. 150 *ff*., 481 *ff*.

their worship that differentiate one from another. No poetic tales of their deeds gave them the distinct individuality of the Homeric deities, and no images represented them in perfect humanity. Religion was a practical concern: it was essential to know what god to address for a particular end, at what time and place, in what words, with what offerings; but the early Romans felt no need for imagining what the gods were like, nor impulse to speculate about the divine nature. Mythology, religious art, and philosophy they learned in time from the Greeks.

The division of nature and human life into neatly delimited provinces which we have observed in the functions of the gods is carried farther: there is not only a god of waters in general, Neptunus, and one of the rolling river, Volturnus, but one of the landing-place, Portunus; not only gods of the fields, the Lares, but a guardian of the bounds between neighbours' fields, Terminus. A much minuter subdivision of functions appears in the pontifical litanies called Indigitamenta. Thus the Flamen Cerealis invoked no less than twelve divinities who presided over the successive steps of the husbandman's labours, from the breaking of the ground to the storing of the grain: Vervactor, Redarator, Imporcitor, Insitor, Obarator, Occator, Sarritor, Subruncinator, Messor, Convector, Conditor, Promitor, whose functions are connected respectively with the ploughing of the fallow, second ploughing, running the furrows, sowing, ploughing under, harrowing, hoeing, weeding, reaping, carting home, storing in the granary, bringing out for use. It is to be observed that the list includes none of the greater deities of agriculture—Tellus, the fruitful soil, Saturnus, the god of the seeding, Consus, of the storing; the functions of the last two are performed by Insitor and Conditor.

Varro collected and classified the names of many such functional deities, whose business he seems frequently to have assigned to them by etymological guesses. The Church Fathers, who found in this aspect of the Roman religion an easy mark for ridicule, have preserved his lists of the *di nuptiales*, and of those which have to do with man from his conception in the womb to his death in decrepit old age. Thus, Levana lifted up the infant at his birth, Cunina took charge of him in the cradle, Edula and Potina taught him to eat and drink, Statilinus to stand, Abeona and Adeona accompanied him going and coming, Domiduca saw him safely home, and so on.[1] Each human being had, further, a personal tutelary deity; a man his Genius, a woman her Juno. This companion and guardian is so peculiarly his own that a man's genius is often spoken of as if it were a kind of a substantivised personality; it is, however, not his soul, though it is as intimately and inseparably linked to him as his soul. It goes with him through life and departs from life with him at the end: Horace calls the genius, "natale comes qui temperat astrum, naturæ deus humanæ mortalis, in unum quodque caput voltu mutabilis, albus et ater." Yet it is so identified with the individual that in funerary inscriptions it is sometimes joined in the dedication with the Di Manes. Of other aspects and developments of the notion of the genius we shall have to speak in a later connection. Here it concerns us as an instance of the subdivision and specialisation of divine functions.

The Roman historians treat religion as an institution of the state. The gods, of course, were in existence before Rome was founded, but they were not the gods of the Roman people until the state had formally made them such, determining what gods should be worshipped, and where and when, and with what rites. This religious constitution of the state they ascribed to Numa, the second king. What was *fas* had a divine sanction independent of the state, but the *jus sacrum* was only a branch of the *jus publicum* of the state, and Cicero, for example, puts *jus divinum* on the same footing with *jus humanum*—both were established by the early communities of men. The legal bent of the Roman mind shows

[1] It may reasonably be questioned whether the Indigitamenta represent a primitive feature of the Roman religion. They make the impression of priestly elaboration and systematisation.

itself in the conception of the relation between the people and its gods—in one word, its religion—as a contractual relation: the Roman people, through its proper representatives, has undertaken to worship these gods, to celebrate certain festivals, to maintain certain priesthoods, to offer certain sacrifices, and so on. And the gods, on their part, in accepting this homage undertake to do for the people the various things which belong to them in their several spheres to do. This conception is evidently a transference to the first establishment of the religion of the form in which new gods and new cults were introduced in historical times and of the legal notions which attach to the obligations of a vow.

In the time of the monarchy the king himself was the head of the state religion. No doubt in early times on solemn occasions he exercised in person priestly functions for the whole people, and he appointed the priests on whom the ordinary service of the gods devolved. Upon the abolition of the kingdom, those rites in which the king had personally officiated were assumed by the priest of Janus, with the title Rex Sacrorum, and to him was accorded the precedence over all others, though in importance he was overshadowed by the pontifices. His wife, the Regina Sacrorum, similarly succeeded to the religious functions of the queen. The establishment of the republic led to a complete separation of the civil and religious authority which had been united in the person of the king; to the former the elected magistrates succeeded, to the latter the college of the pontifices, upon which, accordingly, the responsible oversight over the religion of the state fell. The pontifical college, consisting originally of three members (successively enlarged by law to eight, nine, fifteen), presided over by the Pontifex Maximus, filled its own vacancies; and in the same way the other collegia, such as the augurs, were self-perpetuating corporations. The Pontifex Maximus chose—or as the term was, "laid hold of"—the flamines of the three highest gods (Juppiter, Mars, Quirinus), and presumably the other flamines; also the priestesses of Vesta and the Rex Sacrorum, taking them, at east in mid-republican times, from a list of nominees presented to him.

The flamines were the priests of particular gods on whom the actual conduct of the cultus was incumbent. The old Roman worship was without pomp or extravagance, preserving in these respects the simplicity of its origin; but in the performance of the rites the utmost ceremoniousness prevailed, the smallest departure from the traditional form in word or gesture invalidated the whole. This is, indeed, the underlying idea of religion, and probably the primitive meaning of the word (*relegere* the opposite of *neglegere*).

Offerings, whether private or public, were commonly a gift or tribute to the gods, and were made of the every-day products of a primitive agriculture—dry spelt-grits (pounded, not ground) with salt, or spelt-mush, beans, various kinds of bread and cakes, honey, fruits, milk, and cheese—and of the domestic animals, swine, sheep, neat cattle. In the public cults the sacrifices were on a larger scale; cattle and sheep were preferred to the cheap and common pig, and the tendency of the cereal oblations was to become accessories merely.

Of a different kind were the sacrifices of pregnant cows to Tellus on the Fordicidia (April 15) in the several curiæ and by the pontifices on the Capitol, primarily a magical rite to promote the fertility of the seeded soil and of the impregnated flocks and herds. The fœtus, torn from the victim's womb, was burned by the chief vestal, and the ashes, along with the blood of the October horse, were distributed to shepherds at the Parilia for the expiation and disinfection of their flocks. At the Robigalia (April 25) a dog was offered by the Flamen Quirinalis in a sacred grove five miles from the city to avert the danger to the grain crops from rust, and a red dog was offered for the same end on a day annually fixed by the pontifices (*augurium canarium*); here also the magical origin is plain. Dogs were also favourite piacular victims, as in the Lupercalia (February 15). The sacrifice of the October horse by the Flamen Martialis (October 15), after the campaign season was over, was probably a piacular purification from bloodshed before the conception of a thank offering to the war-god arose. Part of the victim's blood was allowed to run upon the hearth of the Regia, part was preserved in the House of Vesta, and used, as we have seen, in the following spring for the disinfection of the folds and flocks. These instances must suffice to illustrate the numerous survivals in the Roman cult of primitive magic and piacula. Of expiations which demanded the death of a human being there is in the old Roman religion no evidence.

Most of the ancient festivals which had a fixed place in the calendar and some of the *feriæ conceptivæ* which were specially appointed by the pontifices are associated with the two chief occupations, husbandry and war. Sacrifices and lustrations are the central features of the festivals, but with these are connected many other observances—ritual dances such as those of the Salii; the circuit of the Palatine by the Luperci, girt with a goatskin, and the februation of women; processions of priests, magistrates, and people at the Ambarvalia and the Robigalia; races of mules at the Consualia and of horses at the festivals of Mars (Equirria); the New-Year's licence of the feast of Anna Perenna on March 15. Many of the festivals brought together the people of particular neighbourhoods and localities, or the members of political groups like the curiæ, and these naturally had a more popular character than the public ceremonies under the conduct of the priests.

By the side of the pontifical college stood the college of augurs (also originally of three members), the official diviners of the state. They either invited a sign from the gods, as for the inauguration of a priest, or interpreted according to their art the signs which the deity offered unsought. These signs were either celestial phenomena, such as lightning in a certain quarter of the heaven, or the appearance and flight of birds, the way in which domestic fowls ate their corn (a form of divination practised especially in military expeditions), the behaviour of four-footed animals, and portentous occurrences (*dira*).

No important act of public or private life was undertaken without first obtaining the assurance that the act, time, place, and circumstance had the approval of the gods; in particular, the magistrates had to obtain this assurance for all acts on which the public welfare depended; for example, the holding of comitia, the sending out of military expeditions, the crossing of a river by an army, the beginning of an engagement. *Auspicia publica* could be taken only by a magistrate, whose authority is therefore summed up in the attribution to him of *auspicium imperiumque*, and by him only in matters which lay within his legal competence.   Private auspices early fell into disuse; traces of them survive chiefly in connection with weddings.   The taking of the auspices by the magistrates and the interpretation of them were subject to the complicated rules of the art as expounded by the augurs; and this primitive Roman divination must be distinguished from the Disciplina Etrusca, practised by the haruspices, as well as from the consultation of the Sibylline Books, the foreign origin of which was always recognised.

The primitive Roman conception of the gods as the powers operative in certain spheres of nature and life, as it gave rise to no mythology, so had no tendency to represent them in human form.   According to Varro, images of the gods were unknown in the first one hundred and seventy years of the city's existence—that is, down to the establishment of the Capitoline sanctuary with its divine triad.   Nor was any material seat or symbol necessary to realise the presence of deities who were so inseparably connected with localities and activities that they may be said to be embodied in them. For the same reason there were no divine dwellings (temples); the House of Vesta is not really an exception, for it was only a shelter for the ever-burning fire on the hearth of the state. There were, of course, spots particularly associated with certain gods or cults—the wolf's den of Lupercus, a pit (*mundus*) into which the first-fruits were thrown, sacred groves, altars, fanes.   Such spots were holy places, consecrated from public ground.   Some of the gods had several holy places; others seem not to have had any in their own right, but to have shared with their more fortunate fellows.

In the religion of the household the central place in the earliest times was held by Vesta, the fire on the domestic hearth, who corresponds in name and fact to the Greek Hestia. The care of the fire, including the daily cleansing of the hearth, which was the essential part of the cult, was naturally incumbent on the mistress of the house. Vesta presided over the preparation of food and also over the grinding of flour; the Vestalia on the 9th of June was a special holiday of millers and bakers. The disposition to regard the city as a larger household which made Janus, the guardian of the house door, one of the great gods of the state, created a Vesta Publica Populi Romani, and made the perpetual fire on her hearth as prominent in the public religion as in the life of the family. The place of the mistress of the house was filled by six Vestal Virgins under the supervision of the Pontifex Maximus, who were charged also with the preparation of the *mola salsa* and *muries* (salted meal and brine) for the worship of the other gods. The storeroom of the house (*penus*) and its contents were under the protection of the storeroom gods, the Di Penates, who extend their functions to the whole domestic economy; Vesta is sometimes counted among them. As there is a Vesta of the Roman people, so also there are Di Penates Publici, who preside over its economic welfare. They are, in fact, the gods of the state religion considered in this capacity; the oath of office in republican times ran merely, "By Juppiter and the Di Penates." In later times the domestic Penates were chosen at the will of the householder from among the greater gods;[1] but primitively there was no such identification.

To the domestic religion belongs also the cult of the Lares. Originally a guardian of the fields, worshipped at the crossroads or the corners where estates joined, the Lar watched over the house of the owner of the field and over the entire household, and in the city the Lar Familiaris took his place

[1] More exactly, he gave the names of these gods to his Penates.

beside the Penates, and received offerings—ordinarily blood-less—on the Calends, Nones, and Ides of every month, and on all recurring and occasional family festivals. Finally, the Genius of the Pater Familias was worshipped by all the family, together with the Lar and the Penates.

The old Roman calendar sets apart several days in the year for rites directed to deities of the nether world or concerned with the souls or ghosts of the dead: the Larentalia in December, the Feralia in February, the Lemuria in May, the Carnaria on June 1.   To the infernal deities belong Vediovis, Larenta, Carna, and others.   More commonly the powers of death and the underworld are subsumed under the vague euphemistic name, Di Manes, "the kindly deities."   Especially for the dead forefathers the *dies parentales* (February 13–21) were kept, during which the temples were closed, marriages might not be celebrated, the tombs were repaired and adorned, and food offered to the departed.   The spirits of the ancestors, the Di Parentum, were believed to watch over the house and to avenge infractions of the ordinances of the family.   The Romans had no vivid imagination of the state after death, and no notion of a retribution beyond; but they had their share of the world-wide belief in ghosts, spectres, and bogeys, and tried to dissuade or prevent their visitations, partly by offerings, partly by aversive rites, as when in the Lemuria the householder threw out nine black beans at midnight.   Beans are, indeed, so closely associated with death and the underworld that the Flamen Dialis was forbidden to touch or even name them.

The old Roman religion, such as it has been outlined above, was organised and regulated at a very early time, and, established as one of the fundamental institutions of the state, it was perpetuated with no essential change through the whole age of the republic.   It is the religion of a little city-state, whose territories stretched but a few miles beyond its gates, a community subsisting chiefly on agriculture, with domestic industries and no extensive commerce, almost yearly engaged in war with neighbours on the same plane of civilisation and—with the sole exception of the Etruscans—of the same or kindred race. But even this little Rome had grown up by the union and fusion of smaller communities, and numerous cults and festivals in different ways show plainly that they belonged to particular settlements or clans before they were taken up into the common religion of the Roman people. The Roman historians and antiquarians may have gone beyond the evidence in distributing particular gods and cults to the several tribes or to allied and subjected towns, but they were right in recognising the composite character of the religion.

The elements thus fused were, however, of the same sort; the same conceptions of the nature of the deities and of what to do for them appear in them all. Even after the calendar was fixed, and the canon of native gods closed for all time, similar divinities and worships were introduced from other Italic centres—Diana, for instance, and Venus. But the Romans were early brought into contact with alien races and civilisations. Latium bordered on the north on Etruscan territory, and about 600 B. C. the Tarquins became the rulers of Rome. The origin and affinities of the Etruscans are unsolved problems; but long before the southward expansion of their power (which eventually extended as far as Campania) they had been in close commercial relations with the Greeks in southern Italy, and in alliance as well in active trade with Carthage, and their civilisation had been greatly affected by foreign, especially by Greek, influences. Not only native Etruscan gods and cults arrived in this way in Rome, but Tuscanised Greek religions.

In the first years of the republic a strong current of Greek influence direct from southern Italy set in; and again in the latter part of the third century B. C. the Hellenising of religion as well as of the whole Roman civilisation received a fresh impetus, and was carried so far that the native religion fell into decadence. The expansion of Roman dominion in Italy led to the adoption of the gods of allied and of subjected peoples; conquests in foreign lands brought in, especially

under the empire, all manner of Oriental divinities, under
their own names or masquerading in Greek and Roman
characters, and Oriental mysteries with their diverse methods of salvation, until Rome became the Pantheon of the
world.   But, in distinction from the native old Roman gods
(Di Indigetes) all these were classed as newcomers (Noven-
sides).

The history of Roman religion is thus chiefly the history
of the introduction and more or less complete naturalisation
of foreign religions.   The first significant step in this course
was the establishment of the triad, Juppiter, Juno, and Minerva (in the character of defender of the city, which she
borrowed from Athena), upon the Capitol by the Tarquin
kings, pushing into the background the older triad, Juppiter,
Mars, Quirinus.   Another sanctuary of Minerva, on the
Aventine, dating from the same period, shows her in the
character of the deity of artisans and handicrafts.[1]   The temple of Diana, also on the Aventine, is the reflection in religion
of the succession of Rome to Aricia as the centre of the Latin
League, of which the establishment of the worship of the
Alban Juppiter Latiaris and the adoption of the Feriæ Latinæ
is another consequence.   To the time of the kings tradition
ascribes also the acquisition from Cumæ of the Sibylline
Books and the appointment of custodians and interpreters
of these oracles (originally two, subsequently ten and fifteen), the building of the circus, the introduction of the
ceremonial of the triumph, and of the Ludi Romani.

When a city was conquered and its political existence terminated by incorporation in the Roman domain, or if it was
destroyed, it became incumbent on the conquerors to assume
all the obligations of the community to the gods; they became
gods of the Roman people, and their cultus was either perpetuated on the old spot—but now in the name of the Roman
people and under the direction of the pontifices—or a sanctuary was founded in Rome and the worship conducted by the
Roman priesthood.   Natives of other cities who settled in

[1] This character also belongs to Athena; see above, p. 421.

Rome for trade or other reasons were free to maintain the worship of their own gods; and it frequently happened that in time these gods were formally enrolled by the magistrates, with the advice and consent of the Senate, among the gods of the Roman people, which in this manner assumed legal obligations to them.

The gods thus imported into the state were not all treated in the same way. The Greek deities from southern Italy and Sicily were felt to be foreign in a very different degree from those of the Italic neighbours; they were worshipped with rites wholly unlike the old Roman cults. Consequently, while the Italian cults were under the direction of the pontifices, the Greek rites were all put under the keepers of the Sibylline Books, the Duoviri (later, Decemviri, Quindecemviri) Sacris Faciundis; they were ministered to, not by Roman citizens, but by foreign priests, and their temples were all outside the precincts of the sacred city, the pomœrium.

Apollo was the first of the greater Greek gods to be thus received, probably at the same time with the Sibylline oracles, and like them he came from Cumæ. It was particularly in his quality of god of healing that he was first worshipped in Rome (Apollo Medicus), and his temple, in the neighbourhood of the Circus Flaminius, was erected in 431 B. C. in fulfilment of a vow made two years before in time of plague. Other Greek deities were introduced at the instance of the Sibylline oracles. Thus, soon after the expulsion of the kings, the crops failed badly and the import of grain was unsatisfactory. The oracle bade propitiate Demeter, Dionysos, and Korē. A temple was accordingly vowed, which was consecrated to them in 493 B. C. under the Latinised names, Ceres, Liber, Libera. About the same time, perhaps, indeed upon the same occasion, a temple was erected to Hermes, the god of merchants, under the name Mercurius, and in connection with it a kind of corn exchange and a merchants' guild appeared. In similar emergencies in the following centuries the help and protection of other Greek gods were sought: thus, a pestilence in 293 B. C. was the occasion of sending for Æsculapius, the divine physician, from Epidaurus, and the founding of his temple on the island in the Tiber.

Temples were erected in this period, not only for the Greek deities, who had long dwelt in houses made with hands, but for the old Roman gods; and by degrees the latter also came to be represented by images after Greek types and doubtless the work of foreign artists. The Greek forms of worship made a much stronger appeal to the senses than the old Roman rites, and reckoned more upon the presence and participation of the people. The "supplications," whether to avert calamities, or to secure the success of an enterprise such as a campaign, or as thanksgivings after a deliverance or a victory, in which multitudes moved in procession from temple to temple through all the city; the choruses of maidens, or, as in the Secular Festival, of well-born youths and maidens; the games, which, as they multiplied, tended more and more to become mere spectacles for the assembled throngs, were singularly unlike the old-fashioned Roman cults.

Equally foreign were the *lectisternia* in the temples, where, before puppet images of the gods reclining on cushions, tables were spread with food, or, on occasion, companies of gods and goddesses brought together in some public place around the festal board. The first instance of the latter was in 339 B. C., when, in a time of pestilence, an eight-day feast of this kind was given to Apollo and Latona, Hercules and Diana, Mercury and Neptune. In 217 B. C. was held a great *lectisternium* of the twelve gods, Juppiter and Juno, Neptune and Minerva, Mars and Venus, Apollo and Diana, Vulcan and Vesta, Mercury and Ceres. Here Greek and Latin gods mingle indiscriminately, but the circle of twelve gods and the grouping in pairs is purely Greek. It was but one step farther when the gilded statues of the twelve gods were set up in the Forum after the pattern of the Agora in Athens. Thus the old worship was by degrees put completely into the shadow by the more popular, æsthetic, and emotional ritual.

There was a darker side to these foreign improvements in

religion: it was the Sibylline oracles which prescribed the burying alive of a pair of Greeks—man and woman—and a pair of Gauls, as a peculiarly efficacious piaculum in time of great public apprehension; three cases are recorded in which this was done (226, 216, and 114 B. C.). The twenty-seven puppets of rushes annually thrown into the Tiber from the old pile bridge are called Argei, that is, in the oracular cant, Greeks, and are perhaps substitutes for an expiation by human lives; but the matter is obscure.

The Greek gods who came in under their own names were few compared with those who were rebaptised with the names of Latin deities to whom they had some resemblance in attributes or functions. They brought along their own cults and myths—nothing was Latin about them but their appellations. Venus, an old Italian goddess of gardens—especially, it seems, of kitchen and market gardens—had to lend her name, perhaps by association of blooming beauty, to Aphrodite, when from her Sicilian seat in Eryx the cult of that divinity reached Rome. Her first temple was erected on the Capitol in 215 B. C. at the direction of the Sibylline oracles, and others followed. Ceres and Libera, as we have seen, were understood to be Latin for Demeter and Korē; Poseidon figured as Neptunus; Pluto and Persephone as Dis pater and Proserpina, and so on through the catalogue.

Nor was it enough for Roman religion to annex the whole Greek pantheon. In 205 B. C., in the crisis of the war with Hannibal, the custodians of the oracles found it in their books that the sacred stone of the Mother of the Gods (Mater Deum Magna Idæa), the goddess of Pessinus in Phrygia, must be fetched to Rome. A ship was accordingly despatched to Pergamon, whither Attalos had transported the stone, and it reached Rome in 204 B. C., where it was received with exuberant rejoicings. The great temple on the Palatine was dedicated in 191 B. C. Games were held in honour of the goddess, in connection with which, in 194 B. C., the first stage plays were exhibited. The Ludi Megalenses took their place among the annual festivals, beginning on

April 4, on which day the Prætor Urbanus offered sacrifice at the temple. The cult of the Great Mother was conducted by Phrygian priests; and down to the end of the republic it was against the law for a Roman citizen to enter this priesthood. The outlandish garb of the trousered and bonneted priests, the emasculated Galli in woman's dress, the frenzied enthusiasm, gave the Romans their first experience of the religions of the East, and fascinated while it repelled. The Phrygian goddess was the forerunner of a long procession of Oriental deities which streamed toward Rome; but she was the last to get an invitation from the Sibylline Books.

Most of the foreign gods who were brought in by authority were summoned in time of distress, when plague or famine or disastrous war or dire prodigies seemed to demand new and potent expiations; they did not come to supplant the old Roman gods, but their rites were resorted to to rid the state of some strange evil, or, like Mercurius, to preside over interests which had no patron in the old religion.

The principle of specialisation which is characteristic of the Roman religion continued to produce new deities or differentiate old ones. After the Aphrodite of Eryx had come in as Venus Erycina, and the prodigious debauching of three vestals had led to the introduction of Aphrodite Apostrophia as Venus Verticordia (114 B. C.), we find a Venus Felix with the attributes of Fortuna, a Venus Victrix, and Venus Genetrix, to whom the Julian Cæsars traced their lineage through Æneas. Each of these had her own temple, priesthood, and festivals, and was, in spite of the common name, to all intents and purposes a distinct goddess. A glance at a list of the titles of Juppiter will show how many different local and functional deities are comprehended under the one appellation—Juppiter Feretrius, Fulgur, Stator, Victor, Optimus Maximus, are but a few of the multitude.

This is less distinctive, however, than the continual enrichment of the pantheon with deities who bear the names of qualities or conditions, such as Concordia, Spes (Bona Spes), Pietas, all of which were worshipped in the prime of the republic. Such cases are often conceived by modern authors as the deification of abstractions, and thought, therefore, to imply a somewhat advanced stage of religious development. It is only the modern, however, who conceives them as abstract: the power which works harmony among citizens is for the antique apprehension no more abstract than the power that works the germination of grain in the earth. Another group of similar deities seem to be split off from the great gods in specific characters; thus Felicitas comes to stand independently by the side of Juppiter Felix, or Victoria by Juppiter Victor; so also, perhaps, Salus, Fides, Libertas. Another group, in later times, are the virtues of princes, beginning with Clementia Cæsaris (44 B. C.); under the empire this hypostasis of imperial qualities—actual or desiderated—reached great proportions under the impulsion of the emperor worship.

Mention has already been made of the college of augurs who invited, observed, and interpreted signs in heaven and on earth by which the gods indicated their consent or disapproval of public acts in peace or war, and of the Sibylline Books with their official exegetes. A third method of divination was borrowed from the Etruscans, among whom the art had been highly developed. The practitioners of this method, the haruspices, were, until after the fall of the republic, Etruscans, and were summoned to Rome by the Senate when occasion demanded. In earlier centuries little is heard of them, but in the time of the second Punic war they become more prominent; in the second century B. C. they were officially consulted about public prodigies almost as frequently as the Sibylline oracles, and in the first century twice as often. Generals had haruspices on their staff to divine for them concerning the plan and issue of campaigns. They were often resorted to also in private affairs, and seem to have been in especial favour with the aristocracy.

The Disciplina Etrusca was embodied in numerous books dealing with different branches of the art. The haruspices interpreted omens and portents of many kinds; they were the recognised experts in all the freaks of lightning, the science of which was contained in their Libri Fulgurales. Other books treated of the rites to be observed in laying out a city, the definition of its bounds by a pomœrium, the location and dedication of temples, and the like.

The art for which the haruspices were peculiarly famous, however, and from which their name is perhaps derived, was the consultation of the liver of victims. The Romans inspected the entrails of sacrifices to see whether they were normal or not, from which they inferred the assent or dissent of the god to whom the question was directed; but the Etruscans mapped out the liver into regions, and from the size, shape, and markings of the several parts read off specific signs from different gods. Of peculiar significance was the configuration of the *caput jocineris* (called by modern anatomists *processus pyramidalis* or *caudatus*), which is extremely variable; a large *caput* was a good omen; a small, deformed, or missing one spelled disaster; a cleft one, dissension, civil war, and so on. A bronze model of a sheep's liver, laid out as a divining chart and bearing in its numerous fields legends in Etruscan, has been preserved.

Among the Greeks, also, divination by the liver was much employed and the same prominence is given to the *processus pyramidalis* (λοβός).[1] It has been proved beyond question that this pseudoscience is of Babylonian origin; model livers in clay have been found, laid out in regions, and with the *processus pyramidalis* schematised in the same fashion as the bronze liver of Piacenza, and many omen texts interpret the indications given by abnormalities in the various parts of the organ and in the gall-bladder.[2] When and by what route the art reached Italy is unknown.

The influx of Greek gods and the progressive Hellenisation of the Roman religion in the last two centuries of the republic was only part of the triumphant march of Greek culture, which was accelerated by the annexation of Macedonia and the conquest of Corinth (146 B. C.), virtually bringing all

[1] The oldest instances are in Æschylus.   [2] See above, p. 227.

Greece under Roman dominion. Roman literature began with translations and imitations of Greek authors; art and science were not only Greek, but remained for the most part in Greek hands. Education meant the study of the Greek language and literature; increasing numbers of youth of the upper classes completed their education by travel in Greece and study in Greek schools.

The first professors of philosophy and rhetoric who exhibited their wares in Rome were shown the door by decree of the senate (173 B. C.?). A few years after, the censors issued a characteristic edict against the new education: "It has been reported to us that there are men calling themselves Latin rhetoricians, who have introduced a new kind of education, and that young men go to school to them and sit there whole days through. Our forefathers ordained what they wished their children to learn and what schools they wished them to go to. This new business, at variance with the use and custom of our ancestors, we do not approve nor think right. Wherefore we have decided to apprise both those who keep these schools and those who frequent them that we disapprove them." M. Porcius Cato took it for the mission of his life to stem the incoming tide of Greek culture with all its denationalising consequences. But such efforts were like keeping out the sea with a broom.

To those who were ambitious of this new culture, the religion of their fathers, like the old Roman virtues and ideals, seemed irretrievably antiquated and out of mode. In more thoughtful minds acquaintance with Greek philosophy raised questions which went to the root, not of one form of religion, but of all. The poet Ennius (died 169 B. C.) in his Epicharmus reduced the gods to the elements, and he did into Latin the rationalistic Euhemerus who made them dead men. A century later Lucretius (died 55 B. C.), in his De Natura Rerum, set forth the mechanical materialism of Epicurus as a gospel of deliverance from the fear of death and hell. In the last century of the republic Epicureanism was a fashionable philosophy, numbering among its adherents some serious thinkers and many who found its teachings agreeable to their inclinations; after the time of Augustus it sank into insignificance.

The Roman temperament had much greater affinity to Stoicism, especially on its ethical side; and from the days of the younger Scipio many of the noblest spirits were addicted to it. The system of Panætius, however, the first Stoic teacher of note at Rome, was on some points more sceptical than those of his predecessors; he denied the soul even the temporary immortality which the school generally had allowed it (till the next burning up of the world), and doubted or denied the reality of divination, which most of the Stoics treated as a point of orthodoxy. He is also, in all probability, the author of the classification of the gods which his disciple Scævola propounded: There are three classes of gods, those of the poets, those of the philosopher, and those of the statesman. The mythical theology of the poets is full of absurd and degrading fables; the philosophical theology cannot be made the religion of a state, for it is in part beyond the intelligence of the commonalty, in part it would be bad for them—for example, if they should be told that the gods do not look like their images, that in reality god has no age, nor sex, nor limbs. The established religion can, therefore, be nothing but an institution of the state, and its civil theology only a device of wise statesmen, adapted to the needs and capacities of the masses. It is noteworthy that Scævola (died 82 B. C.), who maintained this theory, was himself the official head of the state religion, Pontifex Maximus. The same doctrine is frankly avowed by Varro.

So far as its influence extended, the effect of such teaching was to undermine religion both as belief and observance. The Stoic pantheism might be for individual thinkers a satisfactory substitute for religion; but, as its adherents clearly saw, it was nothing for the man in the street, who could hardly recognise more than the name of his god in their "Juppiter omnipotens, rerum regumque repertor, progenitor genetrixque deum, deus unus et idem." Besides, Stoicism declared the whole public cultus, with its images and sacrifices, not only senseless but harmful.

It must be set down on the other side, however, that the ethics of Panætius did good service in a time when a clarifying of moral notions and a fortifying of conscience was much needed; all the more because he addressed himself not to the wise, but to those who were striving after wisdom. Cicero founded on him his own tractate, De Officiis; Ambrose christianised Cicero, and through him the Stoic may be said to have furnished the basis of the first systematisation of Christian ethics.

Posidonius, the most eminent Stoic teacher in the first half of the century before our era, went back to the common doctrine of the school on the principal points in which Panætius departed from it—the periodical universal conflagrations, demons, and divination. On the other hand, he took a more conciliatory attitude than the older Stoics to other schools, and was disposed to find a large element of truth common to them all. His anthropology, in particular, is influenced by Plato and Aristotle, and this in turn affects his ethics—the heart of his philosophy—and his theology. This drawing together of what may be called the positive schools, in opposition to the Epicureans and to the Sceptics, is one of the signs of the times, and accounts in part for the eclectic tendency which appears on all hands.

The Stoic criticism of the popular religion had itself a religious motive: it offered, at least to the educated, in its own theology something better. The Academic scepticism, on the contrary, was directed against all positive theologies, and especially against the Stoics—their proofs of the existence of gods, their conception of the nature of god, their doctrine of providence, their defence of divination and prophecy. But here also the compromises of the time appear, and a man like Cicero, who, if he had to profess an allegiance, called himself an Academic, is rather a sceptical eclectic than a thorough-going disciple of the New Academy. And for all his theoretical scepticism, he finds probable grounds for believing in the existence of God, the unity of the godhead, the supernatural order and governance of the world, divine providence, and the immortality of the soul.

Many, however, who had only a superficial acquaintance with the matter, rested in the belief that philosophy had somehow disproved religion; while, as for philosophy itself, it was a babel of conflicting opinions, and nothing certain. It was not religion only that suffered from this temper: as in the time of the sophists in Greece, the discussion of ethical questions acted as a solvent on customary morality. It was no longer enough to say of a course of conduct that it was *mos majorum*, the Roman way; the ancestors were allowed no presumption—why, indeed, should it be supposed that they were wiser than the young men of the day? What authority have the traditional notions of virtue? Let us have the reason of it! But in the schools there was much controversy over both the ends and the standards of the moral life, and interest always finds it easy to turn the scales of probability.

The denationalising effect of an alien culture and the mental and moral confusion wrought by an imported philosophy were not, however, the chief cause of the decadence of religion in the last century of the republic. For that we must look to the far-reaching economic and political changes which came over the Roman people in that age, disintegrating the social structure and destroying the moral fibre of all classes. Enormous wealth, gained often by extortion and usury, flowed from the provinces to Italy, and was lavished in insensate and corrupting luxury; the small free landholders were ruined by competition with imported grain and with slave labour, their farms were absorbed in vast latifundia, while they themselves thronged into the cities to swell the hungry and turbulent proletariat. The strife of classes and factions or the insatiate ambition of individuals over and over precipitated bloody civil wars, with their train of proscriptions and distributions, which fill chapter after chapter of Roman history from the Gracchi to the last triumvirate; demagogues reduced political corruption to a science. The virtues that had made Rome great—integrity, frugality, justice, loyalty, piety—belonged to an order that had passed away; the Roman home, with its stern but just paternal discipline, the dignity of the mother, the fidelity of the wife, were part of that bygone order.   Divorce was of every-day occurrence in high society, and was thought no shame; young libertines such as the associates of Catiline made open mock of virtue and honour.

"Italy," it has been said by a recent historian, "was living through the fever of moral disintegration and incoherence which assails all civilised societies that are rich in the manifold resources of culture and enjoyment, but tolerate few restraints on the feverish struggle of contending appetites." Religion was unable to stay this demoralisation, and itself fell more and more into decay.   The cults of the Greek rite suffered less, at least outwardly, from this decay than the old national religion, for they not only possessed greater popular attractions in their showy festivals, but were in the hands of a professional temple priesthood who had a direct interest in the maintenance of worship.   The old Roman gods, on the other hand, were not merely neglected, but in many instances forgotten; their priesthoods died out, and with them all knowledge of their functions and rites.   Varro could only catalogue them as *Di incerti*—gods about whom he could learn nothing definite.   The priestly colleges, the Pontifices and the Augures, were increased in the first century B. C. to fifteen members each, and vacancies were filled, not as before by the members of the college itself, but by a form of popular election from a list made up by the members of the college.   The offices were thus drawn into the turbulent currents of politics, and doubtless men were often chosen who knew little about their duties and cared less.   Under such circumstances, the traditional knowledge of the vast and complex body of ancient ritual and of the augural science which it was the business of these corporations to preserve and apply rapidly declined, and it shortly came to pass that the most diligent students of antiquity found no one who could answer their questions. The pontifices, who had to keep the calendar in order, were so incompetent or so negligent that the agricultural festivals no longer fell in the proper seasons, and it was not until Cæsar's reform that the year was put to rights again.

The ancient offices of the Rex Sacrorum and the great flamines, which were restricted to the dwindling patrician families, were hedged about with so many prescriptions and restrictions that it became difficult or impossible to find any one willing to fill them, in spite of the many honours and privileges that attached to the position. The Rex Sacrorum could hold no political office; the Flamen Dialis, none outside the city. The latter had to wear at all times his priestly vestments, and might never go bareheaded; a table of oblations had to be always spread at the foot of his bed; he must have a wife to whom he was married in the ancient form of *confarreatio*, and whom he might not divorce; if she died, he had to lay down his office; he might not utter an oath, see armed men or mount a horse, leave the city for a single night (in late times, not over three nights), come in contact with a dead body or approach a grave, touch or even name things associated with death and the nether world (goats, dogs, beans, ivy), touch uncooked meat or leavened bread; he might neither wear nor look upon anything that resembled bonds—even his finger-ring must not be completely closed; he must not pass under a vine with long *propagines;* he could be shaved only with a bronze razor, his barber must be a free man, the trimmings of his beard must be buried at the foot of an *arbor felix*, and many more rules of a similar kind, for an infraction of which he was deposed. These restrictions were so vexatious that after 87 B. C. the post remained vacant for three-quarters of a century, until in 11 B. C. Augustus succeeded in filling it again.

The priestly associations, also, in whose hands certain particular ceremonies lay, like the Fratres Arvales and the Sodales Titii, died out, and when Augustus revived them the interrupted tradition could only be in part picked up again. A more conspicuous witness to the general indifference to religion were the many ruinous temples and abandoned holy places. The one religious observance that showed no signs of waning interest was the games. The old Roman *feriæ* were, indeed, put quite into the background by the new-fashioned games given under the direction and at the charges of the magistrates. Beginning with the Ludi Romani (probably in 366 B. C.) and the Ludi Plebeii (216 B. C.), these games multiplied as time went on, and were celebrated with increasing splendour, while their association with religion became looser and looser; the throngs who filled the circus were there to enjoy a great spectacle whose connection with religion was as external and nominal as that of a bull-fight on a saint's day. The ancient household religion was also much neglected—in part consequence, in part cause, of the relaxation of the family tie.

CHAPTER XXII

THE ROMANS

RELIGION UNDER THE EMPIRE

The Reforms of Augustus—Innovations—Deification of Deceased Emperors—Worship of the Living Emperor—Foreign Deities—Syrian Gods—Cybele and Attis—The Mysteries—Taurobolium—Worship and Mysteries of Isis—Initiations—Mysteries of Mithras —The Spelæa—Degrees—Origin of the Religion—The Mithraic Myth—Christianity—Suppression of the Old Religions.

It would be a mistake to infer from the signs of decadence which are so conspicuous in the last century of the republic that religion itself had lost all hold on the hearts and lives of men. It must be remembered that the sources from which our knowledge of religious and moral conditions in that century is drawn disclose to us chiefly the state of things in the capital and among the classes upon which the demoralising influences described above worked with the greatest energy. That the Roman character was not irremediably corrupted, and that the vitality of religion was not wholly exhausted is, indeed, convincingly proved by the history of the following centuries.

Julius Cæsar, who had been a member of the pontifical college since 74 B. C. and became Pontifex Maximus in 63, made some reforms in the state religion, and planned others. Augustus showed his interest in the revival of forms long since fallen into desuetude by declaring war against Cleopatra in 32 B. C. with the ancient priestly rites of the *fetiales* —the first time they had been used, it is said, in a century. When the victory over Antonius at Actium made him master in the state he turned his hand to the filling of priesthoods and the restoration of priestly guilds that had become extinct, such as the Sodales Titii and the Arval Brotherhood. Already for years a member of all three of the great colleges (Pontifices, Augures, Quindecemviri Sacris Faciundis), he had himself enrolled in the revived sodalities, and the leading men of the time were prompt to follow his example. His expressed wish overcame the reluctance of the great families to dedicate their daughters to the service of Vesta, and at last (in 11 B. C.) the long-vacant place of Flamen Dialis was filled again. Beginning in the year 28 B. C., eighty-two temples in the city of Rome were restored, while others had to be completely rebuilt—a striking testimony to the neglect of the last generations.

All these measures had for their end the revival and reform of religion as it was before the century of its decline. But along with this Augustus made innovations which mark an era in the history of Roman religion. The Julian gens regarded Apollo as their peculiar patron and protector; Augustus raised him to the place of the tutelary deity of the monarchy and thus of the state. As a monument of his gratitude for his victories over Sextus Pompeius and Marcus Antonius, he erected for Apollo a new and splendid temple on the Palatine. This edifice stood on ground belonging not to the state but to the dedicator (*in solo privato*), and was, therefore, according to the ancient doctrine of the sacred law, not a public temple; but no such antiquated distinction could prevent the imperial temple from taking rank with the temples of the state, and if the Palatine Apollo with Diana by his side yielded precedence for the sake of history to the Capitoline Juppiter and his companions, Juno and Minerva, his actual importance was second to none. Indeed, the new ritual for the celebration of the Ludi Sæculares in 17 B. C. seems expressly designed to put the Palatine pair upon an equality with the Capitoline triad, while the poets of the time exalt Apollo with their highest praises.

An even bolder innovation was ventured when, after Augustus became Pontifex Maximus (12 B. C.), he consecrated a new temple of Vesta on the Palatine adjoining his palace, thus, as it were, appropriating for the imperial house the sacred hearthfire of the Roman people. In the new Forum Cæsaris a temple was erected to Venus Genetrix as the origin of the Julian house; in the middle of the Forum of Augustus stood a temple of Mars Ultor (dedicated in 2 B. C.). The statutes of this temple ordained that in it members of the imperial family should offer sacrifice upon assuming the *toga virilis;* from it magistrates should set out to the provinces; here the senate should sit when voting to make war or decreeing a triumph; here, after the celebration of a triumph, the *triumphator* should lay down the insignia; here captured standards should be deposited; and here the censors should drive their nail at the expiration of each *lustrum* (five years). In transferring these ceremonies from the temple of the Capitoline Juppiter to this new centre, Augustus pursued his consistent policy of dissociating public acts from the localities with which they had been connected in republican times and attaching them to places which had no memories, and no associations save with the new order of things. The temple of Mars Ultor stood in fact, like that of Apollo on the Palatine, on private ground; it was a foundation not of the Roman people but of the prince personally; and the god thus honoured was, significantly enough, the Avenger of the murder of Julius Cæsar. Venus, as the ancestress of the Julian gens, had a place in this temple also.

Finally, when in 7 B. C. Augustus redivided the city into regions and wards, he prescribed that in every shrine of the Lares Compitales—the patron saints of the parish, one might say—the Genius Augusti should have a place between the two Lares. The reforms of Augustus were thus not merely an antiquarian restoration of the old Roman religion or a revival of the Greek rite, but inaugurated a new epoch; in them was laid the foundation of the religion of the empire.

The most salient feature of this religion as it subsequently developed is the worship of the deified emperors. The first step in this path was taken in 42 B. C., when by formal act of the senate and the people Julius Cæsar was enrolled among the gods. In 29 B. C. a temple was dedicated to him in the Forum; he had a flamen (sacrificial priest) of his own, and a festival (on his birthday) among the public holidays. The example thus set was followed in the case of Augustus (died 14 A. D.); but it was not till the end of the century that the consecration of the deceased emperors became a matter of course. Before Nerva, only Augustus, Claudius, Vespasian, and Titus had been thus honoured.

The senate exercised its right to make gods not only in favour of rulers but of other members of the imperial family, including Livia, the wife of Augustus; Drusilla, sister of Caligula; Nero's daughter Claudia and his wife Poppæa; Titus's daughter Julia; Trajan's father, sister, and wife; Hadrian's wife and mother-in-law; and the wives of Antoninus Pius and Marcus Aurelius. This practice later fell into disuse, but from Nerva on almost every emperor became a god, and the *consecratio*, which at first had followed some time after the ruler's death, was a regular part of the funeral ceremonies.

The Divi Imperatores were not mere titular and complimentary gods. Each of them down to Marcus Aurelius received his own temple and priesthood; and the place they took in the state religion is shown by the form of the oath of office. In republican times magistrates had sworn by Juppiter Optimus Maximus and the Penates; in Domitian's reign the formula ran: "Per Iovem et divom Augustum et divom Claudium et divom Vespasianum Augustum et divom Titum Augustum et genium imperatoris Cæsaris Domitiani Augusti Deosque Penates." The deified empresses had their own priests (or priestesses), and their birthdays were calendar festivals, but they were worshipped in the temples dedicated to their consorts—Livia with Augustus, Plotina with Hadrian, Faustina with Antoninus Pius.

In this way a new class of gods was introduced into the public religion, for whom the name Divi, hitherto equivalent to Dei, was appropriated. They were introduced as a class even into ancient liturgies like that of the Arval Brotherhood which otherwise recognised only the old Roman gods, and in their piacular rites the Arvals offered victims to each of the deified emperors with an invocation by name (inscriptions speak of sixteen or twenty). New sodalities were established for the cult of the Divi, beginning with the Sodales Augustales, who, after the consecration of Claudius, assumed his worship also and the name Augustales Claudiales. A second sodality was formed for Vespasian (Flaviales), which in like manner added the cult of Titus (Flaviales Titiales); the Hadrianales perhaps included Trajan. Each of these, it will be observed, is devoted to the Divi of one family, or at least of closely connected lines. The last of the imperial sodalities, the Antoniniani, however, added to the worship of Antoninus Pius, for which it was originally constituted, not only that of his adoptive sons, Lucius Verus, Marcus Aurelius, and Commodus, but their successors, Pertinax, Caracalla, and Alexander Severus—the assimilation to a gentilic cult is abandoned.

The multiplication of Divi, each with his temple, priesthood, and public festivals celebrated with processions and exhibitions in the circus, became in time a serious burden: not only was the cost of these celebrations a heavy charge on the treasury, but the interruption of public and private business was intolerable. It was plain that, if things went on so, there would soon be more holidays than there were days in the year. Long before it became the custom to deify every dead ruler, the senate had found it necessary to appoint a commission (in 7 A. D.) to go over the calendar and reduce the number of public festivals, if there were to be any working days at all. After M. Aurelius no Divus was honoured with a separate temple; and from the middle of the second century there was a Templum Divorum on the Palatine dedicated to all these deities, with an individual shrine for each.

Beside this public cult of the deceased emperors, the wor-

ship of living emperors established itself. Augustus, as we
have seen, had introduced the worship of the Genius Augusti
along with the Lares Compitales; as the father of the people
he thus takes the place which the genius of the paterfamilias
had in the domestic cult. Only in this form, which was for
the Roman apprehension quite distinct from the worship of
a living man, had the worship of the emperor a place in the
state religion. In the provinces, however, both in the East
and the West, Augustus was worshipped in his lifetime as a
god on earth. In Egypt kings had been divine from time
immemorial. Alexander had gone out of his way to get from
the oracle of Ammon in the great oasis an attestation that
he was the son of the god. The Ptolemies succeeded to the
divinity of the Pharaohs: they were worshipped by the
Egyptians in the temples of the national gods, while in the
Greek cities in Egypt special temples and priesthoods were
dedicated to them. The divine titles Soter, Euergetes,
Epiphanes, with or without the word Theos, speak for themselves. The queens shared this divinity. The first Ptolemy
and Berenice were Θεοὶ Σωτῆρες; Ptolemy II and Arsinoe,
Θεοὶ Ἀδελφοί; Ptolemy III and Berenice II, Θεοὶ Εὐεργέται,
and so on down the line. The Seleucid kings in Syria wore
the same titles; there was a priesthood for the dead kings and
another for the living. The custom of being a god found
imitation not only by the kings of Pergamon but in Commagene and in distant Bactria. Temples were erected, sacrifices offered, festivals and games celebrated in their honour.
In Greece itself the city of Athens honoured its deliverer,
Demetrius Poliorcetes, and his father Antigonus, with a
formal cult, erected an altar to them as Saviours (Σωτῆρες),
and voted them an annual festival with processions and
games.

The modern is likely to take such apotheoses of living
men—often of detestable men—as ignoble flattery or "Oriental servility," and to see in the acceptance of such homage,
not to say in the assumption of divine attributes, an arrogance
bordering on insanity. It must be remembered, however,

that the gods in the popular conception were only magnified men—there was no fundamental difference of kind or character; and that the benefits they bestowed on their worshippers were in great part those which it lay within the power of a ruler to confer on his subjects—protection from their enemies, peace, order, and prosperity. Indeed, for these blessings the dependence of the people on their sovereign was much more immediately manifest than their dependence on the gods; in the collapse of the nationalities the ancient tutelary gods of the cities had proved powerless to secure to their worshippers these blessings. And as for the too human shortcomings of these gods of clay, the popular religions knew nothing of impeccable gods.

It was natural that in the eastern provinces the new ruler should succeed to the divine as well as the human titles of his predecessors. But there were other reasons for the veneration of Augustus—reasons no less strongly felt in Italy than in the provinces. Augustus had put an end to the century of intestine strife, of civil wars and ruthless proscriptions, that had more than once created a veritable reign of terror. He had established a firm peace at home and abroad; the closing of the doors of the temple of Janus was more than the revival of an obsolete rite, it was the inauguration of a new era. The Saviour had appeared, the golden age had begun. The language in which Virgil and Horace extol Augustus is not merely the extravagant flattery of court poets; it expresses a general sentiment. The ills from which he had delivered mankind were so enormous that the achievement seemed superhuman—the man, superman. He is compared to Juppiter and often assimilated to Apollo; the name "god" is given him outright by Virgil, as well as by Propertius and Ovid.

In response to petitions from the Province of Asia and from Bithynia (in 29 B. C.) for permission to establish his worship, Augustus ordained that the temples should be dedicated jointly to the Goddess Rome (the deified city, to whom the Greeks had erected temples as far back as the time of the

Punic wars) and himself; and this conjunction is attested in many municipal and provincial cults both in the East and West. Whether it was modesty or policy which prompted Augustus thus to cling to the skirts of Dea Roma, the fiction was not long maintained; before his death temples were erected to Augustus alone, not only in the provinces, but in Italian cities. In Rome itself, as we have seen, the worship of the Genius of the Emperor was engrafted on the state religion, but the cult of the ruling emperor in his proper person had no place.

Tiberius forbade the foundation of temples and priesthoods to himself, nor would he allow his statue to be set up among the images of the gods. In the provinces he allowed temples to be dedicated to him jointly with the Roman senate and his mother. On the other hand, Caligula took his godhead seriously and demanded divine homage for his person. Nero was more modest; he loved to be hailed in the circus as the new Apollo, but declined a proposal made in the senate to erect a temple to him as Divus—a kind of oblique consecration in his lifetime which may well have seemed to him ominous. Domitian signed himself god in writing to his procurators, but after his death the senate voted him, not the *consecratio*, but a *damnatio memoriæ*. Among the later emperors, Commodus was as much obsessed of his divinity as Caligula. But none of them received the same general worship throughout the empire which had spontaneously been accorded to Augustus. The temples dedicated to him in his lifetime became, upon his death and consecration, temples of Divus Augustus, and did not pass to his successor in the empire. Nor had the reigning emperors after Augustus priesthoods in their own names, at least in the West—some such occur in the East. These senate-made gods did not always abide in their divinity; the worship of some was abolished by decree, as that of Claudius by Nero, others were simply forgotten.

Provinces and municipalities vied with one another in commending themselves to their earthly god by the dedication of temples and images, by festivals and games. These celebrations did more than anything else to make the worship of the divine emperor popular. They survived, indeed, the triumph of Christianity and the suppression of the sacrifices; numerous laws of the Christian emperors are concerned with the regulation of the games, which were still given under the auspices of the provincial priesthoods.

In connection with the worship of the emperors, mention must be made of the establishment of special cults for numerous deities which modern scholars often conceive as personifications of qualities, such as Faith, Hope, Virtue, Honour, and the like, but which Cicero, with truer apprehension, defines, in introducing a list of them, as "res . . . in qua vis inest maior aliqua." Some gods of this class belong to the old Roman religion, others had been added in later times on various occasions; they seem to have multiplied especially in the last century of the republic and the early empire. A new turn and fresh impulse was given to this phase of religion by association with the emperor. Such titles as Salus Augusta, Pax Augusta; Clementia[1] or Providentia Cæsaris, exemplify a category which it would be too long to enumerate. The association varies, but the effect was to link in another way the familiar forms of religion to the person of the ruler.

The worship of the emperors—the Divi and the living ruler—was the one religious bond that united all the diverse peoples and religions of the empire. Other gods were widely worshipped; these universally. However little real faith and reverence there may often have been in it, this universality had more than a mere political significance; it accustomed men to the notion of a public religion in which men of all races and tongues took part. To this extent it prepared the way for the cosmopolitanism of Christianity.

In this rapid sketch of the reforms and institutions of Augustus, our attention had been occupied with the external

---

[1] The senate decreed in 39 A. D. an annual offering to the Clementia of Caligula!

aspects of religion; but it would be a mistake to imagine that we have to do only with a reorganisation of religion from above by a statesman who knew its political value. The power and glory of Rome in the Augustan age wrought an exaltation of the national consciousness which carried in itself a revival of the national religion, so that the measures of Augustus found a response in popular feeling. The revival was, however, short-lived; or perhaps it would be better to say, the decadence was only for a little while arrested.

The religion of the state, established by law, did not make itself the religion of the empire; it remained the religion of the city of Rome. Only the worship of the emperors was universal throughout the provinces, and even that, as we have seen, in a form distinctly provincial.

The incorporation of the multitude of peoples in the empire gave a fresh impulse to that fusion and confusion of gods and cults which had been going on since the conquests of Alexander, and the spontaneous tendency to identify all manner of deities on the ground of superficial resemblances in nature, myth, or function, was artificially promoted by the pantheistic doctrines of priests and philosophers. Greek and Roman gods had to lend their names to Celtic and Teutonic deities, as they had long before done to Egyptian and Oriental, and took in exchange barbarous attributes and rites. The foreign gods themselves were brought to the doors of Rome by merchants and soldiers from all quarters of the world, until the city could be called *templum totius mundi* (Ammianus, XVII, 4, 13), and a Christian controversialist could write that other cities worshipped their own gods, but the Romans worshipped everybody's.

For the first two centuries of the empire these strange gods, whatever popularity they enjoyed, had to content themselves at Rome with private worship, unrecognised by the state, though not molested by it so long as they did not offend against public order and decency. In the third century, however, significantly coincident with the extension of Roman citizenship by Caracalla to all free-born subjects of the empire, the peregrine gods also began to be given the freedom of the state religion. Caracalla admitted Isis to the Roman pantheon, and removed the long-standing rule which kept all these Oriental deities outside the pomœrium. Citizenship, either for gods or men, was after that so little of a distinction that it is often impossible to decide whether a foreign god was formally recognised in the state religion or not.

Among the gods who gain prominence in this period are several Syrian deities: Juppiter Dolichenus of Commagene, Juppiter O. M. Heliopolitanus of Heliopolis (Baalbek), Sol Invictus of Palmyra, Deus Sol Elagabalus of Emesa (Hums), and the Syrian goddess (Atargatis), the most celebrated seat of whose worship was Bambyke-Hierapolis. The Juppiters were gods of heaven—a rank to which the chief gods of many cities in Syria and Phœnicia had been raised in the centuries before the Christian era—and in conformity with another trend in the religions of the time were frequently sun gods; the gods of Palmyra and Emesa are outright identified by the Romans with Sol.

The god of Doliche was an old Anatolian god of warlike attributes, who is represented in reliefs armed with the thunderbolt and double-bitted axe, standing on the back of a bull, and it was in this character that he became a favourite god in the army and the fleet and was in the third century officially enrolled among the *di militares* of the camp. His worship was especially promoted by Commodus and the Severi.

Septimius Severus, himself an African of Punic speech, married Julia Domna, daughter of a priest of Elagabal at Emesa on the Orontes. Their son, Caracalla, was succeeded on the imperial throne by his cousin and pretended son, Elagabalus, a priest of the same god; and he by his cousin on the maternal side and adopted son, Severus Alexander. With a Syrian priestly family wearing the purple, foreign religions were more in vogue than ever. Elagabalus transplanted the holy stone of his eponymous god to Rome with him, where two temples were built for him, one on the Palatine hard by the palace, the other in a suburb near the modern Porta Maggiore. At the midsummer festival the stone was conducted in a car drawn by six white horses to this temple, the priest-emperor walking backward before the car so as not to take his eyes off his god. The emperor took it for his mission to exalt this god to supremacy. All the gods of the state religion were subordinated to him; their images and symbols were set up in his shrine to do him homage; the priest of Elagabal took precedence of the Pontifex Maximus; officials were required, in sacral actions, to name Elagabal before all other deities. The emperor fetched the African Juno Cælestis from Carthage to be formally married to his Syrian god. The historians of the time dilate on the scandalous orgies which characterised the festivals of this deity. Remnants of the old Roman decorum had hitherto held such excesses in restraint or at least kept them in a measure under cover; the police had often in earlier times repressed the delirious fervours of Oriental devotees. But now it was the state itself, in the person of the emperor, which promoted these orgies. The riot of fanaticism and debauch lasted three years; the *damnatio memoriæ* which was launched after the fallen emperor struck his god too; the brief day of Deus Sol Elagabalus was done.

Severus Alexander also had been consecrated in childhood a priest of Elagabal in his native city, Emesa; but he was a man of altogether different character and culture. His reign was in many ways an effort to bring the ship of state back into the old course, and he was zealous in restoring and maintaining the Roman religion. But if in his religious policy he was conservative, in his personal piety he was eclectic; in his private chapel he set up, by the side of the Lares and Penates, images of Apollonius of Tyana, Christ, Abraham, and Orpheus. A generation later, Aurelian, who wore with good right the title *restitutor orbis*, after his victory over the Palmyrene army, not only made the sun god of Palmyra his own patron and protector (Sol Conservator Augusti), but the supreme deity of the empire, Dominus Imperi Romani. His worship was introduced into the state religion; his temple in the Campus Agrippæ was dedicated on December 25, and this was annually celebrated as Natalis Invicti. Aurelian may well have entertained the idea of unifying the multiform religions of his conglomerate dominion in a solar monotheism, such as paganism had been tending toward for a long time. And it is not impossible that an additional motive may have been to present stronger opposition to the growing power of the Christian church. If that was in the emperor's mind, the movement came too late; within a century the vanquished Sol Invictus had to cede his birthday to Christ, Sol Verus (Cyprian), Sol Novus Noster, as Ambrose calls him. Once again, a century after Aurelian, an Oriental sun-god was raised above all the gods when Diocletian officially acknowledged Mithras the protector of the restored empire.

Of much deeper and more lasting significance than these attempts of emperors to graft a foreign supreme god upon the crown of the Roman state religion were the Oriental religions which spread and grew strong in the empire by their own propaganda. Among these the religions of the Magna Mater, of Isis, and of Mithras, far surpass all others in importance; they, and not the effete state and city cults or the political Cæsar worship, were the real rivals and adversaries of Christianity from the second to the fourth centuries.

The Phrygian Mother of the Gods was, as we have seen, the first of the Oriental deities to be admitted to a place in the Roman state religion. Brought to Rome by the senate in 204 B. C. at the bidding of the Sibylline oracles, a temple was soon after erected for her on the Palatine. But notwithstanding their gratitude for deliverance from the Punic peril, the Romans of that day were evidently embarrassed by the manners of their guest. The orgiastic features of the cult were so contrary to the decorum which was for the Roman the sign and spirit of religion, so different, again, from the æsthetic refinement of the Hellenic rites, that assimilation was impossible. The practical sense of the Romans found a compromise. On one day in the year the Prætor Urbanus did the duty of the city by offering sacrifice in the temple; the ceremony of washing the goddess in the brook Almo was also attended by the officials who had charge of foreign cults; at the great festival in the spring Roman gentlemen's clubs (sodalities) dined together in commemoration of the importation of the goddess. To do her public honour, games (Ludi Megalenses) were instituted after the common pattern of the time, with nothing Oriental about them. For the rest, the worship of Magna Mater was left exclusively in the hands of the Asiatic priesthood; Roman citizens were forbidden to enter the priesthood or to take part in the orgies. At certain festivals the priests were allowed to hold processions through the streets and to take up a collection from door to door for the benefit of the temple; the rest of the year they were isolated in their cloister on the Palatine, performing among themselves their strange rites in an unknown tongue.

Down to the end of the republic there is no evidence that the religion had made any considerable impression at Rome or gathered any body of devotees. When the temple burned down in the year 3 B. C., it was rebuilt by Augustus; but with Claudius a new era begins. He introduced—at least to publicity—the festival in March (15–27) which centres about the death and revivification of Attis, of whom, until then, the meagre notices of the worship of Magna Mater at Rome have preserved no mention. These notices, however, tell us nothing about the cult which the Phrygian priests practised within the precincts of their sanctuary; and, in view of all that we otherwise know of the religion, it is not to be imagined that Attis then made his first advent to Rome. In the inscriptions from the time of the empire the priests, including the Archigallus, and priestesses are regularly Roman citizens (frequently freedmen); the earlier restrictions must, therefore, have been repealed.

On the other hand, there is a plain reason why, in the centuries following the beginning of the Christian era, Attis became the outstanding figure in the religion, putting Magna Mater herself into the background. What the senate asked of the Great Mother when they fetched her from Pergamon was by her potent expiations to deliver the state from the danger in which it stood; what men now sought in her mysteries was the salvation of their souls, the earnest and guarantee of the life beyond death. It was in Attis that they had this hope.

The myth of Attis is told by writers of the Hellenistic period in several forms, which differ somewhat widely in detail and circumstance. The differences may be ascribed in part to contamination with cognate myths such as that of Adonis, in part to the euhemeristic rationalism of the sources or to philosophical allegorising; but when all this is subtracted there remain diversities which point to original local variations. Into these it is not pertinent here to go. In all the principal forms of the story, Attis is a youth who is associated in some way with Cybele, the Great Mother, and dies a violent death. In the story which seems to be most closely connected with the cult as we know it, he emasculates himself in an access of fury, and dies of his wounds beneath a pine-tree, violets springing up where his blood drops to earth. That he was restored to life is a secure inference from the sequence of festivals, though it is explicitly attested only by a late author.

The celebration began on March 15, which is designated in the calendar by the words *Canna intrat;* inscriptions acquaint us with corporations of Cannophori (not to be confounded with the Canephoræ of Greek cults), but the significance of the procession of "reed bearers" is unknown. It is a plausible conjecture that it was in some way associated with the discovery of the infant Attis among the bulrushes on the banks of the river Gallos where he had been exposed. About the next act, on March 22, *Arbor intrat*, we are better informed. The corporation of Dendrophori cut down a pine-tree (perhaps in a sacred grove), the branches were decorated with violets, the trunk bound about with woolen fillets like the winding-sheet of the dead. The Attis-tree was carried in procession through the city to the temple of Magna Mater on the Palatine, and set up, "ut aliquod præsens atque augustissimum numen." The 24th of March bears the significant name Sanguis, the day of blood. The mourning for the dead Attis was now at its height; amid a wild music of Phrygian horns, shrill flutes, drums, cymbals, and castanets, with wilder shrieks and furious dances, the Galli worked themselves up to a frenzy of grief, flagellating themselves with armed scourges, slashing their shoulders and arms with knives, sprinkling the altar with their blood, the aspirants to the rank of Gallus castrating themselves with a sharp stone or a potsherd. On the following day, March 25, Hilaria, the frenzied mourning was turned into equal excesses of rejoicing; with feasting, masquerades, and unrestrained ribaldry, they celebrated the resurrection of Attis. A pause of twenty-four hours (Requietio, March 26) succeeded, and the ceremonies ended on the 27th with the Lavatio, the bathing of the image of Cybele in the brook Almo, which gave occasion for another great procession.

The date of the festival, at the vernal equinox, together with its character, makes it plain that the story of Attis is a primitive myth of the death of nature or the impotence of its generative power in winter and its revival in the spring, which, as in other cases, takes the form of the tragedy of a fair young god. The rites were sympathetic means of recalling nature from its winter's death to new life. But, though the original significance did not escape the observation of some of the ancient interpreters, both myth and rite had for those who participated in the mysteries of Attis a wholly different meaning. In the resurrection of Attis they had a convincing demonstration that there was a life after death to which the goddess could raise them as she had raised him. By entering soul and body into the tragedy of the god, by inflicting on themselves the wounds from which he suffered, by becoming Attis in his passion, they became partakers of his risen nature and his immortal life. The hysterical exaltation in which sense, consciousness, and will are paralysed, was for them a divine experience, a foretaste of eternity. Firmicus Maternus describes the mourning by night over a dead god; then a light is brought in, the priest anoints the lips of the company and murmurs to them:

> "Be of good courage, because the god is saved.
> To you also shall be salvation from woes."

It is not certain that he is speaking of Attis, but the words express the gospel of all the mysteries.

With the cult of the Magna Mater is connected another rite which comes into view in the second century of our era, the taurobolium. The oldest inscription thus far known recording a taurobolium was found at Lyons and is dated in 160 A. D., and expressly affirms its derivation from the Roman Vaticanum. During the building of the present church of Saint Peter numerous taurobolium altars of the fourth century were unearthed; the series of inscriptions from the city of Rome extends from 295 A. D. to 390. In Ostia, as well as in the provinces, especially in Gaul, there is much earlier testimony. The rite is vividly described by Prudentius. The man who was to receive its benefits descended into a pit over which was a covering of planks with many holes in them. Upon this a bull was killed, whose blood streamed through the orifices upon the man below, so that every part of his body was drenched with the saving flood and it touched his eyes and ears, his lips and nose; he opened his mouth to receive it, and even swallowed some of it. When, dripping with blood, he emerged from the pit, he was greeted with adoration by the witnesses, a new man, "born again." Once the phrase runs *renatus in æternum;* usually, however, the effect lasted twenty years (*renatus in XX annos*), at the end of which time, presumably, the rite would have to be repeated. The words show plainly enough what those who submitted to this baptism of blood believed it did for them: in it they were reborn to a new and higher, a divine, life.

Other features of the mysteries of Cybele and Attis can be gathered from literary sources. Fasting and chastity and ceremonial ablutions were demanded in the celebration of all the mysteries, and many of them had peculiar restrictions upon the use of specific kinds of food. The emperor Julian, himself an initiate, tells us that in the "sanctification" of the Attis mysteries, contrary to the general rule, the sacred law made it permissible to eat flesh, but prohibited grains; allowed vegetables, but not roots such as turnips; allowed figs, but not pomegranates or fruits like apples. Sacramental rites are attested by Clement of Alexandria and Firmicus Maternus. According to the former the initiate professed: "I have eaten from the timbrel, I have drunk from the cymbal; I have carried the *kernos*,[1] I have gone beneath the *pastos*."[2] It was the symbol of the mystæ.

The taurobolium was perhaps originally a peculiarly drastic purification—*piaculum*, it is, in fact, called by Prudentius—but in the form in which we know it in the inscriptions its effect is clearly positive—it regenerates. With this conception is probably associated a feature of the rite often alluded to, namely, the exsection of the *vires* of the bull (the organs of generation). This also, likely enough, had a quite different origin; but in the mysteries it is most naturally interpreted as has been suggested above.

Of much wider and deeper influence was the religion of Isis. Osiris and Isis were old Egyptian gods; no others were more universally worshipped in Egypt, no myths are met so frequently or in so many connections from the pyramid age to the Ptolemies. The Greeks early identified them with Dionysos and Demeter. When Herodotus speaks of mysteries of Osiris and Isis, his knowledge of which he envelops in pious secrecy, he associates them with the Greek mysteries, Orphic and Eleusinian, in which Dionysos and Demeter were respectively the central figures, and he elsewhere explicitly derives the belief in the immortality of the soul

[1] A peculiar vessel, like a tray with small cups fixed upon it.
[2] The sacred ark.

which is presumed in those mysteries, as well as the trans-migration of souls, from Egypt. This opinion is as un-founded as the rest of Herodotus's theories about the Egyptian origin of Greek religion; nor are the arguments convincing by which Foucart tries to prove that the Eleu-sinian group in fact represented a fusion of the Egyptian triad with the old deities of the place. But the resemblances remain, and are neither superficial nor fortuitous; they spring from the same fundamental conceptions.

Egyptian residents had brought their gods with them into the commercial cities of the eastern Mediterranean long before Alexander. An Athenian law of 333-2 B. C. grants permission to men from Citium in Cyprus to build a temple to Aphrodite at the Piræus, "as the Egyptians have built one to Isis," and oaths by Isis appear in the Middle Comedy. But the great expansion of the religion begins in Ptolemaic times. The Ptolemies, as successors of the Pharaohs not only in royalty but in divinity, patronised the religion of their native subjects; temples of the Greek gods were built and endowed in the new cities whose population was mostly Macedonian and Greek, and spread from them to other cen-tres; but the first king of the line seems also to have had the vision of a religion that should unite the two races. Sarapis was, it is said, originally the Hades of Sinope in Pontus, brought to Alexandria by Ptolemy I in consequence of a dream, but in Egypt he was a fusion of the persons and names of Osiris and Apis (Osar-hapi); we know him only as an Osiris.[1] The priesthood was organised after the Egyptian model, and the worship was offered in the immemorial forms. But the statues of Isis and Sarapis were the work of Greek artists, and the liturgy was translated into Greek, with additions of new pæans by Greek poets. Thus an international future in the Hellenistic and Roman world was made possible.

Enjoying the especial favour of the king, the cult rapidly spread; Serapeums after the pattern of the Alexandrian were erected at Memphis and in numerous other places in Egypt

[1] See above, p. 200.

—a late author counts forty-two. Nor was its success confined to Egypt: political relations with the Ptolemies led to its introduction in Cyprus and Antioch, the islands of the Ægæan—among which Delos became an especially important centre for the dissemination of the religion—Smyrna, and Halicarnassus. In Athens Sarapis had a temple at the foot of the Acropolis; in Bœotia the worship was planted in the third century B. C. at Orchomenus and Tanagra. Merchants and seamen carried it to the ports of Italy: there was a Serapeum in Puteoli as early as 105 B. C.; a temple of Isis in Pompeii was destroyed by the earthquake of 63 B. C., and rebuilt on a larger plan.

The Pastophori of Isis at Rome, according to their tradition, were organised in the time of Sulla. It was not long before the worshippers of the Egyptian goddess fell under the unfavourable notice of the authorities. They had evidently multiplied, and had even presumed to plant a chapel on the Capitoline, in the next neighbourhood to the heads of the state pantheon. In 58 B. C. the altars of Isis were destroyed by command of the senate. Another decree ordaining the demolition of the shrines was passed in 54; but when four years later the consul, L. Æmilius Paulus, undertook to enforce this decree he could not find a workman who dared do such a sacrilege, and had to batter in the doors of the temple with an axe in his own hands. A prodigy in 48 B. C. was interpreted by the augurs as a sign that the gods of Rome were jealous of the intrusion, and to appease them the shrines of Isis and Sarapis were again destroyed.

The frequency of these persecutions is evidence of their futility. The popularity of the religion may be inferred from the fact that only five years later the triumvirs decided to erect a public temple of Isis, an act equivalent to receiving her to the company of the gods of the state religion. In the years of strife that followed it does not appear that any effect was given to this agreement; it seems to have been a bid for public favour which all three made because each was fearful that one of the others might forestall him. In the struggle between Octavian and Antony the Egyptian gods, with Cleopatra, took the wrong side, and Augustus, who in his character of restorer of the Roman religion was unfriendly to all foreign cults, had therefore particular reason to regard the worship of Isis with disfavour. He forbade the erection of private chapels of the Egyptian deities within the pomoerium (28 B. C.), and disregard of this restriction led a few years later to setting the limit a mile farther out. In consequence of a scandal in 19 A. D., in which the custodians of the temple lent their aid to a fraud by which a noble lady was debauched, Tiberius crucified the priests who were implicated, demolished their temple, and threw the image of the goddess into the Tiber. To trust the poets, Isis counted many devotees among women of loose morals, and her temples were frequented by youths in quest of gallant adventures—Ovid recommends them to such equally with synagogues; on the other hand, the elegiac lovers make frequent complaint that their mistresses' piety in keeping "the chaste days of Isis" thwarts their desires. It would be unwarranted, however, to judge the character of her worshippers in general from such testimony.

It was in all probability Caligula who built the first public temple of Isis in the Campus Martius; and thenceforth there was no legal hindrance to the growth of the religion. Lucan (died 65 A. D.) could say: "We have received thine Isis into Roman temples, and the demigod dogs, and the sistra bidding grief, and that Osiris whom by bewailing him thou dost testify to be a man." Vespasian and Titus passed the night before their triumph over the Jews in the temple of Isis, and the triumphal procession set out from it. Domitian, who in the civil war after the death of Nero had saved his life by putting on the dress of a priest of Isis on the Capitol and in this garb making his way unobserved through the city, rebuilt the temple in the Campus Martius after a fire in 80 A. D., and made it one of the most splendid edifices in Rome. Under the Antonine emperors the religion of Isis reached its culmination; Commodus outdid all his predecessors in the extravagance of his devotion, sometimes taking his place in the liturgical processions, shaved bald like an Egyptian priest, and carrying the image of Anubis in his arms.

The repressive measures of Augustus and his successors applied only to the city of Rome, and even there we have seen how fruitless they were. The Egyptian religion progressed unhindered from the south of Italy to the north and through all the western provinces, carried, like other foreign cults, by sailors, traders, discharged soldiers, and slaves. From Carthage it established itself in Africa, from Aquileia it penetrated into the valley of the Danube, by the Rhone valley it spread in Gaul.[1]

There was much in the cult of Isis that touched the æsthetic sense which lies so close to the religious sentiment, and it was free from savage survivals. Of all the foreign religions which were missioning in the Roman world in those centuries it was the most civilised. The imagination could not fail to be impressed by the immemorial antiquity which renewed itself day by day in the liturgy, and the prestige of old-world wisdom attached to the Egyptian theology. The priesthood, unlike those of Greek and Roman temples, was a class apart, wholly devoted to the service of the gods;[2] the worship was not a matter of holidays, but a perpetual round of rites and litanies; every morning the shrine was opened with offerings and prayers; every evening it was closed with like solemn ceremonies. The ancient hymns which the priests intoned were not only venerable forms, they were words of divine efficacy which constrained the very gods. It was not in these features, however, that the strongest attraction of the Egyptian religion lay; it was in the assurance it gave of a blessed immortality.

The Egyptians had concerned themselves more than any other people in the Mediterranean world about the fortunes of man after death. The hope of a new life attached itself to the sun god who dies, and after passing through the gloomy

---

[1] Cumont, The Oriental Religions in Roman Paganism, p. 83.
[2] This was true also, as we have seen, of the priests of Cybele.

realms of night emerges at dawn in new splendour, and to the
myth of Osiris, who, slain by Set, was restored to life and
rules over the realms of the dead.[1]   Once the prerogative of
kings in their quality of divine rulers, these hopes were in
course of time appropriated by the common man.   The Book
of the Underworld and similar texts show the survival—perhaps revival—of the solar salvation in late times, but the
Osirian doctrine was beyond all comparison more popular
and influential.

The myth of Osiris as it is told by Plutarch has been related in another connection.[2]   It is the story of a god who
was dead and is alive again.   In a pyramid text the assembled gods say to him: "Though thou departest, thou comest
again; though thou sleepest, thou wakest again; though thou
diest, thou livest again."   The death and resurrection of
Osiris was represented in a kind of passion play.   A ritual of
the time of the Twelfth Dynasty shows how it was celebrated at Abydos: the god, going forth from his temple,
was attacked and slain by Set; there followed the clamorous
mourning for the dead and the customary funeral rites; Set
was vanquished by Horus, and Osiris, rising triumphant over
death, returned to his temple amid the rejoicing of his
worshippers.

In substantially the same way the drama was enacted at
Rome, beginning on October 28.   With loud wailing and
every expression of passionate grief, in which priests and
people united, Isis, seconded by Nephthys and Anubis,
sought the dismembered body of the slain Osiris.   The cry of
discovery, "We have found him, we rejoice together," gave
its name, Heuresis, to the day (October 31).[3]   Grief suddenly
turns to gladness: the lost is found, the dead is alive again.
The rejoicing was continued for three days, the last of which
bore the name Hilaria, like the great day of rejoicing in the
spring festival of the Magna Mater.   The two festivals, in-

---

[1] See above, pp. 161 ff.   [2] See above, pp. 191 ff.
[3] That the celebration falls in the autumn may perhaps be explained
by the assumption that the rejoicing was originally connected with the
high Nile, on which the prosperity of the coming year depended.

deed, are throughout similar; they are, we might say, independent variations of the same theme, life triumphant over death—in the primitive but long-forgotten sense of the myth, the revival of nature; in the mystery, as in Egyptian religion from remote times, a new, an immortal life for men.

The lament for Osiris, the search, the finding, the loud rejoicing, were enacted openly; they were in themselves adapted to make a deep impression on all beholders, and their significance was not obscure. But there was an esoteric teaching imparted only to the initiated with solemn circumstance and under a veil of profound secrecy. The Oriental religions which sought converts to their salvation in other lands naturally assumed the form of mysteries; but the mysteries of Isis seem to have imitated more closely than the others the Eleusinian type. It is perhaps not without significance that the Eumolpid Timotheus is said to have been called in by Ptolemy to assist in shaping the Alexandrian cult of Sarapis. The resemblances, however, are in external features, and are accompanied by characteristic differences which lie much deeper.

In the mysteries of Isis there were several stages into which the initiates were successively inducted; only to those who had attained the highest degree was the full revelation made. The best account of these mysteries is given by Apuleius in his Metamorphoses (Book XI). To the hero of the story, who by blundering magic had been turned into an ass and in that asinine body with human soul had suffered many things, in answer to his prayer, the goddess herself appears in all the radiance of her divinity, and declares herself:

"Rerum naturæ parens, elementorum omnium domina, sæculorum progenies initialis, summa numinum, regina manium, prima cælitum, deorum dearumque facies uniformis, quæ cæli luminosa culmina, maris salubria flumina, inferum deplorata silentia nutibus meis dispenso: cuius numen unicum, multiformi speciei, ritu vario, nomine multijugo totus veneratur orbis."

The primitive Phrygians, she continues, worshipped her as the Mother of the Gods, the autochthonous Athenians as the Cecropean Minerva, the Cypriotes as the Paphian Venus, the Cretans as Diana Dictynna, the Sicilians as the Stygian Proserpina, the Eleusinians as ancient Ceres, others as Juno, Bellona, Hecate, Rhamnusia; but those who are illumined by the first rays of the nascent sun god, the Æthiopians, and the Arians,[1] and the Egyptians eminent in ancient lore, worshipping her with her own rites, call her by her true name, Queen Isis.

The unity of the godhead is here expressed not in an exclusive but in a comprehensive sense: Isis is all the goddesses. This syncrasy is the tendency of the time: Sarapis, the partner of Isis, is called *pantheus*. An Orphic verse declared that Zeus, Hades, Helios, Dionysos are one; the emperor Julian varies it: Zeus, Hades, Helios are one, and are Sarapis.

The goddess grants Lucius's prayer, and bids him ever remember that all his life belongs to her, adding the promise: "Vives autem beatus, vives in mea tutela gloriosus, et cum spatium sæculi tui permensus ad inferos demearis, ibi quoque in ipso subterraneo semirotundo me quam vides Acherontis tenebris interlucentem Stygiisque penetralibus regnantem, campos Elysios incolens ipse tibi propitiam frequens adorabis."

Apuleius describes at length and vividly the great procession—it is the spring festival of Isis[2]—in the midst of which Lucius, nipping the crown of roses carried by the priest, sheds his ass's skin and is restored to human form, a miracle in which the priest finds a text for an improving address to Lucius and to the beholders: "Videant irreligiosi, videant et errorem suum recognoscant!"

The desire of Lucius to be initiated is not immediately gratified; but at length the day indicated by the goddess approaches, and after a bath and a religious purification by the priest—a kind of baptism by affusion—he is conducted to the temple, where for ten days he lives on meagre diet, abstaining from flesh and wine. When these days of preparation are past, the priest leads him by night into the inmost

[1] East of Parthia.   [2] At the beginning of navigation.

shrine. What he sees and hears there it is not lawful to narrate; yet in mysterious phrase he hints it:

"I approached the confines of death, and, having trod the threshold of Proserpina, borne through all the elements, I returned. I saw the sun in the midst of the night gleaming with white light. I drew near into the presence of the gods of the underworld and the gods of the world above, and adored them all close to." On the following day he was displayed to the multitude on a platform in the temple before the image of the goddess. Dressed in a robe figured with fabulous animals, holding in his hand a lighted torch, wearing a crown of palm leaves projecting like rays—"Thus decked out in the likeness of the sun, and set up like an image, the curtains were suddenly drawn aside, and the people strolled in to see."[1]

This is supposed to have taken place in Corinth. Later, in Rome, by command of the goddess, he was initiated a second and a third time. The third degree is followed by the appearance in a dream of Osiris in his proper form, "Deus deum magnorum potior et maiorumque summus et summorum regnator Osiris." It is a fair inference that in the last initiation Osiris was the chief figure, as Isis was in the first.

The pages of Apuleius not only give us pictures of the cult and glimpses of the mysteries of Isis, and repeat the sounding phrases of her pantheistic theology, but they disclose something of the religious sentiment of her worshippers. The prayers that are put into the mouth of Lucius are, indeed, compositions of a professor of rhetoric, but under the rhetoric is a strain of true piety.

The worship of Mithras first came to the notice of the Romans through the Cilician pirates whom Pompey suppressed in 67 B. C. The conquest of the kingdom of Mithradates, completed by Pompey in the following years, carried

---

[1] This seems to me to be a Mithraic contamination. The figures of the zodiac, the torch, and especially the radiate crown, belong not to Osiris but to Mithras. Observe also that the priest who is his conductor is named Mithra.

the Roman arms into regions where the religion of Mithras prevailed, some of which in the ensuing reorganisation were constituted Roman provinces, while others were ruled by vassal kings. But while the campaigns of Sulla, Pompey, and Cæsar (against Pharnaces), brought to Rome the worship of the Asianic goddess Ma-Bellona, whose cult closely resembled in character that of the Great Mother, Mithras had not the same fortune. It is not till toward the end of the first century after Christ that his mysteries make their appearance in the West, following the annexation of Commagene and Armenia Minor by Vespasian. The oldest Mithræa in Rome date from the reigns of Trajan and Hadrian.

Beginning in the age of the Flavian emperors the religion spread with extraordinary rapidity. No other exotic cult has left so many monuments so widely scattered through the western provinces of the empire. This is doubtless due in part to the fact that, in consequence of the peculiar character of its sanctuaries and their distribution, they have been preserved while others perished; but when full allowance for these accidents is made there can be no question that for two centuries the growth of this religion was one of the most notable phenomena of the age. The often-quoted remark of Renan, that if the expansion of Christianity in the same period had been arrested by some mortal malady the world would have been Mithraist, is doubtless too strong, but that for a time the mysteries of Mithras were in considerable regions the most formidable among the rivals of Christianity is undisputed.

One of the chief agencies in the propagation of this religion was the army. We can follow it from post to post around the frontiers of the empire, up the Danube, along the Rhine, in Britain, and on the margins of the Sahara. The cohorts and alæ raised in Cappadocia or Commagene or Pontus brought it with them to their stations in Dalmatia or Mœsia, or in Africa; the translocation of troops, the transfer of officers from one corps to another on their promotion, and the settlement of discharged soldiers carried it to new centres. That

it made converts among the troops recruited in other quarters
is natural; the virile character of Mithraism pre-eminently
fitted it to be a soldiers' religion. Asiatic slaves, of whom
great numbers came into the markets of the West—serfs sold
by the great landlords of Anatolia or captives enslaved in
mass in the Parthian wars—introduced the religion into Italy
and into the ports and emporia of the provinces, where they
built their little churches and made converts among the lower
classes. Slaves and freedmen employed in government bu-
reaus as clerks and managers reached a somewhat higher
level of society. In these ways the religion was propagated
through all the western parts of the empire; only in Greece
and in the regions where Greek culture was strongest did it
fail to gain a foothold.

In the places of worship called *spelæa*, "grottos," the cella
where the rites were performed was a subterranean hall.
From a pronaos above ground a flight of steps led down to
the cella; at the opposite end, in a niche or apse, was a relief
representing Mithras slaying the bull, and images of other
deities associated with the cult. On either side of the hall,
with a wide aisle in the middle, was a raised podium on which
the worshippers knelt; in the middle aisle stood usually two
altars. These temples are all small; the largest would hardly
hold a hundred worshippers. When the number of converts
outgrew the limits, another Spelæum was built; in Ostia five
are known, in Caruntum four, in Heddernheim three.

The great reliefs not only all represent the same scene, but
all reproduce, sometimes rudely enough, one artistic type, the
composition of a Pergamene sculptor. The god, in Phrygian
costume, has come upon the bull from behind and thrown it
to the ground; with one knee upon its croup, he grasps its
muzzle with his left hand, while with his right he plunges to
its heart a broad, short sword. A dog leaps up to lick the
blood that gushes from the wound, a serpent drinks it as it
streams upon the ground, a scorpion attacks the victim's
scrotum. On either side of the central figures stands a youth,
in garb just like the god's, the one holding a burning torch

aloft, the other an inverted torch; their names, Cautes and Cautopates, are unexplained. Other subsidiary figures sometimes occur in the scene—a lion and a serpent grouped about a vase, for instance; and the central relief is occasionally surrounded by a series of smaller reliefs depicting other chapters in the myth of Mithras. One of these, of which there are also representations in the round, shows a child, naked but for his Phrygian cap, rising out of a rock from which he has two-thirds emerged; in the right hand he holds a short triangular sword, or dirk, in the left a flaming torch. It is the birth of the god—Θεὸς ἐκ πέτρας. Another shows Mithras in converse with the divine sun, whose attributes are the radiate crown and whip; or, again, he shoots an arrow at a rock, from which thereupon a spring of water gushes. In our imperfect knowledge, or rather our complete ignorance, of the myths the interpretation of these reliefs is highly problematical.

In the Mithraic mysteries there were seven degrees, attained by as many successive initiations. The initiates of each degree were designated by a mystifying name. In the first stage the neophyte was a raven (Corax), in the second he became a hidden one (Κρύφιος), in the third a soldier (Miles), in the fourth a lion (Leo). The first three degrees seem to be stages of a catechumenate; a man was not admitted to full participation in the mysteries until he reached the rank of Leo. The three higher degrees were the Persian (Persa), the Sun-courier (Ἡλιοδρόμος) and the Father (Pater). A Pater Patrum perhaps presided over all the organisations in a city as a kind of bishop. The priests (*sacerdotes*) seem generally, but not exclusively, to be of the class of Patres. Candidates prepared themselves by fasting and purifications; in the initiations themselves the courage and fortitude of the candidate were put to the test. Originally these tests may have been as cruel as savage initiations often are, but in Roman times they were probably of a kind by which the candidate was more scared than hurt, as in modern lodges and student fraternities. Some reliefs show men wearing masks in the form of a raven's head or a lion's, in Persian costume or armed as soldiers, and probably such masquerades—a survival of a barbarous cult—had a place in the initiations or in the liturgy.

The Christian Fathers saw in other features of the Mithraic ritual a diabolic travesty of the Christian sacraments. There were baptisms in water which not only purified the body but removed sins; Mithras sealed his soldiers on the forehead as Christians were sealed with the sign of the cross; there was an oblation of bread which corresponded to the Eucharist. A relief published a few years ago represents this mystic meal: before the participants stands a tripod on which are four small loaves of bread, each marked with a cross; one of the participants holds aloft a horn (presumably of wine), while a Persa offers a second to the other communicant. It is not strange that when the Christians came into power they showed peculiar zeal in destroying the Mithræa.

The religion of Mithras had had a long history before it made its appearance in Europe. Mithra was, as we have seen in an earlier chapter, an old Indo-Iranian deity, closely associated in the Vedas with Varuna.[1] In the Zoroastrian Gathas there is no room for any other god beside the one Ahura Mazda; but in the inscriptions of the later Achæmenian kings Mithra's name is joined with Ahura Mazda, and in the Yashts and the younger Avesta generally he is the greatest of the Yazatas, or inferior divinities. Theologically subordinated to Ahura Mazda, for religion he was in his own sphere supreme. He was a god of light, and in the moral world god of truth and good faith, a righteous judge. But, what had more to do with his popularity, Mithra was a heroic god, champion of the true religion and of every good cause, giving victory to the armies of his worshippers. He aided and defended the upright in their conflict with the powers of darkness, human and devilish, and rescued their souls at death from the assaults of demons.

The Persian conquests planted the Zoroastrian religion in

[1] See above, pp. 251, 373.

Asia Minor, where it took a firm root, particularly in Armenia, Pontus, and Cappadocia. Doubtless it acquired there certain local characters from the religions of the country; but that on the whole it remained true to type is manifest from the description Strabo gives of the Magian worship in Cappadocia.

It is in these regions that the peculiar cult of Mithra which is propagated in the mysteries must have had its origin, but of this period of its history nothing is known. The religion was fully developed when it first emerges into our observation, and it is only by inference and comparison that its antecedents can be conjectured. From the native religions of eastern Asia Minor are doubtless derived the barbarous features in the mysteries to which attention has already been called. Indeed, the progressive degrees of initiation, with their terrifying or cruel trials of the neophyte's fortitude, the distinctive masks, some of them representing animals, and the admission of men only to the mysteries, have no connection with the Iranian cult of Mithra, but are of a kind familiar the world over in savage secret societies. Porphyry interprets these degrees as intimations of the transmigration of souls, and it is quite conceivable that the Mithraists themselves in his time gave such an explanation of them; but this symbolism is not their original intent.

In the age when the great gods of western Asia, especially the warrior gods, were being identified with the sun, Mithra followed the fashion; the epithet "invincible" which was given to the sun gods of Palmyra and Emesa was bestowed on him also. *Sol Invictus Mithras* is his common title in Latin inscriptions, and as the day of the Syrian solar Baals waned, Sol Invictus without a name meant Mithras. He usurped the birthday of the sun, December 25; the divine child emerging from the rock is the new-born sun god. In the reliefs in the Mithræa, however, Mithras is distinct from the sun god, with whom he is frequently represented in converse; the myth had been fixed before the identification was thought of.

The astrological doctrines of the Chaldeans, which since Alexander had been working their way westward, and in their threefold character of science, philosophy, and theology invading every sphere of thought, constitute another element in the Mithraic mysteries.[1] That there are just seven degrees is to be attributed to the influence of the astrological system; astral myths and astronomical symbols such as the signs of the zodiac are figured in the monuments. If we were better informed about the ceremonies, we should very likely find that astrology had contributed to the liturgy, and that by a symbolical interpretation an astrological meaning was read into rites of other origin. The Chaldean science plainly combined with Magian theology to produce the monstrous figure of the Mithraic Kronos: this Zervan, with human body and lion's head, wrapped around by the spiral coils of a serpent, with sceptre and thunderbolt for attributes and a key in each hand, sometimes surrounded by a zodiac, is Time, which produces and devours all things by fate.

How much of orthodox Zoroastrianism there was in the composite Mithraic doctrine it is not easy to say. The great figures of the Avestan religion, Ahura Mazda, and his Immortal Beneficent Spirits, have no conspicuous place in the mysteries, though the Cælus Æternus Juppiter of the Roman temples may well be Ahura Mazda. The Mithræa are not equipped for the tendance of the sacred fire, nor are any other of the characteristic features of the Zoroastrian cult to be discovered. It is hard to imagine a Zoroastrian worship, even of a syncretistic sort, without the Haoma ceremonies, and highly improbable, on the other hand, that these rites should have been practised in the mysteries without leaving some trace of themselves—in the Mithraic sacrament, for instance, or by representations of the sacred plant

[1] The extent to which the Chaldean pseudosciences and black arts were appropriated by Zoroastrianism may be inferred from the fact that the Magi gave its very name to magic, and that later writers look upon Babylon as the chief seat of the Magi, whither—with a guileless anachronism—they make Pythagoras resort in his quest for the mysterious wisdom of the East.

in the elaborate symbolical reliefs. It may be added that the monuments give no hint of the peculiar Zoroastrian eschatology. If the conflict of good and evil powers played an important part in the Mithraic doctrine, dualism was in that age not distinctive of Zoroastrianism; it had invaded all the religions and philosophies of the time. Demonology was not a tissue of superstitions to be ashamed of, but a necessary pendant to theology; astrology gave it a new shape and a more terrible power.

What was it that attracted men in such numbers to the service of Mithras? The same motive, doubtless, that drew them to the other mysteries—salvation. But while in the Orphic and Eleusinian mysteries, or in those of Cybele and Isis, the hope of a blessed immortality attached itself to the god who had triumphed over death, the Mithraic gospel is not so evident. It is a natural supposition that the relief which is the invariable altar-piece of the Spelæa, Mithras slaying the bull, represents the supreme moment in a drama of salvation; but even if this inference were entirely certain, the interpretation of the relief is left to conjecture. The scene is thought by many to be a cosmogonic myth: it is the slaying of the primeval cow, from which the whole creation, plants and animals, spring. Others think of the eschatological bull, Hadhayos, which Shaoshyant sacrifices after the resurrection, and of whose fat mingled with the white (celestial) Haoma, is prepared the ambrosia which is given to all men, the food of immortality.[1] The genii, Cautes and Cautopates, figured in the familiar Greek types of Sleep and Death, would not be inappropriate in such a context; but the other common accessories, especially the serpent and the scorpion, Ahrimanian creatures, have no business in the renewed world. Astrological contamination, if not astrological origin, is strongly suggested by the accessories of the central relief.

The church of Mithras was singular among the mysteries of the time in admitting to its communion only men. It is true that Porphyry speaks of Mithraic "lionesses," corre-

[1] See above, p. 402.

sponding to the "lions," and Tertullian writes of *virgines et continentes;* but the testimony of the inscriptions, negative though it is, seems conclusive. It has been surmised that the frequent juxtaposition of Mithræa and temples of the Magna Mater was due to the fact that the wives and daughters of the Mithraists were addicted to the worship of the latter. The exclusion of the religious sex was doubtless a disadvantage in the rivalry of salvations; but in the competition with Christianity Mithraism was at a much greater disadvantage in that it was strongest, not in the great centres, but on the outposts of the empire, and especially because it had never taken root in the lands of Hellenic culture.

By the side of these religions, in which many were seeking the secret and assurance of eternal bliss, Christianity also was spreading in the Roman world. It, too, was an Oriental mystery, which admitted to its most solemn functions only initiates. The gospel of the cross and the resurrection would seem to its hearers another variation of the myth of the youthful demigod who dies a tragic death, and is the way of life to those who are mystically united with him; the baptismal initiation, the *signum*, the sacrament of bread and wine, the body and blood of the redeemer, were all rites of a familiar type. The hierarchical organisation of the clergy, in which each grade had its peculiar forms of consecration, would appear similar to the progressive initiations of the mysteries, whose priests were initiates of the highest class.

It differed from all the rest, however, in its intolerant attitude not only toward other ways of salvation but toward the popular cults and the religion of the state.[1] Persecutions in different regions, and of varying duration and severity, occurred repeatedly in the second and third centuries; but Decius was the first of the emperors to institute general and thorough repressive measures. His death (251 A. D.), after a reign of less than three years, did not end the period of persecution, which was renewed spasmodically by his successors

[1] Judaism, which was equally intolerant, was treated by the law as a national religion.

in the next ten years; and in 303 and 304 Diocletian, who, as we have seen, saluted Mithras as *fautor imperii sui* issued a series of edicts prescribing that the Christians should worship the gods. There followed the worst persecution the church ever suffered, but it was the last. An edict of universal toleration was promulgated in 311 by Galerius, Constantine, and Licinius for the parts of the empire over which they respectively presided. Constantine, when he became sole master of the Roman world, put the church on a parity with other religions recognised by the state, and showed it many marks of personal favour; but did not touch the rights and immunities of other religions.

Under his successors the tables turned. In 341 Constantius and Constans issued an edict closing the temples and forbidding sacrifice: Cesset superstitio sacrificiorum aboleatur insania. It need hardly be said that such a law could not be enforced, and probably no very earnest attempt was made to execute it; but it proclaimed the new spirit of the Christian empire. The reaction under Julian (361–363) was but a momentary check. Gratian (probably in 375) renounced the title Pontifex Maximus, and in 382 confiscated the estates of the temples and did away with all emoluments and immunities of the priests of the Roman state religion. Henceforth the support of the old religions was left to private hands. In Rome, at least, such support was liberally forthcoming; and these very efforts, made by men who felt that they were set to maintain the faith of their fathers, the inheritance of a glorious past, produced in their circle a revival of religious zeal. Jerome's rhetorical exultation over the downfall of heathenism in Rome (Ep. 107; 403 A. D.) is exaggerated; but in the fifth century the old religions decayed and disappeared.

In the East, where Christians were much more numerous, and where there were no such great conservative memories as in Italy, the process of extirpating heathenism went on more rapidly. A vivid picture of the destruction of the great temple of Marnas in Gaza is given by Marcus Diaconus in his life of the bishop Porphyrius—the intrigue and ruse by which Theodosius was brought to order the suppression of the worship of Marnas, and the holy zeal with which the pious bishop demolished the temple, are suggestive of what must have happened unrecorded in many places.

It was easier to raze temples and shatter images than it was to root out of the minds of men, or, if you please, out of human nature, the ideas of which the old religions were the embodiment. The church paid the price of its victory in taking over with the masses it absorbed the vital part of the beliefs and practices they had ostensibly renounced—here too the vanquished gave laws to the victor!

LITERATURE

The aim of the following list is not to give a general bibliography of the subject, but to direct the reader who may desire to inform himself more fully about a particular religion or some aspect of it to the books which he may most profitably consult for that purpose. Books that belong strictly to the specialist are not included, nor, on the other hand, purely popular works, except a few by scholars of high authority. So far as possible, reference is made to books accessible in English; but in this peculiarly international field it is frequently the case that the best works are in other languages. References to foreign literature are confined, however, with one or two exceptions, to French and German. Through the books whose titles are given the student will be able to find his way as far as he chooses into the voluminous and often most important literature on special topics in periodicals and the transactions of learned societies. To enter such articles here, even in the narrowest selection, would not only swell this list to inordinate dimensions but defeat its purpose.

GENERAL

Works of Reference.—*Encyclopædia of Religion and Ethics.* Edited by JAMES HASTINGS. Vol. I. 1908. Planned on a large scale and with a wide scope. The articles are by scholars of acknowledged competence, many of them of eminence in their fields; full and well-chosen bibliographies are as a rule appended to the articles. **Periodicals.**—*Revue de l'histoire des religions.* Vol. I. 1880. Edited by RENÉ DUSSAUD and PAUL ALPHANDÉRY, with the co-operation of many distinguished French scholars. *Archiv für Religionswissenschaft.* Vol. I. 1898. Edited by RICHARD WÜNSCH, with an able company of co-adjutors. Both are publications of high rank, containing, besides original articles, authoritative reviews of current literature, and comprehensive surveys of the progress of learning. **History of Religions.**— *Lehrbuch der Religionsgeschichte.* Herausgegeben unter Redaktion von P. D. CHANTEPIE DE LA SAUSSAYE. 2 vols. 3d ed. 1905. The chapters are written by scholars specially qualified in the respective religions. Of the preceding edition (1897) there is a French translation:

Manuel d'histoire des religions . . . Traduit . . . sous la direction d'Henri Hubert et Isidore Lévy. 1904. The volume, "Die Orientalischen Religionen," in *Die Kultur der Gegenwart* (1906. 2d ed. 1913), contains an introductory sketch of the religions of primitive peoples, and chapters on the religions of Egypt, Babylonia and Assyria, India, Persia, Islam, Lamaism, China, Japan (Shinto and Buddhism), by eminent German scholars. **Translations: Collections.**—*The Sacred Books of the East.* Translated by various scholars and edited by F. MAX MÜLLER. 49 vols. 1879 *seqq.* Vol. L. *General Index to the Names and Subject Matter.* By M. WINTERNITZ. 1910. The most important of the scriptures of India (Vedic, Brahmanic, Jain, Buddhist); China (Confucian, Taoist); the Avesta and later Zoroastrian (Pahlavi) texts; the Koran. The excellent index adds greatly to the usefulness of the work. The volumes of the series will be referred to below in connection with the several religions, with the abbreviation "S. B. E." A volume of selections to illustrate the character and teachings of Chinese, Indian, Zoroastrian, and Mohammedan religions, translated by qualified scholars, is *Religionsgeschichtliches Lesebuch.* Herausgegeben von A. BERTHOLET. 1908. There is a similar work on a somewhat larger scale in Swedish, edited by N. SÖDERBLOM. 1908. LEHMANN, E., *Textbuch zur Religionsgeschichte.* 1912. Smaller in compass, more comprehensive in scope, including texts illustrative of religions which have no canonical scriptures (Egypt, Babylonia, Greece, Rome, the Teutonic peoples). A series of little volumes in English, *The Wisdom of the East,* edited by L. CRAMER-BYNG and S. A. KAPADIA, has the motive and character of an anthology rather than a scientific purpose.

CHINA

History.—WILLIAMS, S. WELLS, *The Middle Kingdom.* 2 vols. Revised edition, 1883. The historical chapters of this work separately, under the title: *A History of China.* Edited by F. W. WILLIAMS. 1897. HIRTH, F., *The Ancient History of China.* To the end of the Chóu Dynasty [249 B. C.]. 1908. CHAVANNES, ÉDOUARD, *Les mémoires historiques de Se-Ma Ts'ien.* Traduits et annotés. 1895 *seqq.* The great Chinese historian. Thus far five volumes. The introduction by the translator is of high value. **Literature.**—GRUBE, W., *Geschichte der chinesischen Litteratur.* 1902. GILES, H. A., *A History of Chinese Literature.* 1901. A popular work on a smaller scale. **Religion: General Works.**—LEGGE, JAMES, *The Religions of China.* Confucianism and Tâoism Described and Compared with Christianity. 1881. EDKINS, JOSEPH, *Religion in China.* Containing a Brief Account of the Three Religions of the Chinese. 2d ed. 1878. Popular introductions. GROOT, J. J. M. DE, *The Religious System of China.* Its Ancient Forms, Evolution, History, and Present Aspect. Part I (vols. I–III), Disposal of the Dead; Part II (vols. IV–VI), On the Soul and Ancestral Worship. 1892–1910. (Other volumes to come.) An immense collection, including custom, folk-lore, demonology, etc. By the same au-

thor: *Sectarianism and Religious Persecution in China.* 2 vols. 1903–4.
The attitude of the state and of the Confucian literati toward Bud-
dhism, Taoism, and the sects. Also: *The Religion of the Chinese.* 1910.
Religion in China. 1912. Two short courses of lectures given in Amer-
ica. PARKER, E. H., *China and Religion.* 1905. *Studies in Chinese
Religion.* 1910. The "Studies" are chiefly reprints of articles pre-
viously published; a translation of the Tao-teh-king is included. GRUBE,
W., *Religion und Kultus der Chinesen.* 1910.

RELIGION OF THE STATE

Texts.—LEGGE, JAMES, *The Chinese Classics.* With a Translation,
Critical and Exegetical Notes, Prolegomena, and Copious Indexes. 5
vols. (in 8). 1861 *seqq.* The introductions and commentary with the
translation make this incomparably the most useful work in its field to
the student. By the same author: *The Texts of Confucianism.* 4 vols.
1879–85. (S. B. E., vols. III, XVI, XXVII, XXVIII.) Comprising
the Shu-king, parts of the Shi-king, the Yih-king, and Li-ki; translation
only, without commentary. HARLEZ, CHARLES DE, *I-li. Cérémonial
de la Chine antique.* Traduit, etc. 1890. **Religion.**—LEGGE, in the
Prolegomena to his edition of the Classics. ROSS, JOHN, *The Original
Religion of China.* 1909. A good description of the religion of the
canonical books, with numerous translations. Like Legge, the author
is convinced that the primitive Chinese were monotheists. On the imperial rites, HARLEZ, CHARLES DE, *La religion et les cérémonies impériales
de la Chine moderne.* 1893. (In Memoirs of the Belgian Academy of
Sciences, vol. LII.)

MORAL AND POLITICAL PHILOSOPHY

Texts.—Confucian Analects, Great Learning, Doctrine of the Mean,
Mencius. See LEGGE, *Classics,* and reprints from them. **Confucius.**—
LEGGE, JAMES, *Life and Teaching of Confucius.* 1867. FABER, ERNST,
Systematical Digest of the Doctrines of Confucius According to the Analects.
Translated by P. G. Moellendorff. 1875. DOUGLAS, R. K., *Confucianism and Taoism.* 1879. Popular. DVOŘÁK, R., *Chinas Re-
ligionen.* Teil I, Confucius und seine Lehre. 1895. An excellent ac-
count and analysis. **Yang Chu and Moh Tih.**—LEGGE, *Classics.* II,
95–102, 103–125. FABER, E., *Grundgedanken des alten chinesischen So-
cialismus; oder die Lehre des Philosophen Micius.* 1877. **Mencius.**—
LEGGE, JAMES, *Life and Works of Mencius.* 1875. FABER, E., *The
Mind of Mencius. Systematic Digest,* etc. Translated by A. B. Hutch-
inson. 1882. **Wang Chung.**—FORKE, A., *Lun Hen. Philosophical
Essays of Wang Chung.* I, 1907; II, 1911. **Chu Hi and Sing-li School.**
—HARLEZ, CHARLES DE, *L'école philosophique moderne de la Chine, ou
système de la nature* (*Sing-li*). 1890. (In Memoirs of the Belgian
Academy of Sciences, vol. XLIX.) For other literature, see GRUBE, *Lit-
teratur,* pp. 333 *ff.*

TAOISM

Texts.—LEGGE, JAMES, *The Texts of Taoism*. 2 vols. 1891. (S. B. E., vols. XXXIX, XL.) Contains the Tao-teh-king, Writings of Chuang-tzsĕ, "Actions and their Retributions." The difficulty of the Tao-teh-king has tempted many translators. STRAUSS, VICTOR VON, *Taò tĕ king*. 1870. With introduction and notes; highly praised by some of the best sinologues. E. H. PARKER, in *Studies*, etc. 1910 (see above), pp. 99–131. A chronological bibliography of the literature, *ibid.*, pp. 92 *ff*. Dr. Paul Carus has published the Chinese text, with translation, etc. 1898. There is a recent German translation by WILHELM. **Lieh-tzse.**—FABER, E., *Der Naturalismus bei den alten Chinesen . . . oder die sämmtlichen Werke des Philosophen Licius übersetzt und erklärt*. 1877. **Chuang-tzse.**—LEGGE, S. B. E., vols. XXXIX, XL; GILES, H. A., *Chuang-tsŭ, Mystic, Moralist, and Social Reformer*. 1899. A very readable translation, with an important introduction. **Taoism as Philosophy and Religion.**—DVOŘAK, R., *Chinas Religionen*. Teil II, Lao-tsï und seine Lehre. 1903. Perhaps the best exposition of the philosophy; instructive comparison with Confucius. PARKER, E. H., *Studies*, etc., see above. DOUGLAS, R. K., *Confucianism and Taouism*. 1879. On the attitude of the government toward Taoism, see DE GROOT, *Sectarianism*. The Taoist popular literature is represented by the "Tractate of Actions and their Retributions" (S. B. E., vol. XL); see also Douglas, *op. cit.*, pp. 256 *ff*.

RELIGION OF THE MASSES

DE GROOT, *Religious System*, etc., *Sectarianism*, etc. (both above). GRUBE, W., *Religion und Kultus*. Many modern works on Chinese life and custom.

BUDDHISM

Texts.—BEAL, SAMUEL, *Catena of Buddhist Scriptures from the Chinese*. 1871. For other Mahayana texts, see below, under INDIA; also JAPAN, Buddhism. **History and Doctrine.**—EDKINS, JOSEPH, *Chinese Buddhism*. A Volume of Sketches, Historical, Descriptive, and Critical. 2d ed. 1893. GROOT, J. J. M. DE, *Le code du Mahâyâna en Chine*. Son influence sur la vie monacale et sur le monde laïque. 1893. Describes modern Buddhism from the author's own observations; contains a translation of the "Sutra of Brahma's Net," the rule for Bodhisattvas. On the relations of the government to Buddhism, see DE GROOT, *Sectarianism*. **Lamaism.**—GRÜNWEDEL, A., "Der Lamaismus," in *Die Kultur der Gegenwart*, I, 3, 1, where additional literature will be found. Of much interest is further, GRÜNWEDEL, A., *Mythologie des Buddhismus in Tibet und der Mongolei*. 1901. Finely illustrated. For literature on Chinese Buddhist sects, see below, under JAPAN.

JAPAN

History.—MURDOCH, JAMES, *A History of Japan*. Vol. I. From the Origins to the Arrival of the Portuguese in 1542 A. D. 1910. MURDOCH, JAMES, and YAMAGATA, ISOH, *A History of Japan during the Century of Early Foreign Intercourse* (1542–1651). 1903. **Literature.**—FLORENZ, KARL, *Geschichte der japanischen Litteratur*, 1905–6. ASTON, W. G., *A History of Japanese Literature*. 1899. A popular work by a very competent hand. **Religion: General Works.**—GRIFFIS, WILLIAM E., *The Religions of Japan*. 1895. Did service in its time by making accessible the results of investigation; now in considerable part superseded by the progress of learning. KNOX, GEORGE W., *The Development of Religion in Japan*. 1907. Six lectures, of which the two on Confucianism deal with a subject in which the author was especially interested.

SHINTO

Texts.—CHAMBERLAIN, B. H., *Kojiki, or Records of Ancient Matters*. 1883. ASTON, W. G., *Nihongi. Chronicles of Japan, from the Earliest Times to A. D. 697*. 2 vols. 1896. FLORENZ, KARL, *Japanische Annalen (Nihongi)*. 2d ed. 1903. FLORENZ, KARL, *Japanische Mythologie*. 1901. SATOW, E., "Ancient Japanese Rituals," in *Transactions of the Asiatic Society of Japan*, vols. VII (1879) and IX (1881); continued by FLORENZ, *ibid.*, vol. XXVI (1899). **Religion.**—ASTON, W. G., *Shinto (The Way of the Gods)*. 1905. The best exposition of the subject, with copious translations and native illustrations. Not to be confounded with a meagre compend under a similar title (Shinto, the Ancient Religion of Japan. 1907).

BUDDHISM

The **History** of Buddhism in Japan, both external and internal, is best read in Murdoch. **Texts.**—See below, under INDIA, Buddhism; also BEAL, *Catena*, under CHINA. The Sukhavati Sutras, which are the foundation of the Pure Land Sects, are translated in S. B. E., vol. XLIX. **Sects and Doctrines.**—NANJIO, BUNYIU, *A Short History of the Twelve Buddhist Sects*. 1887. Substantially a translation of statements by leading priests of various sects. FUJISHIMA, RYAUON, *Le Bouddhisme Japonais*. Doctrines et histoire des douze grandes sectes Bouddhiques du Japon. 1889. French translation of Nanjio. A book written by a learned priest, Gyonen, in 1289, a kind of catechism on the doctrines of the eight older sects is translated in the *Revue de l'histoire des religions*, vols. XXV and XXVI. HAAS, HANS, *Die Sekten des japanischen Buddhismus*. 1905. LLOYD, ARTHUR, "Developments of Japanese Buddhism," in *Transactions of the Asiatic Society of Japan*, vol. XXII, pp. 337–506. On the Jodo and Shin sects particularly, LLOYD, *The Wheat Among the Tares*. 1908. *Shinran and his*

Work. 1910. *The Creed of Half Japan.* 1911. The author tries to prove that the Pure Land doctrine of salvation by faith is in some way derived from Christianity. HAAS, HANS, *"Amida Buddha unsere Zuflucht."* Urkunden zum Verständnis der japanischer Sukhavati Buddhismus. 1910. Translations of texts, with historical and biographical introductions and notes; material of high value and interest.

EGYPT

History.—BREASTED, JAMES H., *History of Egypt from the Earliest Times to the Persian Conquest.* 1905. 2d ed. 1909. MEYER, EDUARD, *Geschichte des Altertums,* 2d ed. I, 2. 1909. From the beginnings to the sixteenth century B. C. The treatment of the religion is one of the conspicuous merits of the work. A French translation is in course of publication. MASPÉRO, G., *Histoire ancienne des peuples de l'Orient classique.* 3 vols. 1895-9. Especially good on Egypt, the author's own province; admirably illustrated. English translation, under volume titles: *Dawn of Civilization, Struggle of the Nations, Passing of the Empires,* 1894 to 1900. **Religion.**—ERMAN, ADOLF, *Handbook of Egyptian Religion.* Translated by A. S. Griffith. 1907. Prepared as one of a series of museum handbooks; illustrated. There is a second German edition, 1909. The same author's *Life in Ancient Egypt,* 1894, may also profitably be consulted. WIEDEMANN, ALFRED, *Religion of the Ancient Egyptians.* 1897. STEINDORFF, G., *The Religion of the Ancient Egyptians.* 1905. BREASTED, JAMES H., *Development of Religion and Thought in Ancient Egypt.* 1912. The large use made for the first time of the pyramid texts gives this book a peculiar value for the early period. **Texts.**—RENOUF, P. LE PAGE, *Book of the Dead.* Translation and Commentary Continued and Completed by É. Naville. 1907.

BABYLONIA AND ASSYRIA

MEYER, E., *Geschichte des Altertums,* I, 2; see remarks under EGYPT. KING, L. W., *History of Babylonia and Assyria from Prehistoric Times to the Persian Conquest.* Part I, History of Sumer and Akkad. 1910. ROGERS, R. W., *History of Babylonia and Assyria.* 2 vols. 1900. The earlier parts to some extent antiquated by the discoveries and researches of the last decade. **Religion.**—JASTROW, MORRIS, JR., *The Religion of Babylonia and Assyria.* 1898. Superseded by the same author's *Die Religion Babyloniens und Assyriens.* 2 vols. 1905-12. The fullest treatment of the subject; deals at great length with the hymns, prayers, incantations, and especially with divination; but leaves the myths, etc., for a future publication. Also, JASTROW, M., JR., *Aspects of Religious Belief and Practice in Babylonia and Assyria.* 1911. A useful introduction to the subject. ZIMMERN, HEINRICH, in SCHRADER, *Die Keilinschriften und das Alte Testament.* 3d ed. 1903. Part II. ZIMMERN is the author also of the article, "Babylonians and Assyrians," in the *Encyclopædia of Religion and Ethics,* where the literature of special topics may be found. ROGERS, ROBERT W., *The Religion of Babylonia and Assyria; Especially in its Relations to Israel*. 1908. DHORME, PAUL, *La religion Assyro-Babylonienne*. 1910. Both popular.

INDIA

History.—SMITH, VINCENT A., *The Early History of India*. From 600 B. C. to the Mohammedan Conquest. 2d ed. 1908. **Literature.**— WINTERNITZ, M., *Geschichte der indischen Litteratur*. I. Der Veda. Die volkstümlichen Epen und die Puranas. 1908. II, 1. Die Buddhistische Litteratur. 1913. The most satisfactory work on the subject. MACDONELL, ARTHUR A., *A History of Sanskrit Literature*. 1900. Elementary. HENRY, V., *Les littératures de l'Inde*. 1904. A well-proportioned and firmly outlined sketch. **Religion: General Works.**— BARTH, A., *The Religions of India*. Authorized translation by J. WOOD. 3d ed. 1891. Comprehensive and admirably lucid; at some points— notably on the relation of Jainism to Buddhism—corrected by later studies. HOPKINS, E. W., *The Religions of India*. 1895. The chapters on the religion of the epics and the law books are of especial value. MONIER-WILLIAMS, MONIER, *Brahmanism and Hinduism*. 4th ed. 1891. LYALL, ALFRED C., *Asiatic Studies*. 1882. Second Series, 1899. DEUSSEN, PAUL, *Allgemeine Geschichte der Philosophie*. Mit besonderer Berücksichtigung der Religionen. I, 1. 1894; 2d ed. 1906; I, 2. 1899; I, 3. 1908. Of the first importance for Indian thought in all its aspects.

RELIGION OF THE VEDA

Texts: Rig-Veda.—WILSON, HORACE HAYMAN, *Rig-Veda-Sanhitá*. 6 vols. 1850–88. (Vols. IV–VI edited by E. B. COWELL and W. F. WEBSTER.) F. MAX MÜLLER, *Vedic Hymns*. Part I. 1891. (S. B. E., vol. XXXII: Hymns to the Maruts, Rudra, Vayu, and Vata.) OLDENBERG, HERMANN, *Vedic Hymns*. Part II. 1897. (S. B. E., vol. XLVI: Hymns to Agni.) MUIR, JOHN, *Original Sanskrit Texts on the Origin and History of the People of India, their Religion and Institutions*. Collected, translated, and illustrated. 5 vols. 2d ed. 1868–73. Digest of materials and discussion. **Atharva-Veda.**—WHITNEY, WILLIAM D., *Atharva-Veda Samhitā*. Translated, with a Critical and Exegetical Commentary. Edited by C. R. LANMAN. 2 vols. 1905. BLOOMFIELD, M., *Hymns of the Atharva-Veda*. 1897. (S. B. E., vol. XLII.) **Brahmanas.**—EGGELING, JULIUS, *Satapatha-Brâhmana*. 5 vols. 1882–1900. (S. B. E., vols. XII, XXVI, XLI, XLIII, XLIV.) **Law Books.**—Translated by various scholars: S. B. E., vols. II, XIV, XXV, XXXIII. **Household Rules and Ritual.**—S. B. E., vols. XXIX, XXX. **Upanishads.**— DEUSSEN, PAUL, *Sechzig Upanishads des Veda*. Aus dem Sanskrit übersetzt. 1897. 2d ed. 1905. The only comprehensive and trustworthy translation. A selection, embracing the most significant and interesting parts of the Upanishads, will be found in DEUSSEN, *Die Geheimlehre des Veda*. Ausgewählte Texte aus dem Sanskrit übersetzt.

1907. **Life and Custom.**—ZIMMER, HEINRICH, *Altindisches Leben.* Die Cultur der vedischen Arier nach den Saṃhitā. 1879. **Mythology.** —MACDONELL, ARTHUR A., *Vedic Mythology.* (In Grundriss der indo-arischen Philologie.) **Religion.**—BERGAIGNE, ABEL, *La religion védique d'après les hymnes du Rig-Véda.* 3 vols. 1878–83. Vol. IV. Index, by M. BLOOMFIELD. 1897. Great digest of materials. OLDENBERG, HERMANN, *Die Religion des Veda.* 1894. There is also a French translation of this excellent book. BLOOMFIELD, M., *The Religion of the Veda.* The Ancient Religion of the Veda (from the Rig-Veda to the Upanishads). 1908. Popular lectures. LÉVI, SYLVAIN, *La doctrine du sacrifice dans les Brâhmanas.* 1898. **Philosophy of the Upanishads.** —GOUGH, A. E., *The Philosophy of the Upanishads and Ancient Indian Metaphysics.* 1882. DEUSSEN, PAUL, *The Philosophy of the Upanishads.* Translated by A. S. Geden. 1906. (=Allgemeine Geschichte der Philosophie, I, 2.) OLTRAMARE, PAUL, *L'histoire des idées théosophiques dans l'Inde.* I. La théosophie Brahmanique. 1906. An excellent introduction to the whole subject. SPEYER, J. S., *De Indische theosophie en hare beteekenis voor ons.* 1910. A discussion of the significance of Indian philosophy and theosophy for the West.

JAINISM

Texts.—JACOBI, HERMANN, *Gaina Sutras.* Translated from the Prakrit. 2 vols. 1884, 1895. (S. B. E., vols. XXII, XLV.) With extremely valuable introductions on the literature and history of the Jains. **Doctrine.**—JACOBI, *u. s.*, BÜHLER, GEORG, *On the Indian Sect of the Jainas.* Translated from the German. Edited with an outline of Jaina mythology by James Burgess. 1903.

BUDDHISM

Texts.—DAVIDS, T. W. RHYS, *Dialogues of the Buddha.* Part I, 1899; Part II, 1910. Translations from the Digha Nikaya. DAVIDS, T. W. RHYS, *Buddhist Suttas.* Translated from the Pali. 1881. (S. B. E., vol. XI.) MÜLLER, F. MAX, *The Dhammapada;* FAUSBÖLL, V., *The Suttanipata.* 1881. (Both in S. B. E., vol. X.) DAVIDS, T. W. RHYS, *The Questions of King Milinda.* 2 vols. 1890, 1894. (S. B. E., vols. XXXV, XXXVI.) DAVIDS, T. W. RHYS, and OLDENBERG, HERMANN, *Vinaya Texts.* 3 vols. 1881–1885. (S. B. E., vols. XIII, XVII, XX.) Buddhist discipline. Translations of Patimokkha, Mahavagga, Chullavagga. KERN, HENDRIK, *The Saddharma Pundarika, or the Lotus of the True Law.* 1884. (S. B. E., vol. XXI.) COWELL, E. V., MÜLLER, F. MAX, and TAKAKUSU, J., *Buddhist Mahâyâna Texts.* 1894. (S. B. E., vol. XLIX.) Translations of the Buddhacarita, Sukhavati Sutras, etc. FORMICHI, CARLO, *Açvaghoṣa. Poeta del Buddhismo.* 1912. With a version of the Buddhacarita. *Jataka, or Stories of Buddha's Former Births.* 6 vols. 1895–1907. Translation edited by E. B. Cowell. WARREN, HENRY C., *Buddhism in Translations.* 1896.

Selections from Pali texts, with explanatory introductions. An excellent guide in this voluminous literature. **Religion: General Works.**
—DAVIDS, T. W. RHYS, *Buddhist India.* 1903. GRÜNWEDEL, ALBERT, *Buddhist Art in India.* Translated by Agnes C. Gibson. Revised and enlarged by James Burgess. 1901. SMITH, VINCENT A., *Asoka.* 1901. KERN, HENDRIK, *Manual of Indian Buddhism.* 1896. (In Grundriss der indo-arischen Philologie.) The same: *Der Buddhismus und seine Geschichte in Indien.* Übersetzt von H. Jacobi. 2 vols. 1882. *Histoire du Bouddhisme dans l'Inde.* Traduit par G. Huet. 2 vols. 1903. OLDENBERG, HERMANN, *Buddha. Sein Leben, seine Lehre, seine Gemeinde.* 5th ed. 1906. English translation: *Buddha; his Life, his Doctrine, his Order.* 1882. This translation, from the first German edition, is out of date in many particulars. MONIER-WILLIAMS, MONIER, *Buddhism.* 1889. Also to a considerable extent antiquated. HARDY, R. SPENCE, *Manual of Buddhism in its Modern Development.* 2d ed. (reprint). 1880. Buddhism in Ceylon, from native sources. The same: *Eastern Monachism.* 1850. Both works are still of high value in their field. COPLESTON, REGINALD S., *Buddhism, Primitive and Present, in Magadha and Ceylon.* 1892. [HALL] H. FIELDING, *The Soul of a People.* 4th ed. 1902. An attractive sketch of modern Burmese Buddhism. By the same author: *The Hearts of Men.* 1901. LA VALLÉE POUSSIN, L. DE, *Bouddhisme. Opinions sur l'histoire de la dogmatique.* 1909. The best discussion, for the general reader, of the development of Buddhist doctrine. The author has also contributed several valuable articles to the Encyclopædia of Religion and Ethics. WALLESER, MAX, *Die philosophische Grundlage des älteren Buddhismus.* 1904. The same: *Die Mittlere Lehre (Mādhyamika-śaṣṭra) des Nagarjuna.* (Translated from the Tibetan) 1911; also from the Chinese version, 1912. The last two highly important for the evolution of the Mahayana. On this period, in which much is still very obscure, see also *Açvaghosha's Awakening of Faith in the Mahâyâna.* Translated by T. Suzuki. 1900. HUBER, É., AÇVAGHOṢA, *Sûtrâlaṃkâra.* Translated from the Chinese. 1908. (See also Sylvain Lévi in Journal Asiatique, 10ième série, XII, 57–184.) LÉVI, SYLVAIN, *Asanga: Mahāyāna-sūtralaṃkāra.* Exposé de la doctrine du grand véhicule selon le système Yogacara. 2 vols. 1907–11.

PHILOSOPHICAL SYSTEMS

General.—COWELL, E. B., and GOUGH, A. E., *The Sarva-darsana-saṃgraha; or Review of the Different Systems of Hindu Philosophy.* By MÁDHAVA ÁCHÁRYA. 1882. Account of sixteen systems or schools. The same work is embodied in Deussen's Allgemeine Geschichte der Philosophie, I, 3. **Vedanta: Texts.**—THIBAUT, GEORGE, *The Vedânta-Sûtras.* With the Commentary of Sankarâkârya [Çankara]. 2 vols. 1890, 1896. (S. B. E., vols. XXXIV, XXXVIII.) The same: *The Vedânta-Sûtras.* With the Commentary of Râmânuga. 1904. (S. B. E., vol. XLVIII.) DEUSSEN, PAUL, *Die Sûtras des Vedânta.* . . . Nebst dem vollständigen Commentar des Çankara. 1887. **The Ve-**

danta System.—DEUSSEN, PAUL, *Das System des Vedânta.* 2d ed. 1906. *The System of the Vedânta.* Translated by Charles Johnston. 1912. An able and thorough exposition of the system of Çankara. A brief and lucid summary of the system is DEUSSEN, P., *Outline of the Vedanta Philosophy.* Translated by J. H. Woods and C. B. Runkle. 1906. On the system of Ramanuja, see especially Thibaut's extended introduction to his translation in S. B. E., XXXIV. **Sankhya: Texts.**—BALLANTYNE, JAMES R., *The Sánkhya Aphorisms of Kapila.* With Extracts from Vijnána Bhikshu's Commentary. Edited by F. E. Hall. 1885. GARBE, RICHARD, *Sâṃkhya-pravacana-bhâshya.* Aus dem Sanskrit übersetzt. 1889. The same: *Der Mondschein der Sâṃkhya-Wahrheit.* Vâcaspatimiçra's *Sâṃkhya-tattva-kaumudî* in deutscher Übersetzung, u. s. w., 1891. For other translations, see GARBE, Sâṃkhya-Philosophie (below), pp. 79 *ff*. **The Sankhya System.**—GARBE, RICHARD, *Die Sâṃkhya-Philosophie.* Eine Darstellung des indischen Rationalismus. 1894. An admirably clear exposition. A full bibliography is included. See also GARBE, *Sâṃkhya und Yoga.* 1896. (In Grundriss der indoarischen Philologie.) **Yoga.**—See GARBE, above. WOODS, JAMES H., *The Yoga System of Patañjali; or the Ancient Hindu Doctrine of Concentration of Mind.* Being the mnemonic rules (Yoga-sūtras) of Patañjali, the comment (Bhāshya) attributed to Vyāsa, and the explanation (Vyākhyā) of Vāchaspati-Miçra. 1913. (Harvard Oriental Series.) The most comprehensive work on the subject. See also OLTRAMARE, *Théosophie,* above. The reader who is curious about genuine modern Yoga practice will find his account in SCHMIDT, RICHARD, *Fakire und Fakirtum im alten und modernen Indien.* Yoga-Lehre und Yoga-Praxis, etc. 1908. Contains a translation of an esteemed practical handbook (Gheraṇḍasaṃhitā), with native illustrations of the postures, etc. See also OMAN, JOHN CAMPBELL, *The Mystics, Ascetics, and Saints of India.* A study of Saddhuism, with an Account of the Yogis, Sanyasis, Bairagis, etc. 1903. Other works of the same author below, under Hinduism. **Vaiçeshika.**—HULTZSCH, E., *Tarkasaṃgraha.* Ein Kompendium der Dialektik und Atomistik. 1907. (In Abhandl. der Götting. Gesellsch. d. Wissensch.) **Other Systems.**—DEUSSEN, *Geschichte der Philosophie,* I, 3; and the *Sarva-darçana-saṃgraha.*

HINDUISM

Mahabharata.—HOPKINS, E. W., *The Great Epic of India; its Character and Origin.* 1901. OMAN, J. C., *The Great Indian Epics.* 1899. More popular. MONIER-WILLIAMS, MONIER, *Indian Wisdom.* 4th ed. 1893. DEUSSEN, PAUL, *Vier philosophische Texte aus dem Mahâbhâratam.* 1906. Translation. **Bhagavad-Gita.**—DEUSSEN, in *Philosophische Texte,* above. GARBE, RICHARD, *Die Bhagavadgîtâ.* Aus dem Sanskrit übersetzt, mit einer Einleitung über ihre ursprüngliche Gestalt, ihre Lehren und ihr Alter. 1905. By the use of different sizes of type, the original poem, as Garbe reconstructs it, is distinguished from later additions. The reader who wishes not merely to admire but to understand will do well to turn first to Garbe. Of English translations that of

TELANG, *The Bhagavadgîtâ, with the Sanatsugâtîya and the Anugîtâ.* 2d ed. 1898. (S. B. E., vol. VIII), is especially commended for its— somewhat prosaic—fidelity. On the religion of the poem, see GARBE, *op. cit.*; also, by the same author, the article, "Bhagavad-Gita," in *Encyclopædia of Religion and Ethics*, II, 535 *ff.*, where the literature will be found more fully. For a different view, see DEUSSEN, *Geschichte der Philosophie*, I, 3 (pp. 8 *ff.*, *cf.* Vorwort, p. vi)—the philosophical inconsistencies of the poem not due to additions and adaptations, but representing a "transitional philosophy." **Hindu Religions.**—WARD, WILLIAM, *A View of the History, Literature and Mythology of the Hindoos.* 3 vols. 1822. WILSON, HORACE HAYMAN, *A Sketch of the Religious Sects of the Hindus.* (Works, edited by R. Rost, vols. I and II. 1862.) MONIER-WILLIAMS, MONIER, *Brahmanism and Hinduism.* 4th ed. 1891. OMAN, J. C., *Cults, Customs, and Superstitions of India.* 1908. *The Brahmans, Theists and Muslims of India.* 2d ed. (London, n. d.) Translations of the **Puranas,** the Hindu scriptures. WILSON, H. H., *The Vishnu Purana.* Edited by F. E. HALL. (Works, etc., vols. VI–X.) BURNOUF, ÉMILE, *Le Bhagavâta Purâna, ou Histoire poétique de Krichna.* 3 vols. 1840–7. Other literature in Winternitz. On the doctrine of salvation by faith in Hinduism, see GRIERSON, G. A., article "Bhakti-Marga," *Encyclopædia of Religion and Ethics*, II, 540 *f.* **Sikhs.**—TRUMPP, E., *Adi Granth.* 1877. MACAULIFFE, M. A., *The Sikh Religion and its Gurus.* Sacred Writings and Authors. 6 vols. 1909. **Akbar.**—BEVERIDGE, H., article, "Akbar," *Encyclopædia of Religion and Ethics*, with literature. BONET-MAURY, G., "La religion d'Akbar, et ses rapports avec l'Islamisme et le Parsisme," *Revue de l'histoire des religions*, LI (1905), 153– 171. **Brahma Samaj.**—OMAN, J. C., *Brahmans, Theists and Muslims of India.* 2d ed., pp. 99–151. For additional literature, see the article in *Encyclopædia of Religion and Ethics.* **Arya Samaj.**—OMAN, *Cults*, etc., pp. 129–181.

ZOROASTRIANISM

History.—MEYER, EDUARD, *Geschichte des Altertums.* Vols. I and III. Early history of the Iranians and of the Achæmenean Empire. The article by MEYER, "Persia: History, Ancient," in *Encyclopædia Britannica*, XXI, 202–224, 11th ed., is a comprehensive outline. **Literature.**—GELDNER, K. F., *Awestalitteratur.* WEST, E. W., *Pahlavi Literature.* (Both in Grundriss der iranischen Philologie.) DARMESTETER, introductions to his French translation. **Texts.**—DARMESTETER, JAMES, *Le Zend-Avesta.* Traduction nouvelle, avec commentaire historique et philologique. 3 vols. 1892–3. The introductions and commentary give this work peculiar value. An earlier translation by the same author: *The Zend-Avesta.* Part I. 2d ed. 1895. Part II. 1883. (S. B. E., vols. IV and XXIII.) MILLS, L. H., *The Zend-Avesta.* Part III (Yasna, Visparad, etc.). (S. B. E., vol. XXXI.) MILLS, L. H., *The Gâthas of Zarathushtra (Zoroaster) in Metre and Rhythm.* 1906. **Pahlavi Texts.**—WEST, E. W., *Pahlavi Texts.* 5 vols.

1880–97. (S. B. E., vols. V, XVIII, XXIV, XXXVII, XLVII.)
With highly valuable introductions. **Life of Zoroaster.**—JACKSON,
A. V. W., *Zoroaster, the Prophet of Ancient Iran.* 1899. The accounts
of Zoroaster's life in native and Greek sources are fully presented and
discussed. **Religion.**—JACKSON, A. V. W., *Die iranische Religion.*
1900, 1904. (In Grundriss der iranischen Philologie, vol. II.)

GREECE

History.—Besides the standard works on Greek history, especial
mention should be made of EDUARD MEYER, *Geschichte des Altertums,*
vols. II–V. (1893–1902.) The religion of the Greeks is here put in
relation with the whole political, social, and economic development;
and the treatment of the religion itself, from the historical point of
view, is the best that has been written. **Literature.**—CROISET, A. ET
M., *Histoire de la littérature grecque.* 5 vols. 1887–99. (I, 2d ed.
1896.) Broad learning and good reading. CHRIST, W., *Geschichte der
griechischen Literatur.* 5th ed. (By WILHELM SCHMIDT, I, 1908; II,
1, 1911.) WILLAMOWITZ-MOELLENDORFF, ULRICH VON, *Die griechische
Literatur des Altertums.* (In Die Kultur der Gegenwart. I, 8. 2d ed.
1907.) A brilliant sketch by an author of genius. MAHAFFY, JOHN P.,
A History of Classical Greek Literature. 2 vols. 1880. JEBB, R. C.,
Classical Greek Poetry. 1894. Lectures. CROISET, A. and M., *An
Abridged History of Greek Literature.* Translated by George Heffel-
bower. 1904. **Religion: General Works.**—MAURY, L.-F. A., *Histoire
des religions de la Grèce antique.* 3 vols. 1857–59. The most readable
general history, distinguished by wealth of material and sanity of judgment. The "comparative" element may now be safely neglected. A
good popular history is ARTHUR FAIRBANKS, *Handbook of Greek Religion,*
1910, with free use of archæological material, and an extensive bibliography. FARNELL, LEWIS R., *The Cults of the Greek States.* 5 vols.
1896–1909. A comprehensive study of the Greek gods, their distribution, cults, etc. By the same author: *The Higher Aspects of Greek
Religion.* 1912. Also, *Greece and Babylon.* 1911. A refutation of the
notion that Greek civilisation and religion are deeply in debt to Babylonia. HARRISON, JANE E., *Prolegomena to the Study of Greek Religion.*
1903. 2d ed. 1908. *Themis; a Study of the Social Origin of Greek
Religion.* 1911. The former work deals chiefly with "some neglected
aspects" of Greek religion—the survivals of the savage stage. The
second volume is a mass of undigested theories. ROHDE, E., *Psyche.
Seelencult und Unsterblichkeitsglauben bei den Griechen.* 1894. 3d ed.
1903. GIRARD, J., *Le sentiment religieux en Grèce d'Homère à Eschyle.*
1879. DECHARME, PAUL, *La critique des traditions religieuses chez les
Grecs des les origines au temps de Plutarque.* 1904. **The Epic Age.**—
SEYMOUR, T. D., *Life in the Homeric Age,* c. xiv. **Poetry and Philosophy.**—CAMPBELL, LEWIS, *Religion in Greek Literature.* 1898. ZELLER,
EDUARD, *Die Philosophie der Griechen in ihrer geschichtlichen Ent-
wickelung.* 5 vols. Classic. English translations from older editions.

GOMPERZ, THEODOR, *Griechische Denker*. 3 vols. 2d ed. 1903–9. English translation: *Greek Thinkers*. A History of Ancient Philosophy. 4 vols. 1901–12. BURNET, JOHN, *Early Greek Philosophy*. 1892. 2d ed. 1908. CAIRD, EDWARD, *The Evolution of Theology in the Greek Philosophers*. 2 vols. 1904. ADAM, JAMES, *The Religious Teachers of Greece*. 1908. Poets and philosophers; Homer to Plato. EUCKEN, RUDOLF, *Lebensanschauungen der grossen Denker*. Eine Entwickelungsgeschichte des Lebensproblems von Plato bis zur Gegenwart. 3d ed. 1905. English translation: *The Problem of Human Life as viewed by the Great Thinkers*. 1910. SCHMEKEL, A., *Die Philosophie der mittleren Stoa in ihrem geschichtlichen Zusammenhang dargestellt*. 1892. OAKESMITH, JOHN, *The Religion of Plutarch*. A Pagan Creed of Apostolic Times. 1902. **Worship.**—STENGEL, P., *Die griechischen Kultusaltertümer*. 2d ed. 1898. GARDNER, PERCY, and JEVONS, F. B., *Manual of Greek Antiquities*. 1895. **Mysteries.**—FARNELL, L. R., *Cults*, etc., vol. III., 127–213.

ROMANS

FRIEDLÄNDER, LUDWIG, *Darstellungen aus der Sittengeschichte Roms von August bis zum Ausgang der Antoninen*. 8th ed. (Bearbeitet von S. HIRZEL.) 1910. DILL, SAMUEL, *Roman Society from Nero to Marcus Aurelius*. 1904. **Religion.**—WISSOWA, GEORG, *Religion und Kultus der Römer*. 1902. 2d ed. 1912. Of fundamental importance to every student. AUST, E., *Die Religion der Römer*. 1899. An excellent book, smaller and more popular in form than Wissowa's, presenting much the same view. FOWLER, W. WARDE, *The Religious Experience of the Roman People*. From the Earliest Times to the Age of Augustus. 1911. The English reader will find this his best guide, and the notes will introduce him to the literature of the subject. The same: *The Roman Festivals of the Republic*. An Introduction to the Study of the Religion of the Romans. 1899. DE MARCHI, *Il culto privato di Roma antica*. 2 vols. 1896–1903. Fundamental for the household religion. CARTER, JESSE B., *The Religion of Numa, and Other Essays on the Religion of Ancient Rome*. 1906. Also, by the same author: *The Religious Life of Ancient Rome*. A Study in the Development of Religious Consciousness from the Foundation of the City until the Death of Gregory the Great. 1911. Lectures, ranging over a wide field. **Philosophy.**—See ZELLER, above. MASSON, JOHN, *Lucretius, Epicurean and Poet*. 2 vols. 1907–9. **Oriental Religions in the Roman World.**—CUMONT, FRANZ, *Textes et monuments figurés relatifs aux mystères de Mithra*, etc. 2 vols. fol. 1896–9. *The Mysteries of Mithra*. Translated by T. J. McCormack. 1903. Translation of a small book setting forth the main results of the author's great work. CUMONT, FRANZ, *The Oriental Religions in Roman Paganism*. Translated by Grant Showerman. 1911. A popular survey. By the same author: *Astrology and Religion Among the Greeks and Romans*. 1912. A timely discussion by a scholar peculiarly expert in this field. LAFAYE, GEORGES, *Histoire du culte des divinités d'Alexandrie . . . hors de l'Égypte*. 1884. TOUTAIN, J., *Les* *cultes païens dans l'empire romain.* I. Les provinces latines. II. Les cultes orientaux. 1911. Not yet completed. **End of the Old Religion.**—Boissier, Gaston, *La fin du paganisme.* Études sur les dernieres luttes religieuses en Occident au quatrième siècle. 2 vols. 6th ed. 1909.

INDEX

617

---

[1] The Mahayana systems, also, admit no permanent soul-entity; but the
masses, incapable of such subtleties, believe in transmigration.

The International Theological Library

ARRANGEMENT OF VOLUMES AND AUTHORS

THEOLOGICAL ENCYCLOPÆDIA. By CHARLES A. BRIGGS, D.D., D.Litt., sometime Professor of Theological Encyclopædia and Symbolics, Union Theological Seminary, New York.

AN INTRODUCTION TO THE LITERATURE OF THE OLD TESTAMENT. By S. R. DRIVER, D.D., D.Litt., Regius Professor of Hebrew and Canon of Christ Church, Oxford. *[Revised and Enlarged Edition.*

CANON AND TEXT OF THE OLD TESTAMENT. By the Rev. JOHN SKINNER, D.D., Principal and Professor of Old Testament Language and Literature, College of the Presbyterian Church of England, Cambridge, England, and the Rev. OWEN WHITEHOUSE, B.A., Principal and Professor of Hebrew, Chestnut College, Cambridge, England.

OLD TESTAMENT HISTORY. By HENRY PRESERVED SMITH, D.D., Librarian, Union Theological Seminary, New York. *[Now Ready.*

CONTEMPORARY HISTORY OF THE OLD TESTAMENT. By FRANCIS BROWN, D.D., LL.D., D.Litt., President and Professor of Hebrew, Union Theological Seminary, New York.

THEOLOGY OF THE OLD TESTAMENT. By A. B. DAVIDSON, D.D., LL.D., sometime Professor of Hebrew, New College, Edinburgh.
[Now Ready.

AN INTRODUCTION TO THE LITERATURE OF THE NEW TESTAMENT. By Rev. JAMES MOFFATT, B.D., Minister United Free Church, Broughty Ferry, Scotland. *[Now Ready.*

CANON AND TEXT OF THE NEW TESTAMENT. By CASPAR RENÉ GREGORY, D.D., LL.D., Professor of New Testament Exegesis in the University of Leipzig. *[Now Ready.*

THE LIFE OF CHRIST. By WILLIAM SANDAY, D.D., LL.D., Lady Margaret Professor of Divinity and Canon of Christ Church, Oxford.

TORY OF CHRISTIANITY IN THE APOSTOLIC AGE. By
R C. McGIFFERT, D.D., Professor of Church History, Union Theo-
Seminary, New York. [Now Ready.

TEMPORARY HISTORY OF THE NEW TESTAMENT. By
K C. PORTER, D.D., Professor of Biblical Theology, Yale University,
Haven, Conn.

EOLOGY OF THE NEW TESTAMENT. By GEORGE B. STEVENS,
D., sometime Professor of Systematic Theology, Yale University, New
Aven, Conn. [Now Ready.

BIBLICAL ARCHÆOLOGY. By G. BUCHANAN GRAY, D.D., Professor
of Hebrew, Mansfield College, Oxford.

THE ANCIENT CATHOLIC CHURCH. By ROBERT RAINEY, D.D.,
LL.D., sometime Principal of New College, Edinburgh. [Now Ready.

THE LATIN CHURCH FROM GREGORY THE GREAT TO THE
COUNCIL OF TRENT. [Author to be announced later.

THE GREEK AND EASTERN CHURCHES. By W. F. ADENEY, D.D.,
Principal of Independent College, Manchester. [Now Ready.

THE REFORMATION. By T. M. LINDSAY, D.D., Principal of the United
Free College, Glasgow. [2 vols. Now Ready.

CHRISTIANITY IN LATIN COUNTRIES SINCE THE COUNCIL OF
TRENT. By PAUL SABATIER, D.Litt., Drome, France.

THEOLOGICAL SYMBOLICS. By CHARLES A. BRIGGS, D.D., D.Litt.,
sometime Professor of Theological Encyclopædia and Symbolics, Union
Theological Seminary, New York. [In Press.

HISTORY OF CHRISTIAN DOCTRINE. By G. P. FISHER, D.D.,
LL.D., sometime Professor of Ecclesiastical History, Yale University,
New Haven, Conn. [Revised and Enlarged Edition.

CHRISTIAN INSTITUTIONS. By A. V. G. ALLEN, D.D., sometime
Professor of Ecclesiastical History, Protestant Episcopal Divinity School,
Cambridge, Mass. [Now Ready.

PHILOSOPHY OF RELIGION. By GEORGE GALLAWAY, D.D., Minister
of United Free Church, Castle Douglas, Scotland.

THE HISTORY OF RELIGIONS. By GEORGE F. MOORE, D.D., LL.D.,
Professor in Harvard University. [Now Ready.

APOLOGETICS. By A. B. BRUCE, D.D., sometime Professor of New
Testament Exegesis, Free Church College, Glasgow.
[Revised and Enlarged Edition.

THE CHRISTIAN DOCTRINE OF GOD. By WILLIAM N. CLARKE, D.D.,
sometime Professor of Systematic Theology, Hamilton Theological Seminary. [Now Ready.

THE DOCTRINE OF MAN. By WILLIAM P. PATERSON, D.D., Professor of Divinity, University of Edinburgh.

THE DOCTRINE OF THE PERSON OF JESUS CHRIST. By H. R. MACKINTOSH, Ph.D., D.D., Professor of Theology, New College, Edinburgh.
[Now Ready.

THE CHRISTIAN DOCTRINE OF SALVATION. By GEORGE B. STEVENS, D.D., sometime Professor of Systematic Theology, Yale University.
[Now Ready.

THE DOCTRINE OF THE CHRISTIAN LIFE. By WILLIAM ADAMS BROWN, D.D., Professor of Systematic Theology, Union Theological Seminary, New York.

CHRISTIAN ETHICS. By NEWMAN SMYTH, D.D., Pastor of Congregational Church, New Haven. *[Revised and Enlarged Edition.*

THE CHRISTIAN PASTOR AND THE WORKING CHURCH. By WASHINGTON GLADDEN, D.D., Pastor of Congregational Church, Columbus, Ohio. *[Now Ready.*

THE CHRISTIAN PREACHER. By A. E. GARVIE, D.D., Principal of New College, London, England.

The International Critical Commentary

ARRANGEMENT OF VOLUMES AND AUTHORS

THE OLD TESTAMENT

GENESIS. The Rev. JOHN SKINNER, D.D., Principal and Professor of Old Testament Language and Literature, College of Presbyterian Church of England, Cambridge, England. [*Now Ready.*

EXODUS. The Rev. A. R. S. KENNEDY, D.D., Professor of Hebrew, University of Edinburgh.

LEVITICUS. J. F. STENNING, M.A., Fellow of Wadham College, Oxford.

NUMBERS. The Rev. G. BUCHANAN GRAY, D.D., Professor of Hebrew, Mansfield College, Oxford. [*Now Ready.*

DEUTERONOMY. The Rev. S. R. DRIVER, D.D., D.Litt., Regius Professor of Hebrew, Oxford. [*Now Ready.*

JOSHUA. The Rev. GEORGE ADAM SMITH, D.D., LL.D., Principal of the University of Aberdeen.

JUDGES. The Rev. GEORGE MOORE, D.D., LL.D., Professor of Theology, Harvard University, Cambridge, Mass. [*Now Ready.*

SAMUEL. The Rev. H. P. SMITH, D.D., Librarian, Union Theological Seminary, New York. [*Now Ready.*

KINGS. The Rev. FRANCIS BROWN, D.D., D.Litt., LL.D., President and Professor of Hebrew and Cognate Languages, Union Theological Seminary, New York City.

CHRONICLES. The Rev. EDWARD L. CURTIS, D.D., Professor of Hebrew, Yale University, New Haven, Conn. [*Now Ready.*

EZRA AND NEHEMIAH. The Rev. L. W. BATTEN, Ph.D., D.D., Professor of Old Testament Literature, General Theological Seminary, New York City. [*Now Ready.*

PSALMS. The Rev. CHAS. A. BRIGGS, D.D., D.Litt., sometime Graduate Professor of Theological Encyclopædia and Symbolics, Union Theological Seminary, New York. [*2 vols. Now Ready.*

PROVERBS. The Rev. C. H. TOY, D.D., LL.D., Professor of Hebrew, Harvard University, Cambridge, Mass. [*Now Ready.*

JOB. The Rev. S. R. DRIVER, D.D., D.Litt., Regius Professor of Hebrew, Oxford.

ISAIAH. Chaps. I–XXVII. The Rev. G. BUCHANAN GRAY, D.D., Professor of Hebrew, Mansfield College, Oxford. [*Now Ready.*

ISAIAH. Chaps. XXVIII–XXXIX. The Rev. G. BUCHANAN GRAY, D.D. Chaps. LX–LXVI. The Rev. A. S. PEAKE, M.A., D.D., Dean of the Theological Faculty of the Victoria University and Professor of Biblical Exegesis in the University of Manchester, England.

JEREMIAH. The Rev. A. F. KIRKPATRICK, D.D., Dean of Ely, sometime Regius Professor of Hebrew, Cambridge, England.

EZEKIEL. The Rev. G. A. COOKE, M.A., Oriel Professor of the Interpretation of Holy Scripture, University of Oxford, and the Rev. CHARLES F. BURNEY, D.Litt., Fellow and Lecturer in Hebrew, St. John's College, Oxford.

DANIEL. The Rev. JOHN P. PETERS, Ph.D., D.D., sometime Professor of Hebrew, P. E. Divinity School, Philadelphia, now Rector of St. Michael's Church, New York City.

AMOS AND HOSEA. W. R. HARPER, Ph.D., LL.D., sometime President of the University of Chicago, Illinois. [*Now Ready.*

MICAH, ZEPHANIAH, NAHUM, HABAKKUK, OBADIAH AND JOEL. Prof. JOHN M. P. SMITH, University of Chicago; W. HAYES WARD, D.D., LL.D., Editor of *The Independent*, New York; Prof. JULIUS A. BEWER, Union Theological Seminary, New York. [*Now Ready.*

HAGGAI, ZECHARIAH, MALACHI AND JONAH. Prof. H. G. MITCHELL, D.D.; Prof. JOHN M. P. SMITH, Ph.D., and Prof. J. A. BEWER, Ph.D. [*Now Ready.*

ESTHER. The Rev. L. B. PATON, Ph.D., Professor of Hebrew, Hartford Theological Seminary. [*Now Ready.*

ECCLESIASTES. Prof. GEORGE A. BARTON, Ph.D., Professor of Biblical Literature, Bryn Mawr College, Pa. [*Now Ready.*

RUTH, SONG OF SONGS AND LAMENTATIONS. Rev. CHARLES A. BRIGGS, D.D., D.Litt., sometime Graduate Professor of Theological Encyclopædia and Symbolics, Union Theological Seminary, New York.

THE NEW TESTAMENT

ST. MATTHEW. The Rev. WILLOUGHBY C. ALLEN, M.A., Fellow and Lecturer in Theology and Hebrew, Exeter College, Oxford. [*Now Ready.*

ST. MARK. Rev. E. P. GOULD, D.D., sometime Professor of New Testament Literature, P. E. Divinity School, Philadelphia. [*Now Ready.*

ST. LUKE. The Rev. ALFRED PLUMMER, D.D., sometime Master of University College, Durham. [*Now Ready.*

ST. JOHN. The Right Rev. JOHN HENRY BERNARD, D.D., Bishop of Ossory, Ireland.

HARMONY OF THE GOSPELS. The Rev. WILLIAM SANDAY, D.D., LL.D., Lady Margaret Professor of Divinity, Oxford, and the Rev. WILLOUGHBY C. ALLEN, M.A., Fellow and Lecturer in Divinity and Hebrew, Exeter College, Oxford.

ACTS. The Rev. C. H. TURNER, D.D., Fellow of Magdalen College, Oxford, and the Rev. H. N. BATE, M.A., Examining Chaplain to the Bishop of London.

ROMANS. The Rev. WILLIAM SANDAY, D.D., LL.D., Lady Margaret Professor of Divinity and Canon of Christ Church, Oxford, and the Rev. A. C. HEADLAM, M.A., D.D., Principal of King's College, London.
[Now Ready.

I. CORINTHIANS. The Right Rev. ARCH ROBERTSON, D.D., LL.D., Lord Bishop of Exeter, and Rev. ALFRED PLUMMER, D.D., late Master of University College, Durham. *[Now Ready.*

II. CORINTHIANS. The Rev. DAWSON WALKER, D.D., Theological Tutor in the University of Durham.

GALATIANS. The Rev. ERNEST D. BURTON, D.D., Professor of New Testament Literature, University of Chicago.

EPHESIANS AND COLOSSIANS. The Rev. T. K. ABBOTT, B.D., D.Litt., sometime Professor of Biblical Greek, Trinity College, Dublin, now Librarian of the same. *[Now Ready.*

PHILIPPIANS AND PHILEMON. The Rev. MARVIN R. VINCENT, D.D., Professor of Biblical Literature, Union Theological Seminary, New York City. *[Now Ready.*

THESSALONIANS. The Rev. JAMES E. FRAME, M.A., Professor of Biblical Theology, Union Theological Seminary, New York City.
[Now Ready.
THE PASTORAL EPISTLES. The Rev. WALTER LOCK, D.D., Warden of Keble College and Professor of Exegesis, Oxford.

HEBREWS. The Rev. JAMES MOFFATT, D.D., Minister United Free Church, Broughty Ferry, Scotland.

ST. JAMES. The Rev. JAMES H. ROPES, D.D., Bussey Professor of New Testament Criticism in Harvard University.

PETER AND JUDE. The Rev. CHARLES BIGG, D.D., sometime Regius Professor of Ecclesiastical History and Canon of Christ Church, Oxford.
[Now Ready.

THE JOHANNINE EPISTLES. The Rev. E. A. BROOKE, B.D., Fellow and Divinity Lecturer in King's College, Cambridge. *[Now Ready.*

REVELATION. The Rev. ROBERT H. CHARLES, M.A., D.D., sometime Professor of Biblical Greek in the University of Dublin.